T0203038

Lecture Notes in Computer Science 11505

More information about this series at http://www.springer.com/series/7410

Editors
Jintai Ding
University of Cincinnati
Cincinnati, OH, USA

Rainer Steinwandt
Department of Mathematical Sciences
Florida Atlantic University
Boca Raton, FL, USA

ISSN 0302-9743   ISSN 1611-3349 (electronic)
Lecture Notes in Computer Science
ISBN 978-3-030-25509-1   ISBN 978-3-030-25510-7 (eBook)
https://doi.org/10.1007/978-3-030-25510-7

LNCS Sublibrary: SL4 – Security and Cryptology

This Springer imprint is published by the registered company Springer Nature Switzerland AG
The registered company address is: Gewerbestrasse 11, 6330 Cham, Switzerland

Jintai Ding · Rainer Steinwandt (Eds.)

Post-Quantum Cryptography

10th International Conference, PQCrypto 2019
Chongqing, China, May 8–10, 2019
Revised Selected Papers

 Springer

Preface

PQCrypto 2019, the 10th International Workshop on Post-Quantum Cryptography, was held in Chongqing, China, during May 8–10, 2019.

The aim of the PQCrypto conference series is to serve as a forum for researchers to present and discuss their work on cryptography in an era with large-scale quantum computers.

Following the same model as its predecessor, PQCrypto 2019 adopted a two-stage submission process in which authors registered their paper(s) one week before the final submission deadline.

The conference received 76 submissions with authors from about 30 countries. Each paper (that had not been withdrawn by the authors) was reviewed in private by at least three Program Committee members. The private review phase was followed by an intensive discussion phase, conducted online. At the end of this process, the Program Committee selected 22 papers for inclusion in the technical program and publication in these proceedings. In some cases, a shepherding phase was imposed to ensure that necessary changes were incorporated by the submitting authors, before the paper was accepted for inclusion in the program and these proceedings. The accepted papers cover a broad spectrum of research within the conference's scope, including both the design and the analysis of cryptographic systems.

In addition to the 22 contributed technical presentations, the program featured outstanding invited talks and a presentation on NIST's ongoing post-quantum cryptography standardization process.

Organizing and running this year's edition of the PQCrypto conference series was a team effort, and we are indebted to everyone who helped make PQCrypto 2019 a success. In particular, we would like to thank all members of the Program Committee and the external reviewers who were a vital part of compiling the technical program. Evaluating and discussing the submissions was a labor-intense task, and we truly appreciate the work that went into this. We also owe a big thank you to Professor Hong Xiang from Chongqing University, who made sure that all local arrangements fell into place as needed.

May 2019

Jintai Ding
Rainer Steinwandt

PQCrypto 2019

The 10th International Conference on Post-Quantum Cryptography

Chongqing, China
May 8–10, 2019

Program Chairs

Jintai Ding · University of Cincinnati, USA
Rainer Steinwandt · Florida Atlantic University, USA

Steering Committee

Daniel J. Bernstein · University of Illinois at Chicago, USA
Johannes Buchmann · Technische Universität Darmstadt, Germany
Claude Crépeau · McGill University, Canada
Jintai Ding · University of Cincinnati, USA
Philippe Gaborit · University of Limoges, France
Tanja Lange · Technische Universiteit Eindhoven, The Netherlands
Daniele Micciancio · University of California at San Diego, USA
Michele Mosca · University of Waterloo, Canada
Nicolas Sendrier · Inria, France
Rainer Steinwandt · Florida Atlantic University, USA
Tsuyoshi Takagi · Kyushu University and University of Tokyo, Japan
Bo-Yin Yang · Academia Sinica, Taiwan

Program Committee

Gorjan Alagic · University of Maryland, USA
Martin R. Albrecht · University of London, UK
Yoshinori Aono · National Institute of Communication Technology, Japan
John B. Baena · University Nacional de Colombia, Colombia
Shi Bai · Florida Atlantic University, USA
Lejla Batina · Radboud University, The Netherlands
Daniel J. Bernstein · University of Illinois at Chicago, USA
Johannes Buchmann · Technische Universität Darmstadt, Germany
Chen-Mou Cheng · Osaka University, Japan
Jung Hee Cheon · Seoul National University, Republic of Korea

External Reviewers

Roberto Araujo
Florian Bache
Ward Beullens
Nina Bindel
Denis Butin
Daniel Cabarcas
Ryann Cartor
Crystal Clough
Edward Eaton
Daniel Escudero
Thomas Espitau
Tim Fritzmann
Qian Guo
Javier Herranz
James Howe
Lei Hu
Shih-Han Hung
Shuichi Katsumata
Natasha Kharchenko
Markus Krausz

Aaron Lye
Pedro Maat Massolino
Khoa Nguyen
Tobias Oder
Angel L. Perez Del Pozo
Federico Pintore
Rachel Player
Eamonn Postlethwaite
Thomas Prest
Youming Qiao
Joost Renes
Angela Robinson
Peter Schwabe
Alan Szepieniec
Rotem Tsabary
Javier Verbel
Weiqiang Wen
Yang Yu
Pavol Zajac

Contents

Lattice-Based Cryptography

Finding Closest Lattice Vectors Using Approximate Voronoi Cells   3
  Emmanouil Doulgerakis, Thijs Laarhoven, and Benne de Weger

Evaluating the Potential for Hardware Acceleration of Four NTRU-Based
Key Encapsulation Mechanisms Using Software/Hardware Codesign   23
  Farnoud Farahmand, Viet B. Dang, Duc Tri Nguyen, and Kris Gaj

Forward-Secure Group Signatures from Lattices   44
  San Ling, Khoa Nguyen, Huaxiong Wang, and Yanhong Xu

Towards Practical Microcontroller Implementation
of the Signature Scheme Falcon   65
  Tobias Oder, Julian Speith, Kira Höltgen, and Tim Güneysu

Learning with Errors

Round5: Compact and Fast Post-quantum Public-Key Encryption   83
  Hayo Baan, Sauvik Bhattacharya, Scott Fluhrer,
  Oscar Garcia-Morchon, Thijs Laarhoven, Ronald Rietman,
  Markku-Juhani O. Saarinen, Ludo Tolhuizen, and Zhenfei Zhang

The Impact of Error Dependencies on Ring/Mod-LWE/LWR
Based Schemes 103
  Jan-Pieter D'Anvers, Frederik Vercauteren, and Ingrid Verbauwhede

Direct CCA-Secure KEM and Deterministic PKE from Plain LWE 116
  Xavier Boyen and Qinyi Li

Cryptanalysis

Recovering Short Secret Keys of RLCE in Polynomial Time 133
  Alain Couvreur, Matthieu Lequesne, and Jean-Pierre Tillich

Cryptanalysis of an NTRU-Based Proxy Encryption Scheme
from ASIACCS'15 153
  Zhen Liu, Yanbin Pan, and Zhenfei Zhang

On the Complexity of "Superdetermined" Minrank Instances 167
  Javier Verbel, John Baena, Daniel Cabarcas, Ray Perlner,
  and Daniel Smith-Tone

Key Establishment

Constant-Round Group Key Exchange from the Ring-LWE Assumption   189
  Daniel Apon, Dana Dachman-Soled, Huijing Gong, and Jonathan Katz

Hybrid Key Encapsulation Mechanisms and Authenticated Key Exchange . . .   206
  *Nina Bindel, Jacqueline Brendel, Marc Fischlin, Brian Goncalves,
  and Douglas Stebila*

Tighter Security Proofs for Generic Key Encapsulation Mechanism
in the Quantum Random Oracle Model   227
  Haodong Jiang, Zhenfeng Zhang, and Zhi Ma

(Tightly) QCCA-Secure Key-Encapsulation Mechanism in the Quantum
Random Oracle Model   249
  Keita Xagawa and Takashi Yamakawa

Isogeny-Based Cryptography

Faster SeaSign Signatures Through Improved Rejection Sampling   271
  Thomas Decru, Lorenz Panny, and Frederik Vercauteren

Genus Two Isogeny Cryptography   286
  E. V. Flynn and Yan Bo Ti

On Lions and Elligators: An Efficient Constant-Time Implementation
of CSIDH   307
  Michael Meyer, Fabio Campos, and Steffen Reith

Hash-Based Cryptography

Quantum Security of Hash Functions and Property-Preservation
of Iterated Hashing   329
  Ben Hamlin and Fang Song

Improved Quantum Multicollision-Finding Algorithm   350
  Akinori Hosoyamada, Yu Sasaki, Seiichiro Tani, and Keita Xagawa

Code-Based Cryptography

Preventing Timing Attacks Against RQC Using Constant Time Decoding
of Gabidulin Codes   371
  Slim Bettaieb, Loïc Bidoux, Philippe Gaborit, and Etienne Marcatel

A Traceable Ring Signature Scheme Based on Coding Theory   387
  Pedro Branco and Paulo Mateus

On the Decoding Failure Rate of QC-MDPC Bit-Flipping Decoders   404
  Nicolas Sendrier and Valentin Vasseur

Author Index   417

Lattice-Based Cryptography

Finding Closest Lattice Vectors Using Approximate Voronoi Cells

Emmanouil Doulgerakis, Thijs Laarhoven$^{(\boxtimes)}$, and Benne de Weger

Eindhoven University of Technology, Eindhoven, The Netherlands
{e.doulgerakis,b.m.m.d.weger}@tue.nl, mail@thijs.co

Abstract. The two traditional hard problems underlying the security of lattice-based cryptography are the shortest vector problem (SVP) and the closest vector problem (CVP). For a long time, lattice enumeration was considered the fastest method for solving these problems in high dimensions, but recent work on memory-intensive methods has resulted in lattice sieving overtaking enumeration both in theory and in practice. Some of the recent improvements [Ducas, Eurocrypt 2018; Laarhoven–Mariano, PQCrypto 2018; Albrecht–Ducas–Herold–Kirshanova–Postlethwaite–Stevens, 2018] are based on the fact that these methods find more than just one short lattice vector, and this additional data can be reused effectively later on to solve other, closely related problems faster. Similarly, results for the preprocessing version of CVP (CVPP) have demonstrated that once this initial data has been generated, instances of CVP can be solved faster than when solving them directly, albeit with worse memory complexities [Laarhoven, SAC 2016].

In this work we study CVPP in terms of approximate Voronoi cells, and obtain better time and space complexities using randomized slicing, which is similar in spirit to using randomized bases in lattice enumeration [Gama–Nguyen–Regev, Eurocrypt 2010]. With this approach, we improve upon the state-of-the-art complexities for CVPP, both theoretically and experimentally, with a practical speedup of several orders of magnitude compared to non-preprocessed SVP or CVP. Such a fast CVPP solver may give rise to faster enumeration methods, where the CVPP solver is used to replace the bottom part of the enumeration tree, consisting of a batch of CVP instances in the same lattice.

Asymptotically, we further show that we can solve an exponential number of instances of CVP in a lattice in essentially the same amount of time and space as the fastest method for solving just one CVP instance. This is in line with various recent results, showing that perhaps the biggest strength of memory-intensive methods lies in being able to reuse the generated data several times. Similar to [Ducas, Eurocrypt 2018], this further means that we can achieve a "few dimensions for free" for sieving for SVP or CVP, by doing $\Theta(d/\log d)$ levels of enumeration on top of a CVPP solver based on approximate Voronoi cells.

Keywords: Lattices · Preprocessing · Voronoi cells · Sieving algorithms · Shortest vector problem (SVP) · Closest vector problem (CVP)

© Springer Nature Switzerland AG 2019
J. Ding and R. Steinwandt (Eds.): PQCrypto 2019, LNCS 11505, pp. 3–22, 2019.
https://doi.org/10.1007/978-3-030-25510-7_1

1   Introduction

Lattice Problems. Lattices are discrete subgroups of $\mathbb{R}^d$: given a basis $B = \{b_1, \ldots, b_d\} \subset \mathbb{R}^d$, the lattice generated by B is defined as $\mathcal{L} = \mathcal{L}(B) := \{\sum_{i=1}^d \lambda_i b_i : \lambda_i \in \mathbb{Z}\}$. Given a basis of $\mathcal{L}$, the shortest vector problem (SVP) is to find a (non-zero) lattice vector s of Euclidean norm $\|s\| = \lambda_1(\mathcal{L}) := \min_{v \in \mathcal{L} \setminus \{0\}} \|v\|$. Given a basis of a lattice and a target vector $t \in \mathbb{R}^d$, the closest vector problem (CVP) is to find a lattice vector $s \in \mathcal{L}$ closest to t. The preprocessing variant of CVP (CVPP) asks to preprocess the lattice $\mathcal{L}$ such that, when later given a target vector t, one can quickly find a closest lattice vector to t.

SVP and CVP are fundamental in the study of lattice-based cryptography, as the security of many schemes is directly related to their hardness. Various other hard lattice problems, such as Learning With Errors (LWE), are closely related to SVP and CVP; see, e.g., [63,74,75] for reductions among lattice problems. These reductions show that understanding the hardness of SVP and CVP is crucial for accurately estimating the security of lattice-based cryptographic schemes.

1.1   Related Work

Worst-Case SVP/CVP Analyses. Although SVP and CVP are both central in the study of lattice-based cryptography, algorithms for SVP have received somewhat more attention, including a benchmarking website to compare different methods [1]. Various SVP algorithms have been studied which can solve CVP as well, such as the polynomial-space, superexponential-time lattice enumeration studied in [14,32,38,40,47,66]. More recently, methods have been proposed which solve SVP/CVP in only single exponential time, but which also require exponential-sized memory [2,6,64]. By constructing the Voronoi cell of the lattice [4,25,64,73], Micciancio–Voulgaris showed that SVP and CVP(P) can provably be solved in time $2^{2d+o(d)}$, and Bonifas–Dadush reduced the complexity for CVPP to only $2^{d+o(d)}$. In high dimensions the best provable complexities for SVP and CVP are currently due to discrete Gaussian sampling [2,3], solving both problems in $2^{d+o(d)}$ time and space in the worst case on arbitrary lattices.

Average-Case SVP/CVP Algorithms. When considering and comparing these methods in practice on random lattices, we get a completely different picture. Currently the fastest heuristic methods for SVP and CVP in high dimensions are based on lattice sieving. After a long series of theoretical works on constructing efficient heuristic sieving algorithms [18–21,50,53,65,68,78,80] as well as applied papers studying how to further speed up these algorithms in practice [28,35,39,46,54,57–61,67,71,72], the best heuristic time complexity for solving SVP (and CVP [52]) currently stands at $2^{0.292d+o(d)}$ [18,59], using $2^{0.208d+o(d)}$ memory. The highest records in the SVP challenge [1] were recently obtained using a BKZ-sieving hybrid [7]. These recent improvements have resulted in a major shift in security estimates for lattice-based cryptography, from estimating the hardness of SVP/CVP using the best enumeration methods, to estimating this hardness based on state-of-the-art sieving results [9,24,26,27,36].

Hybrid Algorithms and Batch-CVP. In moderate dimensions, enumeration-based methods dominated for a long time, and the cross-over point with single-exponential time algorithms like sieving seemed to be far out of reach [66]. Moreover, the exponential memory of, e.g., lattice sieving will ultimately also significantly slow down these algorithms due to the large number of random memory accesses [23], and parallelizing sieving efficiently is less trivial than parallelizing enumeration [7,23,28,46,59,67,79]. Some previous work focused on obtaining a trade-off between enumeration and sieving, using less memory for sieving [17,43,44] or using more memory for enumeration [48].

Another well-known direction for a hybrid between memory-intensive methods and enumeration is to use a fast CVP(P) algorithm as a subroutine within enumeration. As described in, e.g., [40,66], at any given level in the enumeration tree, one is attempting to solve a CVP instance in a lower-rank sublattice, where the target vector is determined by the path from the root to the current node in the tree. Each node at this level in the tree corresponds to a CVP instance in the same sublattice, but with a different target. If we can preprocess this low-dimensional sublattice such that the amortized time complexity of solving a batch of CVP-instances in this sublattice is small, then this may speed up processing the bottom part of the enumeration tree.

A first step in this direction was taken in [52], where it was shown that with a sufficient amount of preprocessing and space, one can achieve better amortized time complexities for batch-CVP than when solving just one instance. The large memory requirement (at least $2^{d/2+o(d)}$ memory is required to improve upon direct CVP approaches) as well as the large number of CVP instances required to get a lower amortized complexity made this approach impractical to date.

1.2   Contributions: Approximate Voronoi Cells

In this paper we revisit the preprocessing approach to CVP of [52], as well as the recent trend of speeding up these algorithms using nearest neighbor searching, and we show how to obtain significantly improved time and space complexities. These results can be viewed as a first step towards a practical, heuristic alternative to the Voronoi cell approach of Micciancio–Voulgaris [66], where instead of constructing the exact Voronoi cell, the preprocessing computes an approximation of it, requiring less time and space to compute and store.

First, our preprocessing step consists of computing a list L of most lattice vectors below a given norm.[1] This preprocessing can be done using either enumeration or sieving. The preprocessed data can best be understood as representing an *approximate* Voronoi cell $\mathcal{V}_L$ of the lattice, where the size of L determines how well $\mathcal{V}_L$ approximates the true Voronoi cell $\mathcal{V}$ of the lattice; see Fig. 1 for an example. Using this approximate Voronoi cell, we then attempt to solve CVP instances by applying the iterative slicing procedure of Sommer–Feder–Shalvi [73], with nearest neighbor optimizations to reduce the search costs [12,18].

---

[1] Heuristically, finding a large fraction of all lattice vectors below a given norm will suffice – one does not necessarily need to run a deterministic preprocessing algorithm to ensure all short lattice vectors are found.

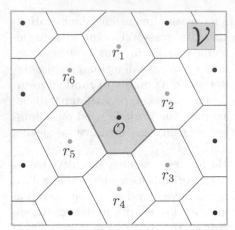 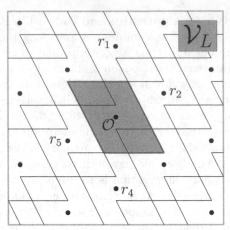

(a) A tiling of $\mathbb{R}^2$ with exact Voronoi cells $\mathcal{V}$ of a lattice $\mathcal{L}$ (red/black points), generated by the set $\mathcal{R} = \{r_1, \dots, r_6\}$ of all *relevant vectors* of $\mathcal{L}$. Here $\mathrm{vol}(\mathcal{V}) = \det(\mathcal{L})$.

(b) An overlapping tiling of $\mathbb{R}^2$ with approximate Voronoi cells $\mathcal{V}_L$ of the same lattice $\mathcal{L}$, generated by a subset of the relevant vectors, $L = \{r_1, r_2, r_4, r_5\} \subset \mathcal{R}$.

Fig. 1. Exact and approximate Voronoi cells of the same two-dimensional lattice $\mathcal{L}$. For the **exact** Voronoi cell $\mathcal{V}$ (Fig. 1a), the cells around the lattice points form a tiling of $\mathbb{R}^2$, covering each point in space exactly once. Given that a point t lies in the Voronoi cell around $s \in \mathcal{L}$, we know that s is the closest lattice point to t. For the **approximate** Voronoi cell $\mathcal{V}_L$ (Fig. 1b), the cells around the lattice points overlap, and cover a non-empty fraction of the space by multiple cells. Given that a vector t lies in an approximate Voronoi cell around a lattice point s, we further do not have the definite guarantee that s is the closest lattice point to t. (Color figure online)

The main difference in our work over [52] lies in generalizing how similar $\mathcal{V}_L$ (generated by the list L) needs to be to $\mathcal{V}$. We distinguish two cases below. As sketched in Fig. 1, a worse approximation leads to a larger approximate Voronoi cell, so $\mathrm{vol}(\mathcal{V}_L) \geq \mathrm{vol}(\mathcal{V})$ with equality iff $\mathcal{V} = \mathcal{V}_L$.

Good approximations: If $\mathcal{V}_L$ is a good approximation of $\mathcal{V}$ (i.e., $\mathrm{vol}(\mathcal{V}_L) \approx \mathrm{vol}(\mathcal{V})$), then with high probability over the randomness of the target vectors, the iterative slicer returns the closest lattice vector to random targets. To guarantee $\mathrm{vol}(\mathcal{V}_L) \approx \mathrm{vol}(\mathcal{V})$ we need $|L| \geq 2^{d/2+o(d)}$, where additional memory can be used to speed up the nearest neighbor part of the iterative slicer. The resulting query complexities are sketched in red in Fig. 2.

Arbitrary approximations: If the preprocessed list contains fewer than $2^{d/2}$ vectors, then $\mathrm{vol}(\mathcal{V}_L) \gg \mathrm{vol}(\mathcal{V})$ and with overwhelming probability the iterative slicer will not return the closest lattice point to a random target vector. However, similar to [40], the running time of this method is decreased by a much more significant factor than the success probability. So if we are able to *rerandomize* the problem instance and try several times, we may still be faster (and more memory-efficient) than when using a larger list L.

1.3   Contributions: Randomized Slicing

To actually find solutions to CVP instances with a "bad" approximation $\mathcal{V}_L$ to the real Voronoi cell $\mathcal{V}$, we need to be able to suitably rerandomize the iterative slicing procedure, so that if the success probability in a single run of the slicer is small, we can repeat the method several times for a high success probability. To do this, we will run the iterative slicer on randomly perturbed vectors $t' \sim D_{t+\mathcal{L},s}$, sampled from a discrete Gaussian over the coset $t + \mathcal{L}$. Here the standard deviation s needs to be sufficiently large to make sampling from $D_{t+\mathcal{L},s}$ efficient and the results of the slicer to be almost independent, and s needs to be sufficiently small to guarantee that the slicer will terminate in a limited number of steps. Algorithm 1 explicitly describes this procedure, given as input an approximate Voronoi cell $\mathcal{V}_L$ (i.e., a list $L \subset \mathcal{L}$ of short lattice vectors defining the facets of this approximate Voronoi cell).

Algorithm 1. The randomized heuristic slicer for finding closest vectors

---

Require: A list $L \subset \mathcal{L}$ and a target $t \in \mathbb{R}^d$
Ensure: The algorithm outputs a closest lattice vector $s \in \mathcal{L}$ to t
   1: $s \leftarrow 0$ ▷ Initial guess s for closest vector to t
   2: **repeat**
   3:     Sample $t' \sim D_{t+\mathcal{L},s}$ ▷ Randomly shift t by a vector $v \in \mathcal{L}$
   4:     **for each** $r \in L$ **do**
   5:         **if** $\|t' - r\| < \|t'\|$ **then**   ▷ New shorter vector $t' \in t + \mathcal{L}$
   6:             Replace $t' \leftarrow t' - r$ and restart the **for**-loop
   7:     **if** $\|t'\| < \|t - s\|$ **then**
   8:         $s \leftarrow t - t'$ ▷ New lattice vector s closer to t
   9: **until** s is a closest lattice vector to t
  10: **return** s

Even though this algorithm requires sampling many vectors from the coset $t + \mathcal{L}$ and running the iterative slicer on all of these, the overall time complexity of this procedure will still be lower, since the iterative slicer needs less time to complete when the input list L is shorter. To estimate the number of iterations necessary to guarantee that the algorithm returns the actual closest vector, we make the following assumption, stating that the probability that the iterative slicer terminates with a vector $t' \in (t + \mathcal{L}) \cap \mathcal{V}$, given that it must terminate to some vector $t' \in (t+\mathcal{L}) \cap \mathcal{V}_L$, is proportional to the ratio of the volumes of these (approximate) Voronoi cells $\mathcal{V}$ and $\mathcal{V}_L$.

Heuristic assumption 1 (Randomized slicing) *For $L \subset \mathcal{L}$ and large s,*

$$\Pr_{t' \sim D_{t+\mathcal{L},s}} \left[\mathrm{Slice}_L(t') \in \mathcal{V} \right] \approx \frac{\mathrm{vol}(\mathcal{V})}{\mathrm{vol}(\mathcal{V}_L)}. \tag{1}$$

This is a new and critical assumption to guarantee that the claimed asymptotic complexities are correct, and we will therefore come back to this assumption later on, to show that experiments indeed suggest this assumption is justified.

1.4   Contributions: Improved CVPP Complexities

For the exact closest vector problem with preprocessing, our improved complexities over [52] mainly come from the aforementioned randomizations. To illustrate this with a simple example, suppose we run an optimized (GaussSieve-based [65]) LDSieve [18], ultimately resulting in a list of $(4/3)^{d/2+o(d)}$ of the shortest vectors in the lattice, indexed in a nearest neighbor data structure of size $(3/2)^{d/2+o(d)}$. Asymptotically, using this list as our approximate Voronoi cell, the iterative slicer succeeds with probability $p = (13/16)^{d/2+o(d)}$ (as shown in the analysis later on), while processing a query with this data structure takes time $(9/8)^{d/2+o(d)}$. By repeating a query $1/p$ times with rerandomizations of the same CVP instance, we obtain the following heuristic complexities for CVPP.

Proposition 1 (Standard sieve preprocessing). *Using the output of the LDSieve [18] as the preprocessed list and encompassing data structure, we can heuristically solve CVPP with the following query space and time complexities:*

$$S = (3/2)^{d/2+o(d)} \approx 2^{0.292d+o(d)}, \qquad T = (18/13)^{d/2+o(d)} \approx 2^{0.235d+o(d)}.$$

This point (S, T) *is highlighted in light blue in Fig. 2.*

If we use a more general analysis of the approximate Voronoi cell approach, varying over both the nearest neighbor parameters and the size of the preprocessed list, we can obtain even better query complexities. For a memory complexity of $(3/2)^{d/2+o(d)} \approx 2^{0.292d+o(d)}$, we can achieve a query time complexity of approximately $2^{0.220d+o(d)}$ by using a shorter list of lattice vectors, and a more memory-intensive parameter setting for the nearest neighbor data structure. The following main result summarizes all the asymptotic time–space trade-offs we can obtain for heuristically solving CVPP in the average case.

Theorem 1 (Optimized CVPP complexities). *Let* $\alpha \in (1.03396, \sqrt{2})$ *and* $u \in (\sqrt{\frac{\alpha^2-1}{\alpha^2}}, \sqrt{\frac{\alpha^2}{\alpha^2-1}})$. *With approximate Voronoi cells we can heuristically solve CVPP with preprocessing space and time* S_1 *and* T_1, *and query space and time* S_2 *and* T_2, *where:*

$$S_1 = \max\left\{S_2, \left(\frac{4}{3}\right)^{d/2+o(d)}\right\}, \qquad T_1 = \max\left\{S_2, \left(\frac{3}{2}\right)^{d/2+o(d)}\right\}, \qquad (2)$$

$$S_2 = \left(\frac{\alpha}{\alpha - (\alpha^2-1)(\alpha u^2 - 2u\sqrt{\alpha^2-1}+\alpha)}\right)^{d/2+o(d)}, \qquad (3)$$

$$T_2 = \left(\frac{16\alpha^4(\alpha^2-1)}{-9\alpha^8+64\alpha^6-104\alpha^4+64\alpha^2-16} \cdot \frac{\alpha+u\sqrt{\alpha^2-1}}{-\alpha^3+\alpha^2u\sqrt{\alpha^2-1}+2\alpha}\right)^{d/2+o(d)}. \qquad (4)$$

The best query complexities (S_2, T_2) *together form the blue curve in Fig. 2.*

Compared to [52], we obtain trade-offs for much lower memory complexities, and we improve upon both the best CVPP complexities of [52] and the best

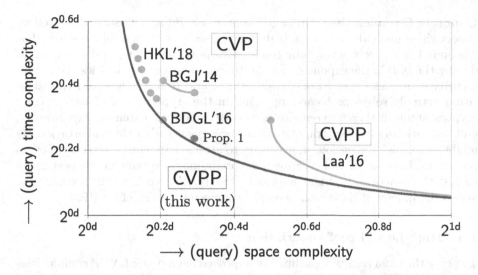

Fig. 2. Query complexities for finding closest vectors, directly (CVP) and with preprocessing (CVPP). The leftmost red points/curve show the best asymptotic SVP/CVP complexities of Becker–Gama–Joux [19], Becker–Ducas–Gama–Laarhoven [18], and Herold–Kirshanova–Laarhoven [44]. The rightmost red point and curve are the previous best CVPP complexities of [52]. The blue curve shows our new CVPP complexities. (Color figure online)

SVP/CVP complexities of [18,44].[2] Observe that our trade-off passes *below* all the best CVP results, i.e., we can always solve an exponentially large batch of $2^{\varepsilon d}$ CVP instances for small $\varepsilon > 0$ in the same amount of time as the current best complexities for solving just one instance, for any memory bound.

Due to the condition that $\alpha > 1.0339\dots$ (which follows from the fact that the denominator in T_2 needs to remain positive), the blue curve in Fig. 2 terminates on the left side at a minimum query space complexity of $1.03396^{d+o(d)} \approx 2^{0.0482d+o(d)}$. One might wonder whether we can obtain a continuous trade-off between the query time and space complexities reaching all the way to $2^{o(d)}$ memory and $2^{\omega(d)}$ query time. The lower bound on α might be a consequence of our analysis, and perhaps a different approach would show this algorithm solves CVPP in $2^{O(d)}$ time even with less memory.

As for the other end of the blue curve, as the available space increases, one can achieve an amortized time complexity for CVP of $2^{\varepsilon d+o(d)}$ at the cost of $(1/\varepsilon)^{O(d)}$ preprocessed space for arbitrary $\varepsilon > 0$. For large query space complexities, i.e., when a lot of memory and preprocessing power is available for speeding up the queries, the blue and red curve converge, and the best parameter choice is to set $\alpha \approx \sqrt{2}$ such that $\mathcal{V}_L \approx \mathcal{V}$, as explained in Sect. 1.2.

---

[2] As detailed in [52], by modifying sieve algorithms for SVP, one can also solve CVP with essentially equivalent heuristic time and space complexities as for SVP.

Concrete Complexities. Although Theorem 1 and Fig. 2 illustrate how well we expect these methods to scale in high dimensions d, we would like to stress that Theorem 1 is a purely asymptotic result, with potentially large order terms hidden by the $o(d)$ in the exponents for the time and space complexities. To obtain security estimates for real-world applications, and to assess how fast this algorithm actually solves problems appearing in the cryptanalysis of lattice-based cryptosystems, it therefore remains necessary to perform extensive experiments, and to cautiously try to extrapolate from these results what the real attack costs might be for high dimensions d, necessary to attack actual instantiations of cryptosystems. Later on we will describe some preliminary experiments we performed to test the practicality of this approach, but further work is still necessary to assess the impact of these results on the concrete hardness of CVPP.

1.5   High-Level Proof Description

To prove the main results regarding the improved asymptotic CVPP complexities compared to [52], we first prove that under certain natural heuristic assumptions, we obtain the following upper bound on the volume of approximate Voronoi cells generated by the $\alpha^{d+o(d)}$ shortest vectors of a lattice. The preprocessing will consist of exactly this: generate the $\alpha^{d+o(d)}$ shortest vectors in the lattice, and store them in a nearest neighbor data structure that allows for fast look-ups of nearby points in space.

Lemma 1 (Relative volume of approximate Voronoi cells). *Let $L \subset \mathcal{L}$ consist of the $\alpha^{d+o(d)}$ shortest vectors of a lattice $\mathcal{L}$, with $\alpha \in (1.03396, \sqrt{2})$. Then heuristically,*

$$\frac{\mathrm{vol}(\mathcal{V}_L)}{\mathrm{vol}(\mathcal{V})} \leq \left(\frac{16\alpha^4 \left(\alpha^2 - 1 \right)}{-9\alpha^8 + 64\alpha^6 - 104\alpha^4 + 64\alpha^2 - 16} \right)^{d/2+o(d)}. \tag{5}$$

Using this lemma and the heuristic assumption stated previously, relating the success probability of the slicer to the volume of the approximate Voronoi cell, this immediately gives us a (heuristic) lower bound on the success probability p_α of the randomized slicing procedure, given as input a preprocessed list of the $\alpha^{d+o(d)}$ shortest vectors in the lattice. Then, similar to [52], the complexity analysis is a matter of combining the costs for the preprocessing phase, the costs of the nearest neighbor data structure, and the cost of the query phase, where now we need to repeat the randomized slicing of the order $1/p_\alpha$ times – the difference in the formulas for the complexities compared to [52] comes exactly from this additional factor $1/p_\alpha \approx \mathrm{vol}(\mathcal{V}_L)/\mathrm{vol}(\mathcal{V})$.

To prove the above lemma regarding the volume of approximate Voronoi cells, we will prove the following statements. First, we show that if the list L contains the $\alpha^{d+o(d)}$ shortest vectors of a random lattice $\mathcal{L}$, then on input a target vector t, we heuristically expect the slicer to terminate on a reduced vector $t' \in t + \mathcal{L}$ of norm at most $\|t'\| \leq \beta \cdot \lambda_1(\mathcal{L})$, where β is determined by the parameter α. The relation between α and β can be succinctly described by the following relation

$$\beta = \alpha^2/\sqrt{4\alpha^2 - 4}. \tag{6}$$

More precisely, we show that as long as $\|t'\| \gg \beta \cdot \lambda_1(\mathcal{L})$, then with high probability we expect to be able to combine t' with vectors in L to form a shorter vector $t'' \in t + \mathcal{L}$ with $\|t''\| < \|t'\|$. On the other hand, if we have a vector $t' \in t + \mathcal{L}$ of norm less than $\beta \cdot \lambda_1(\mathcal{L})$, then we only expect to be able to combine t' with a vector in L to form a shorter vector with exponentially small probability $2^{-\Theta(d)}$. In other words, reducing to a vector of norm $\beta \cdot \lambda_1(\mathcal{L})$ can be done almost "effortlessly", while after that even making small progress in reducing the length of t' comes at an exponential loss in the success probability.

Good Approximations. Next, from the above relation between the size of the input list, $|L|$ (or α), and the reduced norm of the shifted target vector, $\|t'\|$ (or β), the previous result of [52] immediately follows – to achieve $t' \in \mathcal{V}$ we heuristically need $\beta = 1 + o(1)$. This implies that $\alpha = \sqrt{2}$ is the minimal parameter that guarantees we will be able to effortlessly reduce to the exact Voronoi cell, and so L must contain the $\alpha^{d+o(d)} = 2^{d/2+o(d)}$ shortest vectors in the lattice. In that case the success probability is constant, and the costs of the query phase are determined by a single reduction of t with the iterative slicer.

Arbitrary Approximations. However, even if $\alpha < \sqrt{2}$ is smaller, and the corresponding β is therefore larger than 1, the slicer might still succeed with (exponentially) small probability. To analyze the success probability, note that from the Gaussian heuristic we may assume that the closest vector to our target t lies uniformly at random in a ball (or sphere) of radius $\lambda_1(\mathcal{L})$ around t. Then, also for the reduced vector t' of norm at most $\beta \cdot \lambda_1(\mathcal{L})$, the closest lattice vector lies in a ball of radius $\lambda_1(\mathcal{L})$ around it. Since our list L contains all vectors of norm less than $\alpha \cdot \lambda_1(\mathcal{L})$, we will clearly find the closest lattice vector in the list L if the closest lattice vector lies in the intersection of two balls of radii $\lambda_1(\mathcal{L})$ (resp. $\alpha \cdot \lambda_1(\mathcal{L})$) around t' (resp. $\mathbf{0}$). Estimating the volume of this intersection of balls, relative to the volume of the ball of radius $\lambda_1(\mathcal{L})$ around t', then gives us a lower bound on the success probability of the slicer, and a heuristic upper bound on the volume of the corresponding approximate Voronoi cell. This analysis ultimately leads to the aforementioned lemma.

Tightness of the Proof. Note that the above proof technique only gives us a *lower bound* on the success probability, and an *upper bound* on the volume of the approximate Voronoi cell: when the target vector has been reduced to a vector of norm at most $\beta \cdot \lambda_1(\mathcal{L})$, we bound the success probability of the slicer by the probability that the slicer now terminates successfully in a *single* iteration. Since the algorithm might also succeed in more than one additional iteration, the actual success probability may be higher. A tighter analysis, perhaps showing that the given heuristic bound can be improved upon, is left for future work.

1.6   Intermezzo: Another Few Dimensions for Free

Recently, Ducas [35] showed that in practice, one can effectively use the additional vectors found by lattice sieving to solve a few extra dimensions of SVP "for free". More precisely, by running a lattice sieve in a base dimension d, one can solve SVP in dimension $d' = d + \Theta(d/\log d)$ at little additional cost. This is done by taking all vectors returned by a d-dimensional lattice sieve, and running Babai's nearest plane algorithm [16] on all these vectors in the d'-dimensional lattice to find short vectors in the full lattice. If d' is close enough to d, one of these vectors will then be "rounded" to a shortest vector of the full lattice.

On a high level, Ducas' approach can be viewed as a sieving/enumeration hybrid, where the *top* part of enumeration is replaced with sieving, and the bottom part is done regularly as in enumeration, which is essentially equivalent to doing Babai rounding [16]. The approach of using a CVPP-solver inside enumeration is in a sense dual to Ducas' idea, as here the *bottom* part of the enumeration tree is replaced with a (sieving-like) CVPP routine. Since our CVPP complexities are strictly better than the best SVP/CVP complexities, we can also gain up to $\Theta(d/\log d)$ dimensions for free as follows:

1. First, we initialize an enumeration tree in the full lattice $\mathcal{L}$ of dimension $d' = d + k$, and we process the top $k = \varepsilon \cdot d/\log d$ levels as usual in enumeration. This will result in $2^{\Theta(k \log k)} = 2^{\Theta(d)}$ target vectors at level k, and this requires a similar time complexity of $2^{\Theta(d)}$ to generate all these target vectors.
2. Then, we run the CVPP preprocessing on the d-dimensional sublattice of $\mathcal{L}$ corresponding to the bottom part of the enumeration tree. This may for instance take time $2^{0.292d+o(d)}$ and space $2^{0.208d+o(d)}$ using the sieve of [18].
3. Finally, we take the batch of $2^{\Theta(d)}$ target vectors at level k in the enumeration tree, and we solve CVP for each of them with our approximate Voronoi cell and randomized slicing algorithm, with query time $2^{0.220d+o(d)}$ each.

By setting $k = \varepsilon \cdot d/\log d$ as above with small, constant $\varepsilon > 0$, the costs for solving SVP or CVP in dimension d' are asymptotically dominated by the costs of the preprocessing step, which is as costly as solving SVP or CVP in dimension d. So similar to [35], asymptotically we also get $\Theta(d/\log d)$ dimensions "for free". However, unlike for Ducas' idea, in practice the dimensions are likely not quite as free here, as there is more overhead for doing the CVPP-version of sieving than for Ducas' additional batch of Babai nearest plane calls.

Even More Dimensions for Free. A natural question one might ask now is: can both ideas be combined to get even more dimensions "for free"? At first sight, this seems hard to accomplish, as Ducas' idea speeds up SVP rather than CVPP. Furthermore, note that when solving SVP without Ducas' trick, one gets $2^{0.208d+o(d)}$ short lattice vectors when only one shortest vector is needed, and so in a sense one might "naturally" hope to gain something by going for only one short output vector. Here the analysis of the iterative slicer is already based on the fact that ultimately, we hope to reduce a single target vector to its closest neighbor in the lattice. There might be a way of combining both ideas to get even more dimensions for free, but for now this is left as an open problem.

1.7   Contributions: Experimental Results

Besides the theoretical contributions mentioned above, with improved heuristic time and space complexities compared to [52], for the first time we also implemented a (sieving-based) CVPP solver using approximate Voronoi cells. For the preprocessing we used a slight modification of a lattice sieve, returning more vectors than a standard sieve, allowing us to vary the list size in our experiments. Our implementations serve two purposes: validating the additional heuristic assumption we make, and to see how well the algorithm performs.

Validation of the Randomization Assumption. To obtain the aforementioned improved asymptotic complexities for solving CVPP, we required a new heuristic assumption, stating that if the iterative slicer succeeds with some probability p on a CVP instance t, then we can repeat it $1/p$ times with perturbations $t' \sim D_{t+\mathcal{L},s}$ to achieve a high success probability for the same target t. To verify this assumption, we implemented our method and tested it on lattices of dimension 50 with a range of randomly chosen targets to see whether, if the probability of success is small, repeating the method m times will increase the success rate by a factor m. Figure 3 shows performance metrics for various numbers of repetitions and for varying list sizes. In particular, Fig. 3a illustrates the increased success probability as the number of repetitions increases, and Fig. 3c shows that the normalized success probability per trial[3] seems independent of the number of repetitions. Therefore, the "expected time" metric as illustrated in Fig. 3b appears to be independent of the number of trials.

Experimental Performance. Unlike the success probabilities, the time complexity might vary a lot depending on the underlying nearest neighbor data structure. For our experiments we used hyperplane LSH [29] as also used in the HashSieve [50,58], as it is easy to implement, has few parameters to set, and performs better in low dimensions ($d = 50$) than the LDSieve [18,59].

To put the complexities of Fig. 3b into perspective, let us compare the normalized time complexities for CVPP with the complexities of sieving for SVP, which by [52] are comparable to the costs for CVP. First, we note that the HashSieve algorithm solves SVP in approximately 4 s on the same machine. This means that in dimension 50, the expected time complexity for CVPP with the HashSieve (roughly 2 ms) is approximately 2000 times smaller than the time for solving SVP. To explain this gap, observe that the list size for solving SVP is approximately 4000, and so the HashSieve algorithm needs to perform in the order of 4000 reductions of newly sampled vectors with a list of size 4000. For solving CVPP, we only need to reduce 1 target vector, with a slightly larger list of 10 000 to 15 000 vectors. So we save a factor 4000 on the number of reductions, but the searches are more expensive, leading to a speed-up of less than a factor 4000.

---

[3] As the success prob. q for m trials scales as $q = 1-(1-p)^m$ if each trial independently has success prob. p, we computed the success prob. per trial as $p = 1 - (1 - q)^{1/m}$.

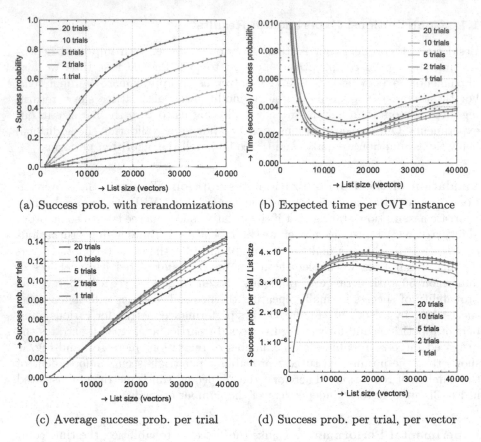

(a) Success prob. with rerandomizations

(b) Expected time per CVP instance

(c) Average success prob. per trial

(d) Success prob. per trial, per vector

Fig. 3. Experimental results for solving CVPP with randomized slicing in dimension 50. Each data point corresponds to 10 000 random target vectors for those parameters.

Predictions and Extrapolations. For solving SVP or CVP, the Hash-Sieve [50] reports time complexities in dimension d of $2^{0.45d-19}$ s, corresponding to 11 s in dimension 50, i.e., a factor 3 slower than here. This is based on doing $n \approx 2^{0.21d}$ reductions of vectors with the list. If doing only one of these searches takes a factor $2^{0.21d}$ less time, and we take into account that for SVP the time complexity is now a factor 3 less than in [50], then we obtain an estimated complexity for CVPP in dimension d of $2^{0.24d-19}/3$, which for $d = 50$ corresponds to approximately 2.6 ms. A rough extrapolation would then lead to a time complexity in dimension 100 of only 11 s. This however seems to be rather optimistic – preliminary experiments in dimensions 60 and 70 suggest that the overhead of using a lot of memory may be rather high here, as the list size is usually even larger than for standard sieving.

1.8   Contributions: Asymptotics for Variants of CVPP

For easier variants of CVP, such as when the target lies closer to the lattice than expected or an approximate solution to CVP suffices as a solution, we obtain considerable gains in both the time and space complexities when using preprocessing. We explicitly consider two variants of CVPP below.

BDDP$_\delta$. For bounded distance decoding with preprocessing (BDDP), we are given a target vector t and a guarantee that t lies within distance $\delta \cdot \lambda_1(\mathcal{L})$ to the nearest lattice vector, for some parameter $\delta > 0$. By the Gaussian heuristic, setting $\delta = 1$ makes this problem as hard as general CVPP without a distance guarantee, while for small $\delta \to 0$ polynomial-time algorithms exist [16].

By adjusting the analysis leading up to Theorem 1 for BDDP, we obtain the same result as Theorem 1 with two modifications: T_2 is replaced by $T_2^{(\delta)}$ below, and the range of admissable values α changes to (α_0, α_1), with α_0 the smallest root larger than 1 of the denominator of the left-most term in $T_2^{(\delta)}$, and α_1 the smallest value larger than 1 such that the left-most term in $T_2^{(\delta)}$ equals 1. The resulting optimized trade-offs for various $\delta \in (0,1)$ are plotted in Fig. 4a.

$$T_2^{(\delta)} = \left(\frac{16\alpha^4 \left(\alpha^2 - 1 \right) \delta^2}{-9\alpha^8 + 8\alpha^6(3+5\delta^2) - 8\alpha^4(2+9\delta^2+2\delta^4) + 32\alpha^2(\delta^2+\delta^4) - 16\delta^4} \cdot [\dots] \right)^{d/2+o(d)}. \quad (7)$$

Note that in the limit of $\delta \to 0$, our algorithm tries to reduce a target close to the lattice to the origin. This is similar to reducing a vector to the **0**-vector in the GaussSieve [65], and even with a long list of all short lattice vectors this does not occur with probability 1. Here also the limiting curve in Fig. 4a shows that for $\delta \to 0$ with suitable parameterization we can do better than just with sieving, but we do not get polynomial time and space complexities.

CVPP$_\kappa$. For the approximate version of CVPP, a lattice vector v qualifies as a solution for t if it lies at most a factor κ further from the real distance of t from the lattice, for some $\kappa \geq 1$. Heuristically, this is essentially equivalent to looking for any lattice vector within radius $\kappa \cdot \lambda_1(\mathcal{L})$ of the target, and similar to BDDP the resulting trade-offs can be summarized by Theorem 1 where T_2 is replaced by $T_2^{(\kappa)}$ below, and the range of admissable values α again changes to (α_0, α_1) as before.

$$T_2^{(\kappa)} = \left(\frac{16\alpha^4 \left(\alpha^2 - 1 \right)}{-9\alpha^8 + 8\alpha^6(3+5\kappa^2) - 8\alpha^4(2+9\kappa^2+2\kappa^4) + 32\alpha^2(\kappa^2+\kappa^4) - 16\kappa^4} \cdot [\dots] \right)^{d/2+o(d)}. \quad (8)$$

For increasing approximation factors $\kappa \to \infty$, our algorithm tries to reduce a target vector to vector of norm less than $\kappa \cdot \lambda_1(\mathcal{L})$. For large κ this is increasingly easy to achieve, and as $\kappa \to \infty$, both the query time and space complexities in our analysis converge to zero as expected. Figure 4b highlights this asymptote, and illustrates the other trade-offs through some examples for small $\kappa > 1$.

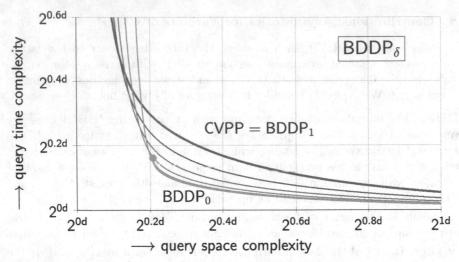

(a) Heuristic complexities for BDDP$_\delta$ for different values $\delta \in \{0, 0.2, \ldots, 0.8, 1\}$. Smaller δ correspond to easier problems but also to a larger lower bound α_0 on α. The trade-off for $\delta \to 0$ is indicated by the thick orange line.

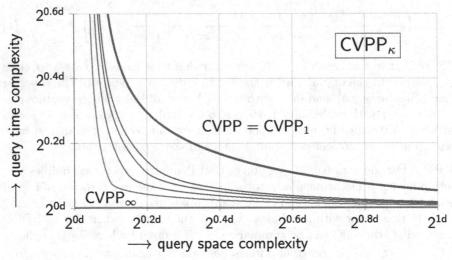

(b) Heuristic query complexities for CVPP$_\kappa$ for different approximation factors $\kappa \in \{\sqrt{4/3}, 1.2, 1.3, 1.5, \infty\}$. The thick green line shows the limit as $\kappa \to \infty$.

Fig. 4. Asymptotics for solving variants of CVP(P) with approximate Voronoi cells: (a) BDDP$_\delta$ and (b) CVPP$_\kappa$. Note that the (tail of the) curve for CVPP$_{\sqrt{4/3}}$ overlaps with the curve for BDDP$_0$.

1.9 Open Problems

Combination with Other Techniques. The focus of this work was on the asymptotic complexities we can achieve for high dimensions d, and therefore we focused only on including techniques from the literature that lead to the best asymptotics. In practice however, there may be various other techniques that can help speed up these methods in moderate dimensions. This for instance includes Ducas' dimensions for free [35], progressive sieving [35,54], the recent sieving-BKZ hybrid [7], and faster NNS techniques [7,11]. Incorporating such techniques will likely affect the experimental performance as well, and future work may show how well the proposed techniques truly perform in practice when all the state-of-the-art techniques are combined into one.

Faster Enumeration with Approximate Voronoi Cells. As explained above, one potential application of our CVPP algorithm is as a subroutine within enumeration, to speed up the searches in the bottom part of the tree. Such an algorithm can be viewed as a trade-off between enumeration and sieving, where the level at which we insert the CVPP oracle determines whether we are closer to enumeration or to sieving. An open question remains whether this would lead to faster algorithms in practice, or if the preprocessing/query costs are too high. Note that depending on at which level of the tree the CVPP oracle is inserted, and on the amount of pruning in enumeration, the hardness of the CVP instances at these levels also changes. Optimizing all parameters involved in such a combination appears to be a complex task, and is left for future work.

Sieving in the Dual Lattice. For the application of CVPP within enumeration, observe that a decisional CVPP oracle, deciding whether a vector lies close to the lattice or not, may actually be sufficient; most branches of the enumeration tree will not lead to a solution, and therefore in most cases running an accurate decision-CVPP oracle is enough to determine that this subtree is not the right subtree. For those few subtrees that potentially do contain a solution, one could then run a full CVP(P) algorithm at a slightly higher cost. Improving the complexities for the decision-version of CVPP may therefore be an interesting future direction, and perhaps one approach could be to combine this with ideas from [5], by running a lattice sieve on the dual lattice to find many short vectors in the dual lattice, which can then be used to check if a target vector lies close to the primal lattice or not.

Quantum Complexities. As one of the strengths of lattice-based cryptography is its conjectured resistance to quantum attacks [22], it is important to study the potential impact of quantum improvements to SVP and CVP algorithms, so that the parameters can be chosen to be secure in a post-quantum world [15,55]. For lattice sieving for solving SVP, the time complexity exponent potentially decreases by approximately 25% [55], and for CVPP we expect the exponents may decrease by approximately 25% as well. Studying the exact quantum asymptotics of solving CVPP with approximate Voronoi cells is left for future work.

1.10 Outline

Due to space restrictions, the remainder of the paper, including full details on all claims, is given in the appendix.[4] Below we briefly outline the contents of these appendices for the interested reader.

Appendix A – Preliminaries
This section describes preliminary results and notation for the technical contents, formally states the main hard problems discussed in the paper, formalizes the heuristic assumptions made throughout the paper, and describes existing results on nearest neighbor searching, lattice sieving algorithms, Voronoi cells, and Voronoi cell algorithms.

Appendix B – Approximate Voronoi cells
In Appendix B we formalize the CVPP approach considered in this paper in terms of our approximate Voronoi cell framework with randomized slicing, and we derive our main results regarding improved asymptotic complexities for exact CVPP. Approximate Voronoi cells are formally introduced, the main results are stated and proved in terms of this framework, and all corresponding algorithms are given in pseudocode.

Appendix C – Experimental results
Appendix C describes the experiments we performed with these methods in more detail, both to verify the (additional) heuristic assumptions we made for this paper, and to assess the practicality of our CVPP algorithm. Here we also briefly compare our results to various published complexities for SVP or CVP(P), to put these numbers into context.

Appendix D – Asymptotics for variants of CVPP
The last appendix finally discusses asymptotic results for variants of CVPP, namely approximate CVPP and BDDP. This section contains a more formal statement of the results given in Sect. 1.8, and explains how the analysis changes compared to the analysis for exact CVPP, and how this leads to improved complexities for these slightly easier variants of (exact) CVPP.

Acknowledgments. The authors are indebted to Léo Ducas, whose ideas and suggestions on this topic motivated work on this paper. The authors are further grateful to the reviewers, whose thorough study of the contents (with one review even exceeding the page limit for the conference) significantly helped improve the contents of the paper, as well as improve the presentation of the results. Emmanouil Doulgerakis is supported by the NWO under grant 628.001.028 (FASOR). At the time of writing a preliminary version of this paper, Thijs Laarhoven was supported by the SNSF ERC Transfer Grant CRETP2-166734 FELICITY. At the time of publishing, Thijs Laarhoven is supported by a Veni Innovational Research Grant from NWO under project number 016.Veni.192.005.

---

[4] The full version of this paper including all appendices will be made available online at https://eprint.iacr.org/2016/888.

References

1. SVP challenge (2018). http://latticechallenge.org/svp-challenge/
2. Aggarwal, D., Dadush, D., Regev, O., Stephens-Davidowitz, N.: Solving the shortest vector problem in 2^n time via discrete Gaussian sampling. In: STOC, pp. 733–742 (2015)
3. Aggarwal, D., Dadush, D., Stephens-Davidowitz, N.: Solving the closest vector problem in 2^n time - the discrete Gaussian strikes again! In: FOCS, pp. 563–582 (2015)
4. Agrell, E., Eriksson, T., Vardy, A., Zeger, K.: Closest point search in lattices. IEEE Transact. Inf. Theor. **48**(8), 2201–2214 (2002)
5. Aharonov, D., Regev, O.: Lattice problems in NP ∩ coNP. In: FOCS, pp. 362–371 (2004)
6. Ajtai, M., Kumar, R., Sivakumar, D.: A sieve algorithm for the shortest lattice vector problem. In: STOC, pp. 601–610 (2001)
7. Albrecht, M., Ducas, L., Herold, G., Kirshanova, E., Postlethwaite, E., Stevens, M.: The general sieve kernel and new records in lattice reduction. Preprint, 2018
8. Alekhnovich, M., Khot, S., Kindler, G., Vishnoi, N.: Hardness of approximating the closest vector problem with pre-processing. In: FOCS, pp. 216–225 (2005)
9. Alkim, E., Ducas, L., Pöppelmann, T., Schwabe, P.: Post-quantum key exchange - a new hope. In: USENIX Security Symposium, pp. 327–343 (2016)
10. Andoni, A., Indyk, P.: Near-optimal hashing algorithms for approximate nearest neighbor in high dimensions. In: FOCS, pp. 459–468 (2006)
11. Andoni, A., Indyk, P., Laarhoven, T., Razenshteyn, I., Schmidt, L.: Practical and optimal LSH for angular distance. In: NIPS, pp. 1225–1233 (2015)
12. Andoni, A., Laarhoven, T., Razenshteyn, I., Waingarten, E.: Optimal hashing-based time-space trade-offs for approximate near neighbors. In: SODA, pp. 47–66 (2017)
13. Andoni, A., Razenshteyn, I.: Optimal data-dependent hashing for approximate near neighbors. In: STOC, pp. 793–801 (2015)
14. Aono, Y., Nguyen, P.Q.: Random sampling revisited: lattice enumeration with discrete pruning. In: Coron, J.-S., Nielsen, J.B. (eds.) EUROCRYPT 2017. LNCS, vol. 10211, pp. 65–102. Springer, Cham (2017). https://doi.org/10.1007/978-3-319-56614-6_3
15. Aono, Y., Nguyen, P.Q., Shen, Y.: Quantum lattice enumeration and tweaking discrete pruning. In: Peyrin, T., Galbraith, S. (eds.) ASIACRYPT 2018. LNCS, vol. 11272, pp. 405–434. Springer, Cham (2018). https://doi.org/10.1007/978-3-030-03326-2_14
16. Babai, L.: On Lovasz lattice reduction and the nearest lattice point problem. Combinatorica **6**(1), 1–13 (1986)
17. Bai, S., Laarhoven, T., Stehlé, D.: Tuple lattice sieving. In: ANTS, pp. 146–162 (2016)
18. Becker, A., Ducas, L., Gama, N., Laarhoven, T.: New directions in nearest neighbor searching with applications to lattice sieving. In: SODA, pp. 10–24 (2016)
19. Becker, A., Gama, N., Joux, A.: A sieve algorithm based on overlattices. In: ANTS, pp. 49–70 (2014)
20. Becker, A., Gama, N., Joux, A.: Speeding-up lattice sieving without increasing the memory, using sub-quadratic nearest neighbor search. Cryptology ePrint Archive, Report 2015/522, pp. 1–14 (2015)

21. Becker, A., Laarhoven, T.: Efficient (ideal) lattice sieving using cross-polytope LSH. In: AFRICACRYPT, pp. 3–23 (2016)
22. Bernstein, D.J., Buchmann, J., Dahmen, E. (eds.): Post-quantum Cryptography. Springer, Heidelberg (2009). https://doi.org/10.1007/978-3-540-88702-7
23. Bernstein, D.J., Chuengsatiansup, C., Lange, T., van Vredendaal, C.: NTRU prime: reducing attack surface at low cost. In: Adams, C., Camenisch, J. (eds.) SAC 2017. LNCS, vol. 10719, pp. 235–260. Springer, Cham (2018). https://doi.org/10.1007/978-3-319-72565-9_12
24. Bhattacharya, S., et al.: Round5: Compact and fast post-quantum public-key encryption. Cryptology ePrint Archive, Report 2018/725 (2018)
25. Bonifas, N., Dadush, D.: Short paths on the Voronoi graph and the closest vector problem with preprocessing. In: SODA, pp. 295–314 (2015)
26. Bos, J., et al.: Frodo: Take off the ring! practical, quantum-secure key exchange from LWE. In: CCS, pp. 1006–1018 (2016)
27. Bos, J., et al.: CRYSTALS - Kyber: a CCA-secure module-lattice-based KEM. In: Euro S&P, pp. 353–367 (2018)
28. Bos, J.W., Naehrig, M., van de Pol, J.: Sieving for shortest vectors in ideal lattices: a practical perspective. Int. J. Appl. Crypt. 3(4), 313–329 (2016)
29. Charikar, M.S.: Similarity estimation techniques from rounding algorithms. In: STOC, pp. 380–388 (2002)
30. Christiani, T.: A framework for similarity search with space-time tradeoffs using locality-sensitive filtering. In: SODA, pp. 31–46 (2017)
31. Conway, J.H., Sloane, N.J.A.: Sphere Packings, Lattices and Groups. Springer, Heidelberg (1999). https://doi.org/10.1007/978-1-4757-6568-7
32. Correia, F., Mariano, A., Proenca, A., Bischof, C., Agrell, E.: Parallel improved Schnorr-Euchner enumeration SE++ for the CVP and SVP. In: PDP, pp. 596–603 (2016)
33. Dadush, D., Regev, O., Stephens-Davidowitz, N.: On the closest vector problem with a distance guarantee. In: CCC, pp. 98–109 (2014)
34. The FPLLL development team. FPLLL, a lattice reduction library (2016). https://github.com/fplll/fplll
35. Ducas, L.: Shortest vector from lattice sieving: a few dimensions for free. In: Nielsen, J.B., Rijmen, V. (eds.) EUROCRYPT 2018. LNCS, vol. 10820, pp. 125–145. Springer, Cham (2018). https://doi.org/10.1007/978-3-319-78381-9_5
36. Ducas, L., Lepoint, T., Lyubashevsky, V., Schwabe, P., Seiler, G., Stehlé, D.: CRYSTALS - Dilithium: Digital signatures from module lattices. CHES **2018**, 238–268 (2018)
37. Feige, U., Micciancio, D.: The inapproximability of lattice and coding problems with preprocessing. In: CCC, pp. 32–40 (2002)
38. Fincke, U., Pohst, M.: Improved methods for calculating vectors of short length in a lattice. Math. Comput. **44**(170), 463–471 (1985)
39. Fitzpatrick, R., et al.: Tuning gausssieve for speed. In: Aranha, D.F., Menezes, A. (eds.) LATINCRYPT 2014. LNCS, vol. 8895, pp. 288–305. Springer, Cham (2015). https://doi.org/10.1007/978-3-319-16295-9_16
40. Gama, N., Nguyen, P.Q., Regev, O.: Lattice enumeration using extreme pruning. In: Gilbert, H. (ed.) EUROCRYPT 2010. LNCS, vol. 6110, pp. 257–278. Springer, Heidelberg (2010). https://doi.org/10.1007/978-3-642-13190-5_13
41. Gentry, C., Peikert, C., Vaikuntanathan, V.: Trapdoors for hard lattices and new cryptographic constructions. In: STOC, pp. 197–206 (2008)

42. Hermans, J., Schneider, M., Buchmann, J., Vercauteren, F., Preneel, B.: Parallel shortest lattice vector enumeration on graphics cards. In: AFRICACRYPT, pp. 52–68 (2010)

43. Herold, G., Kirshanova, E.: Improved algorithms for the approximate k-list problem in euclidean norm. In: Fehr, S. (ed.) PKC 2017. LNCS, vol. 10174, pp. 16–40. Springer, Heidelberg (2017). https://doi.org/10.1007/978-3-662-54365-8_2

44. Herold, G., Kirshanova, E., Laarhoven, T.: Speed-ups and time–memory trade-offs for tuple lattice sieving. In: Abdalla, M., Dahab, R. (eds.) PKC 2018. LNCS, vol. 10769, pp. 407–436. Springer, Cham (2018). https://doi.org/10.1007/978-3-319-76578-5_14

45. Indyk, P., Motwani, R.: Approximate nearest neighbors: towards removing the curse of dimensionality. In: STOC, pp. 604–613 (1998)

46. Ishiguro, T., Kiyomoto, S., Miyake, Y., Takagi, T.: Parallel gauss sieve algorithm: solving the SVP challenge over a 128-dimensional ideal lattice. In: Krawczyk, H. (ed.) PKC 2014. LNCS, vol. 8383, pp. 411–428. Springer, Heidelberg (2014). https://doi.org/10.1007/978-3-642-54631-0_24

47. Kannan, R.: Improved algorithms for integer programming and related lattice problems. In: STOC, pp. 193–206 (1983)

48. Kirchner, P., Fouque, P.-A.: Time-memory trade-off for lattice enumeration in a ball. Cryptology ePrint Archive, Report 2016/222 (2016)

49. Klein, P.: Finding the closest lattice vector when it's unusually close. In: SODA, pp. 937–941 (2000)

50. Laarhoven, T.: Sieving for shortest vectors in lattices using angular locality-sensitive hashing. In: Gennaro, R., Robshaw, M. (eds.) CRYPTO 2015. LNCS, vol. 9215, pp. 3–22. Springer, Heidelberg (2015). https://doi.org/10.1007/978-3-662-47989-6_1

51. Laarhoven, T.: Tradeoffs for nearest neighbors on the sphere. arXiv:1511.07527 [cs.DS], pp. 1–16 (2015)

52. Laarhoven, T.: Sieving for closest lattice vectors (with preprocessing). In: Avanzi, R., Heys, H. (eds.) SAC 2016. LNCS, vol. 10532, pp. 523–542. Springer, Cham (2017). https://doi.org/10.1007/978-3-319-69453-5_28

53. Laarhoven, T., de Weger, B.: Faster sieving for shortest lattice vectors using spherical locality-sensitive hashing. In: Lauter, K., Rodríguez-Henríquez, F. (eds.) LATINCRYPT 2015. LNCS, vol. 9230, pp. 101–118. Springer, Cham (2015). https://doi.org/10.1007/978-3-319-22174-8_6

54. Laarhoven, T., Mariano, A.: Progressive lattice sieving. In: PQCrypto, pp. 292–311 (2018)

55. Laarhoven, T., Mosca, M., van de Pol, J.: Finding shortest lattice vectors faster using quantum search. Des. Codes Crypt. **77**(2), 375–400 (2015)

56. Lagarias, J.C., Lenstra, H.W., Schnorr, C.-P.: Korkin-Zolotarev bases and successive minima of a lattice and its reciprocal lattice. Combinatorica **10**(4), 333–348 (1990)

57. Mariano, A., Bischof, C.: Enhancing the scalability and memory usage of HashSieve on multi-core CPUs. In: PDP, pp. 545–552 (2016)

58. Mariano, A., Laarhoven, T., Bischof, C.: Parallel (probable) lock-free HashSieve: a practical sieving algorithm for the SVP. In: ICPP, pp. 590–599 (2015)

59. Mariano, A., Laarhoven, T., Bischof, C.: A parallel variant of LDSieve for the SVP on lattices. In: PDP, pp. 23–30 (2017)

60. Mariano, A., Dagdelen, Ö., Bischof, C.: A comprehensive empirical comparison of parallel listsieve and gausssieve. In: Lopes, L., et al. (eds.) Euro-Par 2014. LNCS, vol. 8805, pp. 48–59. Springer, Cham (2014). https://doi.org/10.1007/978-3-319-14325-5_5
61. Mariano, A., Timnat, S., Bischof, C.: Lock-free GaussSieve for linear speedups in parallel high performance SVP calculation. In: SBAC-PAD, pp. 278–285 (2014)
62. Micciancio, D.: The hardness of the closest vector problem with preprocessing. IEEE Transact. Inf. Theory **47**(3), 1212–1215 (2001)
63. Micciancio, D.: Efficient reductions among lattice problems. In: SODA, pp. 84–93 (2008)
64. Micciancio, D., Voulgaris, P.: A deterministic single exponential time algorithm for most lattice problems based on Voronoi cell computations. In: STOC, pp. 351–358 (2010)
65. Micciancio, D., Voulgaris, P.: Faster exponential time algorithms for the shortest vector problem. In: SODA, pp. 1468–1480 (2010)
66. Micciancio, D., Walter, M.: Fast lattice point enumeration with minimal overhead. In: SODA, pp. 276–294 (2015)
67. Milde, B., Schneider, M.: A parallel implementation of gausssieve for the shortest vector problem in lattices. In: Malyshkin, V. (ed.) PaCT 2011. LNCS, vol. 6873, pp. 452–458. Springer, Heidelberg (2011). https://doi.org/10.1007/978-3-642-23178-0_40
68. Nguyên, P.Q., Vidick, T.: Sieve algorithms for the shortest vector problem are practical. J. Math. Cryptol. **2**(2), 181–207 (2008)
69. Dagdelen, Ö., Schneider, M.: Parallel enumeration of shortest lattice vectors. In: D'Ambra, P., Guarracino, M., Talia, D. (eds.) Euro-Par 2010. LNCS, vol. 6272, pp. 211–222. Springer, Heidelberg (2010). https://doi.org/10.1007/978-3-642-15291-7_21
70. Regev, O.: Improved inapproximability of lattice and coding problems with preprocessing. IEEE Transact. Inf. Theory **50**(9), 2031–2037 (2004)
71. Schneider, M.: Analysis of Gauss-Sieve for solving the shortest vector problem in lattices. In: Katoh, N., Kumar, A. (eds.) WALCOM 2011. LNCS, vol. 6552, pp. 89–97. Springer, Heidelberg (2011). https://doi.org/10.1007/978-3-642-19094-0_11
72. Schneider, M.: Sieving for shortest vectors in ideal lattices. In: Youssef, A., Nitaj, A., Hassanien, A.E. (eds.) AFRICACRYPT 2013. LNCS, vol. 7918, pp. 375–391. Springer, Heidelberg (2013). https://doi.org/10.1007/978-3-642-38553-7_22
73. Sommer, N., Feder, M., Shalvi, O.: Finding the closest lattice point by iterative slicing. SIAM J. Discret. Math. **23**(2), 715–731 (2009)
74. Stephens-Davidowitz, N.: Dimension-preserving reductions between lattice problems, pp. 1–6 (2016). http://noahsd.com/latticeproblems.pdf
75. van de Pol, J.: Lattice-based cryptography. Master's thesis, Eindhoven University of Technology (2011)
76. Viterbo, E., Biglieri, E.: Computing the voronoi cell of a lattice: the diamond-cutting algorithm. IEEE Transact. Inf. Theory **42**(1), 161–171 (1996)
77. Wang, J., Shen, H.T., Song, J., Ji, J.: Hashing for similarity search: a survey. arXiv:1408.2927 [cs.DS], pp. 1–29 (2014)
78. Wang, X., Liu, M., Tian, C., Bi, J.: Improved Nguyen-Vidick heuristic sieve algorithm for shortest vector problem. In: ASIACCS, pp. 1–9 (2011)
79. Yang, S.-Y., Kuo, P.-C., Yang, B.-Y., Cheng, C.-M.: Gauss sieve algorithm on GPUs. In: Handschuh, H. (ed.) CT-RSA 2017. LNCS, vol. 10159, pp. 39–57. Springer, Cham (2017). https://doi.org/10.1007/978-3-319-52153-4_3
80. Zhang, F., Pan, Y., Hu, G.: A three-level sieve algorithm for the shortest vector problem. In: SAC, pp. 29–47 (2013)

Evaluating the Potential for Hardware Acceleration of Four NTRU-Based Key Encapsulation Mechanisms Using Software/Hardware Codesign

Farnoud Farahmand, Viet B. Dang, Duc Tri Nguyen, and Kris Gaj[✉]

George Mason University, Fairfax, USA
{ffarahma,vdang6,dnguye69,kgaj}@gmu.edu

Abstract. The speed of NTRU-based Key Encapsulation Mechanisms (KEMs) in software, especially on embedded software platforms, is limited by the long execution time of its primary operation, polynomial multiplication. In this paper, we investigate the potential for speeding up the implementations of four NTRU-based KEMs, using software/hardware codesign, when targeting Xilinx Zynq UltraScale+ multiprocessor system-on-chip (MPSoC). All investigated algorithms compete in Round 1 of the NIST PQC standardization process. They include: ntru-kem from the NTRUEncrypt submission, Streamlined NTRU Prime and NTRU LPRime KEMs of the NTRU Prime candidate, and NTRU-HRSS-KEM from the submission of the same name. The most-time consuming operation, polynomial multiplication, is implemented in the Programmable Logic (PL) of Zynq UltraScale+ (i.e., in hardware) using constant-time hardware architectures most appropriate for a given algorithm. The remaining operations are executed in the Processing System (PS) of Zynq, based on the ARM Cortex-A53 Application Processing Unit. The speed-ups of our software/hardware codesigns vs. purely software implementations, running on the same Zynq platform, are determined experimentally, and analyzed in the paper. Our experiments reveal substantial differences among the investigated candidates in terms of their potential to benefit from hardware accelerators, with the special focus on accelerators aimed at offloading to hardware only the most time-consuming operation of a given cryptosystems. The demonstrated speed-ups vs. functionally equivalent purely software implementations vary between 4.0 and 42.7 for encapsulation, and between 6.4 and 149.7 for decapsulation.

Keywords: Software/hardware implementation ·
Hardware accelerator · Key Encapsulation Mechanism ·

This paper is partially based upon work supported by the U.S. Department of Commerce/National Institute of Standards and Technology under Grant no. 70NANB18H218, as well as the National Science Foundation under Grant no. CNS-1801512.

J. Ding and R. Steinwandt (Eds.): PQCrypto 2019, LNCS 11505, pp. 23–43, 2019.
https://doi.org/10.1007/978-3-030-25510-7_2

Post-Quantum Cryptography · NTRU · System on Chip ·
Programmable logic · High-level synthesis ·
Embedded software platforms

1   Introduction

Hardware benchmarking of Post-Quantum Cryptography (PQC) candidates is
extremely challenging due to their high algorithmic complexity, specifications
geared more toward mathematicians than toward engineers, and the lack of
hardware description language libraries containing code of basic building blocks.
As a result, the workload for a single algorithm can easily reach several man-
months. Consequently, due to the Round 1 focus on evaluating security and
software efficiency [20], only a few candidates in the NIST PQC standardization
process have been fully implemented in hardware to date [9,12,15,16,22,24].
To make the matters worse, a substantial number of operations used by PQC
algorithms are both complex and sequential in nature. Porting these operations
to hardware can take a large number of man-hours, and at the same time bring
little benefit in terms of the total execution time.

In this paper, we propose an approach aimed at overcoming these difficulties. This approach is based on the concept of software/hardware codesign. The
majority of the algorithm operations are implemented in software. Only a few
main operations (optimally just one), taking the majority of the execution time,
are offloaded to hardware.

This approach has become very practical in modern embedded systems due
to the emergence of special platforms, integrating the software programmability
of an ARM-based processor with the hardware programmability of FPGA fabric.
Examples include Xilinx Zynq 7000 System on Chip (SoC), Xilinx Zynq Ultra-
Scale+ MPSoC, Intel Arria 10 SoC FPGAs, and Intel Stratix 10 SoC FPGAs.
These devices support hybrid software/hardware codesigns composed of a traditional C program running on an ARM processor, communicating, using an
efficient interface protocol (such as AMBA AXI4), with a hardware accelerator
described manually using a hardware description language such as VHDL, or
generated automatically, using High-Level Synthesis.

Assuming that an implemented algorithm contains a limited number of operations, suitable for parallelization, and these operations contribute 91% or more
to the total execution time, then an order of magnitude (or higher) speed-up is
possible, with the amount of development time reduced from months to weeks
or even days.

An additional benefit of this approach is the possibility to easily estimate
the speed-ups that could be achieved by developing and implementing special
instructions of a general-purpose processor (such as ARM) supporting a specific
PQC algorithm or a group of related-algorithms.

Based on extensive software profiling experiments, conducted using both
ARM and AMD64 platforms, we have determined that all NTRU-based NIST
Round 1 KEMs are very suitable for software/hardware codesign. In particular,

for all of them, no more than three major operations contribute at least 92% of the total execution time to both encapsulation and decapsulation. Additionally, the most time consuming of these operations, polynomial multiplications in $Z_q[x]/P$ and $Z_3[x]/P$, with P selected as a polynomial of the prime degree n, are very easily parallelizable and straightforward to implement in constant time using moderate amount of hardware resources.

In the rest of this paper, we quantify the influence of a dedicated hardware accelerator on the performance and implementation cost of each of the following four Round 1 KEMs: NTRUEncrypt [6], NTRU-HRSS [13], Streamlined NTRU Prime, and NTRU LPRime [5,21]. The speed-ups of the software/hardware codesigns vs. purely software implementations are measured, and their influence on the ranking of candidates is determined.

Table 1. Features of round 1 NTRU-based KEMs.

Feature	NTRUEncrypt	NTRU-HRSS	Streamlined NTRU Prime	NTRU LPRime
Polynomial P	$x^n - 1$	$\Phi_n = (x^n - 1)/(x - 1)$ irreducible in $Z_q[x]$	$x^n - x - 1$ irreducible in $Z_q[x]$	$x^n - x - 1$ irreducible in $Z_q[x]$
Degree n^*	Prime	Prime	Prime	Prime
Modulus q	2^d	$2^{ceil(3.5+log_2(n))}$	Prime	Prime
Weight w	Fixed weight for f and g	N/A	Fixed weight for f and r. $3w \leq 2n$ $16w + 1 \leq q$	Fixed weight for b and a. $3w \leq 2n$ $16w + 2\delta + 3 \leq q$
Quotient rings	R/q: $Z_q[x]/(x^n - 1)$	R/q: $Z_q[x]/(x^n - 1)$ S/3: $Z_3[x]/(\Phi_n)$	R/q: $Z_q[x]/(x^n - x - 1)$ R/3: $Z_3[x]/(x^n - x - 1)$	R/q: $Z_q[x]/(x^n - x - 1)$ R/3: $Z_3[x]/(x^n - x - 1)$
#Poly Mults for encapsulation	1 in R/q	1 in R/q	1 in R/q	2 in R/q
#Poly Mults for decapsulation	2 in R/q	2 in R/q 1 in S/3	2 in R/q 1 in R/3	3 in R/q
Private key f of the form 1+3F	Yes	No	No	No
Invertibility checks in key generation	Yes	No	Yes	No
Decryption failures	Yes	No	No	No

* denoted by N in the specification of NTRUEncrypt and by p in the specifications of Streamlined NTRU Prime and NTRU LPRime

2   Background

Basic features of four investigated Round 1 NTRU-based KEMs are summarized in Table 1. NTRUEncrypt is the only candidate that uses a reducible polynomial, which may potentially increase its attack surface. It is also the only candidate with a non-zero probability of decryption failure, and one of the two (together with Streamlined NTRU Prime) requiring invertibility checks in key generation. All polynomials have a prime degree n. Three features that have primary influence on the area of a corresponding hardware accelerator include: (a) prime vs. power-of-two modulus q for operations on polynomial coefficients; (b) requirement for operations in additional rings, such as $Z_3[x]/(\Phi_n)$ in NTRU-HRSS and $Z_3[x]/(x^n - x - 1)$ in Streamlined NTRU Prime; (c) Private key of the form $1 + 3F$ in NTRUEncrypt.

The execution time of Encapsulation and Decapsulation is affected primarily by the required number of polynomial multiplications (Poly Mults), which is the lowest in case of NTRUEncrypt and the highest in case of NTRU LPRime. The fixed weight of polynomials with small coefficients affects the execution time of a polynomial multiplication only in case of using a rotator-based multiplier [4, 8,14].

In Table 2, the numerical values of parameters in the implemented variants of KEMs are summarized. All investigated KEMs use approximately the same values of the polynomial degree n, which in hardware leads to similar Poly Mult execution times in terms of the number of clock cycles. NTRUEncrypt and NTRU-HRSS have an advantage of using a modulus q being a power of two, which substantially reduces the time of Poly Mult in software, and the area of the Poly Mult accelerator in hardware. Three out of four KEMs are claimed to belong to the security category 5, with the number of pre-quantum security bits estimated to be close to 256. NTRU-HRSS is the only investigated candidate limited to the security category 1, with the number of pre-quantum security bits estimated at 136 (i.e., slightly above 128). It should be stressed that no other sets of parameters, corresponding to any higher security category are provided in the specification of this KEM. Similarly, no other parameter sets, corresponding to any lower security levels, are defined in the specifications of Streamlined NTRU Prime or NTRU LPRime. The public and private key sizes are the smallest for NTRUEncrypt and the largest for Streamlined NTRU Prime.

3   Previous Work

3.1   Hardware Accelerators for NTRUEncrypt

In 2001, Bailey et al. [4] introduced and implemented a Fast Convolution Algorithm for polynomial multiplication, exploiting the sparsity of polynomials. In [14], Kamal et al. analyzed several implementation options for traditional NTRUEncrypt [11] targeting Virtex-E family of FPGAs. In this design, the polynomial multiplier took advantage of the ternary nature of polynomials in NTRUEncrypt and utilized an empirically chosen Barrel shifter (rotator). The results were reported for the parameter set with (n = 251, q = 128). Liu et al. implemented the truncated polynomial ring multiplier using linear feedback shift register (LFSR) in 2015 [17] and an extended LFSR [18] in 2016. Both designs were implemented using Cyclone IV FPGAs. The former paper reported results

Table 2. Numerical values of parameters in the implemented variants of round 1 NTRU-based KEMs.

Feature	NTRUEncrypt	NTRU-HRSS	Streamlined NTRU Prime	NTRU LPRime
Parameter set	NTRU-743	ntruhrss701	sntrup4591761	ntrulpr4591761
Degree n	743	701	761	761
Modulus q	$2048 = 2^{11}$	$8192 = 2^{13}$	$2^{12} < 4591 < 2^{13}$	$2^{12} < 4591 < 2^{13}$
Polynomials with small coefficients	Fixed weight 494 for f and g. Uniform trinary for r and m	Uniform T+ for f and g. Uniform trinary for r and m	Fixed weight 286 for f and r. Uniform trinary for g and m	Fixed weight 250 for b and a.
Expected failure rates	2^{-112}	0	0	0
Security category	5	1	5	5
Pre-quantum security bits	256	136	248	225
Shared key size in bits	384	256	256	256
Public key size*	1023	1140	1218	1047
Secret key size*	1173	1422	1600	1238
Ciphertext size*	1023	1281	1047	1175

* sizes in bytes

for three parameter sets with $(n = 251, q = 128)$, $(n = 347, q = 128)$, and $(n = 503, q = 256)$. The latter paper reported results for 12 parameter sets specified in the IEEE Standard NTRUEncrypt SVES [2]. Out of these parameter sets, the closest one to the cases considered in this paper was the parameter set with $(n = 761, q = 2048)$. None of the aforementioned designs was made open-source. In [8], the first full constant-time implementation of the IEEE Standard NTRU-Encrypt SVES [2] was reported. This implementation supported two parameter sets, with $(n = 1499, q = 2048)$ and $(n = 1087, q = 2048)$, and targeted the Xilinx Virtex UltraScale FPGA. As described above, the results reported in these papers concerned different parameter values and/or different (mostly much older) hardware platforms. Additionally, all aforementioned hardware implementations other than [17] and [8] were not constant time. As a result, their comparison with the results presented in this work is neither practical nor fair.

3.2   Software-Hardware Codesign of PQC Algorithms

Only a few attempts to accelerate software implementations of post-quantum cryptosystems have been made through software/hardware (SW/HW) codesign. A coprocessor consisting of the PicoBlaze softcore and several parallel acceleration units for the McEliece cryptosystem was implemented on Spartan-3AN

FPGAs by Ghosh et al. [10]. No speed-up vs. purely software implementation using PicoBlaze was reported.

In 2015, Aysu et al. [3] built a high-speed implementation of a lattice-based digital signature scheme using SW/HW codesign techniques. The paper focused on the acceleration of signature generation. The design targeted the Cyclone IV FPGA family and consisted of the NIOS2 soft processor, a hash unit, and a polynomial multiplier. Compared to the C implementation running on the NIOS2 processor, the most efficient software/hardware codesign reported in the paper achieved the speed-up of 26,250x at the expense of the increase in the number of Logic Elements by a factor of 20.

Migliore et al. [19] presented a hardware/software codesign for the lattice-based Fan-Vercauteren (FV) homomorphic encryption scheme with the majority of the Karatsuba-based multiplication/relinearization operation performed in hardware. The platform used for hardware acceleration was Stratix V GX FPGA. Software ran on a PC, based on Intel i7-4910MQ, with 4 cores operating at 2.9 GHz, connected with the FPGA-based DE5-450 Terasic board using PCI Express (PCIe) 3.0, with eight lines, capable of handling transfers with the throughput up to 250 MB/s per line in full-duplex. The speed-up compared to the purely software implementation was estimated to be 1.4x.

Wang et al. [23] reported a software/hardware implementation of the PQC digital signature scheme XMSS. The selected platform was an Intel Cyclone V SoC, and the software part of the design was implemented using a soft-core processor RISC-V. Hardware accelerators supported a general-purpose SHA-256 hash function, as well as several XMSS specific operations. The design achieved the speed-up of 23x for signing and 18x for verification over a purely software implementation running on RISC-V.

All the aforementioned platforms were substantially different than the platforms used in this work. The algorithms and their parameters were also substantially different. As a result, limited information could be inferred regarding the optimal software/hardware partitioning, expected speed-up, or expected communication overhead.

4   Methodology

4.1   Platform and Software

The platform selected for our experiments is Xilinx Zynq UltraScale+ MPSoC XCZU9EG-2FFVB1156E, which is fabricated using a 16 nm technology and mounted on the ZCU102 Evaluation Kit from Xilinx. This MPSoC is composed of two major parts sharing the same chip, the PS and PL. The PS (Processing System) includes a quad-core ARM Cortex-A53 Application Processing Unit (APU), a dual-core ARM Cortex-R5 Real-Time Processing Unit (RPU), Graphics Processing Unit, 256 kB On-Chip Memory, and more. Each processor of the APU and RPU is equipped with a 32 kB instruction cache and a 32 kB data cache. In our experiments, we use only one processor of the APU (Core 0 of Cortex-A53) running at the frequency of 1.2 GHz. The PL (Programmable Logic) includes a programmable FPGA fabric similar to that of Virtex UltraScale+ FPGAs. The software used is Xilinx Vivado Design Suite HLx Edition, Xilinx Software Development Kit (XSDK), and Xilinx Vivado HLS, all with the versions no. 2017.2.

A high-level block diagram of the experimental software/hardware codesign platform is shown in Fig. 1. The hardware accelerator, implementing the Polynomial Multiplier unit, is denoted as Poly Mult. This accelerator is extended with the Input and Output FIFOs, as well as AXI DMA, for high-speed communication with the Processing System. The details of the Input and Output FIFO interfaces are shown in Fig. 2. Timing measurements are performed using an AXI Timer, capable of measuring time in clock cycles of the 200 MHz system clock. The Poly Mult unit can operate at a variable frequency different than that of DMA. This frequency can be changed at run time using the Clocking Wizard, controlled from software. As a result, the Input and Output FIFOs use different clocks for their read and write operations.

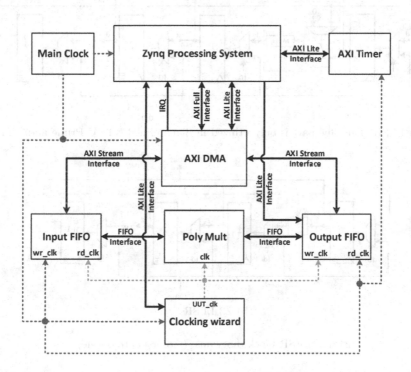

Fig. 1. High-level block diagram of the experimental SW/HW co-design platform.

4.2 Design of Hardware Using the RTL Methodology

The Register-Transfer Level (RTL) designs of hardware accelerators for NTRU-based KEMs follow closely the block diagrams shown in Figs. 3, 4, 5 and 6.

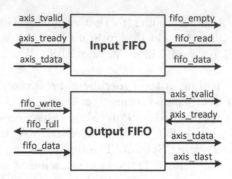

Fig. 2. The input and output FIFO interface.

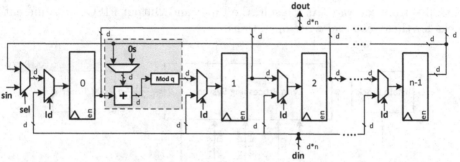

(a) Zq_LFSR. The blue part is only utilized in Streamlined NTRU Prime and NTRU LPRime

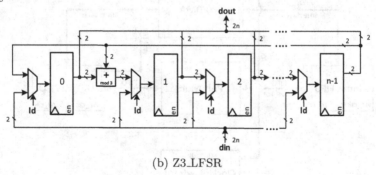

(b) Z3_LFSR

Fig. 3. LFSR block diagrams. (Color figure online)

The Zq_LFSR, used in all KEMs, is initialized with the value of a polynomial $a(x)$ with large coefficients. In each subsequent iteration, the output from LFSR contains the value $a(x) \cdot x^i \bmod P$. In a single clock cycle, a simple multiplication by x, namely $a(x) \cdot x^{i+1} \bmod P = a(x) \cdot x^i \cdot x \bmod P$, is performed. For $P = x^n - 1$, this multiplication is equivalent to rotation. For $P = x^n - x - 1$, an extra addition mod q, marked in Fig. 3a with the blue background is required.

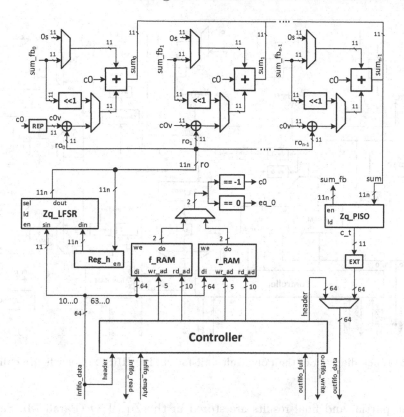

Fig. 4. Block diagram of the Poly Mult unit for NTRUEncrypt.

The multiplication in the ring $S/3$ for NTRU-HRSS and $R/3$ for Streamlined NTRU Prime is performed using the Z3_LFSR, shown Fig. 3b. This circuit operates using the same principle as Zq_LFSR, except all polynomial coefficients are reduced mod 3.

The entire Poly Mult unit for NTRUEncrypt is shown in Fig. 4. The multiplication of a polynomial $a(x)$ with large coefficients by a polynomial $b(x)$ with small coefficients (limited to -1, 0, and 1), involves calculating $a(x) \cdot x^i \bmod P$, multiplying it by b_i, and adding it to the partial sum. The multiplication of each coefficient by -1 is accomplished by calculating their one's complement (using an XOR with c0v, obtained by replicating c0 11 times) and the addition of c0 as carry-in to the following adder, represented by a square with $+$.

Coefficients of the public key h, are preloaded to the NTRUEncrypt Zq_LFSR before an encapsulation starts. All of these coefficients can be stored in Reg_h, and loaded back to Zq_LFSR in a single clock cycle, in case this LFSR is used in-between for any operation not involving h. Similarly, coefficients of the private key f are preloaded to the asymmetric f_RAM, visible at the input as a 32x64 RAM, and at the output as a 1024x2 RAM, before the decryption starts.

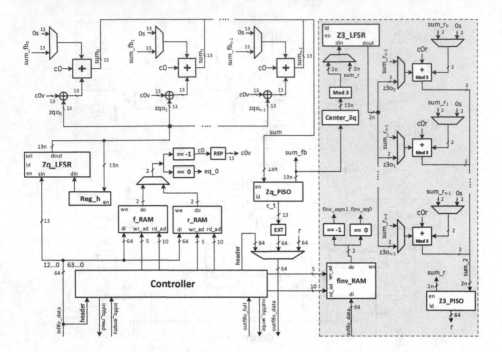

Fig. 5. Block diagram of the Poly Mult unit for NTRU-HRSS. (Color figure online)

The partial and final results are stored in the Zq_PISO (Parallel-In Serial-Out) unit, with the parallel input of the width of $11 \cdot n$ bits, the parallel output of the same width (used to enable the accumulation of intermediate products), and the serial output of the width of 11 bits used to read out the final result to the output FIFO.

The multiplication $t = r * h$, performed during encapsulation and the second part of decapsulation, takes $n = 743$ clock cycles. The multiplication $m' = f * c = (1 + 3 \cdot F) * c$, performed during the first part of decapsulation, requires two additional clock cycles, used respectively for the calculation of $F * c + 2 \cdot F * c$ (with the multiplication of each coefficient of $F * c$ by 2 accomplished using a shift to the left by one, denoted in the diagram as $<< 1$) and $c + 3 \cdot F * c$. In this paper, $a * b$ denotes polynomial multiplication, and $a \cdot b$ denotes regular multiplication, i.e., a multiplication of a polynomial and a constant, or a multiplication of two polynomial terms.

The Controller is responsible for generating suitable select and enable signals, communication with the Input and Output FIFOs, interpreting the input headers with instructions sent by the respective driver, and generating the output header containing the status and error codes that are sent back to the driver.

A block diagram of the hardware accelerator for NTRU-HRSS is shown in Fig. 5. The new part, marked using the blue background, is responsible for operations in the ring S/3. Compared to NTRUEncrypt, the size of all large coefficients increases from 11 to 13 bits. The portion of the circuit responsible for performing

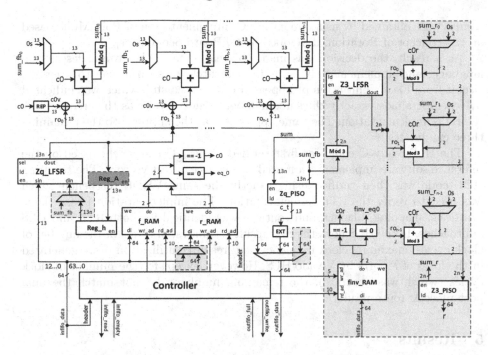

Fig. 6. Block diagram of the Poly Mult units for Streamlined NTRU Prime and NTRU LPRime. The blue parts are used only in the design for Streamlined NTRU Prime and the red part is used only in the design for NTRU LPRime. (Color figure online)

multiplication by $f = (1 + 3 \cdot F)$ is removed. Other than that, the operation of the circuit remains almost identical.

A block diagram of the hardware accelerators for Streamlined NTRU Prime and NTRU LPRime is shown in Fig. 6. The operations in R/3 are necessary only in case of Streamlined NTRU Prime and are similar to operations in S/3 for NTRU-HRSS. Compared to NTRU-HRSS, the main difference is the need for reduction of partial sums, involving large coefficients, mod q. Since now, q is a 13-bit prime, a conditional subtraction is necessary. An additional register A is required for NTRU LPRime only, increasing the number of required flip-flops.

4.3 Design of Hardware Using the HLS Methodology

The reference implementation of NTRUEncrypt in C, for $n = 743$, is based on the grade school algorithm for multiplication (also known as schoolbook, paper-and-pencil, etc.). Only for n equal to a power of 2, the fully recursive Karatsuba multiplication is used. When the grade school implementation of Poly Mult in C was provided at the input of Vivado HLS, the resulting circuit required tens of thousands of clock cycles to complete a single multiplication (even after inserting multiple Vivado HLS directives in the form of pragmas). The similar results were obtained by using an earlier C implementation of Poly Mult, based on the concept of Rotation, developed by OnBoard Security [1].

As a result, the decision was made to treat C like a hardware description language, and implement Poly Mult from scratch, in such a way to infer the circuit from Fig. 4. This attempt appeared to be successful, which was indicated by reaching almost exactly the same number of clock cycles as that required by the RTL implementation. The same approach was then applied to the remaining three candidates.

The HLS-ready C code was first verified using a C testbench, based on the reference software implementation used as a source of test vectors. The resulting HDL code was then verified using exactly the same VHDL testbench which was used to verify the RTL implementation. The implementation phase (logic synthesis, mapping, placing, and routing) was identical for both RTL and HLS approaches. In the HLS flow, the first result estimates, in terms of the number of clock cycles, maximum clock frequency, and resource utilization, were generated in the form of reports by Vivado HLS. However, except for the number of clock cycles (which was accurate), the remaining numbers did not match the final post-place & route results.

5   Results

The results of profiling for the purely software implementations, running on a single core of ARM Cortex-A53, at the frequency of 1.2 GHz, are presented in the left portion of Table 3. For each of the four investigated algorithms and each major operation (Encapsulation and Decapsulation), four most time-consuming functions are identified. In each of the investigated cases, the most time consuming function is poly_mult(), responsible for performing polynomial multiplication in R/q. The contribution of this function varies between 78.2% in case of the NTRUEncrypt encapsulation, up to 99.5% in case of the Streamlined NTRU Prime decapsulation. poly_mult() is the only function listed among the four most time-consuming functions for all 8 investigated operations. It is also a function with a well-known potential for vast parallelization (and thus a very substantial speed-up) in hardware. As a result, poly_mult() was a natural candidate for offloading to hardware, and no other function listed in Table 3 could offer a clear potential for delivering an additional speed-up, especially for multiple algorithms.

The number of clock cycles required by Poly Mult, the maximum clock frequency, and the resource utilization obtained using the RTL and HLS approaches are summarized in Table 4. In both cases, the number of clock cycles is determined using simulation. The maximum clock frequency is obtained by using Vivado in combination with the automated hardware optimization tool called Minerva [7]. The obtained values correspond to the static timing analysis results after placing and routing, and have been confirmed experimentally using our setup shown in Fig. 1. The resource utilization is based on the post-place and route reports of Vivado. Only resources used to implement Poly Mult are listed in

Table 3. Profiling results for the software and software/hardware implementations targeting Zynq UltraScale+ MPSoC. (SW) and (HW) indicate whether poly_mult() is executed in software or in hardware. x2 means that a given function is called twice.

Function	Time [us]	Time [%]	Function	Time [us]	Time [%]
Software			Software/Hardware		
NTRUEncrypt - Encaps					
1. poly_mult (SW)	743.510	78.177	1. generate_r	91.665	38.286
2. generate_r	91.665	9.638	2. mask_m	40.960	17.108
3. mask_m	40.960	4.307	3. poly_mult (HW)	32.115	13.414
4. crypto_hash_sha512 x2	17.650	1.856	4. crypto_hash_sha512 x2	17.650	7.372
NTRUEncrypt - Decaps					
1. poly_mult (SW) x2	1492.870	87.800	1. generate_r	79.890	29.999
2. generate_r	79.890	4.699	2. poly_mult (HW) x2	55.966	21.015
3. unmask_m	40.865	2.403	3. unmask_m	40.865	15.345
4. unpack_secret_key_CCA	17.975	1.057	4. unpack_secret_key_CCA	17.975	6.750
NTRU-HRSS - Encaps					
1. poly_mult (SW)	3091.550	97.585	1. poly_Rq_frommsg	31.570	28.138
2. poly_Rq_frommsg	31.570	0.997	2. poly_mult (HW)	31.521	28.094
3. owcpa_samplemsg	11.445	0.361	3. owcpa_samplemsg	11.445	10.201
4. poly_Rq_getnoise	10.595	0.334	4. poly_Rq_getnoise	10.595	9.443
NTRU-HRSS - Decaps					
1. poly_mult (SW) x2	9302.780	99.211	1. poly_mult (HW) x2	51.333	39.678
2. poly_Rq_frommsg	30.460	0.325	2. poly_Rq_frommsg	30.460	23.544
3. unpack_sk	10.315	0.110	3. unpack_sk	10.315	7.973
4. poly_Rq_getnoise	9.975	0.106	4. poly_Rq_getnoise	9.975	7.710
Streamlined NTRU Prime - Encaps					
1. poly_mult (SW)	11,846.950	92.702	1. small_random_weightw	766.025	77.933
2. small_random_weightw	766.025	5.994	2. FIPS202_SHA3_512	155.080	15.777
3. FIPS202_SHA3_512	155.080	1.214	3. poly_mult (HW)	34.003	3.459
4. rq_decode	10.165	0.080	4. rq_decode	10.165	1.034
Streamlined NTRU Prime - Decaps					
1. poly_mult (SW) x2	35,546.140	99.489	1. FIPS202_SHA3_512	154.535	64.734
2. FIPS202_SHA3_512	154.535	0.433	2. poly_mult (HW) x2	52.428	21.962
3. rq_decode	10.145	0.028	3. rq_decode	10.145	4.250
4. rq_round3	9.045	0.025	4. rq_round3	9.045	3.789
NTRU LPRime - Encaps					
1. poly_mult (SW) x2	23,693.840	97.908	1. small_seeded_weightw	327.195	57.686
2. small_seeded_weightw	327.195	1.352	2. FIPS202_SHA3_512 x2	106.355	18.751
3. FIPS202_SHA3_512 x2	106.355	0.439	3. poly_mult (HW) x2	53.663	9.461
4. rq_fromseed	28.995	0.120	4. rq_fromseed	28.995	5.112
NTRU LPRime - Decaps					
1. poly_mult (SW) x2	35,540.750	98.598	1. small_seeded_weightw	339.285	58.920
2. small_seeded_weightw	339.285	0.941	2. FIPS202_SHA3_512 x2	102.960	17.880
3. FIPS202_SHA3_512 x2	102.960	0.286	3. poly_mult (HW) x2	68.484	11.893
4. rq_fromseed	29.000	0.080	4. rq_fromseed	29.000	5.036

Table 4. Differences in results obtained using the RTL and HLS approaches.

Metric	RTL	HLS	HLS/RTL
NTRUEncrypt			
#cycles for Poly Mult in Encaps	744	743	0.999
#cycles for Poly Mult in Decaps	1,491	1,488	0.971
Maximum Clk Freq [MHz]	330	251	0.761
#LUTs	27,912	42,667	1.529
#Slices	4,431	6,268	1.415
#FFs	24,697	24,756	1.002
#BRAMs	4	3	0.750
NTRU-HRSS			
#cycles for Poly Mult in Encaps	702	703	1.001
#cycles for Poly Mult in Decaps	2,111	2,110	0.999
Maximum Clk Freq [MHz]	300	295	0.983
#LUTs	33,230	32,196	0.969
#Slices	5,476	6,622	1.209
#FFs	32,327	48,792	1.609
#BRAMs	6	4	0.667
Streamlined NTRU prime			
#cycles for Poly Mult in Encaps	762	761	0.998
#cycles for Poly Mult in Decaps	2,291	2,291	1.000
Maximum Clk Freq [MHz]	255	155	0.608
#LUTs	65,207	88,678	1.360
#Slices	9,699	13,690	1.411
#FFs	32,929	31,764	0.965
#BRAMs	6	4	0.667
NTRU LPRime			
#cycles for Poly Mult in Encaps	1,524	1,522	0.998
#cycles for Poly Mult in Decaps	2,287	2,283	0.998
Maximum Clk Freq [MHz]	255	158	0.620
#LUTs	52,297	77,385	1.480
#Slices	8,483	12,215	1.440
#FFs	39,730	39,832	1.002
#BRAMs	4	3	0.750

Table 4. Additional logic implemented in hardware, shown in Fig. 1, such as AXI DMA, Input FIFO, Output FIFO, Clocking Wizard, and AXI Timer, requires additional 7,858 LUTs, 1,593 Slices, 8,794 flip-flops, and 11 BRAMs.

Overall, the HLS-based implementations match very well (or even outperform) manually developed RTL implementations in terms of the number of clock cycles and the number of storage elements (flip-flops and BRAMs). The only exception is NTRU-HRSS, where the number of flip-flops is about 61% larger in case of using HLS. However, the HLS-based implementations require between 36% and 53% of more LUTs, and between 41% and 44% of more Slices. Once again the only exception is NTRU-HRSS, where the number of LUTs is comparable, at the expense of the substantial increase in the number of flip-flops. Additionally, the maximum clock frequency of the HLS-generated designs reached between 61% and 98% of the frequency of the manually-generated RTL designs. The development time was comparable because of the additional learning curve and more frequent trial-and-error tests necessary to develop an optimal HLS-ready C code.

Overall, the RTL approach was demonstrated to be superior, although not by a high margin. This approach is also more mature and more trusted by the cryptographic engineering community. As a result, in the rest of this paper, only results obtained using the RTL approach are reported and analyzed.

In Table 5, area overhead caused by special operations specific to particular KEMs is listed. Overall, Streamlined NTRUPrime and NTRU LPRime pay quite substantial price in terms of both maximum clock frequency and area compared to NTRUEncrypt and NTRU-HRSS. For example, replacing $q = 2^{13}$ by the 13-bit prime $q = 4591$ between NTRU-HRSS and Streamlined NTRU Prime, results in the 15% decrease in the maximum clock frequency, and increase in the number of LUTs by approximately a factor of two. The number of storage elements, flip-flops and BRAMs, remains approximately the same. Supporting operations in S/3 for NTRU-HRSS and R/3 for Streamlined NTRU Prime requires 26.4%

Table 5. Area overhead of special operations of NTRU-based KEMs.

Operations	LUTs	FFs
NTRUEncrypt		
Logic supporting multiplication by 1+3F	12.0%	0%
NTRU-HRSS		
Logic supporting operations in S/3	26.4%	16.4%
Streamlined NTRU Prime		
Logic supporting operations in R/3	8.4%	9.3%
Logic supporting mod q	38.0%	0%
NTRU LPRime		
Logic supporting mod q	53.2%	0%
Logic for register A	0%	24.9%

and 8.4% of the total number of accelerator LUTs, respectively. The percentage is larger in NTRU-HRSS primarily because of the smaller total area required by this KEM. The resource utilization in absolute area units (LUTs, FFs) is comparable. Supporting special multiplication by 1+3F in NTRUEncrypt costs about 12% of the total number of LUTs, and the special register A in NTRU LPRime requires about 25% more flip-flops.

Table 6. Timing results.

Algorithm	Total SW [ms]	Total SW/ HW [ms]	Total speed-up	Poly Mul SW [ms]	Poly Mul HW [ms]	Poly Mul speed-up	SW part Sped up by HW [%]
Encapsulation							
NTRUEncrypt	0.951	0.239	**4.0**	0.744	0.032	23.2	**78.18**
NTRU-HRSS	3.168	0.112	**28.2**	3.092	0.032	98.1	97.58
Strl NTRU Prime	12.780	0.983	**13.0**	11.847	0.034	348.4	92.70
NTRU LPRime	24.200	0.567	**42.7**	23.694	0.054	441.5	97.91
Decapsulation							
NTRUEncrypt	1.700	0.266	**6.4**	1.493	0.056	26.7	87.80
NTRU-HRSS	9.377	0.129	**72.5**	9.303	0.051	181.2	98.95
Strl NTRU Prime	35.729	0.239	**149.7**	35.546	0.052	678.0	**99.49**
NTRU LPRime	36.046	0.576	**62.6**	35.541	0.068	519.0	98.60

Timing results are summarized in Table 6. For each investigated KEM and each major operation (Encapsulation and Decapsulation), we list the total execution time in software (for the reference software implementations in C running on ARM Cortex-A53 of Zynq UltraScale+ MPSoC), the total execution time in software and hardware (after offloading polynomial multiplications to hardware), and the obtained speed-up. The ARM processor runs at 1.2 GHz, DMA for the communication between the processor and the hardware accelerator at 200 MHz, and the hardware accelerators at the maximum frequencies, specific for the RTL implementations of each algorithm, listed in Table 4. All execution times were obtained through experimental measurements using the setup shown in Fig. 1.

The total speed-up varies from 4.0 for encapsulation in NTRUEncrypt to 149.7 for decapsulation in the Streamlined NTRU Prime. The main reason for such big differences is the percentage of time spent by the respective software implementation for operations offloaded to hardware. For the aforementioned two operations, this percentage varies from 78.18% to 99.49%.

The time required for the polynomial multiplication in hardware is similar for all algorithms, to the large extant because a significant percentage of that time is spent for the DMA initialization and data transfer, and only a small percentage on actual computations. The software/hardware communication overhead is quantified in Table 7. It is defined as the percentage of the total number of clock cycles used for the DMA initialization and the input/output data transfer vs. the total number of clock cycles used by the hardware accelerator. As shown in the respective rows of Table 7, this overhead varies between 78% and 89%.

Table 7. Software/hardware communication overhead.

Feature	NTRU Encrypt	NTRU-HRSS	Streamlined NTRU Prime	NTRU LPRime
Encapsulation				
#cycles for transfer (input + output)	25 + 744	23 + 702	25 + 762	25 + 1523
#cycles for Poly Muls	746	702	765	1,531
#cycles for DMA init	4,908	4,877	5,249	7,654
Total #cycles	6,423	6,304	6,801	10,733
Transfer overhead %	88.39	88.86	88.75	85.74
Decapsulation				
#cycles for transfer (input + output)	769 + 1488	725 + 725	763 + 787	787 + 2285
#cycles for Poly Muls	1,494	2,111	2,296	2,295
#cycles for DMA init	7,442	6,706	6,640	8,330
Total #cycles	11,193	10,267	10,486	13,697
Transfer overhead %	86.65	79.44	78.10	83.24

Table 8. Actual speed-up for Zynq UltraScale+ MPSoC (with Proc. Clk =1.2 GHz, Comm. Clk = 200 MHz, Accel. Clk = Max. Clk Freq from Table 3) vs. estimated speed-up for the case of Special Instructions (SI) of ARM Cortex A53 (Proc. Clk = Comm. Clk = Accel. Clk = 1.2 GHz).

Feature	NTRU Encrypt	NTRU-HRSS	Streamlined NTRU Prime	NTRU LPRime
Encapsulation				
Poly Mul speed-up act	24.56	101.92	349.98	444.03
Poly Mul speed-up SI	471.14	2,079.81	7,328.01	7,387.49
Ratio SI/Actual	19.19	20.41	20.94	16.64
Total speed-up act	3.97	28.24	13.00	42.67
Total speed-up SI	4.51	38.01	13.44	46.80
Ratio SI/A	1.14	1.35	1.03	1.10
Decapsulation				
Poly Mul speed-up act	29.03	192.35	682.91	522.98
Poly Mul speed-up SI	382.07	2,507.91	8,872.67	6,357.21
Ratio SI/Actual	13.16	13.04	12.99	12.16
Total speed-up actual	6.38	72.48	149.67	62.60
Total speed-up SI	7.77	110.68	187.38	70.20
Ratio SI/A	1.22	1.53	1.25	1.12

In spite of this communication penalty, the speed-up for the polynomial multiplication itself is very high. For all KEMs other than NTRUEncrypt, this speed-up exceeds 98. For NTRUEncrypt, it is about 23 for encapsulation and 27 for decapsulation. This lower speed-up can be attributed primarily to the faster software implementation (due to the use of $q = 2^{11}$).

Overall, offloading polynomial multiplication to hardware has substantially changed the ranking of investigated KEMs. In pure software, NTRUEncrypt was by far the most efficient, followed by NTRU-HRSS, and trailed by Streamlined NTRU Prime and NTRU LPRime. In the software/hardware implementation, NTRU-HRSS was the fastest for both basic operations. For encapsulation it was followed by NTRUEncrypt, NTRU LPRime, and Streamlined NTRU Prime, and for decapsulation, by Streamlined NTRU Prime, NTRUEncrypt, and NTRU LPRime. However, when analyzing these results, one needs to keep in mind that NTRU-HRSS provides much lower security level compared to all remaining KEMs (the security strength category 1 vs. 5), and the specifications of these KEMs do not support comparing all of them at the same security level.

Using the actual results for the existing modern embedded systems platform, Zynq UltraScale+ MPSoC, we can also estimate the results for a hypothetical future platform, an ARM processor, equipped with special instructions capable of executing polynomial multiplication. We assume that in such platform, the number of clock cycles required for computations and input/output transfer will remain the same. However, both the Poly Mult and the transfer of data will be performed at the same frequency as the frequency of the processor itself (e.g., 1.2 GHz). We also assume that the DMA initialization is not any longer required.

The speed-ups calculated under such assumptions are referred to as speed-ups for the case of Special Instructions (SI). These speed-ups are summarized and compared with the actual speed-ups (obtained for Zynq UltraScale+ MPSoC) in Table 8. The SI speed-ups for Poly Mult itself exceed the actual speed ups by a factor varying between 16.64 and 20.94 for encapsulation, and between 12.16 and 13.16 for decapsulation. At the same time, the total speed-ups improve for the case of special instructions by much smaller factor, varying between 1.03 and 1.35 for encapsulation, and between 1.12 and 1.53 for decapsulation. As a result, our study can be used as a relatively accurate predictor of the improvements possible by extending a modern ARM processor with special instructions capable of performing the respective variants of Poly Mult.

On the other hand, our current study cannot be used to predict the performance and ranking of the investigated candidates when implemented entirely in hardware. Such implementations can benefit from elimination of the communication overhead between a processor and a hardware accelerator. They may also take advantage of an ability to parallelize some additional operations, other than Poly Mult. At the same time for many auxiliary operations, which are sequential in nature, moving from a processor to reconfigurable fabric, operating at much lower clock frequency, may have either negative or at least negligible effect on the overall performance. As a result, the actual full hardware implementations are required to properly rank candidates in terms of their performance in FPGAs and ASICs.

When it comes to alternative software/hardware implementations, the right side of Table 3, may serve as a starting point for future work. This side, presents the results of profiling for our software/hardware implementations. Only for the NTRU-HRSS decapsulation, Poly Mult remains the most time-consuming operation. For all remaining algorithms it moves to the second or third position in the ranking. The new most time consuming functions, such as generate_r for NTRUEncrypt, small_random_weightw for the Streamlined NTRU Prime - Encapsulation, and small_seeded_weightw for NTRU LPRime are likely to be parallalizable and thus suitable for offloading to hardware. On the other hand, FIPS202_SHA3_512 is mostly sequential, and thus it is likely to offer a lower performance gain when implemented in hardware. Additional factors, such as the development effort, the total size of inputs and outputs of a given function, as well as the area/memory requirements may need to be taken into account when investigating any alternative software/hardware partitioning schemes.

6   Conclusions

Using SW/HW codesign allows the implementers of candidates for new cryptographic standards (such as NIST PQC standards) to substantially reduce the development time compared to the use of purely hardware implementations. The implementers avoid reproducing in hardware the cumbersome and mostly sequential operations required for input/output, as well as multiple auxiliary operations that have a negligible influence on the total execution time. Instead, they can focus on major and most time consuming operations, which can easily contribute about 90% to the total execution time, and are suitable for parallelization. In this study, we have clearly demonstrated the viability of this approach in case of four Round 1 NIST PQC candidates and their major operation, Poly Mult. The obtained results shed a light on the correct ranking of the investigated four NTRU-based KEMs when offloading the most time consuming operations to hardware is a design option.

References

1. NTRU Open Source Project. https://github.com/NTRUOpenSourceProject
2. IEEE Standard Specification for Public Key Cryptographic Techniques Based on Hard Problems over Lattices, P1363.1-2008, March 2009
3. Aysu, A., Yuce, B., Schaumont, P.: The future of real-time security: Latency-optimized lattice-based digital signatures. ACM Transact. Embed. Comput. Syst. (TECS) 14(3), 43 (2015)
4. Bailey, D.V., Coffin, D., Elbirt, A., Silverman, J.H., Woodbury, A.D.: NTRU in constrained devices. In: Koç, Ç.K., Naccache, D., Paar, C. (eds.) CHES 2001. LNCS, vol. 2162, pp. 262–272. Springer, Heidelberg (2001). https://doi.org/10.1007/3-540-44709-1_22

5. Bernstein, D.J., Chuengsatiansup, C., Lange, T., van Vredendaal, C.: NTRU Prime, August 2017. https://ntruprime.cr.yp.to/ntruprime-20160511.pdf

6. Chen, C., Hostein, J., Whyte, W., Zhang, Z.: NIST PQ Submission: NTRUEncrypt A lattice based encryption algorithm, May 2018. https://www.onboardsecurity.com/nist-post-quantum-crypto-submission

7. Farahmand, F., Ferozpuri, A., Diehl, W., Gaj, K.: Minerva: automated hardware optimization tool. In: 2017 International Conference on ReConFigurable Computing and FPGAs (ReConFig), pp. 1–8. IEEE, December 2017

8. Farahmand, F., Sharif, M.U., Briggs, K., Gaj, K.: A high-speed constant-time hardware implementation of NTRUEncrypt SVES. In: 2018 International Conference on Field Programmable Technology (ICFPT) (2018)

9. Ferozpuri, A., Gaj, K.: High-speed FPGA implementation of the NIST round 1 rainbow signature scheme. In: International Conference on ReConFigurable Computing and FPGAs (ReConFig 2018), pp. 1–6. IEEE, December 2018

10. Ghosh, S., Delvaux, J., Uhsadel, L., Verbauwhede, I.: A speed area optimized embedded co-processor for McEliece cryptosystem. In: 23rd International Conference on Application-Specific Systems, Architectures and Processors (ASAP), Delft, Netherlands, 9–11 July 2012, pp. 102–108. IEEE (2012). https://doi.org/10.1109/ASAP.2012.16

11. Hoffstein, J., Pipher, J., Silverman, J.H.: NTRU: a ring-based public key cryptosystem. In: Buhler, J.P. (ed.) Algorithmic Number Theory, pp. 267–288. Springer, Heidelberg (1998). https://doi.org/10.1007/BFb0054868

12. Howe, J., Oder, T., Krausz, M., Güneysu, T.: Standard lattice-based key encapsulation on embedded devices. IACR Transact. Cryptogr. Hardw. Embed. Syst. **2018**(3), 372–393 (2018). https://tches.iacr.org/index.php/TCHES/article/view/7279

13. Hülsing, A., Rijneveld, J., Schanck, J.M., Schwabe, P.: NTRU-HRSS-KEM: algorithm specifications and supporting documentation, November 2017. https://csrc.nist.gov/CSRC/media/Projects/Post-Quantum-Cryptography/documents/round-1/submissions/NTRU_HRSS_KEM.zip

14. Kamal, A.A., Youssef, A.M.: An FPGA implementation of the NTRUEncrypt cryptosystem. In: 2009 International Conference on Microelectronics - ICM, pp. 209–212, December 2009

15. Koziel, B., Azarderakhsh, R.: SIKE - supersingular isogeny key encapsulation: VHDL implementation, November 2017. https://sike.org

16. Kuo, P.C., et al.: High performance post-quantum key exchange on FPGAs. Cryptology ePrint Archive, Report 2017/690 (2017). https://eprint.iacr.org/2017/690

17. Liu, B., Wu, H.: Efficient architecture and implementation for NTRUEncrypt system. In: 2015 IEEE 58th International Midwest Symposium on Circuits and Systems (MWSCAS), pp. 1–4, August 2015

18. Liu, B., Wu, H.: Efficient multiplication architecture over truncated polynomial ring for NTRUEncrypt system. In: 2016 IEEE International Symposium on Circuits and Systems (ISCAS), pp. 1174–1177, May 2016

19. Migliore, V., Real, M.M., Lapotre, V., Tisserand, A., Fontaine, C., Gogniat, G.: Hardware/software co-design of an accelerator for FV homomorphic encryption scheme using Karatsuba algorithm. IEEE Transact. Comput. **67**(3), 335–347 (2018)

20. National Institute of Standards and Technology: Post-Quantum Cryptography, December 2017. https://csrc.nist.gov/Projects/Post-Quantum-Cryptography

21. National Institute of Standards and Technology: Post-Quantum Cryptography: Round 1 Submissions, December 2017. https://csrc.nist.gov/projects/post-quantum-cryptography/round-1-submissions
22. Oder, T., Güneysu, T.: Implementing the NewHope-simple key exchange on low-cost FPGAs. In: Fifth International Conference on Cryptology and Information Security, Latin America, La Habana, Cuba, 20–22 September 2017 (2017)
23. Wang, W., et al.: XMSS and embedded systems - XMSS hardware accelerators for RISC-V. Cryptology ePrint Archive, Report 2018/1225 (2017). https://eprint.iacr.org/2017/138.pdf
24. Wang, W., Szefer, J., Niederhagen, R.: FPGA-based Niederreiter cryptosystem using binary Goppa codes. In: Lange, T., Steinwandt, R. (eds.) PQCrypto 2018. LNCS, vol. 10786, pp. 77–98. Springer, Cham (2018). https://doi.org/10.1007/978-3-319-79063-3_4. http://caslab.csl.yale.edu/code/niederreiter/

Forward-Secure Group Signatures
from Lattices

San Ling, Khoa Nguyen, Huaxiong Wang, and Yanhong Xu[✉]

Division of Mathematical Sciences, School of Physical and Mathematical Sciences,
Nanyang Technological University, Singapore, Singapore
{lingsan,khoantt,hxwang,xu0014ng}@ntu.edu.sg

Abstract. Group signature is a fundamental cryptographic primitive, aiming to protect anonymity and ensure accountability of users. It allows group members to anonymously sign messages on behalf of the whole group, while incorporating a tracing mechanism to identify the signer of any suspected signature. Most of the existing group signature schemes, however, do not guarantee security once secret keys are exposed. To reduce potential damages caused by key exposure attacks, Song (ACM-CCS 2001) put forward the concept of forward-secure group signature (FSGS), which prevents attackers from forging group signatures pertaining to past time periods even if a secret group signing key is revealed at the current time period. For the time being, however, all known secure FSGS schemes are based on number-theoretic assumptions, and are vulnerable against quantum computers.

In this work, we construct the first lattice-based FSGS scheme. Our scheme is proven secure under the Short Integer Solution and Learning With Errors assumptions. At the heart of our construction is a scalable lattice-based key evolving mechanism, allowing users to periodically update their secret keys and to efficiently prove in zero-knowledge that key evolution process is done correctly. To realize this essential building block, we first employ the Bonsai tree structure by Cash et al. (EURO-CRYPT 2010) to handle the key evolution process, and then develop Langlois et al.'s construction (PKC 2014) to design its supporting zero-knowledge protocol.

Keywords: Group signatures · Key exposure · Forward-security · Lattice-based cryptography · Zero-knowledge proofs

1 Introduction

GROUP SIGNATURES. Initially suggested by Chaum and van Heyst [19], group signature (GS) allows users of a group controlled by a manager to sign messages anonymously in the name of the group (anonymity). Nevertheless, there is a tracing manager to identify the signer of any signature should the user abuse the anonymity (traceability). These seemingly contractive features, however, allow group signatures to find applications in various real-life scenarios

© Springer Nature Switzerland AG 2019
J. Ding and R. Steinwandt (Eds.): PQCrypto 2019, LNCS 11505, pp. 44–64, 2019.
https://doi.org/10.1007/978-3-030-25510-7_3

such as e-commence systems and anonymous online communications. Unfortunately, the exposure of group signing keys renders almost all the existing schemes unsatisfactory in practice. Indeed, in the traditional models of group signatures, e.g., [6,8,10,29,30,55], the security of the scheme is no longer guaranteed when the key exposure arises. So now let us look closely at the key exposure problem and the countermeasures to it.

EXPOSURE OF GROUP SIGNING KEYS AND FORWARD-SECURE GROUP SIGNATURES. Exposure of users' secret keys is one of the greatest dangers to many cryptographic protocols in practice [56]. Forward-secure mechanisms first introduced by Anderson [4], aim to minimize the damages caused by secret key exposures. More precisely, forward-security protects past uses of private keys in earlier time periods even if a break-in occurs currently. Afterwards, many forward-secure schemes were constructed, such as forward-secure signatures [1,7,26], forward-secure public key encryption systems [9,16,22], and forward-secure signatures with un-trusted update [13,40,41]. At the heart of these schemes is a key evolving technique that operates as follows. It divides the lifetime of the scheme into discrete T time periods. Upon entering a new time period, a subsequent secret key is computed from the current one via a *one-way* key evolution algorithm. Meanwhile, the preceding key is deleted promptly. Due to the one-wayness of the updating algorithm, the security of the previous keys is preserved even though the current one is compromised. Therefore, by carefully choosing a secure scheme that operates well with a key evolving mechanism, forward-security of the scheme can be guaranteed.

As investigated by Song [56], secret key exposure in group signatures is much more damaging than in ordinary digital signatures. In group signatures, if one group member's signing key is disclosed to the attacker, then the latter can sign arbitrary messages. In this situation, if the underlying group signature scheme is not secure against exposure of group signing keys, then the whole system has to be re-initialized, which is obviously inefficient in practice. Besides its inefficiency, this solution is also unsatisfactory. Once there is a break-in of the system, all previously signed group signatures become invalid since we do not have a mechanism to distinguish whether a signature is generated by a legitimate group member or by the attacker. What is worse, one of the easiest way for a misbehaving member Eve to attack the system and/or to repudiate her illegally signed signatures is to reveal her group signing key secretly in the Internet and then claim to be a victim of the key exposure problem [26]. Now the users who had accepted signatures *before* Eve's group signing key is exposed are now at the mercy of all the group members, some of whom (e.g., Eve) would not reissue the signatures with the new key.

The aforementioned problems induced by the exposure of group signing keys motivated Song [56] to put forward the notion of forward-secure group signature (FSGS), in which group members are able to update their group signing keys at each time period via a one-way key evolution algorithm. Therefore, when some group member's singing key is disclosed, all the signatures generated during past periods remain valid, which then prevents dishonest group members from repudiating signatures by simply exposing keys. Later, Nakanishi, Hira, Funabiki [50] defined a rigourous security model of FSGS for static groups, where users are fixed throughout the scheme, and demonstrated a pairing-based construction. Subsequently, Libert and Yung [42] extended Nakanishi et al.'s work to capture the setting of the dynamically growing groups. However, all these schemes are constructions based on number-theoretic assumptions and are fragile in the presence of quantum adversaries. In order not to put all eggs in one basket, it is imperative to consider instantiations based on alternative, post-quantum foundations, e.g., lattice assumptions. In view of this, let us now look at the topic of lattice-based group signatures.

LATTICE-BASED GROUP SIGNATURES. In 2010, Gordon et al. [25] introduced the first lattice-based instantiation of GS. Since then, numerous schemes have been put forward with various improvements on security, efficiency, and functionality. While many of them [11,15,21,31,36,44,52] aim to provide enhancement on security and efficiency, they are solely designed for the static groups and often fall too short for specific needs of real-life applications. With regard to advanced features, there have been proposed several schemes [32,33,39,45–47] and they are still behind their counterparts in the number-theoretic setting. Specifically, [32, 33,45,47] deal with dynamic user enrollments and/or revocations of misbehaving users while [39,46] attempt to restrict the power of the tracing manager or keep his actions accountable. For the time being, the problem of making GS secure against the key exposure problem is still open in the context of lattices. Taking into account the great threat of key exposure to GS and the vulnerability of GS from number-theoretic assumptions in front of quantum computers, it would be tempting to investigate lattice-based instantiations of FSGS. Furthermore, it would be desirable to achieve it with reasonable overhead, e.g., with complexity at most poly-logarithmic in T.

OUR CONTRIBUTIONS. We introduce the first FSGS scheme in the context of lattices. The scheme satisfies the security requirements put forward by Nakanishi et al. [50] in the random oracle model. Assuming the hardness of the Short Integer Solution (SIS) problem and the Learning With Errors (LWE) problem, our scheme achieves full anonymity and a stronger notion of traceability named forward-secure traceability, which captures the traceability in the setting of key exposure problems. Let λ be the security parameter, N be the expected number of group members, and T be total time periods, our construction achieves signature size $\widetilde{\mathcal{O}}(\lambda(\log N + \log T))$, group public key size $\widetilde{\mathcal{O}}(\lambda^2(\log N + \log T))$, and secret key size $\widetilde{\mathcal{O}}(\lambda^2(\log N + \log T)^2 \log T)$. In particular, forward security is achieved with a reasonable cost: the size of keys and signatures are at most $\mathcal{O}(\log^3 T)$ larger than those of the basic GS scheme [32] upon which we build ours.

OVERVIEW OF OUR TECHNIQUES. Typically, designing secure GS requires a combination of digital signature, encryption scheme and zero-knowledge (ZK) protocol. Let us first consider an ordinary GS scheme similar to the template proposed by Bellare et al. [6]. In the scheme, each user is assigned an ℓ bit string id as identity, where $\ell = \log N$. The user's signing key is a signature on his identifier id, generated by the group manager. Specifically, we let the signing key be a short vector $\mathbf{v}_{\mathrm{id}}$ satisfying $\mathbf{A}_{\mathrm{id}} \cdot \mathbf{v}_{\mathrm{id}} = \mathbf{u} \bmod q$ for some public vector $\mathbf{u}$. When signing a message, the user first encrypts his identity id to a ciphertext $\mathbf{c}$ and proves that he possesses a valid signature on his identity that is also correctly encrypted to $\mathbf{c}$. To achieve forward-security, we would need a mechanism to update the group signing key periodically and a ZK protocol to prove that the key updating procedure is done honestly.

Inspired by the HIBE-like key evolving technique from Nakanishi et al. [50] and Libert and Yung [42], which in turn follows from [9,13,16], we exploit the hierarchical structure of the Bonsai tree [18] to enable periodical key updating. To the best of our knowledge, this is the only lattice-based HIBE in the standard model with supporting (Stern-like [57]) ZK proofs by Langlois et al. [32], which seems to be the right stepping stone towards our goal. Let $T = 2^d$ be the total number of time periods. To enable key updating, each user id is associated with a subtree of depth d, where the leaves of the tree correspond to successive time periods in the apparent way. Let the subtree be identified by matrices $\mathbf{A}_{\mathrm{id}}, \mathbf{A}_{\ell+1}^0, \mathbf{A}_{\ell+1}^1, \ldots, \mathbf{A}_{\ell+d}^0, \mathbf{A}_{\ell+d}^1$ and $z = \mathsf{Bin}(t)$ be the binary representation of t. In order to show the key evolution is done correctly, we observe that it suffices to prove possession of a (short) Bonsai signature $\mathbf{v}_{\mathrm{id}\|z}$ satisfying $[\mathbf{A}_{\mathrm{id}}|\mathbf{A}_{\ell+1}^{z[1]}|\cdots|\mathbf{A}_{\ell+d}^{z[d]}] \cdot \mathbf{v}_{\mathrm{id}\|z} = \mathbf{u} \bmod q$. However, proving knowledge of the Bonsai signature departs from the protocol presented in [32]. The matrix $\mathbf{A}_{\mathrm{id}}$ should be secret and the binary string z should be public in our case while it is the other way around in [32]. Nevertheless, analyzing the above equation carefully, it actually reduces to proving knowledge of short vectors $\mathbf{w}_1$ and $\mathbf{w}_2$ and a binary string id such that $\mathbf{A}_{\mathrm{id}} \cdot \mathbf{w}_1 + \mathbf{A}'' \cdot \mathbf{w}_2 = \mathbf{u} \bmod q$, where $\mathbf{v}_{\mathrm{id}\|z} = (\mathbf{w}_1\|\mathbf{w}_2)$ and $\mathbf{A}''$ is built from some public matrices. To prove knowledge of $\mathbf{w}_2$, we can employ the decomposition/extension/permutation techniques by Ling et al. [43] that operate in Stern's framework [57]. Regarding the ZK protocol for proving knowledge of $\mathbf{w}_1$ and id, it indeed depends on the signature scheme used by the group manager to certify users. For simplicity, we employ the Bonsai tree signature [18] as well. Then, by utilizing the ZK protocol in [32], we are able to prove knowledge of $\mathbf{w}_1$ and id and manage to obtain the desired ZK protocol for proving possession of $\mathbf{v}_{\mathrm{id}\|z}$. It is worth mentioning that, besides the Bonsai signature, the Boyen signature [12] is also a plausible candidate, for which a ZK protocol showing the possession of a valid message-signature pair was known [44].

In the above, we have discussed the (Stern-like) ZK protocol showing knowledge of correctly updated signing key $\mathbf{v}_{\mathrm{id}\|\mathsf{Bin}(t)}$, the main technical building block in achieving our FSGS scheme. The next question is then how should the user derive $\mathbf{v}_{\mathrm{id}\|\mathsf{Bin}(t)}$ for all possible t using his group signing key $\mathbf{v}_{\mathrm{id}}$. To this end, we make a minor but significant change to the group signing key. Observe that for the Bonsai tree signature, once a trapdoor matrix $\mathbf{S}_{\mathrm{id}}$ satisfying $\mathbf{A}_{\mathrm{id}} \cdot \mathbf{S}_{\mathrm{id}} = \mathbf{0} \bmod q$ is known, the user id is able to generate $\mathbf{v}_{\mathrm{id}\|\mathsf{Bin}(t)}$ for all possible t. Therefore, we let the user's signing key be $\mathbf{S}_{\mathrm{id}}$ instead. Nevertheless, we then observe user id should not hold $\mathbf{S}_{\mathrm{id}}$ at all times, as the adversary could also generate all possible $\mathbf{v}_{\mathsf{id}\|\mathsf{Bin}(t)}$ once $\mathbf{S}_{\mathsf{id}}$ is known to him. One trivial method is to generate all possible $\mathbf{v}_{\mathsf{id}\|\mathsf{Bin}(t)}$ and then delete all the previous ones upon entering a new period. However, this will incur linear dependency on T, which is undesirable for efficiency purpose.

To achieve logarithmic overhead, we should think of a way to employ the structure of the Bonsai tree. Let $\mathsf{Nodes}_{(t \to T-1)}$ be the set of nodes such that it has size at most $\log T$ and contains exactly one ancestor of each leaf or the leaf itself between t and $T - 1$[1]. Now we let the signing key of user id at time t be trapdoor matrices $\mathbf{S}_{\mathsf{id}\|z}$ for all $z \in \mathsf{Nodes}_{(t \to T-1)}$. The user is then able to produce all possible $\mathbf{v}_{\mathsf{id}\|\mathsf{Bin}(t)}$ by employing $\mathbf{S}_{\mathsf{id}\|z}$ if z is an ancestor of $\mathsf{Bin}(t)$. More importantly, for each $z' \in \mathsf{Nodes}_{(t+1 \to T-1)}$, there exists a unique ancestor $z \in \mathsf{Nodes}_{(t \to T-1)}$, which enables the evolving of the signing key from time t to $t + 1$, thanks to the basis delegation algorithm of the Bonsai signature.

As discussed so far, we have shown how to update the key periodically and identified the ZK protocol for the honest behaviour of update. The thing that remains is to find a public key encryption (PKE) scheme that is compatible with the above ingredients. Furthermore, to achieve full anonymity, it typically requires the PKE scheme to be CCA-secure. To this end, we apply the CHK transform [17] to the identity-based encryption scheme [24]. For the obtained PKE scheme, we observe that there exists a Stern-like ZK protocol (see [44]) for proving knowledge of the plaintext, which is compatible in our setting.

To summarize, we have obtained a lattice-based FSGS scheme by developing several technical building blocks from previous works in a non-trivial way. Our scheme satisfies full anonymity due to the facts that the underlying encryption scheme is CCA-secure and that the underlying ZK protocol is statistically zero-knowledge, and achieves forward-secure traceability due to the security of the Bonsai tree signature [18]. We believe that, our construction - while not being truly novel - would certainly help to enrich the area of lattice-based GS.

RELATED WORK. Recently, Kansal, Dutta and Mukhopadhyay [27] proposed a lattice-based FSGS scheme that operates in the model of Libert and Yung [42]. Unfortunately, it can be observed that their construction does not satisfy the correctness and security requirements of [42]. (For details, see full version of this paper.)

2   Preliminaries

Throughout the paper, all vectors are column vectors. When concatenating two matrices of form $\mathbf{A} \in \mathbb{R}^{n \times m}$ and $\mathbf{B} \in \mathbb{R}^{n \times k}$, we use the notion $[\mathbf{A}|\mathbf{B}] \in \mathbb{R}^{n \times (m+k)}$ while we denote $(\mathbf{x}\|\mathbf{y}) \in \mathbb{R}^{m+k}$ as the concatenation of two vectors of form $\mathbf{x} \in \mathbb{R}^m$ and $\mathbf{y} \in \mathbb{R}^k$. Let $[m]$ be the set $\{1, 2, \cdots, m\}$.

---

[1] This set can be determined by the Nodeselect algorithm presented by Libert and Yung [42].

2.1 Forward-Secure Group Signatures

We now recall the syntax and security requirements of forward-secure group signature (FSGS), as formalized by Nakanishi et al. [50]. An FSGS scheme consists of the following polynomial-time algorithms.

KeyGen: This algorithm takes the tuple (λ, T, N) as input, with λ being security parameter, T being total number of time periods, and N being maximum number of group members. It then returns group public key gpk, secret key msk of group manager (GM), secret key mosk of tracing manager (TM), initial user secret keys usk_0. usk_0 is an array of initial N secret signing key $\{\mathsf{usk}_0[0], \mathsf{usk}_0[1], \cdots, \mathsf{usk}_0[N-1]\}$, with $\mathsf{usk}_0[i]$ being the initial key of user i.

KeyUpdate: On inputs gpk, $\mathsf{usk}_t[i]$, i, and $t+1$, with $\mathsf{usk}_t[i]$ being the secret signing key of user i at time t, this randomized algorithm outputs the secret signing key $\mathsf{usk}_{t+1}[i]$ of user i at time $t+1$.

Sign: On inputs gpk, $\mathsf{usk}_t[i]$, user i, time period t, and message M, this randomized algorithm generates a signature Σ on message M.

Verify: It takes as inputs gpk, time period t, message M and signature Σ, and returns $1/0$ indicating the validity of the signature.

Open: On inputs gpk, mosk, t, M and Σ, this deterministic algorithm returns an index i or $\perp$.

Correctness. For all λ, T, N, $(\mathsf{gpk}, \mathsf{msk}, \mathsf{mosk}, \mathsf{usk}_0) \leftarrow \mathsf{KeyGen}(\lambda, T, N)$, $\forall i \in \{0, 1, \cdots, N-1\}$, all $M \in \{0,1\}^*$, all $\mathsf{usk}_t[i] \leftarrow \mathsf{KeyUpdate}(\mathsf{gpk}, \mathsf{usk}_{t-1}[i], i, t)$ for all $t \in \{0, 1, \cdots T-1\}$, the following equations hold:

$$\mathsf{Verify}(\mathsf{gpk}, t, M, \mathsf{Sign}(\mathsf{gpk}, \mathsf{usk}_t[i], t, M)) = 1,$$

$$\mathsf{Open}(\mathsf{gpk}, \mathsf{mosk}, t, M, \mathsf{Sign}(\mathsf{gpk}, \mathsf{usk}_t[i], t, M)) = i.$$

Forward-Secure Traceability. This requirement demands that any PPT adversary, even if it can corrupt the tracing manager and some (or all) group members, is not able to produce a valid signature (i) that is opened to some non-corrupted user or (ii) that is traced to some corrupted user, but the signature is signed at time period preceding the secret key query of this corrupted user. Note that (i) captures the standard traceability requirement as in [6] while (ii) deals with the new requirement in the context of forward-security.

Full Anonymity. This requirement demands that any PPT adversary is infeasible to figure out which of two signers of its choice signed the challenged message of its choice at time period t of its choice. Details are referred to [50] or the full version of this paper.

2.2 Some Background on Lattices

Let $n \in \mathbb{Z}^+$ and Λ be a lattice of dimension n over $\mathbb{R}^n$. Let $\mathbf{S} = \{\mathbf{s}_1, \cdots, \mathbf{s}_n\} \subset \mathbb{R}^n$ be a basis of Λ. For simplicity, we write $\mathbf{S} = [\mathbf{s}_1| \cdots |\mathbf{s}_n] \in \mathbb{R}^{n \times n}$. Define

$\|\mathbf{S}\| = \mathrm{Max}_i \|\mathbf{s}_i\|$. Let $\widetilde{\mathbf{S}} = [\widetilde{\mathbf{s}}_1| \cdots |\widetilde{\mathbf{s}}_n]$ be the Gram-Schmidt orthogonalization of $\mathbf{S}$. We refer to $\|\widetilde{\mathbf{S}}\|$ as the Gram-Schmidt norm of $\mathbf{S}$. For any $\mathbf{c} \in \mathbb{R}^n$ and $\sigma \in \mathbb{R}^+$, define the following: $\rho_{\sigma,\mathbf{c}}(\mathbf{x}) = \exp(-\pi \frac{\|\mathbf{x}-\mathbf{c}\|^2}{\sigma^2})$ and $\rho_{\sigma,\mathbf{c}}(\Lambda) = \sum_{\mathbf{x} \in \Lambda} \rho_{\sigma,\mathbf{c}}(\mathbf{x})$ for any $\mathbf{x} \in \Lambda$. Define the discrete Gaussian distribution over the lattice Λ with parameter σ and center $\mathbf{c}$ to be $D_{\Lambda,\sigma,\mathbf{c}}(\mathbf{x}) = \rho_{\sigma,\mathbf{c}}(\mathbf{x})/\rho_{\sigma,\mathbf{c}}(\Lambda)$ for any $\mathbf{x} \in \Lambda$. We often omit $\mathbf{c}$ if it is $\mathbf{0}$.

Let $n, m, q \in \mathbb{Z}^+$ with $q \geq 2$. For $\mathbf{A} \in \mathbb{Z}_q^{n \times m}$ and $\mathbf{u} \in \mathbb{Z}_q^n$ that admits a solution to the equation $\mathbf{A} \cdot \mathbf{x} = \mathbf{u} \bmod q$, define

$$\Lambda^\perp(\mathbf{A}) = \{\mathbf{e} \in \mathbb{Z}^m : \mathbf{Ae} = \mathbf{0} \quad \bmod q\}, \Lambda^{\mathbf{u}}(\mathbf{A}) = \{\mathbf{e} \in \mathbb{Z}^m : \mathbf{Ae} = \mathbf{u} \quad \bmod q\}.$$

Define discrete Gaussian distribution over the set $\Lambda^{\mathbf{u}}(\mathbf{A})$ in the following way: $D_{\Lambda^{\mathbf{u}}(\mathbf{A}),\sigma,\mathbf{c}}(\mathbf{x}) = \rho_{\sigma,\mathbf{c}}(\mathbf{x})/\rho_{\sigma,\mathbf{c}}(\Lambda^{\mathbf{u}}(\mathbf{A}))$ for $\mathbf{x} \in \Lambda^{\mathbf{u}}(\mathbf{A})$.

Lemma 1 ([24,53]). *Let $n, m, q \in \mathbb{Z}^+$ with $q \geq 2$ and $m \geq 2n \log q$. Let $\sigma \in \mathbb{R}$ such that $\sigma \geq \omega(\sqrt{\log m})$.*

- *Then for all but a $2q^{-n}$ fraction of all $\mathbf{A} \in \mathbb{Z}_q^{n \times m}$, the distribution of the syndrome $\mathbf{u} = \mathbf{A} \cdot \mathbf{e} \bmod q$ is within negligible statistical distance from uniform over $\mathbb{Z}_q^n$ for $\mathbf{e} \hookleftarrow D_{\mathbb{Z}^m,\sigma}$. Besides, given $\mathbf{A} \cdot \mathbf{e} = \mathbf{u} \bmod q$, the conditional distribution of $\mathbf{e} \hookleftarrow D_{\mathbb{Z}^m,\sigma}$ is $D_{\Lambda^{\mathbf{u}}(\mathbf{A}),\sigma}$.*
- *Let $x \hookleftarrow D_{\mathbb{Z},\sigma}$, $t = \log n$, and $\beta = \lceil \sigma \cdot t \rceil$. Then the probability of $|x| \leq \beta$ is overwhelming.*
- *The distribution $D_{\mathbb{Z}^m,\sigma}$ has min-entropy at least $m - 1$.*

We next present two hard average-case problems: the *Short Integer Solution* (SIS) problem (in the ℓ_∞ norm) and the *Learning With Errors* (LWE) problem.

Definition 1 ([2,24,49], $\mathrm{SIS}_{n,m,q,\beta}^\infty$). *Given $\mathbf{A} \xleftarrow{\$} \mathbb{Z}_q^{n \times m}$, find a vector $\mathbf{e} \in \mathbb{Z}^m$ so that $\mathbf{A} \cdot \mathbf{e} = \mathbf{0} \bmod q$ and $0 < \|\mathbf{e}\|_\infty \leq \beta$.*

Let $q > \beta\sqrt{n}$ be an integer and m, β be polynomials in n, then solving the $\mathrm{SIS}_{n,m,q,\beta}^\infty$ problem (in the ℓ_∞ norm) is no easier than solving the SIVP_γ problem in the worst-case for some $\gamma = \beta \cdot \widetilde{\mathcal{O}}(\sqrt{nm})$ (see [24,48]).

Definition 2 ([54], $\mathrm{LWE}_{n,q,\chi}$). *For $\mathbf{s} \in \mathbb{Z}_q^n$, define a distribution $\mathcal{A}_{\mathbf{s},\chi}$ over $\mathbb{Z}_q^n \times \mathbb{Z}_q$ as follows: it samples a uniform vector $\mathbf{a}$ over $\mathbb{Z}_q^n$ and an element e according to χ, and outputs the pair $(\mathbf{a}, \mathbf{a}^\top \cdot \mathbf{s} + e)$. Then the goal of the $\mathrm{LWE}_{n,q,\chi}$ problem is to distinguish $m = \mathrm{poly}(n)$ samples chosen according to the distribution $\mathcal{A}_{\mathbf{s},\chi}$ for some secret $\mathbf{s} \in \mathbb{Z}_q^n$ from m samples chosen according to the uniform distribution over $\mathbb{Z}_q^n \times \mathbb{Z}_q$.*

Let $B = \widetilde{\mathcal{O}}(\sqrt{n})$ and χ be an efficiently samplable distribution over $\mathbb{Z}$ that outputs samples $e \in \mathbb{Z}$ with $|e| \leq B$ with all but negligible probability in n. If $q \geq 2$ is an arbitrary modulus, then the $\mathrm{LWE}_{n,q,\chi}$ problem is at least as hard as the worst-case problem SIVP_γ with $\gamma = \widetilde{\mathcal{O}}(n \cdot q/B)$ through an efficient quantum reduction [14,54]. Additionally, it is showed that the hardness of the LWE problem is maintained when the secret $\mathbf{s}$ is chosen from the error distribution χ (see [5]).

Now let us recall some algorithms from previous works that will be used extensively in this work.

Lemma 2 ([3]). *Let $n, m, q \in \mathbb{Z}^+$ with $q \geq 2$ and $m = O(n \log q)$. There is a PPT algorithm* TrapGen(n, m, q) *which returns a tuple $(\mathbf{A}, \mathbf{S})$ such that*

- $\mathbf{A}$ *is within negligible statistical distance from uniform over $\mathbb{Z}_q^{n \times m}$,*
- $\mathbf{S}$ *is a basis for $\Lambda^{\perp}(\mathbf{A})$, i.e., $\mathbf{A} \cdot \mathbf{S} = 0 \bmod q$, and $\|\widetilde{\mathbf{S}}\| \leq \mathcal{O}(\sqrt{n \log q})$.*

Lemma 3 ([24]). *Let $\mathbf{S} \in \mathbb{Z}^{m \times m}$ be a basis of $\Lambda^{\perp}(\mathbf{A})$ for some $\mathbf{A} \in \mathbb{Z}_q^{n \times m}$ whose columns expand the entire group $\mathbb{Z}_q^n$. Let $\mathbf{u}$ be a vector over $\mathbb{Z}_q^n$ and $s \geq \omega(\sqrt{\log n}) \cdot \|\widetilde{\mathbf{S}}\|$. There is a PPT algorithm* SampleD$(\mathbf{A}, \mathbf{S}, \mathbf{u}, s)$ *which returns a vector $\mathbf{v} \in \Lambda^{\mathbf{u}}(\mathbf{A})$ from a distribution that is within negligible statistical distance from $D_{\Lambda^{\mathbf{u}}(\mathbf{A}), s}$.*

We also need the following two algorithms to securely delegate basis.

Lemma 4 ([18]). *Let $\mathbf{S} \in \mathbb{Z}^{m \times m}$ be a basis of $\Lambda^{\perp}(\mathbf{A})$ for some $\mathbf{A} \in \mathbb{Z}_q^{n \times m}$ whose columns generate the entire group $\mathbb{Z}_q^n$. Let $\mathbf{A}' \in \mathbb{Z}_q^{n \times m'}$ be any matrix containing $\mathbf{A}$ as a submatrix. There is a deterministic polynomial-time algorithm* ExtBasis$(\mathbf{S}, \mathbf{A}')$ *which returns a basis $\mathbf{S}' \in \mathbb{Z}^{m' \times m'}$ of $\Lambda^{\perp}(\mathbf{A}')$ with $\|\widetilde{\mathbf{S}'}\| = \|\widetilde{\mathbf{S}}\|$.*

Lemma 5 ([18]). *Let $\mathbf{S}$ be a basis of an m-dimensional integer lattice Λ and a parameter $s \geq \omega(\sqrt{\log n}) \cdot \|\widetilde{\mathbf{S}}\|$. There is a PPT algorithm* RandBasis$(\mathbf{S}, s)$ *that outputs a new basis $\mathbf{S}'$ of Λ with $\|\mathbf{S}'\| \leq s \cdot \sqrt{m}$. Moreover, for any two bases $\mathbf{S}_0, \mathbf{S}_1$ of Λ and any $s \geq \max\{\|\widetilde{\mathbf{S}_0}\|, \|\widetilde{\mathbf{S}_1}\|\} \cdot \omega(\sqrt{\log n})$, the outputs of* RandBasis$(\mathbf{S}_0, s)$ *and* RandBasis$(\mathbf{S}_1, s)$ *are statistically close.*

2.3 The Bonsai Tree Signature Scheme

Our construction builds on the Bonsai tree signature scheme [18]. Now we describe it briefly. The scheme takes the following parameters: λ is the security parameter and $n = \mathcal{O}(\lambda)$, ℓ is the message length, integer $q = \mathrm{poly}(n)$ is sufficiently large, $m = \mathcal{O}(n \log q)$, $\widetilde{L} = \mathcal{O}(\sqrt{n \log q})$, $s = \omega(\sqrt{\log n}) \cdot \widetilde{L}$, and $\beta = \lceil s \cdot \log n \rceil$. The verification key is the tuple $(\mathbf{A}_0, \mathbf{A}_1^0, \mathbf{A}_1^1, \ldots, \mathbf{A}_\ell^0, \mathbf{A}_\ell^1, \mathbf{u})$ while the signing key is $\mathbf{S}_0$, where $(\mathbf{A}_0, \mathbf{S}_0)$ is generated by the TrapGen(n, m, q) algorithm as described in Lemma 2 and matrices $\mathbf{A}_1^0, \mathbf{A}_1^1, \ldots, \mathbf{A}_\ell^0, \mathbf{A}_\ell^1$ and vector $\mathbf{u}$ are all uniformly random and independent over $\mathbb{Z}_q^{n \times m}$ and $\mathbb{Z}_q^n$, respectively.

To sign a binary message id $\in \{0, 1\}^\ell$, the signer first computes the matrix $\mathbf{A}_{\mathrm{id}} := [\mathbf{A}_0 | \mathbf{A}_1^{\mathrm{id}[1]} | \cdots | \mathbf{A}_\ell^{\mathrm{id}[\ell]}] \in \mathbb{Z}_q^{n \times (\ell+1)m}$, and then outputs a vector $\mathbf{v} \in \Lambda^{\mathbf{u}}(\mathbf{A}_{\mathrm{id}})$ via the algorithm SampleD(ExtBasis$(\mathbf{S}_0, \mathbf{A}_{\mathrm{id}}), \mathbf{u}, s)$. To verify the validity of $\mathbf{v}$ on message id, the verifier computes $\mathbf{A}_{\mathrm{id}}$ as above and checks if $\mathbf{A}_{\mathrm{id}} \cdot \mathbf{v} = \mathbf{u} \bmod q$ and $\|\mathbf{v}\|_\infty \leq \beta$ hold. They proved that this signature scheme is existential unforgeable under static chosen message attacks based on the hardness of the SIS problem.

2.4   Stern-Like Zero-Knowledge Argument Systems

The statistical zero-knowledge argument of knowledge (ZKAoK) presented in this work are Stern-like [57] protocols. In 1996, Stern [57] suggested a three-move zero-knowledge protocol for the well-known syndrome decoding (SD) problem. It was then later adapted to the lattice setting for a restricted version of Inhomogeneous Short Integer Solution (ISIS$^\infty$) problem by Kawachi et al. [28]. More recently, Ling et al. [43] generalized the protocol to handle more versatile relations that find applications in the designs of various lattice-based constructions (see, e.g., [34–38,51]). Libert et al. [33] put forward an abstraction of Stern's protocol to capture a wider range of lattice-based relations, which we now recall.

An abstraction of Stern's Protocol. Let $K, L, q \in \mathbb{Z}^+$ with $L \geq K$ and $q \geq 2$, and let VALID $\subset \{-1, 0, 1\}^L$. Given a finite set $\mathcal{S}$, associate every $\phi \in \mathcal{S}$ with a permutation Γ_ϕ of L elements so that the following conditions hold:

$$\begin{cases} \mathbf{w} \in \mathsf{VALID} \iff \Gamma_\phi(\mathbf{w}) \in \mathsf{VALID}, \\ \text{If } \mathbf{w} \in \mathsf{VALID} \text{ and } \phi \text{ is uniform in } \mathcal{S}, \text{ then } \Gamma_\phi(\mathbf{w}) \text{ is uniform in } \mathsf{VALID}. \end{cases} \tag{1}$$

The target is to construct a statistical ZKAoK for the abstract relation of the following form:

$$\mathrm{R}_{\mathrm{abstract}} = \left\{ (\mathbf{M}, \mathbf{u}), \mathbf{w} \in \mathbb{Z}_q^{K \times L} \times \mathbb{Z}_q^K \times \mathsf{VALID} : \mathbf{M} \cdot \mathbf{w} = \mathbf{u} \bmod q. \right\}$$

To obtain the desired ZKAoK protocol, one has to prove that $\mathbf{w} \in \mathsf{VALID}$ and $\mathbf{w}$ satisfies the linear equation $\mathbf{M} \cdot \mathbf{w} = \mathbf{u} \bmod q$. To prove the former condition holds in a ZK manner, the prover chooses $\phi \xleftarrow{\$} \mathcal{S}$ and let the verifier check $\Gamma_\phi(\mathbf{w}) \in \mathsf{VALID}$. According to the first condition in (1), the verifier should be convinced that $\mathbf{w}$ is indeed from the set VALID. At the same time, the verifier is not able to learn any extra information about $\mathbf{w}$ due to the second condition in (1). To show in ZK that the linear equation holds, the prover simply chooses $\mathbf{r}_w \xleftarrow{\$} \mathbb{Z}_q^L$ as a masking vector and then shows to the verifier that the equation $\mathbf{M} \cdot (\mathbf{w} + \mathbf{r}_w) = \mathbf{M} \cdot \mathbf{r}_w + \mathbf{u} \bmod q$ holds instead.

It is proved in [33] that there exists a statistical ZKAoK protocol with perfect completeness, soundness error $2/3$, and communication cost $\mathcal{O}(L \log q)$ for the relation $\mathrm{R}_{\mathrm{abstract}}$. The system utilizes a statistically hiding and computationally binding string commitment scheme COM from [28]. Due to space limit, details are referred to [33] or the full version of this paper.

3   Our Lattice-Based Forward-Secure Group Signature

In the description below, for a binary tree of depth k, we identify each node at depth j with a binary vector z of length j such that $z[1]$ to $z[j]$ are ordered from the top to the bottom and a 0 and a 1 indicate the left and right branch respectively in the order of traversal. Let $B \in \mathbb{Z}^+$. For an integer $0 \leq b \leq B$, denote $\mathsf{Bin}(b)$ as the binary representation of b with length $\lceil \log B \rceil$.

In our FSGS scheme, lifetime of the scheme is divided into T discrete periods $0, 1, \cdots, T - 1$. For simplicity, let $T = 2^d$ for some $d \in \mathbb{Z}^+$. Following previous works [13,42], each time period t is associated with leaf $\mathsf{Bin}(t)$.

Following [13], for $j = 1, \cdots, d + 1$, $t \in \{0, 1, \cdots, T - 1\}$, we define a time period's "right sibling at depth j" as

$$\mathsf{sibling}(j, t) = \begin{cases} (1)^\top & \text{if } j = 1 \text{ and } \mathsf{Bin}(t)[j] = 0, \\ (\mathsf{Bin}(t)[1], \cdots, \mathsf{Bin}(t)[j-1], 1)^\top & \text{if } 1 < j \leq d \text{ and } \mathsf{Bin}(t)[j] = 0, \\ \perp & \text{if } j \leq d \text{ and } \mathsf{Bin}(t)[j] = 1, \\ \mathsf{Bin}(t) & \text{if } j = d + 1. \end{cases}$$

Define node set $\mathsf{Nodes}_{(t \to T-1)}$ to be $\{\mathsf{sibling}(1, t), \cdots, \mathsf{sibling}(d + 1, t)\}$. For any $t' > t$, one can check that for any non-$\perp$ $z' \in \mathsf{Nodes}_{(t' \to T-1)}$, there exists a $z \in \mathsf{Nodes}_{(t \to T-1)}$ such that z is an ancestor of z'.

3.1 Description of the Scheme

Our scheme operates in the Nakanishi et al.'s (static) model [50]. Let $T = 2^d$ and $N = 2^\ell$. The group public key consists of (i) a Bonsai tree of depth $\ell + d$ specified by a matrix $\mathbf{A} = [\mathbf{A}_0 | \mathbf{A}_1^0 | \mathbf{A}_1^1 \cdots | \mathbf{A}_{\ell+d}^0 | \mathbf{A}_{\ell+d}^1] \in \mathbb{Z}_q^{n \times (2\ell+2d+1)m}$ and a vector $\mathbf{u} \in \mathbb{Z}_q^n$, which are for issuing certificate; (ii) A public matrix $\mathbf{B} \in \mathbb{Z}_q^{n \times m}$ of the IBE scheme by Gentry et al. [24], which is for encrypting user identities when signing messages. The secret key of GM is a trapdoor matrix of the Bonsai tree while the secret key of the tracing manager is a trapdoor matrix of the IBE scheme.

Each user id $\in \{0, 1\}^\ell$ is assigned a node id. To enable periodical key updating, each user id is associated with a subtree of depth d. In our scheme, all users are assumed to be valid group members from time 0 to $T - 1$. Let z be a binary string of length $d_z \leq d$. Define $\mathbf{A}_{\mathsf{id}\|z} = [\mathbf{A}_0 | \mathbf{A}_1^{\mathsf{id}[1]} | \cdots | \mathbf{A}_\ell^{\mathsf{id}[\ell]} | \mathbf{A}_{\ell+1}^{z[1]} | \cdots | \mathbf{A}_{\ell+d_z}^{z[d_z]}] \in \mathbb{Z}_q^{n \times (\ell+d_z+1)m}$. Specifically, the group signing key of user id at time t is $\{\mathbf{S}_{\mathsf{id}\|z}, z \in \mathsf{Nodes}_{(t \to T-1)}\}$, which satisfies $\mathbf{A}_{\mathsf{id}\|z} \cdot \mathbf{S}_{\mathsf{id}\|z} = \mathbf{0} \bmod q$. Thanks to the basis delegation technique [18], users are able to compute the trapdoor matrices for all the descendent of nodes in the set $\mathsf{Nodes}_{(t \to T-1)}$ and hence are able to derive all the subsequent signing keys. We remark that for leaf nodes, it is sufficient to generate short vectors instead of short bases, since we do not need to perform further delegations.

Once received the group signing key, each user can issue signatures on behalf of the group. When signing a message at time t, user id first generates a one-time signature key pair (ovk, osk), and then encrypts his identity id to a ciphertext $\mathbf{c}$ using the IBE scheme with respect to "identity" ovk. Next, he proves in zero-knowledge that: (i) he is a certified group member; (ii) he has done key evolution honestly; (iii) $\mathbf{c}$ is a correct encryption of id. To prove that facts (i) and (ii) hold, it is sufficient to prove knowledge of a short vector $\mathbf{v}_{\mathsf{id}\|\mathsf{Bin}(t)}$ such that $\mathbf{A}_{\mathsf{id}\|\mathsf{Bin}(t)} \cdot \mathbf{v}_{\mathsf{id}\|\mathsf{Bin}(t)} = \mathbf{u} \bmod q$. The protocol is developed from Langlois et al.'s technique [32] (which was also employed in [20] for designing policy-based signatures) and Ling et al.'s technique [43], and is repeated $\kappa = \omega(\log n)$ times to achieve negligible soundness error, and is made non-interactive via Fiat-Shamir transform [23] as a triple Π. Finally, the user generates a one-time signature sig on the pair $(\mathbf{c}, \Pi)$, and outputs the group signature consisting of $(\mathsf{ovk}, \mathbf{c}, \Pi, \mathsf{sig})$.

To verify a group signature, one checks the validity of sig under the key ovk and Π. In case of dispute, TM can decrypt the ciphertext with respect to the "identity" ovk using his secret key. Details of the scheme are described below.

KeyGen(λ, T, N): On inputs security parameter λ, total number of time periods $T = 2^d$ for some $d \in \mathbb{Z}_+$ and maximum number of group members $N = 2^\ell$ for some $\ell \in \mathbb{Z}^+$, this algorithm does the following:

1. Choose $n = \mathcal{O}(\lambda)$, $q = \text{poly}(n)$, $m = \mathcal{O}(n \log q)$. Let $k = \ell + d$ and $\kappa = \omega(\log n)$.
2. Run TrapGen(n, m, q) as described in Lemma 2 to obtain $\mathbf{A}_0 \in \mathbb{Z}_q^{n \times m}$ and $\mathbf{S}_0 \in \mathbb{Z}^{m \times m}$.
3. Sample $\mathbf{u} \xleftarrow{\$} \mathbb{Z}_q^n$, and $\mathbf{A}_i^b \xleftarrow{\$} \mathbb{Z}_q^{n \times m}$ for all $i \in [k]$ and $b \in \{0,1\}$.
4. Choose a one-time signature scheme $\mathcal{OTS} = (\mathsf{OGen}, \mathsf{OSign}, \mathsf{OVer})$, and a statistically hiding and computationally binding commitment scheme COM from [28] that will be used in our zero-knowledge argument system.
5. Let $\mathcal{H}_0 : \{0,1\}^* \to \mathbb{Z}_q^{n \times \ell}$ and $\mathcal{H}_1 : \{0,1\}^* \to \{1,2,3\}^\kappa$ be collision-resistant hash functions, which will be modelled as random oracles in the security analysis.
6. Let Gaussian parameter s_i be $\mathcal{O}(\sqrt{nk \log q})^{i-\ell+1} \cdot \omega(\sqrt{\log n})^{i-\ell+1}$, which will be used to generate short bases or sample short vectors at level i for $i \in \{\ell, \ell+1, \cdots, k\}$.
7. Choose integer bounds $\beta = \lceil s_k \cdot \log n \rceil$, $B = \widetilde{\mathcal{O}}(\sqrt{n})$, and let χ be a B-bounded distribution over $\mathbb{Z}$.
8. Generate a master key pair $(\mathbf{B}, \mathbf{S}) \in \mathbb{Z}_q^{n \times m} \times \mathbb{Z}^{m \times m}$ for the IBE scheme by Gentry et al. [24] via the TrapGen(n, m, q) algorithm.
9. For user $i \in \{0, 1, \cdots, N-1\}$, let id $= \mathsf{Bin}(i) \in \{0,1\}^\ell$. Let node id be the identifier of user i. Determine the node set Nodes$_{(0 \to T-1)}$.
   For $z \in \mathsf{Nodes}_{(0 \to T-1)}$, if $z = \perp$, set $\mathbf{usk}_0[i][z] = \perp$. Otherwise denote d_z as the length of z with $d_z \leq d$, compute the matrix

   $$\mathbf{A}_{\mathsf{id}\|z} = [\mathbf{A}_0 | \mathbf{A}_1^{\mathsf{id}[1]} | \cdots | \mathbf{A}_\ell^{\mathsf{id}[\ell]} | \mathbf{A}_{\ell+1}^{z[1]} | \cdots | \mathbf{A}_{\ell+d_z}^{z[d_z]}] \in \mathbb{Z}_q^{n \times (\ell+d_z+1)m}.$$

   and proceed as follows:
   - If z is of length d, i.e., $d_z = d$, it computes a vector $\mathbf{v}_{\mathsf{id}\|z} \in \Lambda^\mathbf{u}(\mathbf{A}_{\mathsf{id}\|z})$ via

     $$\mathbf{v}_{\mathsf{id}\|z} \leftarrow \mathsf{SampleD}(\mathsf{ExtBasis}(\mathbf{S}_0, \mathbf{A}_{\mathsf{id}\|z}), \mathbf{u}, s_k).$$

     Set $\mathbf{usk}_0[i][z] = \mathbf{v}_{\mathsf{id}\|z}$.
   - If z is of length less than d, i.e., $1 \leq d_z < d$, it computes a matrix $\mathbf{S}_{\mathsf{id}\|z} \in \mathbb{Z}^{(\ell+d_z+1)m \times (\ell+d_z+1)m}$ via

     $$\mathbf{S}_{\mathsf{id}\|z} \leftarrow \mathsf{RandBasis}(\mathsf{ExtBasis}(\mathbf{S}_0, \mathbf{A}_{\mathsf{id}\|z}), s_{\ell+d_z}).$$

     Set $\mathbf{usk}_0[i][z] = \mathbf{S}_{\mathsf{id}\|z}$.

Let $\mathbf{usk}_0[i] = \{\mathbf{usk}_0[i][z], z \in \text{Nodes}_{(0 \to T-1)}\}$ be the initial secret key of user i.

Let public parameter be pp, group public key be gpk, secret key of GM be msk, secret key of TM be mosk and initial secret key be $\mathbf{usk}_0$, which are defined as follows:

$$\mathsf{pp} = \{n, q, m, \ell, d, k, \kappa, \mathcal{OTS}, \mathsf{COM}, \mathcal{H}_0, \mathcal{H}_1, s_\ell, \ldots, s_k, \beta, B\},$$

$$\mathsf{gpk} = \{\mathsf{pp}, \mathbf{A}_0, \mathbf{A}_1^0, \mathbf{A}_1^1, \ldots, \mathbf{A}_k^0, \mathbf{A}_k^1, \mathbf{u}, \mathbf{B}\},$$

$$\mathsf{msk} = \mathbf{S}_0, \qquad \mathsf{mosk} = \mathbf{S},$$

$$\mathbf{usk}_0 = \{\mathbf{usk}_0[0], \mathbf{usk}_0[1], \ldots, \mathbf{usk}_0[N-1]\}.$$

KeyUpdate($\mathsf{gpk}, \mathbf{usk}_t[i], i, t+1$): Compute the identifier of user i as $\mathsf{id} = \mathsf{Bin}(i)$, parse $\mathbf{usk}_t[i] = \{\mathbf{usk}_t[i][z], z \in \text{Nodes}_{(t \to T-1)}\}$, and determine the node set $\text{Nodes}_{(t+1 \to T-1)}$.

For $z' \in \text{Nodes}_{(t+1 \to T-1)}$, if $z' = \bot$, set $\mathbf{usk}_{t+1}[i][z'] = \bot$. Otherwise, there exists exactly one $z \in \text{Nodes}_{(t \to T-1)}$ as its prefix, i.e., $z' = z\|y$ for some suffix y. Consider the following two cases.

1. If $z' = z$, let $\mathbf{usk}_{t+1}[i][z'] = \mathbf{usk}_t[i][z]$.
2. If $z' = z\|y$ for some non-empty y, then $\mathbf{usk}_t[i][z] = \mathbf{S}_{\mathsf{id}\|z}$. Consider the following two subcases.
   - If z' is of length d, run

   $$\mathbf{v}_{\mathsf{id}\|z'} \leftarrow \mathsf{SampleD}(\mathsf{ExtBasis}(\mathbf{S}_{\mathsf{id}\|z}, \mathbf{A}_{\mathsf{id}\|z'}), \mathbf{u}, s_k),$$

   and set $\mathbf{usk}_{t+1}[i][z'] = \mathbf{v}_{\mathsf{id}\|z'}$.
   - If z' is of length less than d, run

   $$\mathbf{S}_{\mathsf{id}\|z'} \leftarrow \mathsf{RandBasis}(\mathsf{ExtBasis}(\mathbf{S}_{\mathsf{id}\|z}, \mathbf{A}_{\mathsf{id}\|z'}), s_{\ell+d_{z'}}),$$

   and set $\mathbf{usk}_{t+1}[i][z'] = \mathbf{S}_{\mathsf{id}\|z'}$.

Output updated key as $\mathbf{usk}_{t+1}[i] = \{\mathbf{usk}_{t+1}[i][z'], z' \in \text{Nodes}_{(t+1 \to T-1)}\}$.

Sign($\mathsf{gpk}, \mathbf{usk}_t[i], i, t, M$): Compute the identifier $\mathsf{id} = \mathsf{Bin}(i)$. By the structure of the node set $\text{Nodes}_{(t \to T-1)}$, there exists some $z \in \text{Nodes}_{(t \to T-1)}$ such that $z = \mathsf{Bin}(t)$ is of length d and $\mathbf{usk}_t[i][z] = \mathbf{v}_{\mathsf{id}\|z}$.

To sign a message $M \in \{0,1\}^*$, the signer then performs the following steps.

1. First, generate a one-time signature key pair $(\mathsf{ovk}, \mathsf{osk}) \leftarrow \mathsf{OGen}(n)$, and then encrypt id with respect to "identity" ovk as follows. Let $\mathbf{G} = \mathcal{H}_0(\mathsf{ovk}) \in \mathbb{Z}_q^{n \times \ell}$. Sample $\mathbf{s} \hookleftarrow \chi^n$, $\mathbf{e}_1 \hookleftarrow \chi^m$, $\mathbf{e}_2 \hookleftarrow \chi^\ell$, and compute ciphertext $(\mathbf{c}_1, \mathbf{c}_2) \in \mathbb{Z}_q^m \times \mathbb{Z}_q^\ell$ as

$$(\mathbf{c}_1 = \mathbf{B}^\top \cdot \mathbf{s} + \mathbf{e}_1, \quad \mathbf{c}_2 = \mathbf{G}^\top \cdot \mathbf{s} + \mathbf{e}_2 + \lfloor \tfrac{q}{2} \rfloor \cdot \mathsf{id}). \qquad (2)$$

2. Second, compute the matrix $\mathbf{A}_{\text{id}\|z}$ and generate a NIZKAoK Π to demonstrate the possession of a valid tuple

$$\xi = (\text{id}, \mathbf{s}, \mathbf{e}_1, \mathbf{e}_2, \mathbf{v}_{\text{id}\|z}) \tag{3}$$

such that
(a) $\mathbf{A}_{\text{id}\|z} \cdot \mathbf{v}_{\text{id}\|z} = \mathbf{u} \mod q$, and $\|\mathbf{v}_{\text{id}\|z}\|_\infty \leq \beta$.
(b) Equations in (2) hold with $\|\mathbf{s}\|_\infty \leq B$, $\|\mathbf{e}_1\|_\infty \leq B$ and $\|\mathbf{e}_2\|_\infty \leq B$.
This is done by running our argument system described in Sect. 4.2 with public input

$$\gamma = (\mathbf{A}_0, \mathbf{A}_1^0, \mathbf{A}_1^1, \dots, \mathbf{A}_k^0, \mathbf{A}_k^1, \mathbf{u}, \mathbf{B}, \mathbf{G}, \mathbf{c}_1, \mathbf{c}_2, t)$$

and witness tuple ξ as above. The protocol is repeated $\kappa = \omega(\log n)$ times to obtain negligible soundness error and made non-interactive via the Fiat-Shamir heuristic [23] as a triple $\Pi = ((\text{CMT}_i)_{i=1}^\kappa, \text{CH}, (\text{RSP}_i)_{i=1}^\kappa)$ with $\text{CH} = \mathcal{H}_1(M, (\text{CMT}_i)_{i=1}^\kappa, \mathbf{c}_1, \mathbf{c}_2, t)$.
3. Third, compute a one-time signature $\text{sig} = \text{OSign}(\text{osk}; \mathbf{c}_1, \mathbf{c}_2, \Pi)$ and output the signature as $\Sigma = (\text{ovk}, \mathbf{c}_1, \mathbf{c}_2, \Pi, \text{sig})$.

Verify(gpk, t, M, Σ): This algorithm proceeds as follows:
1. Parse Σ as $\Sigma = (\text{ovk}, \mathbf{c}_1, \mathbf{c}_2, \Pi, \text{sig})$. If $\text{OVer}(\text{ovk}; \text{sig}; \mathbf{c}_1, \mathbf{c}_2, \Pi) = 0$, then return 0.
2. Parse Π as $\Pi = ((\text{CMT}_i)_{i=1}^\kappa, (\text{Ch}_1, \dots, \text{Ch}_\kappa), (\text{RSP}_i)_{i=1}^\kappa)$.
If $(\text{Ch}_1, \cdots, \text{Ch}_\kappa) \neq \mathcal{H}_1(M, (\text{CMT}_i)_{i=1}^\kappa, \mathbf{c}_1, \mathbf{c}_2, t)$, then return 0.
3. For $i \in [\kappa]$, run the verification step of the underlying argument protocol to check the validity of RSP_i with respect to CMT_i and Ch_i. If any of the conditions does not hold, then return 0.
4. Return 1.

Open($\text{gpk}, \text{mosk}, t, M, \Sigma$): If Verify($\text{gpk}, t, M, \Sigma$) $= 0$, abort. Otherwise, let mosk be $\mathbf{S} \in \mathbb{Z}^{m \times m}$ and parse Σ as $\Sigma = (\text{ovk}, \mathbf{c}_1, \mathbf{c}_2, \Pi, \text{sig})$. Then it decrypts $(\mathbf{c}_1, \mathbf{c}_2)$ as follows:
1. Compute $\mathbf{G} = \mathcal{H}_0(\text{ovk}) = [\mathbf{g}_1 | \cdots | \mathbf{g}_\ell] \in \mathbb{Z}^{n \times \ell}$. Then use $\mathbf{S}$ to compute a small norm matrix $\mathbf{F}_{\text{ovk}} \in \mathbb{Z}^{m \times \ell}$ such that $\mathbf{B} \cdot \mathbf{F}_{\text{ovk}} = \mathbf{G} \mod q$. This is done by computing $\mathbf{f}_i \leftarrow \text{SampleD}(\mathbf{B}, \mathbf{S}, \mathbf{g}_i, s_\ell)$ for all $i \in [\ell]$ and let $\mathbf{F}_{\text{ovk}} = [\mathbf{f}_1 | \cdots | \mathbf{f}_\ell]$.
2. Use $\mathbf{F}_{\text{ovk}}$ to decrypt $(\mathbf{c}_1, \mathbf{c}_2)$ by computing

$$\text{id}' = \left\lfloor \frac{\mathbf{c}_2 - \mathbf{F}_{\text{ovk}}^\top \cdot \mathbf{c}_1}{\lfloor q/2 \rfloor} \right\rceil \in \{0,1\}^\ell.$$

3. Return $\text{id}' \in \{0,1\}^\ell$.

3.2   Analysis of the Scheme

EFFICIENCY. We first analyze the complexity of the scheme described in Sect. 3.1, with respect to security parameter λ and parameters $\ell = \log N$ and $d = \log T$. Recall $k = \ell + d$.

- The group public key gpk has bit-size $\widetilde{\mathcal{O}}(\lambda^2 \cdot k)$.
- The user secret key $\mathsf{usk}_t[i]$ has at most $d+1$ trapdoor matrices, and has bit-size $\widetilde{\mathcal{O}}(\lambda^2 \cdot k^2 d)$.
- The size of signature Σ is dominated by that of the Stern-like NIZKAoK Π, which is $\widetilde{\mathcal{O}}(|\xi| \cdot \log q) \cdot \omega(\log \lambda)$, where $|\xi|$ denotes the bit-size of the witness-tuple ξ. Overall, Σ has bit-size $\widetilde{\mathcal{O}}(\lambda \cdot k)$.

CORRECTNESS. The correctness of the above scheme follows from the following facts: (i) the underlying argument system is perfectly complete; (ii) the underlying encryption scheme obtained by transforming the IBE scheme in [24] via CHK transformation [17] is correct.

Specifically, for an honest user, when he signs a message at time period t, he is able to demonstrate the possession of a valid tuple ξ of the form (3). Therefore, with probability 1, the resulting signature Π will be accepted by the Verify algorithm, implied by the perfect completeness of the underlying argument system. As for the correctness of the Open algorithm, note that

$$\mathbf{c}_2 - \mathbf{F}_{\mathsf{ovk}}^{\top} \cdot \mathbf{c}_1 = \mathbf{G}^{\top} \cdot \mathbf{s} + \mathbf{e}_2 + \lfloor \tfrac{q}{2} \rfloor \cdot \mathsf{id} - \mathbf{F}_{\mathsf{ovk}}^{\top} \cdot (\mathbf{B}^{\top} \cdot \mathbf{s} + \mathbf{e}_1)$$

$$= \lfloor \tfrac{q}{2} \rfloor \cdot \mathsf{id} + \mathbf{e}_2 - \mathbf{F}_{\mathsf{ovk}}^{\top} \cdot \mathbf{e}_1$$

where $\|\mathbf{e}_1\| \leq B$, $\|\mathbf{e}_2\|_\infty \leq B$, and $\|\mathbf{f}_i\|_\infty \leq \lceil s_\ell \cdot \log m \rceil = \widetilde{\mathcal{O}}(\sqrt{n \cdot k})$, which is implied by Lemma 1. Recall that $q = \mathrm{poly}(n)$, $m = \mathcal{O}(n \log q)$ and $B = \widetilde{\mathcal{O}}(\sqrt{n})$. Hence

$$\|\mathbf{e}_2 - \mathbf{F}_{\mathsf{ovk}}^{\top} \cdot \mathbf{e}_1\|_\infty \leq B + m \cdot B \cdot \widetilde{\mathcal{O}}(\sqrt{n \cdot k}) = \widetilde{\mathcal{O}}(n^2).$$

As long as we choose sufficiently large q, with probability 1, the Open algorithm will recover id and correctness of the Open algorithm holds.

SECURITY. In Theorem 1, we prove that our scheme satisfies the security requirements put forward by Nakanishi et al. [50].

Theorem 1. *In the random oracle model, the forward-secure group signature described in Sect. 3.1 satisfies full anonymity and forward-secure traceability requirements under the LWE and SIS assumptions.*

The proof of Theorem 1 is deferred to the full version of this paper.

4 The Underlying Zero-Knowledge Argument System

In Sect. 4.1, we recall the extension, decomposition, and permutation techniques from [32,43]. Then we describe in Sect. 4.2 our statistical ZKAoK protocol that will be used in generating group signatures.

4.1 Extension, Decomposition, and Permutation

EXTENSIONS. For $m \in \mathbb{Z}$, let B_{3m} be the set of all vectors in $\{-1, 0, 1\}^{3m}$ having exactly m coordinates -1, m coordinates 1, and m coordinates 0 and $\mathcal{S}_m$ be the set of all permutations on m elements. Let $\oplus$ be the addition operation modulo 2. Define the following functions

- ext_3: $\{-1, 0, 1\}^m \to B_{3m}$ that transforms a vector $\mathbf{v} = (v_1, \ldots, v_m)^\top$ to vector $(\mathbf{v} \| (-1)^{m-n_{-1}} \| \mathbf{0}^{m-n_0} \| \mathbf{1}^{m-n_1})^\top$, where n_j is the number of element j in the vector $\mathbf{v}$ for $j \in \{-1, 0, 1\}$.
- enc_2: $\{0, 1\}^m \to \{0, 1\}^{2m}$ that transforms a vector $\mathbf{v} = (v_1, \ldots, v_m)^\top$ to vector $(v_1, 1 - v_1, \ldots, v_m, 1 - v_m)^\top$.

DECOMPOSITIONS AND PERMUTATIONS. We now recall the integer decomposition technique. For any $B \in \mathbb{Z}^+$, define $p_B = \lfloor \log B \rfloor + 1$ and the sequence $B_1, \ldots, B_{p_B}$ as $B_j = \lfloor \frac{B + 2^{j-1}}{2^j} \rfloor$ for each $j \in [p_B]$. As observed in [43], it satisfies $\sum_{j=1}^{p_B} B_j = B$ and any integer $v \in [B]$ can be decomposed to $\mathsf{idec}_B(v) = (v^{(1)}, \ldots, v^{(p_B)})^\top \in \{0, 1\}^{p_B}$ such that $\sum_{j=1}^{p_B} B_j \cdot v^{(j)} = v$. This decomposition procedure is described in a deterministic manner as follows:

1. $v' := v$
2. For $j = 1$ to p_B do:
   (i) If $v' \geq B_j$ then $v^{(j)} := 1$, else $v^{(j)} := 0$;
   (ii) $v' := v' - B_j \cdot v^{(j)}$.
3. Output $\mathsf{idec}_B(v) = (v^{(1)}, \ldots, v^{(p_B)})^\top$.

Next, for any positive integers m, B, we define the function $\mathsf{vdec}_{m,B}$ that transforms a vector $\mathbf{w} = (w_1, \ldots, w_m)^\top \in [-B, B]^m$ to a vector of the following form:

$$\mathbf{w}' = (\sigma(w_1) \cdot \mathsf{idec}_B(|w_1|) \| \cdots \| \sigma(w_m) \cdot \mathsf{idec}_B(|w_m|)) \in \{-1, 0, 1\}^{mp_B},$$

where $\forall j \in [m]$: $\sigma(w_j) = 0$ if $w_j = 0$; $\sigma(w_j) = -1$ if $w_j < 0$; $\sigma(w_j) = 1$ if $w_j > 0$.

Define the matrix $\mathbf{H}_{m,B} = \begin{bmatrix} B_1, \ldots, B_{p_B} & & \\ & \ddots & \\ & & B_1, \ldots, B_{p_B} \end{bmatrix} \in \mathbb{Z}^{m \times mp_B}$ and its extension $\widehat{\mathbf{H}}_{m,B} = [\mathbf{H}_{m,B} | \mathbf{0}^{m \times 2mp_B}] \in \mathbb{Z}^{m \times 3mp_B}$. Let $\widehat{\mathbf{w}} = \mathsf{ext}_3(\mathbf{w}') \in B_{3mp_B}$, then one can see that $\widehat{\mathbf{H}}_{m,B} \cdot \widehat{\mathbf{w}} = \mathbf{w}$ and for any $\psi \in \mathcal{S}_{3mp_B}$, the following equivalence holds:

$$\widehat{\mathbf{w}} \in B_{3mp_B} \Leftrightarrow \psi(\widehat{\mathbf{w}}) \in B_{3mp_B}. \tag{4}$$

Define the following permutation.

- For any $\mathbf{e} = (e_1, \ldots, e_m)^\top \in \{0, 1\}^m$, define $\Pi_{\mathbf{e}} : \mathbb{Z}^{2m} \to \mathbb{Z}^{2m}$ that maps a vector $\mathbf{v} = (v_1^0, v_1^1, \ldots, v_m^0, v_m^1)^\top$ to $(v_1^{e_1}, v_1^{1-e_1}, \ldots, v_m^{e_m}, v_m^{1-e_m})^\top$.

One can see that, for any $\mathbf{z}, \mathbf{e} \in \{0, 1\}^m$, the following equivalence holds:

$$\mathbf{v} = \mathsf{enc}_2(\mathbf{z}) \Leftrightarrow \Pi_{\mathbf{e}}(\mathbf{v}) = \mathsf{enc}_2(\mathbf{z} \oplus \mathbf{e}). \tag{5}$$

4.2   The Underlying Zero-Knowledge Argument System

We now describe a statistical ZKAoK that will be invoked by the signer when generating group signatures. The protocol is developed from Stern-like techniques proposed by Ling et al. [43] and Langlois et al. [32].

Public input γ: $\mathbf{A}_0 \in \mathbb{Z}_q^{n \times m}$, $\mathbf{A}_j^b \in \mathbb{Z}_q^{n \times m}$ for $(b, j) \in \{0, 1\} \times [k]$, $\mathbf{u} \in \mathbb{Z}_q^n$,
  $\mathbf{B} \in \mathbb{Z}_q^{n \times m}$, $\mathbf{G} \in \mathbb{Z}_q^{n \times \ell}$, $(\mathbf{c}_1, \mathbf{c}_2) \in \mathbb{Z}_q^m \times \mathbb{Z}_q^\ell$, $t \in \{0, 1, \cdots, T - 1\}$.
Secret input ξ: $\mathrm{id} \in \{0, 1\}^\ell$, $\mathbf{s} \in \chi^n$, $\mathbf{e}_1 \in \chi^m$, $\mathbf{e}_2 \in \chi^\ell$, $\mathbf{v}_{\mathrm{id}\|z} \in \mathbb{Z}^{(\ell+d+1)m}$ with
$z = \mathsf{Bin}(t)$.
Prover's goal:

$$
\begin{cases}
\mathbf{A}_{\mathrm{id}\|z} \cdot \mathbf{v}_{\mathrm{id}\|z} = \mathbf{u} \bmod q, \ \|\mathbf{v}_{\mathrm{id}\|z}\|_\infty \le \beta; \\
\mathbf{c}_1 = \mathbf{B}^\top \cdot \mathbf{s} + \mathbf{e}_1 \bmod q, \ \mathbf{c}_2 = \mathbf{G}^\top \cdot \mathbf{s} + \mathbf{e}_2 + \lfloor \frac{q}{2} \rfloor \cdot \mathrm{id} \bmod q; \\
\|\mathbf{s}\|_\infty \le B, \ \|\mathbf{e}_1\|_\infty \le B, \ \|\mathbf{e}_2\|_\infty \le B.
\end{cases}
\tag{6}
$$

We first rearrange the above conditions. Let $\mathbf{A}' = [\mathbf{A}|\mathbf{A}_1^0|\mathbf{A}_1^1|\cdots|\mathbf{A}_\ell^0|\mathbf{A}_\ell^1] \in \mathbb{Z}_q^{(2\ell+1)m}$, $\mathbf{A}_{\mathrm{id}} = [\mathbf{A}_0|\mathbf{A}_1^{\mathrm{id}[1]}|\cdots|\mathbf{A}_1^{\mathrm{id}[\ell]}] \in \mathbb{Z}_q^{(\ell+1)m}$ and $\mathbf{A}'' = \mathbf{A}_{\ell+1}^{z[1]}|\cdots|\mathbf{A}_{\ell+1}^{z[d]}] \in \mathbb{Z}_q^{dm}$. Then $\mathbf{A}_{\mathrm{id}\|z} = [\mathbf{A}_{\mathrm{id}}|\mathbf{A}''] \in \mathbb{Z}_q^{(\ell+d+1)m}$. Let $\mathbf{v}_{\mathrm{id}} = (\mathbf{v}_0\|\mathbf{v}_1\|\cdots\|\mathbf{v}_\ell)$, $\mathbf{w}_2 = (\mathbf{v}_{\ell+1}\|\cdots\|\mathbf{v}_{\ell+d})$ with each $\mathbf{v}_i \in \mathbb{Z}^m$. Then $\mathbf{v}_{\mathrm{id}\|z} = (\mathbf{v}_{\mathrm{id}}\|\mathbf{w}_2)$. Therefore $\mathbf{A}_{\mathrm{id}\|z} \cdot \mathbf{v}_{\mathrm{id}\|z} = \mathbf{u} \bmod q$ is equivalent to

$$
\mathbf{A}_{\mathrm{id}} \cdot \mathbf{v}_{\mathrm{id}} + \mathbf{A}'' \cdot \mathbf{w}_2 = \mathbf{u} \bmod q.
\tag{7}
$$

Since id is part of secret input, $\mathbf{A}_{\mathrm{id}}$ should not be explicitly given. We note that Langlois et al. [32] already addressed this problem. The idea is as follows: they first added ℓ suitable zero-blocks of size m to vector $\mathbf{v}_{\mathrm{id}}$ and then obtained the extended vector $\mathbf{w}_1 = (\mathbf{v}_0\|\mathbf{v}_1^0\|\mathbf{v}_1^1\|\cdots\|\mathbf{v}_\ell^0\|\mathbf{v}_\ell^1) \in \mathbb{Z}^{(2\ell+1)m}$, where the added zero-blocks are $\mathbf{v}_1^{1-\mathrm{id}[1]}, \ldots, \mathbf{v}_\ell^{1-\mathrm{id}[\ell]}$ and $\mathbf{v}_i^{\mathrm{id}[i]} = \mathbf{v}_i, \forall i \in [\ell]$. Now one can check that Eq. (7) is equivalent to

$$
\mathbf{A}' \cdot \mathbf{w}_1 + \mathbf{A}'' \cdot \mathbf{w}_2 = \mathbf{u} \bmod q.
\tag{8}
$$

Let $\mathbf{B}' = \begin{bmatrix} \mathbf{B}^\top & \mathbf{I}_m & \mathbf{0}^{m \times \ell} \\ \mathbf{G}^\top & \mathbf{0}^{\ell \times m} & \mathbf{I}_\ell \end{bmatrix}$, $\mathbf{B}'' = \begin{bmatrix} \mathbf{0}^{m \times \ell} \\ \lfloor q/2 \rfloor \mathbf{I}_\ell \end{bmatrix}$, and $\mathbf{w}_3 = (\mathbf{s}\|\mathbf{e}_1\|\mathbf{e}_2) \in \mathbb{Z}^{n+m+\ell}$. Then one can check that $\mathbf{c}_1 = \mathbf{B}^\top \cdot \mathbf{s} + \mathbf{e}_1 \bmod q, \mathbf{c}_2 = \mathbf{G}^\top \cdot \mathbf{s} + \mathbf{e}_2 + \lfloor \frac{q}{2} \rfloor \cdot \mathrm{id} \bmod q$ is equivalent to

$$
\mathbf{B}' \cdot \mathbf{w}_3 + \mathbf{B}'' \cdot \mathrm{id} = (\mathbf{c}_1\|\mathbf{c}_2) \bmod q.
\tag{9}
$$

Using basic algebra, we can transform Eqs. (8) and (9) into one equation of the following form:

$$
\mathbf{M}_0 \cdot \mathbf{w}_0 = \mathbf{u}_0 \quad \bmod q,
$$

where $\mathbf{M}_0$, $\mathbf{u}_0$ are built from $\mathbf{A}', \mathbf{A}'', \mathbf{B}', \mathbf{B}''$ and $\mathbf{u}, (\mathbf{c}_1\|\mathbf{c}_2)$, respectively, and $\mathbf{w}_0 = (\mathbf{w}_1\|\mathbf{w}_2\|\mathbf{w}_3\|\mathrm{id})$.

Now we can use the decomposition and extension techniques described in Sect. 4.1 to handle our secret vectors. Let $L_1 = 3(2\ell + 1)mp_\beta$, $L_2 = 3dmp_\beta$, $L_3 = 3(n + m + \ell)p_B$, and $L = L_1 + L_2 + L_3 + 2\ell$. We transform our secret vector $\mathbf{w}_0$ to vector $\mathbf{w} = (\widehat{\mathbf{w}}_1\|\widehat{\mathbf{w}}_2\|\widehat{\mathbf{w}}_3\|\widehat{\mathrm{id}}) \in \{-1, 0, 1\}^L$ of the following form:

- $\widehat{\mathbf{w}}_1 = (\widehat{\mathbf{v}}_0\|\widehat{\mathbf{v}}_1^0\|\widehat{\mathbf{v}}_1^1\| \cdots \|\widehat{\mathbf{v}}_\ell^0\|\widehat{\mathbf{v}}_\ell^1) \in \{-1,0,1\}^{L_1}$ with $\widehat{\mathbf{v}}_0 = \mathsf{ext}_3(\mathsf{vdec}_{m,\beta}(\mathbf{v}_0)) \in \mathsf{B}_{3mp_\beta}$, $\forall i \in [\ell]$, $\widehat{\mathbf{v}}_i^{1-\mathsf{id}[i]} = \mathbf{0}^{3mp_\beta}$ and $\widehat{\mathbf{v}}_i^{\mathsf{id}[i]} = \mathsf{ext}_3(\mathsf{vdec}_{m,\beta}(\mathbf{v}_i^{\mathsf{id}[i]})) \in \mathsf{B}_{3mp_\beta}$;
- $\widehat{\mathbf{w}}_2 = \mathsf{ext}_3(\mathsf{vdec}_{dm,\beta}(\mathbf{w}_2)) \in \mathsf{B}_{3dmp_\beta}$;
- $\widehat{\mathbf{w}}_3 = \mathsf{ext}_3(\mathsf{vdec}_{n+m+\ell,B}(\mathbf{w}_3)) \in \mathsf{B}_{3(n+m+\ell)p_B}$;
- $\widehat{\mathsf{id}} = \mathsf{enc}_2(\mathsf{id}) \in \{0,1\}^{2\ell}$.

Using basic algebra, we can form public matrix $\mathbf{M}$ such that

$$\mathbf{M} \cdot \mathbf{w} = \mathbf{M}_0 \cdot \mathbf{w}_0 = \mathbf{u}_0 \bmod q.$$

Up to this point, we have transformed the considered relations into equation of the desired form $\mathbf{M} \cdot \mathbf{w} = \mathbf{u} \bmod q$. We now specify the set VALID that contains the secret vector $\mathbf{w}$, the set $\mathcal{S}$ and permutations $\{\varGamma_\phi : \phi \in \mathcal{S}\}$ such that the conditions in (1) hold.

Define VALID to be the set of vectors of the form $\mathbf{z} = (\mathbf{z}_1\|\mathbf{z}_2\|\mathbf{z}_3\|\mathbf{z}_4) \in \{-1,0,1\}^L$ such that there exists $\mathbf{x} \in \{0,1\}^\ell$

- $\mathbf{z}_1 = (\mathbf{y}_0\|\mathbf{y}_1^0\|\mathbf{y}_1^1\| \cdots \|\mathbf{y}_\ell^0\|\mathbf{y}_\ell^1) \in \{-1,0,1\}^{3(2\ell+1)mp_\beta}$ with $\mathbf{y}_0 \in \mathsf{B}_{3mp_\beta}$ and for each $i \in [\ell]$, $\mathbf{y}_i^{1-\mathbf{x}[i]} = \mathbf{0}^{3mp_\beta}$, $\mathbf{y}_i^{\mathbf{x}[i]} \in \mathsf{B}_{3mp_\beta}$;
- $\mathbf{z}_2 \in \mathsf{B}_{3dmp_\beta}$ and $\mathbf{z}_3 \in \mathsf{B}_{3(n+m+\ell)p_B}$;
- $\mathbf{z}_4 = \mathsf{enc}_2(\mathbf{x}) \in \{0,1\}^{2\ell}$.

Clearly, our vector $\mathbf{w}$ belongs to the tailored set VALID.

Now, let $\mathcal{S} = (\mathcal{S}_{3mp_\beta})^{2\ell+1} \times \mathcal{S}_{3dmp_\beta} \times \mathcal{S}_{3(n+m+\ell)p_B} \times \{0,1\}^\ell$. For any

$$\phi = (\psi_0, \psi_1^0, \psi_1^1, \ldots, \psi_\ell^0, \psi_\ell^1, \eta_2, \eta_3, \mathbf{e}) \in \mathcal{S}, \quad \mathbf{e} = (e_1, \ldots, e_\ell)^\top,$$

define the permutation $\varGamma_\phi : \mathbb{Z}^L \to \mathbb{Z}^L$ as follows. When applied to a vector

$$\mathbf{z} = (\mathbf{y}_0\|\mathbf{y}_1^0\|\mathbf{y}_1^1\| \cdots \|\mathbf{y}_\ell^0\|\mathbf{y}_\ell^1\|\mathbf{z}_2\|\mathbf{z}_3\|\mathbf{z}_4) \in \mathbb{Z}^L$$

where the first $2\ell + 1$ blocks are of size $3mp_\beta$ and the last three blocks are of size $3dmp_\beta$, $3(n+m+\ell)p_B$ and 2ℓ, respectively; it transforms $\mathbf{z}$ to vector $\varGamma_\phi(\mathbf{z})$ of the following form:

$$(\psi(\mathbf{y}_0)\|\psi_1^{e_1}(\mathbf{y}_1^{e_1})\|\psi_1^{1-e_1}(\mathbf{y}_1^{1-e_1})\| \cdots \|\psi_\ell^{e_\ell}(\mathbf{y}_\ell^{e_\ell})\|\psi_\ell^{1-e_\ell}(\mathbf{y}_\ell^{1-e_\ell})\| \\ \eta_2(\mathbf{z}_2)\|\eta_3(\mathbf{z}_3)\|\varPi_\mathbf{e}(\mathbf{z}_4)).$$

Based on the equivalences observed in (4) and (5), it can be checked that if $\mathbf{z} \in$ VALID for some $\mathbf{x} \in \{0,1\}^\ell$, then $\varGamma_\phi(\mathbf{z}) \in$ VALID for some $\mathbf{x} \oplus \mathbf{e} \in \{0,1\}^\ell$. In other words, the conditions in (1) hold, and therefore, we can obtain the desired statistical ZKAoK protocol.

Acknowledgements. The research is supported by Singapore Ministry of Education under Research Grant MOE2016-T2-2-014(S). Khoa Nguyen is also supported by the Gopalakrishnan – NTU Presidential Postdoctoral Fellowship 2018.

References

1. Abdalla, M., Reyzin, L.: A new forward-secure digital signature scheme. In: Okamoto, T. (ed.) ASIACRYPT 2000. LNCS, vol. 1976, pp. 116–129. Springer, Heidelberg (2000). https://doi.org/10.1007/3-540-44448-3_10
2. Ajtai, M.: Generating Hard Instances of Lattice Problems (Extended Abstract). In: STOC 1996, pp. 99–108. ACM (1996)
3. Alwen, J., Peikert, C.: Generating shorter bases for hard random lattices. In: STACS 2009, pp. 75–86 (2009)
4. Anderson, R.: Two remarks on public key cryptology. Technical report, University of Cambridge, Computer Laboratory (2002)
5. Applebaum, B., Cash, D., Peikert, C., Sahai, A.: Fast cryptographic primitives and circular-secure encryption based on hard learning problems. In: Halevi, S. (ed.) CRYPTO 2009. LNCS, vol. 5677, pp. 595–618. Springer, Heidelberg (2009). https://doi.org/10.1007/978-3-642-03356-8_35
6. Bellare, M., Micciancio, D., Warinschi, B.: Foundations of group signatures: formal definitions, simplified requirements, and a construction based on general assumptions. In: Biham, E. (ed.) EUROCRYPT 2003. LNCS, vol. 2656, pp. 614–629. Springer, Heidelberg (2003). https://doi.org/10.1007/3-540-39200-9_38
7. Bellare, M., Miner, S.K.: A forward-secure digital signature scheme. In: Wiener, M. (ed.) CRYPTO 1999. LNCS, vol. 1666, pp. 431–448. Springer, Heidelberg (1999). https://doi.org/10.1007/3-540-48405-1_28
8. Bellare, M., Shi, H., Zhang, C.: Foundations of group signatures: the case of dynamic groups. In: Menezes, A. (ed.) CT-RSA 2005. LNCS, vol. 3376, pp. 136–153. Springer, Heidelberg (2005). https://doi.org/10.1007/978-3-540-30574-3_11
9. Boneh, D., Boyen, X., Goh, E.-J.: Hierarchical identity based encryption with constant size ciphertext. In: Cramer, R. (ed.) EUROCRYPT 2005. LNCS, vol. 3494, pp. 440–456. Springer, Heidelberg (2005). https://doi.org/10.1007/11426639_26
10. Boneh, D., Shacham, H.: Group signatures with verifier-local revocation. In: ACM-CCS 2004, pp. 168–177. ACM (2004)
11. Boschini, C., Camenisch, J., Neven, G.: Floppy-sized group signatures from lattices. In: Preneel, B., Vercauteren, F. (eds.) ACNS 2018. LNCS, vol. 10892, pp. 163–182. Springer, Cham (2018). https://doi.org/10.1007/978-3-319-93387-0_9
12. Boyen, X.: Lattice mixing and vanishing trapdoors: a framework for fully secure short signatures and more. In: Nguyen, P.Q., Pointcheval, D. (eds.) PKC 2010. LNCS, vol. 6056, pp. 499–517. Springer, Heidelberg (2010). https://doi.org/10.1007/978-3-642-13013-7_29
13. Boyen, X., Shacham, H., Shen, E., Waters, B.: Forward-secure signatures with untrusted update. In: ACM-CCS 2006, pp. 191–200. ACM (2006)
14. Brakerski, Z., Gentry, C., Vaikuntanathan, V.: (Leveled) fully homomorphic encryption without bootstrapping. In: ITCS 2012, pp. 309–325. ACM (2012)
15. Camenisch, J., Neven, G., Rückert, M.: Fully anonymous attribute tokens from lattices. In: Visconti, I., De Prisco, R. (eds.) SCN 2012. LNCS, vol. 7485, pp. 57–75. Springer, Heidelberg (2012). https://doi.org/10.1007/978-3-642-32928-9_4
16. Canetti, R., Halevi, S., Katz, J.: A forward-secure public-key encryption scheme. In: Biham, E. (ed.) EUROCRYPT 2003. LNCS, vol. 2656, pp. 255–271. Springer, Heidelberg (2003). https://doi.org/10.1007/3-540-39200-9_16
17. Canetti, R., Halevi, S., Katz, J.: Chosen-ciphertext security from identity-based encryption. In: Cachin, C., Camenisch, J.L. (eds.) EUROCRYPT 2004. LNCS, vol. 3027, pp. 207–222. Springer, Heidelberg (2004). https://doi.org/10.1007/978-3-540-24676-3_13

18. Cash, D., Hofheinz, D., Kiltz, E., Peikert, C.: Bonsai trees, or how to delegate a lattice basis. In: Gilbert, H. (ed.) EUROCRYPT 2010. LNCS, vol. 6110, pp. 523–552. Springer, Heidelberg (2010). https://doi.org/10.1007/978-3-642-13190-5_27
19. Chaum, D., van Heyst, E.: Group signatures. In: Davies, D.W. (ed.) EUROCRYPT 1991. LNCS, vol. 547, pp. 257–265. Springer, Heidelberg (1991). https://doi.org/10.1007/3-540-46416-6_22
20. Cheng, S., Nguyen, K., Wang, H.: Policy-based signature scheme from lattices. Des. Codes Cryptography 81(1), 43–74 (2016)
21. del Pino, R., Lyubashevsky, V., Seiler, G.: Lattice-based group signatures and zero-knowledge proofs of automorphism stability. In: ACM-CCS 2018, pp. 574–591. ACM (2018)
22. Dodis, Y., Katz, J., Xu, S., Yung, M.: Key-insulated public key cryptosystems. In: Knudsen, L.R. (ed.) EUROCRYPT 2002. LNCS, vol. 2332, pp. 65–82. Springer, Heidelberg (2002). https://doi.org/10.1007/3-540-46035-7_5
23. Fiat, A., Shamir, A.: How To prove yourself: practical solutions to identification and signature problems. In: Odlyzko, A.M. (ed.) CRYPTO 1986. LNCS, vol. 263, pp. 186–194. Springer, Heidelberg (1987). https://doi.org/10.1007/3-540-47721-7_12
24. Gentry, C., Peikert, C., Vaikuntanathan, V.: How to use a short basis: trapdoors for hard lattices and new cryptographic constructions. In: STOC 2008, pp. 197–206. ACM (2008)
25. Gordon, S.D., Katz, J., Vaikuntanathan, V.: A group signature scheme from lattice assumptions. In: Abe, M. (ed.) ASIACRYPT 2010. LNCS, vol. 6477, pp. 395–412. Springer, Heidelberg (2010). https://doi.org/10.1007/978-3-642-17373-8_23
26. Itkis, G., Reyzin, L.: Forward-secure signatures with optimal signing and verifying. In: Kilian, J. (ed.) CRYPTO 2001. LNCS, vol. 2139, pp. 332–354. Springer, Heidelberg (2001). https://doi.org/10.1007/3-540-44647-8_20
27. Kansal, M., Dutta, R., Mukhopadhyay, S.: Forward Secure Efficient Group Signature in Dynamic Setting using Lattices. IACR Cryptology ePrint Archive, 2017:1128. https://eprint.iacr.org/2017/1128
28. Kawachi, A., Tanaka, K., Xagawa, K.: Concurrently secure identification schemes based on the worst-case hardness of lattice problems. In: Pieprzyk, J. (ed.) ASIACRYPT 2008. LNCS, vol. 5350, pp. 372–389. Springer, Heidelberg (2008). https://doi.org/10.1007/978-3-540-89255-7_23
29. Kiayias, A., Tsiounis, Y., Yung, M.: Traceable signatures. In: Cachin, C., Camenisch, J.L. (eds.) EUROCRYPT 2004. LNCS, vol. 3027, pp. 571–589. Springer, Heidelberg (2004). https://doi.org/10.1007/978-3-540-24676-3_34
30. Kiayias, A., Yung, M.: Secure scalable group signature with dynamic joins and separable authorities. IJSN 1(1), 24–45 (2006)
31. Laguillaumie, F., Langlois, A., Libert, B., Stehlé, D.: Lattice-based group signatures with logarithmic signature size. In: Sako, K., Sarkar, P. (eds.) ASIACRYPT 2013. LNCS, vol. 8270, pp. 41–61. Springer, Heidelberg (2013). https://doi.org/10.1007/978-3-642-42045-0_3
32. Langlois, A., Ling, S., Nguyen, K., Wang, H.: Lattice-based group signature scheme with verifier-local revocation. In: Krawczyk, H. (ed.) PKC 2014. LNCS, vol. 8383, pp. 345–361. Springer, Heidelberg (2014). https://doi.org/10.1007/978-3-642-54631-0_20. http://eprint.iacr.org/2014/033
33. Libert, B., Ling, S., Mouhartem, F., Nguyen, K., Wang, H.: Signature schemes with efficient protocols and dynamic group signatures from lattice assumptions. In: Cheon, J.H., Takagi, T. (eds.) ASIACRYPT 2016. LNCS, vol. 10032, pp. 373–403. Springer, Heidelberg (2016). https://doi.org/10.1007/978-3-662-53890-6_13

34. Libert, B., Ling, S., Mouhartem, F., Nguyen, K., Wang, H.: Zero-knowledge arguments for matrix-vector relations and lattice-based group encryption. In: Cheon, J.H., Takagi, T. (eds.) ASIACRYPT 2016. LNCS, vol. 10032, pp. 101–131. Springer, Heidelberg (2016). https://doi.org/10.1007/978-3-662-53890-6_4

35. Libert, B., Ling, S., Mouhartem, F., Nguyen, K., Wang, H.: Adaptive oblivious transfer with access control from lattice assumptions. In: Takagi, T., Peyrin, T. (eds.) ASIACRYPT 2017. LNCS, vol. 10624, pp. 533–563. Springer, Cham (2017). https://doi.org/10.1007/978-3-319-70694-8_19

36. Libert, B., Ling, S., Nguyen, K., Wang, H.: Zero-knowledge arguments for lattice-based accumulators: logarithmic-size ring signatures and group signatures without trapdoors. In: Fischlin, M., Coron, J.-S. (eds.) EUROCRYPT 2016. LNCS, vol. 9666, pp. 1–31. Springer, Heidelberg (2016). https://doi.org/10.1007/978-3-662-49896-5_1

37. Libert, B., Ling, S., Nguyen, K., Wang, H.: Zero-knowledge arguments for lattice-based PRFs and applications to e-cash. In: Takagi, T., Peyrin, T. (eds.) ASIACRYPT 2017. LNCS, vol. 10626, pp. 304–335. Springer, Cham (2017). https://doi.org/10.1007/978-3-319-70700-6_11

38. Libert, B., Ling, S., Nguyen, K., Wang, H.: Lattice-based zero-knowledge arguments for integer relations. In: Shacham, H., Boldyreva, A. (eds.) CRYPTO 2018. LNCS, vol. 10992, pp. 700–732. Springer, Cham (2018). https://doi.org/10.1007/978-3-319-96881-0_24

39. Libert, B., Mouhartem, F., Nguyen, K.: A lattice-based group signature scheme with message-dependent opening. In: Manulis, M., Sadeghi, A.-R., Schneider, S. (eds.) ACNS 2016. LNCS, vol. 9696, pp. 137–155. Springer, Cham (2016). https://doi.org/10.1007/978-3-319-39555-5_8

40. Libert, B., Quisquater, J.-J., Yung, M.: Forward-secure signatures in untrusted update environments: efficient and generic constructions. In: ACM-CCS 2007, pp. 266–275. ACM (2007)

41. Libert, B., Quisquater, J.-J., Yung, M.: Key evolution systems in untrusted update environments. ACM Trans. Inf. Syst. Secur. (TISSEC) 13(4), 37 (2010)

42. Libert, B., Yung, M.: Dynamic fully forward-secure group signatures. In: Asia-CCS 2010, pp. 70–81. ACM (2010)

43. Ling, S., Nguyen, K., Stehlé, D., Wang, H.: Improved zero-knowledge proofs of knowledge for the ISIS problem, and applications. In: Kurosawa, K., Hanaoka, G. (eds.) PKC 2013. LNCS, vol. 7778, pp. 107–124. Springer, Heidelberg (2013). https://doi.org/10.1007/978-3-642-36362-7_8

44. Ling, S., Nguyen, K., Wang, H.: Group signatures from lattices: simpler, tighter, shorter, ring-based. In: Katz, J. (ed.) PKC 2015. LNCS, vol. 9020, pp. 427–449. Springer, Heidelberg (2015). https://doi.org/10.1007/978-3-662-46447-2_19

45. Ling, S., Nguyen, K., Wang, H., Xu, Y.: Lattice-based group signatures: achieving full dynamicity with ease. In: Gollmann, D., Miyaji, A., Kikuchi, H. (eds.) ACNS 2017. LNCS, vol. 10355, pp. 293–312. Springer, Cham (2017). https://doi.org/10.1007/978-3-319-61204-1_15

46. Ling, S., Nguyen, K., Wang, H., Xu, Y.: Accountable tracing signatures from lattices. In: Matsui, M. (ed.) CT-RSA 2019. LNCS, vol. 11405, pp. 556–576. Springer, Cham (2019). https://doi.org/10.1007/978-3-030-12612-4_28

47. Ling, S., Nguyen, K., Wang, H., Xu, Y.: Constant-size group signatures from lattices. In: Abdalla, M., Dahab, R. (eds.) PKC 2018. LNCS, vol. 10770, pp. 58–88. Springer, Cham (2018). https://doi.org/10.1007/978-3-319-76581-5_3

48. Micciancio, D., Peikert, C.: Hardness of SIS and LWE with small parameters. In: Canetti, R., Garay, J.A. (eds.) CRYPTO 2013. LNCS, vol. 8042, pp. 21–39. Springer, Heidelberg (2013). https://doi.org/10.1007/978-3-642-40041-4_2
49. Micciancio, D., Regev, O.: Worst-case to average-case reductions based on Gaussian measures. SIAM J. Comput. **37**(1), 267–302 (2007)
50. Nakanishi, T., Hira, Y., Funabiki, N.: Forward-secure group signatures from pairings. In: Shacham, H., Waters, B. (eds.) Pairing 2009. LNCS, vol. 5671, pp. 171–186. Springer, Heidelberg (2009). https://doi.org/10.1007/978-3-642-03298-1_12
51. Nguyen, K., Tan, B.H.M., Wang, H.: Zero-knowledge password policy check from lattices. In: Nguyen, P., Zhou, J. (eds.) ISC 2017. LNCS, vol. 10599, pp. 92–113. Springer, Heidelberg (2017). https://doi.org/10.1007/978-3-319-69659-1_6
52. Nguyen, P.Q., Zhang, J., Zhang, Z.: Simpler efficient group signatures from lattices. In: Katz, J. (ed.) PKC 2015. LNCS, vol. 9020, pp. 401–426. Springer, Heidelberg (2015). https://doi.org/10.1007/978-3-662-46447-2_18
53. Peikert, C., Rosen, A.: Efficient collision-resistant hashing from worst-case assumptions on cyclic lattices. In: Halevi, S., Rabin, T. (eds.) TCC 2006. LNCS, vol. 3876, pp. 145–166. Springer, Heidelberg (2006). https://doi.org/10.1007/11681878_8
54. Regev, O.: On lattices, learning with errors, random linear codes, and cryptography. In: STOC 2005, pp. 84–93. ACM (2005)
55. Sakai, Y., Emura, K., Hanaoka, G., Kawai, Y., Matsuda, T., Omote, K.: Group signatures with message-dependent opening. In: Abdalla, M., Lange, T. (eds.) Pairing 2012. LNCS, vol. 7708, pp. 270–294. Springer, Heidelberg (2013). https://doi.org/10.1007/978-3-642-36334-4_18
56. Song, D.X.: Practical forward secure group signature schemes. In: ACM-CCS 2001, pp. 225–234. ACM (2001)
57. Stern, J.: A new paradigm for public key identification. IEEE Trans. Inf. Theory **42**(6), 1757–1768 (1996)

Towards Practical Microcontroller Implementation of the Signature Scheme Falcon

Tobias Oder[1]([✉]), Julian Speith[1], Kira Höltgen[1], and Tim Güneysu[1,2]

[1] Ruhr -University Bochum, Bochum, Germany
{tobias.oder,julian.speith,kira.hoeltgen,tim.gueneysu}@rub.de
[2] DFKI, Bremen, Germany

Abstract. The majority of submissions to NIST's recent call for Post-Quantum Cryptography are encryption schemes or key encapsulation mechanisms. Signature schemes constitute a much smaller group of submissions with only 21 proposals. In this work, we analyze the practicability of one of the latter category – the signature scheme Falcon with respect to its suitability for embedded microcontroller platforms.

Falcon has a security proof in the QROM in combination with smallest public key and signature sizes among all lattice-based signature scheme submissions with decent performance on common x86 computing architectures. One of the specific downsides of the scheme is, however, that according to its specification it is *"non-trivial to understand and delicate to implement"*.

This work aims to provide some new insights on the realization of Falcon by presenting an optimized implementation for the ARM Cortex-M4F platform. This includes a revision of its memory layout as this is the limiting factor on such constrained platforms. We managed to reduce the dynamic memory consumption of Falcon by 43% in comparison to the reference implementation. Summarizing, our implementation requires 682 ms for key generation, 479 ms for signing, and only 3.2 ms for verification for the $n = 512$ parameter set.

Keywords: Ideal lattices · Falcon · Cortex-M · Microcontroller · NIST PQC

1 Introduction

With the progress on quantum computing that has been made in recent years, the possibility of a powerful quantum computer being build in the coming years seems as likely as never before. The impact of the sheer existence of such a machine to current real world cryptography would be disastrous. Of special significance in that regard is Shor's algorithm for prime factorization and discrete logarithms [32], which, given a powerful quantum computer, allows for polynomial time attacks on almost all public-key algorithms that are in use today.

© Springer Nature Switzerland AG 2019
J. Ding and R. Steinwandt (Eds.): PQCrypto 2019, LNCS 11505, pp. 65–80, 2019.
https://doi.org/10.1007/978-3-030-25510-7_4

As a result, research in the area of post-quantum cryptography has significantly picked up in speed for the last couple of years. A lot of work is currently being put into the construction of quantum-secure cryptographic schemes that one day could replace today's most widely distributed algorithms. This effort culminated in the NISTs call for post-quantum cryptographic algorithms [27] that ended in November 2017. While most of the first round submissions focus on key exchange or key encapsulation schemes (KEMs), a few are dealing with the problem of generating cryptographically sound digital signatures. These include the lattice-based schemes pqNTRUsign [10], qTESLA [7], Dilithium [12], DRS [28], and Falcon [15], but also hash-based algorithms such as SPHINCS$^+$ [21] or schemes based on multivariate quadratics.

There are two competing approaches to realize lattice-based signature schemes. While the majority of them is constructed by applying the Fiat-Shamir transform to an authentication scheme, Falcon is based on the so-called hash-and-sign approach. The major difference is that while Fiat-Shamir schemes in general have a better performance, hash-and-sign ones can be proven to be secure in the Random Oracle Model (ROM) and even the Quantum Random Oracle Model (QROM). Another advantage of hash-and-sign signatures is that it is possible to construct identity-based encryption schemes out of a signature scheme like Falcon [13].

In particular in IoT infrastructures with critical requirements for long-term security, it is important to identify solutions that can still be deployed on contemporary small devices. Embedded systems found in automotive, consumer, or medical applications, for instance, demand an alternative solution that can withstand future attacks in the long run. With the implementation presented in this work, we show that Falcon can be a solution in this context.

1.1   Related Work

The majority of practical work on lattice-based NIST PQC candidates for embedded devices focuses on encryption schemes or key encapsulation mechanisms. An implementation of Saber [11] for ARM Cortex-M microcontroller platforms by Karmakar et al. [23] has been published in TCHES'18 and has since then been further optimized by Kannwischer et al. in [22]. There is also a microcontroller and FPGA implementation of Frodo [3] by Howe et al. [20]. Albrecht et al. developed an implementation of Kyber [5] that exploits existing RSA co-processors [2]. Finally, there is a Cortex-M4 implementation of Round5 [6], a scheme that resulted from the merger of Round2 [17] and HILA5 [30], by Saarinen et al. [31].

A detailed list of publications related to microcontroller implementations of NIST PQC candidates is available at the PQCzoo [19]. The most comprehensive collection of ARM Cortex-M4 implementations can be found in the pqm4 [1] library. Most of these implementations are rather straight-forward portings of their respective reference implementations, but it also features implementations that are described in dedicated publications. The library pqm4 contains ten KEMs and only three signature schemes, namely Dilithium, qTESLA, and SPHINCS+. Falcon has not been included in pqm4.

1.2 Contribution

The Falcon web page [16] mentions that the comparatively low memory consumption of Falcon is one of the highlights of the algorithm and states that "Falcon is compatible with small, memory-constrained embedded devices". The reference implementation of the Falcon submission however paints a different picture as it uses 210 kB of dynamic RAM memory during the signing step. In this work, we want to verify the claim of the Falcon submission to be well suited for memory-constrained embedded devices by presenting the first embedded microcontroller implementation of the signature scheme Falcon.

To do so, we apply a number of memory-saving techniques to reduce the dynamic memory consumption in comparison to the reference implementation by 43%. Our implementation on an ARM Cortex-M4 requires 64 kB of RAM and has a runtime of 682 ms for key generation, 479 ms for signing, and only 3.2 ms for verification using Falcon-512.

In its Call for Proposals [27] NIST explicitly states that the flexibility of a proposed scheme is one major evaluation criterion for the standardization process. The document furthermore defines flexibility to include that "algorithms can be implemented securely and efficiently on a wide variety of platforms, including constrained environments". In our work, we show that Falcon fulfills this requirement to some extent and also highlight the limitations of the scheme regarding its implementation on embedded platforms.

2 Preliminaries

In this chapter, we discuss the mathematical background that is crucial for the understanding of this paper.

2.1 Notation

We follow the notation of the Falcon specification [15]. Matrices are written as bold uppercase letter, vectors as bold lowercase letter, and scalars and polynomials as italic letters. An asterisk marks the component-wise adjoint of the transpose of a matrix. Sampling a value a from a Gaussian distribution is written as $a \leftarrow D_{\mathbb{Z},x,\sigma}$ where x denotes the center of the distribution and σ denotes its standard deviation.

2.2 The Falcon Signature Scheme

Due to the complexity of Falcon, a detailed description of all its components is out of the scope of this work. In the following we will broadly describe the key generation, signing, and verification procedures of Falcon and refer to the official specification [15] for more details.

Key generation, as shown in Algorithm 1, can be separated into two distinct parts. First, it generates polynomials $f, g, F, G \in \mathbb{Z}[x]/(\phi)$ that fulfill the NTRU equation $fG - gF = q \bmod \phi$ using the algorithm NTRUGen. The second part deals with the construction of the Falcon tree T using the LDL* decomposition of the matrix $\mathbf{G} = \mathbf{BB}^*$. Since our optimizations strongly depend on the tree generation algorithm, it can be found in Appendix A. Keygen then returns a public key $\mathsf{pk} = h = gf^{-1} \bmod q$ and a secret key $\mathsf{sk} = (\hat{\mathbf{B}}, \mathsf{T})$.

Algorithm 1. Keygen(ϕ, q)

Require: A monic polynomial $\phi \in \mathbb{Z}[x]$, a modulus q
Ensure: A secret key sk, a public key pk
1: $f, g, F, G, \gamma \leftarrow$ NTRUGen(ϕ, q) ▷ Solving the NTRU equation
2: $\mathbf{B} \leftarrow \begin{bmatrix} g & -f \\ \hline G & -F \end{bmatrix}$
3: $\hat{\mathbf{B}} \leftarrow$ FFT$(\mathbf{B})$
4: $\mathbf{G} \leftarrow \hat{\mathbf{B}} \times \hat{\mathbf{B}}^*$
5: $\mathsf{T} \leftarrow$ ffLDL$^*(\mathbf{G})$ ▷ Computing the LDL* tree
6: **if** ϕ is binary **then**
7:      $\sigma \leftarrow 1.55\sqrt{q}$
8: **else if** ϕ is ternary **then**
9:      $\sigma \leftarrow 1.32 \cdot 2^{1/4}\sqrt{q}$
10: **for** each leaf leaf of **T** **do**   ▷ Normalization step
11:      leaf.value $\leftarrow \sigma/\sqrt{\text{leaf.value}}$
12: $\mathsf{sk} \leftarrow (\hat{\mathbf{B}}, \mathsf{T})$
13: $h \leftarrow gf^{-1} \bmod q$
14: $\mathsf{pk} \leftarrow h$
15: **return** sk, pk

For *signature generation*, Algorithm 2 summarizes the required steps. First it computes a hash value $c \in \mathbb{Z}_q[x]/(\phi)$ of the message m and a salt r. It then uses the secret key sk to compute short values s_1, s_2 such that $s_1 + s_2 h = c \bmod q$ by leveraging its knowledge of f, g, F, G. This is done using the ffSampling algorithm, which is also given in Appendix A. Since s_1 can be reconstructed from s_2, the hash c, and public key h, it suffices to output a compressed version of s_2 as the signature, which also includes the random seed r.

Algorithm 2. Sign(m, sk, β)

Require: A message m, a secret key sk, a bound β
Ensure: A signature sig of m
1: $r \leftarrow \{0, 1\}^{320}$ uniformly
2: $c \leftarrow \mathsf{HashToPoint}(r\|m)$
3: $t \leftarrow (\mathsf{FFT}(c), \mathsf{FFT}(0)) \cdot \hat{\mathbf{B}}^{-1}$
4: **do**
5:     $z \leftarrow \mathsf{ffSampling}_n(t, T)$
6:     $s = (t - z)\hat{\mathbf{B}}$
7: **while** $\|s\| > \beta$
8: $(s_1, s_2) \leftarrow \mathsf{invFFT}(s)$
9: $s \leftarrow \mathsf{Compress}(s_2)$
10: **return** $sig = (r, s)$

Signature verification as shown in Algorithm 3 is rather straightforward and starts by hashing m and r into the hash value c again. Next, s_1 is recomputed and the algorithm checks whether $\|(s_1, s_2)\| \le \beta$ is satisfied with β being some predefined acceptance bound. Only if that bound holds for the given signature, it is accepted as valid.

Algorithm 3. Verify(m, sig, pk, β)

Require: A message m, a signature $sig = (r, s)$, a public key $pk = h \in \mathbb{Z}_q[x]/(\phi)$, a
     bound β
Ensure: Accept or reject
1: $c \leftarrow \mathsf{HashToPoint}(r\|m, q, n)$
2: $s_2 \leftarrow \mathsf{Decompress}(s)$
3: $s_1 \leftarrow c - s_2 h \bmod q$
4: **if** $\|(s_1, s_2)\| \le \beta$ **then**
5:     accept
6: **else**
7:     reject

---

3 Microcontroller Implementation

This section deals with two approaches to implement the `Falcon` signature scheme on our target architecture. The first one combines the tree generation with the fast Fourier sampler to reduce memory requirements, while the second one excludes the key generation from the microcontroller entirely and uses precomputed keys instead.

3.1 Target Platform

The STM32F4DISCOVERY board serves as a constrained target platform for our implementation. Its microcontroller has an 32-bit ARM Cortex-M4F core that runs with a clock frequency of up to 168 MHz. The board offers 192 kB of RAM as well as 1 MB of flash memory. Furthermore, it features a true random number generator (TRNG) based on analog circuitry and a floating-point unit (FPU). But as the FPU only works with single-precision floating point values, we cannot employ it for our implementation.

3.2   Analysis of the Reference Implementation

The analysis of the reference implementation from the `Falcon` submission package is our starting point for the development of our optimized ARM Cortex-M4 implementation. We first measured the dynamic memory consumption of the reference implementation in terms of stack and heap usage. We determine the stack usage with the help of stack canaries. To employ this technique, we start by filling the stack with a magic number before the operation to be measured is executed. Afterwards we check up to which point the magic numbers have been overwritten and therefrom conclude the stack usage. We determine the heap usage by counting the `malloc()` calls in the reference implementation manually as there are only a few of them in the source code.

The resulting dynamic memory consumption of the reference implementation can be seen in Table 1. The first point to note is that 210 kB are required for the signing operation for $n = 1024$ what clearly would not fit into the 192 kB RAM of our STM32F4DISCOVERY development board. Another issue is that in most use cases cryptographic algorithms are subcomponents of a main application on the microcontroller that employes the security functions to securely transmit, receive, or store data. As a result it is not sufficient to make the implementation barely fit the memory of our target platform, but we also need to reserve space for the main application that will be also placed the microcontroller.

Table 1. Dynamic memory usage of the reference implementation in bytes for $n = 512$ and $n = 1024$.

Operation	Stack memory	Heap memory	Total memory
$n = 512$			
Key generation	18,624	14,777	33,401
Sign	22,632	94,040	116,672
Verify	13,456	2,464	15,920
$n = 1024$			
Key generation	24,200	29,113	53,313
Sign	28,696	181,080	209,776
Verify	19,080	2,464	21,544

We identify the large `Falcon` tree used in the fast Fourier sampler during signature generation as the memory bottleneck. Considering the case $n = 1024$, that tree takes up 90 kB of the RAM. To execute `Falcon` on the target architecture, we present two possible solutions: We can either adapt the algorithm in a way that is more memory-conserving, or we may implement only the signature generation and verification while using those algorithms in combination with precomputed keys, which include the `Falcon` tree. The keys can then be stored in Flash memory to unburden the RAM. The latter approach is rather straightforward since one only needs to precompute the keys and load them onto the device. However, for many use cases this is not a satisfiable solution, as we may want to generate new keys over time. Therefore we focus on algorithmic changes for the remainder of this section.

To reduce the memory footprint, our implementation will merge the tree generation and the fast Fourier sampling (cf. Appendix A) into a single algorithm ffSampling* that is described in Algorithm 4. Referring to signature generation as shown in Algorithm 2, we then replace ffSampling$_n$ with ffSampling$_n^*$. The `Falcon` tree is therefore no longer part of the secret key sk and is instead computed on-the-fly during sampling. As the matrix $\mathbf{G}$ is required for the computation of the tree, we additionally need to compute it prior to the sampling step. We can therefore exclude the computation of $\mathbf{G}$ from key generation, since it has no use in that algorithm anymore. That way we only need to keep a small subtree in memory, which is generated whenever the respective part of the tree is required. As a consequence of this memory tradeoff we have to recompute the entire tree for each signature generation with a negative impact on the overall performance. Finally, our embedded implementation natively only supports `Falcon-512` and `Falcon-1024`, though the same concepts can be directly applied for `Falcon-768` as well.

3.3   Memory Optimizations

Our fast Fourier sampler with integrated tree generation is the most expensive operation in terms of memory requirements during the signing procedure. We optimized our implementation such that it only needs 8 kB of temporary space (i.e. n double elements), as the in- and outputs alone already take up 56 kB of RAM for $n = 1024$. The flowchart in Fig. 1 shows that it is not possible to perform this operation in-place without overriding the inputs. For the sake of simplicity, the flowchart does not include splitting and merging operations. After the first call to ffSampling$_n^*$, the first output is already calculated and we therefore cannot use its memory to store intermediate results. Hence we leverage the memory, which in the end will contain the second output, to keep the intermediate results in the meantime. However, we still need to store L_{10} as output of the LDL* somewhere. Therefore it is inevitable to use temporary memory within the sampler without major algorithmic changes.

3.4   Timing Analysis

Timing attacks are a fundamental threat to every cryptographic operation involving secret values [25]. With a timing attack an adversary obtains informa-

Algorithm 4. $\text{ffSampling}_n^*(\mathbf{t}, \mathbf{G})$

Require: $\mathbf{t} = (t_0, t_1) \in \text{FFT}(\mathbb{Q}[x](x^n + 1))^2$ and a full-rank Gram matrix $\mathbf{G} \in$ $\text{FFT}(\mathbb{Q}[x](x^n + 1))^{2 \times 2}$, $\sigma \leftarrow 1.55\sqrt{q}$

Ensure: $\mathbf{z} = (z_0, z_1) \in \text{FFT}(\mathbb{Z}[x](x^n + 1))^2$

1: **if** $(n = 1)$ **then**
2:     $\sigma' \leftarrow \sigma\sqrt{G_{00}}$
3:     $z_0 \leftarrow D_{\mathbb{Z}, t_0, \sigma'}$
4:     $z_1 \leftarrow D_{\mathbb{Z}, t_1, \sigma'}$
5:     **return** $\mathbf{z} = (z_0, z_1)$

6: $(\mathbf{L}, \mathbf{D}) \leftarrow \text{LDL}^*(\mathbf{G})$ $\triangleright \mathbf{L} = \begin{bmatrix} 1 & 0 \\ L_{10} & 1 \end{bmatrix}, \mathbf{D} = \begin{bmatrix} D_{00} & 0 \\ 0 & D_{11} \end{bmatrix}$

7: $d_{10}, d_{11} \leftarrow \text{splittfft}_2(D_{11})$ $\triangleright$ Handle right child
8: $\mathbf{t}_1 \leftarrow \text{splittfft}_2(t_1)$
9: $\mathbf{G}_1 \leftarrow \begin{bmatrix} d_{10} & d_{11} \\ xd_{11} & d_{10} \end{bmatrix}$
10: $\mathbf{z}_1 \leftarrow \text{ffSampling}_{n/2}(\mathbf{t}_1, \mathbf{G}_1)$
11: $\mathbf{z}_1 \leftarrow \text{mergefft}_2(\mathbf{z}_1)$
12: $t_0' \leftarrow t_0 + (t_1 - z_1) \odot L_{10}$ $\triangleright$ Handle left child
13: $d_{00}, d_{01} \leftarrow \text{splittfft}_2(D_{00})$
14: $\mathbf{t}_0 \leftarrow \text{splittfft}_2(t_0')$
15: $\mathbf{G}_0 \leftarrow \begin{bmatrix} d_{00} & d_{01} \\ xd_{01} & d_{00} \end{bmatrix}$
16: $\mathbf{z}_0 \leftarrow \text{ffSampling}_{n/2}(\mathbf{t}_0, \mathbf{G}_0)$
17: $\mathbf{z}_0 \leftarrow \text{mergefft}_2(\mathbf{z}_0)$
18: **return** $\mathbf{z} = (z_0, z_1)$

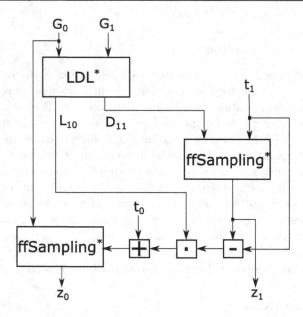

Fig. 1. Flowchart of our fast Fourier sampler with integrated tree generation ffSampling_n^*.

tion about the secret key by observing the execution time of the secret key operation, i.e., the signing operation in signature schemes. Timing attacks even work remotely over networks as shown in [8]. The most basic countermeasure against these attacks is to make sure that the execution time of an implementation is completely independent of the secret key, typically referred to as a *constant-time implementation*. Our implementation is currently designed for being **not** constant-time for two reasons. First, many embedded use-cases only require the verification of signatures (e.g., for the verification of authentic firmware updates or other applications where the embedded device is used as authenticated message sink only). Hence, constant time is not an issue for those embedded implementations for which only public data (i.e., the public key) is used. Second, there are particular components in the design of `Falcon` that make a constant-time implementation of the signature generation challenging:

1. `Falcon` requires to draw samples according to some Gaussian distribution. A lot of research has been focused on developing efficient algorithms for Gaussian sampling [9,14,24,26]. One major difference in comparison to other lattice-based schemes, like KEMs based on the Learning with Errors (LWE) problem, is that in `Falcon` the standard deviation of the Gaussian distribution varies between 1.2 and 1.9 with a precision of 53 bits. Therefore we cannot use constant-time table-based approaches like [24] as a sampling algorithm. Because of the required precision of the sampler, it is also not possible to use the constant-time binomial approach that is utilized in many lattice-based KEMs. The authors of `Falcon` propose to employ a rejection-based approach that is rather inefficient but has an execution time that is independent of the output.

2. Another, more critical obstacle in achieving a constant-time implementation is the use of floating-point arithmetic in `Falcon`. We cannot make use of the floating point unit build into the ARM Cortex-M4F to perform these floating-point operations of `Falcon` as it only works with single precision, while `Falcon` requires double precision operations. Therefore floating point calculations are handled by C runtime library functions, which in turn are usually not constant-time, especially in the case of division or square root operations that are also present in `Falcon`. There are attempts to realize constant-time floating point arithmetic for x86 processors at USENIX'16 [29] and CCS'18 [4]. These works however report a massive performance penalty when their constant-time floating point libraries are utilized resulting in the software being up to one order of magnitude slower than the standard C library functions. However, we are not aware of such libraries for microcontroller platforms and therefore this timing behavior of `Falcon` is one major challenge for its deployment in embedded applications.

4   Results and Comparison

In this section, we discuss the results of our implementation and compare it with others.

4.1 Evaluation Methodology

We evaluate our work by using the *OpenSTM32 System Workbench* (version 2.6), which is based on the development environment `Eclipse` and has specifically been designed to support the development for ARM-based STM32 boards. The IDE uses the GNU ARM Embedded Toolchain (version 7.2) and we set the optimization level to `-O3`. Determining the performance of our implementation is done by using the cycle count register `DWT_CYCCNT` of the *Data Watchpoint and Trace* unit that the Cortex-M4F offers. We assess dynamic RAM consumption by making use of stack canaries as described in Sect. 3.2.

4.2 Results

Table 2 summarizes the cycle counts of our implementations. We can see from the table that the `Falcon` verification is two orders of magnitude faster than the signing operation or the key generation. For comparability with the `pqm4` library [1] the measurements were obtained at 24 MHz. Translated to 168 MHz, verification would take only 3.2 ms while signing takes 479 ms for $n = 512$ without precomputed keys. Key generation even exceeds the signing operation and requires 682 ms to complete. The cost of the signing operation is dominated by the cost of the fast Fourier sampler as this component accounts for 92% of its total cycle count. In turn, the cost of the fast Fourier sampler heavily depends on the performance of the Gaussian sampler that is executed $2n$ times during the fast Fourier sampling. The $2n$ calls to the Gaussian sampler account for 73% of the cycle count of the entire signature generation.

The Gaussian sampler is therefore the main bottleneck in terms of cycle count of the scheme. Using fixed keys increases the performance of the signing by approximately 10%. This is mainly because we do not have to compute the `Falcon` tree in this case. However, fixed keys do not impact the verification. Another observation is that the FFT, which operates on complex double-precision floating point numbers and is required only during signing and key generation, is one order of magnitude more expensive than the NTT that works on plain integers. Nonetheless, the cost of the FFT is still negligible in comparison to the fast Fourier sampling.

In Table 3 we furthermore present the dynamic memory consumption of our implementations. The signing operation has the highest memory consumption and therefore the total memory consumption of the scheme is equal to the memory requirements of the signing operation. In contrast to the reference implementation we do not allocate memory on the heap and the dynamic memory consumption is therefore entirely determined by the stack usage of the implementation. We reduce the memory requirements of the scheme by 43% for $n = 1024$ in comparison to the reference implementation. Using fixed keys further increases the RAM savings to a total of 55% in comparison to the reference implementation as the keys are stored in Flash memory instead.

Table 2. Clock cycle counts for our ARM implementations of `Falcon` at 24 MHz. All results are averaged over 100 runs. The fast Fourier sampling cycle counts marked with † include the generation of the `Falcon` tree.

Operation	Falcon		Falcon with fixed keys	
	$n = 512$	$n = 1024$	$n = 512$	$n = 1024$
Key generation	114,546,135	365,950,978	-	-
Sign	80,503,242	165,800,855	72,261,930	147,330,702
Verify	530,900	1,046,700	529,900	1,083,100
solveNTRU	65,240,266	209,500,594	-	-
Fast Fourier sampling	$74,433,097^\dagger$	$148,600,140^\dagger$	64,354,464	130,468,405
$2n$ Gaussian samples	58,541,540	116,768,948	57,947,926	115,855,189
Compute G	583,800	1,131,800	-	-
FFT	772,200	1,716,300	772,800	1,645,100
NTT	75,900	157,700	75,900	159,700

Table 3. Dynamic memory usage in bytes for our ARM Cortex-M4 implementations in comparison with the reference implementation. For our ARM implementations, we only use the stack. We do not allocate extra memory on the heap.

Operation	Reference		M4		Fixed keys M4	
	$n = 512$	$n = 1024$	$n = 512$	$n = 1024$	$n = 512$	$n = 1024$
Key Gen	33,401	53,313	40,560	51,704	-	-
Sign	116,672	209,776	63,652	120,596	50,508	94,260
Verify	15,920	21,544	6,261	11,893	5,364	10,100

4.3 Comparison

In Table 4 we compare our work with ARM Cortex-M4 implementations of other post-quantum schemes that were either taken from the `pqm4` library [1] or the work of Oder et al. [18]. The security level is given according to the NIST classifications in the Call for Proposals [27]. In this comparison `Falcon` has the lowest execution time for the verification. Even the high-security $n = 1024$ instantiation of `Falcon` verifies signed messages in about the same time as `qTESLA` instantiated at a lower security level. `Dilithium` and `qTESLA` both have a faster signing and key generation. The major advantage of `Falcon` over these schemes however is that `Falcon` comes with a security proof in the ROM and QROM while `Dilithium` does not have such a proof. `qTESLA` can be instantiated with "provably-secure" parameters or "heuristic" parameters. The numbers in Table 4 refer to the heuristic instantiation. The minimal security assumptions of `SPHINCS`$^+$ make it the most conservative choice. The implementation of `SPHINCS`$^+$ is also the only one from the table that has a data-independent execution time. The signing performance however is four orders of magnitude worse than the signing performance of `qTESLA` at the same security level. We therefore consider `Falcon` to be a reasonable trade-off between performance and security.

Table 4. Comparison of our implementation with ARM implementations of other schemes. The given security levels refer to the security categories defined by NIST [27]. For our work, a security level of 1 means that $n = 512$ and level 5 translates to $n = 1024$. The stack memory is given in bytes. The runtime of the key generation, signing, and verification is given in cycles. Our fixed-key implementations are marked by [†].

Impl.	Sec.	Stack	Key Gen	*Sign*	Verify
This work	Level 1	63,652	114,546,135	$80,503,242$	530,900
	Level 5	120,596	365,950,978	$165,800,855$	1,046,700
This work[†]	Level 1	50,508	-	$72,261,930$	529,900
	Level 5	94,260	-	$147,330,702$	1,083,100
Dilithium [12]	Level 2	86,568	2,320,362	$8,348,349$	2,342,191
qTESLA [1]	Level 1	29,336	17,545,901	$6,317,445$	1,059,370
	Level 3	58,112	30,720,411	$11,987,079$	2,225,296
SPHINCS[+] [1]	Level 1	10,768	4,439,815,208	$61,665,898,904$	72,326,283

5   Conclusion

In this work, we presented a microcontroller implementation of the lattice-based signature scheme `Falcon`. Our implementation is memory-efficient and, in contrast to the reference implementation, does fit into the memory of our target platform. We also show that the implementation can be further optimized in terms of performance and memory consumption if the use case does not require to generate a key pair on the device itself. The extremely high performance of the verification makes `Falcon` a suitable scheme for use cases in which the target device does not have to generate a signature, e.g., for the verification of software updates. For future work, optimizations of the Gaussian sampler may result in a huge performance gain during signature generation. One obstacle however is that the signing operation cannot easily be realized in constant-time due to the required floating-point operations.

Acknowledgement. We would also like to thank the anonymous reviewers for their very valuable and helpful feedback. The research in this work was supported in part by the European Unions Horizon 2020 program under project number 644729 SAFEcrypto and 780701 PROMETHEUS.

A   Algorithms

A.1   The Falcon Tree

Please note that there is a typo in the `Falcon` specification [15] in Algorithm 15, Line 3. The description in Algorithm 5 in this section correctly states $n = 2$ instead of $n = 1$.

Algorithm 5. ffLDL*(G)

Require: A full-rank Gram matrix $\mathbf{G} \in \text{FFT}(\mathbb{Q}[x]/(x^n + 1))^{2 \times 2}$
Ensure: A binary tree T

1: $(\mathbf{L}, \mathbf{D}) \leftarrow \text{LDL}^*(\mathbf{G})$ $\triangleright \mathbf{L} = \begin{bmatrix} 1 & 0 \\ L_{10} & 1 \end{bmatrix}, \mathbf{D} = \begin{bmatrix} D_{00} & 0 \\ 0 & D_{11} \end{bmatrix}$

2: T.value $\leftarrow L_{10}$
3: **if** $(n = 2)$ **then**
4:     T.leftchild $\leftarrow D_{00}$
5:     T.rightchild $\leftarrow D_{11}$
6:     **return** T
7: $d_{00}, d_{01} \leftarrow \text{splittfft}_2(D_{00})$
8: $d_{10}, d_{11} \leftarrow \text{splittfft}_2(D_{11})$

9: $\mathbf{G}_0 \leftarrow \begin{bmatrix} d_{00} & d_{01} \\ xd_{01} & d_{00} \end{bmatrix}$

10: $\mathbf{G}_1 \leftarrow \begin{bmatrix} d_{10} & d_{11} \\ xd_{11} & d_{10} \end{bmatrix}$

11: T.leftchild $\leftarrow \text{ffLDL}^*(\mathbf{G}_0)$
12: T.rightchild $\leftarrow \text{ffLDL}^*(\mathbf{G}_1)$
13: **return** T

A.2 Fast Fourier Sampling

The description can be found in Algorithm 6.

Algorithm 6. ffSampling$_n$(t, T)

Require: $\mathbf{t} = (t_0, t_1) \in \text{FFT}(\mathbb{Q}[x]/(x^n + 1))^2$ and a Falcon tree T
Ensure: $\mathbf{z} = (z_0, z_1) \in \text{FFT}(\mathbb{Z}[x]/(x^n + 1))^2$
1: **if** $(n = 1)$ **then**
2:     $\sigma' \leftarrow$ T.value
3:     $z_0 \leftarrow D_{\mathbb{Z}, t_0, \sigma'}$
4:     $z_1 \leftarrow D_{\mathbb{Z}, t_1, \sigma'}$
5:     **return** $\mathbf{z} = (z_0, z_1)$
6: $(\mathsf{T}_0, \mathsf{T}_1) \leftarrow (\text{T.leftchild}, \text{T.rightchild})$
7: $\mathbf{t}_1 \leftarrow \text{splittfft}_2(t_1)$
8: $\mathbf{z}_1 \leftarrow \text{ffSampling}_{n/2}(\mathbf{t}_1, \mathsf{T}_1)$
9: $z_1 \leftarrow \text{mergefft}_2(\mathbf{z}_1)$
10: $t_0' \leftarrow t_0 + (t_1 - z_1) \odot$ T.value
11: $\mathbf{t}_0 \leftarrow \text{splittfft}_2(t_0')$
12: $\mathbf{z}_0 \leftarrow \text{ffSampling}_{n/2}(\mathbf{t}_0, \mathsf{T}_0)$
13: $z_0 \leftarrow \text{mergefft}_2(\mathbf{z}_0)$
14: **return** $\mathbf{z} = (z_0, z_1)$

References

1. pqm4 - post-quantum crypto library for the ARM cortex-M4. https://github.com/mupq/pqm4. Accessed 13 Nov 2018
2. Albrecht, M.R., Hanser, C., Höller, A., Pöppelmann, T., Virdia, F., Wallner, A.: Learning with errors on RSA co-processors. IACR Cryptology ePrint Archive 2018/425 (2018). https://eprint.iacr.org/2018/425
3. Alkim, E., et al.: FrodoKEM learning with errors key encapsulation. https://frodokem.org/files/FrodoKEM-specification-20171130.pdf. Accessed 13 Nov 2018
4. Andrysco, M., Nötzli, A., Brown, F., Jhala, R., Stefan, D.: Towards verified, constant-time floating point operations. In: Lie, D., Mannan, M., Backes, M., Wang, X. (eds.) Proceedings of the 2018 ACM SIGSAC Conference on Computer and Communications Security, CCS 2018, Toronto, ON, Canada, 15–19 October 2018, pp. 1369–1382. ACM (2018). https://doi.org/10.1145/3243734.3243766
5. Avanzi, R., et al.: CRYSTALS-kyber. https://csrc.nist.gov/CSRC/media/Projects/Post-Quantum-Cryptography/documents/round-1/submissions/CRYSTALS_Kyber.zip. Accessed 30 Nov 2018
6. Bhattacharya, S., et al.: Round5: compact and fast post-quantum public-key encryption. IACR Cryptology ePrint Archive 2018/725 (2018). https://eprint.iacr.org/2018/725
7. Bindel, N., et al.: Submission to NIST's post-quantum project: lattice-based digital signature scheme qTESLA. https://csrc.nist.gov/CSRC/media/Projects/Post-Quantum-Cryptography/documents/round-1/submissions/qTESLA.zip. Accessed 26 Nov 2018
8. Brumley, D., Boneh, D.: Remote timing attacks are practical. Comput. Netw. **48**(5), 701–716 (2005). https://doi.org/10.1016/j.comnet.2005.01.010
9. Buchmann, J., Cabarcas, D., Göpfert, F., Hülsing, A., Weiden, P.: Discrete ziggurat: a time-memory trade-off for sampling from a Gaussian distribution over the integers. In: Lange, T., Lauter, K., Lisoněk, P. (eds.) SAC 2013. LNCS, vol. 8282, pp. 402–417. Springer, Heidelberg (2014). https://doi.org/10.1007/978-3-662-43414-7_20
10. Chen, C., Hoffstein, J., Whyte, W., Zhang, Z.: NIST PQ submission: pqN-TRUSign - a modular lattice signature scheme. https://csrc.nist.gov/CSRC/media/Projects/Post-Quantum-Cryptography/documents/round-1/submissions/pqNTRUsign.zip. Accessed 26 Nov 2018
11. D'Anvers, J.P., Karmakar, A., Roy, S.S., Longa, P., Vercauteren, F.: SABER: Mod-LWR based KEM. https://csrc.nist.gov/CSRC/media/Projects/Post-Quantum-Cryptography/documents/round-1/submissions/SABER.zip. Accessed 13 Nov 2018
12. Ducas, L., et al.: CRYSTALS-dilithium: a lattice-based digital signature scheme. IACR Trans. Cryptogr. Hardw. Embed. Syst. **2018**(1), 238–268 (2018). https://doi.org/10.13154/tches.v2018.i1.238-268
13. Ducas, L., Lyubashevsky, V., Prest, T.: Efficient identity-based encryption over NTRU lattices. In: Sarkar, P., Iwata, T. (eds.) ASIACRYPT 2014. LNCS, vol. 8874, pp. 22–41. Springer, Heidelberg (2014). https://doi.org/10.1007/978-3-662-45608-8_2
14. Dwarakanath, N.C., Galbraith, S.D.: Sampling from discrete Gaussians for lattice-based cryptography on a constrained device. Appl. Algebra Eng. Commun. Comput. **25**(3), 159–180 (2014). https://doi.org/10.1007/s00200-014-0218-3

15. Fouque, P.A., et al.: Falcon: Fast-Fourier lattice-based compact signatures over NTRU. https://csrc.nist.gov/CSRC/media/Projects/Post-Quantum-Cryptography/documents/round-1/submissions/Falcon.zip. Accessed 26 Nov 2018
16. Fouque, P.A., et al.: Falcon: Fast-Fourier lattice-based compact signatures over NTRU. https://falcon-sign.info/. Accessed 26 Nov 2018
17. Garcia-Morchon, O., et al.: Round2: KEM and PKE based on GLWR. https://csrc.nist.gov/CSRC/media/Projects/Post-Quantum-Cryptography/documents/round-1/submissions/Round2.zip. Accessed 30 Nov 2018
18. Güneysu, T., Krausz, M., Oder, T., Speith, J.: Evaluation of lattice-based signature schemes in embedded systems. In: 25th IEEE International Conference on Electronics Circuits and Systems (2018)
19. Howe, J.: PQCzoo. https://pqczoo.com/. Accessed 13 Nov 2018
20. Howe, J., Oder, T., Krausz, M., Güneysu, T.: Standard lattice-based key encapsulation on embedded devices. IACR Trans. Cryptogr. Hardw. Embed. Syst. **2018**(3), 372–393 (2018). https://doi.org/10.13154/tches.v2018.i3.372-393
21. Hulsing, A., et al.: SPHINCS+. https://csrc.nist.gov/CSRC/media/Projects/Post-Quantum-Cryptography/documents/round-1/submissions/SPHINCS_Plus.zip. Accessed 26 Nov 2018
22. Kannwischer, M.J., Rijneveld, J., Schwabe, P.: Faster multiplication in $F_2m[x]$ on cortex-M4 to speed up NIST PQC candidates. IACR Cryptology ePrint Archive 2018/1018 (2018). https://eprint.iacr.org/2018/1018
23. Karmakar, A., Mera, J.M.B., Roy, S.S., Verbauwhede, I.: Saber on ARM cca-secure module lattice-based key encapsulation on ARM. IACR Trans. Cryptogr. Hardw. Embed. Syst. **2018**(3), 243–266 (2018). https://doi.org/10.13154/tches.v2018.i3.243-266
24. Karmakar, A., Roy, S.S., Reparaz, O., Vercauteren, F., Verbauwhede, I.: Constant-time discrete Gaussian sampling. IEEE Trans. Comput. **67**(11), 1561–1571 (2018). https://doi.org/10.1109/TC.2018.2814587
25. Kocher, P.C.: Timing attacks on implementations of Diffie-Hellman, RSA, DSS, and other systems. In: Koblitz, N. (ed.) CRYPTO 1996. LNCS, vol. 1109, pp. 104–113. Springer, Heidelberg (1996). https://doi.org/10.1007/3-540-68697-5_9
26. Micciancio, D., Walter, M.: Gaussian sampling over the integers: efficient, generic, constant-time. In: Katz, J., Shacham, H. (eds.) CRYPTO 2017. LNCS, vol. 10402, pp. 455–485. Springer, Cham (2017). https://doi.org/10.1007/978-3-319-63715-0_16
27. National Institute of Standards and Technology: Submission requirements and evaluation criteria for the post-quantum cryptography standardization process. https://csrc.nist.gov/CSRC/media/Projects/Post-Quantum-Cryptography/documents/call-for-proposals-final-dec-2016.pdf. Accessed 14 Nov 2018
28. Plantard, T., Sipasseuth, A., Dumondelle, C., Susilo, W.: DRS: diagonal dominant reduction for lattice-based signature. https://csrc.nist.gov/CSRC/media/Projects/Post-Quantum-Cryptography/documents/round-1/submissions/DRS.zip. Accessed 26 Nov 2018
29. Rane, A., Lin, C., Tiwari, M.: Secure, precise, and fast floating-point operations on x86 processors. In: Holz, T., Savage, S. (eds.) 25th USENIX Security Symposium, USENIX Security 2016, Austin, TX, USA, 10–12 August 2016, pp. 71–86. USENIX Association (2016). https://www.usenix.org/conference/usenixsecurity16/technical-sessions/presentation/rane
30. Saarinen, M.J.O.: HILA5. https://csrc.nist.gov/CSRC/media/Projects/Post-Quantum-Cryptography/documents/round-1/submissions/Hila5.zip. Accessed 30 Nov 2018

31. Saarinen, M.J.O., Bhattacharya, S., García-Morchón, Ó., Rietman, R., Tolhuizen, L., Zhang, Z.: Shorter messages and faster post-quantum encryption with Round5 on Cortex M. IACR Cryptology ePrint Archive 2018/723 (2018). https://eprint. iacr.org/2018/723
32. Shor, P.W.: Polynomial-time algorithms for prime factorization and discrete logarithms on a quantum computer. SIAM Rev. **41**(2), 303–332 (1999). https://doi. org/10.1137/S0036144598347011

Learning with Errors

Round5: Compact and Fast Post-quantum Public-Key Encryption

Hayo Baan[1], Sauvik Bhattacharya[1(✉)], Scott Fluhrer[2],
Oscar Garcia-Morchon[1], Thijs Laarhoven[3], Ronald Rietman[1],
Markku-Juhani O. Saarinen[4], Ludo Tolhuizen[1], and Zhenfei Zhang[5]

[1] Royal Philips N.V., Eindhoven, Netherlands
sauvik.bhattacharya@philips.com
[2] Cisco, San Jose, USA
[3] Eindhoven University of Technology, Eindhoven, Netherlands
[4] PQShield Ltd., Oxford, UK
[5] Algorand, Boston, USA

Abstract. We present the ring-based configuration of the NIST submission Round5, a Ring Learning with Rounding (RLWR)- based IND-CPA secure public-key encryption scheme. It combines elements of the NIST candidates Round2 (use of RLWR as underlying problem, having $1 + x + \ldots + x^n$ with $n + 1$ prime as reduction polynomial, allowing for a large design space) and HILA5 (the constant-time error-correction code XEf). Round5 performs part of encryption, and decryption via multiplication in $\mathbb{Z}_p[x]/(x^{n+1}-1)$, and uses secret-key polynomials that have a factor $(x - 1)$. This technique reduces the failure probability and makes correlation in the decryption error negligibly low. The latter allows the effective application of error correction through XEf to further reduce the failure rate and shrink parameters, improving both security and performance.

We argue for the security of Round5, both formal and concrete. We further analyze the decryption error, and give analytical as well as experimental results arguing that the decryption failure rate is lower than in Round2, with negligible correlation in errors.

IND-CCA secure parameters constructed using Round5 and offering more than 232 and 256 bits of quantum and classical security respectively, under the conservative core sieving model, require only 2144 B of bandwidth. For comparison, similar, competing proposals require over 30% more bandwidth. Furthermore, the high flexibility of Round5's design allows choosing finely tuned parameters fitting the needs of diverse applications – ranging from the IoT to high-security levels.

Keywords: Lattice cryptography · Learning with Rounding ·
Prime cyclotomic ring · Public-key encryption · IND-CPA ·
Error correction

1 Introduction

Standardization bodies such as NIST [30] and ETSI [17,18] are currently in the process of evaluating and standardizing post-quantum cryptography (PQC),

© Springer Nature Switzerland AG 2019
J. Ding and R. Steinwandt (Eds.): PQCrypto 2019, LNCS 11505, pp. 83–102, 2019.
https://doi.org/10.1007/978-3-030-25510-7_5

alternative solutions to RSA and elliptic curve cryptography that are secure against quantum computers. Lattice-based cryptography is a prominent branch of post-quantum cryptography that is based on well-studied problems and offers very good performance characteristics.

Motivation. The choice of the underlying polynomial ring greatly affects the performance of schemes based on ideal lattices, i.e., those based on the Ring Learning with Errors (RLWE) [28] and the Ring Learning with Rounding (RLWR) [6] problems. A common choice [3,10] of the polynomial ring to instantiate an RLWE or RLWR problem is $\mathbb{Z}_q[x]/\Phi_{2n}(x)$ where n is a power of 2. Proposals such as [3,9,11,24] using this ring enjoy lower decryption failure rates due to the sparse nature of the $\Phi_{2n}(x)$ leading to lesser noise propagation. However, requiring that n be a power of 2 restricts the choice of n. Proposals such as [5,35] choose instead the $\mathbb{Z}_q[x]/\Phi_{n+1}(x)$ where $\Phi_{n+1}(x) = x^n + x^{n-1} + \ldots + 1$ for $n+1$ a prime, thus offering a much denser design space. However, due to the worse noise propagation in this polynomial, the decryption failure rate of such schemes suffers.

Error correction has been shown to improve the security and performance of ideal lattice based cryptosystems in [19], and has been practically demonstrated in schemes such as [20,34]. We observe that error correction, when $\mathbb{Z}_q[x]/\Phi_{2n}(x)$ is used, can bring limited reduction in bandwidth requirements if n is limited to powers of two. On the other hand, applying error correction in schemes using $\mathbb{Z}_q[x]/\Phi_{n+1}(x)$ can bring major improvements since, if failure probability is improved, then it is relatively easy to find slightly smaller n values that directly reduce bandwidth requirements. However, as we will see, multiplications in $\mathbb{Z}_q[x]/\Phi_{n+1}(x)$ lead to correlated decryption errors that limit the application of error correction.

Contributions. In this paper, we present the ring version of the Round5 cryptosystem submitted to NIST. Round5 builds upon the rounding-based Round2 [5] scheme, that is constructed based on the prime-order cyclotomic ring, and *XEf*, the constant-time error correction code in HILA5 [34]. Round2 can finely tune its parameter n for each targeted security level, which in combination with rounding and its characteristically small key-sizes leads to efficient performance. However, having a design based on the $\Phi_{n+1}(x)$ polynomial, operational correctness in Round2 suffers from the above mentioned drawbacks.

Our contributions in this work are as follows:

1. We present the RLWR-based Round5 cryptosystem (Sect. 3), that combines the *dense parameter space* offered by the prime-order $\Phi_{n+1}(x)$ cyclotomic polynomial ($n+1$ a prime), with the *low decryption failure rates* typical of the power-of-two $\Phi_{2n}(x)$ polynomial (n a power of two), such as in NewHope [3] and Kyber [9].

   Round5 does this by computing public-keys modulo $\Phi_{n+1}(x)$, such that $n+1$ is a prime (allowing a wide choice for this security parameter), yet computing part of the ciphertext modulo $N_{n+1}(x) = x^{n+1} - 1$ and requiring that secret-keys are polynomials having a factor $(x - 1)$. The latter two ensure that an additional term originating from reductions modulo $\Phi_{n+1}(x)$ in the public-keys vanishes during reduction modulo $N_{n+1}(x)$ in encryption and decryption, leading to a decryption error term that has a noise propagation as low as in the case of the $\Phi_{2n}(x)$ polynomial.

2. We present detailed analytical and experimental results on the decryption error in Round5, especially the occurrence and behavior of correlated errors occurring due to reductions modulo $\Phi_{n+1}(x)$. Our experimental simulations support the claim that the dependence between errors when performing encryption and decryption modulo $N_{n+1}(x)$, although still existent, is negligible; these results are of independent interest and apply also to schemes defined based on the power-of-two $\Phi_{2n}(x)$ polynomial.

3. Based on our above results on independent bit errors when using the $N_{n+1}(x)$ polynomial, we extend the design of Round2 further in Round5 by incorporating the error correction code *XEf*, originally due to [34]. Our choice of this code is motivated by the following.

Firstly, XEf is designed to easily implement constant-time correction of up to f errors, where f is arbitrary, in practice between 2 and 5, and can be chosen based upon the usage scenario. This flexibility of XEf fits the overall design goals of Round5. In comparison, the only other NIST [30] post-quantum candidate utilizing constant-time error correction is ThreeBears [20], however its Melas code can correct only (up to) 2 errors. Another NIST candidate, LAC [27] uses BCH error correction, for which no obvious constant-time implementation exists [26].

Secondly, operations in XEf are based on Boolean logic only, and are therefore simple and fast. XEf's performance is therefore at least at par with, if not better, than the constant-time Melas error correction of the ThreeBears [20] submission, which involves multiplication operations in $\mathbb{F}_{2^q}$. However, we note that the performance overhead of error correction is in general, negligible compared to other, more significant overheads in ideal lattice based cryptosystems, such as polynomial ring multiplications.

Thus, XEf allows Round5 to further drop its decryption failure rate significantly, shrink parameters, and in the process improve security and performance, while remaining flexible enough to optimize its performance when targeting different applications.

2   Background

For each positive integer a, we denote the set $\{0, 1, \ldots, a-1\}$ by $\mathbb{Z}_a$. For a set A, we denote by $a \xleftarrow{\$} A$ that a is drawn uniformly at random from A. For $x \in \mathbb{Q}$, we denote by $\lfloor x \rfloor$ and $\lfloor x \rceil$ rounding downwards to the next smaller integer and rounding to the closest integer (with rounding up in case of a tie) respectively.

Let $n+1$ be prime. The $(n+1)$-th cyclotomic polynomial $\Phi_{n+1}(x)$ then equals $x^n + x^{n-1} + \cdots + x + 1$. We denote the polynomial ring $\mathbb{Z}[x]/\Phi_{n+1}(x)$ by $\mathcal{R}_n$. We denote by $N_{n+1}(x)$ the polynomial $x^{n+1} - 1 = \Phi_{n+1}(x)(x-1)$. For each positive integer a, we write $\mathcal{R}_{n,a}$ for the set of polynomials of degree less than n with all coefficients in $\mathbb{Z}_a$. We call a polynomial in $\mathcal{R}_n$ *ternary* if all its coefficients are 0, 1 or -1. Throughout this document, regular font letters denote elements from $\mathcal{R}_n$. For each $v \in \mathcal{R}_n$, the Hamming weight of v is defined as its number of non-zero coefficients. We denote with $\mathcal{H}_n(h)$ the set of ternary polynomials of degree less than n, with Hamming weight h.

Round5 as presented in this paper relies on the same underlying problem as in [5] tailored to the ring case. Like [5], Round5 as submitted to NIST relies on the General Learning with Rounding problem.

Definition 1 (Ring Learning with Rounding (RLWR)). *Let n, p, q be positive integers such that $q \geq p \geq 2$. Let $\mathcal{R}_{n,q}$ be a polynomial ring, and let D_s be a probability distribution on $\mathcal{R}_n$. The search version of the RLWR problem* $sRLWR_{n,m,q,p}(D_s)$ *is as follows: given m samples of the form* $\left\langle \left\lfloor \frac{p}{q}\langle as \rangle_q \right\rceil \right\rangle_p$ *with $a \in \mathcal{R}_{n,q}$ and a fixed $s \leftarrow D_s$, recover s.*

The decision version of the RLWR problem $dRLWR_{n,m,q,p}(D_s)$ *is to distinguish between the uniform distribution on $\mathcal{R}_{n,q} \times \mathcal{R}_{n,p}$ and the distribution* $\left(a_i, b_i = \left\langle \left\lfloor \frac{p}{q}\langle as \rangle_q \right\rceil \right\rangle_p \right)$ *with $a \xleftarrow{\$} \mathcal{R}_{n,q}$ and a fixed $s \leftarrow D_s$.*

We note that the original decisional RLWR assumption [6] is to distinguish from $\mathcal{R}_{n,q} \times \langle \mathcal{R}_{n,q} \rangle_p$. We simplify it to the uniform case since $p|q$ in our setting.

Round5 uses XEf, an f-bit majority logic error correcting block code, to decrease the decryption failure rate. The code is built using the same strategy as codes used by TRUNC8 [33] (2-bit correction) and HILA5 [34] (5-bit correction). The XEf code is described by $2f$ "registers" r_i of size $|r_i| = l_i$ with $i = 0, \ldots, 2f-1$. We view the κ-bits payload block m as a binary polynomial $m_{\kappa-1}x^{\kappa-1} + \cdots + m_1 x + m_0$ of length κ. Registers are defined via cyclic reduction $r_i = m \bmod x^{l_i} - 1$. A transmitted message consists of the payload m concatenated with register set r (a total of $\mu = \kappa + xe$ bits, where $xe = \sum l_i$).

Upon receiving a message $(m' \mid r')$ one computes the register set r'' corresponding to m' and compares it to the received register set r' – that may also have errors. Errors are in coefficients m'_k where there are parity disagreements for multitude of registers r_i. We use a majority rule and flip bit m'_k if

$$\sum_{i=0}^{2f-1} ((r'_i[\langle k \rangle_{l_i}] - r''_i[\langle k \rangle_{l_i}]) \bmod 2) \geq f + 1 \qquad (1)$$

where the sum is taken as the number of disagreeing register parity bits at k.

3   Round5

The core of Round5 is $r5\_cpa\_pke$, an IND-CPA secure public-key encryption scheme based on the Ring Learning with Rounding (RLWR) problem. r5_cpa_pke is constructed as a *noisy El Gamal encryption* scheme similar to the works in [25] and [4]. Public keys are noisy RLWR samples in $\mathbb{Z}[x]/\Phi_{n+1}(x)$, computed via a lossy rounding down to a smaller modulus.

Algorithm 1. r5_cpa_pke_keygen()	**Algorithm 2.** r5_cpa_pke_encrypt(pk, m)
1 $a \xleftarrow{\$} \mathcal{R}_{n,q}$	1 $r \xleftarrow{\$} \mathcal{H}_n(h)$
2 $s \xleftarrow{\$} \mathcal{H}_n(h)$	2 $u = \left\langle \left\lfloor \frac{p}{q} \left(\langle ar \rangle_{\Phi_{n+1}(x)} + h_1 \right) \right\rceil \right\rangle_p$
3 $b = \left\langle \left\lfloor \frac{p}{q} \left(\langle as \rangle_{\Phi_{n+1}(x)} + h_1 \right) \right\rceil \right\rangle_p$	3 $v = \left\langle \left\lfloor \frac{t}{p} \left(\text{Sample}_\mu \langle br \rangle_{\xi(x)} + h_1 \right) \right\rceil + \right.$
4 **return** $(pk = (a, b), sk = s)$	$\left. \frac{t}{2} \texttt{xef\_compute}_{\kappa,f}(m) \right\rangle_t$
	4 **return** $ct = (u, v)$

Algorithm 3. r5_cpa_pke_decrypt(sk, ct)
1   $v_p = \frac{p}{t} v$
2   $y = \left\langle \left\lfloor \frac{2}{p} \left(v_p - \text{Sample}_\mu \langle su \rangle_{\xi(x)} + h_2 \right) \right\rceil \right\rangle_2$
3   $\hat{m} = \texttt{xef\_correct}_{\kappa,f}(y)$
4   **return** $\hat{m}$

Round5 and its core r5_cpa_pke builds on Round2 [5], specifically the building block CPA-PKE. r5_cpa_pke is thus described in Algorithms 1, 2 and 3, which it inherits from the ring variant of CPA-PKE, along with the cryptosystem parameters, positive integers n, h, p, q, t, μ, f, τ, and a security parameter κ. The moduli q, p, t are powers of 2, such that $t|p|q$. It is required that $p^2 \geq qt$ (see Sect. 5.1), $\mu \leq n$ and $\mu \geq \kappa$. h is the Hamming weight of secret polynomials. r5_cpa_pke also defines a generic polynomial $\xi(x) \in \{N_{n+1}(x), \Phi_{n+1}(x)\}$, which is used to reduce the result of polynomial multiplication during encryption and decryption. In this paper, we discuss performance (in the form of decryption failure behavior) and security trade-offs and requirements for the cases that $\xi(x) = N_{n+1}(x)$ and $\xi(x) = \Phi_{n+1}(x)$.

Algorithm 1 first samples a public polynomial a with coefficients in $\mathbb{Z}_q$, a secret-key polynomial s and computes the public-key polynomial b by rounding its coefficients (to the closest integer) to a smaller modulus $p < q$. Here, rounding is described in terms of rounding downwards, and addition of a rounding constant $h_1 = q/2p$. In Algorithm 2, the encryptor samples an ephemeral secret encryption randomness r and uses it along with a to compute the first ciphertext component u similar to b. The second ciphertext component v is computed using the public-key b and r to obtain a RLWR sample, which is then used as a one-time pad to encrypt the message (which is additionally encoded using an error correction code). Finally, the decryptor in Algorithm 3 computes $\langle su \rangle_{\xi(x)} \approx \langle br \rangle_{\xi(x)}$ and recovers the message. The rounding constant $h_2 = p/2t + p/4 - q/2p$ is used here to remove bias in the decryption error.

Since not all coefficients of v are needed to encrypt a κ bit message, encryption uses the function $\text{Sample}_\mu : c \in \mathcal{R}_{n,p} \rightarrow \mathbb{Z}_p^\mu$, whose output corresponds to the μ lowest order polynomial coefficients of c: $c_0 + c_1 x + \cdots + c_{\mu-1} x^{\mu-1}$. The use of Sample_μ makes encryption and decryption more efficient since only μ coefficients need to be computed in the ciphertext instead of all n. This also improves the failure probability since the encryptor and decryptor need to agree on fewer symbols. Further, this also requires sending fewer symbols, reducing bandwidth required.

The integer f denotes the error-correction capability of a code $Xef_{\kappa,f} \subset \mathbb{Z}_2^{\mu}$. We have an encoding function $\texttt{xef\_compute}_{\kappa,f} : \{0,1\}^{\kappa} \to Xef_{\kappa,f}$ and a decoding function $\texttt{xef\_correct}_{\kappa,f} : \mathbb{Z}_2^{\mu} \to \{0,1\}^{\kappa}$ such that for each $m \in \{0,1\}^{\kappa}$ and each error $e = (e_0, \ldots, e_{\mu-1})$ with at most f bits equal to 1

$$\texttt{xef\_correct}_{\kappa,f}(\texttt{xef\_compute}_{\kappa,f}(m) + e) = m. \tag{2}$$

Secret-keys in Round5 are *sparse*, *ternary* and *balanced*, i.e., they are polynomials of degree at most $(n-1)$, exactly $h/2$ coefficients of which are $+1$, $h/2$ are -1, and the rest zero. Having a fixed weight (sparse) reduces probability of decryption failure and makes computations faster. The latter is also helped by the fact that non-zero components are either $+1$ or -1 (ternary), implying that multiplications can be accomplished using only additions and subtractions. Finally, having an equal number of $+1$'s and -1's (balanced) ensures that the secret-keys have a factor $(x-1)$. Section 4 analyzes how this ensures that decryption errors are not correlated, allowing error correction to be used in Round5. As an additional benefit, the decryption failure rate remains low and at the level of $x^{2^k} + 1$ cyclotomic polynomials, despite using reductions modulo $\Phi_{n+1}(x)$ to compute public-keys.

As a final note, the NIST submission Lizard [11,12] also uses sparse, ternary secret-keys, and similar to our proposal enjoys the resulting benefits in decryption failure probability and computational efficiency. However, Lizard (specifically, its ring-based instantiation RLizard) uses Φ_{2n} (for n a power of 2) as the reduction polynomial. It thus does not require balanced secret-keys and our technique for reducing error correlations; however, its ring choice limits its parameter choices and design space.

4   Correctness Analysis

In this section, the decryption failure behavior of r5_cpa_pke is analyzed. We first present a sufficient condition for correct decryption. We then analyze the probability of this condition not being satisfied and describe how we evaluated this decryption failure probability.

Sufficient Condition for Correctness. Let $\Delta = (h_1 + h_2)1_{\mu} - i_v + \mathrm{Sample}_{\mu}(\langle\langle(br - su)\rangle_{\xi})$, where $\frac{t}{p}i_v(x)$ represents the error introduced in the ciphertext component $v(x)$ due to rounding downwards; each coefficient of $i_v(x)$ is in $\mathbb{Z}_{p/t}$, and 1_a is the polynomial of degree $a - 1$ with all coefficients equal to 1. As shown in Appendix A, if the i-th coefficient of the polynomial y in decryption and the i-th coefficient of $\texttt{xef\_compute}_{\kappa,f}(m)$ do not agree, then

$$\left\langle \frac{q}{p}\Delta_i \right\rangle_q \in \left[\frac{q}{4}, q - \frac{q}{4}\right]. \tag{3}$$

Decryption Failure Probability. The probability of decryption failure in coefficient i before error correction is thus at most the probability that (3) is satisfied. We write $b \equiv \frac{p}{q}(\langle as \rangle_{\varPhi_{n+1}} + h_1 1_n) - i_b$ with all coefficients of i_b in $[0, 1)$. We thus have that $\frac{q}{p} b \equiv \langle as \rangle_{\varPhi_{n+1}} + j_b \pmod{q}$ with all coefficients of $j_b = h_1 1_n - i_b$ in $I = (-\frac{q}{2p}, \frac{q}{2p}] \cap \mathbb{Z}$. Similarly, $\frac{q}{p} u \equiv \langle ar \rangle_{\varPhi_{n+1}} + j_u \pmod{q}$ with all components of j_u in I. We thus can write

$$\frac{q}{p}(br - su) \equiv \langle sa \rangle_{\varPhi_{n+1}} r - s \langle ar \rangle_{\varPhi_{n+1}} + j_b r - s j_u \pmod{q}. \tag{4}$$

Obviously, if $\xi = \varPhi_{n+1}$, then $\langle sa \rangle_{\varPhi_{n+1}} r - s \langle ar \rangle_{\varPhi_{n+1}} \equiv 0 \pmod{\xi}$. The same is true if $\xi = N_{n+1}$ and r and s both are multiples of $(x - 1)$. This is so as there are $\lambda_s, \lambda_r \in \mathbb{Z}[x]$ such that $\langle as \rangle_{\varPhi_{n+1}} r - s \langle ar \rangle_{\varPhi_{n+1}} = \lambda_s \varPhi_{n+1}(x) r(x) - s \lambda_r \varPhi_{n+1}$. As $(x - 1)$ divides s and r, both $\varPhi_{n+1} r$ and $s \varPhi_{n+1}$ are divisible by N_{n+1}. As a result, for $\xi \in \{\varPhi_{n+1}, N_{n+1}\}$ we have that

$$\frac{q}{p}\Delta \equiv j_v + \mathrm{Sample}_\mu \left(\langle j_b r - s j_u \rangle_\xi \right) \pmod{q}. \tag{5}$$

In our analysis below, the coefficients of j_b and j_u are drawn independently and uniformly from I, and the coefficients of j_v are drawn independently and distributed as $\frac{q}{p} y$ with y uniform on $(-\frac{p}{2t}, \frac{p}{2t}] \cap \mathbb{Z}$.

4.1   Computing Failure Probability When $\xi = \varPhi_{n+1}$

We now combine (3) and (5) for the case that $\xi = \varPhi_{n+1}$. As $N_{n+1}(x)$ is a multiple of $\varPhi_{n+1}(x)$, we have that $\langle f \rangle_{\varPhi_{n+1}} = \langle \langle f \rangle_N \rangle_{\varPhi_{n+1}}$. Moreover, if $g(x) = \sum_{i=0}^{n} g_i x^i$, then $\langle g \rangle_{\varPhi_{n+1}} = g - g_n \varPhi_{n+1}$. In particular, for all polynomials s, e,

$$\text{if } \langle se \rangle_N = \sum_{k=0}^{n} c_k(s, e) x^k, \text{ then } \langle se \rangle_{\varPhi_{n+1}} = \sum_{k=0}^{n-1} (c_k(s, e) - c_n(s, e)) x^k, \tag{6}$$

Hence, if the i-th bit is not retrieved correctly, then

$$\langle (j_v(x))_i + c_i(j_b, r) - c_n(j_b, r) - c_i(s, j_u) + c_n(s, j_u) \rangle_q \in \left[\frac{q}{4}, q - \frac{q}{4} \right]. \tag{7}$$

Assuming independence, and taking into account that r and s contain $h/2$ ones and $h/2$ minus ones, $c_k(j_b, r) - c_n(j_b, r) - c_k(s, j_u) + c_n(s, j_u)$ is distributed as the difference of $2h$ independent random variables on I, minus the sum of $2h$ independent random variables on I. The probability that (7) is satisfied thus can be computed explicitly. By the union bound, the probability that at least one of the μ symbols is not retrieved correctly is at most μ times the probability that (7) is satisfied.

4.2   Correlation in Decryption Errors When $\xi = \varPhi_{n+1}$

A basic requirement for using XEf error correction code is that the errors it aims to correct are independent. However, the condition in (7) for a decryption error in position i shows terms $c_n(j_b, r)$ and $c_n(s, j_u)$ that are common to all positions

Failure rate (log_2)

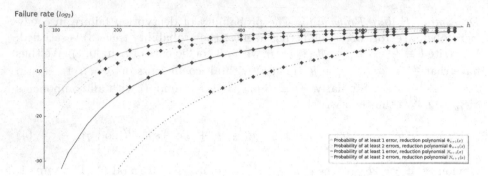

Fig. 1. Probabilities of at least one (continuous lines) and at least two errors (dotted lines) in Round5 ring parameters, plotted against the Hamming weight of secrets (X-axis), for the reduction polynomials $\Phi_{n+1}(x)$ and $N_{n+1}(x)$. Diamonds represent corresponding probabilities computed from actual Round5 simulations for the same parameters. Scripts for analyzing and reproducing these results can be found at www.round5.org.

i. Figure 1 shows the effect of this dependency, by comparing the estimated probabilities of at least one error and that of at least two errors occurring, when the reduction polynomial $\xi = N_{n+1}$ (as in r5_cpa_pke) and when $\xi = \Phi_{n+1}$ (as in Round2 [5]), respectively. It can be seen that due to correlated errors, the probability of at least two errors occurring when the reduction polynomial is $\xi = \Phi_{n+1}$ is much larger than in the case of the $N_{n+1}(x)$ reduction polynomial. As a consequence, the XEf code cannot be directly employed with the reduction polynomial $\xi = \Phi_{n+1}$ as used in Round2.

For any a, (6) can be used to compute $p(i \mid a)$, the probability that bit i is not retrieved correctly, given that $-c_n(j_b, r) + c_n(s, j_u) \equiv a \pmod{q}$. We assume that having a bit error in position i, given that $c_n(s, j_u) - c_n(j_b, r) \equiv a$, is independent of having a bit error in another position j, given that $c_n(s, j_u) - c_n(j_b, r) \equiv a$. The probability of having exactly k bit errors, given that $c_n(s, j_u) - c_n(j_b, r) \equiv a$, then equals $\binom{\mu}{k}(p(0 \mid a))^k(1 - p(0 \mid a))^{\mu-k}$. By summing these probabilities over a, weighted with the probability that $c_n(s, j_u) - c_n(j_b, r) \equiv a$, the probability of having exactly k bit errors is obtained. In Fig. 1, the result of application of this method is also compared with simulations of scaled-down Round5 parameters; Sect. 4.4 contains details.

4.3   Computing Failure Probability When $\xi = N_{n+1}$

Combination of (3) and (5) for $\xi = N_{n+1}$ implies that if an error occurs in position i, then

$$\langle (j_v(x))_i + c_i(j_b, r) - c_i(s, j_u) \rangle_q \in \left[\frac{q}{4}, q - \frac{q}{4} \right]. \tag{8}$$

Note that in order that (8) can be used, it is required that s and r both are multiples of $(x - 1)$, as is the case with Round5.

Assuming independence, and assuming that r and s contain $h/2$ ones and $h/2$ minus ones, $c_i(j_b, r) - c_i(s, j_u)$ is distributed as the sum of h independent uniform random variables on I, minus the sum of h independent uniform random variables on I. The probability that (8) is satisfied thus can be computed explicitly.

Now let the error-correcting code be capable of correcting f symbol errors. Assuming that $c_i(s, e)$ and $c_j(s, e)$ are independent whenever $i \neq j$, the probability of not decoding correctly is at most $\sum_{e \geq f+1} \binom{\mu}{e} p_n^e (1 - p_n)^{\mu - e}$.

4.4   Correlation and Error Correction: Experimental Results

Figure 1 compares the estimated probabilities of at least one error occurring and that of at least two errors occurring, when $\xi = N_{n+1}$ (as in r5_cpa_pke) and when $\xi = \Phi_{n+1}$ (as in Round2 [5]), respectively. These estimates are computed by explicitly convolving probability distributions. Parameters are simulated *without* error correction, and are $n = 800$, $q = 2^{11}$, $p = 2^7$, $t = 2^4$, $\mu = \kappa = 128$, while the Hamming weight varies between 100 and 750 in order to show its effect on both the bit failure rate and error correlation. The influence of the highest-order coefficients $c_n(s, e)$ common to all coefficients in the Φ_{n+1} case is accounted for as explained in Sect. 4.2. Clearly, the probability of at least two errors is much higher when multiplications are done modulo Φ_{n+1} instead of N_{n+1}, and in the latter case, this probability is significantly lower than the probability of at least one error. Figure 1 also shows corresponding probabilities of at least one and at least two errors, obtained from simulations of *actual, scaled-down* r5_cpa_pke parameters, showing that the actual behavior closely matches estimates.

To conclude, the effect of dependency due to polynomial multiplication modulo Φ_{n+1} as in Round2 is made negligible by the combined use of polynomial multiplication modulo N_{n+1} and balanced secrets in Round5, allowing the use of forward error correction, resulting in better security and performance.

5   Security Analysis

In Sect. 5.1, we show that if $\xi = \Phi_{n+1}$, then r5_cpa_pke is IND-CPA secure. Section 5.2 details how Round2's use of the function $Sample_\mu$ prevents known distinguishing attacks such as the *"Evaluate at 1"* attack [21]. Next, Sect. 5.3 extends the IND-CPA security proof in Sect. 5.1 to a RLWE-variant of r5_cpa_pke, which gives strong confidence in Round5's design. Finally, in Sect. 5.4 it is discussed why this proof does not directly translate to an RLWR-based design and a simple design change in Round5 that would make it apply, but which is not introduced since it does not bring major benefits from a concrete security viewpoint.

5.1   IND-CPA Security of r5_cpa_pke When $\xi = \Phi_{n+1}$

When the reduction polynomial $\xi(x)$ in Round5 equals $\Phi_{n+1}(x)$, then r5_cpa_pke is an IND-CPA secure public-key encryption scheme, under the assumption that the decision Ring Learning with Rounding (RLWR) problem with sparse-ternary secrets ($\mathsf{dRLWR}_{\mathrm{spt}}$) is hard for the polynomial ring $\mathbb{Z}[x]/\Phi_{n+1}(x)$. [6, Theorem 3.2] proves that the RLWR problem for any distribution on the secrets is hard assuming that the RLWE problem is hard for the same distribution, for a super-polynomial modulus q. This gives confidence in the asymptotic hardness of our scheme's underlying problem.

The below theorem (informal) gives a tight, classical reduction against classical or quantum adversaries in the standard model:

Theorem 1. *For every adversary $\mathcal{A}$ against r5_cpa_pke, there exist distinguishers $\mathcal{B}$ and $\mathcal{C}$ such that, for $z = \max(p, tq/p)$,*

$$Adv^{IND\text{-}CPA}_{\mathrm{r5\_cpa\_pke}(\xi=\Phi_{n+1})}(\mathcal{A}) \leq Adv^{dRLWR_{spt}}_{n,1,q,p}(\mathcal{B}) + Adv^{dRLWR_{spt}}_{n,2,q,z}(\mathcal{C}). \tag{9}$$

The proof of the above theorem follows a similar approach as [14] to equalize the noise ratios q/p and p/t in (the coefficients of) the two ciphertext components u and v, allowing them to be expressed as two RLWR samples with a common secret and noise distribution (with noise ratio q/z). This technique however does not apply if the reduction polynomial ξ in Round5 is N_{n+1}, as is required for the secure usage of (XEf) error correction in Round5 (see Sect. 4.3).

5.2   Distinguishing Attack at $x = 1$ for $\xi = N_{n+1}$

When $\xi = N_{n+1}$ and $\mu = n+1$, a distinguisher can be built from the evaluation of the ciphertext component $v(x)$ in Algorithm 2 in $x = 1$. This is based on the fact that $(x - 1)$ divides both $r(x)$ and $N_{n+1}(x)$. The attack does not apply if $\mu \leq n$ as in Round5, as the sum of the coefficients of $v(x)$ hidden by Sample_μ is uniformly distributed. Further details can be found in Appendix B.

5.3   IND-CPA Security of r5_cpa_pke with $\xi = N_{n+1}$ and Independent Noise

A variant of r5_cpa_pke where the noise is independently sampled from a given distribution instead of being generated via rounding, is an IND-CPA secure public-key encryption scheme, if the decision Ring LWE problem for $\mathbb{Z}[x]/\Phi_{n+1}(x)$ is hard; this results gives confidence in Round5's RLWR-based design.

Theorem 2. *For every adversary $\mathcal{A}$ against a variant r5_cpa_pke' of r5_cpa_pke where the noise is independently sampled, there exist distinguishers $\mathcal{C}$ and $\mathcal{E}$ such that*

$$Adv^{IND\text{-}CPA}_{\mathrm{r5\_cpa\_pke}'(\xi=N_{n+1})}(\mathcal{A}) \leq Adv^{RLWE(\mathbb{Z}_q[x]/\Phi_{n+1}(x))}_{m=1}(\mathcal{C}) + Adv^{RLWE(\mathbb{Z}_q[x]/\Phi_{n+1}(x))}_{m=2}(\mathcal{E}). \tag{10}$$

where m denotes the number of RLWE samples available to each distinguisher.

A more detailed version of the above theorem and its proof can be found in Appendix C. The proof uses elements of [8, Sect. E1].

Algorithm 4. round_to_root(a, q, p)

---

1 $b \leftarrow \left\lfloor \frac{p}{q} a \right\rceil$

2 **for** $i \leftarrow 0$ **to** $n - 1$ **do**

3 $\quad \Big| \quad e_i \leftarrow \Big(\mathtt{idx} = i \in \mathbb{Z}, \ \mathtt{val} = \frac{p}{q} a - \left\lfloor \frac{p}{q} a \right\rceil \in \mathbb{Q} \Big)$

4 Sort e in descending order of $e.\mathtt{val}$.

5 $k \leftarrow p \left\lceil \frac{b(1)}{p} \right\rceil - b(1)$

6 **for** $i \leftarrow 0$ **to** $k - 1$ **do**

7 $\quad \Big| \quad b_{e_i.\mathtt{idx}} \leftarrow b_{e_i.\mathtt{idx}} + 1$

8 **return** b

5.4 IND-CPA Security of r5_cpa_pke with $\xi = N_{n+1}$ and Rounding Noise

The proof of IND-CPA security for a RLWE variant of r5_cpa_pke in Sect. 5.3 requires both the secrets and also the noise polynomials to be multiples of $(x - 1)$ (this is used in an essential step of the proof, see Appendix C). This last requirement is the reason why this proof does not apply to Round5 with $\xi(x) = x^{n+1} - 1$ using RLWR defined as *component-wise rounding*. This deterministic component-wise rounding does not allow enforcing that the noisy "rounding" polynomials are multiples of $(x - 1)$.

Round5's design can be adapted to use a slightly different type of rounding informally named as "rounding to the root lattice" [15,16,29] – that allows the IND-CPA proof to work. This alternate rounding technique is described in Algorithm 4, that takes as input an $a \in \mathbb{Z}_q[x]$, integer moduli q, p where $p < q$ and returns a $b \in \mathbb{Z}_p[x]$ satisfying $b(1) \equiv 0 \pmod{p}$.

Rounded noise introduced in b using Algorithm 4 is a polynomial whose coefficients sum to zero, so that a direct translation of the IND-CPA proof in Sect. 5.3 to the RLWR case is possible. However, this modification – going from component-wise rounding to rounding to the root lattice – would introduce additional complexity with no clear concrete security benefits. First, Sample$_\mu$ gets rid of $n + 1 - \mu$ coefficients so that knowing k is irrelevant. Second, concrete security attacks use the norm of the noise that hardly changes here. Because of these two reasons, we argue that the current Round5 design (and the rounding used in it) is sound and secure, and further modifications are not required.

6 Parameters, Performance and Comparison

Round5 has a large design space, adding to the parameters available in Round2, namely n, h, q, p, t, also f. If $f > 0$, then $\xi(x) = N(x)$. By searching over the design space, we obtain parameters that minimize bandwidth requirements given a minimum targeted security level and failure probability. The failure probability analysis is done as in Sect. 4. Concrete security is analyzed in the standard manner [5], the primal [4], dual [1], hybrid [23], and sparse secret attacks [1,5] are considered, under both sieving [7] and enumeration [2] cost models. Details are not included due to space limits. A script to verify computations is available at www.round5.org.

Table 1. Parameters: "C" denotes security level against classical adversaries, while "Q" denotes that against quantum ones. Bandwidth is in bytes.

Name Set	Parameters (n, h, q, p, t, f)	Failure rate	Sieving (C/Q)	Enumeration (C/Q)	Bandwidth (pk/ct)
R5ND_1KEM_5c	$490, 162, 2^{10}, 2^7, 2^3, 5$	2^{-88}	128/122	170/135	445 + 549
R5ND_1KEM_0c	$618, 104, 2^{11}, 2^8, 2^4, 0$	2^{-65}	128/122	160/133	634 + 682
R5ND_1KEM_4longkey	$490, 162, 2^{10}, 2^7, 2^3, 4$	2^{-71}	128/122	170/135	453 + 563
R5ND_1PKE_5c	$508, 136, 2^{10}, 2^7, 2^4, 5$	2^{-142}	128/122	166/134	461 + 636
R5ND_5PKE_5c	$940, 414, 2^{12}, 2^8, 2^3, 2$	2^{-144}	256/232	390/307	972 + 1172
R5ND_0KEM_2iot	$372, 178, 2^{11}, 2^7, 2^3, 2$	2^{-41}	96/90	129/96	342 + 394
NewHope1024-CCA-KEM [32]	N/A	2^{-216}	257/233	-	1824 + 2208
Kyber1024 [9]	N/A	2^{-169}	241/218	-	1440 + 1504
FireSaber-KEM [24]	N/A	2^{-165}	270/245	-	1312 + 1472

Table 1 includes a number of exemplary Round5 parameter sets. Also shown are a number of similar proposals for comparison. R5ND_1KEM_5c and R5ND_1KEM_0c both target NIST security category 1 as IND-CPA secure KEMs. However, the second requires around 33% more bandwidth since it does not use error correction ($f = 0$). This demonstrates the benefit of error correction.

R5ND_1KEM_4longkey also targets NIST security category 1 as an IND-CPA secure KEM. However, it uses the flexibility of Sample$_\mu$ to encapsulate a longer key (192 bits instead of 128) so that the (quantum) hardness of attacking the shared secret is as much as (quantum) attacking the underlying lattice problem.

R5ND_1KEM_5c and R5ND_1PKE_5c differ in the target failure probability. The latter is constructed by applying the Fujisaki-Okamoto transform [22] on r5_cpa_-_pke in a standard manner and combining with a secure (one-time) data encapsulation scheme (e.g., AES256); its failure rate is much lower to achieve the IND-CCA security required of public-key encryption (PKE). Comparing the above two parameter sets shows that a more relaxed failure probability target leads to bandwidth savings of more than 100 B.

R5ND_5PKE_5c targets NIST security category 5 as an IND-CCA secure PKE. It requires 2144 B of bandwidth. Among existing proposals targeting the same security category, NewHope1024-CCA-KEM [32] requires 88% more bandwidth, FireSaber [13] requires 30% more, and Kyber1024 requires 37% more. Round5's compact keys fit easily in protocols with a limited (1500 B) MTU.

Finally, parameter set R5ND_0KEM_2iot shows that Round5's design flexibility makes it easy to obtain parameters that offer a reasonable security level, but require relatively little bandwidth enabling security in more resource constrained applications such as IoT.

7 Conclusions and Future Work

In this work, we introduced *Round5*, a lattice-based cryptosystem consisting of a public-key encryption scheme that uses rounding both to introduce noise (for security) and at the same time reduce the key-size, improving performance. Public-keys are computed via ring multiplications in $\mathbb{Z}[x]/\Phi_{n+1}(x)$, thus offering a wide variety of choices for the security parameter n, in turn allowing to finely tune the parameters and performance of Round5. A novel contribution of this work is to compute part of the ciphertext, on the other hand, via ring multiplications in $\mathbb{Z}[x]/N_{n+1}(x)$; this, in combination with the fact that Round5 secret-keys are polynomials with a factor $(x-1)$, allows to have low decryption failure rates similar to schemes constructed using the $x^{2^k}+1$ cyclotomic polynomial, while still allowing to have the above mentioned benefit of the $\mathbb{Z}[x]/\Phi_{n+1}(x)$ polynomial ring.

Further, this leads to very low dependencies between coefficients and independent bit failures, so that error correction can be used to further improve failure rates, performance (since parameters can be shrunk) and security (since more noise can be added). For the latter, r5_cpa_pke uses the XEf f-bit error correcting code originally introduced in the HILA5 scheme [34]. The main advantage of XEf codes is that they avoid table look-ups and conditions altogether and are therefore resistant to timing attacks.

An interesting open question is to investigate a variant of Round5 where component-wise rounding is replaced by the alternate rounding technique described in Algorithm 4 and investigate implications on the resulting scheme's concrete security and decryption failure behavior.

Acknowledgements. We thank Mike Hamburg for helpful discussions on combining features from the prime-order cyclotomic and power-of-two cyclotomic polynomial rings in a lattice based cryptosystem. We thank Léo Ducas for helpful discussions on rounding to the root lattice, and techniques required for proving IND-CPA security for a rounding-based scheme using N_{n+1} as reduction polynomial. Finally, we wish to thank our anonymous reviewers for their helpful comments that led to improving the content and readability of the paper.

A Probability of Decryption Failures in Round5

In decryption, the polynomial $y = \langle\lfloor\frac{2}{p}\zeta\rceil\rangle_2$ is computed, where $\zeta = \langle\frac{p}{t}v -$ Sample$_\mu(\langle su\rangle_\xi) + h_2 1_\mu)\rangle_p$, where 1_μ is the polynomial of degree $\mu-1$ with all coefficients equal to 1. First, a sufficient condition is derived so that y and $\eta = \texttt{xef\_compute}_{\kappa,f}(m)$ agree in a given coefficient. We have that

$$v \equiv \left\langle \frac{t}{p}\text{Sample}_\mu(\langle br\rangle_\xi + h_1 1_n) - \frac{t}{p}i_v \right\rangle_p + \frac{t}{2}\eta \pmod{t},$$

where $\frac{t}{p}i_v$ is the error introduced by the rounding downwards, with each component of i_v in $\mathbb{Z}_{p/t}$. As a result,

$$\zeta \equiv \frac{p}{2}\eta + \Delta \pmod{p} \text{ with } \Delta = (h_1+h_2)1_\mu - i_v + \text{Sample}_\mu(\langle br - su + h_4 j\rangle_\xi). \quad (11)$$

As $y = \lfloor \frac{2}{p}\zeta - \frac{1}{2}\rceil$, it holds that $y \equiv \eta + \lfloor \frac{2}{p}\Delta - \frac{1}{2}1_n\rceil \equiv \eta + \lfloor \frac{2}{p}\{\Delta - \frac{p}{4}1_n\}_p\rceil$ (mod 2). Here $\{w\}_p$ denotes the integer in $(-p/2, p/2)$ that is equivalent to w modulo p. As a consequence, $y_i = \eta_i$ whenever $|\{\Delta_i - \frac{p}{4}\}_p| < \frac{p}{4}$. We infer that $y_i = \eta_i$ whenever

$$\left|\left\{\frac{q}{p}\Delta_i - \frac{q}{4}\right\}_q\right| < \frac{q}{4} \tag{12}$$

Equivalently, as $\frac{q}{p}\Delta_i$ has integer components, if $y_i \neq \eta_i$, then

$$\left\langle \frac{q}{p}\Delta_i \right\rangle_q \in \left[\frac{q}{4}, q - \frac{q}{4}\right] \tag{13}$$

In order to analyze this probability, we work out $\frac{q}{p}\Delta - \frac{q}{4}j$, using (11). We write $j_v = \frac{q}{p}((h_1 + h_2)1_\mu - i_v - \frac{p}{4}1_\mu)$. The definitions of h_1 and h_2 imply that $j_v = \frac{q}{p}(\frac{p}{2t}1_\mu - i_v)$. Each coefficient of i_v is in $\mathbb{Z}_{p/t}$. The value of h_2 thus ensures that the absolute value of each coefficient of $\frac{p}{2t} - i_v$ is at most $\frac{p}{2t}$.

We now analyze $\frac{q}{p}\langle br - su\rangle\rangle_\xi$. Similarly to the expression for v, we write

$$b = \left\langle \frac{p}{q}\left(\langle as\rangle_{\Phi_{n+1}} + h_1 1_n\right) - \frac{p}{q}i_b \right\rangle_p \text{ and } u = \left\langle \frac{p}{q}(\langle ar\rangle_{\Phi_{n+1}} + h_1 1_n) - \frac{p}{q}i_u \right\rangle_p,$$

with all components of i_b and i_u in $\mathbb{Z}_{q/p}$. We thus have

$$\frac{q}{p}(br - su) \equiv \langle sa\rangle_{\Phi_{n+1}}r - s\langle ar\rangle_{\Phi_{n+1}} + j_b r - s j_u \pmod{q} \tag{14}$$

$$\text{where } j_b = h_1 1_n - i_b \text{ and } j_u = h_1 1_n - i_u. \tag{15}$$

As $h_1 = \frac{q}{2p}$, all entries of j_b and of j_u are from the set $I := (-\frac{q}{2p}, \frac{q}{2p}] \cap \mathbb{Z}$. Obviously, if $\xi(x) = \Phi_{n+1}(x)$, then $\langle sa\rangle_{\Phi_{n+1}}r - s\langle ar\rangle_{\Phi_{n+1}} \equiv 0 \pmod{\xi}$. The same is true if $\xi = N_{n+1}$ and r and s both are multiple of $(x-1)$. Indeed, there are $\lambda_s, \lambda_r \in \mathbb{Z}[x]$ such that $\langle sa\rangle_{\Phi_{n+1}} = sa + \lambda_r\Phi_{n+1}$ and $\langle ar\rangle_{\Phi_{n+1}} = ar - \lambda_s\Phi_{n+1}$. As a consequence, $\langle as\rangle_{\Phi_{n+1}}r - s\langle ar\rangle_{\Phi_{n+1}} = \lambda_s\Phi_{n+1}r - s\lambda_r\Phi_{n+1}$. As $(x-1)$ divides s and r, both $\Phi_{n+1}r$ and $s\Phi_{n+1}$ are divisible by N_{n+1}. As a result, for $\xi \in \{\Phi_{n+1}, N_{n+1}\}$

$$\frac{q}{p}\Delta \equiv j_v + \text{Sample}_\mu\left(\langle j_b r - s j_u\rangle_\xi\right) \pmod{q}. \tag{16}$$

The probability of a decryption failure in position i before error correction is at most the probability that (13) is satisfied.

In our analysis of (13) combined with (16), the coefficients of j_b and j_u are drawn independently and uniformly from $I = (-\frac{q}{2p}, \frac{q}{2p}] \cap \mathbb{Z}$, and the coefficients of j_v are drawn independently and distributed as $\frac{q}{p}y$ with y uniform on $(-\frac{p}{2t}, \frac{p}{2t}] \cap \mathbb{Z}$.

B   Distinguishing Attack at $x = 1$ or $\xi = N_{n+1}$

The "Evaluate at $x = 1$" distinguishing attack [21] applies against schemes using the ring $\mathbb{Z}[x]/N_{n+1}(x)$. We argue that this attack cannot be applied in Round5 if $\mu \leq n$.

Consider a pair of polynomials $(b(x), v(x))$ with $b(x)$ uniformly distributed on $\mathbb{Z}_p[x]/(x^{n+1}-1)$ and $v(x) = \langle \text{Sample}_\mu(\lfloor \frac{t}{p}(\langle b(x)r(x)\rangle_{N(x)}+h_1)\rceil) + \frac{t}{2}m(x)\rangle_t$ with $r(x)$ drawn independently and uniformly from the ternary polynomials of degree at most $n-1$ satisfying $r(1) = 0$, and $m(x)$ drawn according to some distribution on $\mathbb{Z}_2[x]/(x^\mu-1)$. We then have that $v(x) \equiv \lfloor \text{Sample}_\mu(\frac{t}{p}(\langle b(x)r(x)\rangle_{N(x)}+h_1))\rceil) + \frac{t}{2}m(x) \pmod{t}$, and so $w(x) = \frac{p}{t}v(x)$ satisfies

$$w(x) \equiv \text{Sample}_\mu(\langle b(x)r(x)\rangle_{N(x)}) + \frac{p}{t} \cdot h_1 \sum_{i=0}^{\mu-1} x^i - \frac{p}{t}\epsilon(x) + \frac{p}{2}m(x) \pmod{p}.$$

where $\epsilon(x)$ is the result of rounding downwards, so all components of $\frac{p}{t}\epsilon(x)$ are in $[0, \frac{p}{t}) \cap \mathbb{Z}$. As $(x-1)$ divides both $r(x)$ and $N(x)$, it follows that $x-1$ divides $\langle b(x)r(x)\rangle_{N(x)}$, and so if $\mu = n+1$, then

$$w(1) \equiv \frac{p}{t} \cdot h_1 \cdot (n+1) - \frac{p}{t}\sum_{i=0}^{n}\epsilon_i + \frac{p}{2}m(1) \pmod{p}.$$

For large n, the value of $\frac{p}{t}\sum_{i=0}^{n}\epsilon_i$ is close to its average, i.e., close to $n\frac{p}{2t}$. As a result, $w(1)$ has maxima at values $\frac{p}{t}h_1(n+1) - n\frac{p}{2t} + \frac{p}{2}k$ for $k \in \{0,1\}$. So $w(1)$ can serve as a distinguisher between the above distribution and the uniform one.

Now assume that $\mu < n+1$. We take $\mu = n$, which is the case giving most information to the attacker. Writing $f(x) = \langle b(x)r(x)\rangle_{N(x)} = \sum_{i=0}^{n}f_ix^i$, it holds that

$$w(1) \equiv \sum_{i=0}^{n-1}f_i + \frac{p}{t} \cdot h_1 \cdot n - \frac{p}{t}\epsilon(1) + \frac{p}{2}m(1) \pmod{p}.$$

As shown above, $f(1) = 0$, and so $\sum_{i=0}^{n-1}f_i = -f_n$. Hence, under the assumption that f_n is distributed uniformly modulo p, also $w(1)$ is distributed uniformly modulo p. The latter assumption is supported by [31].

C   Proof of IND-CPA Security of r5_cpa_pke RLWE Variant

We present the proof of IND-CPA security for an RLWE variant of r5_cpa_pke. The proof uses elements of [8, Sect. E1]. The following notation will be used. We write $\phi(x) = 1 + x + \ldots + x^n$, and $N(x) = x^{n+1} - 1$, where $n+1$ is prime. Moreover, $R_\phi = \mathbb{Z}_q[x]/\phi(x)$, and

$$R_0 = \{f(x) = \sum_{i=0}^{n}f_ix^i \in \mathbb{Z}_q[x] \mid \sum_{i=0}^{n}f_i \equiv 0 \pmod{q}\} \tag{17}$$

As $N(x) = (x-1)\phi(x)$, it holds that $\langle (x-1)f(x)\rangle_{N(x)} = (x-1)\langle f(x)\rangle_{\phi(x)}$ for any $f \in \mathbb{Z}[x]$. As a result, $f(x) \mapsto (x-1)f(x)$ is a bijection from R_ϕ to R_0.

In the proof, the following lemma will be used.

Lemma 1. *Let q and $n+1$ be relatively prime, and let $(n+1)^{-1}$ be the multiplicative inverse of $n+1$ in $\mathbb{Z}_q$. The mapping $\mathcal{F}$ defined as*

$$\mathcal{F} : \left(\sum_{i=0}^{n-1} f_i x^i\right) \mapsto \sum_{i=0}^{n-1} f_i x^i - (n+1)^{-1} \cdot \left(\sum_{i=0}^{n-1} f_i\right) \cdot \phi(x)$$

is a bijection from R_ϕ to R_0.

Proof. It is easy to see that $\mathcal{F}$ maps R_ϕ to R_0. To show that $\mathcal{F}$ is a bijection, let $g(x) = \sum_{i=0}^{n} g_i x^i \in R_0$, and let $f(x) = \sum_{i=0}^{n} \langle g_i - g_n \rangle_q x^i$. Clearly, $f \in \mathbb{Z}_q[x]$ has degree at most $n-1$, and by direct computation, $\mathcal{F}(f(x)) = g(x)$.

In the description below, $\mathcal{S}$ denotes a set of secrets such that

$$\mathcal{S} \subset \{f(x) = \sum_{i=0}^{n-1} f_i x^i \in \mathbb{Z}_q[x] \mid \sum_{i=0}^{n-1} f_i \equiv 0 \pmod{q}\}, \tag{18}$$

Moreover, $\mathcal{M}$ denotes a message space, and ECC_Enc and ECC_Dec are error correcting encoding and decoding algorithms such that

$$\{ECC\_Enc(m) \mid m \in \mathcal{M}\} \subset \{f(x) = \sum_{i=0}^{n} f_i x^i \in \mathbb{Z}_2[x] \mid \sum_{i=0}^{n} f_i \equiv 0 \pmod{2}\}. \tag{19}$$

Moreover, χ denotes a probability distribution on R_ϕ.

For understanding Algorithm 7, note that as $(x-1)|s(x)$, we have that $su' \equiv sa'r + se_1 \pmod{N}$, and, as $(x-1)|r(x)$, that $rb' \equiv ra's + re_0 \pmod{N}$. As a consequence,

$$\zeta \equiv v - su' \equiv \frac{q}{2} ECC\_Enc(m) + (x-1)e_2 + re_0 - se_1 \pmod{N}, \text{ whence}$$

$$\lfloor \frac{2}{q}\zeta \rceil \equiv ECC\_Enc(m) + \lfloor \frac{2}{q}((x-1)e_2 + re_0 - se_1) \rceil \pmod{N}.$$

We are now in a position to prove the following result.

Theorem 3. *For every IND-CPA adversary $\mathcal{A}$ with advantage A, there exist algorithms C and E such that*

$$A \leq Adv_1(C) + Adv_3(E). \tag{20}$$

Here Adv_1 refers to the advantage of distinguishing between the uniform distribution on $(\mathbb{Z}_q[x]/\phi(x))^2$ and the R-LWE distribution

$$(a', b' = \langle a's + e_0 \rangle_\phi) \text{ with } a' \xleftarrow{\$} R_\phi, s \xleftarrow{\$} \mathcal{S}, e_0 \leftarrow \chi \tag{21}$$

Similarly, Adv_3 refers to the advantage of distinguishing between the uniform distribution on $(\mathbb{Z}_q[x]/\phi(x))^4$ and the distribution of two R-LWE samples with a common secret, given by

$$(a', b'', u', v') \text{ with } a', b'' \xleftarrow{\$} \mathbb{Z}_q[x]/\phi(x), u = \langle a'r + e_1 \rangle_\phi, \tag{22}$$

$$v = \langle b''r + e_2 \rangle_\phi \text{ with } r \xleftarrow{\$} \mathcal{S}, e_1, e_2 \leftarrow \chi \tag{23}$$

Algorithm 5. CPA-PKE.Keygen()

---

1 $a' \xleftarrow{\$} R_\phi, s \xleftarrow{\$} \mathcal{S}, e_0 \leftarrow \chi$
2 $b' = \langle a's + e_0 \rangle_\phi$
3 $pk = (a', b')$
4 $sk = s$
5 **return** (pk, sk)

Algorithm 6. CPA-PKE.Enc($pk = (a', b'), m \in \mathcal{M}$)

---

1 $r \xleftarrow{\$} \mathcal{S}, e_1, e_2 \xleftarrow{\$} \chi$
2 $u' = \langle a'r + e_1 \rangle_\phi$
3 $v = \langle \frac{q}{2} ECC\_Enc(m) + b'r + (x-1)e_2 \rangle_N$
4 $c = (u', v)$
5 **return** c

Algorithm 7. CPA-PKE.Dec(sk, c)

---

1 $\zeta = \langle v - su' \rangle_N$
2 $\hat{m} = ECC\_Dec(\lfloor \frac{2\zeta}{q} \rceil_2)$
3 **return** $\hat{m}$

Proof. We prove the theorem using a sequence of IND-CPA games. We denote by S_i the event that the output of game i equals 1.

Game G_0 is the original IND-CPA game. In Game G_1, the public key (a', b') is replaced by a pair (a', b') uniformly drawn from R_ϕ^2. It can be shown that there exists an algorithm $\mathcal{C}$ for distinguishing between the uniform distribution on R_ϕ^2 and the R-LWE distribution of pairs (a', b') with $a' \xleftarrow{\$} R_\phi$, $b' = \langle as' + e_0 \rangle_\phi$ with $s \xleftarrow{\$} \mathcal{S}$ and $e_0 \leftarrow \chi$ such that

$$\mathrm{Adv}_1(\mathcal{C}) = |\mathrm{Pr}(S_0) - \mathrm{Pr}(S_1)|.$$

In Game G_2, the values $u' = \langle a'r + e_1 \rangle_\phi$ and $\hat{v} = \langle b'r + (x-1)e_2 \rangle_N$ used in the generation of v are simultaneously substituted with uniform random variables from R_ϕ and R_0, respectively. It can be shown that there exists an adversary $\mathcal{D}$ with the same running time as that of $\mathcal{A}$ such that

$$\mathrm{Adv}_2(\mathcal{D}) = |\mathrm{Pr}(S_1) - \mathrm{Pr}(S_2)|.$$

Here Adv_2 refers to the advantage of distinguishing between the uniform distribution on $R_\phi^3 \times R_0$ and the distribution

$$(a', b', u', v) = (a', b', \langle a'r + e_1 \rangle_\phi, \langle b'r + (x-1)e_2 \rangle_N) \text{ with } a', b' \xleftarrow{\$} R_\phi, r \xleftarrow{\$} \mathcal{S}, e_1, e_2 \xleftarrow{\$} \chi. \tag{24}$$

Because of (19), the value of the ciphertext v in Game G_2 is independent of bit b, and therefore $\mathrm{Pr}(S_2) = 1/2$. As a final step, we define $\Psi : R_\phi^3 \times R_0 \to R_\phi^4$ as

$$\Psi(a'(x), b'(x), u'(x), v(x)) = (a'(x), b''(x), u'(x), v'(x)) \text{ with} \tag{25}$$

$$b''(x) = \frac{\mathcal{F}(b'(x))}{x-1}, v'(x) = \frac{v(x)}{x-1} \tag{26}$$

As $\mathcal{F}$ is a bijection from R_ϕ to R_0 (see Lemma 1) and $f(x) \mapsto \frac{f(x)}{x-1}$ is a bijection from R_0 to R_ϕ, it follows that Ψ is a bijection. Writing $b(x) = \mathcal{F}(b'(x))$, we infer that

$$b(x)r(x) = b'(x)r(x) - (n+1)^{-1}b'(1)\phi(x)r(x) \equiv b'(x)r(x) \pmod{N(x)},$$

where the latter equivalence holds as $r(x)$ is a multiple of $(x-1)$, and so

$$v(x) = \langle b'(x)r(x) + (x-1)e_2(x)\rangle_N = \langle b(x)r(x) + (x-1)e_2(x)\rangle_N.$$

As $r(x)$ is a multiple of $x - 1$, it follows that $v(x) \in R_0$ and that

$$v'(x) = \frac{v(x)}{x-1} \equiv \langle b''(x)r(x) + e_2(x)\rangle_\phi \text{ where } b''(x) = \frac{b(x)}{x-1}.$$

As a result, the advantage of $\mathcal{E} = \Psi \circ \mathcal{D}$ in distinguishing between the uniform distribution on R_ϕ^4 and the distribution

$$(a', b'', u', v') \text{ with } a, b'' \xleftarrow{\$} R_\phi, u'(x) = \langle a'r + e_1\rangle_\phi \text{ and } v' = \langle b''r + e_2\rangle_\phi$$

is equal to $\mathrm{Adv}_2(D)$. Note that (a, u') and (b'', v') are two R-LWE samples with common secret $r(x) \in \mathcal{S}$, with a', b'' chosen uniformly in R_ϕ and independent noise polynomials $e_1(x)$ and $e_2(x)$.
As $Pr(S_2) = \frac{1}{2}$, we conclude that

$$Adv(\mathcal{A}) = |\mathrm{Pr}(S_0) - \mathrm{Pr}(S_2)| \le \sum_{i=0}^{1} |\mathrm{Pr}(S_i) - \mathrm{Pr}(S_{i+1})| = \mathrm{Adv}_1(\mathcal{C}) + \mathrm{Adv}_2(\mathcal{E}).$$

References

1. Albrecht, M.R.: On dual lattice attacks against small-secret LWE and parameter choices in HElib and SEAL. Cryptology ePrint Archive, Report 2017/047 (2017)
2. Albrecht, M.R., Player, R., Scott, S.: On the concrete hardness of learning with errors. Cryptology ePrint Archive, Report 2015/046 (2015)
3. Alkim, E., Ducas, L., Pöppelmann, T., Schwabe, P.: Post-quantum key exchange - a new hope. Cryptology ePrint Archive, Report 2015/1092 (2015)
4. Alkim, E., Ducas, L., Pöppelmann, T., Schwabe, P.: NewHope without reconciliation. Cryptology ePrint Archive, Report 2016/1157 (2016)
5. Baan, H., et al.: Round2: KEM and PKE based on GLWR. Cryptology ePrint Archive, Report 2017/1183 (2017)
6. Banerjee, A., Peikert, C., Rosen, A.: Pseudorandom functions and lattices. Cryptology ePrint Archive, Report 2011/401 (2011)
7. Becker, A., Ducas, L., Gama, N., Laarhoven, T.: New directions in nearest neighbor searching with applications to lattice sieving. Cryptology ePrint Archive, Report 2015/1128 (2015)

8. Bonnoron, G., Ducas, L., Fillinger, M.: Large FHE gates from tensored homomorphic accumulator. In: Joux, A., Nitaj, A., Rachidi, T. (eds.) AFRICACRYPT 2018. LNCS, vol. 10831, pp. 217–251. Springer, Cham (2018). https://doi.org/10.1007/978-3-319-89339-6_13

9. Bos, J., et al.: CRYSTALS - Kyber: a CCA-secure module-lattice-based KEM. Cryptology ePrint Archive, Report 2017/634 (2017)

10. Bos, J.W., Costello, C., Naehrig, M., Stebila, D.: Post-quantum key exchange for the TLS protocol from the ring learning with errors problem. In: 2015 IEEE Symposium on Security and Privacy, SP 2015, 17–21 May 2015, San Jose, CA, USA, pp. 553–570 (2015)

11. Cheon, J.H., Kim, D., Lee, J., Song, Y.: Lizard: Cut off the Tail! Practical Post-Quantum Public-Key Encryption from LWE and LWR. Cryptology ePrint Archive, Report 2016/1126 (2016)

12. Cheon, J.H., et al.: Lizard. Technical report, National Institute of Standards and Technology (2017). https://csrc.nist.gov/projects/post-quantum-cryptography/round-1-submissions

13. D'Anvers, J.-P., Karmakar, A., Roy, S.S., Vercauteren, F.: SABER. Technical report, National Institute of Standards and Technology (2017). https://csrc.nist.gov/projects/post-quantum-cryptography/round-1-submissions

14. D'Anvers, J.-P., Karmakar, A., Roy, S.S., Vercauteren, F.: Saber: Module-LWR based key exchange, CPA-secure encryption and CCA-secure KEM. Cryptology ePrint Archive, Report 2018/230 (2018)

15. Ducas, L.: Public discussion, August 2018. https://csrc.nist.gov/CSRC/media/Projects/Post-Quantum-Cryptography/documents/round-1/official-comments/Round5-official-comment.pdf. Messages on the NIST PQC mailing list

16. Ducas, L., van Woerden, W.P.J.: The closest vector problem in tensored root lattices of type A and in their duals. Cryptology ePrint Archive, Report 2016/910 (2016). https://eprint.iacr.org/2016/910

17. ETSI. ETSI launches Quantum Safe Cryptography specification group, March 2015

18. ETSI. Terms of reference for ETSI TC cyber working group for quantum-safe cryptography (ETSI TC cyber WG-QSC) (2017). Accessed 15 Feb 2017

19. Fritzmann, T., Pöppelmann, T., Sepulveda, J.: Analysis of error-correcting codes for lattice-based key exchange. Cryptology ePrint Archive, Report 2018/150 (2018)

20. Hamburg, M.: Three Bears. Technical report, National Institute of Standards and Technology (2017). https://csrc.nist.gov/projects/post-quantum-cryptography/round-1-submissions

21. Hoffstein, J., Pipher, J., Silverman, J.H.: NTRU: a ring-based public key cryptosystem. In: Buhler, J.P. (ed.) ANTS 1998. LNCS, vol. 1423, pp. 267–288. Springer, Heidelberg (1998). https://doi.org/10.1007/BFb0054868

22. Hofheinz, D., Hövelmanns, K., Kiltz, E.: A modular analysis of the Fujisaki-Okamoto transformation. Cryptology ePrint Archive, Report 2017/604 (2017)

23. Howgrave-Graham, N.: A hybrid lattice-reduction and meet-in-the-middle attack against NTRU. In: Menezes, A. (ed.) CRYPTO 2007. LNCS, vol. 4622, pp. 150–169. Springer, Heidelberg (2007). https://doi.org/10.1007/978-3-540-74143-5_9

24. d'Anvers, J.P., Karmakar, A., Sinha Roy, S., Vercauteren, F.: Saber: module-LWR based key exchange, CPA-secure encryption and CCA-secure KEM. In: Progress in Cryptology: AfricaCrypt 2018, pp. 282–305 (2018)

25. Lindner, R., Peikert, C.: Better key sizes (and attacks) for LWE-based encryption. Cryptology ePrint Archive, Report 2010/613 (2010)

26. Lu, X.: Public discussion, December 2018. https://csrc.nist.gov/CSRC/media/
    Projects/Post-Quantum-Cryptography/documents/round-1/official-comments/
    LAC-official-comment.pdf. Messages on the NIST PQC mailing list
27. Lu, X., et al.: LAC. Technical report, National Institute of Standards and Tech-
    nology (2017). https://csrc.nist.gov/projects/post-quantum-cryptography/round-
    1-submissions
28. Lyubashevsky, V., Peikert, C., Regev, O.: On ideal lattices and learning with errors
    over rings. Cryptology ePrint Archive, Report 2012/230 (2012)
29. McKilliam, R.G., Clarkson, I.V.L., Quinn, B.G.: An Algorithm to Compute the
    Nearest Point in the Lattice A_n^*. CoRR, abs/0801.1364 (2008)
30. NIST. Submission requirements and evaluation criteria for the post-quantum cryp-
    tography standardization process. POST-QUANTUM CRYPTO STANDARD-
    IZATION. Call For Proposals Announcement (2016)
31. Peikert, C., Regev, O., Stephens-Davidowitz, N.: Pseudorandomness of Ring-LWE
    for Any Ring and Modulus (2017)
32. Pöppelmann, T., et al.: NewHope. Technical report, National Institute of
    Standards and Technology (2017). https://csrc.nist.gov/projects/post-quantum-
    cryptography/round-1-submissions
33. Saarinen, M.-J.O.: Ring-LWE ciphertext compression and error correction: tools
    for lightweight post-quantum cryptography. In: Proceedings of the 3rd ACM Inter-
    national Workshop on IoT Privacy, Trust, and Security, IoTPTS 2017, pp. 15–22.
    ACM, April 2017
34. Saarinen, M.-J.O.: HILA5: on reliability, reconciliation, and error correction for
    ring-LWE encryption. In: Adams, C., Camenisch, J. (eds.) SAC 2017. LNCS, vol.
    10719, pp. 192–212. Springer, Cham (2018). https://doi.org/10.1007/978-3-319-
    72565-9_10
35. Smart, N.P., et al.: LIMA. Technical report, National Institute of Standards and
    Technology (2017). https://csrc.nist.gov/projects/post-quantum-cryptography/
    round-1-submissions

The Impact of Error Dependencies on Ring/Mod-LWE/LWR Based Schemes

Jan-Pieter D'Anvers[✉], Frederik Vercauteren, and Ingrid Verbauwhede

IMEC-COSIC, KU Leuven, Kasteelpark Arenberg 10,
Bus 2452, 3001 Leuven-Heverlee, Belgium
{janpieter.danvers,frederik.vercauteren,
ingrid.verbauwhede}@esat.kuleuven.be

Abstract. Current estimation techniques for the probability of decryption failures in Ring/Mod-LWE/LWR based schemes assume independence of the failures in individual bits of the transmitted message to calculate the full failure rate of the scheme. In this paper we disprove this assumption both theoretically and practically for schemes based on Ring/Mod-Learning with Errors/Rounding. We provide a method to estimate the decryption failure probability, taking into account the bit failure dependency. We show that the independence assumption is suitable for schemes without error correction, but that it might lead to underestimating the failure probability of algorithms using error correcting codes. In the worst case, for LAC-128, the failure rate is 2^{48} times bigger than estimated under the assumption of independence. This higher-than-expected failure rate could lead to more efficient cryptanalysis of the scheme through decryption failure attacks.

Keywords: Lattice cryptography · Ring-LWE · Error correcting codes · Decryption failures

1 Introduction

Due to the recent developments in quantum computing and its threat to current asymmetric key schemes, the cryptographic community has increased its efforts towards the development of post-quantum cryptography, resulting in the NIST Post-Quantum Standardization Process. Several submissions to this process are built on top of the Learning with Errors (LWE) hard problem. These are frequently combined with the usage of polynomial matrix elements, resulting in Ring-LWE or Mod-LWE schemes such as New Hope [1], LAC [15], LIMA [17], R. Emblem [16] and Kyber [2]. Some schemes further reduce their communication bandwidth by replacing the pseudorandomly generated errors terms with rounding errors, resulting in Ring-LWR and Mod-LWR schemes as in Round2 [9] and Saber [3] respectively.

For most of the above encryption schemes there is a small probability of a decryption failure, in which the decryption of the encoded message returns

© Springer Nature Switzerland AG 2019
J. Ding and R. Steinwandt (Eds.): PQCrypto 2019, LNCS 11505, pp. 103–115, 2019.
https://doi.org/10.1007/978-3-030-25510-7_6

a faulty result, where one or more message bits are flipped. As these failure events depend on the secret key, they might compromise the security of the scheme. Therefore, most candidates of the Post-Quantum Standardization Process aim for a failure probability around 2^{-128}. To reduce the failure rate, some schemes utilize error correcting codes (ECC) to make the decryption resilient against a certain number of errors. The NIST candidate LAC [15] relies on extensive error correction, and Fritzmann et al. [7] made a study on the positive impact of the usage of ECC's on the security and bandwidth of lattice-based schemes. Another possibility is to eliminate decryption failures altogether and thus eliminate attacks that exploit them, by selecting the parameter of the scheme accordingly. This comes at the price of a higher bandwidth and computational complexity. Comparing the communication cost, defined as the number of bytes in the public key and the ciphertext, we have 2080 bytes for the original Saber and 3488 bytes for Saber with the same estimated core security level but without decryption failures [4]. However, as most submissions to the NIST Post-Quantum Process have a small decryption failure probability, an analysis of the impact of decryption failures is essential.

A chosen ciphertext attack against Ring-Learning with Errors (Ring-LWE) schemes exploiting decryption failures was reported by Fluhrer [6]. This attack uses knowledge of failing ciphertexts to retrieve the secret. D'Anvers et al. [5] analyzed a decryption failure attack on (Ring/Mod)-LWE/LWR schemes that have protection against chosen ciphertext attacks. The security risk of decryption failures is also reflected in the post-quantum versions [12,13] of the Fujisaki-Okamoto transformation [8], which converts a chosen plaintext secure encryption scheme in a chosen ciphertext secure key encapsulation mechanism (KEM). The security bound of these transformations contains a term considering decryption failures. As this term is quadratic in the failure rate of the underlying scheme, it has an important effect on the security bound.

Consequently, the failure probability is an important factor in the security of these schemes and should be determined precisely. The common approach for computing this probability is calculating the failure rate for one bit of the message, from which the full failure rate is determined assuming the failures between the individual bits are independent. Jin and Zhao [14] proved that for some schemes the failures in individual bits are asymptotically independent if the number of bits goes to infinity. Hamburg [10] did an analysis of the independence of the bits for the NIST Post-Quantum Standardization Process submission ThreeBears [11], which is based on the Integer Module Learning with Errors problem. He identified three sources of correlation: the norm of the secret, the norm of the ciphertext and the correlation between the failures of the individual bits due to the ring structure.

In this paper, we examine the independence assumption for Ring/Mod-LWE/LWR based schemes. First we show both theoretically as well as experimentally that this assumption is not correct. Then, we develop a method to handle the dependency issue in the failure rate calculation. We calculate the failure rate for variants of LAC and validate our method using experimental data[1]. Finally, we discuss the implications of the dependency in different scenarios: for schemes without error correcting codes, we reason that the assumption of independence leads to a slight overestimation of the failure probability. Looking into schemes using error correcting codes to reduce the failure rate, we show that the independence assumption can lead to an underestimation of the failure rate, and thus an overestimation of the security of the underlying scheme. In the most extreme case for LAC-128, the failure rate is overestimated by a factor 2^{48}.

2   Preliminaries

2.1   Notation

Let $\mathbb{Z}_q$ denote the ring of integers modulo q, let R_q represent the ring $\mathbb{Z}_q[X]/(X^n + 1)$ and let $R_q^{l_1 \times l_2}$ designate the ring of $l_1 \times l_2$ matrices over R_q. Polynomials will be written using lowercase letters, vectors with bold lowercase, and matrices with bold uppercase. The l_2-norm of a polynomial x is defined as $\|x\|_2 = \sqrt{\sum_i x_i^2}$ and the l_2-norm of a vector $\boldsymbol{x}$ as $\|\boldsymbol{x}\|_2 = \sqrt{\sum_i \|x_i\|_2^2}$. The rounding operation $\lfloor x \rceil_{q \to p}$ for $x \in \mathbb{Z}_q$, is calculated as $\lfloor p/q \cdot x \rceil \in \mathbb{Z}_p$. The $\mathtt{abs}()$ function takes the absolute value of its input. These operations are extended coefficient-wise for polynomials and vectors. Let a_i, with $a \in R_q$ denote the ith coefficient of a, and denote with $\boldsymbol{a}_i$ for $\boldsymbol{a} \in R_q^{l \times 1}$ the $(i \mod l)^{\text{th}}$ coefficient of the $\lfloor i/l \rfloor^{\text{th}}$ polynomial of $\boldsymbol{a}$.

Let $x \leftarrow \chi(R_q)$ indicate sampling the coefficients of $x \in R_q$ according to distribution χ. The sampling operation is extended coefficient-wise for vectors $\boldsymbol{x} \in R_q^{l \times 1}$ as $\boldsymbol{x} \leftarrow \chi(R_q^{l \times 1})$. Let $\mathtt{Binom}(k, n, p)$ be the cumulative binomial distribution with n draws and probability p, so that $\mathtt{Binom}(k, n, p) = \sum_{i=0}^{\lfloor k \rfloor} \binom{n}{i} p^i (1 - p)^{n-i}$ and let $\mathtt{hypergeom}(k, N, K, n)$ be the hypergeometric distribution with population size N, success states K and draws n as defined by:

$$\mathtt{hypergeom}(k, N, K, n) = \frac{\binom{K}{k} \binom{N - K}{n - k}}{\binom{N}{n}}, \tag{1}$$

$$\text{where:} \quad \binom{a}{b} = \frac{a!}{b!(a - b)!}. \tag{2}$$

2.2   Ring/Mod-LWE/LWR Based Encryption

A general framework for Ring/Mod-LWE-LWR based encryption schemes is provided in Algorithms 1, 2 and 3. The algorithm uses the function $\mathtt{gen}$ to generate the pseudorandom matrix $\boldsymbol{A}$ from a seed $seed_A$, the function $\mathtt{enc}$ to encode

---

[1] The software is available at https://github.com/KULeuven-COSIC/PQCRYPTO-decryption-failures.

Algorithm 1. PKE.KeyGen()

1 $seed_A \leftarrow \mathcal{U}(\{0,1\}^{256})$
2 $\boldsymbol{A} \leftarrow \mathrm{gen}(seed_A) \in R_q^{l \times l}$
3 $\boldsymbol{s}_A \leftarrow \chi_s(R_q^{l \times 1}), \boldsymbol{e}_A \leftarrow \chi_e(R_q^{l \times 1})$
4 $\boldsymbol{b} = \lfloor \boldsymbol{A}\boldsymbol{s}_A + \boldsymbol{e}_A \rceil_{q \to p}$
5 **return** $(pk := (\boldsymbol{b}, seed_A), sk := \boldsymbol{s}_A)$

Algorithm 2. PKE.Enc($pk = (\boldsymbol{b}, seed_A), m, r$)

1 $\boldsymbol{A} \leftarrow \mathrm{gen}(seed_A) \in R_q^{l \times l}$
2 $\boldsymbol{s}'_B \leftarrow \chi_s(R_q^{l \times 1}), \boldsymbol{e}'_B \leftarrow \chi_e(R_q^{l \times 1})$
3 $e''_B \leftarrow \chi_e(R_q)$
4 $\boldsymbol{b}_r = \lfloor \boldsymbol{b} \rceil_{p \to q}$
5 $\boldsymbol{b}' = \lfloor \boldsymbol{A}^T \boldsymbol{s}'_B + \boldsymbol{e}'_B \rceil_{q \to p}$
6 $m_{ecc} = \mathrm{ecc\_enc}(m)$
7 $v' = \lfloor \boldsymbol{b}_r^T \boldsymbol{s}'_B + e''_B + \mathrm{enc}(m_{ecc}) \rceil_{q \to t}$
8 **return** $c = (v', \boldsymbol{b}')$

---

the message m into an element of R_q and the inverse function dec to decode a polynomial back into a message bitstring. The latter decodes coefficients of the polynomial correctly if the deviation from the initial encoded polynomial coefficient is at most $\pm q/4$. If error correcting codes are used in the scheme, the function ecc_enc adds extra redundancy to the bitstring m to enable error correction, while ecc_dec recovers the original message if the number of flipped bits between m_{ecc} and m'_{ecc} is less than a threshold d, which depends on the chosen error correcting code (ECC). When no error correcting codes are used, the functions ecc_enc and ecc_dec act as the identity and return their input. The encryption algorithm PKE.Enc uses the seed r to pseudorandomly generate s'_B, e'_B and e''_B.

By choosing $l = 1$, one obtains a Ring based scheme, while a bigger value of l indicates a module (Mod) based scheme. In Mod/Ring-LWE based schemes, the error distribution χ_e is nonzero, in contrast to Mod/Ring-LWR based schemes where $\chi_e = 0$. In the latter case, parameters p and t are smaller than q, so that the rounding operations $\lfloor \cdot \rceil_{q \to p}$ and $\lfloor \cdot \rceil_{q \to t}$ introduce the errors necessary for security. The rounding additionally compresses the ciphertexts. The rounding operations $\lfloor \cdot \rceil_{p \to q}$ and $\lfloor \cdot \rceil_{t \to q}$ decompress the input back to approximately the original value. The error introduced by these rounding and reconstruction operations will be denoted as follows:

$$\boldsymbol{u}_A = \boldsymbol{A}\boldsymbol{s}_A + \boldsymbol{e}_A - \boldsymbol{b}_r, \tag{3}$$

$$\boldsymbol{u}'_B = \boldsymbol{A}^T \boldsymbol{s}'_B + \boldsymbol{e}'_B - \boldsymbol{b}'_r, \tag{4}$$

$$u''_B = \boldsymbol{b}_r^T \boldsymbol{s}'_B + e''_B + \mathrm{enc}(m_{ecc}) - v'_r. \tag{5}$$

Algorithm 3. PKE.Dec($sk = \boldsymbol{s}_A, c = (v', \boldsymbol{b}')$)

---

1 $\boldsymbol{b}'_r = \lfloor \boldsymbol{b}' \rceil_{p \to q}$
2 $v'_r = \lfloor v' \rceil_{t \to q}$
3 $v = \boldsymbol{b}'^T_r \boldsymbol{s}_A$
4 $m'_{ecc} = \mathsf{dec}(v'_r - v)$
5 $m' = \mathsf{ecc\_dec}(m'_{ecc})$
6 **return** m'

As a first step in determining the error probability of the encryption scheme, we can calculate the value of $v'_r - v$ as follows:

$$v'_r - v = (\boldsymbol{b}^T_r \boldsymbol{s}'_B + e''_B + \lfloor q/2 \rfloor \mathsf{enc}(m_{ecc}) + u''_B) - \boldsymbol{b}'^T_r \boldsymbol{s}_A \tag{6}$$

$$= \lfloor q/2 \rfloor \mathsf{enc}(m_{ecc}) + (\boldsymbol{e}_A + \boldsymbol{u}_A)^T \boldsymbol{s}'_B - (\boldsymbol{e}'_B + \boldsymbol{u}'_B)^T \boldsymbol{s}_A + (u''_B + e''_B) \tag{7}$$

The distribution of one coefficient of $-(\boldsymbol{e}'_B + \boldsymbol{u}'_B)^T \boldsymbol{s}_A + (\boldsymbol{e}_A + \boldsymbol{u}_A)^T \boldsymbol{s}'_B + (u''_B + e''_B)$ can be calculated exhaustively. For the sake of convenience, we will rewrite this as $\boldsymbol{c}^T \boldsymbol{s} + g$, where $\boldsymbol{s}$ is the vector constructed as the concatenation of $-\boldsymbol{s}_A$ and $(\boldsymbol{e}_A + \boldsymbol{u}_A)$, where $\boldsymbol{c}$ is constructed similarly as the concatenation of $(\boldsymbol{e}'_B + \boldsymbol{u}'_B)$ and $\boldsymbol{s}'_B$, and where $g = u''_B + e''_B$:

$$\boldsymbol{s} = \begin{pmatrix} -\boldsymbol{s}_A \\ \boldsymbol{e}_A + \boldsymbol{u}_A \end{pmatrix}, \quad \boldsymbol{c} = \begin{pmatrix} \boldsymbol{e}'_B + \boldsymbol{u}'_B \\ \boldsymbol{s}'_B \end{pmatrix}, \quad g = u''_B + e''_B. \tag{8}$$

A coefficient of the polynomial $v'_r - v$ decodes correctly if the absolute value of the corresponding coefficient of the error term $\boldsymbol{c}^T \boldsymbol{s} + g$ is smaller than $q/4$. A higher value results in a flipped bit after decoding, which will be called a bit error and will be denoted with F_i with i the position of the bit in the message. If the number of bit errors exceeds the threshold for error correction d, a decryption failure occurs, which we will denote with the symbol F. A correct decryption will be denoted with S, so that by definition $P[S] = 1 - P[F]$.

In Table 1, the parameters for LAC-128 and LAC-256 [15] are given. These schemes are used throughout this paper to validate our methodology, as their high failure rate and significant error correction causes their failure rate calculation to be more sensitive to error dependencies. Due to the choices of the moduli q, p and t, the rounding errors $\boldsymbol{u}_A$, $\boldsymbol{u}'_B$ equal the zero vector and u''_B is the zero polynomial.

Table 1. Parameters for LAC

	q	p	t	n	l	d
LAC-128	251	251	251	512	1	29
LAC-256	251	251	251	1024	1	55

2.3   Key Encapsulation Mechanism

From an IND-CPA secure encryption scheme, an IND-CCA secure Key Encapsulation Mechanism (KEM) can be constructed using a post-quantum version [12] of the Fujisaki-Okamoto transformation. The key generation phase is the same as Algorithm 1 and the Encapsulation and Decapsulation functions are defined in Algorithms 4 and 5 respectively, with $\mathcal{G}$ and $\mathcal{H}$ hash functions that model Random Oracles.

Algorithm 4. KEM.Encaps(pk)

1 $m \leftarrow \mathcal{U}(\{0,1\}^{256})$
2 $r = \mathcal{G}(m)$
3 $c = \text{PKE.Enc}(pk, m, r)$
4 $K = \mathcal{H}(r)$
5 **return** (c, K)

Algorithm 5. KEM.Decaps(sk, pk)

1 $m' = \text{PKE.Dec}(sk, c)$
2 $r' = \mathcal{G}(m')$
3 $c' = \text{PKE.Enc}(pk, m', r')$
4 **if** $c = c'$ **then**
5 $\quad$ **return** $K = \mathcal{H}(r)$
6 **else**
7 $\quad$ **return** $K = \perp$

---

3   Error Dependency

The typical method to calculate the failure rate, is to determine the error probability of a single bit of m'_{ecc}, calculated as $p_b = P[|(\boldsymbol{c}^T\boldsymbol{s} + g)_i| > q/4]$, and then assume independence to extend this error probability to the full failure rate. For a scheme that does not use any error correction, this can be expressed as $1 - (1 - p_b)^{l_m}$ or $1 - \text{Binom}(0, l_m, p_b)$, with l_m the length of the encoded message m_{ecc}. For schemes that deploy error correcting codes with a correction capability of d errors, the failure rate amounts to $1 - \text{Binom}(d, l_m, p_b)$.

However, this assumption of independence is not correct. In this section we will show both theoretically and experimentally that there is a positive correlation between the errors of the bits in m'_{ecc}. Intuitively, one can make the following reasoning: $(\boldsymbol{c}^T\boldsymbol{s} + g)$ with high norm for $\boldsymbol{s}$ and $\boldsymbol{c}$ is more likely to produce bit errors, and conversely, bit errors are also more likely to stem from high norm $\boldsymbol{s}$ and $\boldsymbol{c}$. Therefore, a bit error at a certain location, increases the expected norm of $\boldsymbol{s}$ and $\boldsymbol{c}$, therefore increasing the bit error probabilities at other locations. In conclusion, bit errors are expected to be positively correlated.

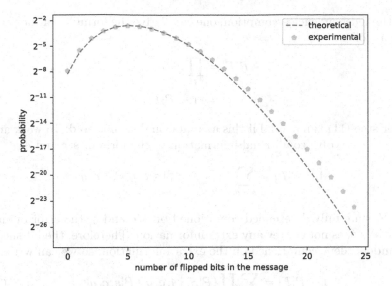

Fig. 1. The probability of a certain number of errors in m'_{ecc}

In Fig. 1, the probability of various number of bit errors in m'_{ecc} is plotted for LAC-256, both experimentally by running the protocol for approximately 2^{31} times, and theoretically under the independence assumption as $1 - \text{Binom}(0, l_m, p_b)$, where p_b is determined experimentally. The choice for LAC stems from the fact that the error probability of a bit of m'_{ecc} is large compared to other schemes, making it possible to experimentally obtain enough errors to get accurate estimations. In Fig. 1, one can see that the errors are clustered: there are more messages without errors and more messages with a high number of errors than predicted by the theoretical model, which confirms our hypothesis that the bit errors are positively correlated. Note that the error probability of a single bit is the same for the model and the experimental data, and that the errors are just more clustered compared to the prediction of the model.

3.1   Handling the Dependency

In this section, we will develop a methodology to calculate the failure rate taking into account the dependency between the errors in the bits of m'_{ecc}. For the sake of simplicity, we will first assume that there is no error correcting code.

$$1 - P[F] = P[S] \tag{9}$$
$$= P[S_0 \cdots S_n] \tag{10}$$

Under the independence assumption, one can derive the formulas of the previous section as follows:

$$1 - P[F] = \prod_i P[S_i] \tag{11}$$

$$= (1 - P[F_0])^n \tag{12}$$

However step (11) is not valid if this assumption does not hold. To work around this issue, we involve conditional information in the form of $\boldsymbol{s}, \boldsymbol{c}$ and g:

$$1 - P[F] = \sum_{\boldsymbol{s},\boldsymbol{c},g} P[S_0 \cdots S_n \,|\, \boldsymbol{s},\boldsymbol{c},g] P[\boldsymbol{s},\boldsymbol{c},g] \tag{13}$$

As the S_i's are fully determined conditioned on $\boldsymbol{s}, \boldsymbol{c}$ and g, the error or success of other bits does not convey any extra information. Therefore, the bit successes S_i are independent conditioned on the extra information, so we can write:

$$1 - P[F] = \sum_{\boldsymbol{s},\boldsymbol{c},g} \prod_i \left(P[S_i \,|\, \boldsymbol{s},\boldsymbol{c},g] \right) P[\boldsymbol{s},\boldsymbol{c},g] \tag{14}$$

$$= \sum_{\boldsymbol{s},\boldsymbol{c},g} \left(1 - P[F_0 \,|\, \boldsymbol{s},\boldsymbol{c},g] \right)^n P[\boldsymbol{s},\boldsymbol{c},g] \tag{15}$$

Unfortunately, this expression is not efficiently computable.

Note that the e_B'' term of g_j does not add any information to S_i if $j \neq i$ and that its coefficients are independent. We will assume that this is also the case for u_B'', so we can write:

$$P[S_i | \boldsymbol{s},\boldsymbol{c},g] \approx P[S_i | \boldsymbol{s},\boldsymbol{c},g_i] \tag{16}$$

From this result we can see that g has little or no contribution to the dependency between the S_i. As discussed in Sect. 3, the norm of $\boldsymbol{s}$ and $\boldsymbol{c}$ is an important cause of dependency. For rings of the form $\mathbb{Z}[X]/(X^n + 1)$ we could assume that this is the main cause of correlation, as different coefficients of $\boldsymbol{c}^T \boldsymbol{s}$ are calculated with different combinations of elements of $\boldsymbol{c}$ and $\boldsymbol{s}$, which can be formalized as follows:

Assumption 1. *For $\boldsymbol{s}, \boldsymbol{c}$ and g as described in Eq. (8), where g and the coefficients of $\boldsymbol{s}$ and $\boldsymbol{c}$ are elements of the ring $\mathbb{Z}[X]/(X^n + 1)$, we can approximate $S_0 \cdots S_n$ to be independent conditioned on $\|\boldsymbol{s}\|_2, \|\boldsymbol{c}\|_2$, which is equivalent to $P[S_0 \cdots S_n \,|\, \|\boldsymbol{s}\|_2, \|\boldsymbol{c}\|_2] \approx \prod_i P[S_i \,|\, \|\boldsymbol{s}\|_2, \|\boldsymbol{c}\|_2]$.*

Using this assumption we write:

$$1 - P[F] = \sum_{\|\boldsymbol{s}\|_2, \|\boldsymbol{c}\|_2} P[S_0 \cdots S_n \mid \|\boldsymbol{s}\|_2, \|\boldsymbol{c}\|_2] P[\|\boldsymbol{s}\|_2, \|\boldsymbol{c}\|_2] \tag{17}$$

$$\approx \sum_{\|\boldsymbol{s}\|_2, \|\boldsymbol{c}\|_2} \prod_i \left(P[S_i \mid \|\boldsymbol{s}\|_2, \|\boldsymbol{c}\|_2] \right) P[\|\boldsymbol{s}\|_2, \|\boldsymbol{c}\|_2] \tag{18}$$

$$\approx \sum_{\|\boldsymbol{s}\|_2, \|\boldsymbol{c}\|_2} \left(P[S_0 \mid \|\boldsymbol{s}\|_2, \|\boldsymbol{c}\|_2] \right)^n P[\|\boldsymbol{s}\|_2] P[\|\boldsymbol{c}\|_2] \tag{19}$$

$$\approx \sum_{\|\boldsymbol{s}\|_2, \|\boldsymbol{c}\|_2} \left(1 - P[F_0 \mid \|\boldsymbol{s}\|_2, \|\boldsymbol{c}\|_2] \right)^n P[\|\boldsymbol{s}\|_2] P[\|\boldsymbol{c}\|_2] \tag{20}$$

Using a similar derivation, the failure rate for schemes with error correction under Assumption 1 can be calculated as:

$$1 - P[F] \approx \sum_{\|\boldsymbol{s}\|_2, \|\boldsymbol{c}\|_2} \left(1 - \texttt{Binom}(d, l_m, p_b) \right) P[\|\boldsymbol{s}\|_2] P[\|\boldsymbol{c}\|_2] \tag{21}$$

$$\text{where: } p_b = P[F_0 \mid \|\boldsymbol{s}\|_2, \|\boldsymbol{c}\|_2] \tag{22}$$

To conclude, one has to calculate the failure rate for every value of $\|\boldsymbol{s}\|_2$ and $\|\boldsymbol{c}\|_2$, after which the failure rate can be found by taking a weighted average. The model from Eq. (20) can be seen as an intermediate between the model from Eq. (12) that was constructed using the independence assumption, and the exact but incalculable model from Eq. (15). In this intermediate model, the main source of correlation between the S_i, following Assumption 1, is taken into account. In the next section we will experimentally assess our intermediate model and observe that it closely represents the experimental data, thus validating our assumption.

3.2   Experiments

To validate the developed methodology, we ran LAC-256 approximately 2^{31} times to get experimental data on the probability of a certain number of failures in m'_{ecc}. We calculated the same probability using the assumption of independence and our dependency aware model.

In general $P[F_0 \mid \|\boldsymbol{s}\|_2, \|\boldsymbol{c}\|_2]$ can be calculated using a Gaussian assumption on the distribution of $\boldsymbol{c}^T \boldsymbol{s} + g$ as described in [5]. For our calculations of LAC we use a more exact algorithm using the fact that the elements of $\boldsymbol{c}, \boldsymbol{s}$ and g are ternary. Intuitively, we first calculate the probability that a certain number l of nonzero coefficients of $\boldsymbol{c}$ and $\boldsymbol{s}$ coincide during the multiplication, expressed as $P[(\texttt{abs}(\boldsymbol{c})^T \texttt{abs}(\boldsymbol{s}))_0 = l \mid \|\boldsymbol{s}\|_2, \|\boldsymbol{c}\|_2]$. Then, we assume the term $(\boldsymbol{c}^T \boldsymbol{s})_0$ given $(\texttt{abs}(\boldsymbol{c})^T \texttt{abs}(\boldsymbol{s}))_0 = l$ to be a sum of l elements randomly picked as plus or minus 1. The full derivation can be expressed as follows:

$$p_b = P[\text{abs}(\boldsymbol{c}^T \boldsymbol{s} + g)_0 > q/4 \,|\, \|\boldsymbol{s}\|_2, \|\boldsymbol{c}\|_2] \tag{23}$$

$$= \sum_l \left(\begin{array}{l} P[\text{abs}(\boldsymbol{c}^T \boldsymbol{s} + g)_0 > q/4 \,|\, (\text{abs}(\boldsymbol{c})^T \text{abs}(\boldsymbol{s}))_0 = l, \|\boldsymbol{s}\|_2, \|\boldsymbol{c}\|_2] \cdot \\ P[(\text{abs}(\boldsymbol{c})^T \text{abs}(\boldsymbol{s}))_0 = l \,|\, \|\boldsymbol{s}\|_2, \|\boldsymbol{c}\|_2] \end{array} \right) \tag{24}$$

$$= \sum_l \left(\begin{array}{l} P[\text{abs}(\boldsymbol{c}^T \boldsymbol{s} + g)_0 > q/4 \,|\, (\text{abs}(\boldsymbol{c})^T \text{abs}(\boldsymbol{s}))_0 = l] \cdot \\ P[(\text{abs}(\boldsymbol{c})^T \text{abs}(\boldsymbol{s}))_0 = l \,|\, \|\boldsymbol{s}\|_2, \|\boldsymbol{c}\|_2] \end{array} \right) \tag{25}$$

$$= \sum_l \sum_{g_0} \left(\begin{array}{l} P[\text{abs}(\boldsymbol{c}^T \boldsymbol{s} + g)_0 > q/4 \,|\, (\text{abs}(\boldsymbol{c})^T \text{abs}(\boldsymbol{s}))_0 = l, g_0] \cdot \\ P[(\text{abs}(\boldsymbol{c})^T \text{abs}(\boldsymbol{s}))_0 = l \,|\, \|\boldsymbol{s}\|_2, \|\boldsymbol{c}\|_2] \cdot P[g_0] \end{array} \right) \tag{26}$$

We can model $P[(\boldsymbol{c}^T \boldsymbol{s})_0 > q/4 - g_0 \,|\, (\text{abs}(\boldsymbol{c})^T \text{abs}(\boldsymbol{s}))_0 = l, g_0]$ as the survival function of a binomial distribution, which can be calculated as $\texttt{Binom}(\frac{l-q/4+g_0}{2}, l, 1/2)$. Similarly, $P[(\boldsymbol{c}^T \boldsymbol{s})_0 < -q/4 - g_0 \,|\, (\text{abs}(\boldsymbol{c})^T \text{abs}(\boldsymbol{s}))_0 = l, g_0]$ can be modelled as $\texttt{Binom}(\frac{l-q/4-g_0}{2}, l, 1/2)$, so that $P[\text{abs}(\boldsymbol{c}^T \boldsymbol{s} + g)_0 > q/4 \,|\, (\text{abs}(\boldsymbol{c})^T \text{abs}(\boldsymbol{s}))_0 = l, g_0]$ is the sum of both probabilities. The distribution $P[(\text{abs}(\boldsymbol{c})^T \text{abs}(\boldsymbol{s}))_0 = l \,|\, \|\boldsymbol{s}\|_2, \|\boldsymbol{c}\|_2]$ can be seen as a hypergeometric distribution $\texttt{hypergeom}(l, n, \|\boldsymbol{s}\|_2, \|\boldsymbol{c}\|_2)$.

The probability of a decryption failure is plotted for various error correction capabilities of the ECC in Fig. 2. We can see that our new dependency aware model outputs a much better estimate of the probabilities of a certain maximum number of errors. Another observation to be made is that the independency based model deviates further from the experimental data as the number of errors increases, which is the case for codes with higher error correction capabilities. This makes the dependency issue especially important for schemes with extensive error correction.

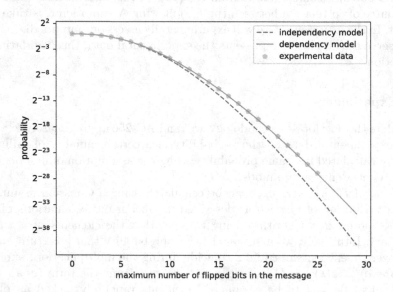

Fig. 2. Probability of failure for various error correction capabilities of ecc_enc

4   Implications

As seen in previous sections, the errors in m'_{ecc} are positively correlated, meaning that an error at a certain position is more likely to happen if another error is present. The inverse is also true: a correct bit of m'_{ecc} enlarges the probability of other bits in m'_{ecc} to be correct. Therefore, due to the dependency, there will be more fully correct messages than one would expect under the assumption of independence. However, as one can see in Fig. 2, the impact of the dependency is small for schemes without error correction. To conclude, an estimate using the assumption of independence will slightly overestimate the failure rate, and thus underestimate the security of the scheme with a small margin. As a result, the approximation using an assumption of independence is legitimate for schemes without an error correction step.

Table 2. The failure rate of different versions of LAC under the different models

	LAC-128	LAC-256
Independency model	2^{-233}	2^{-114}
Dependency model	2^{-185}	2^{-92}
Overestimation factor	2^{48}	2^{22}

In the case of schemes with error correction, one has to be more careful. As can be seen in Fig. 2, the independence model gives an underestimation of the failure rate, which corresponds to an overestimation of the security of the scheme. This overestimation grows as d, the error correction capability of the ECC, becomes larger. In Table 2, the estimated failure rate of different versions of LAC is compared under both models. The discrepancy between both models reaches a factor 2^{48} in case of LAC-128. Therefore, the assumption of independence is not valid for schemes with error correction, and that it could lead to a serious overestimation of the security of the underlying algorithm.

More specifically, a higher failure probability suggests that the scheme might be more vulnerable to a decryption failure attack similar to the attack described by D'Anvers et al. [5], where the secrets are estimated statistically based on failing ciphertexts. Moreover, an attacker can reduce the failure probability by performing a precomputation for weak ciphertexts with higher failure probability. As LAC does not have any security against multi-target attacks that exploit decryption failures, this precomputation only needs to be performed once.

5   Conclusions

In this paper, we challenged the independency assumption of bit errors in messages encrypted with (Ring/Mod)-(LWE/LWR) based schemes. We showed both theoretically and experimentally that the occurrence of errors is positively correlated. Then we devised a method to calculate the failure rate of a scheme, taking into account the dependency of failures. Finally, we showed that the assumption of independence is appropriate for schemes without error correcting codes, but that it might lead to a substantial underestimation of the failure rate for schemes with error correcting codes. This underestimation attains a factor of 2^{48} for LAC-128. A higher-than-expected failure rate could have a serious impact on the security of the scheme through a decryption failure attack.

Acknowledgements. This work was supported in part by the Research Council KU Leuven grants: C16/15/058, C14/18/067 and STG/17/019 and by the European Commission through the Horizon 2020 research and innovation programme Cathedral ERC Advanced Grant 695305.

References

1. Alkim, E., Ducas, L., Pöppelmann, T., Schwabe, P.: Post-quantum key exchange - a New Hope. In: USENIX Security 2016 (2016)
2. Bos, J., etal.: Crystals - Kyber: a CCA-secure module-lattice-based KEM. Cryptology ePrint Archive, Report 2017/634, 2017. http://eprint.iacr.org/2017/634
3. D'Anvers, J.-P., Karmakar, A., Sinha Roy, S., Vercauteren, F.: Saber: module-LWR based key exchange, CPA-secure encryption and CCA-secure KEM. In: Joux, A., Nitaj, A., Rachidi, T. (eds.) AFRICACRYPT 2018. LNCS, vol. 10831, pp. 282–305. Springer, Cham (2018). https://doi.org/10.1007/978-3-319-89339-6_16
4. D'Anvers, J.-P.: Saber without failures parameter estimation (2019). https://github.com/KULeuven-COSIC/PQCRYPTO-decryption-failures
5. D'Anvers, J.-P., Vercauteren, F., Verbauwhede, I.: On the impact of decryption failures on the security of LWE/LWR based schemes. Cryptology ePrint Archive, Report 2018/1089 (2018). https://eprint.iacr.org/2018/1089
6. Fluhrer, S.: Cryptanalysis of ring-LWE based key exchange with key share reuse. Cryptology ePrint Archive, Report 2016/085 (2016). https://eprint.iacr.org/2016/085
7. Fritzmann, T., Pöppelmann, T., Sepulveda, J.: Analysis of error-correcting codes for lattice-based key exchange. Cryptology ePrint Archive, Report 2018/150 (2018). https://eprint.iacr.org/2018/150
8. Fujisaki, E., Okamoto, T.: Secure integration of asymmetric and symmetric encryption schemes. J. Cryptol. 26(1), 80–101 (2013)
9. Garcia-Morchon, O., Zhang, Z., Bhattacharya, S., Rietman, R., Tolhuizen, L., Torre-Arce, J.-L.: Round2. Technical report, National Institute of Standards and Technology (2017). https://csrc.nist.gov/projects/post-quantum-cryptography/round-1-submissions
10. Hamburg, M.: Integer module lwe key exchange and encryption: The three bears - draft 8 (2017). https://www.shiftleft.org/papers/threebears/threebears-draft8.pdf
11. Hamburg, M.: Threebears. Technical report, National Institute of Standards and Technology (2017). https://csrc.nist.gov/projects/post-quantum-cryptography/round-1-submissions
12. Hofheinz, D., Hövelmanns, K., Kiltz, E.: A modular analysis of the Fujisaki-Okamoto transformation. Cryptology ePrint Archive, Report 2017/604 (2017). http://eprint.iacr.org/2017/604

13. Jiang, H., Zhang, Z., Chen, L., Wang, H., Ma, Z.: Post-quantum IND-CCA-secure KEM without additional hash. Cryptology ePrint Archive, Report 2017/1096 (2017). https://eprint.iacr.org/2017/1096

14. Jin, Z., Zhao, Y.: Optimal key consensus in presence of noise. Cryptology ePrint Archive, Report 2017/1058 (2017). https://eprint.iacr.org/2017/1058

15. Lu, X., Liu, Y., Jia, D., Xue, H., He, J., Zhang, Z.: LAC. Technical report, National Institute of Standards and Technology (2017). https://csrc.nist.gov/projects/post-quantum-cryptography/round-1-submissions

16. Seo, M., Park, J.H., Lee, D.H., Kim, S., Lee, S.-J.: Emblem and R. Emblem. Technical report, National Institute of Standards and Technology (2017). https://csrc.nist.gov/projects/post-quantum-cryptography/round-1-submissions

17. Smart, N.P., etal.: LIMA. Technical report, National Institute of Standards and Technology (2017). https://csrc.nist.gov/projects/post-quantum-cryptography/round-1-submissions

Direct CCA-Secure KEM and Deterministic PKE from Plain LWE

Xavier Boyen[1] and Qinyi Li[2(✉)]

[1] QUT, Brisbane, Australia
[2] Griffith University, Brisbane, Australia
qinyi.li@griffith.edu.au

Abstract. We present a particularly simple and efficient CCA-secure public-key encapsulation scheme without random oracles or costly sampling. The construction is direct in the sense that it eschews generic transformations via one-time signatures or MACs typically found in standard-model constructions. This gives us a compact, conceptually simpler, and computationally efficient operation, that in particular does not require any Gaussian sampling. Nevertheless, security is based on the hardness of the plain learning-with-errors (LWE) problem with polynomial modulus-to-noise ratio.

Of further interest, we also show how to obtain CCA-secure *deterministic* public-key encryption (for high-entropy messages), that is more compact and efficient than existing constructions.

1 Introduction

Public-key encryption (PKE) is a central cryptographic primitive to provide secure communication over insecure networks without prior secret-key agreement. In practice, due to its relative inefficiency, it is almost always used in conjunction with a secret-key cipher, where the former encrypts a *random* session key for the latter, which then encrypts the actual data. This flow is the motivation for "hybrid encryption" [8], which consists of a (public-)key encapsulation mechanism (KEM) and a data encapsulation mechanism (DEM). In terms of security, it is well known [8] that if both KEM and DEM are CCA-secure, then the hybrid encryption scheme is CCA-secure, which is the standard notion for security of PKE against active attacks. While DEMs are readily obtained from suitable symmetric-key modes of operation, in the case of KEMs substantial optimisations are to be gained by specialising them to work with random plaintexts only.

Constructing CCA-secure KEMs is easy in principle. Applying the Fujisaki-Okamoto transformations [10] to PKE/KEM schemes with weaker security guarantees (e.g., chosen-plaintext security) results in CCA-secure PKE/KEM

X. Boyen—Research supported in part by ARC Discovery Project grant number DP140103885 and ARC Future Fellowship FT140101145 from the Australian Research Council.

J. Ding and R. Steinwandt (Eds.): PQCrypto 2019, LNCS 11505, pp. 116–130, 2019.
https://doi.org/10.1007/978-3-030-25510-7_7

schemes in the random oracle model. While this approach often leads to practical constructions, one can only make heuristic security arguments for them. Moreover, when it comes to post-quantum security, these heuristic security arguments need to be made in quantum random-oracle models [6] which are not very well understood. For these reasons, designing an efficient and practical post-quantum KEM in the standard model (without random oracles) is already desirable and well motivated.

There are two somewhat generic ways to construct CCA-secure PKE/KEM from lattices in the standard model. The first one is via lossy trapdoor functions [19] (e.g., the constructions from [16,19,21]) and the second one is via the BCHK trasformation [5] from tag-based or identity-based encryption (IBE) (e.g. the constructions from [15]). Both of them require strongly unforgeable one-time signatures or message authentication codes (MACs) as building blocks. This introduces noticeable extra overheads, making the schemes less efficient and less compact.

In this paper, we primarily focus on constructing a KEM that is both conceptually very simple and computationally efficient, but without compromising its provable security. Specifically, we rely on a standard lattice problem (plain learning with errors, a.k.a. LWE [17,20]) in the standard model.[1]

1.1 Our Contributions

Our main contribution is a simple, compact, computationally efficient KEM scheme without random oracles. The construction makes use of identity-based/tag-based lattice trapdoor techniques [1,15]. The public key of our scheme includes two matrices $\mathbf{A} \in \mathbb{Z}_q^{n \times m}$ and $\mathbf{A}_1 \in \mathbb{Z}_q^{n \times w}$, where $w = n \lceil \log q \rceil$, and a target-collision-resistant compression or hash function $f : \mathbb{Z}_q^n \to \{0,1\}^\lambda$, where λ is the security parameter. The private key is a low norm matrix $\mathbf{R} \in \mathbb{Z}^{m \times w}$ such that $\mathbf{A}_1 = \mathbf{AR} \pmod{q}$. The ciphertext of our scheme contains two parts. The first part is $\mathbf{t} = f(\mathbf{s})$ where $\mathbf{s} \in \mathbb{Z}_q^n$ is the randomness of the encapsulation algorithm. The second part is a vector $\mathbf{c}^\top = \lfloor (p/q) \cdot \mathbf{s}^\top \cdot [\mathbf{A}|\mathbf{A}_1 + \varphi(\mathbf{t})\mathbf{G}] \rceil$ where $\varphi : \mathbb{Z}_q^n \to \mathbb{Z}_q^{n \times n}$ is a full-rank difference encoding [1] (here $\mathbf{t}$ is encoded as a vector in $\mathbb{Z}_q^n$) and $\mathbf{G} \in \mathbb{Z}_q^{n \times w}$ is the gadget matrix [15]. The session key is obtained by applying a randomness extractor to $\mathbf{s}$. When $\mathbf{t}$ is non-zero (which happens with overwhelming probability), the lattice trapdoor $(\mathbf{R}, \mathbf{G})$ allows recovering $\mathbf{s}$ and, thus, reproducing the session key. The key idea of our construction is to make the identity/tag the hash value of the secret random vector $\mathbf{s}$ rather than a verification key or a commitment in the BCHK transformation. In terms of security, by using the LWE problem to (computationally) switch the rounding function $\lfloor (p/q) \cdot \mathbf{s}^\top \cdot [\mathbf{A}|\mathbf{A}_1 + \varphi(\mathbf{t})\mathbf{G}] \rceil$ to the so-called "lossy mode" [2], the ran-

---

[1] We note that our approach here departs significantly from the recent NIST Post-Quantum KEM competition, wherein most submitters chose to embrace random oracles and stronger hardness assumptions (e.g., many variants of ring-LWE), to address its rather idiosyncratic rules and success criteria.

dom vector **s** retains sufficient min-entropy (even conditioned on **c** and **t**) that the session key would be random.

Our construction can be seen as a "direct" CCA-secure PKE/KEM construction from identity-based/tag-based encryption in the sense that it does not employ generic transformations. Such kind of direct constructions from pairing-based IBE are known, e.g., [7, 13, 14]. From a high level idea, our KEM construction also has similarities to the CCA-secure PKE scheme from a lossy trapdoor function (LTF) and all-but-one lossy trapdoor function (ABO-LTF) from [19]. In [19], the encryption is roughly done by evaluating a LTF and an ABO-LTF (both are invertible) on the randomness. The well-formness of the ciphertext is guaranteed by signing theses two evaluations with a one-time signature scheme (the verification key also serves as the tag for the ABO-LTF). Our construction "shrinks" this further by using only one (ABO) LTF plus a compression hash function. For our KEM construction, the hash function, which is much lighter than an LTF, is already lossy and enough to ensure that the ciphertext is well-formed. One should also note that our construction is for CCA-secure KEM which is a more specialised primitive than CCA-secure PKE studied in certain earlier constructions.

Our KEM construction is of good computational efficiency. First, the encryption process essentially involves a vector-matrix multiplication, a rounding operation and a target-collision-resistant hash function. In particular, discrete Gaussian sampling is avoided. Second, the decryption can be done efficiently in a parallel fashion by using the so-called "gadget" trapdoor inversion first proposed in [15].

In terms of space efficiency, since our KEM scheme is based on a relatively stronger LWE assumption (but still with polynomial modulus-to-noise ratio), compared to the most efficient existing CCA-secure lattice PKE/KEM constructions in the standard model, e.g., [15], our construction would need relatively larger matrix dimensions (to provide sufficient hardness for the LWE problem). However, since our KEM ciphertext only consists of a single vector over a small field and a small hash value (whose bit-size is the security parameter, e.g., 128), and since our KEM private key is a low-norm matrix with very small entries (-1 and 1), the impact of requiring larger dimensions is rather limited.

As a by-product of our KEM scheme and its structure, we also give a CCA-secure deterministic lattice PKE system. Deterministic PKE has useful direct and indirect applications such as efficient searchable encryption and de-duplication of encrypted databases. Our construction is efficient and compact than what one would get through generic transformations (e.g., [4]). One drawback of our deterministic PKE is that it requires an LWE hardness assumption here with super-polynomial modulus-to-noise ratio, which is stronger than what we need in the (randomised) KEM scheme.

2   Preliminaries

Notation. We denote the security parameter by λ. We use bold lowercase letters (e.g. **a**) to denote vectors and bold capital letters (e.g. **A**) to denote matrices. For a positive integer $q \geq 2$, let $\mathbb{Z}_q$ be the ring of integers modulo q. We denote the group of $n \times m$ matrices in $\mathbb{Z}_q$ by $\mathbb{Z}_q^{n \times m}$. Vectors are treated as column vectors. The transpose of a vector $\mathbf{a}$ is denoted by $\mathbf{a}^\top$. For $\mathbf{A} \in \mathbb{Z}_q^{n \times m}$ and $\mathbf{B} \in \mathbb{Z}_q^{n \times m'}$, let $[\mathbf{A}|\mathbf{B}] \in \mathbb{Z}_q^{n \times (m+m')}$ be the concatenation of $\mathbf{A}$ and $\mathbf{B}$. We denote by $x \leftarrow X$ the process of sampling x according to the distribution X. We denote $s \leftarrow_\$ S$ the process that of sampling element x uniformly from the set S.

For $x \in \mathbb{Z}_p$, define $\mathsf{Transform}_q(x) = \lceil (q/p) \cdot x \rceil$. For $x \in \mathbb{Z}_q$, define the rounding function $\lfloor x \rfloor_p = \lfloor (p/q) \cdot x \rfloor$. The functions $\mathsf{Transform}_q(\cdot)$ and $\lfloor \cdot \rfloor_p$ naturally extend to vectors by applying them component-wise.

For a security parameter λ, a function $\mathsf{negl}(\lambda)$ is negligible in λ if it is smaller than all polynomial fractions for a sufficiently large λ.

Definition 1 (Bounded Distribution, [2]). *For a distribution χ over the reals, and a bound β, we say that χ is β-bounded if the average absolute value of $x \leftarrow \chi$ is less than β, i.e., if $\mathbb{E}[|x|] \leq \beta$.*

Lemma 1. *Let χ be a B-bounded distribution over $\mathbb{Z}$. Let $q \geq p \cdot (2B+1) \cdot n^{\omega(1)}$ be a prime. For $e \leftarrow \chi$, $u \leftarrow_\$ \mathbb{Z}_q$, we have $\lfloor u + e \rfloor_p \neq \lfloor u \rfloor_p$ with probability $\leq (2B+1) \cdot p/q$ which is negligible in n.*

We recall the notion of full-rank-difference encodings (FRD). Agrawal et al. [1] gave an explicit construction of FRD, which we adapt in our construction.

Definition 2. *Let $n \geq 1$ be an integer and q be a prime. We say that a function $\varphi : \mathbb{Z}_q^n \to \mathbb{Z}_q^{n \times n}$ is an encoding with full-rank differences (FRD) if:*

1. *φ is computable in polynomial time;*
2. *for all distinct $\mathbf{u}, \mathbf{v} \in \mathbb{Z}_q^n$, $\varphi(\mathbf{u}) - \varphi(\mathbf{v}) \in \mathbb{Z}_q^{n \times n}$ is full rank (or invertible).*

Definition 3. *Let λ be a security parameter, $n = n(\lambda)$, $\ell = \ell(\lambda)$ and S be a distribution over D. A set of functions $\mathcal{F} = \{f : D \to R\}$ is a family of compression hash functions if (1) There exists a p.p.t algorithm that takes as input a security parameter 1^λ and uniformly samples a function f from $\mathcal{F}$; (2) Given f, $x \in D$, the computation of $f(x)$ can be done in p.p.t; (3) $\log |R| < \log |D|$. We say $\mathcal{F}$ is second pre-image resistant if for all p.p.t algorithm $\mathcal{A}$, the advantage*

$$Adv_{\mathcal{F},\mathcal{A}}^{tcr}(\lambda) = \left[\begin{array}{c} x \neq x^* \\ \text{and } f(x^*) = f(x) \end{array} : \begin{array}{c} f \leftarrow_\$ \mathcal{F} ; x^* \leftarrow S \\ x \leftarrow \mathcal{A}(1^\lambda, f, x^*) \end{array} \right] \leq \mathsf{negl}(\lambda)$$

We say $\mathcal{F}$ is ϵ-hard-to-invert w.r.t S if for all p.p.t algorithm $\mathcal{A}$,

$$\Pr[\mathcal{A}(f(x), f) = x) : f \leftarrow_\$ \mathcal{F}, x \leftarrow S] \leq \epsilon.$$

A collection of compression hash functions is collision-resistant if it is second pre-image resistant and $\mathsf{negl}(\lambda)$-hard-to-invert.

2.1 Public-Key Encapsulation

A public-key encapsulation (KEM) scheme $\Pi = (\mathsf{KeyGen}, \mathsf{Encap}, \mathsf{Decap})$ with key space $\mathcal{K}_\lambda$ consists of three polynomial-time algorithms. The key generation algorithm $\mathsf{KeyGen}(1^\lambda)$ generates a public key Pk and private key Sk. The randomised key encapsulation algorithm $\mathsf{Encap}(\mathsf{Pk})$ generates a session key $K \in \mathcal{K}_\lambda$ and a ciphertext Ct. The decapsulation algorithm $\mathsf{Decap}(\mathsf{Pk}, \mathsf{Sk}, \mathsf{Ct})$ returns the session key K or the error symbol $\bot$. The correctness of a KEM scheme requires that for all $\lambda \in \mathbb{N}$, and all $(K, \mathsf{Ct}) \leftarrow \mathsf{Encap}(\mathsf{Pk})$,

$$\Pr[\mathsf{Decap}(\mathsf{Pk}, \mathsf{Sk}, \mathsf{Ct}) = K] \geq 1 - \mathsf{negl}(\lambda)$$

where the probability is taken over the choice of $(\mathsf{Pk}, \mathsf{Sk}) \leftarrow \mathsf{KeyGen}(1^\lambda)$ and the random coins of Encap and Decap.

We recall the chosen-ciphertext security of KEM. The IND-CCA security of a KEM scheme Π with session key space $\mathcal{K}_\lambda$ is defined by the following security game. The challenger $\mathcal{C}$ runs $(\mathsf{Pk}, \mathsf{Sk}) \leftarrow \mathsf{KeyGen}(1^\lambda)$, chooses a random coin $\mu \leftarrow_\$ \{0, 1\}$, samples $K_0^* \leftarrow_\$ \mathcal{K}_\lambda$, and computes $(K_1^*, \mathsf{Ct}^*) \leftarrow \mathsf{Encap}(\mathsf{Pk})$. Then $\mathcal{C}$ passes $(\mathsf{Pk}, K_\mu^*, \mathsf{Ct}^*)$ to the adversary. The adversary launches adaptive chosen-ciphertext attacks: It repeatedly chooses any $\mathsf{Ct} \neq \mathsf{Ct}^*$ and sends it over to $\mathcal{C}$, to which $\mathcal{C}$ returns $\mathsf{Decap}(\mathsf{Pk}, \mathsf{Sk}, \mathsf{Ct})$. Finally, $\mathcal{A}$ outputs μ' and wins if $\mu' = \mu$. We define $\mathcal{A}$'s advantage in the above security game as

$$\mathsf{Adv}_{\mathcal{A}, \Pi}^{\mathsf{ind\text{-}cca}}(\lambda) = |\Pr[\mu' = \mu] - 1/2|.$$

We say Π is IND-CCA-secure if $\mathsf{Adv}_{\mathcal{A}, \Pi}^{\mathsf{ind\text{-}cca}}(\lambda)$ is negligible in λ.

2.2 Randomness Extraction

The statistical distance between two random variables X and Y over a finite set S is $\mathsf{SD}(X, Y) = \frac{1}{2} \sum_{s \in S} |\Pr[X = s] - \Pr[Y = s]|$. For any $\epsilon > 0$, we say X and Y are ϵ-close if $\mathsf{SD}(X, Y) \leq \epsilon$. The min-entropy of a random variable X is $\mathsf{H}_\infty(X) = -\log(\max_{s \in S} \Pr[X = s])$. The *average-case* conditional min-entropy of X given Y is $\tilde{\mathsf{H}}_\infty(X|Y) = -\log(\mathbb{E}_{y \leftarrow Y}[\max_x \Pr[X = x|Y = y]])$. A distribution (or a random variable) X is called k-source if $\mathsf{H}_\infty(X) \geq k$.

Lemma 2 ([9], Lemma 2.2). *Let X, Y and Z be random variables where Z has at most 2^λ positive-probability values. Then $\tilde{\mathsf{H}}_\infty(X|Y, Z) \geq \tilde{\mathsf{H}}_\infty(X|Y) - \lambda$, and in particular $\tilde{\mathsf{H}}_\infty(X|Z) \geq \mathsf{H}_\infty(X) - \lambda$.*

Definition 4. *A collection of functions $\mathcal{H} = \{h : D \to R\}$ is universal if for any $x_1, x_2 \in D$ such that $x_1 \neq x_2$ it holds that $\Pr_{H \leftarrow \mathcal{H}}[H(x_1) = H(x_2)] = 1/|R|$.*

Lemma 3. *Let X, Y be random variables such that $X \in \{0, 1\}^n$, and $\tilde{\mathsf{H}}_\infty(X|Y) \geq k$. Let $\mathcal{H}$ be a collection of universal hash functions from $\{0, 1\}^n$ to $\{0, 1\}^\ell$ where $\ell \leq k - 2\log(1/\epsilon)$. It holds that for $h \leftarrow_\$ \mathcal{H}$, and $r \leftarrow_\$ \{0, 1\}^\ell$,*

$$\mathsf{SD}\left((h, h(X), Y), (h, r, Y)\right) \leq \epsilon$$

Lemma 4 ([1], **Lemma 4**). *Suppose that $m > (n+1)\log q + \omega(\log n)$ and that $q > 2$ is prime. Let $\mathbf{R}$ be an $m \times k$ matrix chosen uniformly in $\{1, -1\}^{m \times k}$ mod q where $k = k(n)$ is polynomial in n. Let $\mathbf{A}$ and $\mathbf{B}$ be matrices chosen uniformly in $\mathbb{Z}_q^{n \times m}$ and $\mathbb{Z}_q^{n \times k}$ respectively. Then the distribution $(\mathbf{A}, \mathbf{AR})$ is statistically close to the distribution $(\mathbf{A}, \mathbf{B})$.*

2.3   Computational Assumptions

We recall the LWE problem that was introduced by Regev [20].

Definition 5. *Let λ be the security parameter, $n = n(\lambda)$, $m = m(\lambda)$, $q = q(\lambda)$ be integers and $\chi = \chi(\lambda)$ be a distribution over $\mathbb{Z}_q$. The $\mathsf{LWE}_{n,m,q,\chi}$ problem asks for distinguishing the following two distributions:*

$$\mathit{Real} = (\mathbf{A}, \mathbf{s}^{\top}\mathbf{A} + \mathbf{e}^{\top}) \quad and \quad \mathit{Rand} = (\mathbf{A}, \mathbf{c}^{\top})$$

where $\mathbf{A} \leftarrow_{\$} \mathbb{Z}_q^{n \times m}$, $\mathbf{s} \leftarrow_{\$} \mathbb{Z}_q^n$, $\mathbf{e} \leftarrow \chi^m$, and $\mathbf{c} \leftarrow_{\$} \mathbb{Z}_q^n$. We define the advantage that an adversary $\mathcal{A}$ has in solving the LWE problem by

$$\mathit{Adv}_{\mathcal{A}}^{\mathsf{LWE}_{n,m,q,\chi}}(\lambda) = |\Pr[\mathcal{A}(1^{\lambda}, \mathit{Real}) = 1] - \Pr[\mathcal{A}(1^{\lambda}, \mathit{Rand})]|.$$

We say the LWE assumption holds if for every p.p.t. algorithm $\mathcal{A}$, $\mathit{Adv}_{\mathcal{A}}^{\mathsf{LWE}_{n,m,q,\chi}}(\lambda)$ is negligible in λ.

Usually, the distribution χ is the discrete Gaussian distribution $D_{\mathbb{Z},\alpha q}$ where the parameter $\alpha \in (0, 1)$ and $\alpha q \geq \sqrt{n}$. We refer to [11] for details on discrete Gaussian distributions and [17] for the recent result on the hardness of LWE.

In our construction, we consider the amortised LWE problem that asks to distinguish between distributions $(\mathbf{B}, \mathbf{CB} + \mathbf{F})$ and $(\mathbf{B}, \mathbf{A})$ where $\mathbf{B} \leftarrow_{\$} \mathbb{Z}_q^{\ell \times m}$, $\mathbf{C} \leftarrow_{\$} \mathbb{Z}_q^{n \times \ell}$, $\mathbf{F} \leftarrow \chi^{n \times m}$ and $\mathbf{A} \leftarrow \mathbb{Z}_q^{n \times m}$. It was shown, e.g., in [18] (Lemma 7.3), that a p.p.t. algorithm that distinguishes the two distributions of the amortised LWE problem with probability ϵ can be efficiently turned into a p.p.t. algorithm that breaks the $\mathsf{LWE}_{\ell,m,q,\chi}$ problem (per Definition 5) with advantage ϵ/n.

We recall the following Lemma, first proven by Goldwasser et al. [12], and used by Xie et al. [22]. It says that, for certain parameters, the LWE problem remains hard even if the secret is chosen from an arbitrary distribution with sufficient min-entropy in the presence of hard-to-invert auxiliary input.

Lemma 5. *Let $k \geq \log q$ and $\mathcal{F} = \{f : \{0,1\}^n \rightarrow \{0,1\}^*\}$ be a family of one-way functions that are 2^{-k} hard to invert with respect to distribution S over $\{0,1\}^n$. For any super-polynomial $q = q(\lambda)$ and any $m = poly(n)$, any $\beta, \gamma \in (0, 1)$ such that $\gamma/\beta = \mathsf{negl}(n)$, the distributions*

$$(\mathbf{A}, \mathbf{s}^{\top}\mathbf{A} + \mathbf{e}^{\top}, f(\mathbf{s})) \quad and \quad (\mathbf{A}, \mathbf{c}^{\top}, f(\mathbf{s}))$$

are computationally indistinguishable where $\mathbf{A} \leftarrow_{\$} \mathbb{Z}_q^{n \times m}$, $\mathbf{s} \leftarrow S$, $\mathbf{c} \leftarrow_{\$} \mathbb{Z}_q^m$, $\mathbf{e} \leftarrow D_{\mathbb{Z},\beta q}^m$, assuming the $\mathsf{LWE}_{\ell.m,q,D_{\mathbb{Z},\gamma q}}$ assumption holds where $\ell \geq \frac{k - \omega(\log n)}{\log q}$.

2.4 Lattice Trapdoors

Let $n \geq 1$, $q \geq 2$ and $p \leq q$. Set $k = \lceil \log q \rceil$ and $w = nk$, and define the n-by-w gadget matrix $\mathbf{G} = \mathbf{I}_n \otimes [1, 2, 4, ..., 2^{k-1}] \in \mathbb{Z}_q^{n \times w}$. We recall the following lemma that applies the gadget trapdoor [15] to invert the LWE and LWR functions. The lemma stems from Lemma 7.2 of [2] (the algorithm BigInvert). Here we use the fact that the gadget matrix $\mathbf{G}$ has a (publicly known) trapdoor matrix $\mathbf{T} \in \mathbb{Z}^{w \times w}$ s.t. $\mathbf{GT} = \mathbf{0} \bmod q$ and $\|\mathbf{T}\| \leq \sqrt{5}$. (See [15], Proposition 4.2 for details).

Lemma 6 ([3] **Lemma 7.2**). *Let $n \geq 1$, $q \geq 2$, $w = n\lceil \log q \rceil$ and $m = \bar{m} + w$. Set, $\bar{m} > (n+1)\log q + \omega(\log n)$. Let $\mathbf{F} = [\mathbf{A}|\mathbf{AR} + \mathbf{HG}]$ where $\mathbf{A} \in \mathbb{Z}_q^{n \times \bar{m}}$, $\mathbf{R} \leftarrow_\$ \{-1, 1\}^{\bar{m} \times w}$ and $\mathbf{H} \in \mathbb{Z}_q^{n \times n}$ be an invertible matrix. We have for $\mathbf{c}^\top = \lfloor \mathbf{s}^\top \mathbf{F} \rceil_p$ where $\mathbf{s} \in \mathbb{Z}_q^n$, $p \geq O(\bar{m}\sqrt{n \log q})$, there is a p.p.t algorithm Invert(Transform$_q(\mathbf{c}), \mathbf{F}, \mathbf{H}, \mathbf{R}$) that outputs $\mathbf{s}$.*

The following lemma is derived from Lemma 3.3 and Theorem 7.3 of [3].

Lemma 7. *Let λ be the security parameter. Let n, m, ℓ, p, γ be positive integers, χ be a β-bounded distribution, $w = n\lceil \log q \rceil$, and $q \geq \bar{m}\beta\gamma n(\bar{m}+w)p$ be a prime. Then it holds that for $\mathbf{s} \leftarrow_\$ \mathbb{Z}_q^n$, $\mathbf{A} = \mathbf{CB} + \mathbf{F} \in \mathbb{Z}_q^{n \times \bar{m}}$, $\mathbf{R} \leftarrow_\$ \{-1, 1\}^{\bar{m} \times w}$*

$$\tilde{H}_\infty(\mathbf{s}| \lfloor \mathbf{s}^\top [\mathbf{A}|\mathbf{AR}]\rceil_p) \geq n\log(2\gamma) - (\ell + \lambda)\log q$$

where $\mathbf{B} \leftarrow_\$ \mathbb{Z}_q^{\ell \times \bar{m}}$, $\mathbf{C} \leftarrow_\$ \mathbb{Z}_q^{n \times \ell}$ and $\mathbf{F} \leftarrow \chi^{n \times \bar{m}}$.

3 The KEM Scheme

Let λ be the security parameter. The scheme uses a full-rank difference encoding function $\varphi : \mathbb{Z}_q^n \to \mathbb{Z}_q^{n \times n}$ which can be instatiated by the construction given by Agrawal et al. [1]. The scheme also employs a family of hash functions $\mathcal{F} = \{f : \mathbb{Z}_q^n \to \{0, 1\}^\lambda\}$ that is second pre-image resistant, and a family of universal hash functions $\mathcal{H} = \{h : \mathbb{Z}_q^n \to \{0, 1\}^\lambda\}$ for which efficient constructions are known. Let χ be a β-bounded distribution over $\mathbb{Z}_q$. Given the lattice dimension $\ell \geq \lambda$ for LWE problem, we set the parameters for our KEM scheme as follows.

- Let $\delta > 0$ be a constant. Set the matrix dimension n large enough such that $\frac{n-4\lambda}{n^\delta} \geq \ell$ for Lemma 7 (ensuing that $\mathbf{s}$ sufficient leftover min-entropy).
- Set the matrix dimension $\bar{m} = n^{1+\delta}$ to ensure that Lemma 4 applies. Here we assume $n^\delta = 2\log q$.
- The rounding parameter $p = 3\bar{m}^{1.5}$ for Lemma 6.
- The parameter $\gamma = 1$ for Lemma 7
- Set $\beta = \sqrt{\ell}$ as required by the hardness of LWE problem.
- The LWE modulus $q = 12\bar{m}^5$ that satisfies Lemma 7.

KeyGen(1^λ): On input the security parameter λ, the key generation algorithm does:

1. Choose $\mathbf{A} \leftarrow_\$ \mathbb{Z}_q^{n \times \bar{m}}$, $\mathbf{R} \leftarrow_\$ \{-1, 1\}^{\bar{m} \times w}$; Set $\mathbf{A}_1 = \mathbf{AR} \bmod q$.
2. Randomly sample a hash function $f \leftarrow_\$ \mathcal{F}$ and a universal hash function $h \leftarrow_\$ \mathcal{H}$.
3. Set $\mathsf{Pk} = (\mathbf{A}, \mathbf{A}_1, f, h)$ and $\mathsf{Sk} = \mathbf{R}$.

Encap(Pk): On input the public key Pk, the encapsulation algorithm does:
1. Select $\mathbf{s} \leftarrow_\$ \mathbb{Z}_q^n$ and compute $\mathbf{t} \leftarrow f(\mathbf{s})$.
2. Encode $\mathbf{t}$ as a vector in $\mathbb{Z}_q^n$ and compute $\mathbf{c}^\top = \lfloor \mathbf{s}^\top \cdot [\mathbf{A}|\mathbf{A}_1 + \varphi(\mathbf{t})\mathbf{G}] \rceil_p$.
3. Set $K \leftarrow h(\mathbf{s})$ and $\mathsf{Ct} = (\mathbf{c}, \mathbf{t})$.

Decap(Pk, Sk, Ct): On input the private key Sk and a ciphertext $\mathsf{Ct} = (\mathbf{c}, \mathbf{t})$, the decapsulation algorithm does:
1. Runs $\mathsf{Invert}(\mathsf{Transform}_q(\mathbf{c}), [\mathbf{A}|\mathbf{A}_1 + \varphi(\mathbf{t})\mathbf{G}], \mathbf{R})$ to get $\mathbf{s}' \in \mathbb{Z}_q^n$.
2. Compute $\mathbf{t}' = f(\mathbf{s}')$ and return $\bot$ if $\mathbf{t}' \neq \mathbf{t}$.
3. Return $K \leftarrow h(\mathbf{s}')$.

The decryption correctness can be checked by the correctness of Invert as stated in Lemma 6.

Theorem 1. *If the family of hash functions $\mathcal{F}$ is second pre-image resistant and the $\mathsf{LWE}_{\ell, \bar{m}, q, \chi}$ assumption holds, then the KEM scheme is IND-CCA-secure. More specifically, let λ be the security parameter. Given a p.p.t adversary $\mathcal{A}$ that breaks the KEM scheme Π with advantage $\mathsf{Adv}_{\Pi, \mathcal{A}}^{ind\text{-}cca}(\lambda)$, there exist a p.p.t algorithm $\mathcal{B}_1$ that breaks the second pre-image resistance of $\mathcal{F}$ with advantage $\mathsf{Adv}_{\mathcal{F}, \mathcal{B}_1}^{tcr}(\lambda)$ and a p.p.t algorithm $\mathcal{B}_2$ that breaks $\mathsf{LWE}_{\ell, \bar{m}, q, \chi}$ with advantage $\mathsf{Adv}_{\mathcal{B}_2}^{\mathsf{LWE}_{\ell, \bar{m}, q, \chi}}(\lambda)$, such that $\mathsf{Adv}_{\Pi, \mathcal{A}}^{ind\text{-}cca}(\lambda) \leq \mathsf{Adv}_{\mathcal{F}, \mathcal{B}_1}^{tcr}(\lambda) + \mathsf{Adv}_{\mathcal{B}_2}^{\mathsf{LWE}_{\ell, \bar{m}, q, \chi}}(\lambda) + \mathsf{negl}(\lambda)$ where $\mathsf{negl}(\lambda)$ is negligible in λ.*

Proof. We proceed with the proof as a sequence of games. For $i - \{0, 1, 2, 3, 4\}$, we denote the i-th game by $Game_i$. We denote by $Game_i \Rightarrow 1$ the event that the adversary wins the security game, i.e., it outputs μ' such that $\mu' = \mu$.

The first game $Game_0$ is the same as the IND-CCA security game. That is, the adversary $\mathcal{A}$ receives a public key $\mathsf{Pk} = (\mathbf{A}, \mathbf{A}_1, f, h)$ and a challenge ciphertext $\mathsf{Ct}^* = (\mathbf{c}^*, \mathbf{t}^*)$, where

$$\mathbf{t}^* = f(\mathbf{s}^*) \quad ; \quad \mathbf{c}^{*\top} = \lfloor \mathbf{s}^{*\top} \cdot [\mathbf{A}|\mathbf{A}_1 + \varphi(\mathbf{t}^*)\mathbf{G}] \rceil_p$$

for some $\mathbf{s}^* \leftarrow_\$ \mathbb{Z}_q^n$, and a session key K_μ^*, which is either a random value from $\{0, 1\}^\lambda$ or $h(\mathbf{s}^*)$, from the challenger $\mathcal{B}$. Then $\mathcal{A}$ adaptively issues decryption queries $\mathsf{Ct} = (\mathbf{c}, \mathbf{t}) \neq \mathsf{Ct}^*$ and $\mathcal{B}$ runs the real decryption algorithm to return the answers. Finally, $\mathcal{A}$ outputs a bit value μ' indicating that Ct^* encapsulates a real session key or a random session key. According to the definition, we have

$$\Pr[Game_0 \Rightarrow 1] = \Pr[\mu' = \mu] = \mathsf{Adv}_{\Pi, \mathcal{A}}^{ind\text{-}cca}(\lambda) + 1/2$$

In $Game_1$, we make a change in the way of answering decryption queries: $\bot$ is returned if for the given decryption query $\mathsf{Ct} = (\mathbf{c}, \mathbf{t})$, $\mathbf{t} = \mathbf{t}^*$; otherwise, Ct is processed with the real decapsulation algorithm as in $Game_0$. We argue that unless the adversary breaks the second pre-image resistant property of the hash function f, this change is not noticeable.

First of all, we must have $\mathbf{c} \neq \mathbf{c}^*$ (otherwise the decryption query is invalid as it is the challenge ciphertext itself). To make the decryption oracle not to output $\bot$, there must be a unique $\mathbf{s} \neq \mathbf{s}^*$ such that $\mathbf{c}^\top = \lfloor \mathbf{s}^\top \cdot [\mathbf{A}|\mathbf{A}_1 + \varphi(\mathbf{t}^*)\mathbf{G}] \rceil_p$ (and such an $\mathbf{s}$ can be found by the algorithm Invert since the private key $\mathbf{R}$ is known). Therefore we must have $f(\mathbf{s}) = f(\mathbf{s}^*) = \mathbf{t}^*$ which makes $\mathbf{s}$ a valid second pre-image for $\mathbf{t}^*$. So, we have

$$|\Pr[Game_1 \Rightarrow 1] - \Pr[Game_0 \Rightarrow 1]| \leq \mathsf{Adv}_{\mathcal{F},\mathcal{B}_1}^{\mathsf{tcr}}(\lambda)$$

for some proper adversary $\mathcal{B}_1$.

In $Game_2$, we make the following changes on generating the matrix $\mathbf{A}_1$ from the public key Pk. Firstly, we pick $\mathbf{s}^* \leftarrow_\$ \mathbb{Z}_q^n$ and set $\mathbf{t}^* = f(\mathbf{s}^*)$. Then we sample $\mathbf{R} \leftarrow_\$ \{-1,1\}^{\bar{m} \times w}$ and set $\mathbf{A}_1 \leftarrow \mathbf{AR} - \varphi(\mathbf{t}^*)\mathbf{G} \bmod q$. $\mathbf{s}^*$ is also used to construct the challenge ciphertext:

$$\mathbf{t}^* \leftarrow f(\mathbf{s}^*) \quad ; \quad \mathbf{c}^{*\top} \leftarrow \lfloor \mathbf{s}^{*\top} \cdot [\mathbf{A}|\mathbf{A}_1 + \varphi(\mathbf{t}^*)\mathbf{G}] \rceil_p$$

The decryption oracle is implemented as in $Game_1$.

We argue that the adversary's views in $Game_2$ and $Game_1$ are statistically close. First, by Lemma 4, the distributions of $\mathbf{A}_1$ in these two games are statistically close. This means that Pk generated in these two games are statistically indistinguishable for $\mathcal{A}$. Then we note that the decryption queries will be answered properly. This is because by the standard technique of Agrawal et al. [1], knowledge of the binary matrix $\mathbf{R}$ lets us transform the trapdoor for $\mathbf{G}$ into a trapdoor for the whole matrix, as long as $\mathbf{H}$ is invertible. The simulator can thus answer in the same way as the previous games, except for the ciphertexts $\mathsf{Ct} = (\mathbf{c}, \mathbf{t}^*)$, which however, are already excluded:

$$[\mathbf{A}|\mathbf{A}_1 + \varphi(\mathbf{t})\mathbf{G}] = [\mathbf{A}|\mathbf{AR} + (\varphi(\mathbf{t}) - \varphi(\mathbf{t}^*))\mathbf{G}]$$
$$= [\mathbf{A}|\mathbf{AR} + \mathbf{HG}]$$

where, by the property of FRD, $\mathbf{H} \in \mathbb{Z}_q^{n \times n}$ is invertible. So we have

$$|\Pr[Game_2 \Rightarrow 1] - \Pr[Game_1 \Rightarrow 1]| \leq \mathsf{negl}_1(\lambda)$$

for some negligible statistical error $\mathsf{negl}_1(\lambda)$.

In $Game_3$ we change the way that the matrix $\mathbf{A}$ is constructed. In particular, we obtain $\mathbf{A} \leftarrow \mathbf{CB} + \mathbf{F}$ where $\mathbf{B} \leftarrow_\$ \mathbb{Z}_q^{\ell \times \bar{m}}$, $\mathbf{C} \leftarrow_\$ \mathbb{Z}_q^{n \times \ell}$ and $\mathbf{F} \leftarrow \chi^{n \times \bar{m}}$. By the LWE assumption (amortised version) we immediately have

$$\Pr[Game_3 \Rightarrow 1] - \Pr[Game_2 \Rightarrow 1] \leq \mathsf{Adv}_{\mathcal{B}_2}^{\mathsf{LWE}_{\ell,\bar{m},q,\chi}}(\lambda)$$

for some proper adversary $\mathcal{B}_2$.

In $Game_4$, we change the way of generating the challenge session key. In particular, K_1^* is chosen randomly from $\{0,1\}^\lambda$ (recall that K_0^* is chosen uniformly random from $\{0,1\}^\lambda$ in all previous games). We argue that $Game_3$ and $Game_4$ are statistically indistinguishable. First of all, $\mathbf{t}^*$ in the challenge ciphertext has at most 2^λ values. Second, by the construction of the matrix $\mathbf{A}$ and $\mathbf{c}^*$, we have

$$\begin{aligned}
\mathbf{c}^{*\top} &= \left\lfloor \mathbf{s}^{*\top} \cdot [\mathbf{A}|\mathbf{A}_1 + \varphi(\mathbf{t}^*)\mathbf{G}] \right\rceil_p \\
&= \left\lfloor \mathbf{s}^{*\top} \cdot [\mathbf{A}|\mathbf{AR} + (\varphi(\mathbf{t}^*) - \varphi(\mathbf{t}^*))\mathbf{G}] \right\rceil_p \\
&= \left\lfloor \mathbf{s}^{*\top} \cdot [\mathbf{A}|\mathbf{AR}] \right\rceil_p
\end{aligned}$$

By Lemma 2,

$$\begin{aligned}
\tilde{\mathrm{H}}_\infty \left(\mathbf{s}^*|\mathbf{c}^*, \mathbf{t}^*\right) &\geq \tilde{\mathrm{H}}_\infty \left(\mathbf{s}^*|\mathbf{c}^*\right) - \lambda \\
&\geq n \log(2\gamma) - (\lambda + \ell) \log q - \lambda \\
&\geq n - 2\ell \log q - \lambda \\
&= n - \ell \cdot n^\delta - \lambda \\
&\geq 4\lambda - \lambda \\
&= 3\lambda
\end{aligned}$$

Let $\epsilon = 2^{-\lambda}$. So, we have $\tilde{\mathrm{H}}_\infty \left(\mathbf{s}^*|\mathbf{c}^*, \mathbf{t}^*\right) \geq 2\log(1/\epsilon) + \lambda$. Applying Lemma 3 results in $\mathsf{SD}\left((\mathbf{c}^*, \mathbf{t}^*, h, h(\mathbf{s}^*)), (\mathbf{c}^*, \mathbf{t}^*, h, K_1^*)\right) \leq \epsilon = 2^{-\lambda}$ where $K_1^* \leftarrow \{0,1\}^\lambda$. We therefore obtain

$$|\Pr[Game_4 \Rightarrow 1] - \Pr[Game_3 \Rightarrow 1]| \leq 2^{-\lambda}$$

Additionally, in $Game_4$, K_0^* and K_1^* are all random strings chosen from $\{0,1\}^\lambda$. So the adversary $\mathcal{A}$ has exactly probability $1/2$ of correctly guessing μ, i.e.,

$$\Pr[Game_4 \Rightarrow 1] = 1/2$$

Combining the above steps gives us

$$\mathsf{Adv}_{\Pi,\mathcal{A}}^{\mathsf{ind\text{-}cca}}(\lambda) \leq \mathsf{Adv}_{\mathcal{F},\mathcal{B}_1}^{\mathsf{tcr}}(\lambda) + \mathsf{Adv}_{\mathcal{B}_2}^{\mathsf{LWE}_{\ell,\bar{m},q,\chi}}(\lambda) + \mathsf{negl}(\lambda)$$

where $\mathsf{negl}(\lambda) = \mathsf{negl}_1(\lambda) + 2^{-\lambda}$ is negligible. This completes the proof.   □

4   CCA-Secure Deterministic Public-Key Encryption

In this section, we show a construction of CCA-secure deterministic public-key encryption (D-PKE) in the standard model. Deterministic public-key encryption only makes sense for high-min-entropy plaintexts, to preclude the obvious guess-and-encrypt attack, but for such messages it has practical applications ranging from encrypted keyword search to encrypted cloud storage with deduplication.

Our CCA-secure D-PKE has a similar structure as our KEM. We consider the so-called PRIV-CCA security notion for single hard-to-guess message as in

[4].[2] The security of our construction is again based on the hardness of the LWE problem with high-min-entropy secret in the presence of hard-to-invert auxiliary inputs, which is as hard as the standard form of LWE with certain parameters [12]. Our construction is more efficient than the generic constructions by Boldyreva et al. [4] which requires double encryption (e.g., using two lossy trapdoor functions when instantiated with lattice-based primitives).

A D-PKE scheme consists of three algorithms. On input a security parameter 1^λ, the randomised key generation algorithm $\mathsf{KeyGen}(1^\lambda)$ outputs a pair of public and private keys $(\mathsf{Pk}, \mathsf{Sk})$. The *deterministic* encryption algorithm $\mathsf{Enc}(\mathsf{Pk}, \mathsf{m})$ returns a ciphertext Ct. The decryption algorithm $\mathsf{Dec}(\mathsf{Pk}, \mathsf{Sk}, \mathsf{Ct})$ returns the message m or $\perp$. The correctness is required that for all m, $(\mathsf{Pk}, \mathsf{Sk}) \leftarrow \mathsf{KeyGen}(1^\lambda)$,

$$\Pr[\mathsf{Dec}(\mathsf{Pk}, \mathsf{Sk}, \mathsf{Enc}(\mathsf{Pk}, \mathsf{m})) = \mathsf{m}] \geq 1 - \mathsf{negl}(\lambda).$$

We recall the indistinguishability-based security definition of D-PKE for single high-min-entropy messages. Here we consider a stronger version where we require ciphertext pseudorandomness, i.e., that ciphertexts be computationally indistinguishable from random strings. The security game with a D-PKE scheme Π is defined as follows. The adversary $\mathcal{A}$ outputs a distribution M over the message space. Where $\mathrm{H}_\infty(M) \geq k$ (i.e., M is a k-source). The challenger $\mathcal{B}$ runs $(\mathsf{Pk}, \mathsf{Sk}) \leftarrow \mathsf{KeyGen}(1^\lambda)$. It flips a coin $\mu \leftarrow_\$ \{0,1\}$. If $\mu = 0$ it computes $\mathsf{Ct}^* \leftarrow \mathsf{Enc}(\mathsf{Pk}, \mathsf{m}^*)$ where $\mathsf{m}^* \leftarrow M$. Otherwise it chooses Ct^* uniformly at random from the ciphertext space. $\mathcal{B}$ returns $(\mathsf{Pk}, \mathsf{Ct}^*)$ to $\mathcal{A}$. $\mathcal{A}$ then launches adaptive decryption queries $\mathsf{Ct} \neq \mathsf{Ct}^*$ to which $\mathcal{B}$ returns $\mathsf{Dec}(\mathsf{Pk}, \mathsf{Sk}, \mathsf{Ct})$. Finally, $\mathcal{A}$ outputs μ' and wins if $\mu' = \mu$. We define $\mathcal{A}$'s advantage in the security game as

$$\mathsf{Adv}_{\Pi,\mathcal{A}}^{\mathsf{priv1\text{-}cca}}(\lambda) = |\Pr[\mu' = \mu] - 1/2|.$$

We say a D-PKE scheme Π is PRIV-CCA-secure w.r.t. a k-source single message if for every p.p.t. adversary $\mathcal{A}$, the advantage is negligible in λ.

Construction. Our construction uses a full-rank difference encoding function $\varphi : \mathbb{Z}_q^n \to \mathbb{Z}_q^{n \times n}$ as in our construction of KEM. The construction also uses a family of second pre-image resistant functions $\mathcal{F} = \{f : \{0,1\}^n \to \{0,1\}^{2\lambda}\}$ that is universal and 2^{-k}-hard-to-invert with respect to a k-source M over $\{0,1\}^n$. Such a family of functions can be built from the standard Short Integer Solution (SIS) problem.

The security of the construction is based on the hardness of $\mathsf{LWE}_{\ell,q,\bar{m},D_{\mathbb{Z},\gamma q}}$ where we need, for Lemma 5, $\ell \geq \frac{k-\omega(\log n)}{\log q}$, $\gamma \in (0,1)$ such that $\gamma/\beta = \mathsf{negl}(n)$. We set the parameters for decryption correctness and security as follows.

- Set the LWE modulus $q = n^{\omega(1)}$ and parameter $\beta = \sqrt{\ell}/q$ for the LWE hardness results of, e.g. [17,20].

---

[2] It was shown in [4] that such a security notion is equivalent to the PRIV-CCA security notion for multiple messages that form a block source. See [4] for details.

- Set the dimension $\bar{m} = n^{1+\delta}$ where $n^\delta = O(\log q)$ for Lemma 4.
- The rounding parameter $p = 3\bar{m}^{1.5}$, to ensure that Lemma 6 applies.
- Finally, $\beta = 1/(2p\sqrt{n\bar{m}}) \cdot n^{-\omega(1)}$ for applying Lemma 1.

KeyGen(1^λ): On input the security parameter λ, the algorithm does:
1. Choose $\mathbf{A} \leftarrow_\$ \mathbb{Z}_q^{n \times \bar{m}}$, $\mathbf{R} \leftarrow_\$ \{-1, 1\}^{\bar{m} \times w}$; Set $\mathbf{A}_1 = \mathbf{A}\mathbf{R} \bmod q$.
2. Sample a *universal*, second pre-image resistant, 2^k-hard-to-invert hash function $f \leftarrow_\$ \mathcal{F}$.
3. Set $\mathsf{Pk} = (\mathbf{A}, \mathbf{A}_1, f)$ and $\mathsf{Sk} = \mathbf{R}$.

Enc$(\mathsf{Pk}, \mathsf{m})$: On input the public key Pk and message $\mathsf{m} \in \{0,1\}^n$ which comes from some k-source, the algorithm does:
1. Compute $\mathbf{t} \leftarrow f(\mathsf{m})$ and encode $\mathbf{t}$ as a vector in $\mathbb{Z}_q^n$.
2. Compute $\mathbf{c}^\top = \lfloor \mathsf{m}^\top \cdot [\mathbf{A}|\mathbf{A}_1 + \varphi(\mathbf{t})\mathbf{G}] \rceil_p$.
3. Set $\mathsf{Ct} = (\mathbf{c}, \mathbf{t})$.

Dec$(\mathsf{Sk}, \mathsf{Ct})$: On input the private key Sk and a ciphertext $\mathsf{Ct} = (\mathbf{c}, \mathbf{t})$, the decryption algorithm does:
1. Runs $\mathsf{Invert}(\mathsf{Transform}_q(\mathbf{c}), [\mathbf{A}|\mathbf{A}_1 + \varphi(\mathbf{t})\mathbf{G}], \mathbf{R})$ to get $\mathsf{m}' \in \{0,1\}^n$.
2. Compute $\mathbf{t}' = f(\mathsf{m}')$. Return m' if $\mathbf{t}' = \mathbf{t}$ or return $\bot$ otherwise.

Security Proof. Now we give the security proof.

Theorem 2. *Let $k \geq 2\log(1/n^{-\omega(1)}) + \lambda$. If the family of functions $\mathcal{F}$ is universal, 2^{-k}-hard-to-invert, second pre-image resistant, and Lemma 5 holds, the above construction of D-PKE scheme is PRIV-CCA-secure for k-source single message.*

Proof. We proceed the proof by a sequence of games. For $i = \{0, 1, 2, 3, 4\}$, we denote the i-th game by $Game_i$. We denote by $Game_i \Rightarrow 1$ the event that the adversary wins the security game, i.e., it outputs μ' such that $\mu' = \mu$.

The first game $Game_0$ is the original PRIV-CCA security game. That is, the adversary $\mathcal{A}$ generates a k-source distribution M. The challenger samples a challenge message $\mathsf{m}^* \leftarrow M$ and a fair coin $\mu \leftarrow_\$ \{0, 1\}$. It then returns the public key $(\mathbf{A}, \mathbf{A}_1, f)$ and the challnege ciphertext Ct_μ^* to $\mathcal{A}$, where $\mathsf{Ct}_0^* \leftarrow \mathsf{Enc}(\mathsf{Pk}, \mathsf{m}^*)$ and Ct_1^* is uniformly chosen from the ciphertext space. $\mathcal{A}$ then launches adaptive chosen-ciphertext queries Ct subject to the condition that $\mathsf{Ct} \neq \mathsf{Ct}^*$. Finally, $\mathcal{A}$ outputs μ' and it wins if $\mu' = \mu$. By definition we have

$$|\Pr[Game_0 \Rightarrow 1] - 1/2| = \mathsf{Adv}_{\Pi, \mathcal{A}}^{\mathsf{priv1\text{-}cca}}(\lambda).$$

In the second game $Game_1$, we slightly change the way of answering the decryption query: Let the challenge ciphertext $\mathsf{Ct}_\mu^* = (\mathbf{c}^*, \mathbf{t}^*)$. A decryption query $\mathsf{Ct} = (\mathbf{c}, \mathbf{t})$ is rejected if $\mathbf{t} = \mathbf{t}^*$. First, we must have $\mathsf{Ct} \neq \mathsf{Ct}_\mu^*$ by security definition. Second, if $\mathbf{c} \neq \mathbf{c}^*$, there is a $\mathsf{m}' \in \{0,1\}^n$ such that $\mathbf{c}^\top = \lfloor \mathsf{m}'^\top[\mathbf{A}|\mathbf{A}_1 + \varphi(\mathbf{t}^*)] \rceil_p$. (In the case that Ct_0^* was returned, we must have $\mathsf{m}' \neq \mathsf{m}^*$.) Therefore, m' is a valid second pre-image of $\mathbf{t}^*$ on f, and m' can be recovered efficiently through the decryption procedure. So a p.p.t distinguisher between $Game_0$ and $Game_1$ leads to a second-pre-image inversion algorithm for $\mathcal{F}$ and we have

$$|\Pr[Game_1 \Rightarrow 1] - \Pr[Game_0 \Rightarrow 1]| \leq \mathsf{negl}_1(\lambda).$$

In $Game_2$ we set $\mathbf{A}_1 \leftarrow \mathbf{AR} - \varphi(\mathbf{t}^*)\mathbf{G}$. By making this change we have challenge ciphertext $\mathsf{Ct}_0^* = (\mathbf{t}^* = f(\mathsf{m}^*), \ \mathbf{c}^{*T} = \lfloor \mathsf{m}^{*T}[\mathbf{A}|\mathbf{AR}]\rfloor_p)$. By Lemma 4, $\mathbf{A}_1$ is distributed properly except for a negligible statistical error $\mathsf{negl}_1\lambda$. So we have

$$|\Pr[Game_2 \Rightarrow 1] - \Pr[Game_1 \Rightarrow 1]| \leq \mathsf{negl}_2(\lambda).$$

In $Game_3$, we make changes on computing the challenge ciphertext Ct_0^*. Specifically, given the challenge message $\mathsf{m}^* \leftarrow M$, we sample $\mathbf{e} \leftarrow D_{\mathbb{Z},\beta q}^{\bar{m}}$ and compute

$$\begin{aligned}
\mathbf{c}^{*T} &= \left\lfloor \mathsf{m}^{*T}[\mathbf{A}|\mathbf{A}_1 + \varphi(\mathbf{t}^*)\mathbf{G}] + [\mathbf{e}^T|\mathbf{e}^T\mathbf{R}] \right\rfloor_p \\
&= \left\lfloor \mathsf{m}^{*T}[\mathbf{A}|\mathbf{AR}] + [\mathbf{e}^T|\mathbf{e}^T\mathbf{R}] \right\rfloor_p
\end{aligned}$$

where $\mathbf{R}$ is chosen as in the key generation phase. Since m^* is a sample from the distribution M which is chosen independent of $\mathbf{A}$ and $\mathbf{AR}$, so $\mathsf{m}^{*T}[\mathbf{A}|\mathbf{AR}]$ is a random sample from the uniform distribution over $\mathbb{Z}_q^{\bar{m}+w}$ (Recall $\mathbf{A}$ is randomly chosen and $\mathbf{AR}$ statistically close to uniform as per Lemma 4). By Lemma 1 and the fact that $\|\mathbf{e}^T\mathbf{R}\|_\infty \leq \beta q\sqrt{n\bar{m}}$, with all but negligible probability $\mathsf{negl}_3(\lambda)$,

$$\mathbf{c}^{*T} = \left\lfloor \mathsf{m}^{*T}[\mathbf{A}|\mathbf{AR}] \right\rfloor_p$$

as produced in $Game_2$. This shows that

$$|\Pr[Game_3 \Rightarrow 1] - \Pr[Game_2 \Rightarrow 1]| \leq \mathsf{negl}_3(\lambda).$$

In $Game_4$, we set $\mathsf{Ct}_0^* = (\mathbf{t}^* = f(\mathsf{m}^*), \ \mathbf{c}^* = \lfloor[\mathbf{b}^T|\mathbf{b}^T\mathbf{R}]\rfloor_p$ where $\mathbf{b} \leftarrow_\$ \mathbb{Z}_q^{\bar{m}}$ and $\mathsf{m}^* \leftarrow M$. by Lemma 5, the distributions $(\mathbf{A}, \mathbf{b}^T, f(\mathsf{m}^*))$ and $(\mathbf{A}, \mathsf{m}^{*T}\mathbf{A} + \mathbf{e}^T, f(\mathsf{m}^*))$ are computationally indistinguishable under the $\mathsf{LWE}_{\ell,\bar{m},q,D_{\mathbb{Z},\gamma q}}$ assumption, where m^* is from an arbitrary k-source distribution over $\mathbb{Z}_q^n$, $\mathbf{e} \leftarrow D_{\mathbb{Z},\beta q}^{\bar{m}}$ and 2^{-k}-hard-to-invert function f, and $\mathbf{b} \leftarrow \mathbb{Z}_q^{\bar{m}}$. So the challenge ciphertext Ct_0^* in $Game_4$ is indistinguishable from

$$\begin{aligned}
&\left(f(\mathsf{m}^*), \ \lfloor[\mathsf{m}^{*T}\mathbf{A} + \mathbf{e}^T|(\mathsf{m}^{*T}\mathbf{A} + \mathbf{e}^T)\mathbf{R}]\rfloor_p \right) \\
&= \left(f(\mathsf{m}^*), \ \lfloor \mathsf{m}^{*T}[\mathbf{A}|\mathbf{AR}] + [\mathbf{e}^T|\mathbf{e}^T\mathbf{R}]\rfloor_p \right) \\
&= \left(f(\mathsf{m}^*), \ \lfloor \mathsf{m}^{*T}[\mathbf{A}|\mathbf{A}_1 + \varphi(\mathbf{t}^*)\mathbf{G}] + [\mathbf{e}^T|\mathbf{e}^T\mathbf{R}]\rfloor_p \right)
\end{aligned}$$

which is the challenge ciphertext Ct_0^* produced in $Game_3$. We have

$$\Pr[Game_4 \Rightarrow 1] - \Pr[Game_3 \Rightarrow 1] \leq \mathsf{Adv}_{\mathcal{B}}^{\mathsf{LWE}_{\ell,\tilde{m},q,D_{\mathbb{Z},\gamma q}}}(\lambda) + \mathsf{negl}_3(\lambda)$$

for some LWE adversary $\mathcal{B}$.

Furthermore, since the challenge message m^*, a k-source sample, is independent of $\mathbf{c}^*$, $\mathbf{t}^* = f(\mathsf{m}^*)$ is distributed uniformly over $\{0,1\}^{2\lambda}$ except for the negligible probability $\lambda^{-\omega(1)}$ (by the fact that $k \geq 2\log(1/\lambda^{-\omega(1)}) + \lambda$, the universality of f, and Lemma 3). Since $\mathbf{b}$ is chosen uniformly at random from $\mathbb{Z}_q^{\tilde{m}}$, by Lemma 4, $\mathbf{c}^* = \lfloor [\mathbf{b}^\top | \mathbf{b}^\top \mathbf{R}] \rceil_p$ is statistically close to the uniform distribution over $\mathbb{Z}_q^{\tilde{m}+w}$ with up to a negligible distance $p/q = \mathsf{negl}_4(\lambda)$. This shows that Ct_0^* in $Game_5$ is statistically close to a random ciphertext, e.g., Ct_1^*. We have

$$|\Pr[Game_4 \Rightarrow 1] - 1/2| \leq \lambda^{-\omega(1)} + \mathsf{negl}_4(\lambda).$$

To sum up, we have

$$\mathsf{Adv}_{\Pi,\mathcal{A}}^{\mathsf{priv1\text{-}cca}}(\lambda) \leq \mathsf{Adv}_{\mathcal{B}}^{\mathsf{LWE}_{\ell,\tilde{m},q,D_{\mathbb{Z},\gamma q}}}(\lambda) + \mathsf{negl}(\lambda)$$

where $\mathsf{negl}(\lambda)$ accounts for the sum of all negligible terms appeared in the proof. This completes the proof. $\qquad\qquad\square$

References

1. Agrawal, S., Boneh, D., Boyen, X.: Efficient lattice (H)IBE in the standard model. In: Gilbert, H. (ed.) EUROCRYPT 2010. LNCS, vol. 6110, pp. 553–572. Springer, Heidelberg (2010). https://doi.org/10.1007/978-3-642-13190-5_28

2. Alwen, J., Krenn, S., Pietrzak, K., Wichs, D.: Learning with rounding, revisited. In: Canetti, R., Garay, J.A. (eds.) CRYPTO 2013. LNCS, vol. 8042, pp. 57–74. Springer, Heidelberg (2013). https://doi.org/10.1007/978-3-642-40041-4_4

3. Alwen, J., Krenn, S., Pietrzak, K., Wichs, D.: Learning with rounding, revisited: new reduction, properties and applications. Cryptology ePrint Archive, Report 2013/098 (2013). https://eprint.iacr.org/2013/098

4. Boldyreva, A., Fehr, S., O'Neill, A.: On notions of security for deterministic encryption, and efficient constructions without random oracles. In: Wagner, D. (ed.) CRYPTO 2008. LNCS, vol. 5157, pp. 335–359. Springer, Heidelberg (2008). https://doi.org/10.1007/978-3-540-85174-5_19

5. Boneh, D., Canetti, R., Halevi, S., Katz, J.: Chosen-ciphertext security from identity-based encryption. SIAM J. Comput. 36(5), 1301–1328 (2006)

6. Boneh, D., Dagdelen, Ö., Fischlin, M., Lehmann, A., Schaffner, C., Zhandry, M.: Random oracles in a quantum world. In: Lee, D.H., Wang, X. (eds.) ASIACRYPT 2011. LNCS, vol. 7073, pp. 41–69. Springer, Heidelberg (2011). https://doi.org/10.1007/978-3-642-25385-0_3

7. Boyen, X., Mei, Q., Waters, B.: Direct chosen ciphertext security from identity-based techniques. In: Proceedings of the 12th ACM Conference on Computer and Communications Security, pp. 320–329. ACM (2005)

8. Cramer, R., Shoup, V.: Design and analysis of practical public-key encryption schemes secure against adaptive chosen ciphertext attack. SIAM J. Comput. 33(1), 167–226 (2003)

9. Dodis, Y., Ostrovsky, R., Reyzin, L., Smith, A.: Fuzzy extractors: how to generate strong keys from biometrics and other noisy data. SIAM J. Comput. **38**(1), 97–139 (2008)
10. Fujisaki, E., Okamoto, T.: Secure integration of asymmetric and symmetric encryption schemes. J. Cryptol. **26**(1), 80–101 (2013)
11. Gentry, C., Peikert, C., Vaikuntanathan, V.: Trapdoors for hard lattices and new cryptographic constructions. In: Proceedings of the 40th Annual ACM Symposium on Theory of Computing, STOC 2008, pp. 197–206. ACM, New York (2008)
12. Goldwasser, S., Kalai, Y., Peikert, C., Vaikuntanathan, V.: Robustness of the learning with errors assumption. In: Innovations in Computer Science, pp. 230–240 (2010)
13. Kiltz, E., Galindo, D.: Direct chosen-ciphertext secure identity-based key encapsulation without random oracles. Theoret. Comput. Sci. **410**(47–49), 5093–5111 (2009)
14. Lai, J., Deng, R.H., Liu, S., Kou, W.: Efficient CCA-secure PKE from identity-based techniques. In: Pieprzyk, J. (ed.) CT-RSA 2010. LNCS, vol. 5985, pp. 132–147. Springer, Heidelberg (2010). https://doi.org/10.1007/978-3-642-11925-5_10
15. Micciancio, D., Peikert, C.: Trapdoors for lattices: simpler, tighter, faster, smaller. In: Pointcheval, D., Johansson, T. (eds.) EUROCRYPT 2012. LNCS, vol. 7237, pp. 700–718. Springer, Heidelberg (2012). https://doi.org/10.1007/978-3-642-29011-4_41
16. Mol, P., Yilek, S.: Chosen-ciphertext security from slightly lossy trapdoor functions. In: Nguyen, P.Q., Pointcheval, D. (eds.) PKC 2010. LNCS, vol. 6056, pp. 296–311. Springer, Heidelberg (2010). https://doi.org/10.1007/978-3-642-13013-7_18
17. Peikert, C., Regev, O., Stephens-Davidowitz, N.: Pseudorandomness of ring-LWE for any ring and modulus. In: Proceedings of the 49th Annual ACM SIGACT Symposium on Theory of Computing, pp. 461–473. ACM (2017)
18. Peikert, C., Vaikuntanathan, V., Waters, B.: A framework for efficient and composable oblivious transfer. In: Wagner, D. (ed.) CRYPTO 2008. LNCS, vol. 5157, pp. 554–571. Springer, Heidelberg (2008). https://doi.org/10.1007/978-3-540-85174-5_31
19. Peikert, C., Waters, B.: Lossy trapdoor functions and their applications. SIAM J. Comput. **40**(6), 1803–1844 (2011)
20. Regev, O.: On lattices, learning with errors, random linear codes, and cryptography. In: Proceedings of the Thirty-Seventh Annual ACM Symposium on Theory of Computing, STOC 2005, pp. 84–93. ACM, New York (2005)
21. Rosen, A., Segev, G.: Chosen-ciphertext security via correlated products. In: Reingold, O. (ed.) TCC 2009. LNCS, vol. 5444, pp. 419–436. Springer, Heidelberg (2009). https://doi.org/10.1007/978-3-642-00457-5_25
22. Xie, X., Xue, R., Zhang, R.: Deterministic public key encryption and identity-based encryption from lattices in the auxiliary-input setting. In: Visconti, I., De Prisco, R. (eds.) SCN 2012. LNCS, vol. 7485, pp. 1–18. Springer, Heidelberg (2012). https://doi.org/10.1007/978-3-642-32928-9_1

Cryptanalysis

Recovering Short Secret Keys of RLCE
in Polynomial Time

Alain Couvreur[1], Matthieu Lequesne[2,3(✉)], and Jean-Pierre Tillich[3]

[1] Inria and LIX, CNRS UMR 7161 École polytechnique,
91128 Palaiseau Cedex, France
alain.couvreur@lix.polytechnique.fr
[2] Sorbonne Université, UPMC Univ Paris 06, Paris, France
[3] Inria, Paris, France
{matthieu.lequesne,jean-pierre.tillich}@inria.fr

Abstract. We present a key recovery attack against Y. Wang's Random Linear Code Encryption (RLCE) scheme recently submitted to the NIST call for post-quantum cryptography. The public key of this code based encryption scheme is a generator matrix of a generalised Reed Solomon code whose columns are mixed in a certain manner with purely random columns. In this paper, we show that it is possible to recover the underlying structure when there are not enough random columns. The attack reposes on a distinguisher on the dimension of the square code. This process allows to recover the secret key for all the short key parameters proposed by the author in $O(n^5)$ operations. Our analysis explains also why RLCE long keys stay out of reach of our attack.

Keywords: Code based cryptography · McEliece scheme · RLCE ·
Distinguisher · Key recovery attack ·
Generalised Reed Solomon codes · Schur product of codes

1 Introduction

The McEliece encryption scheme dates back to the late 70's [14] and lies among the possible post-quantum alternatives to number theory based schemes using integer factorisation or discrete logarithm. However, the main drawback of McEliece's original scheme is the large size of its keys. Indeed, the classic instantiation of McEliece using binary Goppa codes requires public keys of several hundreds of kilobytes to assert a security of 128 bits. For example, the recent NIST submission *Classic McEliece* [4] proposes public keys of 1.1 to 1.3 megabytes to assert 256 bits security (with a classical computer).

To reduce the size of the keys, two general trends appear in the literature : the first one consists in considering codes with a non trivial automorphism group, the second one in using codes with a higher decoding capacity for encryption. In the last decade, the second trend led to many proposals involving generalised Reed Solomon (GRS) codes, which are well-known to have a large minimum distance

© Springer Nature Switzerland AG 2019
J. Ding and R. Steinwandt (Eds.): PQCrypto 2019, LNCS 11505, pp. 133–152, 2019.
https://doi.org/10.1007/978-3-030-25510-7_8

together with efficient decoding algorithms correcting up to half the minimum distance. On the other hand, the raw use of GRS codes has been proved to be insecure by Sidelnikov and Shestakov [15]. Subsequently, some variations have been proposed as a counter-measure of Sidelnikov and Shestakov's attack. Berger and Loidreau [3] suggested to replace a GRS code by a random subcode of small codimension, Wieschebrink [18] proposed to join random columns in a generator matrix of a GRS code and Baldi *et al.* [1] suggested to mask the structure of the code by right multiplying a generator matrix of a GRS code by the sum of a low rank matrix and a sparse matrix. It turns out that all of these proposals have been subject to efficient polynomial time attacks [8,11,19].

A more recent proposal by Yongge Wang [16] suggests another way of hiding the structure of GRS codes. The outline of Wang's construction is the following: start from a $k \times n$ generator matrix of a GRS code of length n and dimension k over a field $\mathbb{F}_q$, add w additional random columns to the matrix, and mix the columns in a particular manner. The design of this scheme is detailed in Sect. 3.1. This approach entails a significant expansion of the public key size but may resist above-mentioned attacks such as distinguisher and filtration attacks [8,10]. This public key encryption primitive is the core of Wang's recent NIST submission "RLCE-KEM" [17].

Our Contribution: In the present article we give a polynomial time key recovery attack against RLCE. For an $[n, k]$ code with w additional random columns, our attack breaks the system in $O(wk^2n^2)$ operations, when $w < n - k$. This allows us to break half the parameter sets proposed in [17].

2   Notation and Prerequisites

2.1   Generalised Reed Solomon Codes

Notation 1. *Let q be a power of prime and k a positive integer. We denote by $\mathbb{F}_q[X]_{<k}$ the vector space of polynomials over $\mathbb{F}_q$ whose degree is strictly bounded from above by k.*

Definition 1 (Generalised Reed Solomon codes). *Let $x \in \mathbb{F}_q^n$ be a vector whose entries are pairwise distinct and $y \in \mathbb{F}_q^n$ be a vector whose entries are all nonzero. The generalised Reed Solomon (GRS) code with support x and multiplier y of dimension k is defined as*

$$GRS_k(x, y) \overset{def}{=} \{(y_1 f(x_1), \ldots, y_n f(x_n)) \mid f \in \mathbb{F}_q[x]_{<k}\}.$$

2.2   Schur Product of Codes and Square Codes Distinguisher

Notation 2. *The component-wise product of two vectors a and b in $\mathbb{F}_q^n$ is denoted by : $a \star b \overset{def}{=} (a_1 b_1, \ldots, a_n b_n)$. This definition extends to the product of codes where the Schur product of two codes $\mathscr{A}$ and $\mathscr{B} \subseteq \mathbb{F}_q^n$ is defined as*

$$\mathscr{A} \star \mathscr{B} \overset{def}{=} \mathrm{Span}_{\mathbb{F}_q} \{a \star b \mid a \in \mathscr{A}, \ b \in \mathscr{B}\}.$$

In particular, $\mathscr{A}^{*2}$ denotes the square code *of a code $\mathscr{A}$: $\mathscr{A}^{*2} \overset{def}{=} \mathscr{A} \star \mathscr{A}$.*

We recall the following result on the generic behaviour of random codes with respect to this operation.

Proposition 1 *([6, Theorem 2.3], informal). For a linear code $\mathscr{R}$ chosen at random over $\mathbb{F}_q$ of dimension k and length n, the dimension of $\mathscr{R}^{*2}$ is typically $\min(n, \binom{k+1}{2})$.*

This provides a distinguisher between random codes and algebraically structured codes such as generalised Reed Solomon codes [8,19], Reed Muller codes [7], polar codes [2] some Goppa codes [10,12] or algebraic geometry codes [9]. For instance, in the case of GRS codes, we have the following result.

Proposition 2. *Let $n, k, \boldsymbol{x}, \boldsymbol{y}$ be as in Definition 1. Then,*

$$(\boldsymbol{GRS}_k(\boldsymbol{x}, \boldsymbol{y}))^{*2} = \boldsymbol{GRS}_{2k-1}(\boldsymbol{x}, \boldsymbol{y} \star \boldsymbol{y}).$$

In particular, if $k < n/2$, then $\dim(\boldsymbol{GRS}_k(\boldsymbol{x}, \boldsymbol{y}))^{*2} = 2k - 1$.

Thus, compared to a random code $\mathscr{R}$ whose square has a dimension quadratic in $\dim \mathscr{R}$, the square of a GRS code $\mathscr{C}$ has a dimension which is linear in $\dim \mathscr{C}$. This criterion allows to distinguish GRS codes of appropriate dimension from random codes.

2.3   Punctured and Shortened Codes

The notions of *puncturing* and *shortening* are classical ways to build new codes from existing ones. These constructions will be useful for the attack. We recall here their definition. For a codeword $\boldsymbol{c} \in \mathbb{F}_q^n$, we denote $(c_1, \ldots, c_n)$ its entries.

Definition 2 (punctured and restricted codes). *Let $\mathscr{C} \subseteq \mathbb{F}_q^n$ and $\mathcal{L} \subseteq [\![1, n]\!]$. The puncturing of $\mathscr{C}$ at $\mathcal{L}$ is defined as the code*

$$\mathcal{P}_\mathcal{L}(\mathscr{C}) \overset{def}{=} \{(c_i)_{i \in [\![1,n]\!] \setminus \mathcal{L}} \text{ s.t. } \boldsymbol{c} \in \mathscr{C}\}.$$

The restriction of $\mathscr{C}$ to $\mathcal{L}$ is defined as the code $\mathcal{R}_\mathcal{L}(\mathscr{C}) \overset{def}{=} \mathcal{P}_{[\![1,n]\!] \setminus \mathcal{L}}(\mathscr{C})$.

Definition 3 (shortened code). *Let $\mathscr{C} \subseteq \mathbb{F}_q^n$ and $\mathcal{L} \subseteq [\![1, n]\!]$. The shortening of $\mathscr{C}$ at $\mathcal{L}$ is defined as the code*

$$\mathcal{S}_\mathcal{L}(\mathscr{C}) \overset{def}{=} \mathcal{P}_\mathcal{L}(\{\boldsymbol{c} \in \mathscr{C} \text{ s.t. } \forall i \in \mathcal{L}, \ c_i = 0\}).$$

Shortening a code is equivalent to puncturing the dual code, as explained by the following proposition, whose proof can be found in [13, Theorem 1.5.7].

Proposition 3. *Let $\mathscr{C}$ be a linear code over $\mathbb{F}_q^n$ and $\mathcal{L} \subseteq [\![1, n]\!]$. Then,*

$$\mathcal{S}_\mathcal{L}(\mathscr{C}^\perp) = (\mathcal{P}_\mathcal{L}(\mathscr{C}))^\perp \text{ and } (\mathcal{S}_\mathcal{L}(\mathscr{C}))^\perp = \mathcal{P}_\mathcal{L}(\mathscr{C}^\perp),$$

where $\mathscr{A}^\perp$ denotes the dual of the code $\mathscr{A}$.

Notation 3. *Throughout the document, the indexes of the columns (or positions of the codewords) will always refer to the indexes in the original code, although the code has been punctured or shortened. For instance, consider a code $\mathscr{C}$ of length 5 where every word $\boldsymbol{c} \in \mathscr{C}$ is indexed $\boldsymbol{c} = (c_1, c_2, c_3, c_4, c_5)$. If we puncture $\mathscr{C}$ in $\{1, 3\}$, a codeword $\boldsymbol{c}' \in \mathcal{P}_{\{1,3\}}(\mathscr{C})$ will be indexed (c_2', c_4', c_5') and not (c_1', c_2', c_3').*

3   The RLCE Scheme

3.1   Presentation of the Scheme

The RLCE encryption scheme is a code based cryptosystem, inspired by the McEliece scheme. It has been introduced by Wang in [16] and a proposal called "RLCE-KEM" has recently been submitted as a response for the NIST's call for post-quantum cryptosystems [17].

For a message $\boldsymbol{m} \in \mathbb{F}_q^k$, the cipher text is $\boldsymbol{c} = \boldsymbol{m}\boldsymbol{G} + \boldsymbol{e}$ where $\boldsymbol{e} \in \mathbb{F}_q^{n+w}$ is a random error vector of small weight t and $\boldsymbol{G} \in \mathbb{F}_q^{k \times (n+w)}$ is a generator matrix defined as follows, for given parameters n, k and w.

1. Let $\boldsymbol{x}, \boldsymbol{y} \in \mathbb{F}_q^n$ be respectively a support and a multiplier (as in Definition 1).
2. Let $\boldsymbol{G}_0$ denote a random $k \times n$ generator matrix of the generalised Reed Solomon code $\mathbf{GRS}_k(\boldsymbol{x}, \boldsymbol{y})$ of length n and dimension k. Denote by $g_1, \dots, g_n$ the columns of $\boldsymbol{G}_0$.
3. Let $r_1, \dots, r_w$ be column vectors chosen uniformly at random in $\mathbb{F}_q^k$. Denote by $\boldsymbol{G}_1$ the matrix obtained by inserting the random columns between GRS columns at the end of $\boldsymbol{G}_0$ as follows:

$$\boldsymbol{G}_1 \overset{\text{def}}{=} [g_1, \dots, g_{n-w}, g_{n-w+1}, r_1, \dots, g_n, r_w] \in \mathbb{F}_q^{k \times (n+w)}.$$

4. Let $\boldsymbol{A}_1, \dots, \boldsymbol{A}_w$ be 2×2 matrices chosen uniformly at random in $\mathbf{GL}_2(\mathbb{F}_q)$. Let $\boldsymbol{A}$ be the block–diagonal non singular matrix

$$\boldsymbol{A} \overset{\text{def}}{=} \begin{pmatrix} \boldsymbol{I}_{n-w} & & & (0) \\ & \boldsymbol{A}_1 & & \\ & & \ddots & \\ (0) & & & \boldsymbol{A}_w \end{pmatrix} \in \mathbb{F}_q^{(n+w) \times (n+w)}.$$

5. Let $\pi \in \mathfrak{S}_{n+w}$ be a randomly chosen permutation of $[\![1, n+w]\!]$ and $\boldsymbol{P}$ the corresponding $(n+w) \times (n+w)$ permutation matrix.
6. The public key is the matrix $\boldsymbol{G} \overset{\text{def}}{=} \boldsymbol{G}_1 \boldsymbol{A} \boldsymbol{P}$ and the private key is $(\boldsymbol{x}, \boldsymbol{y}, \boldsymbol{A}, \boldsymbol{P})$.

Remark 1. This presentation of the scheme is not exactly the same as in the original specifications of RLCE [17]. It is however equivalent. Indeed, the differences with the original scheme are listed below.

1. The original specifications of RLCE propose as a public key a matrix

$$G = SG_1AP,$$

where S is a $k \times k$ non singular matrix. But, since we chose G_0 to be a *random* generator matrix of the GRS code to which we included random columns, left multiplication by a random nonsingular matrix does not change the probability distribution of the public keys.

2. In [17], the matrix G_0 is called G_s and is a generator matrix of a GRS code but its columns are permuted using a permutation matrix P_1 before including random columns. Actually, if we chose *arbitrary* supports and multipliers, applying a permutation on the columns does not change the probability distribution of the public keys.

3.2 Suggested Sets of Parameters

In [17] the author proposes 2 groups of 3 sets of parameters. The first group (referred to as *odd ID* parameters) corresponds to parameters such that $w \in [0.6(n - k), 0.7(n - k)]$, whereas in the second group (*even ID* parameters) the parameters satisfy $w = n - k$. The parameters of these two groups are listed in Tables 1 and 2.

The attack of the present paper recovers in polynomial time any secret key when parameters lie in the first group.

Table 1. Set of parameters for the first group: $w \in [0.6(n - k), 0.7(n - k)]$.

Security level (bits)	Name in [17]	n	k	t	w	q	Public key size (kB)
128	ID 1	532	376	78	96	2^{10}	118
192	ID 3	846	618	114	144	2^{10}	287
256	ID 5	1160	700	230	311	2^{11}	742

Table 2. Set of parameters for the second group: $w = n - k$.

Security level (bits)	Name in [17]	n	k	t	w	q	Public key size (kB)
128	ID 0	630	470	80	160	2^{10}	188
192	ID 2	1000	764	118	236	2^{10}	450
256	ID 4	1360	800	280	560	2^{11}	1232

4 Distinguishing by Shortening and Squaring

We will show here that it is possible to distinguish some public keys from random codes by computing the square of some shortening of the public code. More precisely, here is our main result.

Theorem 4. *Let $\mathscr{C}$ be a code over $\mathbb{F}_q$ of length $n + w$ and dimension k with generator matrix G which is the public key of an RLCE scheme that is based on a GRS code of length n and dimension k. Let $\mathcal{L} \subset [\![1, n + w]\!]$. Then,*

$$\dim \left(\mathcal{S}_{\mathcal{L}} \left(\mathscr{C} \right) \right)^{*2} \leqslant \min(n + w - |\mathcal{L}|, \; 2(k + w - |\mathcal{L}|) - 1).$$

Remark 2. Actually, according to computer experiments, the inequality established in Theorem 4 seems to be an equality with a probability close to 1 when we are not in the degenerate case described in Sect. 6.7. See Remark 4 for further details.

To prove Theorem 4 we can assume that P is the identity matrix. This is because of the following lemma.

Lemma 1. *For any permutation σ of the code positions $[\![1, n + w]\!]$ we have*

$$\dim \left(\mathcal{S}_{\mathcal{L}} \left(\mathscr{C} \right) \right)^{*2} = \dim \left(\mathcal{S}_{\mathcal{L}^{\sigma}} \left(\mathscr{C}^{\sigma} \right) \right)^{*2},$$

where $\mathscr{C}^{\sigma}$ is the set of codewords in $\mathscr{C}$ permuted by σ, that is $\mathscr{C}^{\sigma} = \{ c^{\sigma} : c \in \mathscr{C} \}$ where $c^{\sigma} \overset{def}{=} (c_{\sigma(i)})_{i \in [\![1, n+w]\!]}$ and $\mathcal{L}^{\sigma} \overset{def}{=} \{ \sigma(i) : i \in \mathcal{L} \}$.

Therefore, for the analysis of the distinguisher, we can make the following assumption which we will use several times the rest of the section, especially to simplify the notation. The general case will follow by using Lemma 1.

Assumption 5. *The permutation matrix P is the identity matrix.*

4.1 Analysis of the Different Kinds of Columns

Notation and Terminology. Before proving the result, let us introduce some notation and terminology. The set of positions $[\![1, n + w]\!]$ splits in a natural way into four sets, whose definitions are given in the sequel

$$[\![1, n + w]\!] = \mathcal{I}_{\text{GRS}}^1 \cup \mathcal{I}_{\text{GRS}}^2 \cup \mathcal{I}_{\text{R}} \cup \mathcal{I}_{\text{PR}}. \tag{1}$$

Definition 4. *The set of GRS positions of the first kind, denoted $\mathcal{I}_{\text{GRS}}^1$, corresponds to GRS columns which have not been associated to a random column. This set has cardinality $n - w$ and is given by*

$$\mathcal{I}_{\text{GRS}}^1 \overset{def}{=} \{ i \in [\![1, n + w]\!] \mid \pi^{-1}(i) \leqslant n - w \}. \tag{2}$$

Under Assumption 5, this becomes: $\mathcal{I}_{\text{GRS}}^1 \overset{def}{=} [\![1, n - w]\!]$.

This set is called this way, because at a position $i \in \mathcal{I}_{\text{GRS}}^1$, any codeword $v \in \mathscr{C}$ has an entry of the form

$$v_i = y_i f(x_i). \tag{3}$$

As we will see later, there might be other code positions that are of this form.

Definition 5. *The set of* twin positions, *denoted* $\mathcal{I}_T$, *corresponds to columns that result in a mix of a random column and a GRS one. This set has cardinality* $2w$ *and is equal to:*

$$\mathcal{I}_T \overset{def}{=} \{i \in [\![1, n+w]\!] \mid \pi^{-1}(i) > n - w\}.$$

Under Assumption 5, this becomes: $\mathcal{I}_T \overset{def}{=} [\![n - w + 1, n + w]\!]$.

The set $\mathcal{I}_T$ can be divided in several subsets as follows.

Definition 6. *Each position in* $\mathcal{I}_T$ *has a unique corresponding twin position which is the position of the column with which it was mixed. For all* $s \in [\![1, w]\!]$, $\pi(n - w + 2s - 1)$ *and* $\pi(n - w + 2s)$ *are twin positions. Under Assumption 5, the positions* $n - w + 2s - 1$ *and* $n - w + 2s$ *are twins for all* s *in* $[\![1, w]\!]$.

For convenience, we introduce the following notation.

Notation 6. *The twin of a position* $i \in \mathcal{I}_T$ *is denoted by* $\tau(i)$.

To any twin pair $\{i, \tau(i)\} = \{\pi(n - w + 2s - 1), \pi(n - w + 2s)\}$ with $s \in \{1, \ldots, w\}$ is associated a unique linear form $\psi_s : \mathbb{F}_q[x]_{<k} \to \mathbb{F}_q$ and a non-singular matrix $\boldsymbol{A}_s$ such that for any codeword $\boldsymbol{v} \in \mathscr{C}$, we have

$$v_i = a_s y_j f(x_j) + c_s \psi_s(f)$$
$$v_{\tau(i)} = b_s y_j f(x_j) + d_s \psi_s(f), \tag{4}$$

where $j = n - w + s$ and

$$\begin{pmatrix} a_s & b_s \\ c_s & d_s \end{pmatrix} = \boldsymbol{A}_s. \tag{5}$$

The linear form ψ_s is the form whose evaluations provides the random column added on the right of the $(n - w + s)$-th column during the construction process of G (see Sect. 3.1, Step 3). From (4), we see that we may obtain more GRS positions: indeed $v_i = a_s y_j f(x_j)$ if $c_s = 0$ or $v_{\tau(i)} = b_s y_j f(x_j)$ if $d_s = 0$. On the other hand if $c_s d_s \neq 0$ the twin pairs are *correlated* in the sense that they behave in a non-trivial way after shortening: Lemma 3 shows that if one shortens the code in such a position its twin becomes a GRS position. We therefore call such a twin pair a *pseudo-random* twin pair and the set of pseudo-random twin pairs forms what we call the set of *pseudo-random* positions.

Definition 7. *The set of* pseudo-random positions *(PR in short), denoted* $\mathcal{I}_{PR}$, *is given by*

$$\mathcal{I}_{PR} \overset{def}{=} \bigcup_{s \in [\![1,w]\!] \ s.t. \ c_s d_s \neq 0} \{\pi(n - w + 2s - 1), \pi(n - w + 2s)\}. \tag{6}$$

Under Assumption 5, this becomes:

$$\mathcal{I}_{PR} = \bigcup_{s \in [\![1,w]\!] \ s.t. \ c_s d_s \neq 0} \{n - w + 2s - 1, n - w + 2s\}. \tag{7}$$

If $c_s d_s = 0$, then a twin pair splits into a GRS position of the second kind and a random position. The GRS position of the second kind is $\pi(n - w + 2s - 1)$ if $c_s = 0$ or $\pi(n - w + 2s)$ if $d_s = 0$ (c_s and d_s can not both be equal to 0 since A_s is invertible).

Definition 8. *The set* GRS *positions of the second kind, denoted* $\mathcal{I}^2_{GRS}$, *is defined as*

$$\mathcal{I}^2_{GRS} \stackrel{def}{=} \{\pi(n - w + 2s - 1) \,|\, c_s = 0\} \cup \{\pi(n - w + 2s) \,|\, d_s = 0\}. \tag{8}$$

Under Assumption 5, this becomes:

$$\mathcal{I}^2_{GRS} = \{n - w + 2s - 1 \,|\, c_s = 0\} \cup \{n - w + 2s \,|\, d_s = 0\}. \tag{9}$$

Definition 9. *The set of* random positions, *denoted* $\mathcal{I}_R$, *is defined as*

$$\mathcal{I}_R \stackrel{def}{=} \{\pi(n - w + 2s - 1) \,|\, d_s = 0\} \cup \{\pi(n - w + 2s) \,|\, c_s = 0\}. \tag{10}$$

Under Assumption 5, this becomes:

$$\mathcal{I}_R = \{n - w + 2s - 1 \,|\, d_s = 0\} \cup \{n - w + 2s \,|\, c_s = 0\}. \tag{11}$$

We also define the *GRS positions* to be the GRS positions of the first or the second kind.

Definition 10. *The set of* GRS *positions, denoted* $\mathcal{I}_{GRS}$, *is defined as*

$$\mathcal{I}_{GRS} \stackrel{def}{=} \mathcal{I}^1_{GRS} \cup \mathcal{I}^2_{GRS}. \tag{12}$$

We finish this subsection with a lemma.

Lemma 2. $|\mathcal{I}^2_{GRS}| = |\mathcal{I}_R|$ *and* $|\mathcal{I}_{PR}| = 2(w - |\mathcal{I}_R|)$.

Proof. Using (7), (9) and (11) we see that, under Assumption 5,

$$[\![n - w + 1, n + w]\!] = \mathcal{I}_{PR} \cup \mathcal{I}^2_{GRS} \cup \mathcal{I}_R \tag{13}$$

and the above union is disjoint. Next, there is a one-to-one correspondence relating $\mathcal{I}^2_{GRS}$ and $\mathcal{I}_R$. Indeed, still under Assumption 5, if $c_s = 0$ for some $s \in [\![1, w]\!]$, then $n - w + 2s - 1 \in \mathcal{I}^2_{GRS}$ and $n - w + 2s \in \mathcal{I}_R$ and conversely if $d_s = 0$. This proves that $|\mathcal{I}^2_{GRS}| = |\mathcal{I}_R|$, which, together with (13) yields the result.   □

4.2   Intermediate Results

Before proceeding to the proof of Theorem 4, let us state and prove some intermediate results. We will start by Lemmas 3 and 4, that will be useful to prove Proposition 4 on the structure of shortened RLCE codes, by induction on the number of shortened positions. This proposition will be the core of the proof of Theorem 4. Then, we will prove a general result on modified GRS codes with additional random columns.

Two Useful Lemmas. The first lemma explains that, after shortening a PR position, its twin will behave like a GRS position. This is actually a crucial lemma that explains why PR columns in G do not really behave like random columns after shortening the code at the corresponding position.

Lemma 3. *Let i be a PR position and $\mathcal{L}$ a set of positions that neither contains i nor $\tau(i)$. Let $\mathscr{C}' \overset{def}{=} \mathcal{S}_{\mathcal{L}}(\mathscr{C})$. The position $\tau(i)$ behaves like a GRS position in the code $\mathcal{S}_{\{i\}}(\mathscr{C}')$. That is, the $\tau(i)$-th column of a generator matrix of $\mathcal{S}_{\{i\}}(\mathscr{C}')$ has entries of the form*

$$\tilde{y}_j f(x_j)$$

for some j in $[\![n - w + 1, n]\!]$ and $\tilde{y}_j$ in $\mathbb{F}_q$.

Proof. Let us assume that $i = n - w + 2s - 1$ for some $s \in \{1, \ldots, w\}$. The case $i = n - w + 2s$ can be proved in a similar way. At position i, for any $c \in \mathscr{C}'$, from (4), we have

$$c_i = ay_j f(x_j) + c\psi_s(f),$$

where $j = n - w + s$. By shortening, we restrict our space of polynomials to the subspace of polynomials in $\mathbb{F}_q[x]_{<k}$ satisfying $c_i = 0$. Since i is a PR position, $c \neq 0$ and therefore

$$\psi_s(f) = -c^{-1}ay_j f(x_j).$$

Therefore, at the twin position $\tau(i) = n - w + 2s$ and for any $c \in \mathcal{S}_{\{i\}}(\mathscr{C}')$, we have

$$c_{\tau(i)} = by_j f(x_j) + d\psi_j(f)$$
$$= y_j(b - dac^{-1})f(x_j).$$

$\square$

Remark 3. This lemma does not hold for a random position, since the proof requires that $c \neq 0$. It is precisely because of this that we have to make a distinction between twin pairs, *i.e.* pairs for which the associated matrix A_s is such that $c_s d_s \neq 0$ and pairs for which it is not the case.

This lemma allows us to get some insight on the structure of the shortened code $\mathcal{S}_{\mathcal{L}}(\mathscr{C})$. Before giving the relevant statement let us first recall the following result.

Lemma 4. *Consider a linear code $\mathscr{A}$ over $\mathbb{F}_q$ whose restriction to a subset $\mathcal{L}$ is a subcode of a k-dimensional GRS code. Let i be an element of $\mathcal{L}$. Then the restriction of $\mathcal{S}_{\{i\}}(\mathscr{A})$ to $\mathcal{L} \setminus \{i\}$ is a subcode of a $(k-1)$-dimensional GRS code.*

Proof. By definition, the restriction $\mathscr{A}'$ to $\mathcal{L}$ is a code of the form

$$\mathscr{A}' \overset{def}{=} \left\{ (y_j f(x_j))_{j \in \mathcal{L}} : f \in L \right\},$$

where the y_j's are nonzero elements of $\mathbb{F}_q$, the x_j's are distinct elements of $\mathbb{F}_q$ and L is a subspace of $\mathbb{F}_q[X]_{<k}$. Clearly the restriction $\mathscr{A}''$ of $S_{\{i\}}(\mathscr{A})$ to $\mathcal{L}\setminus\{i\}$ can be written as

$$\mathscr{A}'' = \left\{(y_j f(x_j))_{j\in\mathcal{L}\setminus\{i\}} : f \in L, f(x_i) = 0\right\}.$$

The polynomials $f(X)$ in L such that $f(x_i) = 0$ can be written as $f(X) = (X - x_i)g(X)$ where $\deg g = \deg f - 1$ and g ranges in this case over a subspace L' of polynomials of degree $< k - 1$. We can therefore write

$$\mathscr{A}'' = \left\{(y_j(x_j - x_i)g(x_j))_{j\in\mathcal{L}\setminus\{i\}} : g \in L'\right\}.$$

This implies our lemma. $\square$

The Key Proposition. Using Lemmas 3 and 4, we can prove the following result by induction. This result is the key proposition for proving Theorem 4.

Proposition 4. *Let $\mathcal{L}$ be a subset of $[\![1, n + w]\!]$ and let $\mathcal{L}_0, \mathcal{L}_1, \mathcal{L}_2$ be subsets of $\mathcal{L}$ defined as*

– $\mathcal{L}_0$ the set of GRS positions (see (2), (8) and (12) for a definition) of $\mathcal{L}$:

$$\mathcal{L}_0 \stackrel{def}{=} \mathcal{L} \cap \mathcal{I}_{\mathrm{GRS}};$$

– $\mathcal{L}_1$ the set of PR positions (see (6)) of $\mathcal{L}$ that do not have their twin in $\mathcal{L}$:

$$\mathcal{L}_1 \stackrel{def}{=} \{i \in \mathcal{L} \cap \mathcal{I}_{\mathrm{PR}} \mid \tau(i) \notin \mathcal{L}\};$$

– $\mathcal{L}_2$ the set of PR positions of $\mathcal{L}$ whose twin position is also included in $\mathcal{L}$:

$$\mathcal{L}_2 \stackrel{def}{=} \{i \in \mathcal{L} \cap \mathcal{I}_{\mathrm{PR}} \mid \tau(i) \in \mathcal{L}\}.$$

Let $\mathscr{C}'$ be the restriction of $S_{\mathcal{L}}(\mathscr{C})$ to $(\mathcal{I}_{\mathrm{GRS}} \setminus \mathcal{L}_0) \cup \tau(\mathcal{L}_1)$. Then, $\mathscr{C}'$ is a subcode of a GRS code of length $|\mathcal{I}_{\mathrm{GRS}}| - |\mathcal{L}_0| + |\mathcal{L}_1|$ and dimension $k - |\mathcal{L}_0| - \frac{|\mathcal{L}_2|}{2}$.

Proof. Let us prove by induction on $\ell = |\mathcal{L}|$ that $\mathscr{C}'$ is a subcode of a GRS code of length $|\mathcal{I}_{\mathrm{GRS}}| - |\mathcal{L}_0| + |\mathcal{L}_1|$ and dimension $k - |\mathcal{L}_0| - \frac{|\mathcal{L}_2|}{2}$.

This statement is clearly true if $\ell = 0$, *i.e.* if $\mathcal{L}$ is the empty set. Assume that the result is true for all $\mathcal{L}$ up to some size $\ell \geqslant 0$. Consider now a set $\mathcal{L}$ of size $\ell + 1$. We can write $\mathcal{L} = \mathcal{L}' \cup \{i\}$ where $\mathcal{L}'$ is of size ℓ.

Let $\mathcal{L}_0, \mathcal{L}_1, \mathcal{L}_2$ be subsets of $\mathcal{L}$ as defined in the statement and $\mathcal{L}'_0, \mathcal{L}'_1, \mathcal{L}'_2$ be the subsets of $\mathcal{L}'$ obtained by replacing in the statement $\mathcal{L}$ by $\mathcal{L}'$. There are now several cases to consider for i.

Case 1: $i \in \mathcal{L}_0$. In this case, $\mathcal{L}_0 = \mathcal{L}'_0 \cup \{i\}$, $\mathcal{L}_1 = \mathcal{L}'_1$ and $\mathcal{L}_2 = \mathcal{L}'_2$.
We can apply Lemma 4 with $\mathscr{A} = S_{\mathcal{L}'}(\mathscr{C})$ because by the induction hypothesis, its restriction to $\mathcal{L}'' \stackrel{def}{=} (\mathcal{I}_{\mathrm{GRS}} \setminus \mathcal{L}'_0) \cup \tau(\mathcal{L}'_1)$ is a subcode of a GRS code of length $|\mathcal{I}_{\mathrm{GRS}}| - |\mathcal{L}'_0| + |\mathcal{L}'_1|$ and dimension $k - |\mathcal{L}'_0| - \frac{|\mathcal{L}'_2|}{2}$.
Therefore the restriction of the shortened code $S_{\mathcal{L}}(\mathscr{C}) = S_{\{i\}}(\mathscr{A})$ to $\mathcal{L}'' \setminus \{i\} = (\mathcal{I}_{\mathrm{GRS}} \setminus \mathcal{L}_0) \cup \tau(\mathcal{L}_1)$ is a subcode of a GRS code of length $|\mathcal{I}_{\mathrm{GRS}}| - |\mathcal{L}_0| + |\mathcal{L}_1|$ and dimension $k - |\mathcal{L}'_0| - \frac{|\mathcal{L}'_2|}{2} - 1 = k - |\mathcal{L}_0| - \frac{|\mathcal{L}_2|}{2}$.

Case 2: $i \in \mathcal{L}_1$. In this case, $\mathcal{L}_0 = \mathcal{L}'_0, \mathcal{L}_1 = \mathcal{L}'_1 \cup \{i\}$ and $\mathcal{L}_2 = \mathcal{L}'_2$. This implies that $\mathcal{L}'$ does not contain i nor $\tau(i)$.

We can therefore apply Lemma 3 with $\mathscr{C}' = \mathcal{S}_{\mathcal{L}'}(\mathscr{C})$. Lemma 3 states that the position $\tau(i)$ behaves like a GRS position in $\mathcal{S}_{\{i\}}(\mathscr{C}') = \mathcal{S}_{\mathcal{L}}(\mathscr{C})$. By induction hypothesis, the restriction of the code $\mathscr{C}'$ to $(\mathcal{I}_{\mathrm{GRS}} \setminus \mathcal{L}'_0) \cup \tau(\mathcal{L}'_1)$ is a subcode of a GRS code of length $|\mathcal{I}_{\mathrm{GRS}}| - |\mathcal{L}'_0| + |\mathcal{L}'_1|$ and dimension $k - |\mathcal{L}'_0| - \frac{|\mathcal{L}'_2|}{2} = k - |\mathcal{L}_0| - \frac{|\mathcal{L}_2|}{2}$.

Therefore the restriction of $\mathcal{S}_{\{i\}}(\mathscr{C}') = \mathcal{S}_{\mathcal{L}}(\mathscr{C})$ to $(\mathcal{I}_{\mathrm{GRS}} \setminus \mathcal{L}_0) \cup \tau(\mathcal{L}_1) = (\mathcal{I}_{\mathrm{GRS}} \setminus \mathcal{L}'_0) \cup \tau(\mathcal{L}'_1) \cup \{\tau(i)\}$ is a subcode of a GRS code of dimension $k - |\mathcal{L}_0| - \frac{|\mathcal{L}_2|}{2}$ and length $|\mathcal{I}_{\mathrm{GRS}}| - |\mathcal{L}'_0| + |\mathcal{L}'_1| + 1 = |\mathcal{I}_{\mathrm{GRS}}| - |\mathcal{L}_0| + |\mathcal{L}_1|$.

Case 3: $i \in \mathcal{L}_2$. In this case, $\mathcal{L}_0 = \mathcal{L}'_0, \mathcal{L}_1 = \mathcal{L}'_1 \setminus \{\tau(i)\}$ and $\mathcal{L}_2 = \mathcal{L}'_2 \cup \{i, \tau(i)\}$. In fact, this case can only happen if $\ell \geqslant 1$ and we will rather consider the induction with respect to the set $\mathcal{L}'' = \mathcal{L} \setminus \{i, \tau(i)\}$ of size $\ell - 1$ and the sets $\mathcal{L}''_0, \mathcal{L}''_1, \mathcal{L}''_2$ such that $\mathcal{L}''_0 = \mathcal{L}_0, \mathcal{L}''_1 = \mathcal{L}_1, \mathcal{L}''_2 = \mathcal{L}_2 \setminus \{i, \tau(i)\}$.

By induction hypothesis on $\mathcal{L}''$, the restriction of $\mathscr{C}'' \overset{\mathrm{def}}{=} \mathcal{S}_{\mathcal{L}''}(\mathscr{C})$ to $(\mathcal{I}_{\mathrm{GRS}} \setminus \mathcal{L}''_0) \cup \tau(\mathcal{L}''_1)$ is a subcode of a GRS code of length $|\mathcal{I}_{\mathrm{GRS}}| - |\mathcal{L}''_0| + |\mathcal{L}''_1| = |\mathcal{I}_{\mathrm{GRS}}| - |\mathcal{L}_0| + |\mathcal{L}_1|$ and dimension $k - |\mathcal{L}''_0| - \frac{|\mathcal{L}''_2|}{2} = k - |\mathcal{L}_0| - \frac{|\mathcal{L}_2|}{2} + 1$.

Following Assumption 5, we can write without loss of generality that $i = n - w + 2s - 1$ for some $s \in \{1, \ldots, w\}$. The case $i = n - w + 2s$ can be proved in a similar way.

Denote $A_s = \begin{pmatrix} a & b \\ c & d \end{pmatrix}$ the non-singular matrix and $j = n - w + s$. For any $c \in \mathscr{C}'$, at positions i and $\tau(i)$ we have

$$c_i = a y_j f(x_j) + c \psi_s(f),$$
$$c_{\tau(i)} = b y_j f(x_j) + d \psi_s(f).$$

Shortening $\mathscr{C}''$ at $\{i, \tau(i)\}$ has the effect of requiring to consider only the polynomials f for which $f(x_j) = \psi_s(f) = 0$. Therefore the restriction of $\mathcal{S}_{\{i, \tau(i)\}}(\mathscr{C}'') = \mathcal{S}_{\mathcal{L}}(\mathscr{C})$ at $(\mathcal{I}_{\mathrm{GRS}} \setminus \mathcal{L}''_0) \cup \tau(\mathcal{L}''_1)$ is a subcode of a GRS code of length $|\mathcal{I}_{\mathrm{GRS}}| - |\mathcal{L}_0| + |\mathcal{L}_1|$ and dimension $k - |\mathcal{L}_0| - \frac{|\mathcal{L}_2|}{2} + 1 - 1 = k - |\mathcal{L}_0| - \frac{|\mathcal{L}_2|}{2}$.

Case 4: $i \in \mathcal{I}_{\mathrm{R}}$. In this case $\mathcal{L}_0 = \mathcal{L}'_0, \mathcal{L}_1 = \mathcal{L}'_1$ and $\mathcal{L}_2 = \mathcal{L}'_2$. Using the induction hypothesis yields directly that $\mathscr{A} = \mathcal{S}_{\mathcal{L}'}(\mathscr{C})$ is a subcode of a GRS code of length $|\mathcal{I}_{\mathrm{GRS}}| - |\mathcal{L}'_0| + |\mathcal{L}'_1| = |\mathcal{I}_{\mathrm{GRS}}| - |\mathcal{L}_0| + |\mathcal{L}_1|$ and dimension $k - |\mathcal{L}'_0| - \frac{|\mathcal{L}'_2|}{2} = k - |\mathcal{L}_0| - \frac{|\mathcal{L}_2|}{2}$. This is also clearly the case for $\mathcal{S}_{\mathcal{L}}(\mathscr{C}) = \mathcal{S}_{\{i\}}(\mathscr{A})$.

This proves that the induction hypothesis also holds for $|\mathcal{L}| = \ell + 1$ and finishes the proof of the proposition. □

A General Result on Modified GRS Codes. Finally, we need a very general result concerning modified GRS codes where some arbitrary columns have been joined to the generator matrix. A very similar lemma is already proved in [8, Lemma 9]. Its proof is repeated below for convenience and in order to provide further details about the equality case.

Lemma 5. *Consider a linear code $\mathscr{A}$ over $\mathbb{F}_q$ with generator matrix of the form $G = (G_{\text{SCGRS}} \ G_{\text{rand}}) P$ of size $k \times (n + r)$ where G_{SCGRS} is a $k \times n$ generator matrix of a subcode of a GRS code of dimension k_{GRS} over $\mathbb{F}_q$, G_{rand} is an arbitrary matrix in $\mathbb{F}_q^{k \times r}$ and P is the permutation matrix of an arbitrary permutation $\sigma \in \mathfrak{S}_{n+r}$. We have*

$$\dim \mathscr{A}^{\star 2} \leqslant 2k_{\text{GRS}} - 1 + r.$$

Moreover, if the equality holds, then for every $i \in [\![n + 1, n + w]\!]$ we have:

$$\dim \mathcal{P}_{\{\sigma(i)\}} \left(\mathscr{A}^{\wedge 2} \right) = \dim \mathscr{A}^{\wedge 2} - 1.$$

Proof. Without loss of generality, we may assume that P is the identity matrix since the dimension of the square code is invariant by permuting the code positions (see Lemma 1). Let $\mathscr{B}$ be the code with generator matrix $(G_{\text{SCGRS}} \ \mathbf{0}_{k \times r})$, where $\mathbf{0}_{k \times r}$ is the zero matrix of size $k \times r$. We also define the code $\mathscr{B}'$ generated by the generator matrix $(\mathbf{0}_{k \times n} \ G_{\text{rand}})$. We obviously have

$$\mathscr{A} \subseteq \mathscr{B} + \mathscr{B}'.$$

Therefore

$$\begin{aligned}
(\mathscr{A})^{\star 2} &\subseteq (\mathscr{B} + \mathscr{B}')^{\star 2} \\
&\subseteq \mathscr{B}^{\star 2} + (\mathscr{B}')^{\star 2} + \mathscr{B} \star \mathscr{B}' \\
&\subseteq \mathscr{B}^{\star 2} + (\mathscr{B}')^{\star 2},
\end{aligned}$$

where the last inclusion comes from the fact that $\mathscr{B} \star \mathscr{B}'$ is the zero subspace since $\mathscr{B}$ and $\mathscr{B}'$ have disjoint supports. The code $\mathscr{B}^{\star 2}$ has dimension $\leqslant 2k_{\text{GRS}} - 1$ whereas $\dim (\mathscr{B}')^{\star 2} \leqslant r$.

Next, if $\dim \mathscr{A}^{\star 2} = 2k_{\text{GRS}} - 1 + r$, then

$$\mathscr{A}^{\star 2} = \mathscr{B}^{\star 2} \oplus (\mathscr{B}')^{\star 2} \quad \text{and} \quad \dim(\mathscr{B}')^{\star 2} = r.$$

Since $\mathscr{B}'$ has length r, this means that $(\mathscr{B}')^{\star 2} = \mathbb{F}_q^r$ and hence, any word of weight 1 supported by the r rightmost positions is contained in $\mathscr{A}^{\star 2}$. Therefore, puncturing this position will decrease the dimension. $\qquad \square$

4.3   Proof of Theorem 4

Proof. By using Proposition 4, we know that the restriction of $\mathcal{S}_{\mathcal{L}}(\mathscr{C})$ to $(\mathcal{I}_{\text{GRS}} \setminus \mathcal{L}_0) \cup \tau(\mathcal{L}_1)$ is a subcode of a GRS code of length $|\mathcal{I}_{\text{GRS}}| - |\mathcal{L}_0| + |\mathcal{L}_1| = n - w + |\mathcal{I}_{\text{GRS}}^2| - |\mathcal{L}_0| + |\mathcal{L}_1|$ and dimension $k_{\text{GRS}} \stackrel{\text{def}}{=} k - |\mathcal{L}_0| - \frac{|\mathcal{L}_2|}{2}$, where:

- $\mathcal{L}_0 \stackrel{\text{def}}{=} \mathcal{I}_{\text{GRS}} \cap \mathcal{L}$;
- $\mathcal{L}_1$ is the set of PR positions of $\mathcal{L}$ that do not have their twin in $\mathcal{L}$;
- $\mathcal{L}_2$ is the union of all twin PR positions that are both included in $\mathcal{L}$.

We also denote by $\mathcal{L}_3$ the set $\mathcal{I}_R \cap \mathcal{L}$. We can then apply Lemma 5 to $\mathcal{S}_\mathcal{L}(\mathscr{C})$ and derive from it the following upper bound:

$$\dim\left(\mathcal{S}_\mathcal{L}(\mathscr{C})\right)^{\star 2} \leqslant 2k_{\mathrm{GRS}} - 1 + |\mathcal{I}_{\mathrm{PR}} \setminus (\mathcal{L} \cup \tau(\mathcal{L}_1))| + |\mathcal{I}_R \setminus \mathcal{L}_3|. \tag{14}$$

Next, using Lemma 2, we get

$$\dim\left(\mathcal{S}_\mathcal{L}(\mathscr{C})\right)^{\star 2}$$

$$\leqslant 2\left(k - |\mathcal{L}_0| - \frac{|\mathcal{L}_2|}{2}\right) - 1 + 2\left(w - |\mathcal{I}_R|\right) - 2|\mathcal{L}_1| - |\mathcal{L}_2| + |\mathcal{I}_R| - |\mathcal{L}_3|$$

$$\leqslant 2\left(k + w - |\mathcal{L}_0| - |\mathcal{L}_1| - |\mathcal{L}_2| - |\mathcal{L}_3|\right) - 1 + (|\mathcal{L}_3| - |\mathcal{I}_R|) \tag{15}$$

$$\leqslant 2\left(k + w - |\mathcal{L}|\right) - 1. \tag{16}$$

The other upper bound on $\dim\left(\mathcal{S}_\mathcal{L}(\mathscr{C})\right)^{\star 2}$ which is $\dim\left(\mathcal{S}_\mathcal{L}(\mathscr{C})\right)^{\star 2} \leqslant n + w - |\mathcal{L}|$ follows from the fact that the dimension of this code is bounded by its length. Putting both bounds together yields the theorem. □

Remark 4. We ran the following simulations using ID 1 parameters (see Table 1): for three hundred random independent public keys, we computed $\dim\left(\mathcal{S}_\mathcal{L}(\mathscr{C})\right)^{\star 2}$ for $|\mathcal{L}|$ ranging over $[\![\ell_{\min}, \ell_{\max}]\!]$, as defined in (21). For more than 99% of the cases, inequality (14) is an equality. In particular, this means that the inequality of Theorem 4 is almost always an equality whenever $\mathcal{I}_R$ is the empty set, *i.e.* when we are not in the degenerate case defined in Sect. 6.7.

5   Reaching the Range of the Distinguisher

For this distinguisher to work we need to shorten the code enough so that its square does not fill in the ambient space, but not too much since the square of the shortened code should have a dimension strictly less than the typical dimension of the square of a random code given by Proposition 1. Namely, we need to have:

$$\dim\left(\mathcal{S}_\mathcal{L}(\mathscr{C})\right)^{\star 2} < \binom{k + 1 - |\mathcal{L}|}{2} \quad \text{and} \quad \dim\left(\mathcal{S}_\mathcal{L}(\mathscr{C})\right)^{\star 2} < n + w - |\mathcal{L}|. \tag{17}$$

Thanks to Theorem 4, we know that (17) is satisfied as soon as

$$2(k + w - |\mathcal{L}|) - 1 < \binom{k + 1 - |\mathcal{L}|}{2} \quad \text{and} \quad 2(k + w - |\mathcal{L}|) - 1 < n + w - |\mathcal{L}|. \tag{18}$$

We will now find the values $|\mathcal{L}|$ for which the inequalities of (18) are satisfied.

First Inequality. In order to determine when the first inequality of (18) is verified, let us denote

$$k' \overset{\text{def}}{=} k - |\mathcal{L}|.$$

Inequality (18) becomes $4k' - 2 + 4w < k'^2 + k'$, or equivalently $k'^2 - 3k' - 4w + 2 > 0$, which after a resolution leads to $k' > \frac{3 + \sqrt{16w + 1}}{2}$.

Hence, we have:

$$|\mathcal{L}| < k - \frac{3 + \sqrt{16w + 1}}{2}. \tag{19}$$

Second Inequality. The second inequality of (18) is equivalent to

$$|\mathcal{L}| \geqslant w + 2k - n. \tag{20}$$

Conditions to Verify Both Inequalities. Putting inequalities (19) and (20) together gives that $|\mathcal{L}|$ should satisfy

$$w + 2k - n \leqslant |\mathcal{L}| < k - \frac{3 + \sqrt{16w + 1}}{2}.$$

We can therefore find an appropriate $\mathcal{L}$ if and only if

$$w + 2k - n < k - \frac{3 + \sqrt{16w + 1}}{2},$$

which is equivalent to

$$n - k > w + \frac{3 + \sqrt{16w + 1}}{2} = w + O(\sqrt{w}).$$

In other words, the distinguisher works up to values of w that are close to the second choice $n - k = w$. From now on, we set

$$\ell_{\min} \stackrel{\text{def}}{=} w + 2k - n \qquad \text{and} \qquad \ell_{\max} \stackrel{\text{def}}{=} \left\lceil k - \frac{3 + \sqrt{16w + 1}}{2} - 1 \right\rceil. \tag{21}$$

Practical Results. We have run experiments using MAGMA [5] and SAGE. For the parameters of Table 1, here are the intervals of possible values of $|\mathcal{L}|$ so that the code $\mathcal{S}_{\mathcal{L}}(\mathscr{C})^{*2}$ has a non generic dimension:

- ID 1: $n = 532, k = 376, w = 96, |\mathcal{L}| \in [\![316, 354]\!]$;
- ID 3: $n = 846, k = 618, w = 144, |\mathcal{L}| \in [\![534, 592]\!]$;
- ID 5: $n = 1160, k = 700, w = 311, |\mathcal{L}| \in [\![551, 663]\!]$.

The interval always coincides with the theoretical interval $[\![\ell_{\min}, \ell_{\max}]\!]$.

6 The Attack

In this section we will show how to find an equivalent private key $(\boldsymbol{x}, \boldsymbol{y}, \boldsymbol{A}, \boldsymbol{P})$ defining the same code.

We assume that all the matrices $\boldsymbol{A}_s = \begin{pmatrix} a_s & b_s \\ c_s & d_s \end{pmatrix}$ appearing in the definition of the scheme in Subsect. 3.1 are such that $c_s d_s \neq 0$. We explain in Sect. 6.7 how to deal with the special case $c_s d_s = 0$. Note that this corresponds to a case where $\mathcal{I}_R = \emptyset$ and $\mathcal{I}_{GRS}^2 = \emptyset$.

Remark 5. In the present section where we the goal is to recover the permutation, we no longer work under Assumption 5.

6.1 Outline of the Attack

In summary, the attack works as follows.

1. Compute the interval $[\![\ell_{\min}, \ell_{\max}]\!]$ of the distinguisher and choose ℓ in the middle of the distinguisher interval. Ensure $\ell < \ell_{\max}$.
2. For several sets of indices $\mathcal{L} \subseteq [\![1, n + w]\!]$ such that $|\mathcal{L}| = \ell$, compute $\mathcal{S}_\mathcal{L}(\mathscr{C})$ and identify pairs of twin positions contained in $[\![1, n+w]\!]$. Repeat this process until identifying all pairs of twin positions, as detailed in Sect. 6.2.
3. Puncture the twin positions in order to get a GRS code and recover its structure using the Sidelnikov Shestakov attack [15].
4. For each pair of twin positions, recover the corresponding 2×2 non-singular matrix A_i, as explained in Sect. 6.6.
5. Finish to recover the structure of the underlying GRS code.

6.2 Identifying Pairs of Twin Positions

Let $\mathcal{L} \subseteq [\![1, n + w]\!]$ be such that both $|\mathcal{L}|$ and $|\mathcal{L}| + 1$ are contained in the distinguisher interval. We compare the dimension of $(\mathcal{S}_\mathcal{L}(\mathscr{C}))^{*2}$ with the dimension of $\left(\mathcal{P}_{\{i\}}(\mathcal{S}_\mathcal{L}(\mathscr{C}))\right)^{*2}$ for all positions i in $[\![1, n + w]\!] \setminus \mathcal{L}$.

- If $i \in \mathcal{I}_{\mathrm{GRS}}$ (see (2), (8) and (12) for the definition), puncturing does not affect the dimension of the square code:

$$\dim (\mathcal{S}_\mathcal{L}(\mathscr{C}))^{*2} = \dim \left(\mathcal{P}_{\{i\}}(\mathcal{S}_\mathcal{L}(\mathscr{C}))\right)^{*2}.$$

- If $i \in \mathcal{I}_{\mathrm{PR}}$ (see (6) for a definition) and $\tau(i) \in \mathcal{L}$, then according to Lemma 3, the position i is "derandomised" in $\mathcal{S}_\mathcal{L}(\mathscr{C})$ and hence behaves like a GRS position in the shortened code. Therefore, very similarly to the previous case, the dimension does not change.
- If $i \in \mathcal{I}_{\mathrm{PR}}$ and $\tau(i) \notin \mathcal{L}$, in $\mathcal{S}_\mathcal{L}(\mathscr{C})$, the two corresponding columns behave like random ones. Assuming that the inequality of Theorem 4 is an equality, which almost always holds when no pair of twin positions is degenerate (see Sect. 6.7 and Remark 4), then, according to Lemma 5, puncturing $\mathcal{S}_\mathcal{L}(\mathscr{C})^{*2}$ at i (resp. $\tau(i)$) reduces its dimension. Therefore,

$$\dim \left(\mathcal{P}_{\{i\}}(\mathcal{S}_\mathcal{L}(\mathscr{C}))\right)^{*2} = \dim \left(\mathcal{P}_{\{\tau(i)\}}(\mathcal{S}_\mathcal{L}(\mathscr{C}))\right)^{*2} = \dim (\mathcal{S}_\mathcal{L}(\mathscr{C}))^{*2} - 1.$$

If some pair of twin positions is degenerate, the non-degenerate ones can be identified in the same way.

This provides a way to identify any position in $[\![1, n + w]\!] \setminus \mathcal{L}$ having a twin which also lies in $[\![1, n + w]\!] \setminus \mathcal{L}$: by searching zero columns in a parity-check matrix of $\mathcal{S}_\mathcal{L}(\mathscr{C})^{*2}$, we obtain the set $\mathcal{T}_\mathcal{L} \subset [\![1, n + w]\!] \setminus \mathcal{L}$ of even cardinality of all the positions having their twin in $[\![1, n + w]\!] \setminus \mathcal{L}$:

$$\mathcal{T}_\mathcal{L} \stackrel{\text{def}}{=} \bigcup_{\{i, \tau(i)\} \subseteq [\![1, n+w]\!] \setminus \mathcal{L}} \{i, \tau(i)\}.$$

Once these positions are identified, we can associate each such position to its twin. This can be done as follows. Take $i \in \mathcal{I}_\mathcal{L}$ and consider the code $\mathcal{S}_{\mathcal{L} \cup \{i\}}(\mathscr{C})$. The column corresponding to the twin position $\tau(i)$ has been derandomised and hence will not give a zero column in a parity-check matrix of $(\mathcal{S}_{\mathcal{L} \cup \{i\}}(\mathscr{C}))^{\star 2}$, so puncturing the corresponding column will not affect the dimension.

This process can be iterated by using various shortening sets $\mathcal{L}$ until obtaining w pairs of twin positions. It is readily seen that considering $O(1)$ such sets is enough to recover all pairs with very large probability.

6.3   Recovering the Remainder of the Code

As soon as all the pairs of twin positions are identified, consider the code $\mathcal{P}_{\mathcal{I}_\mathrm{PR}}(\mathscr{C})$ punctured at $\mathcal{I}_\mathrm{PR}$. Since the randomised positions have been punctured this code is nothing but a GRS code and, applying the Sidelnikov Shestakov attack [15], we recover a pair $\boldsymbol{a}, \boldsymbol{b}$ such that $\mathcal{P}_{\mathcal{I}_\mathrm{PR}}(\mathscr{C}) = \mathbf{GRS}_k(\boldsymbol{a}, \boldsymbol{b})$.

6.4   Joining a Pair of Twin Positions : The Code $\mathscr{C}^{(i)}$

To recover the remaining part of the code we will consider iteratively the pairs of twin positions. We recall that $\mathcal{I}_\mathrm{PR}$ corresponds to the set of positions having a twin. Let $\{i, \tau(i)\}$ be a pair of twin positions and consider the code

$$\mathscr{C}^{(i)} \stackrel{\text{def}}{=} \mathcal{P}_{[\![1,n]\!] \setminus (\mathcal{I}_\mathrm{GRS} \cup \{i, \tau(i)\})}(\mathscr{C}).$$

In this code, any position is GRS but positions i and $\tau(i)$. Hence, for any codeword $\boldsymbol{c} \in \mathscr{C}^{(i)}$ we have:

$$\begin{aligned} c_i &= a y_j f(x_j) + c \psi_j(f) \\ c_{\tau(i)} &= b y_j f(x_j) + d \psi_j(f) \end{aligned} \qquad (22)$$

for some integer $j \in [\![n - w + 1, n]\!]$, where ψ_j and $\boldsymbol{A} = \begin{pmatrix} a & b \\ c & d \end{pmatrix}$ are defined as in (4) and (5).

Note that we do not need to recover exactly $(\boldsymbol{x}, \boldsymbol{y}, \boldsymbol{A}, \boldsymbol{P})$. We need to recover a 4-tuple $(\boldsymbol{x}', \boldsymbol{y}', \boldsymbol{A}', \boldsymbol{P}')$ which describes the same code. Thus, without loss of generality, after possibly replacing a by $a y_j$ and b by $b y_j$, one can suppose that $y_j = 1$. Moreover, after possibly replacing ψ_j by $d \psi_j$, one can suppose that $d = 1$. Recall that in this section we suppose that $cd \neq 0$.

Thanks to these simplifying choices, (22) becomes

$$\begin{aligned} c_i &= a f(x_j) + c \psi_j(f) \\ c_{\tau(i)} &= b f(x_j) + \psi_j(f). \end{aligned}$$

6.5   Shortening $\mathscr{C}^{(i)}$ at the Last Position to Recover x_j

If we shorten $\mathscr{C}^{(i)}$ at the $\tau(i)$-th position, according to Lemma 3, it will "derandomise" the i-th position (it implies $\psi_j(f) = -bf(x_j)$) and any $c \in \mathcal{S}_{\{\tau(i)\}}\left(\mathscr{C}^{(i)}\right)$ verifies

$$c_i = (a - bc)f(x_j).$$

Since the support x_j and multiplier y_j are known at all the positions of $\mathscr{C}^{(i)}$ but the two PR ones, for any codeword $c \in \mathcal{S}_{\{\tau(i)\}}\left(\mathscr{C}^{(i)}\right)$, one can find the polynomial $f \in \mathbb{F}_q[x]_{<k}$ whose evaluation provides c. Therefore, by collecting a basis of codewords in $\mathcal{S}_{\{\tau(i)\}}\left(\mathscr{C}^{(i)}\right)$ and the corresponding polynomials, we can recover the values of x_j and $a - bc$.

6.6   Recovering the 2×2 Matrix

Once we have x_j we need to recover the matrix

$$A = \begin{pmatrix} a & b \\ c & 1 \end{pmatrix}.$$

Note that, its determinant $\det A = a - bc$ has already been obtained in the previous section. First, one can guess b as follows. Let $G^{(i)}$ be a generator matrix of $\mathscr{C}^{(i)}$. As in the previous section, by interpolation, one can compute the polynomials $f_1, \ldots, f_k$ whose evaluations provide the rows of $G^{(i)}$. Consider the column vector

$$v \stackrel{\text{def}}{=} \begin{pmatrix} f_1(x_j) \\ \vdots \\ f_k(x_j) \end{pmatrix}$$

and denote by v_i and $v_{\tau(i)}$ the columns of $G^{(i)}$ corresponding to positions c_i and $c_{\tau(i)}$:

$$v_i = \begin{pmatrix} af_1(x_j) + c\psi_j(f_1) \\ \vdots \\ af_k(x_j) + c\psi_j(f_k) \end{pmatrix} \quad \text{and} \quad v_{\tau(i)} = \begin{pmatrix} bf_1(x_j) + \psi_j(f_1) \\ \vdots \\ bf_k(x_j) + \psi_j(f_k) \end{pmatrix}.$$

Next, search $\lambda \in \mathbb{F}_q$ such that $v_i - \lambda v_{\tau(i)}$ is collinear to v. This relation of collinearity can be expressed in terms of cancellation of some 2×2 determinants which are polynomials of degree 1 in λ. Their common root is nothing but c.

Finally, we can find the pair (a, b) by searching the pairs (λ, μ) such that

(i) $\lambda - c\mu = \det A$;
(ii) $v_i - \lambda v$ and $v_{\tau(i)} - \mu v$ are collinear.

Here the relation of collinearity will be expressed as the cancellation of 2×2 determinants which are linear combinations of λ, μ and $\lambda\mu$ and elementary elimination process provides us with the value of the pair (a, b).

6.7   How to Treat the Case of Degenerate Twin Positions?

Recall that a pair of twin positions $i, \tau(i)$ is such that any codeword $c \in \mathscr{C}$ has i-th and $\tau(i)$-th entries of the form:

$$c_i = a y_j f(x_j) + b \psi_j(f) \qquad c_{\tau(i)} = c y_j f(x_j) + d \psi_j(f).$$

This pair is said to be *degenerate* if either b or d is zero. In such a situation, some of the steps of the attack cannot be applied. In what follows, we explain how this rather rare issue can be addressed.

If either b or d is zero, then one of the positions is actually a pure GRS position while the other one is PR but the process explained in the article does not manage to associate the two twin columns.

Suppose without loss of generality that $b = 0$. In the first part if the attack, when we collect pairs of twin positions, the position $\tau(i)$ will be identified as PR with no twin sister *a priori*. To find its twin sister, we can proceed as follows. For any GRS position j replace the j-th column v_j of a generator matrix G of $\mathscr{C}$ by an arbitrary linear combination of v_j and the $\tau(i)$-th column, this will "pseudo–randomise" this column and if the j-th column is the twin of the $\tau(i)$-th one, this will be detected by the process of shortening, squaring and searching zero columns in the parity check matrix.

7   Complexity of the Attack

The most expensive part of the attack is the step consisting in identifying pairs of twin positions. Recall that, from [8], the computation of the square of a code of length n and dimension k costs $O(k^2 n^2)$ operations in $\mathbb{F}_q$. We need to compute the square of a code $O(w)$ times, because there are w pairs of twin positions. Hence this step has a total complexity of $O(w n^2 k^2)$ operations in $\mathbb{F}_q$. Note that the actual dimension of the shortened codes is significantly less than k and hence the previous estimate is overestimated.

The cost of the Sidelnikov Shestakov attack is that of a Gaussian elimination, namely $O(n k^2)$ operations in $\mathbb{F}_q$ which is negligible compared to the previous step. The cost of the final part is also negligible compared to the computation of the squares of shortened codes. This provides an overall complexity in $O(w n^2 k^2)$ operations in $\mathbb{F}_q$.

Conclusion

We presented a polynomial time key-recovery attack based on a square code distinguisher against the public key encryption scheme RLCE. This attack allows us to break all the so-called *odd ID* parameters suggested in [17]. Namely, the attack breaks the parameter sets for which the number w of random columns was strictly less than $n - k$. Our analysis suggests that, for this kind of distinguisher by squaring shortenings of the code, the case $w = n - k$ is the critical one. The *even ID* parameters of [17], for which the relation $w = n - k$ always holds, remain out of the reach of our attack.

Acknowledgements. The authors are supported by French *Agence nationale de la recherche* grants ANR-15-CE39-0013 *Manta*, ANR-17-CE39-0007 *CBCrypt* and by the Commission of the European Communities through the Horizon 2020 program under project number 645622 (PQCRYPTO). Computer aided calculations have been performed using softwares SAGE and MAGMA [5].

References

1. Baldi, M., Bianchi, M., Chiaraluce, F., Rosenthal, J., Schipani, D.: Enhanced public key security for the McEliece cryptosystem. J. Cryptol. **29**(1), 1–27 (2016). https://doi.org/10.1007/s00145-014-9187-8
2. Bardet, M., Chaulet, J., Dragoi, V., Otmani, A., Tillich, J.-P.: Cryptanalysis of the McEliece public key cryptosystem based on polar codes. In: Takagi, T. (ed.) PQCrypto 2016. LNCS, vol. 9606, pp. 118–143. Springer, Cham (2016). https://doi.org/10.1007/978-3-319-29360-8_9
3. Berger, T.P., Loidreau, P.: Security of the Niederreiter form of the GPT public-key cryptosystem. In: Proceedings IEEE International Symposium on Information Theory - ISIT 2002, p. 267. IEEE, June 2002
4. Bernstein, D.J., et al.: Classic McEliece: conservative code-based cryptography, November 2017. https://csrc.nist.gov/CSRC/media/Projects/Post-Quantum-Cryptography/documents/round-1/submissions/Classic_McEliece.zip, first round submission to the NIST post-quantum cryptography call
5. Bosma, W., Cannon, J., Playoust, C.: The Magma algebra system I: the user language. J. Symbolic Comput. **24**(3/4), 235–265 (1997)
6. Cascudo, I., Cramer, R., Mirandola, D., Zémor, G.: Squares of random linear codes. IEEE Trans. Inform. Theory **61**(3), 1159–1173 (2015)
7. Chizhov, I.V., Borodin, M.A.: Effective attack on the McEliece cryptosystem based on Reed-Muller codes. Discrete Math. Appl. **24**(5), 273–280 (2014)
8. Couvreur, A., Gaborit, P., Gauthier-Umaña, V., Otmani, A., Tillich, J.P.: Distinguisher-based attacks on public-key cryptosystems using Reed-Solomon codes. Des. Codes Cryptogr. **73**(2), 641–666 (2014). https://doi.org/10.1007/s10623-014-9967-z
9. Couvreur, A., Márquez-Corbella, I., Pellikaan, R.: Cryptanalysis of McEliece cryptosystem based on algebraic geometry codes and their subcodes. IEEE Trans. Inform. Theory **63**(8), 5404–5418 (2017)
10. Couvreur, A., Otmani, A., Tillich, J.P.: Polynomial time attack on wild McEliece over quadratic extensions. IEEE Trans. Inform. Theory **63**(1), 404–427 (2017)
11. Couvreur, A., Otmani, A., Tillich, J.-P., Gauthier–Umaña, V.: A polynomial-time attack on the BBCRS scheme. In: Katz, J. (ed.) PKC 2015. LNCS, vol. 9020, pp. 175–193. Springer, Heidelberg (2015). https://doi.org/10.1007/978-3-662-46447-2_8
12. Faugère, J.C., Gauthier, V., Otmani, A., Perret, L., Tillich, J.P.: A distinguisher for high rate McEliece cryptosystems. IEEE Trans. Inform. Theory **59**(10), 6830–6844 (2013)
13. Huffman, W.C., Pless, V.: Fundamentals of Error-Correcting Codes. Cambridge University Press, Cambridge (2003). https://doi.org/10.1017/CBO9780511807077
14. McEliece, R.J.: A Public-Key System Based on Algebraic Coding Theory, pp. 114–116. Jet Propulsion Lab (1978). DSN Progress Report 44
15. Sidelnikov, V.M., Shestakov, S.: On the insecurity of cryptosystems based on generalized Reed-Solomon codes. Discrete Math. Appl. **1**(4), 439–444 (1992)

16. Wang, Y.: Quantum resistant random linear code based public key encryption scheme RLCE. In: Proceedings of the IEEE International Symposium on Information Theory - ISIT 2016, pp. 2519–2523. IEEE, Barcelona, July 2016. https://doi.org/10.1109/ISIT.2016.7541753
17. Wang, Y.: RLCE-KEM (2017). http://quantumca.org, first round submission to the NIST post-quantum cryptography call
18. Wieschebrink, C.: Two NP-complete problems in coding theory with an application in code based cryptography. In: Proceedings IEEE International Symposium Information Theory - ISIT, pp. 1733–1737 (2006)
19. Wieschebrink, C.: Cryptanalysis of the Niederreiter public key scheme based on GRS subcodes. In: Sendrier, N. (ed.) PQCrypto 2010. LNCS, vol. 6061, pp. 61–72. Springer, Heidelberg (2010). https://doi.org/10.1007/978-3-642-12929-2_5

Cryptanalysis of an NTRU-Based Proxy Encryption Scheme from ASIACCS'15

Zhen Liu[1,2,3], Yanbin Pan[1], and Zhenfei Zhang[4(✉)]

[1] Key Laboratory of Mathematics Mechanization, NCMIS,
Academy of Mathematics and Systems Science,
Chinese Academy of Sciences, Beijing 100190, China
panyanbin@amss.ac.cn
[2] State Key Laboratory of Cryptology, P.O. Box 5159, Beijing 100878, China
[3] School of Mathematical Sciences, University of Chinese Academy of Sciences,
Beijing 100049, China
liuzhen16@mails.ucas.ac.cn
[4] Algorand, Boston, USA
zhenfei@algorand.com

Abstract. In ASIACCS 2015, Nuñez, Agudo, and Lopez proposed a proxy re-encryption scheme, NTRUReEncrypt, based on NTRU, which allows a proxy to translate ciphertext under the delegator's public key into a re-encrypted ciphertext that can be decrypted correctly by delegatee's private key. In addition to its potential resistance to quantum algorithm, the scheme was also considered to be efficient. However, in this paper we point out that the re-encryption process will increase the decryption error, and the increased decryption error will lead to a reaction attack that enables the proxy to recover the private key of the delegator and the delegatee. Moreover, we also propose a second attack which enables the delegatee to recover the private key of the delegator when he collects enough re-encrypted ciphertexts from a same message. We reevaluate the security of NTRUReEncrypt, and also give suggestions and discussions on potential mitigation methods.

Keywords: NTRUReEncrypt · NTRU · Decryption failure ·
Reaction attack · Key recovery

1 Introduction

The concept of proxy re-encryption (PRE) scheme was proposed by Blaze, Bleumer and Strauss in 1998 [5]. A re-encryption scheme allows a proxy to translate ciphertext under the delegator's public key into a ciphertext of the same message that can be decrypted correctly by the delegatee's private key, whereas the proxy is given just a re-encryption key and learns nothing about

Yanbin Pan was supported by the NNSF of China (No. 61572490), and by the National Center for Mathematics and Interdisciplinary Sciences, CAS.

© Springer Nature Switzerland AG 2019
J. Ding and R. Steinwandt (Eds.): PQCrypto 2019, LNCS 11505, pp. 153–166, 2019.
https://doi.org/10.1007/978-3-030-25510-7_9

the message. A PRE scheme can be seen as an extension of public-key encryption. It uses same fundamental algorithms as a traditional public key encryption scheme. Additionally, it also requires algorithms to generate re-encryption keys and to re-encrypt ciphertexts.

In the literature, there exit a number of proxy re-encryption schemes, based on number theoretic problems such as the discrete logarithm problem [6]. However, due to Shor's quantum algorithm, the integer factorization problem and the discrete logarithm problem can be solved efficiently [17,18]. It is crucial to have alternatives that are robust against quantum computers. In 2017, NIST [1,7] started a standardization process on post-quantum cryptography. Among all candidate proposals, lattice based solutions are ones of most promising. Although NIST considers only public key encryption and signature schemes at this stage, it is also important to identify lattice based candidate for proxy re-encryption schemes, for examples [3,20].

At AsiaCCS 2015, Nuñez, Agudo and Lopez [16] proposed a new proxy re-encryption scheme, NTRUReEncrypt, based on a well-established lattice-based public-key encryption scheme NTRU. Here the encryption and decryption messages are identical to the classical NTRUEncrypt scheme. With an additional re-encryption mechanism, they achieved an efficient post-quantum PRE scheme.

NTRU [12], introduced by Hoffstein, Pipher and Silverman in 1996, has been standardized by IEEE 1363.1 [19] and ANSI X9.98 [2]. It features high efficiency and low memory requirement. After 20 years of development, there are three mainstreams of the NTRU algorithms. The IEEE standardized version, NTRUEncrypt was later on submitted to NIST-PQC process as [21]. The parameters follow the design principals outlined in [11]. The other two NTRU based submissions are NTRU-prime [4] and NTRU-HRSS [15] schemes.

Similar to other lattice based cryptosystems, the NTRU scheme may admit decryption errors. When a decryption failure occurs, information on private keys may be (partially) leaked. In 2003, Howgrave *et al.* [14] successfully demonstrated an attack that employs large number of queries to a *weak* decryption oracle. Unlike a classical decryption oracle, a weak decryption oracle will only tell whether a valid ciphertext was decrypted correctly or not (see [13]). This attack is later known as the *reaction* attack, and becomes common to lattice based cryptography [8,22]. In practice, to address this attack one may choose optimized parameters so that the decryption error is negligible in security parameter, for example, NTRUEncrypt [11]; or less optimized ones that eliminate the decryption errors, for example, NTRU-HRSS [15].

In NTRUReEncrypt, the delegator first chooses a small polynomial s, and encrypts the message m as $C_A = h_A * s + m$, where delegator's private key is (f_A, g_A) and delegator's public key is $h_A = p * g_A * f_A^{-1}$. After receiving C_A, the proxy chooses small polynomial e and sends $C_B = C_A * rk_{A \to B} + p * e$ to the delegatee, where $rk_{A \to B} = f_A * f_B^{-1}$ is the re-encrypted key of the proxy and f_B is the private key of the delegatee. Finally, the delegatee computes $C_B * f_B$ modulo q and reduces it modulo p to recover the message m.

Our first contribution is to analyze the `NTRUReEncrypt` scheme using the aforementioned reaction attack. Note that the `NTRUReEncrypt` scheme follows the parameter sets in [11, 19, 21]. The probability of decryption failure was set to be negligible in the security parameter for a public key encryption scheme. However, the re-encryption process of `NTRUReEncrypt` significantly increases decryption error[1]. We give a detailed analyze the probability of decryption failure in Table 1, and show how to use a reaction attack to recover private keys, given sufficient many decryption failures. We also note that one can simply mitigate this attack by increasing the modulus (and also the dimensions accordingly to ensure the lattice problem is still hard in practice) so that decryption failure probability becomes negligible again.

Table 1. The probabilities of decryption failure after encryption and re-encryption

Parameter sets	$log_2(P_{dec}(c))$	$log_2(P_{dec}(c'))$
ees1087ep1	-219	-92
ees1171ep1	-245	-117
ees1499ep1	-323	-200
ntru-443	-217	-35
ntru-743	-122	-16

Our other contribution is a new attack in which a curious delegatee receiving a large re-encrypted ciphertexts from a single message can recover the private key of a delegator. Roughly speaking, note that the intermediate polynomial during the delegatee's decryption has the form of $C_{B_i} * f_B = p * g_A * s_i + m * f_A + p * e_i * f_B$. Once the delegatee collects enough (denoted by l) intermediate polynomials for a same message m, he can average them to obtain $p * g_A * \sum_{i=1}^{l} s_i/l + m * f_A + p * f_B * \sum_{i=1}^{l} e_i/l = f_B * \sum_{i=1}^{l} C_{B_i}/l$. Since s_i, e_i are randomly chosen small polynomials, for sufficiently large l, the coefficients of $p * g_A * \sum_{i=1}^{l} s_i/l$ and $p * f_B * \sum_{i=1}^{l} e_i/l$ will be very small. Hence, with overwhelming probability, the equation $m * f_A = Round(\sum_{i=1}^{l} f_B * C_{B_i}/l)$ holds, from which we can efficiently recover the private key f_A. To resist such an attack, some randomized padding scheme should be added carefully (Table 2).

Our second attack indeed bases on the fact that each re-encrypted messages leaks partial information of the secret key. Our attack is a simple illustration of such a leakage. In lattice based signatures schemes, transcript leakages are usually fixed with rejection sampling methods. It is not trivial to apply this method to an re-encryption scheme. We leave secure instantiation of NTRU based re-encryption schemes to future work.

---

[1] Indeed, even if the `NTRUReEncrypt` adopts NTRU-HRSS parameter sets that don't have decryption errors by design, the re-encryption process will introduce decryption errors.

Table 2. The approximate number of required re-encrypted ciphertexts

Parameter sets	Number of ciphertexts
ees1087ep1	$2^{58.5}$
ees1171ep1	$2^{58.7}$
ees1499ep1	$2^{59.7}$
ntru-443	$2^{53.5}$
ntru-743	$2^{57.3}$

Roadmap. The remainder of the paper is organized as follows. In Sect. 2, we recall the original NTRU encryption and explain its decryption failures. In Sect. 3, we present the proxy re-encryption scheme NTRUReEncrypt. In Sect. 4, we give our first attack against NTRUReEncryptand analyze the decryption failure probability. In Sect. 5, we give our second attack against NTRUReEncrypt. Finally, we give a short conclusion in Sect. 6.

2   Notations and Preliminaries

2.1   Notations and Definitions

Let $\mathcal{R}$ denote the ring $Z[X]/(X^N - 1)$, where N is prime. Let $+$ and $*$ denote addition and multiplication in $\mathcal{R}$, respectively. For integer p, q, $\gcd(p, q) = 1$ and $p \ll q$. Let $\mathcal{R}_q$ be the ring $Z_q[X]/(X^N - 1)$ and $\mathcal{R}_p$ be the ring $Z_p[X]/(X^N - 1)$. We use $\|.\|_\infty$ to denote the infinite norm and $\|.\|$ to denote the Euclidean norm.

A polynomial $a(x) = a_0 + a_1 x + \cdots + a_{N-1} x^{N-1}$ is identified with its vector of coefficients $a = [a_0, a_1, \cdots, a_{N-1}]$. The maximum and minimum coefficients of polynomial or vector are denoted by

$$Max(a(x)) = \max_{0 \le i \le N-1}\{a_i\} \quad and \quad Min(a(x)) = \min_{0 \le i \le N-1}\{a_i\}.$$

The width of a polynomial $a(X)$ is the difference between its largest and smallest coefficients

$$Width(a(x)) = Max(a(x)) - Min(a(x)).$$

The reversal polynomial $\bar{a}(x)$ of a polynomial $a(x)$ in $\mathcal{R}$ is defined to be $\bar{a}(x) = a(x^{-1})$. If $a = (a_0, a_1, \cdots, a_{N-1})$, then $\bar{a} = (a_0, a_{N-1}, a_{N-2}, \cdots, a_1)$.

Let $\hat{a}(x) = a(x) * \bar{a}(x)$ in $\mathcal{R}$, a coefficient $\hat{a}_i$ of $\hat{a}(x)$ is the dot products of a with its successive rotations $x^i * a$. We have $\hat{a}_0 = \sum_{i=0}^{N-1} a_i^2 = \|a\|^2$.

For positive integers d_1, d_2, We set the notation:

$$\mathcal{T}_{(d_1,d_2)} = \left\{ \begin{array}{c} \text{trinary polynomials of } \mathcal{R} \text{ with } d_1 \text{ entries} \\ \text{equal to 1 and } d_2 \text{ entries equal to } -1 \end{array} \right\}.$$

2.2 Overview of NTRU

We now briefly present the basic NTRU encryption scheme, for more details see [12]. The polynomials used in NTRU are selected from four sets $\mathcal{L}_f, \mathcal{L}_g, \mathcal{L}_s, \mathcal{L}_m$, where $\mathcal{L}_f = \{f : f \in \mathcal{T}_{(d_f, d_f - 1)}\}$, $\mathcal{L}_g = \{g : g \in \mathcal{T}_{(d_g, d_g)}\}$, $\mathcal{L}_s = \{s : s \in \mathcal{T}_{(d_s, d_s)}\}$, and $\mathcal{L}_m = \{m \in \mathcal{R}$: every coefficient of m lies between $\frac{p-1}{2}$ and $\frac{p-1}{2}\}$.

- **KeyGen(1^k):** On input security parameter k, the key generation algorithm KenGen first chooses $f \in \mathcal{L}_f$, such that f has inverse f_q^{-1} in R_q and f_p^{-1} in R_p, $g \in \mathcal{L}_g$, then computes $h = p * g * f_q^{-1}$ mod q and outputs public key $pk = h$ and private key $sk = (f, g)$.

- **Enc(pk, m):** On input the public key pk and a message $m \in \mathcal{L}_m$, the encryption algorithm Enc chooses $s \in \mathcal{L}_s$ and outputs the ciphertext $c = h * s + m$ mod q.

- **Dec(sk, c):** On input the private key sk and the ciphertext c, the decryption algorithm Dec computes $a = c * f$ mod q, and place the coefficient of a in the interval $(-q/2, q/2]$. Outputs $m = a * f_p^{-1}$ mod p.

2.3 Decryption Failures

When decrypting a ciphertext c, one caluates

$$a = c * f = p * g * s + m * f \quad \text{mod } q. \tag{1}$$

Since the polynomials f, g, s and m are small, the coefficients of polynomial $p * g * s + m * f$ lie in $(-q/2, q/2]$ with high probability. If the equality mod q in Eq. (1) also holds over $\mathbb{Z}$. Then, we have

$$a * f_p^{-1} = p * g * s * f_p^{-1} + m * f * f_p^{-1} = m \quad \text{mod } p.$$

Hence decryption works if Eq. (1) also holds over $\mathbb{Z}$. A warp failure occurs if $\|p * g * s + m * f\|_\infty \geq q/2$ and a gap failure occurs if the width of $p * g * s + m * f$ is greater than or equal to q.

Howgrave et al. [14] presented the attack based on decryption failure. The attacker selected (m, s_i) with fixed m, such that $\|p * g * s_i + m * f\|_\infty \geq q/2$. Once the attacker collected sufficiently large (m, s_i), the attacker can recover the private key (g, f).

3 NTRUReEncrypt

3.1 Presentation of the Scheme

In [16], Nuñez et al. proposed a proxy re-encryption scheme NTRUReEncrypt based on NTRU, where a proxy is given re-encryption key $rk_{A \to B}$ that allows him to translate a message m encrypted under Alice's public key pk_A into a re-encrypted ciphertext of the same message m decryptable by Bob's private key sk_B.

The NTRUReEncrypt scheme consists of five algorithms:

- **KeyGen(1^k):** On input the security parameter k, the output of key generation algorithm for Alice is (sk_A, pk_A), where $sk_A = (f_A, g_A)$ and $pk_A = h_A$. Let f_A^{-1} denote the inverse of f_A in the ring R_q.

- **ReKeyGen(sk_A, sk_B):** On input the secret key sk_A and the secret key sk_B, the re-encryption algorithm ReKeyGen computes the re-encryption key between Alice and Bob as $rk_{A \to B} = f_A * f_B^{-1} \mod q$. The re-encryption key can be computed by a simple three-party protocol originally proposed in [6], is as follows: Alice selects $r \in \mathcal{R}_q$ and sends $r * f_A \mod q$ to Bob and r to the proxy, then Bob sends $r * f_A * f_B^{-1} \mod q$ to the proxy, so the proxy can compute $rk_{A \to B} = f_A * f_B^{-1} \mod q$.

- **Enc(pk_A, m):** On input the public key pk_A and the message m, the encryption algorithm Enc generates $s \in \mathcal{T}_{d_s, d_s}$, and outputs $C_A = h_A * s + m \mod q$.

- **ReEnc($rk_{A \to B}, C_A$):** On input a re-encryption key $rk_{A \to B}$ and a ciphertext C_A, the re-encryption algorithm ReEnc generates $e \in \mathcal{T}_{d_s, d_s}$ and outputs $C_B = C_A * rk_{A \to B} + p * e \mod q$.

- **Dec(sk_A, C_A):** On input the secret key sk_A and the ciphertext C_A, the decryption algorithm computes $C_A' = C_A * f_A \mod q$ and outputs $m = C_A' \mod p$.

Next, We would like to point out that

- In order to decrypt the re-encrypted ciphertext correctly, the private polynomial f_B has to be congruent to 1 modulo p. So the difference between NTRU and NTRUReEncrypt of the key generation is that the private key f has the form of $1 + p * F$, where $F \in \mathcal{T}_{(d_f, d_f)}$.
- In practical, the message m is padded with random bits and masked according to a hamming weight restriction, which means message representatives are trinary polynomials with the number of $+1s$, $-1s$, and $0s$ each be greater than d_m. So for simplicity, m satisfies the hamming weight restriction in this paper.
- The error term e is chosen randomly from the ring $\mathcal{R}$ during the re-encryption in [16], which is unreasonable. In fact, e should be small, we therefore assume that e is sampled from the same set as s.

For the correctness of Bob's decryption, when Bob gets the re-encryption ciphertext C_B, he first computes

$$
\begin{aligned}
C_B * f_B &= (C_A * f_A * f_B^{-1} + p * e) * f_B \\
&= (h_A * s + m) * f_A + p * e * f_B \\
&= p * g_A * s + m * f_A + p * e * f_B \mod q
\end{aligned}
\tag{2}
$$

If the last part of Eq. (2) also holds over $\mathbb{Z}$, then we have $C'_B = p * g_A * s + m * f_A + p * e * f_B$. After taking modulo p, Bob can obtain the original message m.

Remark 1. *The scheme is also bidirectional and multihop, namely it's trivial to obtain $rk_{B \to A}$ from $rk_{A \to B}$ and the re-encryption process can be repeated multiple times.*

3.2 Parameter Sets

The author of [16] implemented NTRUReEncrypt scheme on ees439ep1, ees1087ep1, ees1171ep1, ees1499ep1 parameter sets following the IEEE P1363.1 standards [19]. They also used the product form polynomials for optimization of each set. However, some specific parameters are not clear in [16], so we only list ees1087ep1, ees1171ep1, ees1499ep1 in Table 3.

Note that the NTRU project has proposed new parameter sets ntru-443 and ntru-743, which are submitted to NIST PQC competition [21]. For completeness, we also list them in Table 3 to analyze the security of the scheme.

For ees1087ep1, ees1171ep1, ees1499ep1, ntru-443, ntru-743, the private key is $(f, g) = (1 + p * F)$ with $F \in \mathcal{T}_{(d_f, d_f)}$ and $g \in \mathcal{T}_{(dg, dg)}$, the polynomial $s \in \mathcal{T}_{(d_s, d_s)}$.

Table 3. Some instances of trinary polynomials

Instance	N	p	q	dg	df=ds=dm
ees1087ep1	1087	3	2048	362	120
ees1171ep1	1171	3	2048	390	106
ees1499ep1	1499	3	2048	499	79
ntru-443	443	3	2048	143	143
ntru-743	743	3	2048	247	247

4   Reaction Attack Against NTRUReEncrypt

Recall that in Bob's decryption, the intermediate polynomial is $p * g_A * s + m * f_A + p * e * f_B$ and the additional term $p * e * f_B$ produces an increased error. Hence, the decryption failure probability is expected to significantly increase. On the other hand, the attacks based on the decryption failures has been studied well in [14]. Therefore, we employ their attack to analyze the security of the NTRUReEncrypt scheme.

More precisely, it is assume that the attacker has access to an oracle to determine whether a validly created ciphertext can be decrypted correctly or not. The attack takes as follows. The first stage is that the attacker uses the oracle to collect (m, s, e), which generates the re-encrypted ciphertext C_B that can not be decrypted correctly. The second stage is that the attacker fixes (m, s) and randomly searches e_i, where (m, s, e_i) causes decryption failure. The final stage is that the attacker uses those $\widehat{e}_i$ correlated with $\widehat{f_B}$ to determine the private key f_B. Note that the proxy can create C_{A_i} by encrypting random m_i with random s_i and C_{B_i} by re-encrypting C_{A_i} with random e_i, we therefore assume that a corrupt proxy can act as an attacker.

Before explaining our attack, we first show that the decryption failure probability of NTRUReEncrypt significantly increases for Bob.

4.1   Estimating Decryption Failure Probability of C_A

We use the method introduced in [10] to estimate the decryption failure probability. Recall that in Alice's decryption, she computes

$$C_A' = p * g_A * s + f_A * m$$
$$= p * g_A * s + p * F_A * m + m \quad \text{mod } q,$$

Decryption works, if

$$\|C_A'\|_\infty = \|p * (g_A * s + F_A * m) + m\|_\infty < q/2.$$

Therefore, the decryption failure probability P_{dec} can be bounded by the probability that one or more coefficients of $g_A * s + F_A * m$ has an absolute value greater than $c = (q - 2)/(2p)$. So we have

$$P_{dec}(c) = \Pr[\|g_A * s + F_A * m\|_\infty \geq c].$$

For trinary $F_A \in \mathcal{T}_{(d_f, d_f)}$, $g_A \in \mathcal{T}_{(d_g, d_g)}$, $s \in \mathcal{T}_{(d_s, d_s)}$. Let X_j denote a cofficient of $g_A * s + F_A * m$, then X_j has the form

$$(g_A * s + F_A * m)_j = (s * g_A)_j + (F_A * m)_j,$$

and each term in the sum is a sum of either $2d_s$ or $2d_f$ coefficients of g_A or m. Note that each term in the sum has mean 0.

For instance, let $\varepsilon(i) \in \{1, -1\}$ and $a(i)$ represents index, we have

$$(s * g_A)_j = \sum_{i=1}^{2d_s} \varepsilon(i)(g_A)_{a(i)}.$$

We assume that the coefficients of g_A are independent random variables taking the value 1 with probability $\frac{d_g}{N}$, -1 with probability $\frac{d_g}{N}$ and 0 with probability $\frac{N - 2d_g}{N}$. Hence, the variance σ_1^2 of $(g_A * s)_j$ is computed as:

$$\sigma_1^2 = E((s * g_A)_j^2) = \sum_{i=1}^{2d_s} E((g_A)_{a(i)}^2) = \frac{4d_s d_g}{N}.$$

Recall that the message m is sampled uniformly from the set of trinary polynomials, which restrains that the number of non-zero coefficients can not exceed $N - d_m$. We also assume that the coefficient of m is chosen as ± 1 with the probability $\frac{N-d_m}{N}$ and 0 with the probability $\frac{d_m}{N}$. Similarly, the variance σ_2^2 of $(F_A * m)_j$ is

$$\sigma_2^2 = E((F_A * m)_j^2) = 2d_f \cdot \frac{N - d_m}{N}.$$

Suppose $2d_s$, $2d_g$ are large, the central limit theorem suggests that the distribution of X_j has the normal distribution with mean 0 and variance σ^2:

$$\sigma^2 = \sigma_1^2 + \sigma_2^2 = \frac{4d_s d_g + 2d_f \cdot (N - d_m)}{N}$$

With complementary error function $\mathbf{erfc}(\cdot)$, the probability that a coefficient X_j has absolute value exceeds c is given by

$$\Pr[|X_j| \geq c] = \mathbf{erfc}(c/\sqrt{2}\sigma).$$

After applying the union bound, the probability $P_{dec}(c)$ is bounded by

$$P_{dec}(c) = N \cdot \mathbf{erfc}(c/\sqrt{2}\sigma),$$

where

$$\mathbf{erfc}(c/\sqrt{2}\sigma) = \frac{2}{\sqrt{\pi}} \cdot \int_{c/\sqrt{2}\sigma}^{\infty} e^{-x^2} \, dx.$$

4.2 Estimating Decryption Failure Probability of C_B

When Bob receives the re-encrypt ciphertext C_B, the intermediate process is to compute

$$C_B{}' = p * g_A * s + m * f_A + p * e * f_B,$$

and the failure occurs if

$$\|p \cdot (g_A * s + F_A * m + p * F_B * e) + pe + m\|_\infty \geq q/2.$$

Similarly, for trinary $F_B \in \mathcal{T}_{(d_f, d_f)}$, we get the probability

$$P_{dec}(c') = N \cdot \mathbf{erfc}(c'/\sqrt{2}\sigma'),$$

where

$$\sigma'^2 = \sigma^2 + \frac{p^2 \cdot 4d_s d_f}{N},$$

and

$$c' = c - 1.$$

We estimate decryption failure probabilities with the parameters specified in Sect. 3.2 and list them below (Table 4).

As we can see, the probability that the re-encrypted ciphertext C_B fails to decrypt is much greater than that of C_A. What's more, the decryption failures lead to reaction attack.

Table 4. The probabilities of decryption failure during encryption and re-encryption

Instance	σ^2	σ'^2	$log_2(P_{dec}(c))$	$log_2(P_{dec}(c'))$
ees1087ep1	373	850	-219	-92
ees1171ep1	334	679	-245	-117
ees1499ep1	255	405	-323	-200
ntru-443	378	2040	-217	-35
ntru-743	658	3614	-122	-16

4.3 Description of the Attack

For completeness, we simply describe the attack as below. See [14] for more details about the reaction attack based on the decryption failure.

- **Stage 1:** The attacker first collects (m, s, e), which will generate the re-encrypted ciphertext C_B that can not be decrypted correctly. Moreover, the triplet (m, s, e) should satisfy two conditions: there must be a coefficient of $p * g_A * s + m * f_A$ that is both abnormally far from its expected value and further from the expected value than any other coefficient, and the distances between the two coefficients of $p * g_A * s + m * f_A$ furthest from their expected value, which is known as the gap of $p * g_A * s + m * f_A$, should be large enough.

- **Stage 2:** For fixed (m, s) found in Stage 1, the attacker randomly chooses e_i and collects (m, s, e_i) that causes decryption failure for Bob. Suppose the i−th coefficient of $p * g_A * s + m * f_A$ is abnormally far from its expected value, then it is most likely that the absolute value of the i−th coefficient of $p * g_A * s + m * f_A + p * e_i * f_B$ exceeds $q/2$. The strength of this bias towards the i−th coefficient of the $p * g_A * s + m * f_A + p * e_i * f_B$ will depend on the gap of $p * g_A * s + m * f_A$. What's more, it suggests that e_i is correlated with $x^i * \overline{f_B}$. Since the reversal of $x^i * \overline{f_B}$ equals to $x^{-i} * f_B$, $\widehat{e_i}$ is corrected with $\widehat{f_B}$.

- **Stage 3:** For sufficiently large k, the value of $\widehat{f_B}$ can be derived from the average of the polynomials $\widehat{e_1}, \widehat{e_2}, \cdots, \widehat{e_k}$. Furthermore, f_B can be recovered from $\widehat{f_B}$ according to the algorithm introduced in [9].
  Since the proxy has the re-encryption key $rk_{A \to B} = f_A * f_B^{-1} \mod q$ and the public key of Alice is $h_A = p * g_A * f_A^{-1} \mod q$. Once the attaker recovers the private key f_B, f_A can be found by computing $f_A = rk_{A \to B} * f_B \mod q$ and g_A can be found by computing $g_A = p * g_A * h_A \mod q$.

5   Key Recovery Attack Against NTRUReEncrypt

In this section, we show that curious Bob can recover Alice's secret keys f_A when collecting enough ciphertexts from a single message.

5.1   Key Idea of Recovering f_A for Bob

For simplicity, suppose a message m could be encrypted l times using the same public key f_A of Alice, and the ciphertexts are computed as

$$C_{A_i} = h_A * s_i + m \quad i = 1, \cdots, l.$$

When Bob receives C_{B_i} corresponding to C_{A_i}, he can first computes the following relation

$$f_B * C_{B_i} = p * g_A * s_i + p * f_B * e_i + m * f_A.$$

Next, Bob obtains

$$f_B * \sum_{i=1}^{l} C_{B_i} = p * g_A * \left(\sum_{i=1}^{l} s_i \right) + p * f_B * \left(\sum_{i=1}^{l} e_i \right) + l * m * f_A.$$

Note that p, g_A, s_i, f_B, and e_i are small. We can expect that for sufficiently large l, $p * g_A * \sum_{i=1}^{l} s_i/k$ and $p * f_B * \sum_{i=1}^{l} e_i/k$ are small enough. Since the coefficients of $m * f_A$ are integer, the following equation holds with high probability,

$$m * f_A = Round\left(\sum_{i=1}^{l} f_B * C_{B_i}/l \right).$$

where $Round(\cdot)$ is a rounding function.

Since Bob can decrypt correctly to obtain the message m, so the unknown private key f_A will be recovered by solving the above linear equations.

5.2   Analyze the Size of l

For the attack, we need l that satisfies

$$\left\| p * g_A * \sum_{i=1}^{l} s_i/l \right\|_{\infty} \leq \frac{1}{4}, \quad \left\| p * f_B * \sum_{i=1}^{l} e_i/l \right\|_{\infty} \leq \frac{1}{4},$$

to ensure $m * f_A = Round(\sum_{i=1}^{l} f_B * C_{B_i}/l)$.

For any $s_i \in T_{(d_s, d_s)}$, let $X = \sum_{i=1}^{l} s_i/l = (X_0, \cdots, X_{N-1})$. For sufficiently large l, the central limit theorem states that X has the N dimension normal distribution $\mathcal{N}(0, \Sigma)$, where the diagonal elements of Σ are $\frac{2d_s}{lN}$ and the rest are $\frac{-2d_s}{lN(N-1)}$.

We define $\|\Sigma\|_{\infty} = \max_i \sum_{j=1}^{N} |\sigma_{ij}|$, where σ_{ij} is the component of Σ. Now we have $\|\Sigma\|_{\infty} = \frac{4d_s}{lN}$. Let λ denote the maximal eigenvalue of Σ, then we have $\lambda \leq \|\Sigma\|_{\infty} = \frac{4d_s}{lN}$.

On the other hand, there exists $Y = (Y_0, Y_1, \cdots, Y_{N-1})$ and an orthogonal matrix D, such that

$$X = YD,$$

where $Y_0, \cdots, Y_{N-1}$ are independent variables and the covariance matrix of Y is a diagonal matrix in which the elements on the diagonal are the eigenvalues of the covariance matrix Σ of X. Hence, let $Var(Y_j)$ denote the variance of Y_j, we know

$$\lambda = \max_j Var(Y_j) \leq \frac{4d_s}{lN}.$$

To estimate the probability $\Pr\left[\left\|p * g_A * \sum_{i=1}^{l} s_i/l\right\|_\infty \leq \frac{1}{4}\right]$, we can consider the probability $\Pr\left[\bigcap_{j=1}^{N} |X_j| \leq \epsilon\right]$, where ϵ satifies

$$\left\|p * g_A * \left(\sum_{i=1}^{l} s_i/l\right)\right\|_\infty \leq 2d_g p\epsilon \leq \frac{1}{4}.$$

Since $X_0, \cdots, X_{N-1}$ are not independent, we can consider the probability $\Pr\left[\bigcap_{j=1}^{N} |Y_j| \leq \epsilon/N\right]$ instead, where

$$\Pr\left[\bigcap_{j=1}^{N} |Y_j| \leq \epsilon/N\right] = \prod_{i=0}^{N-1} \Pr[|Y_j| \leq \epsilon/N].$$

By the Chebyshev inequality, we know that

$$\Pr[|Y_j| \leq \epsilon/N] \geq 1 - \frac{Var(Y_j)}{(\epsilon/N)^2}.$$

Finally we obtain

$$\Pr\left[\bigcap_{j=1}^{N} |Y_j| \leq \epsilon/N\right] \geq (1 - \frac{\lambda}{(\epsilon/N)^2})^N \geq (1 - \frac{4d_s N}{l\epsilon^2})^N.$$

Recall that e_i has the same distribution, a similar analysis applies. So, for simplicity, we compute the value of l that makes $\frac{4d_s N}{l\epsilon^2}$ as small as possible by setting $\epsilon = \frac{1}{8pd_g}$. We roughly give the l needed to recover the private key with overwhelming probability (0.8 for the following table) in ees1087ep1, ees1171ep1, ees1499ep1, ntru-443 and ntru-743 (Table 5).

Table 5. The approximate number of received re-encrypted ciphertexts

Instance	l
ees1087ep1	$4.06 \cdot 10^{17}$
ees1171ep1	$4.83 \cdot 10^{17}$
ees1499ep1	$9.67 \cdot 10^{17}$
ntru-443	$1.26 \cdot 10^{16}$
ntru-743	$1.82 \cdot 10^{17}$

6   Conclusion

In this paper, we presented two key recovery attacks against NTRUReEncrypt to show the weakness of the scheme.

- The first one is based on the attack introduced in [14]. The attacker has access to an oracle that can detect whether the valid ciphertext can be decrypted correctly or not. The countermeasures to mitigate this attack is by tuning the parameters to ensure that the decryption failure probability is negligible, i.e., $< 2^{-128}$.
- The second one is based on the fact that Bob knows the original message m, so he can compute an equation in the form of $p * g_A * \sum_{i=1}^{l} s_i/l + m * f_A + p * f_B * \sum_{i=1}^{l} e_i/l = f_B * \sum_{i=1}^{l} C_{B_i}/l$. For sufficiently large l, $p * g_A * \sum_{i=1}^{l} s_i/l$ and $p * f_B * \sum_{i=1}^{l} e_i/l$ converge to 0. Hence f_A can be recovered by solving $m * f_A = Round(f_B * \sum_{i=1}^{l} C_{B_i}/l)$.

Acknowledgement. The authors would like to thank David Nuñez for his helpful discussions.

References

1. NIST post-quantum cryptography project. https://csrc.nist.gov/Projects/Post-Quantum-Cryptography/Round-1-Submissions
2. ANSI X 98: Lattice-based polynomial public key establishment algorithm for the financial services industry. Technical report, ANSI (2010)
3. Aono, Y., Boyen, X., Phong, L.T., Wang, L.: Key-private proxy re-encryption under LWE. In: Paul, G., Vaudenay, S. (eds.) INDOCRYPT 2013. LNCS, vol. 8250, pp. 1–18. Springer, Cham (2013). https://doi.org/10.1007/978-3-319-03515-4_1
4. Bernstein, D.J., Chuengsatiansup, C., Lange, T., van Vredendaal, C.: NTRU prime: reducing attack surface at low cost. In: Adams, C., Camenisch, J. (eds.) SAC 2017. LNCS, vol. 10719, pp. 235–260. Springer, Cham (2018). https://doi.org/10.1007/978-3-319-72565-9_12
5. Blaze, M., Bleumer, G., Strauss, M.: Divertible protocols and atomic proxy cryptography. In: Nyberg, K. (ed.) EUROCRYPT 1998. LNCS, vol. 1403, pp. 127–144. Springer, Heidelberg (1998). https://doi.org/10.1007/BFb0054122
6. Canetti, R., Hohenberger, S.: Chosen-ciphertext secure proxy re-encryption. In: Proceedings of the 14th ACM Conference on Computer and Communications Security, pp. 185–194. ACM (2007)
7. Chen, L., et al.: Report on post-quantum cryptography. Technical report (2016). https://nvlpubs.nist.gov/nistpubs/ir/2016/NIST.IR.8105.pdf
8. Fluhrer, S.R.: Cryptanalysis of ring-LWE based key exchange with key share reuse. IACR Cryptology ePrint Archive 2016, p. 85 (2016). http://eprint.iacr.org/2016/085
9. Gentry, C., Szydlo, M.: Cryptanalysis of the revised NTRU signature scheme. In: Knudsen, L.R. (ed.) EUROCRYPT 2002. LNCS, vol. 2332, pp. 299–320. Springer, Heidelberg (2002). https://doi.org/10.1007/3-540-46035-7_20

10. Hirschhorn, P.S., Hoffstein, J., Howgrave-Graham, N., Whyte, W.: Choosing NTRUEncrypt parameters in light of combined lattice reduction and MITM approaches. In: Abdalla, M., Pointcheval, D., Fouque, P.-A., Vergnaud, D. (eds.) ACNS 2009. LNCS, vol. 5536, pp. 437–455. Springer, Heidelberg (2009). https://doi.org/10.1007/978-3-642-01957-9_27

11. Hoffstein, J., Pipher, J., Schanck, J.M., Silverman, J.H., Whyte, W., Zhang, Z.: Choosing parameters for NTRUEncrypt. In: Handschuh, H. (ed.) CT-RSA 2017. LNCS, vol. 10159, pp. 3–18. Springer, Cham (2017). https://doi.org/10.1007/978-3-319-52153-4_1

12. Hoffstein, J., Pipher, J., Silverman, J.H.: NTRU: a ring-based public key cryptosystem. In: Buhler, J.P. (ed.) ANTS 1998. LNCS, vol. 1423, pp. 267–288. Springer, Heidelberg (1998). https://doi.org/10.1007/BFb0054868

13. Hoffstein, J., Silverman, J.H.: Reaction attacks against the NTRU public key cryptosystem. Technical report, NTRU Cryptosystems Technical Report (1999)

14. Howgrave-Graham, N., et al.: The impact of decryption failures on the Security of NTRU encryption. In: Boneh, D. (ed.) CRYPTO 2003. LNCS, vol. 2729, pp. 226–246. Springer, Heidelberg (2003). https://doi.org/10.1007/978-3-540-45146-4_14

15. Hülsing, A., Rijneveld, J., Schanck, J., Schwabe, P.: High-speed key encapsulation from NTRU. In: Fischer, W., Homma, N. (eds.) CHES 2017. LNCS, vol. 10529, pp. 232–252. Springer, Cham (2017). https://doi.org/10.1007/978-3-319-66787-4_12

16. Nuñez, D., Agudo, I., Lopez, J.: NTRUReEncrypt: an efficient proxy re-encryption scheme based on NTRU. In: Proceedings of the 10th ACM Symposium on Information, Computer and Communications Security, pp. 179–189. ACM (2015)

17. Shor, P.W.: Algorithms for quantum computation: discrete logarithms and factoring. In: 1994 Proceedings of 35th Annual Symposium on Foundations of Computer Science, pp. 124–134. IEEE (1994)

18. Shor, P.W.: Polynomial-time algorithms for prime factorization and discrete logarithms on a quantum computer. SIAM Rev. 41(2), 303–332 (1999)

19. Whyte, W., Howgrave-Graham, N., Hoffstein, J., Pipher, J., Silverman, J., Hirschhorn, P.: IEEE P1363. 1: draft standard for public-key cryptographic techniques based on hard problems over lattices. Technical report, IEEE (2008)

20. Xagawa, K., Tanaka, K.: Proxy re-encryption based on learning with errors (mathematical foundation of algorithms and computer science) (2010)

21. Zhang, Z., Chen, C., Hoffstein, J., Whyte, W.: NTRUencrypt. Technical report (2017). https://csrc.nist.gov/projects/post-quantum-cryptography/round-1-submissions

22. Zhang, Z., Plantard, T., Susilo, W.: Reaction attack on outsourced computing with fully homomorphic encryption schemes. In: Kim, H. (ed.) ICISC 2011. LNCS, vol. 7259, pp. 419–436. Springer, Heidelberg (2012). https://doi.org/10.1007/978-3-642-31912-9_28

On the Complexity of "Superdetermined" Minrank Instances

Javier Verbel[1(✉)], John Baena[1], Daniel Cabarcas[1], Ray Perlner[2], and Daniel Smith-Tone[2,3]

[1] Universidad Nacional de Colombia, Sede Medellín, Medellín, Colombia
{javerbelh,jbbaena,dcabarc}@unal.edu.co
[2] National Institute of Standards and Technology, Gaithersburg, USA
ray.perlner@nist.gov
[3] University of Louisville, Louisville, USA
daniel-c.smith@louisville.edu

Abstract. The Minrank (MR) problem is a computational problem closely related to attacks on code- and multivariate-based schemes. In this paper we revisit the so-called Kipnis-Shamir (KS) approach to this problem. We extend previous complexity analysis by exposing non-trivial syzygies through the analysis of the Jacobian of the resulting system, with respect to a group of variables. We focus on a particular set of instances that yield a very overdetermined system which we refer to as "superdetermined". We provide a tighter complexity estimate for such instances and discuss its implications for the key recovery attack on some multivariate schemes. For example, in HFE the speedup is roughly a square root.

Keywords: Minrank problem · Multivariate · Cryptanalysis · HFE

1 Introduction

The post-quantum cryptography initiative emerges in response to Shor's factoring algorithm [25], to identify quantum hard problems to support cryptographic constructions. This major endeavor has come to a climax in recent years with NIST's ongoing post-quantum "competition."

One central problem is the Minrank problem (MR). Its decisional version is, given m matrices $M_1, M_2, \ldots, M_m \in \mathcal{M}_{n \times n}(\mathbb{F})$, and a target rank r, to determine whether there exists a linear combination of these matrices with rank at most r. It is important both in multivariate public key cryptography [4,21,23,26], and in code-based cryptography [19]. Buss et al. first introduced the MR problem and proved it NP-complete [3]. In the context of cryptography, MR first appeared as part of an attack against the HFE cryptosystem by Kipnis and Shamir [21]. There are three well known approaches to solve the Minrank problem, namely, Kipnis-Shamir (KS), minors [16], and linear algebra search [20].

The complexity of the minors approach and of the linear algebra search are well understood. However, the complexity of the KS approach is not so clear. In

© Springer Nature Switzerland AG 2019
J. Ding and R. Steinwandt (Eds.): PQCrypto 2019, LNCS 11505, pp. 167–186, 2019.
https://doi.org/10.1007/978-3-030-25510-7_10

[16], the authors assume that a generic instance of KS yields a "generic enough" bilinear system (see Sect. 2.2), and under this assumption, using the results in [17], they estimate the solving degree at $d = \min(m, r(n - r)) + 1$ and so the complexity of KS as $O\left(\binom{m+r(n-r)+d-1}{d}^{\omega}\right)$, with $2 \leq \omega \leq 3$. Experimental evidence shows that this estimate wildly overestimates the true solving degree [4].

An important technical contribution of this paper is to show that the assumption that the KS system is generic bilinear is unrealistic. The system is indeed bilinear in two sets of variables that we call the linear variables and the kernel variables. However, we expose the structure in the system beyond bilinearity. It can be seen as having a sequence of generic bilinear blocks. Such a structure implies that the Jacobians with respect to the linear and kernel variables have particular forms. This is important because left kernel vectors of the Jacobian are syzygies. Thus, through the Jacobian with respect to the linear variables, we show how to construct some non-trivial syzygies, yielding non-trivial degree falls.

The degree of these syzygies suggests a crucial distinction between two cases of the MR problem. If $m > nr$, these syzygies typically have degree $r + 2$. However, if $m < nr$, we can construct a number of lower degree syzygies. We refer to instances where $m < nr$ as "superdetermined." This property applies to several multivariate schemes and it is in contrast to instances of the minrank problem that occur in other contexts, like rank-based cryptography.

The exposed structure of the KS system leads to tighter complexity estimates for the superdetermined MR instances. Using the XL algorithm and multiplying only by monomials from kernel variables, the complexity of solving uniformly random instances of KS systems is $O\left((r\kappa)^{(d_{KS}+2)\omega}\right)$, where $2 < \omega \leq 3$,

$$d_{KS} = \min\left\{d \mid \left[\binom{r}{d}n > \binom{r}{d+1}m\right], 1 \leq d \leq r - 1\right\},$$

and κ can be chosen so that $\max\left\{\frac{m}{n-r}, d_{KS} + 1\right\} \leq \kappa \leq n - r$. This is much lower than previous estimates. For example, if $m = n$ and $r < \sqrt{n}$, then $d_{KS} \leq r/2 + 1$, and we can choose $\kappa = \sqrt{n}$, so that, $r\kappa < n$, and hence, our complexity estimate is $O(n^{(r/2)\omega})$, compared to $O(n^{r\omega})$ from previous estimates, c.f. [1].

Since a key recovery attack based on the MR problem can be performed on several multivariate schemes, we revise the complexity of the KS method for some multivariate schemes such as HFE, ZHFE, and HFEv-. The speedup in each case depends on the ratio of m to n and on the relation between n and r. For example, in HFE the speedup is roughly a square root.

The paper is organized as follows. In Sect. 2 we present background material. In Sect. 3 we describe the structure of the KS system. In Sect. 4 we provide the main results of the paper, including the construction of the syzygies. In Sect. 5 we revise the complexity of the KS method based on the new findings. In Sect. 6 we provide some experimental data supporting the theoretical results. Finally, in Sect. 7 we discuss the implications of our findings for some multivariate schemes.

2 Preliminaries

2.1 Solving Multivariate Systems of Equations

Let $\mathbb{F}$ be a finite field, and consider the polynomial system $F = \mathbf{a}$, where $\mathbf{a}$ is an element in the image of $F = (f_1, \ldots, f_m) : \mathbb{F}^n \to \mathbb{F}^m$, and the f_i's are multivariate polynomials in the unknowns $x_1, \ldots, x_n$, with coefficients in $\mathbb{F}$. The first effective algorithm for solving nonlinear multivariate systems did so by computing a Gröbner basis for the ideal generated by the equations [2]. Since the late 90s, however, far superior algorithms have been developed such as Faugère's F4 and F5 [14,15], and the XL family of algorithms inspired by [22] and popularized in [6,21].

The XL algorithm simply computes an echelon form of the Macaulay matrix in degree d of F for high enough d. This is the matrix whose columns represent the monomials of degree at most d with rows representing each polynomial of degree less than or equal to d of the tf_i, where t is a monomial. It can be shown that there exists some degree d such that this echelon form is a Gröbner basis of the ideal. The algorithms F4 and F5 are similar but more efficient in removing redundant rows a priori. The first fall degree d_{ff} is the smallest degree such that some polynomial drops in degree after echelonizing the Macaulay matrix. It is widely accepted that d_{ff} is a good parameter to measure the complexity of solving polynomial systems [10–13]. The reason is that often the solving degree is not much larger than the first fall degree. Our experiments confirm this is the case for KS systems, as shown below in Sect. 6.

2.2 Bilinear Systems

Consider two tuples of unknowns $\mathbf{x} = (x_1, x_2, \ldots, x_{n_1})$ and $\mathbf{y} = (y_1, y_2, \ldots, y_{n_2})$. Let $\mathbb{F}[\mathbf{x}, \mathbf{y}]$ denote the ring of multivariate polynomials with coefficients in $\mathbb{F}$ and variables $x_1, x_2, \ldots, x_{n_1}, y_1, y_2, \ldots, y_{n_2}$. A *bilinear polynomial* $f(\mathbf{x}, \mathbf{y})$ is a quadratic polynomial in $\mathbb{F}[\mathbf{x}, \mathbf{y}]$ which is affine in each set of variables. If we can write $f(\mathbf{x}, \mathbf{y}) = \mathbf{x}^\top A \mathbf{y}$ for some $A \in \mathcal{M}_{n_1 \times n_2}(\mathbb{F})$, we say f is a *homogeneous bilinear polynomial*.

Throughout this work, sequences of polynomials are considered as column vectors of polynomials. Suppose $f_i \in \mathbb{F}[\mathbf{x}, \mathbf{y}]$ is a bilinear polynomial for $i = 1, 2, \ldots, m$. The sequence $\mathcal{F} = (f_1, f_2, \ldots, f_m)$ is called a *bilinear sequence* on $\mathbb{F}[\mathbf{x}, \mathbf{y}]$. In the particular case when each f_i is also homogeneous, we say $\mathcal{F}$ is a *homogeneous bilinear sequence* on $\mathbb{F}[\mathbf{x}, \mathbf{y}]$.

Definition 1. *Given a sequence $\mathcal{F} = (f_1, f_2, \ldots, f_m)$ on $\mathbb{F}[\boldsymbol{x}, \boldsymbol{y}]$, the Jacobian of $\mathcal{F}$ with respect to the set $\boldsymbol{x}$, is given by $\mathsf{jac}_{\boldsymbol{x}}(\mathcal{F}) = \left[\frac{\partial f_i}{\partial x_j} \right]_{1 \leq i \leq m, 1 \leq j \leq n_1}$. Likewise we define $\mathsf{jac}_{\boldsymbol{y}}(\mathcal{F})$, the Jacobian of $\mathcal{F}$ with respect to the set $\boldsymbol{y}$.*

When $\mathcal{F}$ is a bilinear sequence, each entry of $\mathsf{jac}_{\mathbf{x}}(\mathcal{F})$ (*resp.* $\mathsf{jac}_{\mathbf{y}}(\mathcal{F})$) is a linear form in the $\mathbf{y}$ (*resp.* $\mathbf{x}$) variables. A *syzygy* of $\mathcal{F}$ is a sequence $\mathcal{G} = (g_1, g_2, \ldots, g_m) \in \mathbb{F}[\mathbf{x}, \mathbf{y}]^m$ such that $\sum_{i=1}^m g_i f_i = 0$.

Proposition 1. *Let* $\mathcal{F} = (f_1, f_2, \ldots, f_m)$ *be a homogeneous bilinear sequence on* $\mathbb{F}[x, y]$. *Suppose* $\mathcal{G} = (g_1, g_2, \ldots, g_m)$ *is a sequence on* $\mathbb{F}[y]$, *then*

$$\sum_{i=1}^{m} g_i f_i = 0 \tag{1}$$

if and only if $\mathcal{G}^{\top}$ *belongs to the left-kernel of* $jac_x(\mathcal{F})$.

Proposition 2. *Suppose that* $\mathcal{F}$ *is a homogeneous bilinear sequence on* $\mathbb{F}[x, y]$. *If a sequence* $\mathcal{G}$ *on* $\mathcal{F}[x]$ *is a syzygy of* $\mathcal{F}$, *then* $\mathcal{G}$ *is not a trivial syzygy*[1].

2.3   Minrank Problem

One complexity theoretic problem related to the hardness of solving certain multivariate systems is the MinRank (MR) problem. The computational MR problem can be stated as follows.

Problem 1 (MinRank (Search Version)). *Given a positive integer* r, *and* m *matrices* $M_1, M_2, \ldots, M_m \in \mathcal{M}_{s \times t}(\mathbb{F})$, *find* $x_1, x_2, \ldots, x_m \in \mathbb{F}$ *such that* $\mathsf{Rank}(\sum_{\ell=1}^{m} x_\ell M_\ell) \leq r$.

The decisional version of the MR problem is known to be NP-complete even if we insist that $s = t = n$, see [3], and seems difficult in practice. There are three main methods in the literature for solving the MR problem, Kipnis-Shamir modeling, minors modeling [1] and linear algebra search [20].

Introduced by Kipnis and Shamir in [21], the KS method stands on the following fact: if $p < n$, $M \in \mathcal{M}_{n \times n}(\mathbb{F})$, $K' \in \mathcal{M}_{n \times p}(\mathbb{F})$ has rank p and $MK' = 0$, then $\mathsf{Rank}(M) \leq n - p$. Thus, the MR problem can be solved by finding $x_1, \ldots, x_m, k_1, \ldots, k_{r(n-r)} \in \mathbb{F}$ such that

$$\left(\sum_{\ell=1}^{m} x_\ell M_\ell\right) \begin{bmatrix} I_{n-r} \\ K^{\top} \end{bmatrix} = \mathbf{0}, \tag{2}$$

where

$$K = \begin{bmatrix} k_1 & k_2 & \cdots & k_r \\ \vdots & \vdots & \ddots & \vdots \\ k_{r(n-r-1)+1} & k_{r(n-r-1)+2} & \cdots & k_{r(n-r)} \end{bmatrix} \tag{3}$$

and I_{n-r} is the identity matrix of size $n - r$. If there exists a matrix in the span of the M_i's such that its column space is generated by its r rightmost columns, then the system (2) has a solution. This system is bilinear in the variables $\mathbf{x} = (x_1, \ldots, x_m)$ and the unknown entries $\mathbf{k} = (k_1, k_2, \ldots, k_{r(n-r)})$ of K. Throughout this work we will refer to the first group as the *linear variables*, and to the second one as the *kernel variables*. Therefore, (2) can be seen as a bilinear system of $n(n-r)$ equations in $m + r(n-r)$ variables. The complexity

---

[1] For a formal definition of a trivial syzygy see [13].

of solving this kind of system has been studied by Faugère et al. in [16,17]. They upper bound the complexity of KS modeling by that of solving a generic bilinear system with $n(n-r)$ equations, where one group of variables has m elements and the other has $r(n-r)$ elements. In that case, the given bound is

$$O\left(\left(\frac{m+r(n-r)+\min(m,r(n-r))+1}{\min(m,r(n-r))+1}\right)^{\omega}\right),$$

where $2 \leq \omega \leq 3$ is the linear algebra constant.

3   The Structure of the KS System

In this section we describe the basic structure of the system given in (2). First, in Sect. 3.1, we show that such a matrix equation can be seen as a set of $n-r$ chained bilinear subsystems, where each subsystem has generic quadratic part and linear part involving only the $\mathbf{x}$ variables. Then, in Sect. 3.2, we describe the Jacobian of the system with respect to the kernel variables. We show that if a KS instance $\mathcal{F}$ is chosen uniformly at random, then, with high probability, the syzygies of $\mathcal{F}$ that only involve linear variables have degree at least r.

3.1   KS and Bilinear System

Set $M = \sum_{\ell=1}^{m} x_\ell M_\ell$, where each $M_\ell \in \mathcal{M}_{n \times n}(\mathbb{F})$. Let $M_{(i,j)}$ and $M_{\ell,(i,j)}$ denote the (i,j) entry of the matrices M and M_ℓ, respectively. Under this setting, the (i,j) entry of $M \cdot [I_{n-r} \ K]^{\top}$ is given by the polynomial

$$f_j^{(i)} = \sum_{t=1}^{r} M_{(i,n-r+t)} \cdot k_{(t-1)r+j} + M_{(i,j)} \in \mathbb{F}[\mathbf{x}, \mathbf{k}], \qquad (4)$$

where $1 \leq i \leq n$, $1 \leq j \leq n-r$, and $k_{(t-1)r+j}$ is located at the (t,j) entry of K. The sequence $\mathcal{F}$ formed by the $n(n-r)$ polynomials given in (4) is called a KS *sequence* with parameters n, m, r. The sequence $\mathcal{F}$ is bilinear in the sets of unknowns $\mathbf{x} = (x_1, \ldots, x_m)$ and $\mathbf{k} = (k_1, k_2, \ldots, k_{r(n-r)})$. Recall that we refer to $\mathbf{x}$ and $\mathbf{k}$ as the linear and kernel variables, respectively. We also denote as $\mathsf{KS}(n,m,r)$ the set of KS sequences with parameters n, m, r. A KS *system* is a system of the form $\mathcal{F} = \mathbf{0}$, where $\mathcal{F}$ is a KS sequence.

Even though a sequence $\mathcal{F} \in \mathsf{KS}(n,m,r)$ is bilinear, it is not a generic one. Notice that each polynomial $f_j^{(i)}$ only involves r variables of the set $\mathbf{k}$ and its linear part only contains variables from $\mathbf{x}$. For $t = 1, 2, \ldots, n-r$, let $\mathcal{F}_t$ denote the subsequence of $\mathcal{F}$ given by $\mathcal{F}_t = (f_t^{(1)}, f_t^{(2)}, \ldots, f_t^{(n)})$. This sequence is bilinear in the set of variables $\mathbf{x}$ and $\mathbf{k}^{(t)} = (k_{(t-1)r+1}, k_{(t-1)r+2}, \ldots, k_{tr})$. Notice that the coefficient of every quadratic monomial in $\mathcal{F}$ can be any element in $\mathbb{F}$. On the contrary, the linear part of the polynomials in $\mathcal{F}$ only contains linear variables, so the coefficients of the kernel variables in the linear part of the polynomials in $\mathcal{F}$ are forced to be zero. Thus, a sequence $\mathcal{F} \in \mathsf{KS}(n,m,r)$ can be seen as $\mathcal{F} = (\mathcal{F}_1, \mathcal{F}_2, \ldots, \mathcal{F}_{n-r})$, where the quadratic part of $\mathcal{F}_t$ is generic (no restrictions at all) and the linear part is a generic linear form in the linear variables.

3.2   Jacobian with Respect to Kernel Variables

Let us begin by showing the structure of the Jacobian with respect to the kernel variables for KS sequences. Here we set $\mathcal{F}_t = (f_t^{(1)}, f_t^{(2)}, \ldots, f_t^{(n)})$, $f_t^{(i)}$, M as in Sect. 3.1 and $\otimes$ will denote the Kronecker product.

Lemma 1. *Suppose $\mathcal{F} = (\mathcal{F}_1, \mathcal{F}_2, \ldots, \mathcal{F}_{n-r}) \in \mathsf{KS}(n, m, r)$. Let I_{n-r} be the identity matrix of size $n - r$. Then for $j \in \{1, 2, \ldots, n - r\}$, we have that $\mathsf{jac}_{\mathbf{k}^{(1)}}(\mathcal{F}_1) = \mathsf{jac}_{\mathbf{k}^{(j)}}(\mathcal{F}_j)$, and $\mathsf{jac}_{\mathbf{k}}(\mathcal{F}) = I_{n-r} \otimes \mathsf{jac}_{\mathbf{k}^{(1)}}(\mathcal{F}_1)$.*

Remark 1. Assume $\mathcal{F}$ denotes the quadratic part of a sequence in $\mathsf{KS}(n, m, r)$. By Proposition 1 and Lemma 1, $\mathcal{F}$ has a degree d syzygy $\mathcal{G} \in \mathbb{F}[\mathbf{x}]^{n(n-r)}$ if and only if $\mathcal{F}_1$ has a degree d syzygy $\mathcal{G}_1 \in \mathbb{F}[\mathbf{x}]^n$. Explicitly, each syzygy $\mathcal{G}$ of $\mathcal{F}$ can be written as $(\mathcal{G}_1, \mathcal{G}_2, \ldots, \mathcal{G}_{n-r})$, where each $\mathcal{G}_j$ is a syzygy of $\mathcal{F}_1$.

Now suppose that the matrices $M_1, M_2, \ldots, M_m \in \mathcal{M}_{n \times n}(\mathbb{F})$ are chosen uniformly at random. Each entry of the matrix $M = \sum_{i=1}^m x_i M_i$ is a uniformly chosen linear form in the linear variables. In particular, its r rightmost columns are the Jacobian of a uniformly chosen homogeneous bilinear sequence. This is a bilinear sequence with $m + r$ variables and n equations. Assume $\mathcal{F}_1$ is underdetermined $(n < m + r)$ and that $r < n$. If Conjecture 1 in Sect. 4.2 of [17] is true, with high probability the left kernel of $\mathsf{jac}_{\mathbf{k}^{(1)}}(\mathcal{F}_1)$ is generated by

$$\text{Ker} := \left\{ \left(\text{minor}(\tilde{M}_T, 1), -\text{minor}(\tilde{M}_T, 2), \ldots, (-1)^n \text{minor}(\tilde{M}_T, n) \right) \mid T \in \mathcal{T} \right\},$$

where $\tilde{M}_T = [\tilde{M} \; T]$ with $\tilde{M} = \mathsf{jac}_{\mathbf{k}^{(1)}}(\mathcal{F}_1)$, $\text{minor}(\tilde{M}_T, j)$ denotes the determinant of $\tilde{M}_T$ after removing its j-th row, and $\mathcal{T}$ is the set of $n \times (n - r - 1)$ matrices such that

- each column of T has exactly a 1 and the rest of its entries are 0,
- each row of T has at most a 1 and the remaining entries 0,
- if i_j denotes the number of the row containing the only 1 of the j−th column and if $j < t$, then $i_j < i_t$.

Notice that Ker has $\binom{n}{r+1}$ elements. Each of them has exactly $r + 1$ nonzero components and every nonzero component is a different minor of $\tilde{M}$ of size r. Since each entry of $\tilde{M}$ is a homogeneous linear polynomial in the $\mathbf{x}$ variables, $\text{Ker} \subset \mathbb{F}[\mathbf{x}]_r^n$ [2]. Consequently, if Conjecture 1 in [17] is true, then we do not expect to find an element in Ker having degree less than r.

The following theorem summarizes these results. We include a proof for completeness.

Theorem 1. *Suppose Conjecture 1 in [17] is true, $\mathcal{F} \in \mathsf{KS}(n, m, r)$ is chosen uniformly at random. Then, using only monomials in the linear variables in the XL algorithm, with high probability the first fall degree is $r + 2$.*

---

[2] $\mathbb{F}[\mathbf{x}]_r$ denotes the vector space formed by the degree d homogeneous polynomials in $\mathbb{F}[\mathbf{x}]$.

Proof. By Proposition 1 and Lemma 1, we only need to prove that with high probability there is not $\mathcal{G}_1 \in \mathbb{F}[\mathbf{x}]^n$ having degree less than r and $\mathcal{G}_1^\top \mathrm{jac}_{\mathbf{k}^{(1)}}(\mathcal{F}_1) = 0$. Assuming that Conjecture 1 in [17] is true, if $\mathcal{F} \in \mathsf{KS}(n, m, r)$ is chosen uniformly at random, then with high probability Ker generates the left kernel of $\mathrm{jac}_{\mathbf{k}^{(1)}}(\mathcal{F}_1)$. Therefore, with high probability, each syzygy of $\mathcal{F}_1$, only involving $\mathbf{x}$ variables, has degree at least $r + 2$.

4   Jacobian with Respect to the Linear Variables

The Jacobian of a KS system with respect to the linear variables deserves a section of its own. We provide a detailed description here and describe non-trivial syzygies that arise from this structure. We show that if $m < nr$ non-trivial syzygies of the quadratic part of $\mathcal{F}$ can be explicitly built, having degree less than r. In Sect. 4.1 we use a small example to motivate the notation thereafter. We then provide a general construction in Sect. 4.2 for square matrices, and further generalize in Sect. 4.3 to non-square matrices and fewer kernel vectors.

Let us consider an MR instance with m matrices $M_1, \ldots, M_m \in \mathcal{M}_{n \times n}(\mathbb{F})$ and target rank r. Recall that the KS system is given by $\left(\sum_{i=1}^m x_i M_i \right) K' = \mathbf{0}$, where the kernel matrix is $K' = \begin{bmatrix} I_{n-r} & K \end{bmatrix}^\top$ with K as in (3). The Jacobian with respect to the linear variables of the corresponding sequence $\mathcal{F} \in \mathsf{KS}(n, m, r)$ can be written as $\mathrm{jac}_{\mathbf{x}}(\mathcal{F}) = (I_n \otimes K) L + C$, where $C \in \mathcal{M}_{n(n-r) \times m}(\mathbb{F})$, L is an $nr \times m$ matrix whose rows $L_1, L_2, \ldots, L_{rn}$ are given by the expression $L_{r(i-1)+j} = \begin{bmatrix} M_{1,(i,n-r+j)} & M_{2,(i,n-r+j)} & \cdots & M_{m,(i,n-r+j)} \end{bmatrix}$ for $i = 1, 2, \ldots, n$ and $j = 1, 2, \ldots, r$.

The approach we follow here to find syzygies of a KS sequence $\mathcal{F}$ is the same used in Sect. 3.2, i.e., we find elements in the left-kernel of the Jacobian of the quadratic part of $\mathcal{F}$, but now with respect to the linear variables. By Proposition 1, those kernel elements correspond to syzygies of the quadratic part of $\mathcal{F}$. In order to simplify the notation, throughout this section, we assume that the sequence $\mathcal{F} \in \mathsf{KS}(n, m, r)$ only contains its quadratic part. Under such assumption, the Jacobian with respect to the $\mathbf{x}$ variables of the sequence $\mathcal{F}$ is given by $\mathrm{jac}_{\mathbf{x}}(\mathcal{F}) = (I_n \otimes K) L$.

From now on $\ker_l(B)$ will denote the left-kernel of a matrix B. A naïve way to find elements in $\ker_l(\mathrm{jac}_{\mathbf{x}}(\mathcal{F}))$ is by finding elements in $\ker_l(I_n \otimes K)$. Those kernel elements have degree r and can be built analogously as we did in Sect. 3.2 for $\mathrm{jac}_{\mathbf{k}}(\mathcal{F})$. A natural question is whether it is possible to get degree falls at a smaller degree from $\mathrm{jac}_{\mathbf{x}}(\mathcal{F})$. The answer to this question is affirmative under certain conditions. In Sect. 4.2 we show how it can be done for general sequences in $\mathsf{KS}(n, m, r)$, with $m < nr$. We now show a small example to introduce the general process.

4.1   A Small Example $n = 4$, $M = 4$ and $r = 2$

Here we show how to build degree one syzygies of a sequence $\mathcal{F} \in \mathsf{KS}(4, 4, 2)$, which involve only the kernel variables. In this particular case, the Jacobian $\mathrm{jac}_{\mathbf{x}}(\mathcal{F})$ is given by

$$\mathsf{jac}_{\mathbf{x}}(\mathcal{F}) = \left(\begin{bmatrix} 1\,0\,0\,0 \\ 0\,1\,0\,0 \\ 0\,0\,1\,0 \\ 0\,0\,0\,1 \end{bmatrix} \otimes \begin{bmatrix} k_1 & k_2 \\ k_3 & k_4 \end{bmatrix} \right) \cdot L.$$

Suppose $(a_1, a_2, \ldots, a_8) \in \ker_l(L)$, $\mathbf{v}_0 = (a_2, a_4, a_6, a_8) \otimes (-k_3, k_1)$ and $\mathbf{v}_1 = (a_1, a_3, a_5, a_7) \otimes (k_4, -k_2)$. Then $\mathbf{v}_0 (I_4 \otimes K) = \det(K) [(0, 1) \otimes (a_2, a_4, a_6, a_8)]$ and $\mathbf{v}_1 (I_4 \otimes K) = \det(K) [(1, 0) \otimes (a_1, a_3, a_5, a_7)]$. Thus

$$(\mathbf{v}_0 + \mathbf{v}_1)\mathsf{jac}_{\mathbf{x}}(\mathcal{F}) = \det(K)(a_1, a_2, \ldots, a_8) \cdot L = \mathbf{0},$$

and $\mathbf{v}_0 + \mathbf{v}_1$ is a syzygy of $\mathcal{F}$ of degree one.

We just saw how to build a syzygy of degree one, namely $\mathbf{v}_0 + \mathbf{v}_1$. If we consider $\mathbf{b} \in \ker_l(L)$, linearly independent with $\mathbf{a} = (a_1, \ldots, a_8)$, and repeat the process described above, then we end up with a degree one syzygy $\tilde{\mathbf{v}}_0 + \tilde{\mathbf{v}}_1$ linearly independent with $\mathbf{v}_0 + \mathbf{v}_1$. Indeed, since $\mathbf{v}_0, \mathbf{v}_1$ do not share monomials componentwise, neither do $\tilde{\mathbf{v}}_0$ and $\tilde{\mathbf{v}}_1$. Thus, we have that

$$x(\mathbf{v}_0 + \mathbf{v}_1) + y(\tilde{\mathbf{v}}_0 + \tilde{\mathbf{v}}_1) = \mathbf{0} \quad \text{if and only if} \quad x\mathbf{v}_0 + y\tilde{\mathbf{v}}_0 = 0 \text{ and } x\mathbf{v}_1 + y\tilde{\mathbf{v}}_1 = 0,$$

and the right-hand implication happens if and only if $x\mathbf{a} + y\mathbf{b} = 0$. Consequently, $\mathbf{v}_1 + \mathbf{v}_2$ and $\tilde{\mathbf{v}}_1 + \tilde{\mathbf{v}}_2$ are linearly independent if and only if $\mathbf{a}$ and $\mathbf{b}$ are.

As a consequence of the previous analysis, we can build a set of linearly independent degree one syzygies in $\mathcal{F}[\mathbf{k}]$ with as many elements as the dimension of $\ker_l(L)$. Thus, if $\mathcal{F} \in \mathsf{KS}(4, 4, 2)$ is chosen uniformly at random, so are the matrices M_1, M_2, M_3, M_4 used to build $\mathcal{F}$. In particular, L is a uniformly random matrix of size 8×4, so with high probability, the left kernel of L has dimension 4, which is the maximum number of linearly independent syzygies of degree one that we can construct as above.

4.2   First Degree Fall for Any n, m, r, with $m < rn$

We now describe a general method to find syzygies of degree d_{KS} of a sequence $\mathcal{F} \in \mathsf{KS}(n, m, r)$, where d_{KS} is some particular integer less than r.

Let us begin by introducing the notation using throughout this section. Here $k_1, k_2, \ldots, k_{r(n-r)}$ are the entries of the matrix K, as shown in (3). Given two vectors of integers $\mathbf{l} = (l_1 + 1, \ldots, l_\ell + 1)$ and $\mathbf{c} = (c_1, \ldots, c_\ell)$, where $1 \le c_i \le r$ and $1 \le l_i + 1 \le n - r$ for $i = 1, \ldots, r$, we define $K_{\mathbf{l}, \mathbf{c}}$ as

$$K_{\mathbf{l}, \mathbf{c}} = \begin{vmatrix} k_{rl_1 + c_1} & k_{rl_1 + c_2} & \cdots & k_{rl_1 + c_\ell} \\ k_{rl_2 + c_1} & k_{rl_2 + c_2} & \cdots & k_{rl_2 + c_\ell} \\ \vdots & \vdots & \ddots & \vdots \\ k_{rl_\ell + c_1} & k_{rl_\ell + c_2} & \cdots & k_{rl_\ell + c_\ell} \end{vmatrix}.$$

Let d be an integer such that $0 < d + 1 \le \min\{n - r, r\}$. We set $\mathcal{C}_d = \{(t_1, \ldots, t_d) \mid t_k \in \mathbb{N}, 1 \le t_k < t_{k+1} \le r\}$ and $\mathcal{R}_d = \{(j_1 + 1, \ldots, j_{d+1} + 1) \mid j_k \in \mathbb{N}, 0 \le j_k < j_{k+1} \le n - r - 1\}$. The sets $\mathcal{C}_d, \mathcal{R}_d$ represent, respectively, all possible sets of d columns and sets of $d+1$ rows of K in ascending order. For any $\mathbf{t} = (t_1, \ldots, t_d) \in \mathcal{C}_d$ and $\mathbf{j} = (j_1 + 1, \ldots, j_{d+1} + 1) \in \mathcal{R}_d$, let $\mathbf{j}_s$ denote the vector resulting from removing the s-th entry from $\mathbf{j}$, and $V_{\mathbf{j}}^{\mathbf{t}}$ denote the column vector in $\mathbb{F}[\mathbf{k}]^{n-r}$ which has values $(-1)^1 K_{\mathbf{j}_1, \mathbf{t}}, \ldots, (-1)^{d+1} K_{\mathbf{j}_{d+1}, \mathbf{t}}$ in positions numbered by $j_1 + 1, \ldots, j_{d+1} + 1$, respectively, and zeros elsewhere. More precisely, $V_{\mathbf{j}}^{\mathbf{t}} = \sum_{i=1}^{d+1} (-1)^i K_{\mathbf{j}_i, \mathbf{t}} \, \mathbf{e}_{j_i+1}$, where $\mathbf{e}_i$ denotes the i-th standard basis vector of $\mathbb{F}^{n-r}$. Notice that if $\hat{\mathbf{e}}_1, \hat{\mathbf{e}}_2, \ldots, \hat{\mathbf{e}}_r$ are the canonical vectors in $\mathbb{F}^r$, then it can be shown that

$$\left(V_{\mathbf{j}}^{\mathbf{t}}\right)^{\top} K = \sum_{s \in \mathcal{S}_{\mathbf{t}}} K_{\mathbf{j}, (\mathbf{t}, s)} \, \hat{\mathbf{e}}_s^{\top}, \tag{5}$$

where $\mathcal{S}_{\mathbf{t}} := \{s \in \mathbb{N} \mid 1 \leq s \leq r, \; s \text{ is not an entry of } \mathbf{t}\}$. For $\mathbf{t} \in \mathcal{C}_d$ and $\mathbf{j} \in \mathcal{R}_d$, let $E_{\mathbf{j}, \mathbf{t}}$ be the subspace of $\mathbb{F}[\mathbf{k}]_d^{n(n-r)}$ spanned by $\left\{ \tilde{\mathbf{e}}_1 \otimes V_{\mathbf{j}}^{\mathbf{t}}, \ldots, \tilde{\mathbf{e}}_n \otimes V_{\mathbf{j}}^{\mathbf{t}} \right\}$, where $\tilde{\mathbf{e}}_i$ denotes the i-th standard vector basis of $\mathbb{F}^n$. It can be shown that if $\mathbf{j} \neq \mathbf{j}'$ or $\mathbf{t} \neq \mathbf{t}'$ then $E_{\mathbf{j}, \mathbf{t}} \cap E_{\mathbf{j}', \mathbf{t}'} = \{\mathbf{0}\}$.

Lemma 2. *Suppose $\mathbf{j}, \mathbf{j}' \in \mathcal{R}_d$, and $\mathbf{t}, \mathbf{t}' \in \mathcal{C}_d$. If $\mathbf{j} \neq \mathbf{j}'$ or $\mathbf{t} \neq \mathbf{t}'$ then $E_{\mathbf{j}, \mathbf{t}} \cap E_{\mathbf{j}', \mathbf{t}'} = \{\mathbf{0}\}$.*

Proof. First of all, note that if $\mathbf{e}_{\ell}'$ denotes the ℓ-th vector in the standard basis of $\mathbb{F}^{n(n-r)}$, then the following set is a basis for the $\mathbb{F}$-vector space $\mathbb{F}[\mathbf{k}]_d^{n(n-r)}$

$$\mathcal{B} = \{\mathbf{m} \, \mathbf{e}_{\ell}' \mid \mathbf{m} \in \mathbb{F}[\mathbf{k}]_d \text{ a monomial and } \ell = 1, \ldots, n(n-r)\}.$$

In particular, any basis element $\tilde{\mathbf{e}}_s \otimes V_{\mathbf{j}}^{\mathbf{t}}$ of $E_{\mathbf{j}, \mathbf{t}}$ can be seen as an $\mathbb{F}$-linear combination of elements in $\mathcal{B}$. Notice that if $\mathbf{j} = (j_1 + 1, j_2 + 2, \ldots, j_{d+1} + 2)$, by definition we have $V_{\mathbf{j}}^{\mathbf{t}} = \sum_{i=1}^{d+1} (-1)^i K_{\mathbf{j}_i, \mathbf{t}} \, \mathbf{e}_{j_i+1}$, hence

$$\tilde{\mathbf{e}}_s \otimes V_{\mathbf{j}}^{\mathbf{t}} = \sum_{i=1}^{d+1} (-1)^i K_{\mathbf{j}_i, \mathbf{t}} \, (\tilde{\mathbf{e}}_s \otimes \mathbf{e}_{j_i+1})$$

$$= \sum_{i=1}^{d+1} (-1)^i K_{\mathbf{j}_i, \mathbf{t}} \, \mathbf{e}_{(s-1)(n-r)+j_i+1}'.$$

Let us set

$$\mathcal{B}_{\mathbf{j}, \mathbf{t}}^s := \{\mathbf{m} \, \mathbf{e}_{(s-1)(n-r)+j_i+1}' \mid \mathbf{m} \text{ is a monomial of } K_{\mathbf{j}_i, \mathbf{t}} \text{ and } i = 1, \ldots, d+1\},$$

i.e., $\mathcal{B}_{\mathbf{j}, \mathbf{t}}^s$ contains the basis vectors from $\mathcal{B}$ whose $\mathbb{F}$-linear combination produces $\tilde{\mathbf{e}}_s \otimes V_{\mathbf{j}}^{\mathbf{t}}$. For this reason

$$E_{\mathbf{j}, \mathbf{t}} \subset \mathrm{Span}_{\mathbb{F}} \left\{ \bigcup_{s=1}^{n} \mathcal{B}_{\mathbf{j}, \mathbf{t}}^s \right\}.$$

Finally we show that in any case, $\mathbf{t} \neq \mathbf{t}'$ or $\mathbf{j} \neq \mathbf{j}'$, we have

$$\left\{\bigcup_{s=1}^{n} \mathcal{B}_{\mathbf{j},\mathbf{t}}^{s}\right\} \cap \left\{\bigcup_{s=1}^{n} \mathcal{B}_{\mathbf{j}',\mathbf{t}'}^{s}\right\} = \emptyset. \tag{6}$$

In the first case, there is some integer t which is a component of $\mathbf{t}$, but not a component of $\mathbf{t}'$. Because of the structure of K, it is clear that each monomial in the polynomial $K_{\mathbf{j}_i,\mathbf{t}}$ has a factor of the form k_{2j+t}. Since t does not appear as a component in $\mathbf{t}'$, no monomial in $K_{\mathbf{j}_i',\mathbf{t}'}$ has a factor of the form $k_{2j'+t}$. Consequently, Eq. (6) holds.

In the other case, $\mathbf{j} \neq \mathbf{j}'$, there is at least one index i for which $j_i + 1$ is a component of $\mathbf{j}$ and it is not a component of $\mathbf{j}'$. So each element in $\bigcup_{s=1}^{n} \mathcal{B}_{\mathbf{j},\mathbf{t}}^{s}$ has as a factor either a monomial of the form mk_{2j_i+t}, for some t, or the vector $\mathbf{e}'_{(s-1)(n-r)+j_i+1}$ for some s, and no element with such factors belongs to $\bigcup_{s=1}^{n} \mathcal{B}_{\mathbf{j}',\mathbf{t}'}^{s}$. Consequently, Eq. (6) holds.

Fix $\mathbf{t} = (t_1, \ldots, t_d) \in \mathcal{C}_d$ and $s \in \mathcal{S}_{\mathbf{t}}$. Let i be the only integer satisfying $t_i < s < t_{i+1}$ and σ the permutation that sends $(t_1, \ldots, t_i, s, t_{i+1}, \ldots, t_d)$ to $(t_1, \ldots, t_d, s)$. For each $s \in \{1, 2, \ldots, r\}$ define $\mathsf{sgn}(\mathbf{t}, s)$ to be $\mathsf{sgn}(\sigma)$ if $s \in \mathcal{S}_{\mathbf{t}}$ and zero otherwise[3]. Notice that, if $\tilde{\mathbf{t}} := (t_1, \ldots, t_i, s, t_{i+1}, \ldots, t_d)$, then $K_{\mathbf{j},\tilde{\mathbf{t}}}$ is a minor of K of size $d+1$. Moreover, for any $\mathbf{j} \in \mathcal{R}_d$ it holds that $\mathsf{sgn}(\mathbf{t}, s) \cdot K_{\mathbf{j},(\mathbf{t},s)}$ is equal to $K_{\mathbf{j},\tilde{\mathbf{t}}}$ if $s \in \mathcal{S}_{\mathbf{t}}$, or equal to 0 otherwise.

We now address the main theorem of this section. For some fixed $\mathbf{j} \in \mathcal{R}_d$ we establish a one-to-one correspondence between elements in the left-kernel of certain matrix $\tilde{B}_{\mathbf{j}}$ and certain elements in the left-kernel of $(I_n \otimes K)L$, where K is as in (3) and $L \in \mathcal{M}_{rn \times m}(\mathbb{F})$, see Theorem 2 below.

Before stating the mentioned theorem, let us describe the matrix $\tilde{B}_{\mathbf{j}}$ for a given $\mathbf{j} \in \mathcal{R}_d$. This is a column block matrix of size $\binom{r}{d}n \times \binom{r}{d+1}m$, with blocks $B_{\mathbf{t}_1}, B_{\mathbf{t}_2}, \ldots, B_{\mathbf{t}_\ell}$, where $\ell = \binom{r}{d}$ and each $B_{\mathbf{t}_i}$ is an $n \times \binom{r}{d+1}m$ matrix over $\mathbb{F}$. To define each block $B_{\mathbf{t}_i}$, we introduce one more notation. We denote by $\mathrm{MINORS}_{d+1}(K(\mathbf{j}))$ the set of minors of size $d + 1$ of the matrix $K(\mathbf{j})$, which is simply the matrix whose rows are the rows of K with indexes in $\mathbf{j}$. Let us fix an enumeration on that set of minors, say $\mathrm{MINORS}_{d+1}(K(\mathbf{j})) = \{\mathsf{m}_1, \mathsf{m}_2, \ldots, \mathsf{m}_{\ell'}\}$, with $\ell' = \binom{r}{d+1}$. For each $\mathbf{t}_i \in \mathcal{C}_d$, the block $B_{\mathbf{t}_i}$ is also a block matrix of the form $B_{\mathbf{t}_i} = [B_{\mathbf{t}_i,1} B_{\mathbf{t}_i,2} \cdots B_{\mathbf{t}_i,\ell'}]$, where $B_{\mathbf{t}_i,k}$ is a matrix of size $n \times m$, for $k = 1, 2, \ldots, \ell'$. A particular $B_{\mathbf{t}_i,k}$ is given by

$$B_{\mathbf{t}_i,k} := \mathsf{sgn}(\mathbf{t}_i, s) \left(L_s^{\top} L_{r+s}^{\top} \cdots L_{r(n-1)+s}^{\top}\right)^{\top}, \text{ where } L_1, L_2, \ldots, L_{rn} \text{ are the}$$

rows of L, if s is the unique integer such that $\mathsf{sgn}(\mathbf{t}_i, s)K_{\mathbf{j},(\mathbf{t}_i,s)} = \mathsf{m}_k$. Otherwise, $B_{\mathbf{t}_i,s}$ is the $n \times m$ zero matrix.

From now on we set $\mathcal{C}_d = \{\mathbf{t}_1, \mathbf{t}_2, \ldots, \mathbf{t}_\ell\}$.

Theorem 2. *Let $\mathbb{F}$ be a field, $L \in \mathcal{M}_{rn \times m}(\mathbb{F})$, d be an integer such that $0 < d + 1 \leq \min\{n - r, r\}$, $\mathbf{j} \in \mathcal{R}_d$, and $\mathbf{a} \in \mathbb{F}^{\ell n}$. If $\mathbf{a}_{\mathbf{t}_1}, \mathbf{a}_{\mathbf{t}_2}, \ldots, \mathbf{a}_{\mathbf{t}_\ell} \in \mathbb{F}^n$ are*

---

[3] $\mathsf{sgn}(\sigma)$ denotes the sign of the permutation σ.

such that $\boldsymbol{a} = (\boldsymbol{a}_{t_1}, \boldsymbol{a}_{t_2}, \ldots, \boldsymbol{a}_{t_\ell})$, then $\boldsymbol{a} \in \ker_l(\tilde{B}_j)$ if and only if $\sum_{k=1}^{\ell} \boldsymbol{a}_{t_k} \otimes V_j^{t_k} \in \ker_l[(I_n \otimes K)L]$. Moreover, assume $A = \{\boldsymbol{a}^1, \ldots, \boldsymbol{a}^h\}$ for some $1 \leq h \leq n|\mathcal{C}_d|$ and $\boldsymbol{a}^i := (\boldsymbol{a}_{t_1}^i, \ldots, \boldsymbol{a}_{t_\ell}^i)$, with $\boldsymbol{a}_{t_k}^i \in \mathbb{F}^n$ for $i = 1, \ldots, h$. Then, $\tilde{\mathcal{S}}_j := \left\{ \sum_{k=1}^{\ell} \boldsymbol{a}_{t_k}^i \otimes V_j^{t_k} \mid i = 1, \ldots, h \right\}$ is $\mathbb{F}$-linearly independent if and only if A is $\mathbb{F}$-linearly independent.

Proof. For each $\mathbf{t} \in \mathcal{C}_d$, we set $\mathbf{a_t} = (a_{1,t}, \ldots, a_{n,t}) \in \mathbb{F}^n$. So that $\mathbf{a_t} = \sum_{i=1}^{n} a_{i,t} \, \tilde{e}_i$, where $\tilde{e}_i$ denotes the i-th element in the standard basis of $\mathbb{F}^n$. By Eq. (5) we have

$$\sum_{\mathbf{t} \in \mathcal{C}_d} \left(\mathbf{a_t} \otimes V_{\mathbf{j}}^{\mathbf{t}} \right)^{\top} (I_n \otimes K) L = \sum_{\mathbf{t} \in \mathcal{C}_d} \left(\mathbf{a_t^{\top}} \otimes (V_{\mathbf{j}}^{\mathbf{t}})^{\top} K \right) L$$

$$= \sum_{\mathbf{t} \in \mathcal{C}_d} \left(\mathbf{a_t^{\top}} \otimes \left[\sum_{s \in \mathcal{S}_t} K_{\mathbf{j},(\mathbf{t},s)} \, \hat{\mathbf{e}}_s^{\top} \right] \right) L$$

$$= \sum_{\mathbf{t} \in \mathcal{C}_d} \left[\sum_{s \in \mathcal{S}_t} K_{\mathbf{j},(\mathbf{t},s)} \sum_{i=1}^{n} a_{it} \, (\tilde{e}_i \otimes \hat{e}_s)^{\top} L \right]$$

$$= \sum_{\substack{\mathbf{t} \in \mathcal{C}_d \\ s \in \mathcal{S}_t}} \mathrm{sgn}(\mathbf{t}, s) \left[\mathbf{a_t^{\top}} \begin{pmatrix} L_s \\ L_{r+s} \\ \vdots \\ L_{r(n-1)+s} \end{pmatrix} \right] \mathrm{sgn}(\mathbf{t}, s) K_{\mathbf{j},(\mathbf{t},s)},$$

where $L_1, \ldots, L_{rn}$ are the rows of L. For each $\mathsf{m}_k \in \mathrm{MINORS}_{d+1}(K(\mathbf{j}))$ let $(\tilde{\mathbf{t}}_1, s_1), (\tilde{\mathbf{t}}_2, s_2), \ldots, (\tilde{\mathbf{t}}_e, s_e)$ be the sequence of $(d+1)$-tuples with $\tilde{\mathbf{t}}_i \in \mathcal{C}_d$ and $s_i \in \mathcal{S}_{\tilde{\mathbf{t}}_i}$ such that $\mathrm{sgn}(\tilde{\mathbf{t}}_j, s_j) K_{(\tilde{\mathbf{t}}_j, s_j)} = \mathsf{m}_k$ for $j = 1, 2, \ldots, e$. Thus

$$\sum_{\mathbf{t} \in \mathcal{C}_d} \left(\mathbf{a_t} \otimes V_{\mathbf{j}}^{\mathbf{t}} \right)^{\top} (I_n \otimes K) L = \sum_{k=1}^{\ell'} \left[\sum_{j=1}^{e} \mathrm{sgn}(\tilde{\mathbf{t}}_j, s_j) \mathbf{a}_{\tilde{\mathbf{t}}_j}^{\top} \begin{pmatrix} L_{s_j} \\ L_{r+s_j} \\ \vdots \\ L_{r(n-1)+s_j} \end{pmatrix} \right] \mathsf{m}_k$$

$$= \sum_{k=1}^{\ell'} \left(\sum_{\mathbf{t} \in \mathcal{C}_d} \mathbf{a_t} \mathbf{B}_{\mathbf{t},k} \right) \mathsf{m}_k.$$

The last equality holds because any $\mathbf{t} \in \mathcal{C}_d - \{\tilde{\mathbf{t}}_1, \tilde{\mathbf{t}}_2, \ldots, \tilde{\mathbf{t}}_e\}$ leads to a $\mathbf{B}_{\mathbf{t},k} = \mathbf{0}$. Since the minors of K do not have monomials in common, $\mathbf{a} = (\mathbf{a}_{t_1}, \ldots, \mathbf{a}_{t_\ell})$ is a vector such that $\sum_{i=1}^{\ell} \left(\mathbf{a}_{t_i} \otimes V_{\mathbf{j}}^{t_i} \right)^{\top} \in \ker_l[(I_n \otimes K)L]$ if and only if we have that $\sum_{i=1}^{\ell} \mathbf{a}_{t_i} \mathbf{B}_{t_i,k} = \mathbf{0}$ for each minor m_k. Equivalently, if and only if

$$\sum_{i=1}^{\ell} \mathbf{a}_{t_i} [\mathbf{B}_{t_i,1} \, \mathbf{B}_{t_i,2} \cdots \mathbf{B}_{t_i,\ell'}] = \mathbf{0}, \quad \sum_{i=1}^{\ell} \mathbf{a}_{t_i} \mathbf{B}_{t_i} = \mathbf{0},$$

$$(\mathbf{a}_{t_1}, \mathbf{a}_{t_2}, \ldots, \mathbf{a}_{t_\ell}) [\mathbf{B}_{t_1}^{\top} \, \mathbf{B}_{t_2}^{\top} \cdots \mathbf{B}_{t_\ell}^{\top}]^{\top} = \mathbf{0}, \quad \text{and } \mathbf{a}\tilde{B}_j = \mathbf{0}.$$

Now we prove the last statement of the theorem. Suppose $\mathbf{a}^1, \mathbf{a}^2, \ldots, \mathbf{a}^h \in \mathbb{F}^{\ell n}$ are linearly independent and $\mathbf{a}^i = (\mathbf{a}^i_{\mathbf{t}_1}, \mathbf{a}^i_{\mathbf{t}_2}, \ldots, \mathbf{a}^i_{\mathbf{t}_\ell})$, for each $i = 1, 2, \ldots, h$. Assume $x_1, x_2, \ldots, x_h \in \mathbb{F}$ are such that $\sum_{i=1}^h x_i \left(\sum_{j=1}^\ell \mathbf{a}^i_{\mathbf{t}_j} \otimes V_{\mathbf{j}}^{\mathbf{t}_j} \right) = \mathbf{0}$. Since each $\mathbf{a}^i_{\mathbf{t}_j} \otimes V_{\mathbf{j}}^{\mathbf{t}_j} \in E_{\mathbf{j},\mathbf{t}_j}$, so does every $\sum_{i=1}^h x_i \left(\mathbf{a}^i_{\mathbf{t}_j} \otimes V_{\mathbf{j}}^{\mathbf{t}_j} \right)$. By Lemma 2 the previous equation holds if and only if $\sum_{i=1}^h x_i \left(\mathbf{a}^i_{\mathbf{t}_j} \otimes V_{\mathbf{j}}^{\mathbf{t}_j} \right) = \mathbf{0}$, for each $j = 1, 2, \ldots, \ell$. Equivalently, $\sum_{i=1}^h x_i \mathbf{a}^i_{\mathbf{t}_j} = \mathbf{0}$ for each j. That is, $\sum_{i=1}^h x_i \mathbf{a}^i = \mathbf{0}$.

Remember that we are only considering the quadratic part of sequences $\mathcal{F} \in \mathsf{KS}(n, m, r)$, so that $\mathsf{jac}_{\mathbf{x}}(\mathcal{F}) = (I_n \otimes K) L$, where K is given in (3). Consequently, the previous theorem shows a way to build syzygies of $\mathcal{F}$ (see Proposition 1). For a fixed $j \in \mathcal{R}_d$, Theorem 2 also says that we can build as many syzygies as the dimension of the left-kernel of the matrix $\tilde{B}_{\mathbf{j}}$. For a matrix $L \in \mathcal{M}_{rn \times m}(\mathbb{F})$ chosen uniformly at random, we conjecture that the probability that $\tilde{B}_{\mathbf{j}}$ is full rank is very high and it depends on the size of $\mathbb{F}$.

Conjecture 1. Suppose $\binom{r}{d} n > \binom{r}{d+1} m$, $d + 1 \le \min\{n - r, r\}$, $m \le rn$, and $\mathbf{j} \in \mathcal{R}_d$. If $L \in \mathcal{M}_{rn \times m}(\mathbb{F})$ is chosen uniformly at random, then with overwhelming probability in the size of $\mathbb{F}$, the rank of $\tilde{B}_{\mathbf{j}}$ is $\binom{r}{d+1} m$.

We experimentally tested this conjecture for values of $20 \le n \le 25$, $n - 3 \le m \le 2n$, $6 \le r \le 10$ and $|\mathbb{F}| = 13$; and for $8 \le n \le 16$, $2 \le r \le 8$, $n - 4 \le m \le rn$ and $|\mathbb{F}| = 2$. Assuming that Conjecture 1 is true, we have the following corollary.

Corollary 1. *Suppose $\binom{r}{d} n > \binom{r}{d+1} m$, $d + 1 \le \min\{n - r, r\}$, $m < rn$, and $\mathbf{j} \in \mathcal{R}_d$. If $\mathcal{F} \in \mathsf{KS}(n, m, r)$ is chosen uniformly at random, and assuming Conjecture 1 holds, then with overwhelming probability, there is a set $\tilde{S}_{\mathbf{j}}$ of $\binom{r}{d} n - \binom{r}{d+1} m$ syzygies of $\mathcal{F}$ of degree d. Moreover, $\tilde{S}_{\mathbf{j}}$ is $\mathbb{F}$-linearly independent.*

Proof. Suppose $\mathcal{F} \in \mathsf{KS}(n, m, r)$ is chosen uniformly at random. Recall that $\mathsf{jac}_x(\mathcal{F}) = (I_n \otimes K) L$, so $L \in \mathcal{M}_{rn \times m}(\mathbb{F})$ can be seen as chosen uniformly at random as well. Let us set $A = \{\mathbf{a}^1, \mathbf{a}^2, \ldots, \mathbf{a}^h\}$ and define $\tilde{S}_{\mathbf{j}}$ and $\tilde{B}_{\mathbf{j}}$ as in Theorem 2. By this theorem, $A \subset \ker_l(\tilde{B}_{\mathbf{j}})$ is $\mathbb{F}$-linearly independent if and only if $\tilde{S}_{\mathbf{j}} \subset \ker_l[(I_n \otimes K)L]$ is linearly independent. By Conjecture 1, with overwhelming probability the dimension of $\ker_l(\tilde{B}_{\mathbf{j}})$ is $\binom{r}{d} n - \binom{r}{d+1} m$. Finally, by Proposition 1, each element in $\tilde{S}_{\mathbf{j}}$ is a syzygy of $\mathcal{F}$.

It can be shown that for different $\mathbf{j}, \mathbf{j}' \in \mathcal{R}_d$, $\tilde{S}_{\mathbf{j}} \cup \tilde{S}_{\mathbf{j}'}$ is a linearly independent set of syzygies of $\mathcal{F}$.

Proposition 3. *Suppose $j, j' \in \mathcal{R}_d$ are distinct and that $L \in \mathcal{M}_{rn \times m}(\mathbb{F})$. Let $A = \{a^1, \ldots, a^{\ell_1}\}$ and $B = \{b^1, \ldots, b^{\ell_2}\}$ be two sets not necessarily different, with $a^i = (a^i_{t_1}, a^i_{t_2}, \ldots, a^i_{t_{\ell'}})$ and $b^i = (b^i_{t_1}, b^i_{t_2}, \ldots, b^i_{t_\ell})$ as described in Theorem 2. If we set*

$$\tilde{S}_j = \left\{ \sum_{j=1}^\ell a^i_{t_j} \otimes V_j^{t_j} \mid i = 1, \ldots, \ell_1 \right\}, \quad \tilde{S}_{j'} = \left\{ \sum_{j=1}^\ell b^i_{t_j} \otimes V_j^{t_j} \mid i = 1, \ldots, \ell_2 \right\},$$

then $\mathcal{S}_j \cup \mathcal{S}_{j'}$ is a set of linearly independent vectors in $\ker_l[(I_n \otimes K)L]$ if and only if A and B are both linearly independent in $\ker_l(L)$.

Proof. By Theorem 2 we have that $A, B \subset \ker_l(\tilde{B}_j)$ and are $\mathbb{F}$-linearly independent if and only if $\mathcal{S}_j, \mathcal{S}_{j'} \subset \ker_l[(I_n \otimes K)L]$ and are both $\mathbb{F}$-linearly independent. Suppose there are $x_1, x_2, \ldots, x_{\ell_1}, y_1, y_2, \ldots, y_{\ell_2} \in \mathbb{F}$ such that

$$\sum_{i=1}^{\ell_1} x_i \left(\sum_{j=1}^{\ell} \mathbf{a}_{\mathbf{t}_j}^i \otimes V_j^{\mathbf{t}_j} \right) + \sum_{i=1}^{\ell_2} y_i \left(\sum_{j=1}^{\ell} \mathbf{b}_{\mathbf{t}_j}^i \otimes V_{j'}^{\mathbf{t}_j} \right) = 0, \quad \text{i.e.,}$$

$$\sum_{j=1}^{\ell} \left[\sum_{i=1}^{\ell_1} x_i \left(\mathbf{a}_{\mathbf{t}_j}^i \otimes V_j^{\mathbf{t}_j} \right) + \sum_{i=1}^{\ell_2} y_i \left(\mathbf{b}_{\mathbf{t}_j}^i \otimes V_{j'}^{\mathbf{t}_j} \right) \right] = 0.$$

Notice that each of the 2ℓ sums in the previous equation belongs to a different $E_{j,t}$ subspace. By Lemma 2, those subspaces have trivial intersection pairwise. Consequently, last equation holds if and only if each of those sums is zero, that is, for $j = 1, 2, \ldots, \ell$,

$$\sum_{i=1}^{\ell_1} x_i \left(\mathbf{a}_{\mathbf{t}_j}^i \otimes V_j^{\mathbf{t}_j} \right) = 0 \quad \text{and} \quad \sum_{i=1}^{\ell_2} y_i \left(\mathbf{b}_{\mathbf{t}_j}^i \otimes V_{j'}^{\mathbf{t}_j} \right) = 0,$$

which is true if and only if

$$\sum_{i=1}^{\ell_1} x_i \mathbf{a}^i = 0 \quad \text{and} \quad \sum_{i=1}^{\ell_2} y_i \mathbf{b}^i = 0.$$

As a consequence and assuming that Conjecture 1 is true, we can calculate a number of degree falls that we know for sure will happen at degree $d+2$, for a particular $d < r$.

Corollary 2. *Suppose Conjecture 1 is true, $\binom{r}{d}n > \binom{r}{d+1}m$, $d+1 \le \min\{n - r, r\}$ and $m < rn$. If $\mathcal{F} \in KS(n, m, r)$ is chosen uniformly at random, then with overwhelming probability there is a set of*

$$\binom{n-r}{d+1} \left[\binom{r}{d}n - \binom{r}{d+1}m \right]$$

linearly independent syzygies of $\mathcal{F}$ of degree d.

4.3 Analysis for Non-square MR and κ Kernel Vectors

In this part we adapt the analysis performed in Sect. 4.2 to MR instances with non-square matrices. We also see how the results of that section are affected if we consider a KS system with only κ kernel vectors.

Suppose p, q, m, r, κ are integers such that $m < rp$ and $\frac{m}{p-r} < \kappa \le q - r$. We can consider an MR instance with matrices $M_1, M_2, \ldots, M_m \in \mathcal{M}_{p \times q}(\mathbb{F})$ and target rank r. When we say that we are considering κ kernel vectors in the KS modeling, what we mean is that we are dealing with the system

$$\left(\sum_{i=1}^{m} x_i M_i\right) K'_\kappa = \mathbf{0}_{p \times \kappa}, \tag{7}$$

where K'_κ is the matrix consisting of the first κ columns of K', that is, $K'_\kappa = [\tilde{I}_\kappa \ K_\kappa]^\top$, $\tilde{I}_\kappa$ is formed by the first κ rows of the identity matrix I_{q-r} and

$$K_\kappa = \begin{bmatrix} k_1 & k_2 & \cdots & k_r \\ k_{r+1} & k_{r+2} & \cdots & k_{2r} \\ \vdots & \vdots & \ddots & \vdots \\ k_{r(\kappa-1)+1} & k_{r(\kappa-1)+2} & \cdots & k_{r\kappa} \end{bmatrix}.$$

Let us set $\mathbf{k} = (k_1, k_2, \ldots, k_{r\kappa})$, and let $\mathsf{KS}_\kappa(p \times q, m, r)$ be the set of all sequences in $\mathbb{F}[\mathbf{x}, \mathbf{k}]$ that are formed by the entries of any matrix that has the shape of the one on the left-hand side of (7). For each $\mathcal{F} \in \mathsf{KS}_\kappa(p \times q, m, r)$ its Jacobian is given by

$$\mathrm{jac}_{\mathbf{x}}(\mathcal{F}) = (I_p \otimes K_\kappa) L + C, \tag{8}$$

where $C \in \mathcal{M}_{p\kappa \times m}(\mathbb{F})$, L is an $rp \times m$ matrix with rows $L_1, L_2, \ldots, L_{rp}$ and $L_{r(i-1)+j} = \begin{bmatrix} M_{1,(i,p-r+j)} & M_{2,(i,p-r+j)} & \cdots & M_{m,(i,p-r+j)} \end{bmatrix}$ for $i = 1, 2, \ldots, p$ and $j = 1, 2, \ldots, r$.

Let $\mathcal{C}_d$ be like in Sect. 4.2 and $\mathcal{R}_{\kappa,d} := \{(j_1+1, \ldots, j_{d+1}+1) \mid j_k \in \mathbb{N}, \ 0 \le j_k < j_{k+1} \le \kappa - 1\}$. Provided an integer d, with $0 \le d \le \min\{\kappa-1, r-1\}$, and $\mathbf{j} \in \mathcal{R}_{\kappa,d}$, the matrix $\tilde{B}_{\mathbf{j}}$ is now of size $\binom{r}{d}p \times \binom{r}{d+1}m$. Such a matrix is constructed as in the square MR case, but setting $n = p$. The polynomial vector $V_{\mathbf{j}}^{\mathbf{t}}$ is defined like in the full kernel vector case, with the only difference that now it has length κ instead of $q - r$. The proof of the following theorem is analogous to the proof of Theorem 2.

Theorem 3. *Let $\mathbb{F}$ be a field, $L \in \mathcal{M}_{rp \times m}(\mathbb{F})$, d be an integer such that $0 < d+1 \le \min\{\kappa, r\}$, $\mathbf{j} \in \mathcal{R}_{\kappa,d}$, and $\mathbf{a} \in \mathbb{F}^{\ell p}$. If $\mathbf{a}_{t_1}, \mathbf{a}_{t_2}, \ldots, \mathbf{a}_{t_\ell} \in \mathbb{F}^p$ are such that $\mathbf{a} = (\mathbf{a}_{t_1}, \mathbf{a}_{t_2}, \ldots, \mathbf{a}_{t_\ell})$, then $\mathbf{a} \in \ker_l(\tilde{B}_{\mathbf{j}})$ if and only if $\sum_{k=1}^{\ell} \mathbf{a}_{t_k}^i \otimes V_{\mathbf{j}}^{t_k} \in \ker_l[(I_p \otimes K)L]$. Moreover, if $A = \{\mathbf{a}^1, \ldots, \mathbf{a}^h\}$ for some $1 \le h \le n|\mathcal{C}_d|$ and $\mathbf{a}^i := (\mathbf{a}_{t_1}^i, \mathbf{a}_{t_2}^i, \ldots, \mathbf{a}_{t_\ell}^i)$, with $\mathbf{a}_{t_k}^i \in \mathbb{F}^p$ for $i = 1, \ldots, h$, then*

$$\tilde{\mathcal{S}}_{\mathbf{j}} := \left\{ \sum_{k=1}^{\ell} \mathbf{a}_{t_k}^i \otimes V_{\mathbf{j}}^{t_k} \mid i = 1, \ldots, h \right\}$$

is $\mathbb{F}$- linearly independent if and only if A is $\mathbb{F}$- linearly independent.

If Conjecture 1 is true, we have the following two corollaries.

Corollary 3. *Suppose Conjecture 1 is true, $\binom{r}{d}p > \binom{r}{d+1}m$, $d+1 \le \min\{\kappa, r\}$, $m < rp$, and $\mathbf{j} \in \mathcal{R}_{\kappa,d}$. If $\mathcal{F} \in \mathsf{KS}_\kappa(p \times q, m, r)$ is chosen uniformly at random, then with overwhelming probability the rank of $\tilde{B}_{\mathbf{j}}$ is $\binom{r}{d+1}m$.*

Proof. Given $\mathbf{j} \in \mathcal{R}_{\kappa,d} \subset \mathcal{R}_d$, if Conjecture 1 is true, with high probability the rank of $\tilde{B}_{\mathbf{j}}$ is $\binom{r}{d+1}m$.

Corollary 4. *Suppose Conjecture 1 is true, $\binom{r}{d}p > \binom{r}{d+1}m$, $d+1 \leq \min\{\kappa, r\}$, $m < rp$, and $\mathbf{j} \in \mathcal{R}_{\kappa,d}$. If $\mathcal{F} \in KS_\kappa(p \times q, m, r)$ is chosen uniformly at random, then with high probability there is a set $\tilde{S}_{\mathbf{j}}$ of $\binom{r}{d}p - \binom{r}{d+1}m$ syzygies of $\mathcal{F}$ of degree d. Moreover, $\tilde{S}_{\mathbf{j}}$ is $\mathbb{F}$-linearly independent.*

Proposition 4. *Let $\mathbf{j}, \mathbf{j}'$ be two different elements in $\mathcal{R}_{\kappa,d}$ and $L \in \mathcal{M}_{rp \times m}(\mathbb{F})$. Let $A = \{\mathbf{a}^1, \ldots, \mathbf{a}^{\ell_1}\}$, $B = \{\mathbf{b}^1, \ldots, \mathbf{b}^{\ell_2}\}$, $\tilde{S}_{\mathbf{j}}$ and $\tilde{S}_{\mathbf{j}'}$ be as in Proposition 3. Then, $\tilde{S}_{\mathbf{j}} \cup \tilde{S}_{\mathbf{j}'}$ is a set of linearly independent vectors in $\ker_l\left[(I_p \otimes K)L\right]$ if and only if A and B are both linearly independent in $\ker_l(L)$.*

Similarly to the square case and full kernel case, we expect to have the following result.

Corollary 5. *Suppose Conjecture 1 is true, $\binom{r}{d}p > \binom{r}{d+1}m$, $d+1 \leq \min\{\kappa, r\}$ and $m < rp$. If $\mathcal{F} \in KS_\kappa(p \times q, m, r)$ is chosen uniformly at random, then with high probability there is a set with*

$$\binom{\kappa}{d+1}\left[\binom{r}{d}p - \binom{r}{d+1}m\right]$$

linearly independent syzygies of $\mathcal{F}$ of degree d.

5   Complexity of the KS Modeling Revisited

Proposition 4 and Corollary 5 (Corollary 2 for square matrices) naturally lead to a new algorithm to solve systems of the form $\mathcal{F} = \mathbf{0}$, where $\mathcal{F}$ is randomly chosen in $KS_\kappa(p \times q, m, r)$, and $m < rp$. Let p, q, m, r be positive integers. The following number

$$d_{KS} = \min\left\{d \mid \left[\binom{r}{d}p > \binom{r}{d+1}m\right], 1 \leq d \leq r-1\right\} \qquad (9)$$

is well defined if $m < rp$. Assuming $d_{KS} + 1 \leq \kappa$, by Corollary 5, with high probability we can build degree drops from $d_{KS} + 2$ to $d_{KS} + 1$, for a randomly given $\mathcal{F} \in KS_\kappa(p \times q, m, r)$. By Proposition 2, such degree falls are not produced by trivial syzygies. Thus $D_{KS} := d_{KS} + 2$ is an upper bound for the first fall degree D_{ff}. Then, we construct the Macaulay matrix at degree $d_{KS} + 1$, append the degree falls, and row reduce this augmented matrix. If there are not enough polynomials to solve, we continue the XL algorithm up to degree $d_{KS} + 2, d_{KS} + 3, \ldots$ until we solve the system.

Based on these observations, we now estimate the complexity of solving such a system, by means of the first fall degree D_{ff} of the system, which is the smallest degree needed so that the Macaulay matrix of the system of that degree exhibits a degree fall when reduced [9].

We can further improve the complexity by multiplying only by monomials from kernel variables **k** in the XL algorithm. It can be proved that for this particular kind of equations, the XL algorithm restricted in this manner, still finds a solution. This follows from the facts that the ideal generated by $\mathcal{F}$ is radical [18], that the system $\mathcal{F} = 0$ has a unique solution, and that each polynomial in $\mathcal{F}$ has only linear variables in its linear part.

Consequently, using the XL algorithm and multiplying only by monomials from kernel variables, the complexity of solving instances of KS that are chosen uniformly at random is

$$O\left(\binom{r\kappa + d_{KS} + 1}{d_{KS} + 2}^{w}\right) = O\left(\binom{r\kappa + D_{KS} - 1}{D_{KS}}^{w}\right) = O\left((r\kappa)^{D_{KS}w}\right),$$

where $2 < \omega \leq 3$ and κ is the number of kernel vectors that we choose in order to keep the system overdetermined, that is, $\kappa \geq \frac{m}{p-r}$.

This is much lower than previous estimates. For example, if $m = p = q = n$ and $r < \sqrt{n}$, then $d_{KS} \leq r/2 + 1$, and we can choose $\kappa = \sqrt{n}$, so that, $r\kappa < n$, and hence, our complexity estimate is $O(n^{(r/2)\omega})$, compared to $O(n^{r\omega})$ from previous estimates, c.f. [1].

6   Experimental Results

In this section we present some experimental data to confront our theoretical findings. The results are summarized in Tables 1 and 2.

Table 1 shows that for $\mathcal{F} \in \mathsf{KS}(n \times n, m, r)$, and different values of r, $D_{KS} = d_{KS} + 2$ is a tight bound on the first fall degree. It also shows that D_{KS} is not far from the solving degree, which the maximum degree reached during the Gröbner basis computation. The solving degree was exactly D_{KS} in most cases, and it was $D_{KS} + 1$ in the worst case. Also, in Table 1 we can see that the KS system can be solved by using the XL algorithm multiplying only by kernel variables. This leads to much smaller matrices.

Table 2 addresses the question of how to choose κ. In Sect. 4.3, we showed that as long as $d_{KS} + 1 \leq \kappa$, we would find nontrivial relations for a sequence $\mathcal{F} \in \mathsf{KS}_\kappa(n \times n, m, r)$ at degree $d_{KS} + 2$. We also saw that if $\kappa \geq \frac{m}{n-r}$, the system is overdetermined, so we do not expect spurious solutions. In all the experiments presented in Table 2, we indeed obtained only true solutions. However, choosing the smallest possible κ is not necessarily the best choice, because for very small κ the solving degree increases. The experiments suggest there is an optimal κ around $d_{KS} + 2$. In Table 2, $d_{KS} + 2 = 5$ for $r = 6$ or $r = 5$, and $d_{KS} + 2 = 4$ when $r = 4$.

7   Implications in Multivariate Cryptography

A key recovery attack can be performed on several multivariate schemes by solving some MR problem instances [4,7,21,23,26]. In this section, we review

Table 1. Experimental result for KS method on uniformly chosen MR instances over $GF(13)$. For different values of r, a sequence $\mathcal{F} \in \mathsf{KS}(10 \times 10, 10, r)$ is chosen considering $n-r$ kernel vectors. In each case $F4$ and a version of the XL algorithm, in which we only multiply by kernel variables, are run over $\mathcal{F}$. Measures of the first fall degree D_{ff}, the solving degree D_{slv} and size of the largest matrix L.matrix. For each r in the first column shows the F4 data and in the second one the XL data.

r	2		3		4		5		6	
D_{KS}	3		4		4		5		5	
	F4	XL	F4	XL	F4	XL	F4	XL	F4	XL
D_{ff}	3	3	4	4	4	4	5		5	
D_{slv}	3	3	4	4	4		5			
L.matrix	2217	1530	24582	20240	38586		341495		>2035458	

Table 2. Experimental results for the KS method on uniformly chosen MR instances over $GF(13)$. A sequence $F \in KS(12 \times 12, 12, r)$ is chosen considering κ kernel vectors. The variable x_1 is set to 1 in F. $F4$ is used to find the variety of the resulting system. Measures of the first fall degree D_{ff}, the solving degree D_{slv}, time and memory are presented.

r	κ	D_{ff}	D_{slv}	Time [s]	Mem [MB]	r	κ	D_{ff}	D_{slv}	Time [s]	Mem [MB]
6	6	4	5	20079	25547	4	8	4	4	58	194
	5	4	5	42858	20928		7	4	4	38	128
	4	4	5	95768	34573		6	4	4	21	107
5	7	4	4	756	1984		5	4	4	13	104
	6	4	4	367	1199		4	4	4	11	64
	5	4	4	377	758		3	4	4	6	64
	4	4	4	108	352		2	4	5	14	160
	3	5	5	795	1648						

the complexity of the KS method for some of the most common multivariate schemes. We are not including Rainbow in this analysis, since the improvement that we are proposing for KS is still way slower than the linear algebra techniques used to perform the MR attack against this particular signature scheme [8].

HFE: A key recovery attack on the HFE encryption scheme with parameters $(n, D, |\mathbb{F}|)$ can be performed by solving a KS system $\mathcal{F} = \mathbf{0}$, where $\mathcal{F} \in \mathsf{KS}(n \times n, n, r)$ and $r = \lceil \log_{|\mathbb{F}|} D \rceil$. In this case, $d_{KS} = \lceil \frac{r-1}{2} \rceil$ or $d_{KS} = \frac{r-1}{2}+1$, depending on whether $r-1$ is odd or even. The complexity of solving an MR instance with parameters $n \times n, n, r$, using κ kernel vectors is

$$O\left(\binom{r\kappa + d_{KS} + 1}{d_{KS} + 2}^{w}\right),$$

where $d_{KS} = \lceil \frac{r-1}{2} \rceil$ or $\frac{r-1}{2} + 1$.

For example, for the parameters $n = 128, D = 192, |\mathbb{F}| = 2$ analyzed in [1], we have $r = 8$, and $d_{KS} = 4$. Using $\kappa = 10$ kernel vectors, we need to deal with a KS system of $n\kappa = 1280$ equations in $n + r\kappa = 208$ variables. Assuming $\omega = 2.4$, the complexity of solving such a system is 2^{69}, which is way better than the 2^{108} complexity of the minors method approach estimated in [1] .

ZHFE: To perform a key recovery attack on the ZHFE encryption scheme with parameters $(n, D, |\mathbb{F}|)$, we need to solve a KS instance $\mathcal{F} = \mathbf{0}$, where $\mathcal{F} \in$ $KS(n \times n, 2n, r)$ and $r = \lceil \log_{|\mathbb{F}|} D \rceil + 1$, see [4]. In this case d_{KS} is either $\lceil \frac{2r-1}{3} \rceil$ or $\frac{2r-1}{3} + 1$.

For the proposed parameters $n = 55$, $D = 105$, $|\mathbb{F}| = 7$ [24], we have that $r = 4$ and $d_{KS} = 3$. Thus, by considering $\kappa = 14$ kernel vectors, the estimated complexity is then 2^{63}, with $\omega = 2.8$. This is better than the estimated 2^{76} with $\omega = 2.8$ provided in [4] based on the minors method.

HFEv-: In HFEv- with parameters $(|\mathbb{F}|, n, D, a, v)$ the system to solve is $\mathcal{F} = \mathbf{0}$, where $\mathcal{F} \in KS((n + v) \times (n + v), n - a, r + a + v)^4$ and $r = \lceil \log_{|\mathbb{F}|} D \rceil$ [23]. The parameter for complexity d_{KS} is given by $\left\lceil \frac{(r+a+v)(n-a)-(n+v)}{2n+v-a} \right\rceil$ or $\frac{(r+a+v)(n-a)-(n+v)}{2n+v-a} + 1$, depending if the value inside $\lceil \cdot \rceil$ is even or odd.

GeMMS and Gui: GeMMS and Gui are HFEv- based multivariate signature schemes proposed in the NIST's ongoing post-quantum "competition" [5,23]. A key recovery attack to GeMMS or Gui with parameters $(|\mathbb{F}|, n, D, a, v, k)$ reduces to a key recovery attack to the underlying HFEv- instances with parameters $(|\mathbb{F}|, n, D, a, v)$. We use the sets of parameters proposed for the NIST's competition to analyze the complexity of such an attack and set $\omega = 2.3$, which is the one used in the Gui submission. The main improvement in the key recovery attack is derived from reducing the number of kernel vectors. For the parameter sets Gui-184(2,184,33,16,16,2), Gui-312(2,312,129,24,20,2) and Gui-448(2,448,513,32,28,2) we may set $\kappa = 18$, $\kappa = 25$ and $\kappa = 34$, respectively, producing key recovery complexities of 2^{281}, 2^{429} and 2^{598} steps, respectively. For comparison, the estimates provided in [23] via minors modeling were 2^{323}, 2^{480} and 2^{665}, respectively. A similar effect applies to the GeMMS security estimates as well.

Acknowledgements. We would like to thank Daniel Escudero, Albrecht Petzoldt, Rusydi Makarim, and Karan Khathuria for useful discussions. The author Javier Verbel is supported by "Fondo Nacional de Financiamiento para la Ciencia, la Tecnología y la Innovación Francisco José de Caldas" , Colciencias (Colombia). Some of the experiments were conducted on the Gauss Server, financed by "Proyecto Plan 150x150 Fomento de la cultura de evaluación continua a través del apoyo a planes de mejoramiento de los programas curriculares".

---

[4] When $r + v + a$ is odd the target rank is $r + a + v - 1$.

References

1. Bettale, L., Faugère, J.C., Perret, L.: Cryptanalysis of HFE, multi-HFE and variants for odd and even characteristic. Des. Codes Crypt. **69**(1), 1–52 (2013)
2. Buchberger, B.: A theoretical basis for the reduction of polynomials to canonical forms. SIGSAM Bull. **10**(3), 19–29 (1976)
3. Buss, J.F., Frandsen, G.S., Shallit, J.O.: The computational complexity of some problems of linear algebra. J. Comput. Syst. Sci. **58**(3), 572–596 (1999)
4. Cabarcas, D., Smith-Tone, D., Verbel, J.A.: Key recovery attack for ZHFE. In: Lange, T., Takagi, T. (eds.) PQCrypto 2017. LNCS, vol. 10346, pp. 289–308. Springer, Cham (2017). https://doi.org/10.1007/978-3-319-59879-6_17
5. Casanova, A., Faugère, J.C., Macario-Rat, G., Patarin, J., Perret, L., Ryckeghem, J.: GeMSS: a great multivariate short signature. NIST CSRC (2017). https://csrc.nist.gov/CSRC/media/Projects/Post-Quantum-Cryptography/documents/round-1/submissions/GeMSS.zip
6. Courtois, N., Klimov, A., Patarin, J., Shamir, A.: Efficient algorithms for solving overdefined systems of multivariate polynomial equations. In: Preneel, B. (ed.) EUROCRYPT 2000. LNCS, vol. 1807, pp. 392–407. Springer, Heidelberg (2000). https://doi.org/10.1007/3-540-45539-6_27
7. Courtois, N.T.: Efficient zero-knowledge authentication based on a linear algebra problem MinRank. In: Boyd, C. (ed.) ASIACRYPT 2001. LNCS, vol. 2248, pp. 402–421. Springer, Heidelberg (2001). https://doi.org/10.1007/3-540-45682-1_24
8. Ding, J., Chen, M.S., Petzoldt, A., Schmidt, D., Yang, B.Y.: Rainbow. NIST CSRC (2017). https://csrc.nist.gov/CSRC/media/Projects/Post-Quantum-Cryptography/documents/round-1/submissions/Rainbow.zip
9. Ding, J., Hodges, T.J.: Inverting HFE systems is quasi-polynomial for all fields. In: Rogaway, P. (ed.) CRYPTO 2011. LNCS, vol. 6841, pp. 724–742. Springer, Heidelberg (2011). https://doi.org/10.1007/978-3-642-22792-9_41
10. Ding, J., Kleinjung, T.: Degree of regularity for HFE-. Cryptology ePrint Archive, Report 2011/570 (2011). https://eprint.iacr.org/2011/570
11. Ding, J., Schmidt, D.: Solving degree and degree of regularity for polynomial systems over a finite fields. In: Fischlin, M., Katzenbeisser, S. (eds.) Number Theory and Cryptography. LNCS, vol. 8260, pp. 34–49. Springer, Heidelberg (2013). https://doi.org/10.1007/978-3-642-42001-6_4
12. Ding, J., Yang, B.-Y.: Degree of regularity for HFEv and HFEv-. In: Gaborit, P. (ed.) PQCrypto 2013. LNCS, vol. 7932, pp. 52–66. Springer, Heidelberg (2013). https://doi.org/10.1007/978-3-642-38616-9_4
13. Dubois, V., Gama, N.: The degree of regularity of HFE systems. In: Abe, M. (ed.) ASIACRYPT 2010. LNCS, vol. 6477, pp. 557–576. Springer, Heidelberg (2010). https://doi.org/10.1007/978-3-642-17373-8_32
14. Faugere, J.C.: A new efficient algorithm for computing Grobner bases (F4). J. Pure Appl. Algebra **139**, 61–88 (1999)
15. Faugere, J.C.: A new efficient algorithm for computing Grobner bases without reduction to zero (F5). In: ISSAC 2002, pp. 75–83. ACM Press (2002)
16. Faugère, J.-C., El Din, M.S., Spaenlehauer, P.J.: Computing loci of rank defects of linear matrices using Gröbner bases and applications to cryptology. In: Proceedings of Symbolic and Algebraic Computation, International Symposium, ISSAC 2010, 25–28 July 2010, Munich, Germany, pp. 257–264 (2010)
17. Faugère, J.-C., El Din, M.S., Spaenlehauer, P.J.: Groebner bases of bihomogeneous ideals generated by polynomials of bidegree (1, 1): algorithms and complexity. J. Symb. Comput. **46**(4), 406–437 (2011)

18. Faugère, J.-C., Levy-dit-Vehel, F., Perret, L.: Cryptanalysis of MinRank. In: Wagner, D. (ed.) CRYPTO 2008. LNCS, vol. 5157, pp. 280–296. Springer, Heidelberg (2008). https://doi.org/10.1007/978-3-540-85174-5_16
19. Gaborit, P., Ruatta, O., Schrek, J.: On the complexity of the rank syndrome decoding problem. IEEE Trans. Inf. Theory **62**(2), 1006–1019 (2016)
20. Goubin, L., Courtois, N.T.: Cryptanalysis of the TTM cryptosystem. In: Okamoto, T. (ed.) ASIACRYPT 2000. LNCS, vol. 1976, pp. 44–57. Springer, Heidelberg (2000). https://doi.org/10.1007/3-540-44448-3_4
21. Kipnis, A., Shamir, A.: Cryptanalysis of the HFE public key cryptosystem by relinearization. In: Wiener, M. (ed.) CRYPTO 1999. LNCS, vol. 1666, pp. 19–30. Springer, Heidelberg (1999). https://doi.org/10.1007/3-540-48405-1_2
22. Lazard, D.: Gröbner bases, Gaussian elimination and resolution of systems of algebraic equations. In: van Hulzen, J.A. (ed.) EUROCAL 1983. LNCS, vol. 162, pp. 146–156. Springer, Heidelberg (1983). https://doi.org/10.1007/3-540-12868-9_99
23. Petzoldt, A., Chen, M.-S., Yang, B.-Y., Tao, C., Ding, J.: Design principles for HFEv- based multivariate signature schemes. In: Iwata, T., Cheon, J.H. (eds.) ASIACRYPT 2015. LNCS, vol. 9452, pp. 311–334. Springer, Heidelberg (2015). https://doi.org/10.1007/978-3-662-48797-6_14
24. Porras, J., Baena, J., Ding, J.: ZHFE, a new multivariate public key encryption scheme. In: Mosca, M. (ed.) PQCrypto 2014. LNCS, vol. 8772, pp. 229–245. Springer, Cham (2014). https://doi.org/10.1007/978-3-319-11659-4_14
25. Shor, P.W.: Polynomial-time algorithms for prime factorization and discrete logarithms on a quantum computer. SIAM J. Comput. **26**(5), 1484–1509 (1997)
26. Vates, J., Smith-Tone, D.: Key recovery attack for all parameters of HFE-. In: Lange, T., Takagi, T. (eds.) PQCrypto 2017. LNCS, vol. 10346, pp. 272–288. Springer, Cham (2017). https://doi.org/10.1007/978-3-319-59879-6_16

Key Establishment

Constant-Round Group Key Exchange from the Ring-LWE Assumption

Daniel Apon[1], Dana Dachman-Soled[2], Huijing Gong[2(✉)], and Jonathan Katz[2]

[1] National Institute of Standards and Technology, Gaithersburg, USA
daniel.apon@nist.gov
[2] University of Maryland, College Park, USA
danadach@ece.umd.edu, {gong,jkatz}@cs.umd.edu

Abstract. Group key-exchange protocols allow a set of N parties to agree on a shared, secret key by communicating over a public network. A number of solutions to this problem have been proposed over the years, mostly based on variants of Diffie-Hellman (two-party) key exchange. To the best of our knowledge, however, there has been almost no work looking at candidate *post-quantum* group key-exchange protocols.

Here, we propose a constant-round protocol for unauthenticated group key exchange (i.e., with security against a passive eavesdropper) based on the hardness of the Ring-LWE problem. By applying the Katz-Yung compiler using any post-quantum signature scheme, we obtain a (scalable) protocol for *authenticated* group key exchange with post-quantum security. Our protocol is constructed by generalizing the Burmester-Desmedt protocol to the Ring-LWE setting, which requires addressing several technical challenges.

Keywords: Ring learning with errors · Post-quantum cryptography · Group key exchange

1 Introduction

Protocols for (authenticated) key exchange are among the most fundamental and widely used cryptographic primitives. They allow parties communicating over an insecure public network to establish a common secret key, called a *session key*, permitting the subsequent use of symmetric-key cryptography for encryption and authentication of sensitive data. They can be used to instantiate so-called "secure channels" upon which higher-level cryptographic protocols often depend.

Most work on key exchange, beginning with the classical paper of Diffie and Hellman, has focused on two-party key exchange. However, many works have also explored extensions to the *group* setting [1,2,5,6,8,9,11–17,21,22,24,25,29–31] in which N parties wish to agree on a common session key that they can each then use for encrypted/authenticated communication with the rest of the group.

The recent effort by NIST to evaluate and standardize one or more quantum-resistant public-key cryptosystems is entirely focused on digital signatures and

© Springer Nature Switzerland AG 2019
J. Ding and R. Steinwandt (Eds.): PQCrypto 2019, LNCS 11505, pp. 189–205, 2019.
https://doi.org/10.1007/978-3-030-25510-7_11

two-party key encapsulation/key exchange,[1] and there has been an extensive amount of research over the past decade focused on designing such schemes. In contrast, we are aware of almost no[2] work on *group* key-exchange protocols with post-quantum security beyond the observation that a post-quantum group key-exchange protocol can be constructed from any post-quantum two-party protocol by having a designated group manager run independent two-party protocols with the $N - 1$ other parties, and then send a session key of its choice to the other parties encrypted/authenticated using each of the resulting keys. Such a solution is often considered unacceptable since it is highly asymmetric, requires additional coordination, is not contributory, and puts a heavy load on a single party who becomes a central point of failure.

1.1   Our Contributions

In this work, we propose a constant-round group key-exchange protocol based on the hardness of the Ring-LWE problem [27], and hence with (plausible) post-quantum security. We focus on constructing an *unauthenticated* protocol—i.e., one secure against a passive eavesdropper—since known techniques such as the Katz-Yung compiler [24] can then be applied to obtain an *authenticated* protocol secure against an active attacker.

The starting point for our work is the two-round group key-exchange protocol by Burmester and Desmedt [15,16,24], which is based on the decisional Diffie-Hellman assumption. Assume a group $\mathbb{G}$ of prime order q and a generator $g \in \mathbb{G}$ are fixed and public. The Burmester-Desmedt protocol run by parties $P_0, \ldots, P_{N-1}$ then works as follows:

1. In the first round, each party P_i chooses uniform $r_i \in \mathbb{Z}_q$ and broadcasts $z_i = g^{r_i}$ to all other parties.
2. In the second round, each party P_i broadcasts $X_i = (z_{i+1}/z_{i-1})^{r_i}$ (where the parties' indices are taken modulo N).

Each party P_i can then compute its session key sk_i as

$$\mathsf{sk}_i = (z_{i-1})^{N r_i} \cdot X_i^{N-1} \cdot X_{i+1}^{N-2} \cdots X_{i+N-2}.$$

One can check that all the keys are equal to the same value $g^{r_0 r_1 + \cdots + r_{N-1} r_0}$.

In attempting to adapt their protocol to the Ring-LWE setting, we could fix a ring R_q and a uniform element $a \in R_q$. Then:

1. In the first round, each party P_i chooses "small" secret value $s_i \in R_q$ and "small" noise term $e_i \in R_q$ (with the exact distribution being unimportant in the present discussion), and broadcasts $z_i = a s_i + e_i$ to the other parties.

---

[1] Note that CPA-secure key encapsulation is equivalent to two-round key-exchange (with passive security).

[2] The protocol of Ding et al. [19] has no security proof; the work of Boneh et al. [10] shows a framework for constructing a group key-exchange protocol with plausible post-quantum security but without a concrete instantiation.

2. In the second round, each party P_i chooses a second "small" noise term $e_i' \in R_q$ and broadcasts $X_i = (z_{i+1} - z_{i-i}) \cdot s_i + e_i'$.

Each party can then compute a session key b_i as

$$b_i = N \cdot s_i \cdot z_{i-1} + (N-1) \cdot X_i + (N-2) \cdot X_{i+1} + \cdots + X_{i+N-2}.$$

The problem, of course, is that (due to the noise terms) these session keys computed by the parties will *not* be equal. They will, however, be "close" to each other if the $\{s_i, e_i, e_i'\}$ are all sufficiently small, so we can add an additional reconciliation step to ensure that all parties agree on a common key k.

This gives a protocol that is correct, but proving security (even for a passive eavesdropper) is more difficult than in the case of the Burmester-Desmedt protocol. Here we informally outline the main difficulties and how we address them. First, we note that trying to prove security by direct analogy to the proof of security for the Burmester-Desmedt protocol (cf. [24]) fails; in the latter case, it is possible to use the fact that, for example,

$$(z_2/z_0)^{r_1} = z_1^{r_2 - r_0},$$

whereas in our setting the analogous relation does not hold. In general, the natural proof strategy here is to switch all the $\{z_i\}$ values to uniform elements of R_q, and similarly to switch the $\{X_i\}$ values to uniform subject to the constraint that their sum is approximately 0 (i.e., subject to the constraint that $\sum_i X_i \approx 0$). Unfortunately this cannot be done by simply invoking the Ring-LWE assumption $O(N)$ times; in particular, the first time we try to invoke the assumption, say on the pair $(z_1 = as_1 + e_1, \ X_1 = (z_2 - z_0) \cdot s_1 + e_1')$, we need $z_2 - z_0$ to be uniform—which, in contrast to the analogous requirement in the Burmester-Desmedt protocol (for the value z_2/z_0), is not the case here. Thus, we must somehow break the circularity in the mutual dependence of the $\{z_i, X_i\}$ values.

Toward this end, let us look more carefully at the distribution of $\sum_i X_i$. We may write

$$\sum_i X_i = \sum_i (e_{i+1} s_i - e_{i-1} s_i) + \sum_i e_i'.$$

Consider now changing the way X_0 is chosen: that is, instead of choosing $X_0 = (z_1 - z_{N-1})s_0 + e_0'$ as in the protocol, we instead set $X_0 = -\sum_{i=1}^{N-1} X_i + e_0'$ (where e_0' is from the same distribution as before). Intuitively, as long as the standard deviation of e_0' is large enough, these two distributions of X_0 should be "close" (as they both satisfy $\sum_i X_i \approx 0$). This, in particular, means that we need the distribution of e_0' to be different from the distribution of the $\{e_i'\}_{i>0}$, as the standard deviation of the former needs to be larger than the latter.

We can indeed show that when we choose e_0' from an appropriate distribution then the Rényi divergence between the two distributions of X_0, above, is bounded by a polynomial. With this switch in the distribution of X_0, we have broken the circularity and can now use the Ring-LWE assumption to switch the distribution of z_0 to uniform, followed by the remaining $\{z_i, X_i\}$ values.

Unfortunately, bounded Rényi divergence does not imply statistical closeness. However, polynomially bounded Rényi divergence *does* imply that any event occurring with negligible probability when X_0 is chosen according to the second distribution also occurs with negligible probability when X_0 is chosen according to the first distribution. For these reasons, we change our security goal from an "indistinguishability-based" one (namely, requiring that, given the transcript, the real session key is indistinguishable from uniform) to an "unpredictability-based" one (namely, given the transcript, it should be infeasible to compute the real session key). In the end, though, once the parties agree on an unpredictable value k they can hash it to obtain the final session key $\mathsf{sk} = \mathcal{H}(k)$; this final value sk will be indistinguishable from uniform if $\mathcal{H}$ is modeled as a random oracle.

2   Preliminaries

2.1   Notation

Let $\mathbb{Z}$ be the ring of integers, and let $[N] = \{0, 1, \dots, N-1\}$. If χ is a probability distribution over some set S, then $x_0, x_1, \dots, x_{\ell-1} \leftarrow \chi$ denotes independently sampling each x_i from distribution χ. We let $\mathrm{Supp}(\chi) = \{x : \chi(x) \neq 0\}$. Given an event E, we use $\overline{E}$ to denote its complement. Let $\chi(E)$ denote the probability that event E occurs under distribution χ. Given a polynomial p_i, let $(p_i)_j$ denote the jth coefficient of p_i. Let $\log(X)$ denote $\log_2(X)$, and $\exp(X)$ denote e^X.

2.2   Ring Learning with Errors

Informally, the (decisional) version of the Ring Learning with Errors (Ring-LWE) problem is: for some secret ring element s, distinguish many random "noisy ring products" with s from elements drawn uniform from the ring. More precisely, the Ring-LWE problem is parameterized by (R, q, χ, ℓ) as follows:

1. R is a ring, typically written as a polynomial quotient ring $R = \mathbb{Z}[X]/(f(X))$ for some irreducible polynomial $f(X)$ in the indeterminate X. In this paper, we restrict to the case of that $f(X) = X^n + 1$ where n is a power of 2. In later sections, we let R be parameterized by n.
2. q is a modulus defining the quotient ring $R_q := R/qR = \mathbb{Z}_q[X]/(f(X))$. We restrict to the case that q is prime and $q = 1 \mod 2n$.
3. $\chi = (\chi_s, \chi_e)$ is a pair of noise distributions over R_q (with χ_s the *secret key* distribution and χ_e the *error* distribution) that are concentrated on "short" elements, for an appropriate definition of "short" (e.g., the Euclidean distance metric on the integer-coefficients of the polynomials s or e drawn from R_q); and
4. ℓ is the number of samples provided to the adversary.

Formally, the Ring-LWE problem is to distinguish between ℓ samples independently drawn from one of two distributions. The first distribution is generated by fixing a random secret $s \leftarrow \chi_s$ then outputting

$$(a_i, b_i = s \cdot a_i + e_i) \in R_q \times R_q,$$

for $i \in [\ell]$, where each $a_i \in R_q$ is drawn uniformly at random and each $e_i \leftarrow \chi_e$ is drawn from the error distribution. For the second distribution, each sample $(a_i, b_i) \in R_q \times R_q$ is simply drawn uniformly at random.

Let A_{n,q,χ_s,χ_e} be the distribution that outputs the Ring-LWE sample $(a_i, b_i = s \cdot a_i + e_i)$ as above. We denote by $\mathsf{Adv}^{\mathsf{RLWE}}_{n,q,\chi_s,\chi_e,\ell}(\mathcal{B})$ the advantage of algorithm $\mathcal{B}$ in distinguishing distributions $A^\ell_{n,q,\chi_s,\chi_e}$ and $\mathcal{U}^\ell(R_q^2)$.

We define $\mathsf{Adv}^{\mathsf{RLWE}}_{n,q,\chi_s,\chi_e,\ell}(t)$ to be the maximum advantage of any adversary running in time t. Note that in later sections, we write as $\mathsf{Adv}_{n,q,\chi,\ell}$ when $\chi = \chi_s = \chi_e$ for simplicity.

The Ring-LWE Noise Distribution. The noise distribution χ (here we assume $\chi_s = \chi_e$, though this is not necessary) is usually a discrete Gaussian distribution on $R_q^\vee$ or in our case R_q (see [18] for details of the distinction, especially for concrete implementation purposes). Formally, in case of power of two cyclotomic rings, the discrete Gaussian distribution can be sampled by drawing each coefficient independently from the 1-dimensional discrete Gaussian distribution over $\mathbb{Z}$ with parameter σ, which is supported on $\{x \in \mathbb{Z} : -q/2 \leq x \leq q/2\}$ and has density function

$$D_{\mathbb{Z}_q,\sigma}(x) = \frac{e^{\frac{-\pi x^2}{\sigma^2}}}{\sum_{x=-\infty}^{\infty} e^{\frac{-\pi x^2}{\sigma^2}}}.$$

2.3 Rényi Divergence

The Rényi divergence (RD) is a measure of closeness of two probability distributions. For any two discrete probability distributions P and Q such that $\mathrm{Supp}(P) \subseteq \mathrm{Supp}(Q)$, we define the Rényi divergence of order 2 as

$$\mathrm{RD}_2(P\|Q) = \sum_{x \in \mathrm{Supp}(P)} \frac{P(x)^2}{Q(x)}.$$

Rényi divergence has a probability preservation property that can be considered the multiplicative analogues of statistical distance.

Proposition 1. *Given discrete distributions P and Q with $\mathrm{Supp}(P) \subseteq \mathrm{Supp}(Q)$, let $E \in \mathrm{Supp}(Q)$ be an arbitrary event. We have*

$$Q(E) \geq P(E)^2 / \mathrm{RD}_2(P\|Q).$$

This property implies that as long as $\mathrm{RD}_2(P\|Q)$ is bounded by $\mathrm{poly}(\lambda)$, any event E that occurs with negligible probability $Q(E)$ under distribution Q also occurs with negligible probability $P(E)$ under distribution P. We refer to [26,27] for the formal proof.

Theorem 2.1 ([7]). *Fix $m, q \in \mathbb{Z}$, a bound B, and the 1-dimensional discrete Gaussian distribution $D_{\mathbb{Z}_q,\sigma}$ with parameter σ such that $B < \sigma < q$. Moreover, let $e \in \mathbb{Z}$ be such that $|e| \leq B$. If $\sigma = \Omega(B\sqrt{m/\log\lambda})$, then*

$$\mathrm{RD}_2((e + D_{\mathbb{Z}_q,\sigma})^m \| D_{\mathbb{Z}_q,\sigma}^m) \leq \exp(2\pi m(B/\sigma)^2) = \mathrm{poly}(\lambda),$$

where X^m denotes m independent samples from X.

2.4   Generic Key Reconciliation Mechanism

In this subsection, we define a generic, one round, two-party key reconciliation mechanism which allows both parties to derive the same key from an approximately agreed upon ring element. A key reconciliation mechanism KeyRec consists of two algorithms recMsg and recKey, parameterized by security parameter 1^λ as well as β_{Rec}. In this context, Alice and Bob hold "close" keys – b_A and b_B, respectively – and wish to generate a shared key k so that $k = k_A = k_B$. The abstract mechanism KeyRec is defined as follows:

1. Bob computes $(K, k_B) = \mathsf{recMsg}(b_B)$ and sends the reconciliation message K to Alice.
2. Once receiving K, Alice computes $k_A = \mathsf{recKey}(b_A, K) \in \{0,1\}^\lambda$.

CORRECTNESS. Given $b_A, b_B \in R_q$, if each coefficient of $b_B - b_A$ is bounded by β_{Rec} – namely, $|b_B - b_A| \leq \beta_{\mathsf{Rec}}$ – then it is guaranteed that $k_A = k_B$.

SECURITY. A key reconciliation mechanism KeyRec is secure if the subsequent two distribution ensembles are computationally indistinguishable. (First, we describe a simple, helper distribution).

$\mathsf{Exe}_{\mathsf{KeyRec}}(\lambda)$: A draw from this helper distribution is performed by initiating the key reconciliation protocol among two honest parties and outputting (K, k_B); i.e. the reconciliation message K and (Bob's) key k_B of the protocol execution.

We denote by $\mathsf{Adv}_{\mathsf{KeyRec}}(\mathcal{B})$ the advantage of adversary $\mathcal{B}$ distinguishing the distributions below.

$$\{(K, k_B) : b_B \leftarrow \mathcal{U}(R_q), (K, k_B) \leftarrow \mathsf{Exe}_{\mathsf{KeyRec}}(\lambda, b_B)\}_{\lambda \in \mathbb{N}},$$

$$\{(K, k') : b_B \leftarrow \mathcal{U}(R_q), (K, k_B) \leftarrow \mathsf{Exe}_{\mathsf{KeyRec}}(\lambda, b_B), k' \leftarrow U_\lambda\}_{\lambda \in \mathbb{N}},$$

where U_λ denotes the uniform distribution over λ bits.

We define $\mathsf{Adv}_{\mathsf{KeyRec}}(t)$ to be the maximum advantage of any adversary running in time t.

Key Reconciliation Mechanisms from the Literature. The notion of key reconciliation was first introduced by Ding et al. [19]. in his work on two-party, lattice-based key exchange. It was later used in several important works on two-party key exchange, including [4,28,32].

   In the key reconciliation mechanisms of Peikert [28], Zhang et al. [32] and Alkim et al. [4], the initiating party sends a small amount of information about its secret, b_B, to the other party. This information is enough to allow the two parties to agree upon the same key $k = k_A = k_B$, while revealing no information about k to an eavesdropper. When instantiating our GKE protocol with this type of key reconciliation (specifically, one of [4,28,32]), our final GKE protocol is "contributory," in the sense that all parties contribute entropy towards determining the final key.

Another method for the two parties to agree upon the same joint key $k = k_A = k_B$, given that they start with keys b_A, b_B that are "close," was first introduced in [3] (we refer to their technique as a key reconciliation mechanism, although it is technically not referred to as such in the literature). Here, the initiating party uses its private input to generate a Regev-style encryption of a random bit string k_B of its choice under secret key b_B. and then sends to the other party, who decrypts with its approximate secret key b_A to obtain k_A. Due to the inherent robustness to noise of Regev-style encryption, it is guaranteed that $k = k_A = k_B$ with all but negligible probability. Instantiating our GKE protocol with this type of key reconciliation (specifically, that in [3]) is also possible, but does not lead to the preferred "contributory GKE," since the initiating party's entropy completely determines the final group key.

3 Group Key Exchange Security Model

A group key-exchange protocol allows a session key to be established among $N > 2$ parties. Following prior work [12–14,23], we will use the term group key exchange (GKE) to denote a protocol secure against a *passive* (eavesdropping) adversary and will use the term authenticated group key exchange (GAKE) to denote a protocol secure against an *active* adversary, who controls all communication channels. Fortunately, the work of Katz and Yung [23] presents a compiler that takes any GKE protocol and transforms it into a GAKE protocol. The underlying tool required for this transform is any digital signature scheme which is strongly unforgeable under adaptive chosen message attack (EUF-CMA). We may thus focus our attention on achieving GKE in the remainder of this work.

In GKE, the adversary gets to see a single transcript generated by an execution of the GKE protocol. Given the transcript, the adversary must distinguish the real key from a fake key that is generated uniformly at random and independently of the transcript.

Formally, for security parameter $\lambda \in \mathbb{N}$, we define the following distribution:

$\mathsf{Execute}_\Pi^{\mathcal{O}_H}(\lambda)$: A draw from this distribution is performed by sampling a classical random oracle $\mathcal{H}$ from distribution $\mathcal{O}_H$, initiating the GKE protocol Π among N honest parties with security parameter λ relative to $\mathcal{H}$, and outputting $(\mathsf{trans}, \mathsf{sk})$ the transcript trans and key sk of the protocol execution.

Consider the following distributions:

$$\{(\mathsf{trans}, \mathsf{sk}) : (\mathsf{trans}, \mathsf{sk}) \leftarrow \mathsf{Execute}_\Pi^{\mathcal{O}_H}(\lambda)\}_{\lambda \in \mathbb{N}},$$
$$\{(\mathsf{trans}, \mathsf{sk}') : (\mathsf{trans}, \mathsf{sk}) \leftarrow \mathsf{Execute}_\Pi^{\mathcal{O}_H}(\lambda), \mathsf{sk}' \leftarrow U_\lambda\}_{\lambda \in \mathbb{N}},$$

where U_λ denotes the uniform distribution over λ bits. Let $\mathsf{Adv}^{\mathsf{GKE},\mathcal{O}_H}(\mathcal{A})$ denote the advantage of adversary $\mathcal{A}$, with classical access to the sampled oracle $\mathcal{H}$, distinguishing the distributions above.

To enable a concrete security analysis, we define $\mathsf{Adv}^{\mathsf{GKE},\mathcal{O}_H}(t, q_{\mathcal{O}_H})$ to be the maximum advantage of any adversary running in time t and making at most $q_{\mathcal{O}_H}$ queries to the random oracle. Security holds even if the adversary sees multiple executions by a hybrid argument.

In the next section we will define our GKE scheme and prove that it satisfies the notion of GKE.

4 A Group Key-Exchange Protocol

In this section, we present our group key exchange construction, GKE, which runs key reconciliation protocol KeyRec as a subroutine. Let KeyRec be parametrized by β_{Rec}. The protocol has two security parameters λ and ρ. λ is the computational security parameter, which is used in the security proof. ρ is the statistical security parameter, which is used in the correctness proof. σ_1, σ_2 are parameters of discrete Gaussian distributions. In this setting, N players $P_0, \ldots, P_{N-1}$ plan to generate a shared session key. The players' indices are taken modulo N.

The structure of the protocol is as follows: All parties agree on "close" keys $b_0 \approx \cdots \approx b_{N-1}$ after the second round. Player $N-1$ then initiates a key reconciliation protocol to allow all users to agree on the same key $k = k_0 = \cdots = k_{N-1}$. Since we are only able to prove that k is difficult to compute for an eavesdropping adversary (but may not be indistinguishable from random), we hash k using random oracle $\mathcal{H}$ to get the final shared key sk.

Public parameter: $R_q = \mathbb{Z}_q[x]/(x^n + 1)$, $a \leftarrow \mathcal{U}(R_q)$.

Round 1: Each player P_i samples $s_i, e_i \leftarrow \chi_{\sigma_1}$ and broadcasts $z_i = as_i + e_i$.
Round 2: Player P_0 samples $e_0' \leftarrow \chi_{\sigma_2}$ and each of the other players P_i samples $e_i' \leftarrow \chi_{\sigma_1}$, broadcasts $X_i = (z_{i+1} - z_{i-1})s_i + e_i'$.
Round 3: Player P_{N-1} proceeds as follows:
  1. Samples $e_{N-1}'' \leftarrow \chi_{\sigma_1}$ and computes $b_{N-1} = z_{N-2}Ns_{N-1} + e_{N-1}'' + X_{N-1} \cdot (N-1) + X_0 \cdot (N-2) + \cdots + X_{N-3}$.
  2. Computes $(K_{N-1}, k_{N-1}) = \mathsf{recMsg}(b_{N-1})$ and broadcasts K_{N-1}.
  3. Obtains session key $\mathsf{sk}_{N-1} = \mathcal{H}(k_{N-1})$.
Key Computation: Each player P_i (except P_{N-1}) proceeds as follows:
  1. Computes $b_i = z_{i-1}Ns_i + X_i \cdot (N-1) + X_{i+1} \cdot (N-2) + \cdots + X_{i+N-2}$.
  2. Computes $k_i = \mathsf{recKey}(b_i, K_{N-1})$, and obtains session key $\mathsf{sk}_i = \mathcal{H}(k_i)$.

4.1 Correctness

The following claim states that each party derives the same session key sk_i, with all but negligible probability, as long as $\chi_{\sigma_1}, \chi_{\sigma_2}$ satisfy the constraint $(N^2 + 2N) \cdot \sqrt{n}\rho^{3/2}\sigma_1^2 + (\frac{N^2}{2} + 1)\sigma_1 + (N-2)\sigma_2 \leq \beta_{\mathsf{Rec}}$, where β_{Rec} is the parameter from the KeyRec protocol.

Theorem 4.1. *Given* β_{Rec} *as the parameter of* KeyRec *protocol,* $N, n, \rho, \sigma_1, \sigma_2$ *as parameters of GKE protocol* Π, *as long as* $(N^2 + 2N) \cdot \sqrt{n}\rho^{3/2}\sigma_1^2 + (\frac{N^2}{2} + 1)\sigma_1 + (N - 2)\sigma_2 \leq \beta_{\mathsf{Rec}}$ *is satisfied, if all players honestly execute the group key exchange protocol described above, then each player derives the same key as input of* $\mathcal{H}$ *with probability* $1 - 2 \cdot 2^{-\rho}$.

Proof. We refer to Sect. A of Appendix for the detailed proof. $\qquad\square$

5   Security Proof

The following theorem shows that protocol Π is a passively secure group key-exchange protocol. We remark that we prove security of the protocol for a classical attacker only; in particular, we allow the attacker only classical access to $\mathcal{H}$. We believe the protocol can be proven secure even against attackers that are allowed to make quantum queries to $\mathcal{H}$, but leave proving this to future work.

Theorem 5.1. *If the parameters in the group key exchange protocol* Π *satisfy the constraints* $2N\sqrt{n}\lambda^{3/2}\sigma_1^2 + (N-1)\sigma_1 \leq \beta_{\mathsf{Rényi}}$ *and* $\sigma_2 = \Omega(\beta_{\mathsf{Rényi}}\sqrt{n/\log\lambda})$, *and if* $\mathcal{H}$ *is modeled as a random oracle, then for any algorithm* $\mathcal{A}$ *running in time* t, *making at most* q *queries to the random oracle, we have:*

$$\mathsf{Adv}_\Pi^{\mathsf{GKE},\mathcal{O}_H}(t, \mathsf{q}) \leq 2^{-\lambda+1}$$

$$+ \sqrt{\left(N \cdot \mathsf{Adv}_{n,q,\chi_{\sigma_1},3}^{\mathsf{RLWE}}(t_1) + \mathsf{Adv}_{\mathsf{KeyRec}}(t_2) + \frac{\mathsf{q}}{2^\lambda}\right) \cdot \frac{\exp\left(2\pi n\left(\beta_{\mathsf{Rényi}}/\sigma_2\right)^2\right)}{1 - 2^{-\lambda+1}}},$$

where $t_1 = t + \mathcal{O}(N) \cdot t_{\mathsf{ring}}, t_2 = t + \mathcal{O}(N) \cdot t_{\mathsf{ring}}$ *and where* t_{ring} *is defined as the (maximum) time required to perform operations in* R_q.

Proof. Consider the joint distribution of $(\mathsf{T}, \mathsf{sk})$, where $\mathsf{T} = (\{z_i\}, \{X_i\}, K_{k\ 1})$ is the transcript of an execution of the protocol Π, and k is the final shared session key. The distribution of $(\mathsf{T}, \mathsf{sk})$ is denoted as Real. Proceeding via a sequence of experiments, we will show that under the Ring-LWE assumption, if an efficient adversary queries the random oracle on input k_{N-1} in the Ideal experiment (to be formally defined) with at most negligible probability, then it also queries the random oracle on input k_{N-1} in the Real experiment with at most negligible probability.

Furthermore, in Ideal, the input k_{N-1} to the random oracle is uniform random, which means that the adversary has $\mathsf{negl}(\lambda)$ probability of guessing k_{N-1} in Ideal when $\mathsf{q} = \mathsf{poly}(\lambda)$. Finally, we argue that the above is sufficient to prove the GKE security of the scheme, because in the random oracle model, the output of the random oracle on k_{N-1} – i.e. the agreed upon key – looks uniformly random to an adversary who does not query k_{N-1}. We now proceed with the formal proof.

Let Query be the event that k_{N-1} is among the adversary $\mathcal{A}$'s random oracle queries and denote by $\Pr_i[\mathsf{Query}]$ the probability that event Query happens in *Experiment i*. Note that we let $e_0' = \hat{e}_0$ in order to distinguish this from the other e_i''s sampled from a different distribution.

Experiment 0. This is the original experiment. In this experiment, the distribution of $(\mathsf{T}, \mathsf{sk})$ is as follows, denoted Real:

$$
\mathrm{Real} := \left\{
\begin{aligned}
& a \leftarrow R_q; s_0, s_1, \ldots, s_{N-1}, e_0, e_1, \ldots, e_{N-1} \leftarrow \chi; \\
& z_0 = as_0 + e_0, z_1 = as_1 + e_1, \ldots, z_{N-1} = as_{N-1} + e_{N-1}; \\
& e'_1, \ldots, e'_{N-1} \leftarrow \chi_{\sigma_1}; \hat{e}_0 \leftarrow \chi_{\sigma_2}; \\
& X_0 = (z_1 - z_{N-1})s_0 + \hat{e}_0, X_1 = (z_2 - z_0)s_1 + e'_1, \ldots, \\
& X_{N-1} = (z_0 - z_{N-2})s_{N-1} + e'_{N-1}; e''_{N-1} \leftarrow \chi_{\sigma_1}; \\
& b_{N-1} = z_{N-2}Ns_{N-1} + e''_{N-1} + X_{N-1} \cdot (N-1) + \\
& \quad X_0 \cdot (N-2) + \cdots + X_{N-3}; \\
& (K_{N-1}, k_{N-1}) = \mathsf{recMsg}(b_{N-1}); \mathsf{sk} = \mathcal{H}(k_{N-1}); \\
& \mathsf{T} = (z_0, \ldots, z_{N-1}, X_0, \ldots, X_{N-1}, K_{N-1}).
\end{aligned}
\right\} : (\mathsf{T}, \mathsf{sk}) \; .
$$

Since $\Pr[\mathcal{A} \text{ succeeds}] = \frac{1}{2} + \mathsf{Adv}_\Pi^{\mathsf{GKE}, \mathcal{O}_H}(t, \mathsf{q}) = \Pr_0[\mathsf{Query}] \cdot 1 + \Pr_0(\overline{\mathsf{Query}}) \cdot \frac{1}{2}$, we have

$$
\mathsf{Adv}_\Pi^{\mathsf{GKE}, \mathcal{O}_H}(t, \mathsf{q}) \leq \Pr_0[\mathsf{Query}]. \tag{1}
$$

In the remainder of the proof, we focus on bounding $\Pr_0[\mathsf{Query}]$.

Experiment 1. In this experiment, X_0 is replaced by $X'_0 = -\sum_{i=1}^{N-1} X_i + \hat{e}_0$. The remainder of the experiment is exactly the same as *Experiment 0*. The corresponding distribution of $(\mathsf{T}, \mathsf{sk})$ is as follows, denoted Dist_1:

$$
\mathrm{Dist}_1 := \left\{
\begin{aligned}
& a \leftarrow \mathcal{U}(R_q); s_0, s_1, \ldots, s_{N-1}, e_0, e_1, \ldots, e_{N-1} \leftarrow \chi_{\sigma_1}; \\
& z_0 = as_0 + e_0, z_1 = as_1 + e_1, \ldots, z_{N-1} = as_{N-1} + e_{N-1}; \\
& e'_0, e'_1, \ldots, e'_{N-1} \leftarrow \chi_{\sigma_1}; \hat{e}_0 \leftarrow \chi_{\sigma_2} \\
& X'_0 = -\sum_{i=1}^{N-1} X_i + \hat{e}_0, X_1 = (z_2 - z_0)s_1 + e'_1, \ldots, \\
& X_{N-1} = (z_0 - z_{N-2})s_{N-1} + e'_{N-1}; e''_{N-1} \leftarrow \chi_{\sigma_1}; \\
& b_{N-1} = z_{N-2}Ns_{N-1} + e''_{N-1} + X_{N-1} \cdot (N-1) + \\
& \quad X_0 \cdot (N-2) + \cdots + X_{N-3}; \\
& (K_{N-1}, k_{N-1}) = \mathsf{recMsg}(b_{N-1}); \mathsf{sk} = \mathcal{H}(k_{N-1}); \\
& \mathsf{T} = (z_0, \ldots, z_{N-1}, X_0, \ldots, X_{N-1}, K_{N-1}).
\end{aligned}
\right\} : (\mathsf{T}, \mathsf{sk}) \; .
$$

Claim. Given $a \leftarrow \mathcal{U}(R_q)$, $s_0, s_1, \ldots, s_{N-1}, e_0, e_1, \ldots, e_{N-1}, e'_1, \ldots, e'_{N-1} \leftarrow \chi_{\sigma_1}$, $\hat{e}_0 \leftarrow \chi_{\sigma_2}$, $X_0 = (z_1 - z_{N-1})s_0 + \hat{e}_0$, $X'_0 = -\sum_{i=1}^{N-1} X_i + \hat{e}_0$, where $R_q, \chi_{\sigma_1}, \chi_{\sigma_2}$, $z_1, z_{N-1}, X_1, \ldots, X_{N-1}$ are defined as above, and the constraint $2N\sqrt{n}\lambda^{3/2}\sigma_1^2 + (N-1)\sigma_1 \leq \beta_{\mathsf{Rényi}}$ is satisfied, we have

$$
\Pr_0[\mathsf{Query}] \leq \sqrt{\Pr_1[\mathsf{Query}] \cdot \frac{\exp(2\pi n(\beta_{\mathsf{Rényi}}/\sigma_2)^2)}{1 - 2^{-\lambda+1}}} + 2^{-\lambda+1}. \tag{2}
$$

Proof. Let $\mathsf{Error} = \sum_{i=0}^{N-1}(s_ie_{i+1} + s_ie_{i-1}) + \sum_{i=1}^{N-1} e_i'$. We begin by showing that the absolute value of each coefficient of Error is bounded by $\beta_{\mathsf{Rényi}}$ with all but negligible probability. Then by adding a "bigger" error $\hat{e}_0 \leftarrow \chi_{\sigma_2}$, the small difference between distributions $\mathsf{Error} + \chi_{\sigma_2}$ (corresponding to Experiment 0) and χ_{σ_2} (corresponding to Experiment 1) can be "washed" away by applying Theorem 2.1.

For all coefficient indices j, note that $|\mathsf{Error}_j| = |(\sum_{i=0}^{N-1}(s_ie_{i+1} + s_ie_{i-1}) + \sum_{i=1}^{N-1} e_i')_j|$. Let bound_λ denote the event that for all i and all coordinate indices j, $|(s_i)_j| \leq c\sigma_1$, $|(e_i)_j| \leq c\sigma_1$, $|(e_i')_j| \leq c\sigma_1$, $|(e_{N-1}'')_j| \leq c\sigma_1$, and $|(\hat{e}_0)_j| \leq c\sigma_2$, where $c = \sqrt{\frac{2\lambda}{\pi \log e}}$. By replacing ρ with λ in Lemmas A.1 and A.2 and by a union bound, we have – conditioned on bound_λ – that $|\mathsf{Error}_j| \leq 2N\sqrt{n}\lambda^{3/2}\sigma_1^2 + (N-1)\sigma_1$ for all j, with probability at least $1 - 2N \cdot 2n2^{-2\lambda}$. Since, under the assumption that $4Nn \leq 2^\lambda$, we have that $\Pr[\mathsf{bound}_\lambda] \geq 1 - 2^{-\lambda}$, we conclude that

$$\Pr[|\mathsf{Error}_j| \leq \beta_{\mathsf{Rényi}}, \forall j] \geq 1 - 2^{-\lambda+1}. \tag{3}$$

For a fixed $\mathsf{Error} \in R_q$, we denote by D_1 the distribution of $\mathsf{Error} + \chi_{\sigma_2}$ and note that D_1, χ_{σ_2} are n-dimension distributions.

Since $\sigma_2 = \Omega(\beta_{\mathsf{Rényi}}\sqrt{n/\log \lambda})$, assuming that for all j, $|\mathsf{Error}_j| \leq \beta_{\mathsf{Rényi}}$, by Theorem 2.1, we have

$$\mathrm{RD}_2(D_1 \| \chi_{\sigma_2}) \leq \exp(2\pi n(\beta_{\mathsf{Rényi}}/\sigma_2)^2) = \mathrm{poly}(\lambda). \tag{4}$$

Then it is straightforward to verify that the distribution of X_0 in *Experiment 0* is

$$\left(as_1s_0 - as_{N-1}s_0 - \sum_{i=0}^{N-1}(e_{i+1}s_i + e_{i-1}s_i) - \sum_{i=1}^{N-1} e_i' \right) + D_1,$$

and the distribution of X_0' in *Experiment 1* is

$$\left(as_1s_0 - as_{N-1}s_0 - \sum_{i=0}^{N-1}(e_{i+1}s_i + e_{i-1}s_i) - \sum_{i=1}^{N-1} e_i' \right) + \chi_{\sigma_2}.$$

In addition, the remaining part of Dist_1 is identical to Real. Therefore we may view Real in *Experiment 0* as a function of a random variable sampled from D_1 and take Dist_1 in *Experiment 1* as a function of a random variable sampled from χ_{σ_2}.

Recall that Query is the event that k_{N-1} is contained in the set of random oracle queries issued by adversary $\mathcal{A}$. We denote by Xbound the event that $|\mathsf{Error}_j| \leq \beta_{\mathsf{Rényi}}, \forall j$. Note that computation of Error_j is available in both *Experiment 0* and *Experiment 1*. We denote by $\Pr_0[\mathsf{Xbound}]$ (resp. $\Pr_1[\mathsf{Xbound}]$) the probability that event Xbound occurs in *Experiment 0* (resp. *Experiment 1*) and define $\Pr_0[\overline{\mathsf{Xbound}}]$, $\Pr_1[\overline{\mathsf{Xbound}}]$ analogously. Let Real' (resp. Dist_1') denote the random variable Real (resp. Dist_1), conditioned on the event Xbound. Therefore, we have

$$\Pr{}_0[\text{Query}] = \Pr{}_0[\text{Query}|\text{Xbound}] \cdot \Pr{}_0[\text{Xbound}] + \Pr{}_0[\text{Query}|\overline{\text{Xbound}}] \cdot \Pr{}_0[\overline{\text{Xbound}}]$$
$$\leq \Pr{}_0[\text{Query}|\text{Xbound}] + \Pr{}_0[\overline{\text{Xbound}}]$$
$$\leq \Pr{}_0[\text{Query}|\text{Xbound}] + 2^{-\lambda+1}$$
$$\leq \sqrt{\Pr{}_1[\text{Query}|\text{Xbound}] \cdot \text{RD}_2(\text{Real}'||\text{Dist}_1')} + 2^{-\lambda+1}$$
$$\leq \sqrt{\Pr{}_1[\text{Query}|\text{Xbound}] \cdot \text{RD}_2(D_1||\chi_{\sigma_2})} + 2^{-\lambda+1}$$
$$\leq \sqrt{\Pr{}_1[\text{Query}|\text{Xbound}] \cdot \exp(2\pi n(\beta_{\text{Rényi}}/\sigma_2)^2)} + 2^{-\lambda+1}$$
$$\leq \sqrt{\Pr{}_1\left[\text{Query} \cdot \frac{\exp(2\pi n(\beta_{\text{Rényi}}/\sigma_2)^2)}{\Pr{}_1[\text{Xbound}]}\right]} + 2^{-\lambda+1}$$
$$\leq \sqrt{\Pr{}_1[\text{Query}] \cdot \frac{\exp(2\pi n(\beta_{\text{Rényi}}/\sigma_2)^2)}{1 - 2^{-\lambda+1}}} + 2^{-\lambda+1},$$

where the second and last inequalities follow from (3), the third inequality follows from Proposition 1 and the fifth inequality follows from (4). □

Due to page restriction, we defer the proof of showing

$$\Pr{}_1[\text{Query}] \leq \left(N \cdot \text{Adv}_{n,q,\chi_{\sigma_1},3}^{\text{RLWE}}(t_1) + \text{Adv}_{\text{KeyRec}}(t_2) + \frac{q}{2^\lambda}\right),$$

to the full version. □

5.1 Parameter Constraints

Beyond the parameter settings recommended for instantiating Ring-LWE with security parameter λ, parameters $N, n, \sigma_1, \sigma_2, \lambda, \rho$ of the protocol above are also required to satisfy the following inequalities:

$$(N^2 + 2N) \cdot \sqrt{n}\rho^{3/2}\sigma_1^2 + (\frac{N^2}{2} + 1)\sigma_1 + (N-2)\sigma_2 \leq \beta_{\text{Rec}} \quad \text{(Correctness)} \quad (5)$$

$$2N\sqrt{n}\lambda^{3/2}\sigma_1^2 + (N-1)\sigma_1 \leq \beta_{\text{Rényi}} \quad \text{(Security)} \quad (6)$$

$$\sigma_2 = \Omega(\beta_{\text{Rényi}}\sqrt{n/\log\lambda}) \quad \text{(Security)} \quad (7)$$

We comment that once the ring, the noise distributions, and the security parameters λ, ρ are fixed, the maximum number of parties is fixed.

Acknowledgments. This material is based on work performed under financial assistance award 70NANB15H328 from the U.S. Department of Commerce, National Institute of Standards and Technology. Work by Dana Dachman-Soled was additionally supported in part by NSF grants #CNS-1840893 and #CNS-1453045, and by a research partnership award from Cisco.

A   Correctness of the Group Key-Exchange Protocol

Theorem 4.1. *Given* β_{Rec} *as parameter of* KeyRec *protocol,* $N, n, \rho, \sigma_1, \sigma_2$ *as parameters of GKE protocol* Π, $(N^2+2N)\cdot\sqrt{n}\rho^{3/2}\sigma_1^2+(\frac{N^2}{2}+1)\sigma_1+(N-2)\sigma_2 \leq \beta_{\mathsf{Rec}}$ *is satisfied, if all players honestly execute the group key exchange protocol as described above, then each player derive the same key as input of* $\mathcal{H}$ *with probability* $1 - 2 \cdot 2^{-\rho}$.

Proof. Given $s_i, e_i, e'_i, e''_{N-1} \leftarrow \chi_{\sigma_1}, \hat{e}_0 \leftarrow \chi_{\sigma_2}$ for all i as specified in protocol Π, we begin by introducing the following lemmas to analyze probabilities that each coordinate of $s_i, e_i, e'_i, e''_{N-1}, \hat{e}_0$ are "short" for all i, and conditioned on the first event, $s_i e_i$ are "short".

Lemma A.1. *Given* $s_i, e_i, e'_i, e''_{N-1}, \hat{e}_0$ *for all* i *as defined above, let* bound *denote the event that for all* i *and all coordinate indices* j, $|(s_i)_j| \leq c\sigma_1$, $|(e_i)_j| \leq c\sigma_1$, $|(e'_i)_j| \leq c\sigma_1$, $|(e''_{N-1})_j| \leq c\sigma_1$, *and* $|(\hat{e}_0)_j| \leq c\sigma_2$, *where* $c = \sqrt{\frac{2\rho}{\pi \log e}}$, *we have* $\Pr[\text{bound}] \geq 1 - 2^{-\rho}$.

Proof. Using the fact that complementary error function $\mathrm{erfc}(x) = \frac{2}{\sqrt{\pi}}\int_x^\infty e^{-t^2}\,dt \leq e^{-x^2}$, we obtain

$$\Pr[|v| \geq c\sigma + 1; v \leftarrow D_{\mathbb{Z}_q,\sigma}] \leq 2 \sum_{x=\lfloor c\sigma+1\rfloor}^{\infty} D_{\mathbb{Z}_q,\sigma}(x) \leq \frac{2}{\sigma}\int_{c\sigma}^\infty e^{-\frac{\pi x^2}{\sigma^2}}\,dx$$

$$= \frac{2}{\sqrt{\pi}}\int_{\frac{\sqrt{\pi}}{\sigma}(c\sigma)}^\infty e^{-t^2}\,dt \leq e^{-c^2\pi}.$$

Note that there are $3nN$ number of coordinates sampled from distribution $D_{\mathbb{Z}_q,\sigma_1}$, and n number of coordinates sampled from distribution $D_{\mathbb{Z}_q,\sigma_2}$ in total. Assume $3nN + n \leq e^{c^2\pi/2}$, since all the coordinates are sampled independently, we bound $\Pr[\text{bound}]$ as follow:

$$\Pr[\text{bound}] = \big(1 - \Pr[|v| \geq c\sigma_1 + 1; v \leftarrow D_{\mathbb{Z}_q,\sigma_1}]\big)^{3nN}$$
$$\cdot \big(1 - \Pr[|\hat{e}_0| \geq c\sigma_2 + 1; \hat{e}_0 \leftarrow D_{\mathbb{Z}_q,\sigma_2}]\big)^n$$
$$\geq 1 - (3nN + n)e^{-c^2\pi} \geq 1 - e^{-c^2\pi/2} \geq 1 - 2^{-\rho}.$$

The last inequality follows as $c = \sqrt{\frac{2\rho}{\pi \log e}}$.   □

Lemma A.2. *Given* $s_i, e_i, e'_i, e''_{N-1}, \hat{e}_0$ *for all* i *as defined above, and* bound *as defined in Lemma A.1, let* $\text{product}_{\mathsf{s_i,e_j}}$ *denote the event that, for all coefficient indices* v, $|(s_i e_j)_v| \leq \sqrt{n}\rho^{3/2}\sigma_1^2$. *we have*

$$\Pr[\text{product}_{\mathsf{s_i,e_j}}|\text{bound}] \geq 1 - 2n \cdot 2^{-2\rho}.$$

Proof. For $t \in \{0, \ldots, n-1\}$, Let $(s_i)_t$ denote the tth coefficient of $s_i \in R_q$, namely, $s_i = \sum_{t=0}^{n-1}(s_i)_t X^i$. $(e_j)_t$ is defined analogously. Since we have $X^n + 1$ as modulo of R, it is easy to see that $(s_i e_j)_v = c_v X^v$, where $c_v = \sum_{u=0}^{n-1}(s_i)_u(e_j)_{v-u}^*$, and $(e_j)_{v-u}^* = (e_j)_{v-u}$ if $v - u \geq 0$, $(e_j)_{v-u}^* = -(e_j)_{v-u+n}$, otherwise. Thus, conditioned on $|(s_i)_t| \leq c\sigma_1$ and $|(e_j)_t| \leq c\sigma_1$ (for all i, j, t) where $c = \sqrt{\frac{2\rho}{\pi \log e}}$, by Hoeffding's Inequality [20], we derive

$$\Pr[|(s_i e_j)_v| \geq \delta] = \Pr\left[\left|\sum_{u=0}^{n-1}(s_i)_u(e_j)_{v-u}^*\right| \geq \delta\right] \leq 2\exp\left(\frac{-2\delta^2}{n(2c^2\sigma_1^2)^2}\right),$$

as each product $(s_i)_u(e_j)_{v-u}^*$ in the sum is an independent random variable with mean 0 in the range $[-c^2\sigma_1^2, c^2\sigma_1^2]$. By setting $\delta = \sqrt{n}\rho^{3/2}\sigma_1^2$, we obtain

$$\Pr[|(s_u e_v)_i| \geq \sqrt{n}\rho^{3/2}\sigma_1^2] \leq 2^{-2\rho+1}. \tag{8}$$

Finally, by Union Bound,

$$\Pr[\text{product}_{s_i,e_j}|\text{bound}] = \Pr[|(s_i e_j)_v| \leq \sqrt{n}\rho^{3/2}\sigma_1^2, \forall v] \geq 1 - 2n \cdot 2^{-2\rho}. \tag{9}$$

$\square$

Now we begin analyzing the chance that not all parties agree on the same final key. The correctness of KeyRec guarantees that this group key exchange protocol has agreed session key among all parties $\forall i, k_i = k_{N-1}$, if $\forall j$, the jth coefficient of $|b_{N-1} - b_i| \leq \beta_{\text{Rec}}$.

For better illustration, we first write $X_0, \ldots, X_{N-1}$ in form of linear system as follows. $\boldsymbol{X} = [X_0 \ X_1 \ X_2 \ \cdots \ X_{N-1}]^T$

$$= \underbrace{\begin{bmatrix} 1 & 0 & 0 & 0 & \ldots & 0 & -1 \\ -1 & 1 & 0 & 0 & \ldots & 0 & 0 \\ 0 & -1 & 1 & 0 & \ldots & 0 & 0 \\ 0 & 0 & -1 & 1 & \ldots & 0 & 0 \\ \vdots & \vdots & \vdots & & \ddots & & \vdots \\ 0 & 0 & 0 & 0 & \ldots & -1 & 1 \end{bmatrix}}_{M} \underbrace{\begin{bmatrix} as_0 s_1 \\ as_1 s_2 \\ as_2 s_3 \\ as_3 s_4 \\ \vdots \\ as_{N-2} s_{N-1} \\ as_{N-1} s_0 \end{bmatrix}}_{S} + \underbrace{\begin{bmatrix} s_0 e_1 - s_0 e_{N-1} + e_0' \\ s_1 e_2 - s_1 e_0 + e_1' \\ s_2 e_3 - s_2 e_1 + e_2' \\ s_3 e_4 - s_3 e_2 + e_3' \\ \vdots \\ s_{N-2} e_{N-3} - s_{N-2} e_{N-3} + e_{N-2}' \\ s_{N-1} e_0 - s_{N-1} e_{N-2} + e_{N-1}' \end{bmatrix}}_{E}.$$

$$\tag{10}$$

We denote the matrices above by $\boldsymbol{M}, \boldsymbol{S}, \boldsymbol{E}$ from left to right and have the linear system as $\boldsymbol{X} = \boldsymbol{MS} + \boldsymbol{E}$. By setting $\boldsymbol{B}_i = [i-1 \ i-2 \ \cdots \ 0 \ N-1 \ N-2 \ \cdots \ i]$ as a N-dimensional vector, we can then write b_i as $\boldsymbol{B}_i \cdot \boldsymbol{X} + N(as_i s_{i-1} + s_i e_{i-1}) = \boldsymbol{B}_i \boldsymbol{MS} + \boldsymbol{B}_i \boldsymbol{E} + N(as_i s_{i-1} + s_i e_{i-1})$, for $i \neq N-1$ and write b_{N-1} as $\boldsymbol{B}_{N-1} \boldsymbol{MS} + \boldsymbol{B}_{N-1} \boldsymbol{E} + N(as_{N-1} s_{N-2} + s_{N-1} e_{N-2}) + e_{N-1}''$. It is straightforward to see that, entries of $\boldsymbol{MS}$ and $Nas_i s_{i-1}$ are eliminated through the process of computing $b_{N-1} - b_i$. Thus we get

$$b_{N-1} - b_i = (\boldsymbol{B}_{N-1} - \boldsymbol{B}_i)\,\boldsymbol{E} + N(s_{N-1}e_{N-2} - s_i e_{i-1}) + e''_{N-1}$$

$$= (N - i - 1)\cdot\left(\sum_{\substack{j\in\mathbb{Z}\cap[0,i-1]\\ \text{and } j=N-1}} s_j e_{j+1} - s_j e_{j-1} + e'_j\right) + e''_{N-1}$$

$$+ (-i - 1)\left(\sum_{j=i}^{N-2} s_j e_{j+1} - s_j e_{j-1} + e'_j\right) + N(s_{N-1}e_{N-2} - s_i e_{i-1})$$

Observe that for an arbitrary $i \in [N]$, there are at most $(N^2 + 2N)$ terms in form of $s_u e_v$, at most $N^2/2$ terms in form of e'_w where $e'_w \leftarrow \chi_{\sigma_1}$, at most $N - 2$ terms of e'_0, where $e'_0 \leftarrow \chi_{\sigma_2}$, and one term in form of e''_{N-1} in any coordinate of the sum above. Let $\text{product}_{\mathsf{ALL}}$ denote the event that for all the terms in form of $s_u e_v$ observed above, each coefficient of such term is bounded by $\sqrt{n}\rho^{3/2}\sigma_1^2$. By Union Bound and by assuming $2n(N^2 + 2N) \leq 2^\rho$, it is straightforward to see $\Pr[\overline{\text{product}_{\mathsf{ALL}}}|\text{bound}] \leq (N^2 + 2N)\cdot 2n 2^{-2\rho} \leq 2^{-\rho}$.

Let bad be the event that not all parties agree on the same final key. Given the constraint $(N^2 + 2N)\cdot\sqrt{n}\rho^{3/2}\sigma_1^2 + (\frac{N^2}{2} + 1)\sigma_1 + (N - 2)\sigma_2 \leq \beta_{\mathsf{Rec}}$ satisfied, we have

$$\Pr[\text{bad}] = \Pr[\text{bad}|\text{bound}]\cdot\Pr[\text{bound}] + \Pr[\text{bad}|\overline{\text{bound}}]\cdot\Pr[\overline{\text{bound}}] \tag{11}$$

$$\leq \Pr[\overline{\text{product}_{\mathsf{ALL}}}]\cdot 1 + 1\cdot\Pr[\overline{\text{bound}}] \leq 2\cdot 2^{-\rho}, \tag{12}$$

which completes the proof. $\qquad\qquad\qquad\qquad\qquad\qquad\qquad\qquad\qquad\square$

References

1. Abdalla, M., Bresson, E., Chevassut, O., Pointcheval, D.: Password-based group key exchange in a constant number of rounds. In: Yung, M., Dodis, Y., Kiayias, A., Malkin, T. (eds.) PKC 2006. LNCS, vol. 3958, pp. 427–442. Springer, Heidelberg (2006). https://doi.org/10.1007/11745853_28
2. Abdalla, M., Pointcheval, D.: A scalable password-based group key exchange protocol in the standard model. In: Lai, X., Chen, K. (eds.) ASIACRYPT 2006. LNCS, vol. 4284, pp. 332–347. Springer, Heidelberg (2006). https://doi.org/10.1007/11935230_22
3. Alkim, E., Ducas, L., Pöppelmann, T., Schwabe, P.: NewHope without reconciliation. Cryptology ePrint Archive, Report 2016/1157 (2016). http://eprint.iacr.org/2016/1157
4. Alkim, E., Ducas, L., Pöppelmann, T., Schwabe, P.: Post-quantum key exchange— a new hope. In: 25th USENIX Security Symposium (USENIX Security 2016), pp. 327–343. USENIX Association, Austin (2016)
5. Becker, K., Wille, U.: Communication complexity of group key distribution. In: Proceedings of the 5th ACM Conference on Computer and Communications Security, CCS 1998, pp. 1–6. ACM, New York (1998)
6. Bellare, M., Rogaway, P.: Provably secure session key distribution: the three party case. In: 27th Annual ACM Symposium on Theory of Computing, Las Vegas, NV, USA, 29 May–1 June, pp. 57–66. ACM Press (1995)

7. Bogdanov, A., Guo, S., Masny, D., Richelson, S., Rosen, A.: On the hardness of learning with rounding over small modulus. In: Kushilevitz, E., Malkin, T. (eds.) TCC 2016. LNCS, vol. 9562, pp. 209–224. Springer, Heidelberg (2016). https://doi.org/10.1007/978-3-662-49096-9_9

8. Bohli, J.-M., Vasco, M.I.G., Steinwandt, R.: Password-authenticated constant-round group key establishment with a common reference string. Cryptology ePrint Archive, Report 2006/214 (2006). http://eprint.iacr.org/2006/214

9. Bohli, J.-M., Vasco, M.I.G., Steinwandt, R.: Secure group key establishment revisited. Int. J. Inf. Secur. 6(4), 243–254 (2007)

10. Boneh, D., et al.: Multiparty non-interactive key exchange and more from isogenies on elliptic curves. arXiv preprint arXiv:1807.03038 (2018)

11. Bresson, E., Catalano, D.: Constant round authenticated group key agreement via distributed computation. In: Bao, F., Deng, R., Zhou, J. (eds.) PKC 2004. LNCS, vol. 2947, pp. 115–129. Springer, Heidelberg (2004). https://doi.org/10.1007/978-3-540-24632-9_9

12. Bresson, E., Chevassut, O., Pointcheval, D.: Provably authenticated group Diffie-Hellman key exchange—the dynamic case. In: Boyd, C. (ed.) ASIACRYPT 2001. LNCS, vol. 2248, pp. 290–309. Springer, Heidelberg (2001). https://doi.org/10.1007/3-540-45682-1_18

13. Bresson, E., Chevassut, O., Pointcheval, D.: Dynamic group Diffie-Hellman key exchange under standard assumptions. In: Knudsen, L.R. (ed.) EUROCRYPT 2002. LNCS, vol. 2332, pp. 321–336. Springer, Heidelberg (2002). https://doi.org/10.1007/3-540-46035-7_21

14. Bresson, E., Chevassut, O., Pointcheval, D., Quisquater, J.-J.: Provably authenticated group Diffie-Hellman key exchange. In: 8th Conference on Computer and Communications Security, ACM CCS 2001, Philadelphia, PA, USA, 5–8 November, pp. 255–264. ACM Press (2001)

15. Burmester, M., Desmedt, Y.: A secure and efficient conference key distribution system. In: De Santis, A. (ed.) EUROCRYPT 1994. LNCS, vol. 950, pp. 275–286. Springer, Heidelberg (1995). https://doi.org/10.1007/BFb0053443

16. Burmester, M., Desmedt, Y.: A secure and scalable group key exchange system. Inf. Process. Lett. 94(3), 137–143 (2005)

17. Choi, K.Y., Hwang, J.Y., Lee, D.H.: Efficient ID-based group key agreement with bilinear maps. In: Bao, F., Deng, R., Zhou, J. (eds.) PKC 2004. LNCS, vol. 2947, pp. 130–144. Springer, Heidelberg (2004). https://doi.org/10.1007/978-3-540-24632-9_10

18. Crockett, E., Peikert, C.: Challenges for ring-LWE. Cryptology ePrint Archive, Report 2016/782 (2016). http://eprint.iacr.org/2016/782

19. Ding, J., Xie, X., Lin, X.: A simple provably secure key exchange scheme based on the learning with errors problem. Cryptology ePrint Archive, Report 2012/688 (2012). http://eprint.iacr.org/2012/688

20. Hoeffding, W.: Probability inequalities for sums of bounded random variables. J. Am. Stat. Assoc. 58(301), 13–30 (1963)

21. Ingemarsson, I., Tang, D., Wong, C.: A conference key distribution system. IEEE Trans. Inf. Theor. 28(5), 714–720 (1982)

22. Katz, J., Shin, J.S.: Modeling insider attacks on group key-exchange protocols. In: Proceedings of the 12th ACM Conference on Computer and Communications Security, CCS 2005, pp. 180–189. ACM, New York (2005)

23. Katz, J., Yung, M.: Scalable protocols for authenticated group key exchange. In: Boneh, D. (ed.) CRYPTO 2003. LNCS, vol. 2729, pp. 110–125. Springer, Heidelberg (2003). https://doi.org/10.1007/978-3-540-45146-4_7

24. Katz, J., Yung, M.: Scalable protocols for authenticated group key exchange. J. Cryptol. **20**(1), 85–113 (2007)
25. Kim, Y., Perrig, A., Tsudik, G.: Simple and fault-tolerant key agreement for dynamic collaborative groups. In: Proceedings of the 7th ACM Conference on Computer and Communications Security, CCS 2000, pp. 235–244. ACM, New York (2000)
26. Langlois, A., Stehlé, D., Steinfeld, R.: GGHLite: more efficient multilinear maps from ideal lattices. In: Nguyen, P.Q., Oswald, E. (eds.) EUROCRYPT 2014. LNCS, vol. 8441, pp. 239–256. Springer, Heidelberg (2014). https://doi.org/10.1007/978-3-642-55220-5_14
27. Lyubashevsky, V., Peikert, C., Regev, O.: On ideal lattices and learning with errors over rings. In: Gilbert, H. (ed.) EUROCRYPT 2010. LNCS, vol. 6110, pp. 1–23. Springer, Heidelberg (2010). https://doi.org/10.1007/978-3-642-13190-5_1
28. Peikert, C.: Lattice cryptography for the internet. Cryptology ePrint Archive, Report 2014/070 (2014). http://eprint.iacr.org/2014/070
29. Steer, D.G., Strawczynski, L.: A secure audio teleconference system. In: 21st Century Military Communications - What's Possible?'. Conference Record. Military Communications Conference, MILCOM 1988, October 1988
30. Steiner, M., Tsudik, G., Waidner, M.: Key agreement in dynamic peer groups. IEEE Trans. Parallel Distrib. Syst. **11**(8), 769–780 (2000)
31. Wu, Q., Mu, Y., Susilo, W., Qin, B., Domingo-Ferrer, J.: Asymmetric group key agreement. In: Joux, A. (ed.) EUROCRYPT 2009. LNCS, vol. 5479, pp. 153–170. Springer, Heidelberg (2009). https://doi.org/10.1007/978-3-642-01001-9_9
32. Zhang, J., Zhang, Z., Ding, J., Snook, M., Dagdelen, Ö.: Authenticated key exchange from ideal lattices. In: Oswald, E., Fischlin, M. (eds.) EUROCRYPT 2015. LNCS, vol. 9057, pp. 719–751. Springer, Heidelberg (2015). https://doi.org/10.1007/978-3-662-46803-6_24

Hybrid Key Encapsulation Mechanisms and Authenticated Key Exchange

Nina Bindel[1], Jacqueline Brendel[1(✉)], Marc Fischlin[1], Brian Goncalves[2], and Douglas Stebila[3]

[1] Technische Universität Darmstadt, Darmstadt, Germany
jacqueline.brendel@crisp-da.de
[2] Ryerson University, Toronto, ON, Canada
[3] University of Waterloo, Waterloo, ON, Canada

Abstract. Concerns about the impact of quantum computers on currently deployed public key cryptography have instigated research into not only quantum-resistant cryptographic primitives but also how to transition applications from classical to quantum-resistant solutions. One approach to mitigate the risk of quantum attacks and to preserve common security guarantees are *hybrid* schemes, which combine classically secure and quantum-resistant schemes. Various academic and industry experiments and draft standards related to the Transport Layer Security (TLS) protocol already use some form of hybrid key exchange; however sound theoretical approaches to substantiate the design and security of such hybrid key exchange protocols are missing so far.

We initiate the modeling of hybrid authenticated key exchange protocols, considering security against adversaries with varying levels of quantum power over time, such as adversaries who may become quantum in the future or are quantum in the present. We reach our goal using a three-step approach: First, we introduce security notions for key encapsulation mechanisms (KEMs) that enable a fine-grained distinction between different quantum scenarios. Second, we propose several combiners for constructing hybrid KEMs that correspond closely to recently proposed Internet-Drafts for hybrid key exchange in TLS 1.3. Finally, we present a provably sound design for hybrid key exchange using KEMs as building blocks.

Keywords: Key exchange · Hybrid key exchange · Combiners · KEMs

1 Introduction

The construction of cryptographic algorithms that could resist attacks by quantum computers is a significant field of current research. However, even after new (quantum-resistant)algorithms have been agreed upon, history shows that transitioning applications and protocols to use new algorithms can be a long and difficult process: backwards compatibility has to be maintained without introducing the risk of downgrade attacks, and the adoption rate of new versions is very

© Springer Nature Switzerland AG 2019
J. Ding and R. Steinwandt (Eds.): PQCrypto 2019, LNCS 11505, pp. 206–226, 2019.
https://doi.org/10.1007/978-3-030-25510-7_12

slow. An additional obstacle for the post-quantum transition is the uncertainty about the hardness of post-quantum assumptions due to their relative novelty. Parameter choices for post-quantum schemes are not yet reliable (cf. e.g. [2]) and evolving cryptanalysis may yet show them to be vulnerable even against classical attacks. So we find ourselves in a predicament: the demand to protect today's communication from the potential threat posed by quantum computers and the expected lengthy time frame to complete widespread deployment of new algorithms, call for beginning the transition sooner rather than later; but we are not sufficiently confident in the concrete security of post-quantum schemes for immediate deployment.

Hybrid Schemes and Robust Combiners. So-called hybrid schemes offer a solution for the dilemma: they combine two or more algorithms of the same kind such that the combined scheme is secure as long as one of the two components remains secure. The study of such schemes in the symmetric setting dates back to work by Even and Goldreich [25]. In the public key setting, work by Zhang et al. [42] and Dodis and Katz [24] examined the security of using multiple public key encryption schemes. Harnik et al. [27] defined the term *robust combiner* to formalize such combinations, and the case of combiners for oblivious transfer, with a sketch of a combiner for key agreement. Combiners for other primitives have since followed, including hybrid digital signatures by Bindel et al. [12]. Most relevant to our setting of key exchange and KEMs is the work by Giacon et al. [26] which considers various KEM combiners. While this work on KEM combiners is an important first step towards constructing hybrid KEMs, their solutions focus solely on classical adversaries. Since the advent of quantum computing and thus the introduction of more powerful adversaries is an important motivation for investigating hybrid key exchange, quantum security analyses of hybrid schemes is not to be neglected; in particular because most of the constructions of [26] use idealized assumptions such as random oracles that might not immediately transfer to the quantum setting [13]. Moreover, the (quantum) security of hybrid authenticated key exchange remains unresolved in [26]. An alternative recent approach to model security of protocols in which a component fails is the breakdown-resilience model of Brendel, Fischlin, and Günther [20].

There is appetite in academia [16,17] and industry for hybrid key exchange in particular. In 2016 Google temporarily tested a hybrid key exchange ciphersuite "CECPQ1" combining elliptic curve Diffie–Hellman (ECDH) and ring-LWE key exchange (specifically, NewHope [3]) in the Transport Layer Security (TLS) stack of an experimental build of its Chrome browser [19,33]. Microsoft Research [23] and Cloudflare [38] have also expressed interest in hybrid key exchange, and several Internet-Drafts have been submitted to the IETF's TLS working group on hybrid key exchange [37,40].

Quantum Security. Designing quantum-resistant cryptographic schemes requires not only quantum-hard mathematical assumptions, but also appropriate security definitions and proofs. Boneh et al. [13] initiated the study of the security of classical public key primitives in the quantum random oracle model, where the locally quantum adversary can access the random oracle in superposition.

A line of subsequent work [14, 15, 41] extends security definitions of various cryptographic primitives to the case of fully quantum adversaries, i.e., where the adversary's interaction with any oracle (e.g., the decryption oracle for indistinguishability under chosen-ciphertext-attacks of public key encryption, the signing oracle for unforgeability of digital signatures) can also be in superposition. Bindel et al. [12] give a hierarchy of intermediate security notions, where the adversary may be classical during some parts of the security experiment, and quantum in others, to capture the transition from classical to fully quantum security.

Our Contributions. We observe that, despite the strong interest by industry in hybrid key exchange, there has been little academic investigation of the design and security of such schemes. Since early prototypes often become de facto standards, it is important to develop solid theoretical foundations for hybrid key exchange and KEMs at an early stage, especially considering the presence of quantum adversaries. Our work bridges the gap for quantum-resistant hybrid KEMs and extends the foundations to treat hybrid authenticated key exchange protocols: we give new security models both for KEMs and authenticated key exchange protocols that account for adversaries with different levels of quantum capabilities in the security experiment. Furthermore, we examine several combiners for KEMs and prove their robustness, i.e., we prove that the security holds if at least one KEM is secure among possibly other assumptions. These include a new combiner, called XOR-then-MAC combiner, which is based on minimal assumptions and is—to the best of our knowledge—the first KEM combiner construction which is provably secure against fully quantum adversaries. We also discuss dual-PRF-based combiners that are closely related to the key schedule used in TLS 1.3 [35]. We then proceed to show how hybrid KEMs can be used to construct hybrid authenticated key exchange protocols. Our detailed contributions are as follows.

Hierarchy of KEM Security Definitions. We define a family of new security notions for KEMs. Following the approach of [12] for signature schemes, we adapt the security experiment for indistinguishability under chosen-ciphertext attack (IND-CCA) to distinguish between classical and quantum adversarial capabilities at several key points: the adversary's local computational power during interaction with the decapsulation oracle; whether or not an adversary can make decapsulation queries in superposition; and the adversary's local computational power later, after it can no longer interact with the decapsulation oracle. We represent the three choices as X, y, and Z, respectively, and abbreviate a combination as X^yZ-ind-cca. This leads to four different levels: fully classical adversaries (denoted $X^yZ = C^cC$); "future-quantum" (C^cQ), where the adversary is classical today but gains quantum power later; "post-quantum" (Q^cQ) where the locally quantum adversary still interacts classically with the decapsulation oracle; and "fully quantum" (Q^qQ), where all computation and interaction can be quantum. As summarized in Fig. 1, we show that these different security notions form a strict hierarchy. Unless stated otherwise, the following constructions in the paper focus on providing security against Q^cQ adversaries, excluding the fully-quantum scenario. This "restriction" is natural as hybrid solutions are intended to secure the transition to the post-quantum setting.

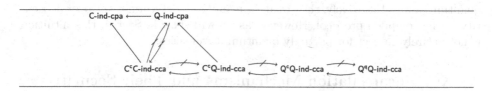

Fig. 1. Implications $(\rightarrow)$ and separations $(\nrightarrow)$ between indistinguishability-based security notions for KEMs wrt. two-stage adversaries.

KEM Combiners. We present three KEM combiners and show their robustness for C^cC, C^cQ, and Q^cQ adversaries; all the proofs are in the standard model.

- XtM: The XOR-then-MAC combiner XtM computes the session key k of the resulting hybrid KEM as the left half of $k_1 \oplus k_2$, where k_1 and k_2 are the session keys of the input KEMs. Additionally, the XtM combiner augments the ciphertexts with a message authentication code (MAC) tag $\text{MAC}_{K_{\text{mac}}}(c_1\|c_2)$, where K_{mac} is built from the right halves of k_1 and k_2, and c_1 and c_2 are the ciphertexts of the two input KEMs. XtM uses the lowest number of cryptographic assumptions, as it relies solely on the security of one of the two combined KEMs and the (one-time) existential unforgeability of the MAC scheme; such a MAC can be built unconditionally and efficiently using universal hash functions [39]. We also discuss that the XtM combiner achieves full quantum resistance (Q^qQ) if one of the input KEMs has this property and if the MAC is Q^cQ secure, where the MAC can again be built unconditionally. To the best of our knowledge this is the first security proof for a KEM combiner in this setting.
- dualPRF: The dual PRF combiner computes k as $\text{PRF}(\text{dPRF}(k_1, k_2), c_1\|c_2)$. In a dual pseudorandom function (PRF), the partial functions $\text{dPRF}(k_1, \cdot)$ and $\text{dPRF}(\cdot, k_2)$ are both assumed to be PRFs (and thus indistinguishable from random functions).
  This combiner is motivated by the key derivation function used in TLS 1.3 [35], which acts both as an extractor (like HKDF's extraction algorithm) and as a pseudorandom function (like HMAC in HKDF), and models how Whyte et al.'s hybrid TLS 1.3 proposal derives the combined session key [40] by concatenating both session keys prior to key derivation.
- The nested combiner N computes k as $\text{PRF}(\text{dPRF}(F(k_1), k_2), c_1\|c_2)$. It is motivated by Schanck and Stebila's hybrid TLS 1.3 proposal which derives the combined session key by feeding each component into an extended TLS 1.3 key schedule [37].

Hybrid Authenticated Key Exchange. Our third contribution is to show how to build hybrid authenticated key exchange from hybrid KEMs. Our construction relies on Krawczyk's SigMA-compiler [32] using signatures and MACs to authenticate and lift the protocol to one that is secure against active adversaries. The intriguing question here is which security properties the involved primitives need to have in order to achieve resistance against the different levels of adversarial quantum power. Intuitively, the "weakest primitive" determines the overall security of the compiled protocol. However, as we will show in Sect. 4, this intuition is not entirely correct for partially quantum adversaries.

2   Key Encapsulation Mechanisms and Their Security

We adjust the basic definitions for KEMs and their indistinguishability-based security notions to the partially and fully quantum adversary setting.

A *key encapsulation mechanism* $\mathcal{K}$ consists of three algorithms KeyGen, Encaps, Decaps and a corresponding key space K. The *key generation* algorithm KeyGen() returns a public/secret-key pair (pk, sk). The *encapsulation* algorithm Encaps(pk) takes as input a public key pk and outputs a ciphertext c and a key $k \in K$, whereas Decaps(sk, c) takes as input a secret key sk and a ciphertext c and returns a key $k \in K$ or $\bot$, denoting failure.

A KEM $\mathcal{K}$ is *ϵ-correct* if for all $(sk, pk) \leftarrow$ KeyGen() and $(c, k) \leftarrow$ Encaps(pk), it holds that $\Pr[\text{Decaps}(sk, c) \neq k] \leq \epsilon$. We say it is *correct* if $\epsilon = 0$. The security of KEMs is defined in terms of the indistinguishability of the session key against chosen-plaintext (IND-CPA) and chosen-ciphertext (IND-CCA) adversaries. The adversary $\mathcal{A}$ is given c^*, κ_b^*, and pk, and is asked to output a bit b', indicating whether κ_b^* equals Decaps(sk, c^*) or a random value. $\mathcal{A}$ wins if $b' = b$. In the IND-CCA experiment $\mathcal{A}$ additionally has access to a decapsulation oracle, which returns the decapsulation of any ciphertext not equal to the challenge ciphertext c^*. We adapt the traditional definitions of IND-CPA and IND-CCA security of KEMs for quantum adversaries. Here we only treat the case of IND-CCA security, the definition of IND-CPA security against quantum adversaries can be found in the full version of this paper [11].

IND-CCA Security Against Partially or Fully Quantum Adversaries. Previous works on security of KEMs against quantum adversaries, such as that of Hofheinz, Hövelmanns, and Kiltz [28], consider a quantum adversary that has local quantum power and can query the random oracle in superposition. Bindel et al. [12] however, consider partially quantum adversaries to model the security of signature schemes against quantum adversaries. We consider the latter approach in the context of IND-CCA security of KEMs to enable distinctions when modeling chosen-ciphertext attacks for KEMs. In particular, our model allows to distinguish between adversaries with evolving quantum capabilities over time. To capture these cases for hybrid signatures, [12] introduced a two-stage security notion for unforgeability of signature schemes; we transfer this notion to KEMs.

We consider a two-stage adversary $\mathcal{A} = (\mathcal{A}_1, \mathcal{A}_2)$, in which $\mathcal{A}_1$ has access to the decapsulation oracle, then terminates and passes a state to the second-stage adversary $\mathcal{A}_2$, which does not have access to the decapsulation oracle. Let

$X, Z \in \{C, Q\}$ and $y \in \{c, q\}$. We will use the terminology "$X^y Z$ adversary" to denote that $\mathcal{A}_1$ is either classical ($X = C$) or quantum ($X = Q$), that $\mathcal{A}_1$'s access to its decapsulation oracle is either classical ($y = c$) or quantum ($y = q$), and that $\mathcal{A}_2$ is either classical ($Z = C$) or quantum ($Z = Q$). In the random oracle model, the adversary can query the random oracle in superposition, if it is quantum; this is independent of y but depends on X and Z. Not all combinations of two-stage We consider the following configurations of $X^y Z$ adversaries to be relevant:

$C^c C$ *security* corresponds to a purely **classical** adversary with classical access to all oracles. This corresponds to the traditional IND-CCA security notion. $C^c Q$ *security* refers to a scenario with a currently classical but potentially **future quantum** adversary. In particular, the adversary is classical as long as it has access to the decapsulation oracle; eventually the adversary gains local quantum computing power, but by this time the adversary relinquishes access to the decapsulation. $Q^c Q$ *security* models an adversary that always has local quantum computing power, but interacts with the active system (in the first stage) only using classical queries. This kind of setting is for example considered in [28] and is commonly referred to as the **post-quantum** setting. $Q^q Q$ *security* models a **fully quantum** adversary with quantum access to all oracles in the first stage.[1]

It is notation-wise convenient to define an order for the notions, with $Q \geq C$ and $q \geq c$, consequently implying a partial order $X^y Z \geq U^v W$ if $X \geq U$, $y \geq v$, and $Z \geq W$, i.e., $Q^q Q \geq Q^c Q \geq C^c Q \geq C^c C$. Let $\max S$ (resp., $\min S$) denote the set of maximal (resp., minimal) elements of S according to this partial order. Since we usually have a total order on S, i.e., $S \subseteq \{C^c C, C^c Q, Q^c Q, Q^q Q\}$, we often simply speak of *the* maximal element. For example, it holds that $C^c Q = \max\{C^c C, C^c Q\}$.

Figure 2 shows the security experiment for indistinguishability of keys in a key encapsulation mechanism $\mathcal{K} = (\mathsf{KeyGen}, \mathsf{Encaps}, \mathsf{Decaps})$ under chosen-ciphertext attacks for a two-stage $X^y Z$ adversary $\mathcal{A} = (\mathcal{A}_1, \mathcal{A}_2)$ in the classical or quantum random oracle model; the standard model notion can be obtained by omitting the hash oracles. For every notion $X^y Z$-ind-cca, we define the corresponding advantage to be $\mathsf{Adv}_{\mathcal{K}}^{X^y Z\text{-ind-cca}}(\mathcal{A}) = \left| \Pr\left[\mathsf{Expt}_{\mathcal{K}}^{X^y Z\text{-ind-cca}}(\mathcal{A}) \Rightarrow 1 \right] - \frac{1}{2} \right|$.

Similarly to [12], and as depicted in Fig. 1, we can show that the various indistinguishability notions for KEMs are related to each other through a series of implications and separations. The proposition statements and proofs of these results can be found in the full version [11].

3   Practical Combiners for Hybrid Key Encapsulation

In this section, we discuss the use of robust combiners to construct hybrid key encapsulation mechanisms. We propose three combiners motivated by practical applications of hybrid KEMs. The first combiner, the XOR-then-MAC combiner XtM, uses a simple exclusive-or of the two keys k_1, k_2 of the KEMs but adds a message authentication over the ciphertexts (with a key derived from the encapsulated the keys). Hence, this solution relies solely on the additional assumption

---

[1] Our fully quantum $Q^q Q$ model is different from [1] since our challenge ciphertext c^* is classical, whereas [1] considers quantum challenge ciphertexts.

$\mathrm{Expt}_{\mathcal{K}}^{\mathrm{XYZ\text{-}ind\text{-}cca}}(\mathcal{A})$:	$\mathsf{Decaps}^{\perp}(sk, c, c^*)$:
1 $H \leftarrow_{\$} \mathcal{H}_{\mathcal{K}}$	1 if $c = c^*$: return $\perp$
2 $q_D \leftarrow 0, q_H \leftarrow 0$	2 else: return $\mathsf{Decaps}(sk, c)$
3 $(sk, pk) \leftarrow \mathsf{KeyGen}()$	$\mathcal{O}_H^{\mathsf{c}}(x)$:
4 $(c^*, \kappa_0^*) \leftarrow \mathsf{Encaps}(pk)$	1 $q_H \leftarrow q_H + 1$
5 $\kappa_1^* \leftarrow_{\$} K$	2 return $H(x)$
6 $b \leftarrow_{\$} \{0,1\}$	$\mathcal{O}_H^{\mathsf{Q}}(\sum_{x,t,z} \psi_{x,t,z} \,|x,t,z\rangle)$:
7 $st \leftarrow \mathcal{A}_1^{\mathcal{O}_H^{\mathsf{X}}(\cdot), \mathcal{O}_D^{\mathsf{Y}}(\cdot)}(pk, c^*, \kappa_b^*)$	1 $q_H \leftarrow q_H + 1$
8 $b' \leftarrow \mathcal{A}_2^{\mathcal{O}_H^{\mathsf{Z}}(\cdot)}(st)$	2 return $\sum_{x,t,z} \psi_{x,t,z} \,|x, t \oplus H(x), z\rangle$
9 return $[\![b = b']\!]$	$\mathcal{O}_D^{\mathsf{c}}(c)$:
	1 $q_D \leftarrow q_D + 1$
	2 return $\mathsf{Decaps}^{\perp}(sk, c, c^*)$
	$\mathcal{O}_D^{\mathsf{q}}(\sum_{c,t,z} \psi_{c,t,z} \,|c,t,z\rangle)$:
	1 $q_D \leftarrow q_D + 1$
	2 return $\sum_{c,t,z} \psi_{c,t,z} \,|c, t \oplus \mathsf{Decaps}^{\perp}(sk, c, c^*), z\rangle$

Fig. 2. Two-Stage IND-CCA security of KEM $\mathcal{K}$ in the classical or quantum random oracle model.

of a secure one-time MAC which, in turn, can be instantiated unconditionally. The second combiner, dualPRF, relies on the existence of dual pseudorandom functions (PRFs) [4,5,8] which provide security if either the key material or the label carries entropy. The HKDF key derivation function is, for example, based on this dual principle. The third combiner, N, is a nested variant of the dual-PRF combiner inspired by the key derivation procedure in TLS 1.3 and the proposal how to augment it for hybrid schemes in [37].

Throughout we let $\mathcal{K}_1 = (\mathsf{KeyGen}_1, \mathsf{Encaps}_1, \mathsf{Decaps}_1)$ and $\mathcal{K}_2 = (\mathsf{KeyGen}_2, \mathsf{Encaps}_2, \mathsf{Decaps}_2)$ be two KEMs. We write $\mathcal{C}[\mathcal{K}_1, \mathcal{K}_2] = (\mathsf{KeyGen}_{\mathcal{C}}, \mathsf{Encaps}_{\mathcal{C}}, \mathsf{Decaps}_{\mathcal{C}})$ for the hybrid KEM constructed by one of the three proposals $\mathcal{C} \in \{\mathsf{XtM}, \mathsf{dualPRF}, \mathsf{N}\}$. In all our schemes, $\mathsf{KeyGen}_{\mathcal{C}}$ simply returns the concatenation of the two public keys ($pk \leftarrow (pk_1, pk_2)$) and the two secret keys ($sk \leftarrow (sk_1, sk_2)$).

In the following, we focus on proving security against at most post-quantum $\mathsf{Q}^{\mathsf{c}}\mathsf{Q}$ adversaries, i.e., adversaries with classical access to the decapsulation oracle only, omitting $\mathsf{Q}^{\mathsf{q}}\mathsf{Q}$-ind-cca security. This is due to the fact that hybrid KEMs and key exchange solutions are designed to secure the transitional phase until quantum computers become first available. The eventually following widespread deployment of quantum computers and cryptography, and thus security against $\mathsf{Q}^{\mathsf{q}}\mathsf{Q}$ adversaries, is outside the scope of the post-quantum setting.

3.1   XtM: XOR-then-MAC Combiner

Giacon et al. [26] demonstrate that the plain XOR-combiner, which concatenates the ciphertexts and XORs the individual keys, preserves ind-cpa security. They show that, in general, it does not preserve ind-cca security, e.g., the combiner may become insecure if one of the KEMs is insecure. We note that it is easy to see that this is even true if *both* KEMs are ind-cca secure: given a challenge ciphertext (c_1^*, c_2^*) the adversary can make two decapsulation requests for (c_1^*, c_2) and (c_1, c_2^*) with fresh ciphertexts $c_1 \neq c_1^*$, $c_2 \neq c_2^*$ for which it knows the encapsulation keys. This allows the adversary to easily recover the challenge key κ_0^* from the answers.

The XOR-then-MAC Combiner. Our approach is to prevent the adversary from mix-and-match attacks by computing a message authentication code over the ciphertexts and attaching it to the encapsulation. For this we require a strongly robust MAC combiner, i.e., a combiner which takes two keys $k_{mac,1}, k_{mac,2}$ as input and provides one-time unforgeability, even if one of the keys is chosen adversarially. We discuss the construction of such MACs later. The combined KEM key is derived as an exclusive-or of the leading parts of the two encapsulated keys, $k_{kem} \leftarrow k_{kem,1} \oplus k_{kem,2}$, and the MAC key $k_{mac} = (k_{mac,1}, k_{mac,2})$ consisting of the remaining parts of both encapsulated keys. If necessary, the encapsulated keys can be stretched pseudorandomly by the underlying encapsulation schemes first to achieve the desired output length. We depict the resulting hybrid KEM in Fig. 3.

$\mathsf{Encaps}_{\mathsf{XtM}}(pk_1, pk_2)$:
1 $(c_1, k_{kem,1} \| k_{mac,1}) \leftarrow \mathsf{Encaps}_1(pk_1)$
2 $(c_2, k_{kem,2} \| k_{mac,2}) \leftarrow \mathsf{Encaps}_2(pk_2)$
3 $k_{kem} \leftarrow k_{kem,1} \oplus k_{kem,2}$
4 $k_{mac} \leftarrow (k_{mac,1}, k_{mac,2})$
5 $c \leftarrow (c_1, c_2)$
6 $\tau \leftarrow \mathsf{MAC}_{k_{mac}}(c)$
7 return $((c, \tau), k_{kem})$

$\mathsf{Decaps}_{\mathsf{XtM}}((sk_1, sk_2), ((c_1, c_2), \tau))$:
1 $k'_{kem,1} \| k'_{mac,1} \leftarrow \mathsf{Decaps}_1(sk_1, c_1)$,
2 $k'_{kem,2} \| k'_{mac,2} \leftarrow \mathsf{Decaps}_2(sk_2, c_2)$
3 $k'_{kem} \leftarrow k'_{kem,1} \oplus k'_{kem,2}$
4 $k'_{mac} \leftarrow (k'_{mac,1}, k'_{mac,2})$
5 if $\mathsf{MVf}_{k'_{mac}}((c_1, c_2), \tau) = 0$: return $\bot$
6 else: return k'_{kem}

Fig. 3. KEM constructed by the XOR-then-MAC combiner $\mathsf{XtM}[\mathcal{K}_1, \mathcal{K}_2, \mathcal{M}]$.

Security of MACs. It suffices to use one-time MACs with multiple verification queries. This means that the adversary can initially choose a message, receives the MAC, and can then make multiple verification attempts for other messages. We require strong unforgeability, meaning the adversary wins if it creates any new valid message-tag pair, even for the same initial message. We use a two-stage version of the definition with an $\mathsf{X^yZ}$ adversary who is of type X while it has y access to the verification oracle and receives the challenge ciphertext. The adversary is of type Z after it no longer has access to the verification oracle.

To capture the strong combiner property of MACs, where the adversary $\mathcal{A}$ tries to win for a key $k_{mac} = (k_{mac,1}, k_{mac,2})$ where either $k_{mac,1}$ or $k_{mac,2}$ is chosen by $\mathcal{A}$, we allow $\mathcal{A}$ to specify one of the two keys for computing the challenge and for each verification query and in the forgery attempt. The security experiment for $\mathsf{X^yZ\text{-}OT\text{-}sEUF}$ security of such two-key MACs is given in the full version of this paper [11].

Security of the XOR-then-MAC Combiner. We can now show that the XOR-then-MAC combiner is a robust KEM combiner, in the sense that the resulting KEM is as secure as the strongest of the two input KEMs (assuming the MAC is also equally secure). In particular, we show in Theorem 1 that $\mathsf{XtM}[\mathcal{K}_1, \mathcal{K}_2, \mathcal{M}]$ is IND-CCA secure in the post-quantum setting (Q^cQ) if the MAC $\mathcal{M}$ and at least one of the two KEMs is post-quantum IND-CCA secure. In fact, the security offered by the MAC is only required in case of IND-CCA attacks, yielding an even better bound for the IND-CPA case. In what follows, atk is a variable for either cca or cpa.

Theorem 1 (XOR-then-MAC is robust). *Let $\mathcal{K}_1$ be a $\mathsf{X}^c\mathsf{Z}$-ind-atk secure KEM, $\mathcal{K}_2$ a $\mathsf{U}^c\mathsf{W}$-ind-atk secure KEM, and $\mathcal{M}$ is an $\mathsf{R}^c\mathsf{T}$-OT-sEUF secure MAC, where $\mathsf{R}^c\mathsf{T} = \max\{\mathsf{X}^c\mathsf{Z}, \mathsf{U}^c\mathsf{W}\}$. Then $\mathsf{XtM}[\mathcal{K}_1, \mathcal{K}_2, \mathcal{M}]$ as defined in Fig. 3 is also $\mathsf{R}^c\mathsf{T}$-ind-atk secure. More precisely, for any efficient adversary $\mathcal{A}$ of type $\mathsf{R}^c\mathsf{T}$ against the combined KEM $\mathcal{K}' = \mathsf{XtM}[\mathcal{K}_1, \mathcal{K}_2, \mathcal{M}]$, there exist efficient adversaries $\mathcal{B}_1$, $\mathcal{B}_2$, and $\mathcal{B}_3$ such that*

$$\mathsf{Adv}_{\mathsf{XtM}[\mathcal{K}_1, \mathcal{K}_2, \mathcal{M}]}^{\mathsf{R}^c\mathsf{T}\text{-ind-atk}}(\mathcal{A}) \leq 2 \cdot \min\left\{\mathsf{Adv}_{\mathcal{K}_1}^{\mathsf{R}^c\mathsf{T}\text{-ind-atk}}(\mathcal{B}_1), \mathsf{Adv}_{\mathcal{K}_2}^{\mathsf{R}^c\mathsf{T}\text{-ind-atk}}(\mathcal{B}_2)\right\}$$
$$+ \mathsf{Adv}_{\mathcal{M}}^{\mathsf{R}^c\mathsf{T}\text{-OT-sEUF}}(\mathcal{B}_3).$$

Moreover, the run times of $\mathcal{B}_1$, $\mathcal{B}_2$, and $\mathcal{B}_3$ are approximately the same as that of $\mathcal{A}$, and $\mathcal{B}_3$ makes at most as many verification queries as $\mathcal{A}$ makes decapsulation queries.

The corresponding proof can be found in the full version of this paper [11].

Instantiating the MAC. We use a strong form of combiner for MACs where the adversary can choose one of the two MAC keys. It is easy to build secure MAC combiners of this type by concatenating two MACs, each computed under one of the keys. For specific constructions carious improvements may apply. For instance, for deterministic MACs in which verification is performed via re-computation, one may aggregate the two MACs via exclusive-or [30] to reduce the communication overhead.

MACs satisfying the Q^cQ-OT-sEUF notion can be constructed based on the Carter-Wegman paradigm using universal hash functions [39], without relying on cryptographic assumptions. Our construction of course uses that the input, consisting of the ciphertexts holding the keys, is larger then the keys, such that we need to extend the domain of the universal hash function. For a pairwise-independent hash function with bound ϵ, it is clear that an adversary cannot win with a single verification query after seeing one MAC, except with probability at most ϵ. Since verification is deterministic and consists of re-computing the tag, it follows that the adversary cannot win with probability more than $q\epsilon$ with q verification queries [7].

The Carter-Wegman paradigm allows for another potential improvement. Suppose one uses hashing of the form $am+b$ over some finite field $\mathbf{F}$ with addition $+$ and multiplication $\cdot$, where m is the message and $k_{\mathsf{mac}} = (a, b)$ is the MAC key.

Then, instead of computing one MAC for each key part $k_{\text{mac},1}$ and $k_{\text{mac},2}$, one can compute a single MAC over the key $k_{\text{mac}} = k_{\text{mac},1} + k_{\text{mac},2} = (a_1 + a_2, b_1 + b_2)$. This combiner provides strong unforgeability as required above, since for known keys $k_{\text{mac},2} = (a_2, b_2)$ and $k'_{\text{mac},2} = (a'_2, b'_2)$ one can transform a MAC for message m under unknown key $k_{\text{mac},1} + k_{\text{mac},2}$ into one for $k_{\text{mac},1} + k'_{\text{mac},2}$, simply by adding $(a'_2 - a_2) \cdot m + (b'_2 - b_2)$ to the tag. By symmetry this holds analogously for known keys $k_{\text{mac},1}$ and $k'_{\text{mac},1}$.

Alternatively to Carter-Wegman MACs, one could use HMAC [5] for instantiating the MAC directly, or rely on the HKDF paradigm of using HMAC as an extractor. Namely, one applies the extraction step of HKDF, HKDF.Ext, with the ciphertexts acting as the salt and the MAC key as the keying material. This approach is based on the idea that HMAC is a good extractor. We discuss such issues in more detail next, when looking at the TLS-like combiners.

Resistance Against Fully-Quantum Attacks. We have shown that the combiner $\text{XtM}[\mathcal{K}_1, \mathcal{K}_2, \mathcal{M}]$ inherits security of the underlying KEMs if the MAC is secure, for classical queries to the decapsulation oracle (which is the setting we also consider for key exchange). We outline here that the result can be easily extended to fully quantum adversaries with superposition queries to the decapsulation oracle. This only assumes that one of the individual KEMs achieves this level of security. Interestingly, the MAC $\mathcal{M}$ only needs to be $Q^c Q$-OT-sEUF secure for a single classical verification query. The reason is that the MAC in the challenge is still computed classically, and in the security reduction we measure a potential forgery in a decapsulation superposition query and output this classical MAC.

The approach for showing security is very similar to the proof in the post-quantum case. The only difference lies in the final game hop, where we cannot simply read off a potential MAC forgery from a decapsulation query of the form $(c_1^*, *, *)$ for the value c_1^* in the challenge, because the query is in superposition. But we can adapt the "measure-and-modify" technique of Boneh et al. [13] for proving the quantum-resistance of Bellare-Rogaway style encryptions. In our case, if the amplitudes of entries (c_1^*, c_2, τ) with a valid MAC and fresh $(c_2, \tau) \neq (c_2^*, \tau^*)$ in the quantum decapsulation queries would be non-negligible, then we could measure for a randomly chosen query among the polynomial many decapsulation queries to get a (classical) MAC forgery with non-negligible probability. This would contradict the $Q^c Q$-OT-sEUF security of $\mathcal{M}$. If, on the other hand, the query probability of such forgeries is negligible, then we can change the function $\text{Decaps}^\perp$ into $\text{Decaps}^{\perp\perp}$ which now also outputs $\perp$ for any query of the form $(c_1^*, *, *)$. Following the line of reasoning as in [13], based on the results of Bennett et al. [10], this cannot change the adversary's output behavior significantly. Again, since we can instantiate the MAC for classical queries information-theoretically, we get a secure KEM combiner in the fully quantum case, without requiring an extra assumption beyond full quantum resistance of one of the KEMs.

3.2   dualPRF: Dual-PRF Combiner

Our second combiner is based on dual PRFs [4,5,8]. The definitions of (dual) PRF security can be found in the full version [11]. Informally, a dual PRF $\mathsf{dPRF}(k, x)$ is a PRF when either the key material k is random (i.e., $\mathsf{dPRF}(k, \cdot)$ is a PRF), or alternatively when the input x is random (i.e., $\mathsf{dPRF}(\cdot, x)$ is a PRF). HMAC has been shown to be a secure MAC under the assumption it is a dual PRF, and Bellare and Lysyanskaya [8] have given a generic validation of the dual PRF assumption for HMAC and therefore HKDF.

To construct a hybrid KEM from a dual PRF, the naive approach of directly using a dual PRF to compute the session key of the combined KEM as $\mathsf{dPRF}(k_1, k_2)$ is not sufficient. If, say, $\mathcal{K}_1$ is secure and $\mathcal{K}_2$ is completely broken, then an adversary might be able to transform the challenge ciphertext (c_1^*, c_2^*) into (c_1^*, c_2), where $c_2 \neq c_2^*$ but encapsulates the same key k_2 as c_2^*. With a single decapsulation query the adversary would be able to recover the key $\mathsf{dPRF}(k_1, k_2)$ and distinguish it from random. Our approach, shown in Fig. 4, is to apply another pseudorandom function with the output of the dual PRF as the PRF key and the ciphertexts as the input label: $\mathsf{PRF}(\mathsf{dPRF}(k_1, k_2), (c_1, c_2))$.

Our dualPRF combiner is inspired by the key derivation in TLS 1.3 [35] and models Whyte et al.'s proposal for supporting hybrid key exchange in TLS 1.3 [40]. In TLS 1.3, HKDF's extract function is applied to the raw ECDH shared secret; the result is then fed through HKDF's expand function with the (hashed) transcript as (part of) the label. In Whyte et al.'s hybrid proposal, the session keys from multiple KEMs are concatenated as a single shared secret input to HKDF extract as shown in Fig. 5. The dualPRF combiner models this by taking dPRF as HKDF extract and PRF as HKDF expand (cf. Fig. 4).

Security of the Dual-PRF Combiner. We show that $\mathsf{dualPRF}[\mathcal{K}_1, \mathcal{K}_2, \mathsf{dPRF}, \mathsf{PRF}]$ is IND-CCA secure in the post-quantum setting if dPRF is a post-quantum secure dual PRF, PRF is a post-quantum secure PRF, and at least one of the two KEMs is post-quantum IND-CCA secure. The proof can be found in the full version [11].

Theorem 2 (Dual-PRF is robust). *Let $\mathcal{K}_1$ be an $\mathsf{X^c Z}$-ind-atk secure KEM, $\mathcal{K}_2$ be a $\mathsf{U^c W}$-ind-atk secure KEM, and $\mathsf{R^c T} = \max\{\mathsf{X^c Z}, \mathsf{U^c W}\}$. Moreover, let $\mathsf{dPRF} : K_1 \times K_2 \to K'$ be a $\mathsf{R^c T}$ secure dual PRF, and $\mathsf{PRF} : K' \times \{0,1\}^* \to K_{\mathsf{dualPRF}}$ be a $\mathsf{R^c T}$ secure PRF. Then $\mathsf{dualPRF}[\mathcal{K}_1, \mathcal{K}_2, \mathsf{dPRF}, \mathsf{PRF}]$ as defined in Fig. 4 is $\mathsf{R^c T}$-ind-atk secure.*

More precisely, for any ind-atk *adversary $\mathcal{A}$ of type $\mathsf{R^c T}$ against the combiner* $\mathsf{dualPRF}[\mathcal{K}_1, \mathcal{K}_2, \mathsf{dPRF}, \mathsf{PRF}]$, *we derive efficient adversaries $\mathcal{B}_1$, $\mathcal{B}_2$, $\mathcal{B}_3$, and $\mathcal{B}_4$ such that* $\mathsf{Adv}_{\mathsf{dualPRF}[\mathcal{K}_1, \mathcal{K}_2, \mathsf{dPRF}, \mathsf{PRF}]}^{\mathsf{R^c T}\text{-ind-atk}}(\mathcal{A}) \leq 2 \cdot \mathsf{Adv}_{\mathsf{dPRF}}^{\mathsf{R^c T}\text{-dprf-sec}}(\mathcal{B}_3) + 2 \cdot \mathsf{Adv}_{\mathsf{PRF}}^{\mathsf{R^c T}\text{-prf-sec}}(\mathcal{B}_4) + \min\left\{\mathsf{Adv}_{\mathcal{K}_1}^{\mathsf{R^c T}\text{-ind-atk}}(\mathcal{B}_1), \mathsf{Adv}_{\mathcal{K}_2}^{\mathsf{R^c T}\text{-ind-atk}}(\mathcal{B}_2)\right\}.$

The theorem relies on two-stage security notions for PRFs and dual PRFs, which are the natural adaptation of PRF and dual-PRF security: a two-stage

$\mathsf{Encaps}_{\mathsf{dualPRF}}(pk_1, pk_2)$:

1 $(c_1, k_1) \leftarrow \mathsf{Encaps}_1(pk_1)$
2 $(c_2, k_2) \leftarrow \mathsf{Encaps}_2(pk_2)$
3 $c \leftarrow (c_1, c_2)$
4 $k_d \leftarrow \mathsf{dPRF}(k_1, k_2)$
5 $k \leftarrow \mathsf{PRF}(k_d, c)$
6 return (c, k)

$\mathsf{Decaps}_{\mathsf{dualPRF}}(sk_1, sk_2, c_1, c_2)$:

1 $k_1' \leftarrow \mathsf{Decaps}_1(sk_1, c_1)$
2 $k_2' \leftarrow \mathsf{Decaps}_2(sk_2, c_2)$
3 $k_d' \leftarrow \mathsf{dPRF}(k_1', k_2')$
4 return $\mathsf{PRF}(k_d', (c_1, c_2))$

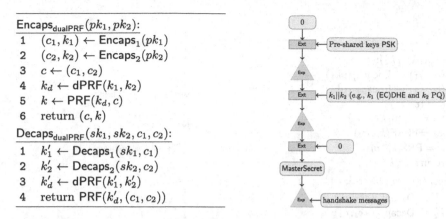

Fig. 4. KEM constructed by the dual PRF combiner $\mathsf{dualPRF}[\mathcal{K}_1, \mathcal{K}_2, \mathsf{dPRF}, \mathsf{PRF}]$.

Fig. 5. Excerpt from altered TLS 1.3 key schedule as proposed in [40] to incorporate an additional secret k_2, enabling a hybrid mode.

$\mathsf{X}^y\mathsf{Z}$ adversary for PRF is classical or quantum (X) while it has access to the PRF oracle (which it accesses classically or in superposition depending on y). After this, in the second stage, it runs classically or quantumly (Z) without oracle access, before outputting a guess as to whether its oracle was real or random. We give the formal definitions of two-stage security notions for PRFs and dual PRFs in the full version of the paper [11].

3.3 N: Nested Dual-PRF Combiner

We augment the dualPRF combiner in the previous section by an extra prepro-cessing step for the key k_1: $k_e \leftarrow \mathsf{Ext}(0, k_1)$, where Ext is another PRF. This is the nested dual-PRF combiner N shown in Fig. 6. Our nested dual-PRF com-biner N models Schanck and Stebila's proposal for hybrid key exchange in TLS 1.3 [37]. In their proposal, as depicted in Fig. 7, one stage of the TLS 1.3 key schedule is applied for each of the constituent KEMs in the hybrid KEM con-struction: each stage in the key schedule applies the HKDF extract function with one input being the output from the previous stage of the key schedule and the other input being the shared secret from this stage's KEM. Finally, HKDF expand incorporates the (hash of the) transcript, including all ciphertexts. Mod-eling the extraction function Ext as a PRF, our nested combiner N captures this scenario.

Security of the Nested Dual-PRF Combiner. We show in Theorem 3 that $\mathsf{N}[\mathcal{K}_1, \mathcal{K}_2, \mathsf{dPRF}, \mathsf{PRF}, \mathsf{Ext}]$ is IND-CCA secure in the post-quantum setting if dPRF is a post-quantum secure dual PRF, PRF and Ext are post-quantum secure PRFs, and at least one of the two KEMs is post-quantum IND-CCA secure.

Encaps$_N(pk_1, pk_2)$:
1 $(c_1, k_1) \leftarrow$ Encaps$_1(pk_1)$
2 $(c_2, k_2) \leftarrow$ Encaps$_2(pk_2)$
3 $c = (c_1, c_2)$
4 $k_e = $ Ext$(0, k_1)$
5 $k_d = $ dPRF(k_e, k_2)
6 $k = $ PRF(k_d, c)
7 return (c, k)

Decaps$_N(sk_1, sk_2, c_1, c_2)$:
1 $k_1' \leftarrow$ Decaps$_1(sk_1, c_1)$
2 $k_2' \leftarrow$ Decaps$_2(sk_2, c_2)$
3 $k_e' = $ Ext$(0, k_1)$
4 $k_d' = $ dPRF(k_e', k_2)
5 return PRF$(k_d', (c_1, c_2))$

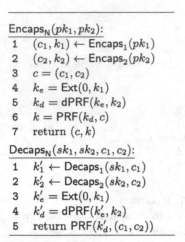

Fig. 6. KEM constructed by the nested dual-PRF combiner $N[\mathcal{K}_1, \mathcal{K}_2, \text{dPRF}, \text{PRF}, \text{Ext}]$.

Fig. 7. Excerpt from altered TLS 1.3 key schedule as proposed in [37] to incorporate an additional secret k_2, effectively enabling a hybrid mode.

Theorem 3 (Nested dual-PRF is robust). *Let $\mathcal{K}_1$ be an X^cZ-ind-atk secure KEM, $\mathcal{K}_2$ be a U^cW-ind-atk secure KEM, dPRF : $K' \times K_2 \to K''$ be a $R^cT = \max\{X^cZ, U^cW\}$ secure dual PRF, PRF : $K'' \times \{0,1\}^* \to K_N$ be an R^cT secure PRF, and Ext : $\{0,1\}^* \times K_1 \to K'$ be an R^cT secure PRF. Then the combiner $N[\mathcal{K}_1, \mathcal{K}_2, \text{dPRF}, \text{PRF}, \text{Ext}]$ as defined in Fig. 4 is R^cT-ind-atk secure.*

More precisely, for any ind-atk adversary $\mathcal{A}$ of type R^cT against the combined KEM $N[\mathcal{K}_1, \mathcal{K}_2, \text{dPRF}, \text{PRF}, \text{Ext}]$, we derive efficient adversaries $\mathcal{B}_1, \mathcal{B}_2, \mathcal{B}_3, \mathcal{B}_4$, and $\mathcal{B}_5$ such that

$$\text{Adv}_{N[\mathcal{K}_1, \mathcal{K}_2, \text{dPRF}, \text{PRF}, \text{Ext}]}^{R^cT\text{-ind-atk}}(\mathcal{A}) \leq \min\left\{\text{Adv}_{\mathcal{K}_1}^{R^cT\text{-ind-atk}}(\mathcal{B}_1), \text{Adv}_{\mathcal{K}_2}^{R^cT\text{-ind-atk}}(\mathcal{B}_2)\right\}$$
$$+ 2 \cdot \text{Adv}_{\text{dPRF}}^{R^cT\text{-dprf-sec}}(\mathcal{B}_3) + 2 \cdot \text{Adv}_{\text{PRF}}^{R^cT\text{-prf-sec}}(\mathcal{B}_4)$$
$$+ 2 \cdot \text{Adv}_{\text{Ext}}^{R^cT\text{-prf-sec}}(\mathcal{B}_5).$$

The proof follows easily from the proof of the dualPRF combiner. Only here we make one more intermediate step in which we use the pseudorandomness of Ext to argue that the output of Ext$(0, k_1)$ is pseudorandom.

4 Authenticated Key Exchange from Hybrid KEMs

We now turn towards the question of how to achieve hybrid authenticated key exchange from hybrid KEMs. There exists a vast body of literature on compilers for authenticated key exchange [6,18,29,31,34,36]. In the following we consider secure AKE protocols from key encapsulation mechanisms combined with SigMA-style authentication [32]. As for KEMs, we consider a two-stage adversary and adjust the commonly used model for authenticated key exchange by Bellare and Rogaway [9] to this setting.

4.1 Security Model

We begin by establishing the security definition for authenticated key exchange against active attackers, starting from the model of Bellare and Rogaway [9].

Parties and Sessions. Let KE be a key exchange protocol. We denote the set of all participants in the protocol by $\mathcal{U}$. Each participant $U \in \mathcal{U}$ is associated with a long-term key pair (pk_U, sk_U), created in advance; we assume every participant receives an authentic copy of every other party's public key through some trusted out-of-band mechanism. In a single run of the protocol (referred to as a *session*), U may act as either initiator or responder. Any participant U may execute multiple sessions in parallel or sequentially.

We denote by $\pi_{U,V}^j$ the jth session of user $U \in \mathcal{U}$ (called the session *owner*) with intended communication partner V. Associated to each session are the following per-session variables; we often write $\pi_{U,V}^j.\mathsf{var}$ to refer to the variable var of session $\pi_{U,V}^j$.

- role $\in \{\mathsf{initiator}, \mathsf{responder}\}$ is the role of the session owner in this session.
- $\mathsf{st_{exec}} \in \{\mathsf{running}, \mathsf{accepted}, \mathsf{rejected}\}$ reflects the current status of execution. The initial value at session creation is running.
- sid $\in \{0,1\}^* \cup \{\bot\}$ denotes the session identifier. The initial value is $\bot$.
- $\mathsf{st_{key}} \in \{\mathsf{fresh}, \mathsf{revealed}\}$ indicates the status of the session key K. The initial value is fresh.
- $\mathsf{K} \in \mathcal{D} \cup \{\bot\}$ denotes the established session key. The initial value is $\bot$.
- tested $\in \{\mathsf{true}, \mathsf{false}\}$ marks whether the session key K has been tested or not. The initial value is false.

To identify related sessions which might compute the same session key, we rely on the notion of partnering using session identifiers. Two sessions $\pi_{S,T}^i$ and $\pi_{U,V}^j$ are said to be *partnered* if $\pi_{S,T}^i.\mathsf{sid} = \pi_{U,V}^j.\mathsf{sid} \neq \bot$. We assume that if the adversary has not interfered, sessions in a protocol run between two honest participants are partnered.

Adversary Model. The adversary interacts with honest parties running AKE protocol instances via oracle queries, which ultimately allow the adversary to fully control all network communications (injecting messages and scheduling if and when message delivery occurs) and compromise certain secret values; the goal of the adversary is to distinguish the session key of an uncompromised session of its choice from random. We model the adversary as a two-stage potentially quantum adversary with varying levels of quantum capabilities. As in Sect. 3, we only consider adversaries that interact with parties using classical oracle queries, omitting Q^qQ adversaries. The following queries model the adversary's control over normal operations by honest parties:

NewSession($U, V, role$): Creates a new session $\pi_{U,V}^j$ for U (with j being the next unused counter value for sessions between U and intended communication partner $V \in \mathcal{U} \cup \{\star\}$) and sets $\pi_{U,V}^j.\text{role} \leftarrow role$.

Send($\pi_{U,V}^j, m$): Sends the message m to the session $\pi_{U,V}^j$. If no session $\pi_{U,V}^j$ exists or does not have $\pi_{U,V}^j.\text{st}_{\text{exec}} = \text{running}$, return $\bot$. Otherwise, the party U executes the next step of the protocol based on its local state, updates the execution status $\pi_{U,V}^j.\text{st}_{\text{exec}}$, and returns any outgoing messages. If st_{exec} changes to accepted and the intended partner V has previously been corrupted, we mark the session key as revealed: $\pi_{U,V}^j.\text{st}_{\text{key}} \leftarrow \text{revealed}$.

The next queries model the adversary's ability to compromise secret values:

Reveal($\pi_{U,V}^j$): If $\pi_{U,V}^j.\text{st}_{\text{exec}} = \text{accepted}$, Reveal($\pi_{U,V}^j$) returns the session key $\pi_{U,V}^j.\text{K}$ and marks the session key as revealed: $\pi_{U,V}^j.\text{st}_{\text{key}} \leftarrow \text{revealed}$. Otherwise, it returns $\bot$.

Corrupt(U): Returns the long-term secret key sk_U of U. Set $\pi_{V,W}^j.\text{st}_{\text{key}} \leftarrow \text{revealed}$ in all sessions where $V = U$ or $W = U$. (If the security definition is meant to capture forward secrecy, this last operation is omitted.)

The final query is used to define the indistinguishability property of session keys:

Test($\pi_{U,V}^j$): At the start of the experiment, a test bit b_{test} is chosen uniformly and random and fixed through the experiment. If $\pi_{U,V}^j.\text{st}_{\text{exec}} \neq \text{accepted}$, the query returns $\bot$. Otherwise, sets $\pi_{U,V}^j.\text{tested} \leftarrow \text{true}$ and proceeds as follows. If $b_{\text{test}} = 0$, a key $\text{K}^* \leftarrow_\$ \mathcal{D}$ is sampled uniformly at random from the session key distribution $\mathcal{D}$. If $b_{\text{test}} = 1$, K^* is set to the real session key $\pi_{U,V}^j.\text{K}$. Return K^*. The Test query may be asked only once.

4.2   Security Definitions

We provide the specific security experiment and definition for AKE security, following the approach of Brzuska et al. [21,22] and divide Bellare–Rogaway-style AKE security into the sub-notions of BR-Match security and BR key secrecy. We only state the definition for two-stage BR key secrecy and security here. The definition for two-stage BR-Match security can be found in the full version [11].

Definition 1 (Two-Stage BR Key Secrecy and Security). *Let* KE *be a key exchange protocol with key distribution* $\mathcal{D}$ *and let* $\mathcal{A} = (\mathcal{A}_1, \mathcal{A}_2)$ *be a two-stage* X^cZ *adversary interacting with* KE *via the queries defined in Sect. 4.1 within the following security experiment* $\text{Expt}_{\text{KE},\mathcal{D}}^{X^cZ\text{-BR}}(\mathcal{A})$:

Setup. *The challenger generates long-term public/private-key pairs for each participant* $U \in \mathcal{U}$, *chooses the test bit* $b_{\text{test}} \leftarrow_\$ \{0,1\}$ *at random, and sets* lost $\leftarrow$ false.

Query Phase 1. *Adversary* $\mathcal{A}_1$ *receives the generated public keys and may (classically) query* NewSession, Send, Reveal, Corrupt, *and* Test.

Stage Change. *At some point,* $\mathcal{A}_1$ *terminates and outputs some state* st *to be passed to the second stage adversary* $\mathcal{A}_2$.

Query Phase 2. $\mathcal{A}_2$ *may now perform local computations on state* st, *but may query only* Reveal *and* Corrupt.

Guess. *At some point,* $\mathcal{A}_2$ *terminates and outputs a guess bit* b_{guess}.

Finalize. *The challenger sets* lost $\leftarrow$ true *if there exist two (not necessarily distinct) sessions* π, π' *such that* $\pi.$sid $= \pi'.$sid, $\pi.$st$_{\mathsf{key}}$ = revealed, *and* $\pi'.$tested = true. *(That is, the adversary has tested and revealed the key in a single session or in two partnered sessions.) If* lost = true, *the challenger outputs a random bit; otherwise the challenger outputs* $[\![b_{\mathsf{guess}} = b_{\mathsf{test}}]\!]$. *Note that forward secrecy, if being modelled, is incorporated into the* Corrupt *query and need not be stated in the Finalize step.*

We say that $\mathcal{A}$ wins the game if $b_{\mathsf{guess}} = b_{\mathsf{test}}$ and lost = false. We say KE provides $\mathsf{X}^c\mathsf{Z}$-BR key secrecy (with/without forward secrecy) if for all QPT $\mathsf{X}^c\mathsf{Z}$ adversaries $\mathcal{A}$ the advantage function $\mathsf{Adv}_{\mathsf{KE},\mathcal{D}}^{\mathsf{X}^c\mathsf{Z}\text{-}\mathsf{BR}}(\mathcal{A}) = \left| \Pr\left[\mathsf{Expt}_{\mathsf{KE},\mathcal{D}}^{\mathsf{X}^c\mathsf{Z}\text{-}\mathsf{BR}}(\mathcal{A}) \Rightarrow 1\right] - \frac{1}{2} \right|$ is negligible in the security parameter.

We call KE $\mathsf{X}^c\mathsf{Z}$-BR secure (with/without forward secrecy) if KE provides BR-Match security and $\mathsf{X}^c\mathsf{Z}$-BR key secrecy (with/without forward secrecy).

Implications. Similarly to the two-stage security notions of indistinguishability for KEMs, the following implications hold for two-stage BR security. The proof of Theorem 4 can be found in the full version [11].

Theorem 4 ($\mathsf{Q}^c\mathsf{Q}$-BR $\Longrightarrow$ $\mathsf{C}^c\mathsf{Q}$-BR $\Longrightarrow$ $\mathsf{C}^c\mathsf{C}$-BR). *Let* KE *be an authenticated key exchange protocol. If* KE *is* $\mathsf{Q}^c\mathsf{Q}$-BR *secure, then* KE *is also* $\mathsf{C}^c\mathsf{Q}$-BR *secure. If* KE *is* $\mathsf{C}^c\mathsf{Q}$-BR *secure then it also is* $\mathsf{C}^c\mathsf{C}$-BR *secure.*

4.3 Compilers for Hybrid Authenticated Key Exchange

In the following we present a compiler for authenticated key exchange in the two-stage adversary setting. The compiled protocol, denoted by $\mathcal{C}_{\mathsf{SigMA}}$, combines a passively secure key encapsulation mechanisms (KEMs) with SigMA-style authentication [32]. Figure 8 in the appendix shows the compiled protocol between Alice and Bob. It takes as input an IND-CPA-secure KEM $\mathcal{K}$, a signature scheme $\mathcal{S}$, a message authentication scheme $\mathcal{M}$—both existentially unforgeable under chosen-message attack—and a KDF-secure key derivation function KDF, where security is considered with respect to two-stage adversaries. To obtain hybrid authenticated key exchange, the KEM $\mathcal{K}$ may then be instantiated with any hybrid KEM.

Security Analysis. We now show that the compiled protocol $\mathcal{C}_{\mathsf{SigMA}}$ achieves *two-stage* BR security (cf. Definition 1). In the theorem below we assume that the

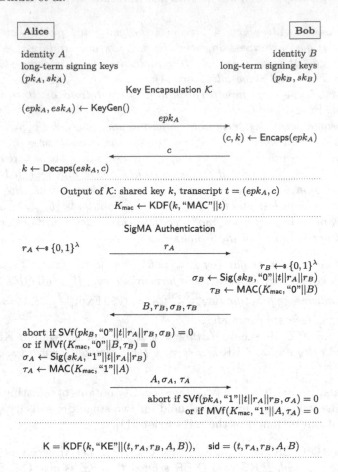

Fig. 8. Compiled protocol $\mathcal{C}_{\mathsf{SigMA}}$ - AKE from signatures and MACs

key encapsulation mechanism $\mathcal{K}$ is either classically secure or quantum resistant against passive adversaries, i.e., R-ind-cpa = C-ind-cpa or R-ind-cpa = Q-ind-cpa and that the remaining primitives achieve either C^cC, C^cQ, or Q^cQ security.

One would generally assume that the "weakest primitive" determines the overall security of the compiled protocol. However, it turns out this intuition is not quite correct. Naturally, in case either the unauthenticated key agreement $\mathcal{K}$ or the key derivation function KDF are only classically secure, we cannot expect more than classical C^cC-BR security of the compiled protocol. Similarly, full post-quantum Q^cQ-BR security can only be achieved if *all* components of the protocol provide this level of security. Interestingly though, for the compiled protocol to guarantee security against future-quantum adversaries (C^cQ-BR security) it suffices for the signature and MAC scheme to be classically secure when combined with Q-ind-cpa-secure key encapsulation and at least C^cQ-secure key derivation.

Theorem 5. *Let $\mathcal{K}$ be an* R-ind-cpa *key encapsulation mechanism, $\mathcal{S}$ be an* $\mathsf{S^cT}$-*unforgeable signature scheme, $\mathcal{M}$ be a* $\mathsf{U^cV}$-*unforgeable message authentication scheme, and* KDF *be a* $\mathsf{W^cX}$-*secure key derivation function. Then the compiled protocol $\mathcal{C}_{\mathsf{SigMA}}$ is* $\mathsf{Y^cZ}$-BR *secure with forward secrecy, where*

- $\mathsf{Y^cZ} = \mathsf{C^cC}$, *if either the key encapsulation mechanism $\mathcal{K}$ or the key derivation function* KDF *are only classically secure, i.e., if either* $\mathsf{R} = \mathsf{C}$ *or* $\mathsf{W^cX} = \mathsf{C^cC}$.
- $\mathsf{Y^cZ} = \mathsf{Q^cQ}$, *if all components are resistant against fully quantum adversaries, i.e, $\mathsf{S^cT} = \mathsf{U^cV} = \mathsf{W^cX} = \mathsf{Q^cQ}$ (and $\mathsf{R} = \mathsf{Q}$).*
- $\mathsf{Y^cZ} = \mathsf{C^cQ}$, *if the employed signature and MAC scheme are at most future-quantum secure, i.e., if $\mathsf{S^cT}, \mathsf{U^cV} \in \{\mathsf{C^cC}, \mathsf{C^cQ}\}$ (and $\mathsf{R} = \mathsf{Q}$, $\mathsf{W^cX} \geq \mathsf{C^cQ}$).*

More precisely, for any efficient two-stage $\mathsf{Y^cZ}$ adversary $\mathcal{A}$ there exist efficient adversaries $\mathcal{B}_1, \mathcal{B}_2, \ldots, \mathcal{B}_4$ such that $\mathsf{Adv}_{\mathcal{C}_{\mathsf{SigMA}},\mathcal{D}}^{\mathsf{Y^cZ}\text{-BR}}(\mathcal{A}) \leq n_s^2 \cdot 2^{-|nonce|} + n_s \Big(n_u \cdot$

$\mathsf{Adv}_{\mathcal{S}}^{\mathsf{S^cT}\text{-eufcma}}(\mathcal{B}_1) + n_s \cdot \Big(\mathsf{Adv}_{\mathcal{K}}^{\mathsf{R}\text{-ind-cpa}}(\mathcal{B}_2) + \mathsf{Adv}_{\mathsf{KDF}}^{\mathsf{W^cX}\text{-kdf-sec}}(\mathcal{B}_3) + \mathsf{Adv}_{\mathcal{M}}^{\mathsf{U^cV}\text{-eufcma}}(\mathcal{B}_4) \Big) \Big)$

where n_s denotes the maximum number of sessions, $|nonce|$ the length of the nonces, and n_u the maximum number of participants.

The corresponding proofs for Key Secrecy and Match Security can be found in the full version [11].

Acknowledgments. We thank the anonymous reviewers for valuable comments. N.B. and J.B. have been supported by the German Research Foundation (DFG) as part of the projects P1 and S4, respectively, within the CRC 1119 CROSSING. J.B. has been funded as part of project D.2 within the DFG RTG 2050 "Privacy and Trust for Mobile Users". B.G. and D.S. have been supported in part by NSERC Discovery grant RGPIN-2016-05146 and an NSERC Discovery Accelerator Supplement.

References

1. Alagic, G., Gagliardoni, T., Majenz, C.: Unforgeable quantum encryption. In: Nielsen, J.B., Rijmen, V. (eds.) EUROCRYPT 2018. LNCS, vol. 10822, pp. 489–519. Springer, Cham (2018). https://doi.org/10.1007/978-3-319-78372-7_16
2. Albrecht, M.R., et al.: Estimate all the {LWE, NTRU} schemes!. In: Catalano, D., De Prisco, R. (eds.) SCN 2018. LNCS, vol. 11035, pp. 351–367. Springer, Cham (2018). https://doi.org/10.1007/978-3-319-98113-0_19
3. Alkim, E., Ducas, L., Pöppelmann, T., Schwabe, P.: Post-quantum Key Exchange—a new hope. In: 25th USENIX Security Symposium (USENIX Security 2016), pp. 327–343. USENIX Association, Austin (2016)
4. Bellare, M.: New proofs for NMAC and HMAC: security without collision-resistance. In: Dwork, C. (ed.) CRYPTO 2006. LNCS, vol. 4117, pp. 602–619. Springer, Heidelberg (2006). https://doi.org/10.1007/11818175_36
5. Bellare, M., Canetti, R., Krawczyk, H.: Keying hash functions for message authentication. In: Koblitz, N. (ed.) CRYPTO 1996. LNCS, vol. 1109, pp. 1–15. Springer, Heidelberg (1996). https://doi.org/10.1007/3-540-68697-5_1
6. Bellare, M., Canetti, R., Krawczyk, H.: A modular approach to the design and analysis of authentication and key exchange (extended abstract). In: 30th ACM STOC, pp. 419–428. ACM Press, May 1998

7. Bellare, M., Goldreich, O., Mityagin, A.: The power of verification queries in message authentication and authenticated encryption. Cryptology ePrint Archive, Report 2004/309 (2004). http://eprint.iacr.org/2004/309

8. Bellare, M., Lysyanskaya, A.: Symmetric and dual PRFs from standard assumptions: a generic validation of an HMAC assumption. Cryptology ePrint Archive, Report 2015/1198 (2015). http://eprint.iacr.org/2015/1198

9. Bellare, M., Rogaway, P.: Entity authentication and key distribution. In: Stinson, D.R. (ed.) CRYPTO 1993. LNCS, vol. 773, pp. 232–249. Springer, Heidelberg (1994). https://doi.org/10.1007/3-540-48329-2_21

10. Bennett, C.H., Bernstein, E., Brassard, G., Vazirani, U.V.: Strengths and weaknesses of quantum computing. SIAM J. Comput. **26**(5), 1510–1523 (1997). https://doi.org/10.1137/S0097539796300933

11. Bindel, N., Brendel, J., Fischlin, M., Goncalves, B., Stebila, D.: Hybrid key encapsulation mechanisms and authenticated key exchange. Cryptology ePrint Archive, Report 2018/903 (2018). https://eprint.iacr.org/2018/903

12. Bindel, N., Herath, U., McKague, M., Stebila, D.: Transitioning to a quantum-resistant public key infrastructure. In: Lange, T., Takagi, T. (eds.) PQCrypto 2017. LNCS, vol. 10346, pp. 384–405. Springer, Cham (2017). https://doi.org/10.1007/978-3-319-59879-6_22

13. Boneh, D., Dagdelen, Ö., Fischlin, M., Lehmann, A., Schaffner, C., Zhandry, M.: Random oracles in a quantum world. In: Lee, D.H., Wang, X. (eds.) ASIACRYPT 2011. LNCS, vol. 7073, pp. 41–69. Springer, Heidelberg (2011). https://doi.org/10.1007/978-3-642-25385-0_3

14. Boneh, D., Zhandry, M.: Quantum-secure message authentication codes. In: Johansson, T., Nguyen, P.Q. (eds.) EUROCRYPT 2013. LNCS, vol. 7881, pp. 592–608. Springer, Heidelberg (2013). https://doi.org/10.1007/978-3-642-38348-9_35

15. Boneh, D., Zhandry, M.: Secure signatures and chosen ciphertext security in a quantum computing world. In: Canetti, R., Garay, J.A. (eds.) CRYPTO 2013. LNCS, vol. 8043, pp. 361–379. Springer, Heidelberg (2013). https://doi.org/10.1007/978-3-642-40084-1_21

16. Bos, J.W., et al.: Frodo: take off the ring! practical, quantum-secure key exchange from LWE. In: Weippl, E.R., Katzenbeisser, S., Kruegel, C., Myers, A.C., Halevi, S. (eds.) ACM CCS 2016, pp. 1006–1018. ACM Press, October 2016

17. Bos, J.W., Costello, C., Naehrig, M., Stebila, D.: Post-quantum key exchange for the TLS protocol from the ring learning with errors problem. In: 2015 IEEE Symposium on Security and Privacy, pp. 553–570. IEEE Computer Society Press, May 2015

18. Boyd, C., Cliff, Y., Gonzalez Nieto, J., Paterson, K.G.: Efficient one-round key exchange in the standard model. In: Mu, Y., Susilo, W., Seberry, J. (eds.) ACISP 2008. LNCS, vol. 5107, pp. 69–83. Springer, Heidelberg (2008). https://doi.org/10.1007/978-3-540-70500-0_6

19. Braithwaite, M.: Google Security Blog: Experimenting with post-quantum cryptography, July 2016. https://security.googleblog.com/2016/07/experimenting-with-post-quantum.html

20. Brendel, J., Fischlin, M., Günther, F.: Breakdown resilience of key exchange protocols and the cases of NewHope and TLS 1.3. Cryptology ePrint Archive, Report 2017/1252 (2017). https://eprint.iacr.org/2017/1252

21. Brzuska, C.: On the foundations of key exchange. Ph.D. thesis, Technische Universität Darmstadt, Darmstadt, Germany (2013). http://tuprints.ulb.tu-darmstadt.de/3414/

22. Brzuska, C., Fischlin, M., Warinschi, B., Williams, S.C.: Composability of Bellare-Rogaway key exchange protocols. In: Chen, Y., Danezis, G., Shmatikov, V. (eds.) ACM CCS 2011, pp. 51–62. ACM Press, October 2011
23. Costello, C., Easterbrook, K., LaMacchia, B., Longa, P., Naehrig, M.: SIDH Library, April 2016. Peace-of-mind hybrid key exchange mode https://www.microsoft.com/en-us/research/project/sidh-library/
24. Dodis, Y., Katz, J.: Chosen-ciphertext security of multiple encryption. In: Kilian, J. (ed.) TCC 2005. LNCS, vol. 3378, pp. 188–209. Springer, Heidelberg (2005). https://doi.org/10.1007/978-3-540-30576-7_11
25. Even, S., Goldreich, O.: On the power of cascade ciphers. ACM Trans. Comput. Syst. **3**(2), 108–116 (1985)
26. Giacon, F., Heuer, F., Poettering, B.: KEM combiners. In: Abdalla, M., Dahab, R. (eds.) PKC 2018. LNCS, vol. 10769, pp. 190–218. Springer, Cham (2018). https://doi.org/10.1007/978-3-319-76578-5_7
27. Harnik, D., Kilian, J., Naor, M., Reingold, O., Rosen, A.: On robust combiners for oblivious transfer and other primitives. In: Cramer, R. (ed.) EUROCRYPT 2005. LNCS, vol. 3494, pp. 96–113. Springer, Heidelberg (2005). https://doi.org/10.1007/11426639_6
28. Hofheinz, D., Hövelmanns, K., Kiltz, E.: A modular analysis of the Fujisaki-Okamoto transformation. In: Kalai, Y., Reyzin, L. (eds.) TCC 2017. LNCS, vol. 10677, pp. 341–371. Springer, Cham (2017). https://doi.org/10.1007/978-3-319-70500-2_12
29. Jager, T., Kohlar, F., Schäge, S., Schwenk, J.: On the security of TLS-DHE in the standard model. In: Safavi-Naini, R., Canetti, R. (eds.) CRYPTO 2012. LNCS, vol. 7417, pp. 273–293. Springer, Heidelberg (2012). https://doi.org/10.1007/978-3-642-32009-5_17
30. Katz, J., Lindell, A.Y.: Aggregate message authentication codes. In: Malkin, T. (ed.) CT-RSA 2008. LNCS, vol. 4964, pp. 155–169. Springer, Heidelberg (2008). https://doi.org/10.1007/978-3-540-79263-5_10
31. Katz, J., Yung, M.: Scalable protocols for authenticated group key exchange. J. Cryptol. **20**(1), 85–113 (2007)
32. Krawczyk, H.: SIGMA: the "SIGn-and-MAc" approach to authenticated Diffie-Hellman and its use in the IKE protocols. In: Boneh, D. (ed.) CRYPTO 2003. LNCS, vol. 2729, pp. 400–425. Springer, Heidelberg (2003). https://doi.org/10.1007/978-3-540-45146-4_24
33. Langley, A.: Intent to Implement and Ship: CECPQ1 for TLS, July 2016. Google group https://groups.google.com/a/chromium.org/forum/#!topic/security-dev/DS9pp2U0SAc
34. Li, Y., Schäge, S., Yang, Z., Bader, C., Schwenk, J.: New modular compilers for authenticated key exchange. In: Boureanu, I., Owesarski, P., Vaudenay, S. (eds.) ACNS 2014. LNCS, vol. 8479, pp. 1–18. Springer, Cham (2014). https://doi.org/10.1007/978-3-319-07536-5_1
35. Rescorla, E.: The Transport Layer Security (TLS) Protocol Version 1.3. RFC 8446, August 2018. https://rfc-editor.org/rfc/rfc8446.txt
36. de Saint Guilhem, C., Smart, N.P., Warinschi, B.: Generic forward-secure key agreement without signatures. In: Nguyen, P., Zhou, J. (eds.) ISC 2017. LNCS, vol. 10599, pp. 114–133. Springer, Cham (2017). https://doi.org/10.1007/978-3-319-69659-1_7
37. Schank, J., Stebila, D.: A Transport Layer Security (TLS) Extension For Establishing An Additional Shared Secret draft-schanck-tls-additional-keyshare-00, April 2017. https://tools.ietf.org/html/draft-schanck-tls-additional-keyshare-00

38. de Valence, H.: SIDH in Go for quantum-resistant TLS 1.3, September 2017. https://blog.cloudflare.com/sidh-go/
39. Wegman, M.N., Carter, L.: New hash functions and their use in authentication and set equality. J. Comput. Syst. Sci. **22**(3), 265–279 (1981). https://doi.org/10.1016/0022-0000(81)90033-7
40. Whyte, W., Fluhrer, S., Zhang, Z., Garcia-Morchon, O.: Quantum-Safe Hybrid (QSH) Key Exchange for Transport Layer Security (TLS) version 1.3 draft-whyte-qsh-tls13-06, October 2017. https://tools.ietf.org/html/draft-whyte-qsh-tls13-06
41. Zhandry, M.: How to construct quantum random functions. In: 53rd FOCS, pp. 679–687. IEEE Computer Society Press, October 2012
42. Zhang, R., Hanaoka, G., Shikata, J., Imai, H.: On the security of multiple encryption or CCA-security+CCA-security=CCA-security? In: Bao, F., Deng, R., Zhou, J. (eds.) PKC 2004. LNCS, vol. 2947, pp. 360–374. Springer, Heidelberg (2004). https://doi.org/10.1007/978-3-540-24632-9_26

Tighter Security Proofs for Generic Key Encapsulation Mechanism in the Quantum Random Oracle Model

Haodong Jiang[1,2,4], Zhenfeng Zhang[2,3(✉)], and Zhi Ma[1,4(✉)]

[1] State Key Laboratory of Mathematical Engineering and Advanced Computing,
Zhengzhou, Henan, China
hdjiang13@gmail.com, ma_zhi@163.com
[2] TCA Laboratory, State Key Laboratory of Computer Science,
Institute of Software, Chinese Academy of Sciences, Beijing, China
zfzhang@tca.iscas.ac.cn
[3] University of Chinese Academy of Sciences, Beijing, China
[4] Henan Key Laboratory of Network Cryptography Technology,
Zhengzhou, Henan, China

Abstract. In (TCC 2017), Hofheinz, Hövelmanns and Kiltz provided a fine-grained and modular toolkit of generic key encapsulation mechanism (KEM) constructions, which were widely used among KEM submissions to NIST Post-Quantum Cryptography Standardization project. The security of these generic constructions in the quantum random oracle model (QROM) has been analyzed by Hofheinz, Hövelmanns and Kiltz (TCC 2017), Saito, Xagawa and Yamakawa (Eurocrypt 2018), and Jiang et al. (Crypto 2018). However, the security proofs from standard assumptions are far from tight. In particular, the factor of security loss is q and the degree of security loss is 2, where q is the total number of adversarial queries to various oracles.

In this paper, using semi-classical oracle technique recently introduced by Ambainis, Hamburg and Unruh (ePrint 2018/904), we improve the results in (Eurocrypt 2018, Crypto 2018) and provide tighter security proofs for generic KEM constructions from standard assumptions. More precisely, the factor of security loss q is reduced to be $\sqrt{q}$. In addition, for transformation T that turns a probabilistic public-key encryption (PKE) into a determined one by derandomization and re-encryption, the degree of security loss 2 is reduced to be 1. Our tighter security proofs can give more confidence to NIST KEM submissions where these generic transformations are used, e.g., CRYSTALS-Kyber etc.

Keywords: Quantum random oracle model ·
Key encapsulation mechanism · Generic construction

1 Introduction

Indistinguishability against chosen-ciphertext attacks (IND-CCA) [1] is widely accepted as a standard security notion for a key encapsulation mechanism

© Springer Nature Switzerland AG 2019
J. Ding and R. Steinwandt (Eds.): PQCrypto 2019, LNCS 11505, pp. 227–248, 2019.
https://doi.org/10.1007/978-3-030-25510-7_13

(KEM). Random oracle model (ROM) [2] is an idealized model, where a hash function is idealized to be a publicly accessible random oracle (RO). Generic constructions of IND-CCA-secure KEMs in the ROM are well studied by Dent [3] and Hofheinz, Hövelmanns and Kiltz [4]. Essentially, these generic constructions are categorized as variants of Fujisaki-Okamoto (FO) transformation (denote these transformations by FO transformations for brevity) [5,6], including $FO^{\not\perp}$, $FO^{\perp}$, $FO_m^{\not\perp}$, $FO_m^{\perp}$, $QFO_m^{\not\perp}$ and $QFO_m^{\perp}$, where m^1 (without m) means $K = H(m)$ ($K = H(m,c)$), $\not\perp$ ($\perp$) means implicit (explicit) rejection, FO denotes the class of transformations that turn a PKE with standard security (one-wayness against chosen-plaintext attacks (OW-CPA) or indistinguishability against chosen-plaintext attacks (IND-CPA)) into an IND-CCA KEM, Q means an additional Targhi-Unruh hash [7] (a length-preserving hash function that has the same domain and range size) is added into the ciphertext, and variants of REACT/GEM transformation [8,9] (denote these transformations by modular FO transformations), including $U^{\not\perp}$, $U^{\perp}$, $U_m^{\not\perp}$, $U_m^{\perp}$, $QU_m^{\not\perp}$ and $QU_m^{\perp}$, where U denotes the class of transformations that turn a PKE with non-standard security (e.g., OW-PCA, one-way against plaintext checking attack [8,9]) or a deterministic PKE (DPKE, where the encryption algorithm is deterministic) into an IND-CCA-secure KEM.

Recently, post-quantum security of these generic transformations has gathered great interest [4,10–15] due to the widespread adoption [11, Table 1] in KEM submissions to NIST Post-Quantum Cryptography Standardization Project [16], of which the goal is to standardize new public-key cryptographic algorithms with security against quantum adversaries. Quantum adversaries may execute all offline primitives such as hash functions on arbitrary superpositions, which motivated the introduction of quantum random oracle model (QROM) [17]. As Boneh et al. have argued [17], for fully evaluating the post-quantum security, the analysis in the QROM is crucial.

When proving a security of a cryptographic scheme S under a hardness assumption of a problem P, we usually construct a reduction algorithm $\mathcal{A}$ against P that uses an adversary $\mathcal{B}$ against S as a subroutine. Let (T, ϵ) and (T', ϵ') denote the running times and advantages of $\mathcal{A}$ and $\mathcal{B}$, respectively. The reduction is said to be tight if $T \approx T'$ and $\epsilon \approx \epsilon'$. Otherwise, if $T \gg T'$ or $\epsilon \ll \epsilon'$, the reduction is non-tight. Generally, the tightness gap, (informally) defined by $\frac{T\epsilon'}{T'\epsilon}$ [18], is used to measure the quality of a reduction. Tighter reductions with smaller tightness gap are desirable for practice cryptography especially in large-scale scenarios, since the tightness of a reduction determines the strength of the security guarantees provided by the security proof.

In [4,10,11] and this work, all the security reductions for (modular) FO transformations in the QROM satisfy (1) T is about T', i.e., $T \approx T'$; (2) $\epsilon' \approx \kappa\epsilon^{\frac{1}{\tau}}$, where κ and τ in the following are respectively denoted as the factor and degree

---

[1] The message m here is picked at random from the message space of underlying PKE.

of security loss[2]. Let q be the total number of adversarial queries to various oracles.

- In [4], Hofheinz et al. presented QROM security reductions for $\text{QFO}_m^{\not\perp}$ and $\text{QFO}_m^{\perp}$ with $\kappa = q^{\frac{3}{2}}$ and $\tau = 4$, for $\text{QU}_m^{\not\perp}$ and $\text{QU}_m^{\perp}$ with $\kappa = q$ and $\tau = 2$.
- In [10], Saito, Xagawa and Yamakawa presented a tight security proof (i.e., $\kappa = 1$ and $\tau = 1$) for $\text{U}_m^{\not\perp}$ under a new (non-standard) security assumption called disjoint simulatability (DS). Moreover, two generic transformation, TPunc and KC, were given to construct a DS-secure DPKE from standard assumptions, with security reductions $\kappa = q$ and $\tau = 2$.
- In [11], Jiang et al. presented security reductions for $\text{FO}^{\not\perp}$, $\text{FO}_m^{\not\perp}$, T, $\text{U}^{\not\perp}$, $\text{U}^{\perp}$, $\text{U}_m^{\not\perp}$ and $\text{U}_m^{\perp}$ with $\kappa = q$ and $\tau = 2$.

As seen above, above security proofs of (modular) FO transformations from standard assumptions are far from tight. Recently, To better assess the security of lattice-based submissions, Ducas and Stehlé [19] suggested 10 questions that NIST should be asking the community. The 10-th question [19, Problem 10] is on this non-tightness in the QROM. To better understand this, they asked that

Can the tightness of those reductions be improved?

1.1   Our Contributions

In this paper, we give a **positive** answer and show that tightness of these reductions can be improved. Specifically, we provide tighter security proofs for these generic transformations in [4, 10] by using semi-classical oracle technique recently introduced by Ambainis, Hamburg and Unruh [20]. The improvements of the factor κ and the degree τ of security loss are summarized in Table 1. The detailed comparison with previous results in [10,11] is shown in Table 2, where ϵ (ϵ') is the advantage of an adversary against security of underlying (resulting) cryptographic primitive and δ is the correctness error (the probability of decryption failure in a legitimate execution of a scheme).

Table 1. Improvements of the factor κ and the degree τ of security loss.

(κ, τ)	TPunc, KC	T	$\text{FO}_m^{\not\perp}, \text{FO}^{\not\perp}, \text{U}^{\not\perp}, \text{U}^{\perp}, \text{U}_m^{\not\perp}, \text{U}_m^{\perp}$
SXY18 [10]	$(q, 2)$	–	–
JZC[+]18 [11]	–	$(q, 2)$	$(q, 2)$
Our work	$(\sqrt{q}, 2)$	$(q, 1)$	$(\sqrt{q}, 2)$

---

[2] When comparing the tightness of different reductions, we assume perfect correctness of underlying scheme for brevity.

Table 2. Comparisons between previous works [10,11] and our work.

Transformations	SXY18 [10]	Our results
$PKE'=TPunc(PKE, G)$	IND-CPA$\Rightarrow$DS $\epsilon' \approx q\sqrt{\epsilon}$	IND-CPA$\Rightarrow$DS $\epsilon' \approx \sqrt{q\epsilon}$
$DPKE'=KC(DPKE, H)$	OW-CPA$\Rightarrow$DS $\epsilon' \approx q\sqrt{\epsilon}$	OW-CPA$\Rightarrow$DS $\epsilon' \approx \sqrt{q\epsilon}$

Transformations	JZC$^+$18 [11]	Our results
$PKE'-T(PKE, G)$	OW-CPA$\Rightarrow$OW-qPCA $\epsilon' \approx q\sqrt{\epsilon}+q\sqrt{\delta}$	IND-CPA$\Rightarrow$OW-qPCA $\epsilon' \approx q\epsilon+q\sqrt{\delta}$
$KEM\text{-}I=FO_m^{\not\perp}(PKE, G, H, f)$	OW-CPA$\Rightarrow$IND-CCA $\epsilon' \approx q\sqrt{\epsilon}+q\sqrt{\delta}$	IND-CPA$\Rightarrow$IND-CCA $\epsilon' \approx \sqrt{q\epsilon}+q\sqrt{\delta}$
$KEM\text{-}II=FO^{\not\perp}(PKE, G, H)$	OW-CPA$\Rightarrow$IND-CCA $\epsilon' \approx q\sqrt{\epsilon}+q\sqrt{\delta}$	IND-CPA$\Rightarrow$IND-CCA $\epsilon' \approx \sqrt{q\epsilon}+q\sqrt{\delta}$
$KEM\text{-}III=U^{\not\perp}(PKE', H)$	OW-qPCA$\Rightarrow$IND-CCA $\epsilon' \approx q\sqrt{\epsilon}$	OW-qPCA$\Rightarrow$IND-CCA $\epsilon' \approx \sqrt{q\epsilon+q\delta}$
$KEM\text{-}IV=U^{\perp}(PKE', H)$	OW-qPVCA$\Rightarrow$IND-CCA $\epsilon' \approx q\sqrt{\epsilon}$	OW-qPVCA$\Rightarrow$IND-CCA $\epsilon' \approx \sqrt{q\epsilon+q\delta}$
$KEM\text{-}V=U_m^{\not\perp}(DPKE', H)$	OW-CPA$\Rightarrow$IND-CCA $\epsilon' \approx q\sqrt{\epsilon}+q\sqrt{\delta}$	OW-CPA$\Rightarrow$IND-CCA $\epsilon' \approx \sqrt{q\epsilon+q\delta}$
$KEM\text{-}VI=U_m^{\perp}(DPKE', H)$	OW-VA$\Rightarrow$IND-CCA $\epsilon' \approx q\sqrt{\epsilon}+q\sqrt{\delta}$	OW-VA$\Rightarrow$IND-CCA $\epsilon' \approx \sqrt{q\epsilon+q\delta}$

1. For $FO_m^{\not\perp}$ and $FO^{\not\perp}$, the security loss factor q in [11] is reduced to be $\sqrt{q}$. Specifically, we give a reduction from IND-CPA security of underlying PKE to IND-CCA security of resulting KEM with $\epsilon' \approx \sqrt{q\epsilon}+q\sqrt{\delta}$, which is tighter than $\epsilon' \approx q\sqrt{\epsilon}+q\sqrt{\delta}$ in [11] from OW-CPA security of underlying PKE.

2. For T, the quadratic security loss is reduced to be a linear one. Particularly, we provide a reduction from IND-CPA security of underlying PKE to OW-qPCA security of resulting PKE with $\epsilon' \approx q\epsilon+q\sqrt{\delta}$, while previous reduction in [11] is from OW-CPA security of underlying PKE with $\epsilon' \approx q\sqrt{\epsilon}+q\sqrt{\delta}$.

3. For TPunc and KC, the security loss factor q in [10] is reduced to be $\sqrt{q}$. Both IND-CPA security of underlying PKE and OW-CPA of underlying DPKE can be reduced to DS security of DPKE by TPunc and KC with $\epsilon' \approx \sqrt{q\epsilon}^3$, respectively. While, under the same assumptions, previous reductions [10] are with $\epsilon' \approx q\sqrt{\epsilon}$.

4. For $U^{\not\perp}$, $U^{\perp}$, $U_m^{\not\perp}$ and $U_m^{\perp}$, the security loss factor q in [11] is also reduced to $\sqrt{q}$. Particularly, OW-qPCA (one-way against quantum plaintext attacks) security and OW-qPVCA (one-way against quantum plaintext and (classical) validity checking attacks) security of underlying PKE, OW-CPA security and OW-VA (one-way against validity checking attacks) security of

---

[3] Here, for TPunc and KC, we just follow [10] and assume the perfect correctness of underlying PKE.

underlying DPKE can be reduced to IND-CCA security of resulting KEM with $\epsilon' \approx \sqrt{q\epsilon + q\delta}$. While, under the same assumptions, previous reductions in [11] are with $\epsilon' \approx q\sqrt{\epsilon}$ or $\epsilon' \approx q\sqrt{\epsilon} + q\sqrt{\delta}$.

According to [11, Table 1], our results directly apply to the NIST KEM submissions [16], including CRYSTALS-Kyber, LAC, SABER, SIKE and LEDAkem, and provide tighter reductions than previous known [4,11]. For the submissions [16] where $\text{QFO}_m^{\not\perp}$ and $\text{QFO}^{\not\perp}$ are adopted, including FrodoKEM, KINDI, Lizard, NewHope, OKCN-AKCN-CNKE, Round2, Titanium, BIG QUAKE and LEDAkem, our results also provide tighter reductions than [11] without requiring the additional Targhi-Unruh hash.

1.2   Technique

In security proofs of (modular) FO transformations [4,10,11], reprogramming random oracle is an important trick. The security loss in current proofs [4,10,11] arises from the reprogramming of quantum random oracle. Here, we focus on the techniques of improving the analysis of quantum random oracle programming.

One way to hiding (OW2H) lemma [21, Lemma 6.2] is a practical tool to prove the indistinguishability between games where the random oracles are reprogrammed. Roughly speaking, OW2H lemma states that the distinguishing advantage $|P_{left} - P_{right}|$ of an oracle algorithm $A^{\mathcal{O}}$ that issuing at most q queries to an oracle $\mathcal{O}$ distinguishes Left ($\mathcal{O}$ is not reprogrammed) from Right ($\mathcal{O}$ is reprogrammed at x^*), can be bounded by $2q\sqrt{P_{guess}}$, that is

$$|P_{left} - P_{right}| \leq 2q\sqrt{P_{guess}}, \tag{1}$$

where P_{guess} is the success probability of another oracle algorithm B guessing x^* by running $A^{\mathcal{O}}$ and measuring one of $A^{\mathcal{O}}$'s query uniformly at random. To apply OW2H lemma to prove the security of some certain cryptographic schemes, [10,11,13] generalized the OW2H lemma. However, these generalizations do not give tighter bounds.

Very recently, Ambainis et al. [20] further improved the OW2H lemma by giving higher flexibility as well as tighter bounds. Specifically, a new technique called semi-classical oracle was developed, and semi-classical OW2H lemma was given with tighter bounds. Informally, a semi-classical oracle $\mathcal{O}_{x^*}^{SC}$ measures the output $|f_{x^*}(x)\rangle$ instead of $|x\rangle$, where $f_{x^*}(x) = 1$ if $x = x^*$ and 0 otherwise. Let $\mathcal{O}\backslash x^*$ be an oracle that first queries semi-classical $\mathcal{O}_{x^*}^{SC}$ and then $\mathcal{O}$. Semi-classical OW2H lemma shows that above $|P_{left} - P_{right}|$ can be bounded by $2\sqrt{qP_{find}}$, i.e.,

$$|P_{left} - P_{right}| \leq 2\sqrt{qP_{find}}, \tag{2}$$

where P_{find} is the probability of the event Find that semi-classical oracle $\mathcal{O}_{x^*}^{SC}$ ever outputs 1 during the execution $A^{\mathcal{O}\backslash x^*}$.

Next, we show how to use above semi-classical OW2H lemma to improve the security proofs of (modular) FO transformations [10,11]. The primal obstacle is the simulation of the semi-classical oracle $\mathcal{O}_{x^*}^{SC}$, which is quantumly accessible. In particular, the key is simulation of f_{x^*}. We overcome this by making the best of specific properties of different FO-like KEM constructions. Specifically, in security proofs of (modular) FO transformations, x^* is instantiated with m^* of which the encryption is exactly challenge ciphertext c^*.

- For KC, $U_m^{\not\perp}$ and $U_m^\perp$, underlying PKE is deterministic. $f_{m^*}(m)$ can be simulated by verifying whether the encryption of m is c^*.
- For $U^{\not\perp}$ and $U^\perp$, underlying PKE satisfies OW-qPCA or OW-qPVCA security. $f_{m^*}(m)$ can be simulated by verifying whether $\text{PCO}(m,c^*) = 1$, where $\text{PCO}(m,c)$ is the plaintext checking oracle that returns 1 iff decryption of ciphertext c yields message m.
- For TPunc, underlying PKE satisfies IND-CPA security. We note that in IND-CPA security game, $m^* \in \{m_0, m_1\}$, where m_0 and m_1 are chosen by the adversary. Thus, the simulator can simulate f_{m^*} by setting $m^* = m_0$ or $m^* = m_1$. This trick comes from [20, Sect. 4.2], where Ambainis et al. argued the hardness of inverting a random oracle with leakage.
- For T, $\text{FO}_m^{\not\perp}$, $\text{FO}^{\not\perp}$, OW-CPA security of underlying PKE is assumed in previous security proofs in [4,11], where OW2H lemma is used. When using semi-classical OW2H lemma, we need to a stronger assumption of underlying PKE, IND-CPA security, to follow above mentioned trick to simulate f_{m^*}.

Directly utilizing semi-classical OW2H lemma with bound (2) instead of OW2H lemma with bound (1), we improve the security reductions for $\text{FO}_m^{\not\perp}$, $\text{FO}^{\not\perp}$, TPunc, KC, $U^{\not\perp}$, $U^\perp$, $U_m^{\not\perp}$ and $U_m^\perp$, and reduce security loss factor from q to $\sqrt{q}$.

By introducing Bures distance, Ambainis et al. [20] also gave another tighter bound,

$$\left| \sqrt{P_{left}} - \sqrt{P_{right}} \right| \leq 2\sqrt{q P_{find}}. \tag{3}$$

Apparently, as pointed by [20], if P_{right} is negligible, i.e., $P_{right} \approx 0$, we can *approximately* have $|P_{left}| \lessapprox 4q P_{find}$. In the security proofs of (modular) FO transformations, roughly speaking, P_{left} is the success probability of an adversary against resulting cryptographic scheme, P_{right} is the corresponding "target probability" (typically, 0 or 1/2) specified by concrete security definition, and P_{find} is the success probability of another adversary against underlying primitive. Note that for OW-qPCA security, the "target probability" $P_{right} = 0$. Thus, using semi-classical OW2H lemma with bound (3), we can further reduce quadratic security loss in the proof of T in [11] to a linear one.

2   Preliminaries

Symbol description λ is denoted as a security parameter. $\mathcal{K}$, $\mathcal{M}$, $\mathcal{C}$ and $\mathcal{R}$ are denoted as key space, message space, ciphertext space and randomness space, respectively. Denote the sampling of a uniformly random element x in a finite set X by $x \xleftarrow{\$} X$. Denote the sampling from some distribution D by $x \leftarrow D$. $x =?y$ is denoted as an integer that is 1 if $x = y$, and otherwise 0. $\Pr[P : G]$ is the probability that the predicate P holds true where free variables in P are assigned according to the program in G. Denote deterministic (probabilistic) computation of an algorithm A on input x by $y := A(x)$ ($y \leftarrow A(x)$). Let $|X|$ be the cardinality of set X. A^H means that the algorithm A gets access to the oracle H. $f \circ g(\cdot)$ means $f(g(\cdot))$. Following the work [4], we also make the convention that the number q_H of the adversarial queries to an oracle H counts the total number of times H is executed in the experiment.

Note: All cryptographic primitives and corresponding security and correctness definitions used in this paper are presented in Appendix A.

2.1   Quantum Random Oracle Model

In this section, we will present several existing lemmas that we need in our security proofs.

Lemma 1 (Simulating the random oracle [22, Theorem 6.1]). *Let H be an oracle drawn from the set of $2q$-wise independent functions uniformly at random. Then the advantage any quantum algorithm making at most q queries to H has in distinguishing H from a truly random function is identically 0.*

Lemma 2 (Generic search problem [11,23,24]). *Let $\gamma \in [0,1]$. Let Z be a finite set. $F : Z \rightarrow \{0,1\}$ is the following function: For each z, $F(z) = 1$ with probability p_z ($p_z \leq \gamma$), and $F(z) = 0$ else. Let N be the function with $\forall z : N(z) = 0$. If an oracle algorithm A makes at most q quantum queries to F (or N), then $\left| \Pr[b = 1 : b \leftarrow A^F] - \Pr[b = 1 : b \leftarrow A^N] \right| \leq 2q\sqrt{\gamma}$.*

Semi-classical oracle. Roughly speaking, semi classical oracle O_S^{SC} only measures the output $|f_S(x)\rangle$ but not the input $|x\rangle$, where f_S is the indicator function such that $f_S(x) = 1$ if $x \in S$ and 0 otherwise. Formally, for a query to O_S^{SC} with $\sum_{x,z} a_{x,z}|x\rangle|z\rangle$, O_S^{SC} does the following
1. initialize a single qubit L with $|0\rangle$,
2. transform $\sum_{x,z} a_{x,z}|x\rangle|z\rangle|0\rangle$ into $\sum_{x,z} a_{x,z}|x\rangle|z\rangle|f_S(x)\rangle$,
3. measure L.

Then, after performing this semi-classical measurement, the query state will become $\sum_{x,z:f_S(x)=y} a_{x,z}|x\rangle|z\rangle$ (non-normalized) if the measurement outputs y ($y \in 0,1$).

Lemma 3 (Semi-classical OW2H [20, Theorem 1]). *Let $S \subseteq X$ be random. Let $\mathcal{O}_1, \mathcal{O}_2$ be oracles with domain X and codomain Y such that $\mathcal{O}_1(x) = \mathcal{O}_2(x)$ for any $x \notin S$. Let z be a random bitstring. ($\mathcal{O}_1, \mathcal{O}_2, S$ and z may have arbitrary joint distribution D.) Let $\mathcal{O}_S^{SC}$ be an oracle that performs the semi-classical measurements corresponding to the projectors M_y, where $M_y := \sum_{x \in X: f_S(x)=y} |x\rangle\langle x|$ ($y \in 0,1$). Let $\mathcal{O}_2 \backslash S$ ("$\mathcal{O}_2$ punctured on S") be an oracle that first queries $\mathcal{O}_S^{SC}$ and then $\mathcal{O}_2$. Let $A^{\mathcal{O}_1}(z)$ be an oracle algorithm with query depth q. Denote*

Find as the event that in the execution of $A^{\mathcal{O}_2 \backslash S}(z)$, $\mathcal{O}_S^{SC}$ ever outputs 1 during semi-classical measurements. Let

$$P_{left} := \Pr[b = 1 : (\mathcal{O}_1, \mathcal{O}_2, S, z) \leftarrow D, b \leftarrow A^{\mathcal{O}_1}(z)]$$

$$P_{right} := \Pr[b = 1 : (\mathcal{O}_1, \mathcal{O}_2, S, z) \leftarrow D, b \leftarrow A^{\mathcal{O}_2}(z)]$$

$$P_{find} := \Pr[\textit{Find} : (\mathcal{O}_1, \mathcal{O}_2, S, z) \leftarrow D, A^{\mathcal{O}_2 \backslash S}(z)].$$

Then $|P_{left} - P_{right}| \le 2\sqrt{(q+1)P_{find}}$, $|\sqrt{P_{left}} - \sqrt{P_{right}}| \le 2\sqrt{(q+1)P_{find}}$. The lemma also holds with bound $\sqrt{(q+1)P_{find}}$ for alternative definition of $P_{right} = \Pr[b = 1 \wedge \neg\textit{Find} : (\mathcal{O}_1, \mathcal{O}_2, S, z) \leftarrow D, b \leftarrow A^{\mathcal{O}_2 \backslash S}(z)]$.

Lemma 4 (Search in semi-classical oracle [20, Corollary 1]). *Suppose that S and z are independent, and that A is a q-query algorithm. Let $P_{max} := \max_{x \in X} \Pr[x \in S]$. Then $\Pr[\textit{Find} : A^{\mathcal{O}_S^{SC}}(z)] \le 4q \cdot P_{max}$.*

3   Improved Security Proofs for (Modular) FO Transformations

In [4], Hofheinz et al. proposed several (modular) FO transformations, including T, $\mathrm{U}^{\not\perp}$, $\mathrm{U}^{\perp}$, $\mathrm{U}_m^{\not\perp}$, $\mathrm{U}_m^{\perp}$, $\mathrm{FO}_m^{\not\perp}$ and $\mathrm{FO}^{\not\perp}$, of which the security in the QROM was proven by [10,11]. However, except the one for $\mathrm{U}_m^{\not\perp}$ from DS security of underlying DPKE to IND-CCA security of resulting KEM [10], all the reductions are non-tight due to the usage of OW2H lemma. To achieve a DS-secure DPKE, [10] also gave two transformations, TPunc and KC, from an IND-CPA-secure PKE and a OW-CPA-secure DPKE, respectively. But, the security reductions for TPunc and KC are also non-tight due to the utilization of OW2H lemma.

In this section, we will show that if the underlying PKE is assumed to be IND-CPA-secure, tighter reductions for $\mathrm{FO}_m^{\not\perp}$ and T can be achieved by using semi-classical oracle technique in [20]. As discussed in Sect. 1.2, we can also use semi-classical oracle technique to obtain tighter security reductions for $\mathrm{FO}^{\not\perp}$, TPunc, KC, $\mathrm{U}^{\not\perp}$, $\mathrm{U}^{\perp}$, $\mathrm{U}_m^{\not\perp}$ and $\mathrm{U}_m^{\perp}$. We present them in the full version.

To a public-key encryption scheme PKE = (*Gen, Enc, Dec*) with message space $\mathcal{M}$ and randomness space $\mathcal{R}$, hash functions $G : \mathcal{M} \to \mathcal{R}$, $H : \mathcal{M} \to \mathcal{K}$ and a pseudorandom function (PRF) f with key space $\mathcal{K}^{prf}$, we associate KEM-I=$\mathrm{FO}_m^{\not\perp}$[PKE,$G$,$H$,$f$], see Fig. 1.

Theorem 1 (PKE IND-CPA $\overset{QROM}{\Rightarrow}$ KEM-I IND-CCA). *If PKE is δ-correct, for any IND-CCA $\mathcal{B}$ against KEM-I, issuing at most q_D queries to the decapsulation oracle DECAPS, at most q_G (q_H) queries to the random oracle G (H) (($q_G + q_H$) $\ge$ 1), there exist an IND-CPA adversary $\mathcal{A}$ against PKE and an adversary $\mathcal{A}'$ against the security of PRF with at most q_D classical queries*

Gen'	Encaps(pk)	Decaps(sk', c)
1: $(pk, sk) \leftarrow Gen$	1: $m \xleftarrow{\$} \mathcal{M}$	1: Parse $sk' = (sk, k)$
2: $k \xleftarrow{\$} \mathcal{K}^{prf}$	2: $c = Enc(pk, m; G(m))$	2: $m := Dec(sk, c)$
3: $sk' := (sk, k)$	3: $K := H(m)$	3: if $Enc(pk, m; G(m)) = c$
4: **return** (pk, sk')	4: **return** (K, c)	4: **return** $K := H(m)$
		5: **else return**
		6: $K := f(k, c)$

Fig. 1. IND-CCA-secure KEM-I=FO$_m^{\not{\perp}}$[PKE,G,H,f]

such that $\mathrm{Adv}_{\mathrm{KEM\text{-}I}}^{\mathrm{IND\text{-}CCA}}(\mathcal{B}) \leq 2\sqrt{(q_G + q_H + 1)\mathrm{Adv}_{\mathrm{PKE}}^{\mathrm{IND\text{-}CPA}}(\mathcal{A})} + 2\frac{(q_G + q_H + 1)^2}{|\mathcal{M}|} + \mathrm{Adv}_{\mathrm{PRF}}(\mathcal{A}') + 4q_G\sqrt{\delta}$ and the running time of $\mathcal{A}$ is about that of $\mathcal{B}$.

Proof. Here, we follow the proof skeleton of [11, Theorem 2]. Let $\mathcal{B}$ be an adversary against the IND-CCA security of KEM-I, issuing at most q_D queries to the decapsulation oracle DECAPS, at most q_G (q_H) queries to the random oracle G (H). Denote Ω_G, Ω_H and Ω_{H_q} as the sets of all functions $G : \mathcal{M} \to \mathcal{R}$, $H : \mathcal{M} \times \mathcal{C} \to \mathcal{K}$ and $H_q : \mathcal{C} \to \mathcal{K}$, respectively. Consider the games $G_0 - G_9$ in Fig. 2. Although the games $G_0 - G_5$ are essentially the same with the games $G_0 - G_5$ in prior proof of [11, Theorem 2], we still outline them here for readability and completeness. In particular, to apply the semi-classical oracle techniques in [20], we introduce games $G_6 - G_9$, which are different from the proof of [11, Theorem 2], and essential for the improvement of tightness in this paper.

GAME G_0. Since game G_0 is exactly the IND-CCA game,

$$\left|\Pr[G_0^{\mathcal{B}} \Rightarrow 1] - 1/2\right| = \mathrm{Adv}_{\mathrm{KEM\text{-}I}}^{\mathrm{IND\text{-}CCA}}(\mathcal{B}).$$

GAME G_1. In game G_1, the DECAPS oracle is changed that the pseudorandom function f is replaced by a random function H_q'. Obviously, any distinguisher between G_0 and G_1 can be converted into a distinguisher $\mathcal{A}'$ between f and H_q' with at most q_D classical queries. Thus,

$$\left|\Pr[G_0^{\mathcal{B}} \Rightarrow 1] - \Pr[G_1^{\mathcal{B}} \Rightarrow 1]\right| \leq \mathrm{Adv}_{\mathrm{PRF}}(\mathcal{A}').$$

Let G' be a random function such that $G'(m)$ is sampled according to the uniform distribution over $\mathcal{R}_{\mathrm{good}}(pk, sk, m) := \{r \in \mathcal{R} : Dec(sk, Enc(pk, m; r)) = m\}$. Let $\Omega_{G'}$ be the set of all functions G'. Define $\delta(pk, sk, m) = \frac{|\mathcal{R}\backslash\mathcal{R}_{\mathrm{good}}(pk,sk,m)|}{|\mathcal{R}|}$ as the fraction of bad randomness and $\delta(pk, sk) = \max_{m \in \mathcal{M}} \delta(pk, sk, m)$. With this notation $\delta = \mathbf{E}[\delta(pk, sk)]$, where the expectation is taken over $(pk, sk) \leftarrow Gen$.

GAME G_2. In game G_2, we replace G by G' that uniformly samples from "good" randomness at random, i.e., $G' \xleftarrow{\$} \Omega_{G'}$. Following the same analysis as in the proof of [11, Theorem 1], we can show that the distinguishing problem between G_1 and G_2 is essentially the distinguishing problem between G and G', which can be converted into a distinguishing problem between F_1 and F_2, where F_1 is a function such that $F_1(m)$ is sampled according to Bernoulli distribution $B_{\delta(pk,sk,m)}$, i.e., $\Pr[F_1(m) = 1] = \delta(pk, sk, m)$ and $\Pr[F_1(m) = 0] = 1 - \delta(pk, sk, m)$, and F_2 is a constant function that always outputs 0 for any input. Thus, conditioned on a fixed (pk, sk) we obtain by Lemma 2, $\left| \Pr[G_1^{\mathcal{B}} \Rightarrow 1 : (pk, sk)] - \Pr[G_2^{\mathcal{B}} \Rightarrow 1 : (pk, sk)] \right| \leq 2q_G\sqrt{\delta(pk, sk)}$. By averaging over $(pk, sk) \leftarrow Gen$ we finally obtain

$$\left| \Pr[G_1^{\mathcal{B}} \Rightarrow 1] - \Pr[G_2^{\mathcal{B}} \Rightarrow 1] \right| \leq 2q_G\mathbf{E}[\sqrt{\delta(pk, sk)}] \leq 2q_G\sqrt{\delta}.$$

GAME G_3. In G_3, H is substituted with $H_q \circ g$, where $g(\cdot) = Enc(pk, \cdot; G(\cdot))$. Since the G in this game only samples "good" randomness, the function g is injective. Thus, $H_q \circ g$ is a perfect random function. Therefore, G_2 and G_3 are statistically indistinguishable and we have $\Pr[G_2^{\mathcal{B}} \Rightarrow 1] = \Pr[G_3^{\mathcal{B}} \Rightarrow 1]$.

GAME G_4. In game G_4, the DECAPS oracle is changed that it makes no use of the secret key sk' any more. When $\mathcal{B}$ queries the DECAPS oracle on c ($c \neq c^*$), $K := H_q(c)$ is returned as the response. Let $m' := Dec(sk, c)$ and consider the following two cases.

Case 1: $Enc(pk, m'; G(m')) = c$. In this case, $H(m') = H_q(c)$ and both DECAPS oracles in G_3 and G_4 return the same value.

Case 2: $Enc(pk, m'; G(m')) \neq c$. In this case, $H_q'(c)$ and $H_q(c)$ are respectively returned in G_3 and G_4. In G_3, $H_q'(c)$ is uniformly random and independent of the oracles G and H in $\mathcal{B}$'s view. In G_4, queries to H can only reveal $H_q(\hat{c})$, where $\hat{c}$ satisfies $g(\hat{m}) = \hat{c}$ for some $\hat{m}$. If there exists a $\hat{m}$ such that $Enc(pk, \hat{m}; G(\hat{m})) = c$, $\hat{m} = m'$ since G in this game only samples from "good" randomness. Thus, $Enc(pk, m'; G(m')) = c$ will contradict the condition $Enc(pk, m'; G(m')) \neq c$. Consequently, $H_q(c)$ is also a fresh random key just like $H_q'(c)$ in $\mathcal{B}$'s view. Hence, in this case, the output distributions of the DECAPS oracles in G_3 and G_4 are identical in $\mathcal{B}$'s view.

As a result, the output distributions of G_3 and G_4 are statistically indistinguishable and we have $\Pr[G_3^{\mathcal{B}} \Rightarrow 1] = \Pr[G_4^{\mathcal{B}} \Rightarrow 1]$.

GAME G_5. In game G_5, we replace G' by G, that is, G in this game is reset to be an ideal random oracle. Then, following the same analysis as in bounding the difference between G_1 and G_2, we can have

$$\left| \Pr[G_4^{\mathcal{B}} \Rightarrow 1] - \Pr[G_5^{\mathcal{B}} \Rightarrow 1] \right| \leq 2q_G\sqrt{\delta}.$$

GAMES $G_0 - G_9$

1: $(pk, sk') \leftarrow Gen'; G \xleftarrow{\$} \Omega_G$

2: $G' \xleftarrow{\$} \Omega_{G'}; G := G'$ $\quad //G_2 - G_4$

3: $g(\cdot) = Enc(pk, \cdot; G(\cdot))$

4: $H \xleftarrow{\$} \Omega_H$ $\quad //G_0 - G_2$

5: $H_q, H_q' \xleftarrow{\$} \Omega_{H_q}; m^* \xleftarrow{\$} \mathcal{M}; r^* := G(m^*)$

6: $r^* \xleftarrow{\$} \mathcal{R}$ $\quad //G_7 - G_9$

7: $c^* := Enc(pk, m^*; r^*)$ $\quad //G_0 - G_8$

8: $m'^* \xleftarrow{\$} \mathcal{M}$ $\quad //G_9$

9: $c^* := Enc(pk, m'^*; r^*)$ $\quad //G_9$

10: $k_0^* := H(m^*); k_1^* \xleftarrow{\$} \mathcal{K}; b \xleftarrow{\$} \{0, 1\}$

11: $k_0^* \xleftarrow{\$} \mathcal{K}$ $\quad //G_7 - G_9$

12: $b' \leftarrow \mathcal{B}^{G, H, \text{DECAPS}}(pk, c^*, k_b^*)$ $\quad //G_0 - G_5$

13: $\ddot{G} := G; \ddot{G}(m^*) \xleftarrow{\$} \mathcal{R}$ $\quad //G_6 - G_7$

14: $\ddot{H} := H; \ddot{H}(m^*) \xleftarrow{\$} \mathcal{K}$ $\quad //G_6 - G_7$

15: $g(\cdot) = Enc(pk, \cdot; \ddot{G}\backslash m^*(\cdot))$ $\quad //G_6 - G_7$

16: $b' \leftarrow \mathcal{B}^{\ddot{G}\backslash m^*, \ddot{H}\backslash m^*, \text{DECAPS}}(pk, c^*, k_b^*) //G_6 - G_7$

17: $g(\cdot) = Enc(pk, \cdot; G\backslash m^*(\cdot))$ $\quad //G_8 - G_9$

18: $b' \leftarrow \mathcal{B}^{G\backslash m^*, H\backslash m^*, \text{DECAPS}}(pk, c^*, k_b^*) //G_8 - G_9$

19: **return** $b' =?b$

DECAPS $(c \neq c^*)$ $\quad //G_0 - G_3$	**$H(m)$** $\quad //G_3 - G_9$

1: Parse $sk' = (sk, k)$ $\qquad\qquad$ 1: **return** $H_q(g(m))$

2: $m' := Dec(sk, c)$

3: if $Enc(pk, m'; G(m')) = c$ $\qquad$ **DECAPS** $(c \neq c^*)$ $\quad //G_4 - G_9$

4: $\quad K := H(m')$ $\qquad\qquad\qquad\qquad$ 1: **return** $K := H_q(c)$

5: **else return**

6: $\quad$ **return** $K := f(k, c)//G_0$

7: $\quad$ **return** $K := H_q'(c)//G_1 - G_3$

Fig. 2. Games G_0-G_9 for the proof of Theorem 1

Let $\ddot{G}$ ($\ddot{H}$) be the function such that $\ddot{G}(m^*)$ ($\ddot{H}(m^*)$) is picked uniformly at random from $\mathcal{R}$ ($\mathcal{K}$), and $\ddot{G} = G$ ($\ddot{H} = H$) everywhere else. In the proof of [11, Theorem 2], G and H in game G_5 are directly reprogrammed to $\ddot{G}$ and $\ddot{H}$, respectively, and then the OW2H lemma is used to argue the indistinguishability.

Here, in order to use the semi-classical OW2H lemma, we reprogram G and H in game G_5 with an additional semi-classical oracle. Thereby, we need to consider the simulation of such a semi-classical oracle, which is unnecessary in the proof of [11, Theorem 2]. As discussed in Sect. 1.2, this semi-classical oracle can be simulated under the IND-CPA security assumption. Thus, we present following gamehops from G_6 to G_9.

GAME G_6. In game G_6, replace G and H by $\ddot{G}\backslash m^*$ and $\ddot{H}\backslash m^*$ respectively. For $\mathcal{B}$'s query to $\ddot{G}\backslash m^*$ ($\ddot{H}\backslash m^*$), $\ddot{G}\backslash m^*$ ($\ddot{H}\backslash m^*$) will first query a semi-classical oracle $\mathcal{O}_{m^*}^{SC}$, i.e., perform a semi-classical measurement, and then query $\ddot{G}$ ($\ddot{H}$). Let Find be the event that $\mathcal{O}_{m^*}^{SC}$ ever outputs 1 during semi-classical measurements of $\mathcal{B}'s$ queries to $\ddot{G}\backslash m^*$ and $\ddot{H}\backslash m^*$. Note that if the event $\neg$Find that $\mathcal{O}_{m^*}^{SC}$ always outputs 0 happens, $\mathcal{B}$ never learns the values of $G(m^*)$ and $H(m^*)$ and bit b is independent of $\mathcal{B}$'s view. That is, $\Pr[G_6^{\mathcal{B}} \Rightarrow 1 : \neg\text{Find}] = 1/2$. Hence,

$$\Pr[G_6^{\mathcal{B}} \Rightarrow 1 \wedge \neg\text{Find} : G_6] = 1/2\Pr[\neg\text{Find} : G_6] = 1/2(1 - \Pr[\text{Find} : G_6]).$$

Let $(G \times H)(\cdot) = (G(\cdot), H(\cdot))$, $(\ddot{G} \times \ddot{H})(\cdot) = (\ddot{G}(\cdot), \ddot{H}(\cdot))$, and $(\ddot{G} \times \ddot{H})\backslash m^*(\cdot) = (\ddot{G}\backslash m^*(\cdot), \ddot{H}\backslash m^*(\cdot))$. If one wants to make queries to G (or H) by accessing to $G \times H$, he just needs to prepare a uniform superposition of all states in the output register responding to H (or G). The number of total queries to $G \times H$ is at most $q_G + q_H$.

$A^{G \times H}(pk, c^*, H(m^*), H_q)$	DECAPS $(c \neq c^*)$
1: $k_0^* = H(m^*); k_1^* \xleftarrow{\$} \mathcal{K}; b \xleftarrow{\$} \{0,1\}$	1: **return** $K := H_q(c)$
2: $b' \leftarrow \mathcal{B}^{G,H,\text{DECAPS}}(pk, c^*, k_b^*)$	
3: **return** $b' =?b$	

Fig. 3. $A^{G \times H}$ for the proof of Theorem 1.

Let $A^{G \times H}$ be an oracle algorithm on input $(pk, c^*, H(m^*), H_q)$[4] in Fig. 3. Sample pk, m^*, G, H_q, H and c^* in the same way as G_5 and G_6, i.e., $(pk, sk) \leftarrow Gen$, $m^* \xleftarrow{\$} \mathcal{M}$, $G \xleftarrow{\$} \Omega_G$, $H_q \xleftarrow{\$} \Omega_{H_q}$, $H := H_q \circ g$ and $c^* = Enc(pk, m^*; G(m^*))$. Then, $A^{G \times H}(pk, c^*, H(m^*), H_q)$ perfectly simulates G_5, and $A^{(\ddot{G} \times \ddot{H})\backslash m^*}(pk, c^*, H(m^*), H_q)$ perfectly simulates G_6. Applying Lemma 3

---

[4] Although H_q here is the whole truth table of H_q, it is just taken as an oracle to make queries (with at most q_H times) in algorithm A. Thus, we can also take H_q as an accessible oracle instead of a whole truth table.

with $X = \mathcal{M}$, $Y = (\mathcal{R}, \mathcal{K})$, $S = \{m^*\}$, $\mathcal{O}_1 = G \times H$, $\mathcal{O}_2 = \ddot{G} \times \ddot{H}$ and $z = (pk, c^*, H(m^*), H_q)$ and A, we can have

$$\left| \Pr[G_5^{\mathcal{B}} \Rightarrow 1] - \Pr[G_6^{\mathcal{B}} \Rightarrow 1 \wedge \neg \mathsf{Find} : G_6] \right| \leq \sqrt{(q_G + q_H + 1)\Pr[\mathsf{Find} : G_6]}.$$

GAME G_7. In game G_7, replace $r^* := G(m^*)$ and $k_0^* := H(m^*)$ by $r^* \xleftarrow{\$} \mathcal{R}$ and $k_0^* \xleftarrow{\$} \mathcal{K}$. We do not care about $\mathcal{B}$'s output, but only whether the event Find happens. Note that in G_6 and G_7, there is no information of $(G(m^*), H(m^*))$ in the oracle $\ddot{G} \times \ddot{H}$. Thus, apparently, $\Pr[\mathsf{Find} : G_6] = \Pr[\mathsf{Find} : G_7]$.

GAME G_8. In game G_8, replace $\ddot{G}$ and $\ddot{H}$ by G and H. Since $G(m^*)$ and $H(m^*)$ are never used in simulating $\mathcal{B}$'s view, such a replacement causes no difference from $\mathcal{B}$'s view and we have $\Pr[\mathsf{Find} : G_7] = \Pr[\mathsf{Find} : G_8]$.

GAME G_9. In game G_9, replace m^* by m'^*. Note that the information of m^* in this game only exists in the oracles $G \backslash m^*$ and $H \backslash m^*$. By Lemma 4,

$$\Pr[\mathsf{Find} : G_9] \leq 4(q_G + q_H / |\mathcal{M}|).$$

$\mathcal{A}(1^\lambda, pk)$	$H(m)$
1: $\quad m^*, m'^* \xleftarrow{\$} \mathcal{M}; m_0 = m^*; m_1 = m'^*; k^* \xleftarrow{\$} \mathcal{K}$	
2: $\quad b'' \xleftarrow{\$} \{0,1\}; r^* \xleftarrow{\$} \mathcal{R}; c^* = Enc(pk, m_{b''}; r^*)$	1: $\quad g(\cdot) := Enc(pk, \cdot; G\backslash m_0(\cdot))$
3: $\quad$ Pick a $2q_G(2q_H)$-wise function $G(H_q)$	2: $\quad$ **return** $H_q \circ g(m)$
4: $\quad b' \leftarrow \mathcal{B}^{G\backslash m_0, H\backslash m_0, \mathrm{DECAPS}}(pk, c^*, k^*)$	DECAPS $(c \neq c^*)$
5: $\quad$ **return** Find	1: $\quad$ **return** $K := H_q(c)$

Fig. 4. Adversary $\mathcal{A}$ for the proof of Theorem 1

Next, we show that any adversary distinguishing G_8 from G_9 can be converted into an adversary against the IND-CPA security of underlying PKE. Construct an adversary $\mathcal{A}$ on input $(1^\lambda, pk)$ as in Fig. 4. Then, according to Lemma 1, if $b'' = 0$, $\mathcal{A}$ perfectly simulates G_8 and $\Pr[\mathsf{Find} : G_8] = \Pr[1 \leftarrow \mathcal{A} : b'' = 0]$. If $b'' = 1$, $\mathcal{A}$ perfectly simulates G_9 and $\Pr[\mathsf{Find} : G_9] = \Pr[1 \leftarrow \mathcal{A} : b'' = 1]$. Since $\mathsf{Adv}_{\mathrm{PKE}}^{\mathrm{IND\text{-}CPA}}(\mathcal{A}) = 1/2 \left| \Pr[1 \leftarrow \mathcal{A} : b'' = 0] - \Pr[1 \leftarrow \mathcal{A} : b'' = 1] \right|$,

$$\left| \Pr[\mathsf{Find} : G_8] - \Pr[\mathsf{Find} : G_9] \right| = 2\mathsf{Adv}_{\mathrm{PKE}}^{\mathrm{IND\text{-}CPA}}(\mathcal{A}).$$

Finally, combing this with the bounds derived above, we have $\mathsf{Adv}_{\mathrm{KEM\text{-}I}}^{\mathrm{IND\text{-}CCA}}(\mathcal{B})$

$$\leq \text{Adv}_{\text{PRF}}(\mathcal{A}') + 4q_G\sqrt{\delta} + 1/2\Pr[\text{Find} : G_6] + \sqrt{(q_G + q_H + 1)\Pr[\text{Find} : G_6]}$$

$$\leq \text{Adv}_{\text{PRF}}(\mathcal{A}') + 4q_G\sqrt{\delta} + \sqrt{2(q_G + q_H + 1)\Pr[\text{Find} : G_6]}$$

$$\leq \text{Adv}_{\text{PRF}}(\mathcal{A}') + 4q_G\sqrt{\delta} + 2\sqrt{(q_G + q_H + 1)\text{Adv}_{\text{PKE}}^{\text{IND-CPA}}(\mathcal{A}) + 2\frac{(q_G + q_H + 1)^2}{|\mathcal{M}|}}.$$

$\square$

The transformation T [4, 25] turns a probabilistic PKE into a determined one by derandomization and re-encryption [25, 26]. To a PKE=(Gen, Enc, Dec) with message space $\mathcal{M}$ and randomness space R, and a random oracle $G : \mathcal{M} \rightarrow \mathcal{R}$, we associate PKE$' = (Gen, Enc', Dec') = $ T[PKE, G], see Fig. 5. As discussed in Sect. 1.2, for T, using semi-classical OW2H lemma with bound (3), we can improve the reduction in [11] and reduce the quadratic security loss to a linear one. The complete proof of Theorem 2 is presented in Appendix B.

$Enc'(pk, m)$	$Dec'(sk, c)$
1 : $\quad c = Enc(pk, m; G(m))$	1 : $\quad m' := Dec(sk, c)$
2 : $\quad$ **return** c	2 : $\quad$ **if** $Enc(pk, m'; G(m')) = c$
	3 : $\qquad$ **return** m'
	4 : $\quad$ **else return** $\perp$

Fig. 5. OW-qPCA-secure PKE$' = $ T[PKE, G]

Theorem 2 (PKE IND-CPA $\overset{QROM}{\Rightarrow}$ PKE$'$ OW-qPCA). *If PKE is δ-correct, for any OW-qPCA $\mathcal{B}$ against* PKE$'$, *issuing at most q_G quantum queries to the random oracle G and at most q_P quantum queries to the plaintext checking oracle* PCO, *there exists an IND-CPA adversary $\mathcal{A}$ against PKE such that* $\text{Adv}_{\text{PKE}'}^{\text{OW-qPCA}}(\mathcal{B}) \leq 4q_G\sqrt{\delta} + 2(q_G + 2)\text{Adv}_{\text{PKE}}^{\text{IND-CPA}}(\mathcal{A}) + 4\frac{(q_G+2)^2}{|\mathcal{M}|}$ *and the running time of $\mathcal{A}$ is about that of $\mathcal{B}$.*

Acknowledgements. We would like to thank Rainer Steinwandt, Fang Song, and anonymous reviewers of PQCrypto 2019 for their comments and suggestions. We are also grateful to Dominique Unruh for helpful discussions on the one way to hiding lemma. This work is supported by the National Key Research and Development Program of China (No. 2017YFB0802000), the National Natural Science Foundation of China (No. U1536205, 61472446, 61701539), and the National Cryptography Development Fund (mmjj20180107, mmjj20180212).

A   Cryptographic Primitives

Definition 1 (Public-key encryption). *A public-key encryption scheme* PKE *consists of three algorithms. The key generation algorithm,* Gen, *is a proba-bilistic algorithm which on input 1^λ outputs a public/secret key-pair (pk, sk). The encryption algorithm* Enc, *on input pk and a message $m \in \mathcal{M}$, outputs a cipher-text $c \leftarrow Enc(pk, m)$. If necessary, we make the used randomness of encryption explicit by writing $c := Enc(pk, m; r)$, where $r \xleftarrow{\$} \mathcal{R}$ ($\mathcal{R}$ is the randomness space). The decryption algorithm* Dec, *is a deterministic algorithm which on input sk and a ciphertext c outputs a message $m := Dec(sk, c)$ or a rejection symbol $\perp \notin \mathcal{M}$. A PKE is determined if Enc is deterministic. We denote* DPKE *to stand for a determined PKE.*

Definition 2 (Correctness [4]). *A public-key encryption scheme* PKE *is δ-correct if $E[\max_{m \in \mathcal{M}} \Pr[Dec(sk, c) \neq m : c \leftarrow Enc(pk, m)]] \leq \delta$, where the expecta-tion is taken over $(pk, sk) \leftarrow$ Gen. A PKE is perfectly correct if $\delta = 0$.*

Definition 3 (DS-secure DPKE [10]). *Let $D_\mathcal{M}$ denote an efficiently sam-pleable distribution on a set $\mathcal{M}$. A DPKE scheme (Gen,Enc,Dec) with plaintext and ciphertext spaces $\mathcal{M}$ and $\mathcal{C}$ is $D_\mathcal{M}$-disjoint simulatable if there exists a PPT algorithm S that satisfies the following,*

(1) Statistical disjointness:

$$\text{DISJ}_{\text{PKE},S} := \max_{(pk, sk) \in Gen(1^\lambda; \mathcal{R}_{gen})} \Pr[c \in Enc(pk, \mathcal{M}) : c \leftarrow S(pk)]$$

is negligible, where $\mathcal{R}_{gen}$ denotes a randomness space for Gen.
(2) Ciphertext indistinguishability: For any PPT adversary $\mathcal{A}$,

$$\text{Adv}^{\text{DS-IND}}_{\text{PKE}, D_\mathcal{M}, S}(\mathcal{A}) := \left| \Pr\left[\mathcal{A}(pk, c^*) \to 1 : \begin{array}{c} (pk, sk) \leftarrow Gen; m^* \leftarrow D_\mathcal{M}; \\ c^* = Enc(pk, m^*) \end{array} \right] \\ - \Pr[\mathcal{A}(pk, c^*) \to 1 : (pk, sk) \leftarrow Gen; c^* \leftarrow S(pk)] \right|$$

is negligible.

Definition 4 (OW-ATK-secure PKE). *Let* PKE $= (Gen, Enc, Dec)$ *be a public-key encryption scheme with message space $\mathcal{M}$. For ATK $\in \{$CPA, VA, qPCA, qPVCA$\}$ [11], we define OW-ATK games as in Fig. 6, where*

$$O_{ATK} := \begin{cases} \perp & \text{ATK} = \text{CPA} \\ \text{VAL}(\cdot) & \text{ATK} = \text{VA} \\ \text{PCO}(\cdot, \cdot) & \text{ATK} = \text{qPCA} \\ \text{PCO}(\cdot, \cdot), \text{VAL}(\cdot) & \text{ATK} = \text{qPVCA}. \end{cases}$$

Define the OW-ATK advantage function of an adversary $\mathcal{A}$ against PKE *as $\text{Adv}^{\text{OW-ATK}}_{\text{PKE}}(\mathcal{A}) := \Pr[\text{OW-ATK}^{\mathcal{A}}_{\text{PKE}} = 1]$.*

Game OW-ATK	Pco(m,c)	Val(c)
1 : $(pk, sk) \leftarrow Gen$	1 : **if** $m \notin \mathcal{M}$	1 : $m := Dec(sk, c)$
2 : $m^* \xleftarrow{\$} \mathcal{M}$	2 : **return** $\perp$	2 : **if** $m \in \mathcal{M}$
3 : $c^* \leftarrow Enc(pk, m^*)$	3 : **else return**	3 : **return** 1
4 : $m' \leftarrow \mathcal{A}^{O_{ATK}}(pk, c^*)$	4 : $Dec(sk, c) =?m$	4 : **else return** 0
5 : **return** $m' =?m^*$		

Fig. 6. Games OW-ATK (ATK $\in$ {CPA, VA, qPCA, qPVCA}) for PKE, where O_{ATK} is defined in Definition 4. In games qPCA and qPVCA, the adversary $\mathcal{A}$ can query the Pco oracle with quantum state.

IND-CPA for PKE	IND-CCA for KEM	Decaps(sk, c)
1 : $(pk, sk) \leftarrow Gen$	1 : $(pk, sk) \leftarrow Gen$	1 : **if** $c = c^*$
2 : $b \leftarrow \{0, 1\}$	2 : $b \xleftarrow{\$} \{0, 1\}$	2 : **return** $\perp$
3 : $(m_0, m_1) \leftarrow \mathcal{A}(pk)$	3 : $(K_0^*, c^*) \leftarrow Encaps(pk)$	3 : **else return**
4 : $c^* \leftarrow Enc(pk, m_b)$	4 : $K_1^* \xleftarrow{\$} \mathcal{K}$	4 : $K := Decaps(sk, c)$
5 : $b' \leftarrow \mathcal{A}(pk, c^*)$	5 : $b' \leftarrow \mathcal{A}^{Decaps}(pk, c^*, K_b^*)$	
6 : **return** $b' =?b$	6 : **return** $b' =?b$	

Fig. 7. IND-CPA game for PKE and IND-CCA game for KEM.

Definition 5 (IND-CPA-secure PKE). *Define* IND $-$ CPA *game of PKE as in Fig. 7 and the* IND $-$ CPA *advantage function of an adversary $\mathcal{A}$ against PKE as* $\mathtt{Adv}_{PKE}^{IND\text{-}CPA}(\mathcal{A}) := \left| \Pr[\text{IND-CPA}_{PKE}^{\mathcal{A}} = 1] - 1/2 \right|$.

Definition 6 (Key encapsulation). *A key encapsulation mechanism KEM consists of three algorithms. The key generation algorithm Gen outputs a key pair (pk, sk). The encapsulation algorithm Encaps, on input pk, outputs a tuple (K, c), where $K \in \mathcal{K}$ and c is said to be an encapsulation of the key K. The deterministic decapsulation algorithm Decaps, on input sk and an encapsulation c, outputs either a key $K := Decaps(sk, c) \in \mathcal{K}$ or a rejection symbol $\perp \notin \mathcal{K}$.*

Definition 7 (IND-CCA-secure KEM). *We define the* IND $-$ CCA *game as in Fig. 7 and the* IND $-$ CCA *advantage function of an adversary $\mathcal{A}$ against KEM as* $\mathtt{Adv}_{KEM}^{IND\text{-}CCA}(\mathcal{A}) := \left| \Pr[\text{IND-CCA}_{KEM}^{\mathcal{A}} = 1] - 1/2 \right|$.

B   Proof of Theorem 2

Proof. Let $\mathcal{B}$ be an adversary against the OW-qPCA security of PKE', issuing at most q_{PC} queries to the oracle PCO, at most q_G queries to the random oracle G. Denote Ω_G as the sets of all functions $G : \mathcal{M} \to \mathcal{R}$. Let G' be a random function such that $G'(m)$ is sampled according to the uniform distribution in $\mathcal{R}_{\text{good}}(pk, sk, m)$, where $\mathcal{R}_{\text{good}}(pk, sk, m) := \{r \in \mathcal{R} : Dec(sk, Enc(pk, m; r)) = m\}$. Let $\Omega_{G'}$ be the set of all functions G'. Let $\delta(pk, sk, m) = \frac{|\mathcal{R}_{\text{bad}}(pk,sk,m)|}{|\mathcal{R}|}$ as the fraction of bad randomness, where $\mathcal{R}_{\text{bad}}(pk, sk, m) = \mathcal{R} \setminus \mathcal{R}_{\text{good}}(pk, sk, m)$. $\delta(pk, sk) = \max_{m \in \mathcal{M}} \delta(pk, sk, m)$. $\delta = \mathbf{E}[\delta(pk, sk)]$, where the expectation is taken over $(pk, sk) \leftarrow Gen$. Consider the games in Figs. 8 and 9.

GAME G_0. Since game G_0 is exactly the OW-qPCA game,

$$\Pr[G_0^{\mathcal{B}} \Rightarrow 1] = \text{Adv}_{\text{PKE}'}^{OW-qPCA}(\mathcal{B}).$$

GAMES $G_0 - G_6$

1: $(pk, sk) \leftarrow Gen; G \xleftarrow{\$} \Omega_G$

2: $G' \xleftarrow{\$} \Omega_{G'}; G := G' \quad //G_1 - G_2$

3: $m^* \xleftarrow{\$} \mathcal{M}; r^* := G(m^*)$

4: $r^* \xleftarrow{\$} \mathcal{R} \quad //G_6$

5: $c^* := Enc(pk, m^*; r^*) //G_0 - G_6$

6: $g(\cdot) := Enc(pk, \cdot; G(\cdot)) //G_0 - G_4$

7: $m' \leftarrow \mathcal{B}^{G,\text{PCO}}(pk, c^*) //G_0 - G_4$

8: $\ddot{G} = G; \ddot{G}(m^*) \xleftarrow{\$} \mathcal{R} //G_5 - G_6$

9: $g(\cdot) := Enc(pk, \cdot; \ddot{G}\backslash m^*(\cdot)) //G_5 - G_6$

10: $m' \leftarrow \mathcal{B}^{\ddot{G}\backslash m^*,\text{PCO}}(pk, c^*) //G_5 - G_6$

11: Query G with input $m' //G_4 - G_6$

12: **return** $m' =?m^*$

$\underline{\text{Pco}(m,c) \quad //G_0 - G_1}$

1: **if** $m \notin \mathcal{M}$

2:     **return** $\perp$

3: **else return**

4:     $Dec'(sk,c) =?m$

$\underline{\text{PCO} (m,c) \quad //G_2 - G_6}$

1: **if** $m \notin \mathcal{M}$

2:     **return** $\perp$

3: **else return**

4:     $g(m) =?c$

Fig. 8. Games G_0-G_6 for the proof of Theorem 2

GAME G_1. In game G_1, we replace G by G' that uniformly samples from "good" randomness at random, i.e., $G' \xleftarrow{\$} \Omega_{G'}$. Following the same analysis as in the proof of Theorem 1, we can have

$$|\Pr[G_0^{\mathcal{B}} \Rightarrow 1] - \Pr[G_1^{\mathcal{B}} \Rightarrow 1]| \leq 2q_G\sqrt{\delta}.$$

GAMES G_6	GAMES G_7
1: $(pk, sk) \leftarrow Gen; G \overset{\$}{\leftarrow} \Omega_G$	1: $(pk, sk) \leftarrow Gen; G \overset{\$}{\leftarrow} \Omega_G$
2: $m^* \overset{\$}{\leftarrow} \mathcal{M}; r^* \overset{\$}{\leftarrow} \mathcal{R}$	2: $m^*, m_1^* \overset{\$}{\leftarrow} \mathcal{M}; r^* \overset{\$}{\leftarrow} \mathcal{R}$
3: $c^* := Enc(pk, m^*; r^*)$	3: $c^* := Enc(pk, m_1^*; r^*)$
4: $g(\cdot) := Enc(pk, \cdot; G\backslash m^*(\cdot))$	4: $g(\cdot) := Enc(pk, \cdot; G\backslash m^*(\cdot))$
5: $m' \leftarrow \mathcal{B}^{G\backslash m^*, \mathrm{PCO}}(pk, c^*)$	5: $m' \leftarrow \mathcal{B}^{G\backslash m^*, \mathrm{PCO}}(pk, c^*)$
6: Query G with input m'	6: Query G with input m'
7: **return** $m' =?m^*$	7: **return** $m' =?m^*$

PCO (m, c) $//G_6 - G_7$

1: **if** $m \notin \mathcal{M}$ **return** $\perp$

2: **else return**

3:     $g(m) =?c$

Fig. 9. Game G_6 and game G_7 for the proof of Theorem 2

GAME G_2. In game G_2, the PCO oracle is changed that it makes no use of the secret key any more. Particularly, when $\mathcal{B}$ queries PCO oracle, $Enc(pk, m; G(m)) =?c$ is returned instead of $Dec'(sk, c) =?m$. It is easy to verify that $Dec'(sk, c) =?m$ is equal to $Dec(sk, c) =?m \wedge Enc(pk, m; G(m)) =?c$. Thus, the outputs of the PCO oracles in G_1 and G_2 merely differs for the case of $Dec(sk, c) \neq m$ and $Enc(pk, m; G(m)) = c$. But, such a case does not exist since G in this game only samples from "good" randomness. That is, the PCO oracle in G_2 always has the identical output with the one in G_1. Therefore, we have

$$\Pr[G_1^{\mathcal{B}} \Rightarrow 1] = \Pr[G_2^{\mathcal{B}} \Rightarrow 1].$$

GAME G_3. In game G_3, we switch the G that only samples from "good" randomness back to an ideal random oracle G. Then, similar to the case of G_0 and G_1, the distinguishing problem between G_2 and G_3 can also be converted to the distinguishing problem between G and G'. Using the same analysis method in bounding the difference between G_0 and G_1, we can have

$$\left|\Pr[G_2^{\mathcal{B}} \Rightarrow 1] - \Pr[G_3^{\mathcal{B}} \Rightarrow 1]\right| \leq 2q_G\sqrt{\delta}.$$

GAME G_4. In game G_4, an additional query to G with **classical** state $|m'\rangle|0\rangle$ is performed after $\mathcal{B}$ returns m'. Obviously, G_4 has the same output as G_3 and we have

$$\Pr[G_3^{\mathcal{B}} \Rightarrow 1] = \Pr[G_4^{\mathcal{B}} \Rightarrow 1].$$

Let $\ddot{G}$ be the function that $\ddot{G}(m^*) = \ddot{r}^*$, and $\ddot{G} = G$ everywhere else, where $\ddot{r}^*$ is picked uniformly at random from $\mathcal{R}$.

GAME G_5. In game G_5, we replace G by a semi-classical oracle $\ddot{G}\backslash m^*$. For a query input, $\ddot{G}\backslash m^*$ will first query $\mathcal{O}_{m^*}^{SC}$, i.e., perform a semi-classical measurement, and then query $\ddot{G}$. Let Find be the event that $\mathcal{O}_{m^*}^{SC}$ ever outputs 1 during semi-classical measurements of the queries to $\ddot{G}\backslash m^*$. We note that

$$\Pr[G_5^{\mathcal{B}} \Rightarrow 1 \wedge \neg\mathsf{Find} : G_5] = 0$$

since $G_5^{\mathcal{B}} \Rightarrow 1$ implies that $m' = m^*$ in G_5, and $\ddot{G}$ is **classically** queried at m' in G_5[5]. Applying Lemma 3 with $X = \mathcal{M}$, $Y = \mathcal{R}$, $S = \{m^*\}$, $\mathcal{O}_1 = G$, $\mathcal{O}_2 = \ddot{G}$ and $z = (pk, c^*)$, we can have

$$\left| \sqrt{\Pr[G_4^{\mathcal{B}} \Rightarrow 1]} - \sqrt{\Pr[G_5^{\mathcal{B}} \Rightarrow 1 \wedge \neg\mathsf{Find} : G_5]} \right| \leq \sqrt{(q_G + 2)\Pr[\mathsf{Find} : G_5]}.$$

GAME G_6. In game G_6, we replace $r^* := G(m^*)$ by $r^* \overset{\$}{\leftarrow} \mathcal{R}$. Since $G(m^*)$ is only used once and independent of the oracles $\ddot{G}$ and PCO,

$$\Pr[\mathsf{Find} : G_5] = \Pr[\mathsf{Find} : G_6].$$

Note that $G(m^*)$ is never used in G_6, we can just replace $G \overset{\$}{\leftarrow} \Omega_G; \ddot{G} = G; \ddot{G}(m^*) \overset{\$}{\leftarrow} \mathcal{R}$ by $\ddot{G} \overset{\$}{\leftarrow} \Omega_G$. For brevity and readability, we will substitute the notation $\ddot{G}$ with notation G. Then, game G_6 can be rewritten as in Fig. 9.

GAME G_7. In game G_7, we replace $c^* = Enc(pk, m^*; r^*)$ by $c^* = Enc(pk, m_1^*; r^*)$, where $m_1^* \overset{\$}{\leftarrow} \mathcal{M}$. Note that the information of m^* in this game only exists in the oracle $G\backslash m^*$, by Lemma 4 we have

$$\Pr[\mathsf{Find} : G_7] \leq 4\frac{q_G + 1}{|\mathcal{M}|}.$$

Next, we show that any adversary distinguishing G_6 from G_7 can be converted into an adversary against the IND-CPA security of underlying PKE scheme. Construct an adversary $\mathcal{A}$ on input $(1^\lambda, pk)$ as in Fig. 10, where Find is 1 iff the event Find that $\mathcal{O}_{m_0}^{SC}$ ever outputs 1 during semi-classical measurements of the queries to $G\backslash m_0$ happens. Then, according to Lemma 1, if $b'' = 0$, $\mathcal{A}$ perfectly simulates G_6 and $\Pr[\mathsf{Find} : G_6] = \Pr[1 \leftarrow \mathcal{A} : b'' = 0]$. If $b'' = 1$, $\mathcal{A}$ perfectly simulates G_7 and $\Pr[\mathsf{Find} : G_7] = \Pr[1 \leftarrow \mathcal{A} : b'' = 1]$. Since $\mathbf{Adv}_{\mathrm{PKE}}^{\mathrm{IND\text{-}CPA}}(\mathcal{A}) = 1/2 |\Pr[1 \leftarrow \mathcal{A} : b'' = 0] - \Pr[1 \leftarrow \mathcal{A} : b'' = 1]|$,

$$|\Pr[\mathsf{Find} : G_6] - \Pr[\mathsf{Find} : G_7]| = 2\mathbf{Adv}_{\mathrm{PKE}}^{\mathrm{IND\text{-}CPA}}(\mathcal{A}).$$

---

[5] For a classical query input m^*, $\mathcal{O}_{m^*}^{SC}$ always outputs 1.

$\mathcal{A}(1^\lambda, pk)$

		PCO (m,c)
1:	$m^*, m_1^* \xleftarrow{\$} \mathcal{M}; m_0 = m^*; m_1 = m_1^*$	
2:	$b'' \xleftarrow{\$} \{0,1\}; r^* \xleftarrow{\$} \mathcal{R}$	1: if $m \notin \mathcal{M}$
3:	$c^* = Enc(pk, m_{b''}; r^*)$	2: return $\perp$
4:	Pick a $2q_G$-wise function G	3: else return
5:	$g(\cdot) := Enc(pk, \cdot; G \backslash m_0(\cdot))$	4: $g(m) =?c$
6:	$m' \leftarrow \mathcal{B}^{G \backslash m_0, \mathrm{PCO}}(pk, c^*)$	
7:	Query G with input m'	
8:	return Find	

Fig. 10. Adversary $\mathcal{A}$ for the proof of Theorem 2

Finally, combing this with the bounds derived above, we can conclude that

$$\mathrm{Adv}_{\mathrm{PKE'}}^{\mathrm{OW}-q\mathrm{PCA}}(\mathcal{B}) \leq 4q_G\sqrt{\delta} + 2(q_G + 2)\mathrm{Adv}_{\mathrm{PKE}}^{\mathrm{IND\text{-}CPA}}(\mathcal{A}) + 4\frac{(q_G + 2)^2}{|\mathcal{M}|}.$$

□

References

1. Rackoff, C., Simon, D.R.: Non-interactive zero-knowledge proof of knowledge and chosen ciphertext attack. In: Feigenbaum, J. (ed.) CRYPTO 1991. LNCS, vol. 576, pp. 433–444. Springer, Heidelberg (1992). https://doi.org/10.1007/3-540-46766-1_35
2. Bellare, M., Rogaway, P.: Random oracles are practical: a paradigm for designing efficient protocols. In: Denning, D.E., Pyle, R., Ganesan, R., Sandhu, R.S., Ashby, V. (eds.) Proceedings of the 1st ACM Conference on Computer and Communications Security, CCS 1993, pp. 62–73. ACM (1993)
3. Dent, A.W.: A designer's guide to KEMs. In: Paterson, K.G. (ed.) Cryptography and Coding 2003. LNCS, vol. 2898, pp. 133–151. Springer, Heidelberg (2003). https://doi.org/10.1007/978-3-540-40974-8_12
4. Hofheinz, D., Hövelmanns, K., Kiltz, E.: A modular analysis of the Fujisaki-Okamoto transformation. In: Kalai, Y., Reyzin, L. (eds.) TCC 2017. LNCS, vol. 10677, pp. 341–371. Springer, Cham (2017). https://doi.org/10.1007/978-3-319-70500-2_12
5. Fujisaki, E., Okamoto, T.: Secure integration of asymmetric and symmetric encryption schemes. In: Wiener, M. (ed.) CRYPTO 1999. LNCS, vol. 1666, pp. 537–554. Springer, Heidelberg (1999). https://doi.org/10.1007/3-540-48405-1_34
6. Fujisaki, E., Okamoto, T.: Secure integration of asymmetric and symmetric encryption schemes. J. Cryptol. **26**(1), 1–22 (2013)
7. Targhi, E.E., Unruh, D.: Post-quantum security of the Fujisaki-Okamoto and OAEP transforms. In: Hirt, M., Smith, A. (eds.) TCC 2016. LNCS, vol. 9986, pp. 192–216. Springer, Heidelberg (2016). https://doi.org/10.1007/978-3-662-53644-5_8

8. Okamoto, T., Pointcheval, D.: REACT: rapid enhanced-security asymmetric cryptosystem transform. In: Naccache, D. (ed.) CT-RSA 2001. LNCS, vol. 2020, pp. 159–174. Springer, Heidelberg (2000). https://doi.org/10.1007/3-540-45353-9_13

9. Jean-Sébastien, C., Handschuh, H., Joye, M., Paillier, P., Pointcheval, D., Tymen, C.: GEM: a generic chosen-ciphertext secure encryption method. In: Preneel, B. (ed.) CT-RSA 2002. LNCS, vol. 2271, pp. 263–276. Springer, Heidelberg (2002). https://doi.org/10.1007/3-540-45760-7_18

10. Saito, T., Xagawa, K., Yamakawa, T.: Tightly-secure key-encapsulation mechanism in the quantum random oracle model. In: Nielsen, J.B., Rijmen, V. (eds.) EUROCRYPT 2018. LNCS, vol. 10822, pp. 520–551. Springer, Cham (2018). https://doi.org/10.1007/978-3-319-78372-7_17

11. Jiang, H., Zhang, Z., Chen, L., Wang, H., Ma, Z.: IND-CCA-secure key encapsulation mechanism in the quantum random oracle model, revisited. In: Shacham, H., Boldyreva, A. (eds.) CRYPTO 2018. LNCS, vol. 10993, pp. 96–125. Springer, Cham (2018). https://doi.org/10.1007/978-3-319-96878-0_4. https://eprint.iacr.org/2017/1096

12. Bernstein, D.J., Persichetti, E.: Towards KEM unification. Cryptology ePrint Archive, Report 2018/526 (2018). https://eprint.iacr.org/2018/526

13. Szepieniec, A., Reyhanitabar, R., Preneel, B.: Key encapsulation from noisy key agreement in the quantum random oracle model. Cryptology ePrint Archive, Report 2018/884 (2018). https://eprint.iacr.org/2018/884

14. Hövelmanns, K., Kiltz, E., Schäge, S., Unruh, D.: Generic authenticated key exchange in the quantum random oracle model. Cryptology ePrint Archive, Report 2018/928 (2018). https://eprint.iacr.org/2018/928

15. Xagawa, K., Yamakawa, T.: (Tightly) QCCA-secure key-encapsulation mechanism in the quantum random oracle model. Cryptology ePrint Archive, Report 2018/838 (2018). https://eprint.iacr.org/2018/838

16. NIST: National institute for standards and technology. Post quantum crypto project (2017). https://csrc.nist.gov/projects/post-quantum-cryptography/round-1-submissions

17. Boneh, D., Dagdelen, Ö., Fischlin, M., Lehmann, A., Schaffner, C., Zhandry, M.: Random oracles in a quantum world. In: Lee, D.H., Wang, X. (eds.) ASIACRYPT 2011. LNCS, vol. 7073, pp. 41–69. Springer, Heidelberg (2011). https://doi.org/10.1007/978-3-642-25385-0_3

18. Menezes, A.: Another look at provable security (2012). Invited Talk at EUROCRYPT 2012: https://www.iacr.org/cryptodb/archive/2012/EUROCRYPT/presentation/24260.pdf

19. Ducas, L., Stehlé, D.: Assessing the security of lattice-based submissions: the 10 questions that NIST should be asking the community (2018). http://prometheuscrypt.gforge.inria.fr/2018-06-04.assessing-security.html

20. Ambainis, A., Hamburg, M., Unruh, D.: Quantum security proofs using semi-classical oracles. Cryptology ePrint Archive, Report 2018/904 (2018). https://eprint.iacr.org/2018/904

21. Unruh, D.: Revocable quantum timed-release encryption. J. ACM 62(6), 49:1–49:76 (2015)

22. Zhandry, M.: Secure identity-based encryption in the quantum random oracle model. In: Safavi-Naini, R., Canetti, R. (eds.) CRYPTO 2012. LNCS, vol. 7417, pp. 758–775. Springer, Heidelberg (2012). https://doi.org/10.1007/978-3-642-32009-5_44

23. Ambainis, A., Rosmanis, A., Unruh, D.: Quantum attacks on classical proof systems: the hardness of quantum rewinding. In: 55th IEEE Annual Symposium on Foundations of Computer Science, FOCS 2014, pp. 474–483. IEEE (2014)
24. Hülsing, A., Rijneveld, J., Song, F.: Mitigating multi-target attacks in hash-based signatures. In: Cheng, C.-M., Chung, K.-M., Persiano, G., Yang, B.-Y. (eds.) PKC 2016. LNCS, vol. 9614, pp. 387–416. Springer, Heidelberg (2016). https://doi.org/10.1007/978-3-662-49384-7_15
25. Bellare, M., Boldyreva, A., O'Neill, A.: Deterministic and efficiently searchable encryption. In: Menezes, A. (ed.) CRYPTO 2007. LNCS, vol. 4622, pp. 535–552. Springer, Heidelberg (2007). https://doi.org/10.1007/978-3-540-74143-5_30
26. Bellare, M., Halevi, S., Sahai, A., Vadhan, S.: Many-to-one trapdoor functions and their relation to public-key cryptosystems. In: Krawczyk, H. (ed.) CRYPTO 1998. LNCS, vol. 1462, pp. 283–298. Springer, Heidelberg (1998). https://doi.org/10.1007/BFb0055735

(Tightly) QCCA-Secure
Key-Encapsulation Mechanism in the
Quantum Random Oracle Model

Keita Xagawa[✉] and Takashi Yamakawa

NTT Secure Platform Laboratories, 3-9-11, Midori-cho,
Musashino-shi, Tokyo 180-8585, Japan
{keita.xagawa.zv,takashi.yamakawa.ga}@hco.ntt.co.jp

Abstract. This paper studies indistinguishability against *quantum* chosen-ciphertext attacks (IND-qCCA security) of key-encapsulation mechanisms (KEMs) in quantum random oracle model (QROM). We show that the SXY conversion proposed by Saito, Yamakawa, and Xagawa (EUROCRYPT 2018) and the HU conversion proposed by Jiang, Zhang, and Ma (PKC 2019) turn a weakly-secure deterministic public-key encryption scheme into an IND-qCCA-secure KEM scheme in the QROM. The proofs are very similar to that for the IND-CCA security in the QROM, easy to understand, and as tight as the original proofs.

Keywords: Tight security · Quantum chosen-ciphertext security · Post-quantum cryptography · KEM

1 Introduction

Quantum Superposition Attacks: Scalable quantum computers will threaten classical cryptography because of efficient quantum algorithms, e.g., Grover's algorithm for DB search [Gro96] and Shor's algorithms for factorization and discrete logarithms [Sho97]. Hence, we study classical cryptography secure against quantum adversaries (see e.g., the technical report from NIST [CJL+16]). Moreover, several researchers studied stronger quantum adversaries that can mount *quantum superposition attacks*, that is, quantum adversaries that can obtain the result of quantum computations with secret. For example, the adversary can obtain $\sum_c \psi_c \ket{c, D(k, c)}$ by querying $\sum_c \psi_c \ket{c}$, where D is a decryption circuit of a symmetric-key encryption scheme and k is a secret key. There are several quantum superposition attacks that break classically-secure cryptographic primitives: Kuwakado and Morii [KM12] presented a quantum chosen-plaintext attack against the Even-Mansour construction of a block cipher if the inner permutation is publicly available as quantum oracle, which employed Simon's algorithm [Sim97] neatly. Kaplan, Leurent, Leverrier, and Naya-Plasencia [KLLN16] also studied quantum superposition attacks against several block ciphers and

© Springer Nature Switzerland AG 2019
J. Ding and R. Steinwandt (Eds.): PQCrypto 2019, LNCS 11505, pp. 249–268, 2019.
https://doi.org/10.1007/978-3-030-25510-7_14

modes.[1] Boneh and Zhandry [BZ13b] also gave a block cipher that is secure against chosen-plaintext-and-ciphertext attacks but vulnerable against quantum chosen-ciphertext attacks.

The stronger attack model in which adversaries can issue quantum queries is worth investigating. We motivate to investigate this model from following arguments:

- If a source code containing secret information is available, then a quantum adversary can implement a quantum machine containing secret information by itself and mount quantum superposition attacks. For example, a reverse engineering of a physical machine containing secret information allows an adversary to obtain an obfuscated code containing secret information. Moreover, white-box cryptography and obfuscation allows us to publish an obfuscated code containing secret information [GHS16].[2]
- In the future, quantum machines and quantum channels will be ubiquitous. Protocols and primitives will handle quantum data as discussed in Damgård, Funder, Nielsen, and Salvail [DFNS14].
- Even if they handle classical data, we can consider the quantum-ubiquitous world as Boneh and Zhandry discussed [BZ13a, BZ13b]. In this world, the end-user device is quantum and, thus, the device should measure the final quantum state and output a classical information, which prevents the quantum superposition attacks. This last step would be eventually avoided by an implementation bug or be circumvented by a neat hack of a quantum adversary in the future.
- Moreover, if they handle classical data and are implemented in classical machines, one can consider special techniques that force the classical machines behave quantumly. For example, Damgård, Funder, Nielsen, and Salvail [DFNS14] and Gagliardoni, Hülsing, and Schaffner [GHS16] discussed the 'frozen smart-card' scenario.

Security of PKE and KEM against Quantum Chosen-Ciphertext Attacks: Boneh and Zhandry [BZ13b] introduced the security against quantum chosen-ciphertext attacks (QCCA security in short) for public-key encryption (PKE), which is the security against quantum adversaries that make quantum decryption queries. Boneh and Zhandry [BZ13b] showed that a PKE scheme obtained by applying the Canetti-Halevi-Katz conversion [BCHK07] to an identity-based encryption (IBE) scheme and one-time signature is IND-QCCA-secure if the underlying IBE scheme is selectively-secure against quantum chosen-identity queries and the underlying one-time signature scheme is (classically) strongly, existentially unforgeable against chosen-message attacks. They also showed that if there exists

---

[1] We also note that Anand, Targhi, Tabia, and Unruh [ATTU16] showed several modes are secure against quantum superposition attacks if the underlying block cipher is quantumly-secure PRF.

[2] This means that if there is quantum chosen-plaintext or quantum chosen-ciphertext attack that breaks a cryptographic scheme easily, we should not publish an obfuscated code by the white-box cryptography or obfuscation.

an IND-CCA-secure PKE, then there exists an ill-formed PKE that is IND-CCA-secure but not IND-qCCA-secure [BZ13b].

As far as we know, this is the only known PKE scheme that is proven to be IND-qCCA secure (excluding the concurrent work by Zhandry [Zha18, 2018-08-14 ver.]).

1.1 Our Contribution

We show that the SXY conversion in Saito, Yamakawa, and Xagawa [SXY18] and the HU conversion proposed by Jiang, Zhang, and Ma [JZM19] turn a PKE scheme into an IND-qCCA-secure KEM scheme in the QROM, if the underlying PKE scheme is perfectly-correct and disjoint-simulatable. We also observed that the perfect correctness can be relaxed as δ-correctness with negligible δ [HHK17].

Our idea is summarized as follows: In the last step of the IND-CCA security proofs of the above conversions, the challenger should simulate the decapsulation oracle on a query of any ciphertext c except the challenge ciphertext c^*. Roughly speaking, we observe that, if this simulation is "history-free," i.e., if the simulation does not depend on previously made queries at all, this procedure can be quantumly simulated by implementing this procedure in the quantum way.[3] For example, in the last step of the IND-CCA security proof in [SXY18], the decapsulation oracle on input c returns $K = H_q(c)$ if $c \neq c^*$, where H_q is a random function chosen by the reduction algorithm. Therefore, intuitively speaking, this simulation is "history-free" and can be implemented quantumly.

1.2 Concurrent Works

Zhandry [Zha18, 2018-08-14 ver.] showed that the PKE scheme obtained by applying the Fujisaki-Okamoto conversion [FO13] to a PKE scheme PKE and a DEM scheme DEM is IND-qCCA-secure in the QROM, if PKE is OW-CPA-secure and well-spread, DEM is OT-secure[4]. Zhandry proposed recording and testing techniques to simulate the decryption oracles. We note that his security proof is non-tight unlike ours.

1.3 Organizations

Section 2 reviews basic notations and definitions. Section 3 reviews security notions of PKE and KEM. Section 4 gives our new qCCA-security proof for the KEM in [SXY18] as known as the SXY conversion. Section 5 gives our new qCCA-security proof for the KEM in [JZM19] as known as the HU conversion.

---

[3] Boneh et al. [BDF+11] defined history-free reductions for signature schemes. They also discussed the difficulties to model history-free reductions in the case of (public-key) encryption schemes. We also do not define history-free property of reductions for KEMs.

[4] Any efficient adversary cannot distinguish $E(k, m_0)$ from $E(k, m_1)$ even if it chooses m_0 and m_1 with $|m_0| = |m_1|$.

2 Preliminaries

2.1 Notation

A security parameter is denoted by κ. We use the standard O-notations: O, Θ, Ω, and ω. DPT and PPT stand for deterministic polynomial time and probabilistic polynomial time. A function $f(\kappa)$ is said to be *negligible* if $f(\kappa) = \kappa^{-\omega(1)}$. We denote a set of negligible functions by $\mathsf{negl}(\kappa)$. For two finite sets X and Y, $\mathsf{Map}(X, Y)$ denote a set of all functions whose domain is X and codomain is Y.

For a distribution χ, we often write "$x \leftarrow \chi$," which indicates that we take a sample x from χ. For a finite set S, $U(S)$ denotes the uniform distribution over S. We often write "$x \leftarrow S$" instead of "$x \leftarrow U(S)$." For a set S and a deterministic algorithm A, A(S) denotes the set $\{\mathsf{A}(x) \mid x \in S\}$.

If inp is a string, then "out $\leftarrow$ A(inp)" denotes the output of algorithm A when run on input inp. If A is deterministic, then out is a fixed value and we write "out := A(inp)." We also use the notation "out := A(inp; r)" to make the randomness r explicit.

For the Boolean statement P, $\mathsf{boole}(P)$ denotes the bit that is 1 if P is true, and 0 otherwise. For example, $\mathsf{boole}(b' \overset{?}{=} b)$ is 1 if and only if $b' = b$.

2.2 Quantum Computation

We refer to [NC00] for basic of quantum computation.

Quantum Random Oracle Model. Roughly speaking, the quantum random oracle model (QROM) is an idealized model where a hash function is modeled as a publicly and quantumly accessible random oracle. See [BDF+11] for a more detailed description of the model.

Lemma. We review useful lemmas regarding the quantum oracles.

Lemma 2.1. *Let ℓ be an integer. Let* $\mathsf{H}\colon \{0,1\}^\ell \times X \to Y$ *and* $\mathsf{H'}\colon X \to Y$ *be two independent random oracles. If an unbounded time quantum adversary $\mathcal{A}$ makes a query to* H *at most q_H times, then we have*

$$\left| \Pr[s \leftarrow \{0,1\}^\ell : \mathcal{A}^{\mathsf{H},\mathsf{H}(s,\cdot)}() \to 1] - \Pr[\mathcal{A}^{\mathsf{H},\mathsf{H'}}() \to 1] \right| \leq q_\mathsf{H} \cdot 2^{\frac{-\ell+1}{2}}$$

where all oracle accesses of $\mathcal{A}$ can be quantum.

Though this seems to be a folklore, Saito et al. [SXY18] and Jiang et al. [JZC+18] gave the proof.

The second one is the hardness of generic search problem. If the oracle F rarely returns 1, then it is hard to distinguish F from the zero oracle N.

Lemma 2.2 (Generic Search Problem ([ARU14, Lemma 37], [HRS16, Thm.1], [JZC+18])**).** *Let $\gamma \in [0, 1]$. Let $\mathcal{Z}$ be a finite set. Let $F\colon \mathcal{Z} \to \{0, 1\}$ be the following function: For each z, $F(z) = 1$ with probability p_z at most γ and $F(z) = 0$ else. Let N be the zero function, that is, $N(z) = 0$ for any $z \in \mathcal{Z}$. If an oracle algorithm $\mathcal{A}$ makes at most Q quantum queries to F (or N), then*

$$\left|\Pr[\mathcal{A}^F() \to 1] - \Pr[\mathcal{A}^N() \to 1]\right| \le 2q\sqrt{\gamma}.$$

Particularly, the probability that $\mathcal{A}$ finds a z satisfying $F(z) = 1$ is at most $2q\sqrt{\gamma}$.

Simulation of Random Oracle. In the original quantum random oracle model introduced by Boneh et al. [BDF+11], they do not allow a reduction algorithm to access a random oracle, so it has to simulate a random oracle by itself. In contrast, in this paper, we give a random oracle access to a reduction algorithm. We remark that this is just a convention and not a modification of the model since we can simulate a random oracle against quantum adversaries in several ways; (1) $2q$-wise independent hash function [Zha12], where q is the maximum number of queries to the random oracle, (2) quantumly-secure PRF [BDF+11], and (3) hash function modeled as quantum random oracle [KLS18]. In addition, Zhandry proposed a new technique to simulate the quantum random oracle, the compressed oracle technique [Zha18]. His new simulation of the quantum random oracle is perfect even for *unbounded* number of queries. In what follows, we use t_{RO} to denote a time needed to simulate a quantum random oracle.

3 Definitions

3.1 Public-Key Encryption (PKE)

The model for PKE schemes is summarized as follows:

Definition 3.1. *A PKE scheme* PKE *consists of the following triple of polynomial-time algorithms* (Gen, Enc, Dec).

- Gen$(1^\kappa; r_g) \to (ek, dk)$: *a key-generation algorithm that on input 1^κ, where κ is the security parameter, outputs a pair of keys (ek, dk). ek and dk are called the encryption key and decryption key, respectively.*
- Enc$(ek, m; r_e) \to c$: *an encryption algorithm that takes as input encryption key ek and message $m \in \mathcal{M}$ and outputs ciphertext $c \in \mathcal{C}$.*
- Dec$(dk, c) \to m/\bot$: *a decryption algorithm that takes as input decryption key dk and ciphertext c and outputs message $m \in \mathcal{M}$ or a rejection symbol $\bot \notin \mathcal{M}$.*

Definition 3.2. *We say a PKE scheme* PKE *is deterministic if* Enc *is deterministic. DPKE stands for deterministic public key encryption.*

We review δ-correctness in Hofheinz, Hövelmanns, and Kiltz [HHK17].

Definition 3.3 (δ-**Correctness** [HHK17]). *Let* $\delta = \delta(\kappa)$. *We say that* PKE $=$ (Gen, Enc, Dec) *is* δ-*correct if*

$$\underset{(ek,\,dk)\leftarrow\mathsf{Gen}(1^\kappa)}{\mathrm{Ex}}\left[\max_{m\in\mathcal{M}}\Pr[c\leftarrow\mathsf{Enc}(ek,m):\mathsf{Dec}(dk,c)\neq m]\right]\leq\delta(\kappa).$$

In particular, we say that PKE *is* perfeclty *correct if* $\delta = 0$.

We also define key's accuracy.

Definition 3.4 (Accuracy). *We say that a key pair* (ek, dk) *is* accurate *if for any* $m \in \mathcal{M}$,
$$\Pr[c\leftarrow\mathsf{Enc}(ek,m):\mathsf{Dec}(dk,c)=m]=1.$$

Remark 3.1. We observe that if PKE is deterministic, then δ-correctness implies that
$$\underset{(ek,\,dk)\leftarrow\mathsf{Gen}(1^\kappa)}{\mathrm{Ex}}[(ek,dk)\text{ is inaccurate}]\leq\delta(\kappa).$$

In other words, if PKE is deterministic and δ-correct, then a key pair is accurate with probability $\geq 1 - \delta$. We finally stress that, if PKE is deterministic but derandomized by the random oracle, then we cannot apply the above argument.

Disjoint Simulatability. Saito et al. defined *disjoint simulatability* of DPKE [SXY18]. Intuitively speaking, a DPKE scheme is disjoint-simulatable if there exists a simulator that is only given an encryption key and generates a "fake ciphertext" that is computationally indistinguishable from a real ciphertext of a random message. Moreover, we require that a fake ciphertext falls in a valid ciphertext space with negligible probability. The formal definition is as follows.

Definition 3.5 (Disjoint simulatability [SXY18]). *Let* $\mathcal{D}_\mathcal{M}$ *denote an efficiently sampleable distribution on a set* $\mathcal{M}$. *A deterministic PKE scheme* PKE $=$ (Gen, Enc, Dec) *with plaintext and ciphertext spaces* $\mathcal{M}$ *and* $\mathcal{C}$ *is* $\mathcal{D}_\mathcal{M}$-*disjoint-simulatable if there exists a PPT algorithm* S *that satisfies the followings.*

– *(Statistical disjointness:)*

$$\mathsf{Disj}_{\mathsf{PKE},S}(\kappa):=\max_{(ek,dk)\in\mathsf{Gen}(1^\kappa;\mathcal{R})}\Pr[c\leftarrow S(ek):c\in\mathsf{Enc}(ek,\mathcal{M})]$$

is negligible, where $\mathcal{R}$ *denotes a randomness space for* Gen.
– *(Ciphertext-indistinguishability:) For any PPT adversary* $\mathcal{A}$,

$$\mathsf{Adv}^{\mathrm{ds\text{-}ind}}_{\mathsf{PKE},\mathcal{D}_\mathcal{M},\mathcal{A},S}(\kappa):=\left|\begin{array}{l}\Pr\left[\begin{array}{l}(ek,dk)\leftarrow\mathsf{Gen}(1^\kappa);m^*\leftarrow\mathcal{D}_\mathcal{M};\\c^*:=\mathsf{Enc}(ek,m^*):\mathcal{A}(ek,c^*)\to1\end{array}\right]\\-\Pr\left[(ek,dk)\leftarrow\mathsf{Gen}(1^\kappa);c^*\leftarrow S(ek):\mathcal{A}(ek,c^*)\to1\right]\end{array}\right|$$

is negligible.

IND-QCCA. Boneh and Zhandry showed that if we consider a quantum challenge oracle, then there exists a quantum adversary that can distinguish the superposition of plaintexts [BZ13b]. They showed that indistinguishability against fully-quantum chosen-plaintext attack (IND-FQCPA) and indistinguishability against fully-quantum chosen-left-right-plaintext attack (IND-FQLRCPA) is impossible. (For the details, see their paper [BZ13b].) Thus, we only consider a classical challenge oracle.

$$\text{Expt}_{\text{PKE},\mathcal{A}}^{\text{ind-qcca}}(\kappa)$$

$b \leftarrow \{0,1\}$

$(ek, dk) \leftarrow \text{Gen}(1^\kappa)$

$(m_0, m_1, st) \leftarrow \mathcal{A}_1^{\text{QDec}_\perp(\cdot)}(ek)$

$c^* \leftarrow \text{Enc}(ek, m_b)$

$b' \leftarrow \mathcal{A}_2^{\text{QDec}_{c^*}(\cdot)}(c^*, st)$

return $\text{boole}(b' \overset{?}{=} b)$

$$\text{QDec}_a(\textstyle\sum_{c,z} \phi_{c,z} |c,z\rangle)$$

return $\displaystyle\sum_{c,z} \phi_{c,z} |c, z \oplus f_a(c)\rangle$

$f_a(c)$

$m := \text{Dec}(dk, c)$

if $c = a$, set $m := \perp$

return m

Fig. 1. Game for PKE schemes

We need to define the result of $m \oplus \perp$, where $\perp \notin \mathcal{M}$. In order to do so, we encode $\perp$ as a bit string outside of the message space. The security definition follows:

Definition 3.6 (IND-QCCA for PKE [BZ13b]). *For any adversary $\mathcal{A}$, we define its IND-QCCA advantages against a PKE scheme* PKE = (Gen, Enc, Dec) *as follows:*

$$\text{Adv}_{\text{PKE},\mathcal{A}}^{\text{ind-qcca}}(\kappa) := \left| \Pr[\text{Expt}_{\text{PKE},\mathcal{A}}^{\text{ind-qcca}}(\kappa) = 1] - 1/2 \right|,$$

where $\text{Expt}_{\text{PKE},\mathcal{A}}^{\text{ind-qcca}}(\kappa)$ *is an experiment described in Fig. 1. We say that* PKE *is* IND-QCCA-*secure if* $\text{Adv}_{\text{PKE},\mathcal{A}}^{\text{ind-qcca}}(\kappa)$ *is negligible for any PPT adversary $\mathcal{A}$.*

3.2 Key Encapsulation Mechanism (KEM)

The model for KEM schemes is summarized as follows:

Definition 3.7. *A KEM scheme* KEM *consists of the following triple of polynomial-time algorithms* (Gen, Encaps, Decaps):

- Gen$(1^\kappa; r_g) \to (ek, dk)$: *a key-generation algorithm that on input 1^κ, where κ is the security parameter, outputs a pair of keys (ek, dk). ek and dk are called the encapsulation key and decapsulation key, respectively.*
- Encaps$(ek; r_e) \to (c, K)$: *an encapsulation algorithm that takes as input encapsulation key ek and outputs ciphertext $c \in C$ and key $K \in \mathcal{K}$.*

- $\mathsf{Decaps}(dk, c) \to K/\bot$: a decapsulation algorithm that takes as input decapsulation key dk and ciphertext c and outputs key K or a rejection symbol $\bot \notin \mathcal{K}$.

Definition 3.8 (δ-Correctness). Let $\delta = \delta(\kappa)$. We say that KEM = (Gen, Encaps, Decaps) is δ-correct if

$$\Pr[(ek, dk) \leftarrow \mathsf{Gen}(1^\kappa); (c, K) \leftarrow \mathsf{Encaps}(ek) : \mathsf{Decaps}(dk, c) \neq K] \leq \delta(\kappa).$$

In particular, we say that KEM is perfeclty correct if $\delta = 0$.

$\mathsf{Expt}^{\text{ind-qcca}}_{\mathsf{KEM},\mathcal{A}}(\kappa)$	$\mathrm{QDEC}_a(\sum_{c,z} \phi_{c,z} \lvert c, z\rangle)$
$b \leftarrow \{0,1\}$	**return** $\sum_{c,z} \phi_{c,z} \lvert c, z \oplus f_a(c)\rangle$
$(ek, dk) \leftarrow \mathsf{Gen}(1^\kappa)$	
$(c^*, K_0^*) \leftarrow \mathsf{Encaps}(ek);$	$f_a(c)$
$K_1^* \leftarrow \mathcal{K}$	
$b' \leftarrow \mathcal{A}^{\mathrm{QDEC}_{c^*}(\cdot)}(ek, c^*, K_b^*)$	$K := \mathsf{Decaps}(dk, c)$
	if $c = a$, set $K := \bot$
return $\mathsf{boole}(b' \stackrel{?}{=} b)$	**return** K

Fig. 2. Game for KEM schemes

IND-qCCA. We also define indistinguishability under *quantum chosen-ciphertext attacks* (denoted by IND-QCCA) for KEM by following [BZ13b].

Definition 3.9 (IND-QCCA for KEM). For any adversary $\mathcal{A}$, we define its IND-QCCA advantage against a KEM scheme KEM = (Gen, Encaps, Decaps) as follows:

$$\mathsf{Adv}^{\text{ind-qcca}}_{\mathsf{KEM},\mathcal{A}}(\kappa) := \left\lvert \Pr[\mathsf{Expt}^{\text{ind-qcca}}_{\mathsf{KEM},\mathcal{A}}(\kappa) = 1] - 1/2 \right\rvert,$$

where $\mathsf{Expt}^{\text{ind-qcca}}_{\mathsf{KEM},\mathcal{A}}(\kappa)$ is an experiment described in Fig. 2.

We say that KEM is IND-QCCA-secure if $\mathsf{Adv}^{\text{ind-qcca}}_{\mathsf{KEM},\mathcal{A}}(\kappa)$ is negligible for any PPT adversary $\mathcal{A}$.

4   IND-qCCA Security of SXY

Let $\mathsf{PKE}_1 = (\mathsf{Gen}_1, \mathsf{Enc}_1, \mathsf{Dec}_1)$ be a deterministic PKE scheme and let $\mathsf{H}: \mathcal{M} \to \mathcal{K}$ and $\mathsf{H}': \{0,1\}^\ell \times \mathcal{C} \to \mathcal{K}$ be random oracles. We review the conversion SXY in Fig. 3. We show that KEM := $\mathsf{SXY}[\mathsf{PKE}_1, \mathsf{H}, \mathsf{H}']$ is IND-QCCA-secure if the underlying PKE_1 is a disjoint-simulatable DPKE.

$\overline{\text{Gen}}(1^K)$	$\overline{\text{Enc}}(ek)$	$\overline{\text{Dec}}(\overline{dk}, c)$, where $\overline{dk} = (dk, ek, s)$
$(ek, dk) \leftarrow \text{Gen}_1(1^K)$	$m \leftarrow \mathcal{D_M}$	$m := \text{Dec}_1(dk, c)$
$s \leftarrow \{0, 1\}^\ell$	$c := \text{Enc}_1(ek, m)$	if $m = \perp$, return $K := H'(s, c)$
$\overline{dk} \leftarrow (dk, ek, s)$	$K := H(m)$	if $c \neq \text{Enc}_1(ek, m)$, return $K := H'(s, c)$
return $(ek, \overline{dk})$	return (K, c)	else return $K := H(m)$

Fig. 3. KEM := SXY[PKE_1, H, H'].

Theorem 4.1 (IND-QCCA security of SXY in the QROM). *Let* PKE_1 *be a δ-correct DPKE scheme. Suppose that PKE_1 is $\mathcal{D_M}$-disjoint-simulatable with a simulator S. For any IND-QCCA quantum adversary $\mathcal{A}$ against KEM issuing q_H and $q_{H'}$ quantum random oracle queries to H and H' and $q_{\overline{\text{Dec}}}$ decapsulation queries, there exists an adversary $\mathcal{B}$ against the disjoint simulatability of PKE_1 such that*

$$\text{Adv}_{\text{KEM}, \mathcal{A}}^{\text{ind-qcca}}(\kappa) \leq \text{Adv}_{\text{PKE}_1, \mathcal{D_M}, S, \mathcal{B}}^{\text{ds-ind}}(\kappa) + \text{Disj}_{\text{PKE}_1, S}(\kappa) + q_{H'} \cdot 2^{\frac{-\ell+1}{2}} + 2\delta$$

and $\text{Time}(\mathcal{B}) \approx \text{Time}(\mathcal{A}) + q_H \cdot \text{Time}(\text{Enc}_1) + (q_H + q_{H'} + q_{\overline{\text{Dec}}}) \cdot t_{\text{RO}}$.

We note that the proof of Theorem 4.1 is essentially equivalent to that of the CCA security in the QROM in [SXY18] except that at the final game we require quantum simulation of decapsulation oracle.

Table 1. Summary of games for the Proof of Theorem 4.1

Game	H	c^*	K_0^*	K_1^*	Decryption of valid c	invalid c	justification
Game_0	$H(\cdot)$	$\text{Enc}_1(ek, m^*)$	$H(m^*)$	random	$H(m)$	$H'(s, c)$	
Game_1	$H(\cdot)$	$\text{Enc}_1(ek, m^*)$	$H(m^*)$	random	$H(m)$	$H_q(c)$	Lemma 2.1
$\text{Game}_{1.5}$	$H_q'(\text{Enc}_1(ek, \cdot))$	$\text{Enc}_1(ek, m^*)$	$H(m^*)$	random	$H(m)$	$H_q(c)$	if key is accurate
Game_2	$H_q(\text{Enc}_1(ek, \cdot))$	$\text{Enc}_1(ek, m^*)$	$H(m^*)$	random	$H(m)$	$H_q(c)$	if key is accurate
Game_3	$H_q(\text{Enc}_1(ek, \cdot))$	$\text{Enc}_1(ek, m^*)$	$H_q(c^*)$	random	$H_q(c)$	$H_q(c)$	if key is accurate
Game_4	$H_q(\text{Enc}_1(ek, \cdot))$	$S(ek)$	$H_q(c^*)$	random	$H_q(c)$	$H_q(c)$	DS-IND

Security Proof. We use a game-hopping proof. The overview of all games is given in Table 1.

Game_0: This is the original game, $\text{Expt}_{\text{KEM}, \mathcal{A}}^{\text{ind-qcca}}(\kappa)$.

Game_1: This game is the same as Game_0 except that $H'(s, c)$ in the decapsulation oracle is replaced with $H_q(c)$ where $H_q : C \rightarrow \mathcal{K}$ is another random oracle. We remark that $\mathcal{A}$ is not given direct access to H_q.

$\mathsf{Game}_{1.5}$: This game is the same as Game_1 except that the random oracle $\mathsf{H}(\cdot)$ is simulated by $\mathsf{H}'_q(\mathsf{Enc}_1(ek,\cdot))$ where H'_q is yet another random oracle. We remark that a decapsulation oracle and generation of K_0^* also use $\mathsf{H}'_q(\mathsf{Enc}_1(ek,\cdot))$ as $\mathsf{H}(\cdot)$ and that $\mathcal{A}$ is not given direct access to H'_q.

Game_2: This game is the same as $\mathsf{Game}_{1.5}$ except that the random oracle $\mathsf{H}(\cdot)$ is simulated by $\mathsf{H}_q(\mathsf{Enc}_1(ek,\cdot))$ instead of $\mathsf{H}'_q(\mathsf{Enc}_1(ek,\cdot))$. We remark that the decapsulation oracle and generation of K_0^* also use $\mathsf{H}_q(\mathsf{Enc}_1(ek,\cdot))$ as $\mathsf{H}(\cdot)$.

Game_3: This game is the same as Game_2 except that K_0^* is set as $\mathsf{H}_q(c^*)$ and the decapsulation oracle always returns $\mathsf{H}_q(c)$ as long as $c \neq c^*$. We denote the modified decapsulation oracle by QDEC'.

Game_4: This game is the same as Game_3 except that c^* is set as $\mathcal{S}(ek)$.

The above completes the descriptions of games. We clearly have

$$\mathsf{Adv}_{\mathsf{KEM},\mathcal{A}}^{\mathsf{ind\text{-}qcca}}(\kappa) = |\Pr[\mathsf{Game}_0 = 1] - 1/2|$$

by the definition. We upperbound this by the following lemmas.

Lemma 4.1. *We have*

$$|\Pr[\mathsf{Game}_0 = 1] - \Pr[\mathsf{Game}_1 = 1]| \leq q_{\mathsf{H}'} \cdot 2^{\frac{-\ell+1}{2}}.$$

Proof. This is obvious from Lemma 2.1. □

Lemma 4.2. *Let* Acc *and* $\overline{\mathsf{Acc}}$ *denote the event that the key pair* (ek, dk) *is accurate and inaccurate, respectively. We have*

$$|\Pr[\mathsf{Game}_1 = 1] - 1/2| \leq |\Pr[\mathsf{Acc}] \cdot \Pr[\mathsf{Game}_1 = 1 \mid \mathsf{Acc}] - 1/2| + \delta.$$

Proof. By the definition, we have

$$\Pr[\mathsf{Acc}] \geq 1 - \delta \text{ and } \Pr[\overline{\mathsf{Acc}}] \leq \delta.$$

We have

$$|\Pr[\mathsf{Game}_1 = 1] - 1/2|$$
$$= \left|\Pr[\overline{\mathsf{Acc}}] \cdot \Pr[\mathsf{Game}_1 = 1 \mid \overline{\mathsf{Acc}}] + \Pr[\mathsf{Acc}] \cdot \Pr[\mathsf{Game}_1 = 1 \mid \mathsf{Acc}] - 1/2\right|$$
$$\leq \Pr[\overline{\mathsf{Acc}}] \cdot \Pr[\mathsf{Game}_1 = 1 \mid \overline{\mathsf{Acc}}] + |\Pr[\mathsf{Acc}] \cdot \Pr[\mathsf{Game}_1 = 1 \mid \mathsf{Acc}] - 1/2|$$
$$\leq \Pr[\overline{\mathsf{Acc}}] + |\Pr[\mathsf{Acc}] \cdot \Pr[\mathsf{Game}_1 = 1 \mid \mathsf{Acc}] - 1/2|$$
$$\leq |\Pr[\mathsf{Acc}] \cdot \Pr[\mathsf{Game}_1 = 1 \mid \mathsf{Acc}] - 1/2| + \delta$$

as we wanted. □

Lemma 4.3. *We have*

$$\Pr[\mathsf{Game}_1 = 1 \mid \mathsf{Acc}] = \Pr[\mathsf{Game}_{1.5} = 1 \mid \mathsf{Acc}].$$

Proof. Since we assume that the key pair (ek, dk) of PKE_1 is accurate, $\mathsf{Enc}_1(ek, \cdot)$ is injective. Therefore, if $\mathsf{H}'_q(\cdot)$ is a random function, then $\mathsf{H}'_q(\mathsf{Enc}_1(ek, \cdot))$ is also a random function. Remarking that access to H'_q is not given to $\mathcal{A}$, it causes no difference from the view of $\mathcal{A}$ if we replace $\mathsf{H}(\cdot)$ with $\mathsf{H}'_q(\mathsf{Enc}_1(ek, \cdot))$. □

Lemma 4.4. *We have*

$$\Pr[\mathsf{Game}_{1.5} = 1 \mid \mathsf{Acc}] = \Pr[\mathsf{Game}_2 = 1 \mid \mathsf{Acc}].$$

Proof. We say that a ciphertext c is valid if we have $\mathsf{Enc}_1(ek, \mathsf{Dec}_1(dk, c)) = c$ and invalid otherwise. We remark that H_q is used only for decrypting an invalid ciphertext c as $\mathsf{H}_q(c)$ in $\mathsf{Game}_{1.5}$. This means that a value of $\mathsf{H}_q(c)$ for a valid c is not used at all in $\mathsf{Game}_{1.5}$.

On the other hand, any output of $\mathsf{Enc}_1(ek, \cdot)$ is valid due to the accuracy of (ek, dk). Since H'_q is only used for evaluating an output of $\mathsf{Enc}_1(ek, \cdot)$, a value of $\mathsf{H}'_q(c)$ for an invalid c is not used at all in $\mathsf{Game}_{1.5}$.

Hence, it causes no difference from the view of $\mathcal{A}$ if we use the same random oracle H_q instead of two independent random oracles H_q and H'_q. □

Lemma 4.5. *We have*

$$\Pr[\mathsf{Game}_2 = 1 \mid \mathsf{Acc}] = \Pr[\mathsf{Game}_3 = 1 \mid \mathsf{Acc}].$$

Proof. Since we set $\mathsf{H}(\cdot) := \mathsf{H}_q(\mathsf{Enc}_1(ek, \cdot))$, for any valid c and $m := \mathsf{Dec}_1(dk, c)$, we have $\mathsf{H}(m) = \mathsf{H}_q(\mathsf{Enc}_1(ek, m)) = \mathsf{H}_q(c)$. Therefore, responses of the decapsulation oracle are unchanged. We also have $\mathsf{H}(m^*) = \mathsf{H}_q(c^*)$. □

Lemma 4.6. *We have*

$$|\Pr[\mathsf{Acc}] \cdot \Pr[\mathsf{Game}_3 = 1 \mid \mathsf{Acc}] - 1/2| \le |\Pr[\mathsf{Game}_3 = 1] - 1/2| + \delta.$$

Proof. We have

$$
\begin{aligned}
&|\Pr[\mathsf{Acc}] \cdot \Pr[\mathsf{Game}_3 = 1 \mid \mathsf{Acc}] - 1/2| \\
&\le \left| \begin{array}{c} \Pr[\mathsf{Acc}] \cdot \Pr[\mathsf{Game}_3 = 1 \mid \mathsf{Acc}] + \Pr[\overline{\mathsf{Acc}}] \cdot \Pr[\mathsf{Game}_3 = 1 \mid \overline{\mathsf{Acc}}] \\ - \Pr[\overline{\mathsf{Acc}}] \cdot \Pr[\mathsf{Game}_3 = 1 \mid \overline{\mathsf{Acc}}] - 1/2 \end{array} \right| \\
&\le \left| \Pr[\mathsf{Game}_3 = 1] - 1/2 - \Pr[\overline{\mathsf{Acc}}] \cdot \Pr[\mathsf{Game}_3 = 1 \mid \overline{\mathsf{Acc}}] \right| \\
&\le |\Pr[\mathsf{Game}_3 = 1] - 1/2| + \Pr[\overline{\mathsf{Acc}}] \cdot \Pr[\mathsf{Game}_3 = 1 \mid \overline{\mathsf{Acc}}] \\
&\le |\Pr[\mathsf{Game}_3 = 1] - 1/2| + \Pr[\overline{\mathsf{Acc}}] \\
&\le |\Pr[\mathsf{Game}_3 = 1] - 1/2| + \delta.
\end{aligned}
$$

In the third inequality, we use the fact that for any reals a, b, and c with $c \ge 0$, we have $|a - b - c| \le |a - b| + c$. (See Lemma A.1 for the proof.) We use this inequality by setting $a = \Pr[\mathsf{Acc}] \cdot \Pr[\mathsf{Game}_3 = 1 \mid \mathsf{Acc}]$, $b = 1/2$ and $c = \Pr[\overline{\mathsf{Acc}}] \cdot \Pr[\mathsf{Game}_3 = 1 \mid \overline{\mathsf{Acc}}]$. □

Lemma 4.7. *There exists a quantum adversary $\mathcal{B}$ such that*

$$|\Pr[\mathsf{Game}_3 = 1] - \Pr[\mathsf{Game}_4 = 1]| \le \mathsf{Adv}^{\text{ds-ind}}_{\mathsf{PKE}_1, \mathcal{D}_M, \mathcal{S}, \mathcal{B}}(\kappa).$$

and $\mathsf{Time}(\mathcal{B}) \approx \mathsf{Time}(\mathcal{A}) + q_H \cdot \mathsf{Time}(\mathsf{Enc}_1) + (q_H + q_{H'} + q_{\overline{\mathsf{Dec}}}) \cdot t_{RO}$.

Proof. We construct an adversary $\mathcal{B}$, which is allowed to access two random oracles H_q and H', against the disjoint simulatability as follows[5].

$\mathcal{B}^{H_q, H'}(ek, c^*)$: It picks $b \leftarrow \{0, 1\}$, sets $K_0^* := H_q(c^*)$ and $K_1^* \leftarrow \mathcal{K}$, and invokes $b' \leftarrow \mathcal{A}^{H, H', \text{QDEC}'}(ek, c^*, K_b^*)$ where $\mathcal{A}'s$ oracles are simulated as follows.
  - $H(\cdot)$ is simulated by $H_q(\mathsf{Enc}_1(ek, \cdot))$.
    H' can be simulated because $\mathcal{B}$ has access to an oracle H'.
  - $\text{QDEC}'(\cdot)$ is simulated by filtering c^* and using $H_q(\cdot)$; that is, on input $\sum_{c,z} \phi_{c,z} |c, z\rangle$, $\mathcal{B}$ returns $\sum_{c \ne c^*, z} \phi_{c,z} |c, z \oplus H_q(c)\rangle + \sum_z \phi_{c^*, z} |c^*, z \oplus \bot\rangle$.

Finally, $\mathcal{B}$ returns $\mathsf{boole}(b \overset{?}{=} b')$.

This completes the description of $\mathcal{B}$. It is easy to see that $\mathcal{B}$ perfectly simulates Game_3 if $c^* = \mathsf{Enc}_1(ek, m^*)$ and Game_4 if $c^* = \mathcal{S}(ek)$. Therefore, we have

$$|\Pr[\mathsf{Game}_3 = 1] - \Pr[\mathsf{Game}_4 = 1]| \le \mathsf{Adv}^{\text{ds-ind}}_{\mathsf{PKE}_1, \mathcal{D}_M, \mathcal{S}, \mathcal{B}}(\kappa)$$

as wanted. Since H is simulated by one evaluation of Enc_1 plus one evaluation of a random oracle H_q, and H' and QDEC' are simulated by one evaluation of random oracles, we have $\mathsf{Time}(\mathcal{B}) \approx \mathsf{Time}(\mathcal{A}) + q_H \cdot \mathsf{Time}(\mathsf{Enc}_1) + (q_H + q_{H'} + q_{\overline{\mathsf{Dec}}}) \cdot t_{RO}$. □

Lemma 4.8. *We have*

$$|\Pr[\mathsf{Game}_4 = 1] - 1/2| \le \mathsf{Disj}_{\mathsf{PKE}_1, \mathcal{S}}(\kappa).$$

Proof. Let Bad denote the event that c^* is in $\mathsf{Enc}_1(ek, \mathcal{M})$ in Game_4. It is easy to see that we have

$$\Pr[\mathsf{Bad}] \le \mathsf{Disj}_{\mathsf{PKE}_1, \mathcal{S}}(\kappa).$$

When Bad does not occur, i.e., $c^* \notin \mathsf{Enc}_1(ek, \mathcal{M})$, $\mathcal{A}$ obtains no information about $K_0^* = H_q(c^*)$. This is because queries to H only reveal $H_q(c)$ for $c \in \mathsf{Enc}_1(ek, \mathcal{M})$, and $\text{QDEC}'(c)$ returns $\bot$ if $c = c^*$. Therefore, we have

$$\Pr[\mathsf{Game}_4 = 1 \mid \overline{\mathsf{Bad}}] = 1/2.$$

Combining the above, we have

$$|\Pr[\mathsf{Game}_4 = 1] - 1/2|$$
$$= \left| \Pr[\mathsf{Bad}] \cdot (\Pr[\mathsf{Game}_4 = 1 \mid \mathsf{Bad}] - 1/2) + \Pr[\overline{\mathsf{Bad}}] \cdot (\Pr[\mathsf{Game}_4 = 1 \mid \overline{\mathsf{Bad}}] - 1/2) \right|$$
$$\le \Pr[\mathsf{Bad}] + \left| \Pr[\mathsf{Game}_4 = 1 \mid \overline{\mathsf{Bad}}] - 1/2 \right|$$
$$\le \mathsf{Disj}_{\mathsf{PKE}_1, \mathcal{S}}(\kappa)$$

as we wanted.   □

---

[5] We allow a reduction algorithm to access the random oracles. See Subsect. 2.2 for details.

Proof (Proof of Theorem 4.1). Combining all lemmas in this section, we obtain the following inequality:

$$\mathsf{Adv}_{\mathsf{KEM},\mathcal{A}}^{\mathrm{ind\text{-}qcca}}(\kappa) = |\Pr[\mathsf{Game}_0 = 1] - 1/2|$$

$$\leq |\Pr[\mathsf{Game}_1 = 1] - 1/2| + q_{\mathsf{H}'} \cdot 2^{\frac{-\ell+1}{2}}$$

$$\leq |\Pr[\mathsf{Acc}] \cdot \Pr[\mathsf{Game}_1 = 1 \mid \mathsf{Acc}] - 1/2| + \delta + q_{\mathsf{H}'} \cdot 2^{\frac{-\ell+1}{2}}$$

$$= |\Pr[\mathsf{Acc}] \cdot \Pr[\mathsf{Game}_{1.5} = 1 \mid \mathsf{Acc}] - 1/2| + \delta + q_{\mathsf{H}'} \cdot 2^{\frac{-\ell+1}{2}}$$

$$= |\Pr[\mathsf{Acc}] \cdot \Pr[\mathsf{Game}_2 = 1 \mid \mathsf{Acc}] - 1/2| + \delta + q_{\mathsf{H}'} \cdot 2^{\frac{-\ell+1}{2}}$$

$$= |\Pr[\mathsf{Acc}] \cdot \Pr[\mathsf{Game}_3 = 1 \mid \mathsf{Acc}] - 1/2| + \delta + q_{\mathsf{H}'} \cdot 2^{\frac{-\ell+1}{2}}$$

$$\leq |\Pr[\mathsf{Game}_3 = 1] - 1/2| + 2\delta + q_{\mathsf{H}'} \cdot 2^{\frac{-\ell+1}{2}}$$

$$\leq |\Pr[\mathsf{Game}_4 = 1] - 1/2| + \mathsf{Adv}_{\mathsf{PKE}_1, \mathcal{D}_{\mathcal{M}}, \mathcal{S}, \mathcal{B}}^{\mathrm{ds\text{-}ind}}(\kappa) + 2\delta + q_{\mathsf{H}'} \cdot 2^{\frac{-\ell+1}{2}}$$

$$\leq \mathsf{Disj}_{\mathsf{PKE}_1, \mathcal{S}}(\kappa) + \mathsf{Adv}_{\mathsf{PKE}_1, \mathcal{D}_{\mathcal{M}}, \mathcal{S}, \mathcal{B}}^{\mathrm{ds\text{-}ind}}(\kappa) + 2\delta + q_{\mathsf{H}'} \cdot 2^{\frac{-\ell+1}{2}}.$$

□

$\underline{\mathsf{Gen}(1^\kappa)}$	$\underline{\mathsf{Enc}(ek)}$	$\underline{\mathsf{Dec}(\overline{dk}, (c_1, c_2))}$, where $\overline{dk} = (dk, ek)$
$(ek, dk) \leftarrow \mathsf{Gen}_1(1^\kappa)$	$m \leftarrow \mathcal{D}_{\mathcal{M}}$	$m := \mathsf{Dec}_1(dk, c_1)$
$\overline{dk} \leftarrow (dk, ek)$	$c_1 := \mathsf{Enc}_1(ek, m)$	if $m = \perp$, return $K := \perp$
return $(ek, \overline{dk})$	$c_2 := \mathsf{H}'(m)$	if $c_1 \neq \mathsf{Enc}_1(ek, m)$, return $K := \perp$
	$K := \mathsf{H}(m)$	if $c_2 \neq \mathsf{H}'(m)$, return $K := \perp$
	return $(K, (c_1, c_2))$	else return $K := \mathsf{H}(m)$

Fig. 4. KEM $:= \mathsf{HU}[\mathsf{PKE}_1, \mathsf{H}, \mathsf{H}']$.

5   IND-QCCA Security of HU

Very recently, Jiang, Zhang, and Ma [JZM19] proposed a conversion HU, which allows an explicit rejection but requires additional hash value c_2 of m. Let $\mathsf{PKE}_1 = (\mathsf{Gen}_1, \mathsf{Enc}_1, \mathsf{Dec}_1)$ be a deterministic PKE scheme and let $\mathsf{H} \colon \mathcal{M} \to \mathcal{K}$ and $\mathsf{H}' \colon \mathcal{M} \to \mathcal{H}$ be random oracles. We review the conversion HU in Fig. 4. We show that $\mathsf{KEM} := \mathsf{HU}[\mathsf{PKE}_1, \mathsf{H}, \mathsf{H}']$ is IND-QCCA-secure if the underlying PKE_1 is a disjoint-simulatable DPKE.

Theorem 5.1 (IND-QCCA security of HU in the QROM). *Let* PKE_1 *be a* δ-*correct DPKE scheme. Suppose that* PKE_1 *is* $\mathcal{D}_{\mathcal{M}}$-*disjoint-simulatable with a simulator* $\mathcal{S}$. *For any* IND-QCCA *quantum adversary* $\mathcal{A}$ *against* KEM *issuing* q_{H} *and* $q_{\mathsf{H}'}$ *quantum random oracle queries to* H *and* H' *and* $q_{\overline{\mathsf{Dec}}}$ *decapsulation* *queries, there exists an adversary* $\mathcal{B}$ *against the disjoint simulatability of* PKE_1 *such that*

$$\mathsf{Adv}^{\text{ind-qcca}}_{\mathsf{KEM},\mathcal{A}}(\kappa) \le \mathsf{Adv}^{\text{ds-ind}}_{\mathsf{PKE}_1,\mathcal{D}_M,\mathcal{S},\mathcal{B}}(\kappa) + \mathsf{Disj}_{\mathsf{PKE}_1,\mathcal{S}}(\kappa) + 2q_{\overline{\mathsf{Dec}}} \cdot |\mathcal{H}|^{-1/2} + 2\delta$$

and $\mathsf{Time}(\mathcal{B}) \approx \mathsf{Time}(\mathcal{A}) + (q_{\mathsf{H}} + q_{\mathsf{H}'}) \cdot \mathsf{Time}(\mathsf{Enc}_1) + (q_{\mathsf{H}} + q_{\mathsf{H}'} + 2q_{\overline{\mathsf{Dec}}}) \cdot t_{\mathsf{RO}}.$

The proof of Theorem 5.1 follows.

Table 2. Summary of games for the Proof of Theorem 5.1. We let $g(\cdot) = \mathsf{Enc}_1(ek, \cdot)$.

Game	H	H'	c_1^*	c_2^*	K_0^*	K_1^*	Decryption K	condition	justification
Game$_0$	H	H'	$\mathsf{Enc}_1(ek, m^*)$	$\mathsf{H}'(m^*)$	$\mathsf{H}(m^*)$	random	$\mathsf{H}(m)$	if $c_1 = \mathsf{Enc}_1(ek, m)$ and $c_2 = \mathsf{H}'(m)$	
Game$_1$	$\mathsf{H}_q \circ g$	$\mathsf{H}'_q \circ g$	$\mathsf{Enc}_1(ek, m^*)$	$\mathsf{H}'_q(c_1^*)$	$\mathsf{H}_q(c_1^*)$	random	$\mathsf{H}(m)$	if $c_1 = \mathsf{Enc}_1(ek, m)$ and $c_2 = \mathsf{H}'(m)$	if key is accurate
Game$_2$	$\mathsf{H}_q \circ g$	$\mathsf{H}'_q \circ g$	$\mathsf{Enc}_1(ek, m^*)$	$\mathsf{H}'_q(c_1^*)$	$\mathsf{H}_q(c_1^*)$	random	$\mathsf{H}_q(c_1)$	if $c_1 = \mathsf{Enc}_1(ek, m)$ and $c_2 = \mathsf{H}'_q(c_1)$	if key is accurate
Game$_3$	$\mathsf{H}_q \circ g$	$\mathsf{H}'_q \circ g$	$\mathsf{Enc}_1(ek, m^*)$	$\mathsf{H}'_q(c_1^*)$	$\mathsf{H}_q(c_1^*)$	random	$\mathsf{H}_q(c_1)$	if $c_2 = \mathsf{H}'_q(c_1)$	Statistical
Game$_3$	$\mathsf{H}_q \circ g$	$\mathsf{H}'_q \circ g$	$\mathcal{S}(ek)$	$\mathsf{H}'_q(c_1^*)$	$\mathsf{H}_q(c_1^*)$	random	$\mathsf{H}_q(c_1)$	if $c_2 = \mathsf{H}'_q(c_1)$	DS-IND

Security Proof. We use a game-hopping proof. The overview of all games is given in Table 2.

Game$_0$: This is the original game, $\mathsf{Expt}^{\text{ind-qcca}}_{\mathsf{KEM},\mathcal{A}}(\kappa)$.

Game$_1$: This game is the same as Game$_0$ except that the random oracle $\mathsf{H}(\cdot)$ and $\mathsf{H}'(\cdot)$ are simulated by $\mathsf{H}_q(\mathsf{Enc}_1(ek, \cdot))$ and $\mathsf{H}'_q(\mathsf{Enc}_1(ek, \cdot))$, respectively, where $\mathsf{H}_q : C \to \mathcal{K}$ and $\mathsf{H}'_q : C \to \mathcal{H}$ are random oracles. We remark that a decapsulation oracle and generation of K_0^* also use $\mathsf{H}_q(\mathsf{Enc}_1(ek, \cdot))$ as $\mathsf{H}(\cdot)$, and generation of c_2^* uses $\mathsf{H}'_q(\mathsf{Enc}_1(ek, \cdot))$ as $\mathsf{H}'(\cdot)$. We also remark that $\mathcal{A}$ is not given direct access to H_q and H'_q.

Game$_2$: This game is the same as Game$_1$ except that the decapsulation oracle returns $K := \mathsf{H}_q(c_1)$ if $c_1 = \mathsf{Enc}_1(ek, m)$ and $\mathsf{H}'_q(c_1) = c_2$, instead returns $K := \mathsf{H}(m)$ if $c_1 = \mathsf{Enc}_1(ek, m)$ and $\mathsf{H}'(m) = c_2$.

Game$_3$: This game is the same as Game$_2$ except that the decapsulation oracle returns $K := \mathsf{H}_q(c_1)$ if $\mathsf{H}'_q(c_1) = c_2$. That is, the decapsulation oracle never use the re-encryption check.

Game$_4$: This game is the same as Game$_3$ except that c_1^* is set as $\mathcal{S}(ek)$.
The above completes the descriptions of games. We clearly have

$$\mathsf{Adv}^{\text{ind-qcca}}_{\mathsf{KEM},\mathcal{A}}(\kappa) = |\Pr[\mathsf{Game}_0 = 1] - 1/2|$$

by the definition. We upperbound this by the following lemmas.

Lemma 5.1. *Let* Acc *denote the event that the key pair* (ek, dk) *is accurate. We have*

$$|\Pr[\mathsf{Game}_0 = 1] - 1/2| \leq |\Pr[\mathsf{Acc}] \cdot \Pr[\mathsf{Game}_0 = 1 \mid \mathsf{Acc}] - 1/2| + \delta.$$

We omit the proof, since the proof is the same as that of Lemma 4.2.

Lemma 5.2. *We have*

$$\Pr[\mathsf{Game}_0 = 1 \mid \mathsf{Acc}] = \Pr[\mathsf{Game}_1 = 1 \mid \mathsf{Acc}].$$

Proof. Since we assume that the key pair is accurate, $\mathsf{Enc}_1(ek, \cdot)$ is injective. Therefore, if $H_q(\cdot)$ (and $H'_q(\cdot)$, resp.) is a random function, then $H_q(\mathsf{Enc}_1(ek, \cdot))$ (and $H'_q(\mathsf{Enc}_1(ek, \cdot))$, resp.) is also a random function. Remarking that access to H_q and H'_q is not given to $\mathcal{A}$, it causes no difference from the view of $\mathcal{A}$ if we replace $H(\cdot)$ (and $H'(\cdot)$, resp.) with $H_q(\mathsf{Enc}_1(ek, \cdot))$ (and $H'_q(\mathsf{Enc}_1(ek, \cdot))$, resp.). □

Lemma 5.3. *We have*

$$\Pr[\mathsf{Game}_1 = 1 \mid \mathsf{Acc}] = \Pr[\mathsf{Game}_2 = 1 \mid \mathsf{Acc}].$$

Proof. This change is just conceptual. Suppose that $c_1 = \mathsf{Enc}_1(ek, m)$. We have that $c_2 = H'(m)$ holds if and only if $c_2 = H'_q(c_1)$ and $K = H(m) = H_q(c_1)$. □

Lemma 5.4. *We have*

$$|\Pr[\mathsf{Game}_2 = 1 \mid \mathsf{Acc}] - \Pr[\mathsf{Game}_3 = 1 \mid \mathsf{Acc}]| \leq 2q_{\overline{\mathsf{Dec}}}|\mathcal{H}|^{-1/2}.$$

Proof. Recall that we have $H'(m) = H'_q(\mathsf{Enc}(ek, m))$ and $H'_q(c_1) = c_2$.

Let us see the details how the decapsulation oracle treats the query $|c_1, c_2, z\rangle$. Let $m = \mathsf{Dec}_1(dk, c_1)$.

- Case 1 that $c_1 = \mathsf{Enc}_1(ek, m)$: in this case, the decapsulation oracles in both games return $|c_1, c_2, z \oplus K\rangle$, where $K := H_q(c_1)$ or $\perp$ depending on that $c_2 = H'_q(c_1)$.
- Case 2 that $c_1 \neq \mathsf{Enc}_1(ek, m)$ and $c_2 \neq H'_q(c_2)$: In this case, the decapsulation oracles in both games return $|c_1, c_2, z \oplus \perp\rangle$.
- Case 3 that $c_1 \neq \mathsf{Enc}_1(ek, m)$ and $c_2 = H'_q(c_1)$: In this case, the decapsulation oracle in Game_2 returns $|c_1, c_2, z \oplus \perp\rangle$, but the decapsulation oracle in Game_3 returns $|c_1, c_2, z \oplus H_q(c_1)\rangle$.

If the query is classical, we can argue the difference as in [JZM19]: Since the adversary cannot access to H'_q directly, it cannot know the value of $H'_q(c_1)$ if c_1 lies outside of $\mathsf{Enc}(ek, \cdot)$. Therefore, any c_2 hits the value $H'_q(c_1)$ with probability at most $1/|\mathcal{H}|$.

Even if the query is quantum, the problem is distinguishing problem and we invoke Lemma 2.2. We now reduce from generic search problem to distinguishing

Game_2 with Game_3. We define the distribution $\mathcal{D}_F$ over $F := \{f : C \times \mathcal{H} \to \{0,1\}\}$ as follows: for each $c_1 \in C$, choose $h_{c_1} \leftarrow \mathcal{H}$ uniformly at random and set

$$f(c_1, h) := \begin{cases} 1 & \text{if } h = h_{c_1} \\ 0 & \text{otherwise.} \end{cases}$$

For each (c_1, h), we have $\Pr[f(c_1, h) = 1] \le |\mathcal{H}|^{-1}$.

The reduction algorithm is defined as follows: Suppose that we are given $f : C \times \mathcal{H} \to \{0,1\}$, which is chosen according to $\mathcal{D}_F$ or set as the zero function N. We construct H, H', and the decapsulation oracle as follows:

- H_q and H'_q: we choose $\mathsf{H}_q|_{\mathsf{Enc}_1(ek,\mathcal{M})}$ and $\mathsf{H}'_q|_{\mathsf{Enc}_1(ek,\mathcal{M})}$ uniformly at random.
- H: on input $|m, z\rangle$, it returns $|m, z \oplus \mathsf{H}_q(\mathsf{Enc}_1(ek, m))\rangle$.
- H': on input $|m, z\rangle$, it returns $|m, z \oplus \mathsf{H}'_q(\mathsf{Enc}_1(ek, m))\rangle$.
- QDEC_{c^*}: On input $|c_1, c_2, z\rangle$, it computes $m = \mathsf{Dec}_1(dk, c_1)$ and computes K as follows:
  - if $c_1 = c_1^*$ and $c_2 = c_2^*$, then let $K = \bot$.
  - if $c_1 = \mathsf{Enc}_1(ek, m)$ and $c_2 = \mathsf{H}'_q(c_1)$, then let $K = \mathsf{H}_q(c_1)$.
  - if $c_1 = \mathsf{Enc}_1(ek, m)$ and $c_2 \ne \mathsf{H}'_q(c_1)$, then let $K = \bot$.
  - if $c_1 \ne \mathsf{Enc}_1(ek, m)$ and $f(c_1, c_2) = 1$, then let $K = \mathsf{H}_q(c_1)$.
  - if $c_1 \ne \mathsf{Enc}_1(ek, m)$ and $f(c_1, c_2) = 0$, then let $K = \bot$.

  it returns $|c_1, c_2, z \oplus K\rangle$.

If $f = N$, then this algorithm perfectly simulates Game_2. On the other hand, if $f \leftarrow \mathcal{D}_F$, then this algorithm perfectly simulates Game_3, since any adversary cannot access H'_q on $C \setminus \mathsf{Enc}(ek, \mathcal{M})$. Thus, according to Lemma 2.2, we have upperbound $2q_{\overline{\mathsf{Dec}}}|\mathcal{H}|^{-1/2}$ as we wanted. $\square$

Lemma 5.5. *We have*

$$|\Pr[\mathsf{Acc}] \cdot \Pr[\mathsf{Game}_3 = 1 \mid \mathsf{Acc}] - 1/2| \le |\Pr[\mathsf{Game}_3 = 1] - 1/2| + \delta.$$

We omit the proof, since the proof is the same as that of Lemma 4.6.

Lemma 5.6. *There exists an adversary $\mathcal{B}$ such that*

$$|\Pr[\mathsf{Game}_3 = 1] - \Pr[\mathsf{Game}_4 = 1]| \le \mathsf{Adv}^{\mathsf{ds\text{-}ind}}_{\mathsf{PKE}_1, \mathcal{D}_M, S, \mathcal{B}}(\kappa).$$

and $\mathsf{Time}(\mathcal{B}) \approx \mathsf{Time}(\mathcal{A}) + q_{\mathsf{H}} \cdot \mathsf{Time}(\mathsf{Enc}_1) + (q_{\mathsf{H}} + q_{\mathsf{H}'} + q_{\overline{\mathsf{Dec}}}) \cdot t_{\mathsf{RO}}.$

Proof. Let $g(\cdot) := \mathsf{Enc}_1(ek, \cdot)$. For ease of notation, we define a new function $f_{\mathsf{H}_q, \mathsf{H}'_q} : C \times \mathcal{H} \to \mathcal{K} \cup \{\bot\}$ as follows:

$$f_{\mathsf{H}_q, \mathsf{H}'_q}(c_1, c_2) := \begin{cases} \mathsf{H}_q(c_1) & \text{if } \mathsf{H}'_q(c_1) = c_2 \\ \bot & \text{otherwise.} \end{cases}$$

We construct an adversary $\mathcal{B}$, which is allowed to access two random oracles H_q and H'_q, against the disjoint simulatability as follows (See footnote 5).

$\mathcal{B}^{H_q,H'_q}(ek,c_1^*)$: It picks $b \leftarrow \{0,1\}$, sets $K_0^* := H_q(c_1^*)$ and $K_1^* \leftarrow \mathcal{K}$, and invokes
$b' \leftarrow \mathcal{A}^{H,H',\overline{\text{Dec}}}(ek,c_1^*,K_b^*)$ where $\mathcal{A}$'s oracles are simulated as follows.
- $H(\cdot)$ is simulated by $H_q(\text{Enc}_1(ek,\cdot))$.
- $H'(\cdot)$ is simulated by $H'_q(\text{Enc}_1(ek,\cdot))$.
- $\overline{\text{Dec}}'(\cdot)$ is simulated by filtering c_1^*; on input $\sum_{c_1,c_2,z}\phi_{c_1,c_2,z}|c_1,c_2,z\rangle$, $\mathcal{B}$ returns

$$\sum_{c_1 \neq c_1^*,z}\phi_{c_1,c_2,z}|c_1,c_2,z \oplus f_{H_q,H'_q}(c_1,c_2)\rangle + \sum_{c_2,z}\phi_{c_1^*,c_2,z}|c_1^*,c_2,z \oplus \perp\rangle$$

Finally, $\mathcal{B}$ returns $\text{boole}(b \overset{?}{=} b')$.

This completes the description of $\mathcal{B}$.

Since $c_2^* := H_q(c_1^*)$, if $c_2 \neq c_2^*$, then the decapsulation oracle in both games and f_{H_q,H'_q} return $\perp$ on input (c_1^*,c_2). Thus, we have

$$\sum_{c_2,z}\phi_{c_1^*,c_2,z}|c_1^*,c_2,z \oplus \perp\rangle = \sum_{c_2 \neq c_2^*,z}\phi_{c_1^*,c_2,z}|c_1^*,c_2,z \oplus \perp\rangle + \phi_{c_1^*,c_2^*,z}|c_1^*,c_2^*,z \oplus \perp\rangle$$

and $\mathcal{B}$ perfectly simulate the decapsulation oracle.

It is easy to see that $\mathcal{B}$ perfectly simulates Game_3 if $c_1^* = \text{Enc}_1(ek,m^*)$ and Game_4 if $c_1^* \leftarrow \mathcal{S}(ek)$. Therefore, we have

$$|\Pr[\text{Game}_3 = 1] - \Pr[\text{Game}_4 = 1]| \leq \text{Adv}_{\text{PKE}_1,\mathcal{D}_M,\mathcal{S},\mathcal{B}}^{\text{ds-ind}}(\kappa)$$

as wanted. We have $\text{Time}(\mathcal{B}) \approx \text{Time}(\mathcal{A}) + (q_H + q_{H'}) \cdot \text{Time}(\text{Enc}_1) + (q_H + q_{H'} + 2q_{\overline{\text{Dec}}}) \cdot t_{\text{RO}}$, since $\mathcal{B}$ invokes $\mathcal{A}$ once, H is simulated by one evaluation of Enc_1 plus one evaluation of a random oracle, and H' and $\overline{\text{Dec}}'$ are simulated by two evaluations of random oracles. □

Lemma 5.7. *We have*

$$|\Pr[\text{Game}_4 = 1] - 1/2| \leq \text{Disj}_{\text{PKE}_1,\mathcal{S}}(\kappa).$$

Proof. Let Bad denote the event that $c_1^* \in \text{Enc}_1(ek,\mathcal{M})$ happens in Game_4. It is easy to see that we have

$$\Pr[\text{Bad}] \leq \text{Disj}_{\text{PKE}_1,\mathcal{S}}(\kappa).$$

When Bad does not occur, i.e., $c_1^* \notin \text{Enc}_1(ek,\mathcal{M})$, $\mathcal{A}$ obtains no information about $K_0^* = H_q(c_1^*)$. This is because queries to H only reveal $H_q(c)$ for $c \in \text{Enc}_1(ek,\mathcal{M})$, and $\overline{\text{Dec}}'(c)$ returns $\perp$ if $c = c_1^*$. Therefore, we have

$$\Pr[\text{Game}_4 = 1 \mid \overline{\text{Bad}}] = 1/2.$$

Combining the above, we have

$$|\Pr[\text{Game}_4 = 1] - 1/2|$$

$$= \left| \Pr[\text{Bad}] \cdot (\Pr[\text{Game}_4 = 1 \mid \text{Bad}] - 1/2) + \Pr[\overline{\text{Bad}}] \cdot (\Pr[\text{Game}_4 = 1 \mid \overline{\text{Bad}}] - 1/2) \right|$$

$$\le \Pr[\text{Bad}] + \left| \Pr[\text{Game}_4 = 1 \mid \overline{\text{Bad}}] - 1/2 \right|$$

$$\le \text{Disj}_{\text{PKE}_1, \mathcal{S}}(\kappa)$$

as we wanted.   □

Proof (Proof of Theorem 5.1). Combining all lemmas in this section, we obtain the following inequality:

$$\text{Adv}_{\text{KEM}, \mathcal{A}}^{\text{ind-qcca}}(\kappa) = |\Pr[\text{Game}_0 = 1] - 1/2|$$

$$\le |\Pr[\text{Acc}] \cdot \Pr[\text{Game}_0 = 1 \mid \text{Acc}] - 1/2| + \delta$$

$$= |\Pr[\text{Acc}] \cdot \Pr[\text{Game}_1 = 1 \mid \text{Acc}] - 1/2| + \delta$$

$$= |\Pr[\text{Acc}] \cdot \Pr[\text{Game}_2 = 1 \mid \text{Acc}] - 1/2| + \delta$$

$$\le |\Pr[\text{Acc}] \cdot \Pr[\text{Game}_3 = 1 \mid \text{Acc}] - 1/2| + 2q_{\overline{\text{Dec}}} |\mathcal{H}|^{-1/2} + \delta$$

$$\le |\Pr[\text{Game}_3 = 1] - 1/2| + 2q_{\overline{\text{Dec}}} |\mathcal{H}|^{-1/2} + 2\delta$$

$$\le |\Pr[\text{Game}_4 = 1] - 1/2| + \text{Adv}_{\text{PKE}_1, \mathcal{D}_M, \mathcal{S}, \mathcal{B}}^{\text{ds-ind}}(\kappa) + 2q_{\overline{\text{Dec}}} |\mathcal{H}|^{-1/2} + 2\delta$$

$$\le \text{Disj}_{\text{PKE}_1, \mathcal{S}}(\kappa) + \text{Adv}_{\text{PKE}_1, \mathcal{D}_M, \mathcal{S}, \mathcal{B}}^{\text{ds-ind}}(\kappa) + 2q_{\overline{\text{Dec}}} |\mathcal{H}|^{-1/2} + 2\delta.$$

□

Acknowledgments. We would like to thank Haodong Jiang and anonymous reviewers of PQCrypto 2019 for insightful comments.

A   Simple Lemma

Lemma A.1. *For any reals a, b, and c with $c \ge 0$, we have*

$$|a - b - c| \le |a - b| + c.$$

Proof. We consider the three cases below:

– Case $a - b \ge c \ge 0$: In this case, we have $a - b - c \ge 0$. Thus, we have $|a - b - c| = a - b - c \le a - b + c = |a - b| + c$.
– Case $a - b \le 0 \le c$: In this case, we have $a - b - c \le 0$. We have $|a - b - c| = -(a - b - c) = -(a - b) + c = |a - b| + c$.
– Case $0 \le a - b \le c$: Again, we have $a - b - c \le 0$. We have $|a - b - c| = -(a - b - c) = -(a - b) + c \le a - b + c = |a - b| + c$.

In all three cases, we have $|a - b - c| \le |a - b| + c$ as we wanted.   □

References

[ARU14] Ambainis, A., Rosmanis, A., Unruh, D.: Quantum attacks on classical proof systems: the hardness of quantum rewinding. In: 55th FOCS, pp. 474–483. IEEE Computer Society Press, October 2014

[ATTU16] Anand, M.V., Targhi, E.E., Tabia, G.N., Unruh, D.: Post-quantum security of the CBC, CFB, OFB, CTR, and XTS modes of operation. In: Takagi, T. (ed.) PQCrypto 2016. LNCS, vol. 9606, pp. 44–63. Springer, Cham (2016). https://doi.org/10.1007/978-3-319-29360-8_4

[BCHK07] Boneh, D., Canetti, R., Halevi, S., Katz, J.: Chosen-ciphertext security from identity-based encryption. SIAM J. Comput. **36**(5), 1301–1328 (2007)

[BDF+11] Boneh, D., Dagdelen, Ö., Fischlin, M., Lehmann, A., Schaffner, C., Zhandry, M.: Random oracles in a quantum world. In: Lee, D.H., Wang, X. (eds.) ASIACRYPT 2011. LNCS, vol. 7073, pp. 41–69. Springer, Heidelberg (2011). https://doi.org/10.1007/978-3-642-25385-0_3

[BZ13a] Boneh, D., Zhandry, M.: Quantum-secure message authentication codes. In: Johansson, T., Nguyen, P.Q. (eds.) EUROCRYPT 2013. LNCS, vol. 7881, pp. 592–608. Springer, Heidelberg (2013). https://doi.org/10.1007/978-3-642-38348-9_35

[BZ13b] Boneh, D., Zhandry, M.: Secure signatures and chosen ciphertext security in a quantum computing world. In: Canetti, R., Garay, J.A. (eds.) CRYPTO 2013. LNCS, vol. 8043, pp. 361–379. Springer, Heidelberg (2013). https://doi.org/10.1007/978-3-642-40084-1_21

[CJL+16] Chen, L., et al.: Report on post-quantum cryptography. Technical report, National Institute of Standards and Technology (NIST) (2016)

[DFNS14] Damgård, I., Funder, J., Nielsen, J.B., Salvail, L.: Superposition attacks on cryptographic protocols. In: Padró, C. (ed.) ICITS 2013. LNCS, vol. 8317, pp. 142–161. Springer, Cham (2014). https://doi.org/10.1007/978-3-319-04268-8_9

[FO13] Fujisaki, E., Okamoto, T.: Secure integration of asymmetric and symmetric encryption schemes. J. Cryptol. **26**(1), 80–101 (2013)

[GHS16] Gagliardoni, T., Hülsing, A., Schaffner, C.: Semantic security and indistinguishability in the quantum world. In: Robshaw, M., Katz, J. (eds.) CRYPTO 2016. LNCS, vol. 9816, pp. 60–89. Springer, Heidelberg (2016). https://doi.org/10.1007/978-3-662-53015-3_3

[Gro96] Grover, L.K.: A fast quantum mechanical algorithm for database search. In: 28th ACM STOC, pp. 212–219. ACM Press, May 1996

[HHK17] Hofheinz, D., Hövelmanns, K., Kiltz, E.: A modular analysis of the Fujisaki-Okamoto transformation. In: Kalai, Y., Reyzin, L. (eds.) TCC 2017. LNCS, vol. 10677, pp. 341–371. Springer, Cham (2017). https://doi.org/10.1007/978-3-319-70500-2_12

[HRS16] Hülsing, A., Rijneveld, J., Song, F.: Mitigating multi-target attacks in hash-based signatures. In: Cheng, C.-M., Chung, K.-M., Persiano, G., Yang, B.-Y. (eds.) PKC 2016. LNCS, vol. 9614, pp. 387–416. Springer, Heidelberg (2016). https://doi.org/10.1007/978-3-662-49384-7_15

[JZC+18] Jiang, H., Zhang, Z., Chen, L., Wang, H., Ma, Z.: IND-CCA-secure key encapsulation mechanism in the quantum random oracle model, revisited. In: Shacham, H., Boldyreva, A. (eds.) CRYPTO 2018. LNCS, vol. 10993, pp. 96–125. Springer, Cham (2018). https://doi.org/10.1007/978-3-319-96878-0_4

[JZM19]   Jiang, H., Zhang, Z., Ma, Z.: Key encapsulation mechanism with explicit rejection in the quantum random oracle model. In: Lin, D., Sako, K. (eds.) PKC 2019. LNCS, vol. 11443, pp. 618–645. Springer, Cham (2019). https://doi.org/10.1007/978-3-030-17259-6_21

[KLLN16] Kaplan, M., Leurent, G., Leverrier, A., Naya-Plasencia, M.: Breaking symmetric cryptosystems using quantum period finding. In: Robshaw, M., Katz, J. (eds.) CRYPTO 2016. LNCS, vol. 9815, pp. 207–237. Springer, Heidelberg (2016). https://doi.org/10.1007/978-3-662-53008-5_8

[KLS18]   Kiltz, E., Lyubashevsky, V., Schaffner, C.: A concrete treatment of fiat-shamir signatures in the quantum random-oracle model. In: Nielsen, J.B., Rijmen, V. (eds.) EUROCRYPT 2018. LNCS, vol. 10822, pp. 552–586. Springer, Cham (2018). https://doi.org/10.1007/978-3-319-78372-7_18

[KM12]   Kuwakado, H., Morii, M.: Security on the quantum-type even-mansour cipher. In: Proceedings of the International Symposium on Information Theory and its Applications, ISITA 2012, Honolulu, HI, USA, 28–31 October 2012, pp. 312–316. IEEE (2012)

[NC00]   Nielsen, M.A., Chuang, I.L.: Quantum Computation and Quantum Information. Cambridge University Press, Cambridge (2000)

[Sho97]   Shor, P.W.: Polynomial-time algorithms for prime factorization and discrete logarithms on a quantum computer. SIAM J. Comput. 26(5), 1484–1509 (1997)

[Sim97]   Simon, D.R.: On the power of quantum computation. SIAM J. Comput. 26(5), 1474–1483 (1997)

[SXY18]   Saito, T., Xagawa, K., Yamakawa, T.: Tightly-secure key-encapsulation mechanism in the quantum random oracle model. In: Nielsen, J.B., Rijmen, V. (eds.) EUROCRYPT 2018. LNCS, vol. 10822, pp. 520–551. Springer, Cham (2018). https://doi.org/10.1007/978-3-319-78372-7_17

[Zha12]   Zhandry, M.: Secure identity-based encryption in the quantum random oracle model. In: Safavi-Naini, R., Canetti, R. (eds.) CRYPTO 2012. LNCS, vol. 7417, pp. 758–775. Springer, Heidelberg (2012). https://doi.org/10.1007/978-3-642-32009-5_44

[Zha18]   Zhandry, M.: How to record quantum queries, and applications to quantum indifferentiability. Cryptology ePrint Archive, Report 2018/276 (2018). https://eprint.iacr.org/2018/276

Isogeny-Based Cryptography

Faster SeaSign Signatures Through Improved Rejection Sampling

Thomas Decru[1](✉), Lorenz Panny[2], and Frederik Vercauteren[1]

[1] imec-COSIC, ESAT, KU Leuven, Leuven, Belgium
{thomas.decru,frederik.vercauteren}@kuleuven.be
[2] Department of Mathematics and Computer Science,
Technische Universiteit Eindhoven, Eindhoven, The Netherlands
lorenz@yx7.cc

Abstract. We speed up the isogeny-based "SeaSign" signature scheme recently proposed by De Feo and Galbraith. The core idea in SeaSign is to apply the "Fiat–Shamir with aborts" transform to the parallel repeated execution of an identification scheme based on CSIDH. We optimize this general transform by allowing the prover to *not* answer a limited number of said parallel executions, thereby lowering the overall probability of rejection. The performance improvement ranges between factors of approximately 4.4 and 65.7 for various instantiations of the scheme, at the expense of roughly doubling the signature sizes.

Keywords: Isogeny-based cryptography · Signatures · SeaSign ·
Rejection sampling · Group actions

1 Introduction

Elliptic curves have become a staple in various cryptographic applications in the past decades. In 1994, however, it was pointed out by Shor that a quantum computer could solve the *Discrete Logarithm Problem* (DLP), which is the core hardness assumption in elliptic-curve cryptography, in polynomial time [12]. For that reason, some of the recent research has shifted towards isogeny-based cryptography. In essence, the underlying mathematical problem is to find an isogeny between two given elliptic curves over a finite field. According to current knowledge, this problem can generally be assumed to be hard, even with the possible advent of quantum computers in mind.

The first instances of isogeny-based cryptosystems were proposed by Couveignes in 1997 [2], including a non-interactive key exchange protocol. His paper

Author list in alphabetical order; see https://www.ams.org/profession/leaders/culture/CultureStatement04.pdf. This work was supported in part by the Commission of the European Communities through the Horizon 2020 program under project number 643161 (ECRYPT-NET) and in part by the Research Council KU Leuven grants C14/18/067 and STG/17/019. Date of this document: 2019.01.24.

J. Ding and R. Steinwandt (Eds.): PQCrypto 2019, LNCS 11505, pp. 271–285, 2019.
https://doi.org/10.1007/978-3-030-25510-7_15

was not published at that time, and the idea was independently rediscovered in 2006 by Rostovtsev and Stolbunov [11]. More recently, Jao and De Feo proposed the so-called *Supersingular Isogeny Diffie–Hellman* (SIDH) scheme in 2011 [7]. This key-exchange protocol is the basis for SIKE [6], which was submitted to the post-quantum standardization project led by NIST [10]. SIDH is inherently different from the scheme of Couveignes and Rostovtsev–Stolbunov, mostly due to the fact that the endomorphism rings of supersingular elliptic curves are noncommutative. However, in 2018, Castryck, Lange, Martindale, Panny and Renes adapted the Couveignes–Rostovtsev–Stolbunov scheme to supersingular elliptic curves, which yields big efficiency improvements, and named the resulting protocol "CSIDH" [1]. In essence, this variation is made possible by restricting the family of curves under consideration to supersingular elliptic curves *defined over* $\mathbb{F}_p$ instead of $\mathbb{F}_{p^2}$.

CSIDH's small key sizes prompted De Feo and Galbraith to transform it into a signature scheme called *SeaSign* in the same year [4]. The construction uses the *Fiat–Shamir with aborts* framework, a technique commonly used in lattice-based cryptography [8], together with an isogeny-based identification scheme going back to Couveignes [2] and Rostovtsev–Stolbunov [11]. Their paper presents three different versions of SeaSign featuring various trade-offs between signature size, public-key size, and secret-key size. One of these versions attains 128 bits of security with signatures of less than one kilobyte. An issue impacting all of these schemes, however, is that the signing and verification times are rather substantial. Indeed, the basic SeaSign scheme takes (on average) almost two days to sign a message on a typical CPU, whereas the variants with smaller signatures or public keys still take almost ten minutes to sign (on average).

In this paper we tackle this performance issue in the more general setting of using group actions in a "Fiat–Shamir with aborts" scheme. We first discuss two (unfortunately mutually exclusive) adjustments that reduce the likelihood of rejections, which decreases the expected number of failed signing attempts before a success and hence makes signing more efficient. Next, we describe a modification that significantly speeds up the signing process at the cost of a small increase in signature size. The basic idea is to allow the prover to refuse answering a small fixed number of challenges, thereby reducing the overall probability of aborting. To attain a given security level, the total number of challenges—and correspondingly the signature size—will be somewhat larger than for standard Fiat–Shamir with aborts. As an application of these general techniques, we analyze the resulting speed-up for the various versions of the SeaSign signature scheme. The improvement is most noticeable when applied to the basic scheme: the original signing cost goes down from almost two days to just over half an hour. The other two, more advanced variants are still sped up by a factor of four to roughly two minutes per signature. Even though this is still too slow for most (if not all) applications, it is a significant improvement over the state of the art, and the underlying ideas of these speed-ups might be useful for other cryptographic schemes as well.

1.1   Notation

The notation $[a; b]$ denotes the integer range $\{a, ..., b\}$.

Fix $n \geq 1$. Throughout, we will consider a transitive action of the abelian group $\mathbb{Z}^n$ on a finite set X, with a fixed element $E_0 \in X$. We will assume that "short" vectors in $\mathbb{Z}^n$ are enough to reach "almost all" elements of X.[1] Moreover, we assume that the cost of computing the action $[\mathbf{v}]E$ of a vector $\mathbf{v} \in \mathbb{Z}^n$ on an element $E \in X$ is linear in the 1-norm $\|\mathbf{v}\|_1 = \sum_{j=1}^{n} |v_j|$ of $\mathbf{v}$. (We will argue in Sect. 2.1 that these assumptions are satisfied in the CSIDH setting.)

2   Preliminaries

A good introductory reference for the applications of elliptic-curve isogenies in cryptography are the lecture notes by De Feo [3].

2.1   CSIDH

Consider a supersingular elliptic curve E defined over $\mathbb{F}_p$, where p is a large prime. While the endomorphism ring $\mathrm{End}(E)$ of E over the algebraic closure of $\mathbb{F}_p$ is noncommutative, the ring $\mathrm{End}_{\mathbb{F}_p}(E)$ of endomorphisms defined over $\mathbb{F}_p$ is an order $\mathcal{O}$ in the imaginary quadratic field $\mathbb{Q}(\sqrt{-p})$.

The ideal class group of $\mathrm{End}_{\mathbb{F}_p}(E) = \mathcal{O}$ is the quotient of the group of fractional invertible ideals in $\mathcal{O}$ by the principal fractional invertible ideals in $\mathcal{O}$, and will be denoted $\mathrm{cl}(\mathcal{O})$. The group $\mathrm{cl}(\mathcal{O})$ acts on the set of $\mathbb{F}_p$-isomorphism classes of elliptic curves with $\mathbb{F}_p$-rational endomorphism ring $\mathcal{O}$ through isogenies. More specifically, when given an $\mathcal{O}$-ideal $\mathfrak{a}$ and an elliptic curve E with $\mathrm{End}_{\mathbb{F}_p}(E) = \mathcal{O}$, we define $[\mathfrak{a}]E$ as the codomain of the isogeny $\varphi_{\mathfrak{a}} \colon E \to E/\mathfrak{a}$ whose kernel is $\bigcap_{\alpha \in \mathfrak{a}} \ker \alpha$. This isogeny is well-defined and unique up to $\mathbb{F}_p$-isomorphism.

There are formulas for computing $[\mathfrak{a}]E$. However, for general $\mathfrak{a}$, this computation requires large field extensions and hence has superpolynomial time complexity. To avoid this, CSIDH restricts to ideals of the form $\mathfrak{a} = \prod_{i=1}^{n} \mathfrak{l}_i^{e_i}$, where all $\mathfrak{l}_i$ are prime ideals of small norm ℓ_i, and such that the action of $\mathfrak{l}_i$ can be computed entirely over the base field $\mathbb{F}_p$. The curve $[\mathfrak{a}]E$ can then be computed by chaining isogenies of degrees ℓ_i. In principle the cost of computing the action of $\mathfrak{l}_i$ is in $\Theta(\ell_i)$, but for small values of ℓ_i it is dominated by a full-size scalar multiplication, which is why assuming cost $|e_1| + \cdots + |e_n|$ for computing the action of $\prod_{i=1}^{n} \mathfrak{l}_i^{e_i}$, as mentioned in Sect. 1.1, comes close to the truth. (Moreover, in our setting, the $|e_i|$ are all identically distributed, hence the differences in costs between various ℓ_i disappear on average.)

The CSIDH group action is defined as follows.

---

[1] In other words: The action of $\mathbb{Z}^n$ on X factors through the quotient $Q = \mathbb{Z}^n/S$, where $S \leq \mathbb{Z}^n$ is the stabilizer of any $E \in X$, and we assume that Q is "sufficiently" covered by "short" vectors in $\mathbb{Z}^n$ under the quotient map $\mathbb{Z}^n \twoheadrightarrow Q$.

Parameters. Integers $n \geq 1$, $B \geq 0$. A prime p of the form $4 \cdot \ell_1 \cdots \ell_n - 1$, with ℓ_i small distinct odd primes. The elliptic curve $E_0 \colon y^2 = x^3 + x$ over $\mathbb{F}_p$. Write X for the set of ($\mathbb{F}_p$-isomorphism classes of) elliptic curves over $\mathbb{F}_p$ with $\mathrm{End}_{\mathbb{F}_p}(E) = \mathcal{O} = \mathbb{Z}[\pi]$, where π is the $\mathbb{F}_p$-Frobenius endomorphism.

Group Action. A group element is represented[2] by a vector $(e_1, ..., e_n) \in \mathbb{Z}^n$ sampled uniformly random from $[-B; B]^n$, which defines the ideal $\mathfrak{a} = \prod_{i=1}^{n} \mathfrak{l}_i^{e_i}$ with $\mathfrak{l}_i = \langle \ell_i, \pi-1 \rangle$. A public element is represented by a single coefficient $A \in \mathbb{F}_p$, describing the curve $E_A \colon y^2 = x^3 + Ax^2 + x$. The result of the action of an ideal $\mathfrak{a}$ on a public element $A \in \mathbb{F}_p$, assuming that E_A has the right endomorphism ring $\mathcal{O}$, is the coefficient B of the curve $[\mathfrak{a}]E_A \colon y^2 = x^3 + Bx^2 + x$.

The security assumption of the group action is that it is essentially a black-box version of the group $\mathrm{cl}(\mathcal{O})$ on which anyone can efficiently act by translations. In particular, given two elliptic curves $E, E' \in X$, it should be hard to find an ideal $\mathfrak{a}$ of $\mathcal{O}$ such that $E' = [\mathfrak{a}]E$.

Notice that it is not clear in general that the vectors in $[-B; B]^n$ cover the whole group, or even a "large" fraction. Unfortunately, sampling uniformly random from $\mathrm{cl}(\mathcal{O})$ is infeasible for large enough parameters, since there is no known efficient way to compute the structure of $\mathrm{cl}(\mathcal{O})$ in that case. In fact, knowing the exact class group structure would be sufficient to obtain much more efficient signatures, since no rejection sampling would be required [4]. Under the right assumptions however, the elements represented by vectors in $[-B; B]^n$ are likely to cover a large fraction of the group as long as $(2B + 1)^n \geq \#\mathrm{cl}(\mathcal{O})$. The values suggested for (n, B) in [1] are $(74, 5)$, which aim to cover a group of size approximately 2^{256}. This results in group elements of 32 bytes, public elements of 64 bytes, and a performance of about 40 ms per group action computation. For more details, see [1].

As stated in Sect. 1.1, we will from now on abstract away the underlying isogeny-based constructions and work in the setting of the group $(\mathbb{Z}^n, +)$ acting on a finite set X.

2.2 SeaSign

SeaSign [4] is a signature scheme based on a sketch of an isogeny-based identification scheme by Couveignes [2] and Stolbunov [13], in combination with the "Fiat–Shamir with aborts" construction [8] from lattice-based cryptography to avoid leakage. The identification part of SeaSign works as follows. Note that our exposition differs from [4] for consistency with the following sections.

Parameters. Like CSIDH, and additionally integers $\delta \geq 1$ and $S \geq 2$.[3]

---

[2] Note this representation matches the assumptions in Sect. 1.1.

[3] Technically there is no reason for δ to be an integer: it is sufficient that $\delta \in \frac{1}{B} \cdot \mathbb{Z}$, but we will assume $\delta \in \mathbb{Z}$ throughout for simplicity.

Keys. Alice's private key is a list $\underline{a} = (a^{(1)}, ..., a^{(S-1)})$ of $S - 1$ vectors sampled uniformly random from $[-B; B]^n \subseteq \mathbb{Z}^n$.

For $i \in \{1, ..., S - 1\}$, write $E_i := [a^{(i)}]E_0$, that is, the result of applying the group element represented by $a^{(i)} \in \mathbb{Z}^n$; then Alice's public key is the list $[\underline{a}]E_0 := (E_1, ..., E_{S-1})$ of her secret vectors applied to the starting element E_0.

This situation is summarized in Fig. 1.

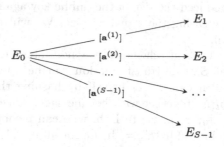

Fig. 1. Structure of Alice's key pair.

Identification. Alice samples an ephemeral vector b uniformly random from the set $[-(\delta+1)B; (\delta+1)B]^n \subseteq \mathbb{Z}^n$. She then computes $E = [b]E_0$ and commits to E. On challenge $c \in \{0, ..., S - 1\}$, she computes $r = b - a^{(c)}$ (where $a^{(0)}$ is defined as 0). If $r \in [-\delta B; \delta B]^n$, she reveals r; else she rejects the challenge. Bob verifies that $[r]E_c = E$.

See Fig. 2 for a visual representation of this protocol.

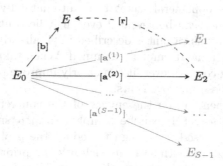

Fig. 2. The identification scheme in the scenario $c = 2$.

Since an attacker (who cannot break the underlying isogeny problems) has a $1/S$ chance of winning, this identification scheme provides $\log_2 S$ bits of security. In order to amplify the security level, Alice typically computes $t \geq 1$ independent vectors $b_1, ..., b_t$ instead of just one. The verifier responds with t challenges $c_1, ..., c_t \in \{0, ..., S - 1\}$. Alice then computes $r_i = b_i - a^{(c_i)}$ for all $1 \leq i \leq t$ and reveals them if all of them are in $[-\delta B; \delta B]^n$; else she rejects the challenge. In order to not have to reject too often, δ must be rather large; more specifically, δ was chosen as nt in [4] to achieve a success probability of roughly $1/e$.

As mentioned in the introduction, [4] gives three SeaSign constructions. The original idea is the scheme above with $S = 2$, i.e., the public key is a single public element. This results in a large t and therefore a very large signature. The second scheme lets the number of private keys S range from 2 up to 2^{16}, which results in smaller, faster signatures at the expense of larger public-key sizes.[4]

The final scheme reduced the size of the public key again by using a Merkle tree, at the cost of increasing the signature size. We will not elaborate on all those variants in detail.

To turn this identification scheme into a non-interactive signature protocol, the standard Fiat–Shamir transformation can be applied [5]. In essence, Alice obtains the challenges $c_1, ..., c_t$ herself by hashing the ephemeral public elements $[\mathbf{b}_1]E_0, ..., [\mathbf{b}_t]E_0$ together with her message. Alice then sends her signature $([\mathbf{b}_1]E_0, ..., [\mathbf{b}_t]E_0; \mathbf{r}_1, ..., \mathbf{r}_t)$ to Bob, who can recompute the challenges $c_1, ..., c_t$ to verify that indeed $[\mathbf{r}_i]E_{c_i} = [\mathbf{b}_i]E_0$ for all $i \in \{1, ..., t\}$.

3   The Improved Signature Scheme

In this section we describe our improvements.

3.1   Core Ideas

1. The first improvement is minor (but still significant) and concerns the identification scheme itself: the following observations result in two variants of the scheme that are more efficient than the basic scheme.[5]
   - Variant $\mathcal{F}$: The ephemeral secret $\mathbf{b}$ is automatically independent of all secrets $\mathbf{a}^{(i)}$, hence can be revealed even if it lies outside of $[-\delta B; \delta B]^n$. We remark that this variant is described in [4] already but disregarded as only a single signing attempt is examined. When taking into account the average signing cost however, it can clearly improve performance, and we will quantify these improvements.
   - Variant $\mathcal{T}$: Depending on the entries of the concrete private keys $\mathbf{a}^{(i)}$, the ephemeral secret $\mathbf{b}$ can be sampled from a smaller set than the worst-case range used in SeaSign to reduce the probability of rejection. Indeed, although the j-th entry in each $\mathbf{a}^{(i)}$ is a priori sampled uniformly in $[-B; B]$, which gives rise to the interval $[-(\delta + 1)B; (\delta + 1)B]$ for the j-th coefficient of each ephemeral vector $\mathbf{b}$, it is obviously useless (since it will *always* be rejected) to sample the j-th coefficient outside the interval $[-\delta B + m_j; \delta B + M_j]$ with $m_j = \min\{0, a_j^{(1)}, ..., a_j^{(S-1)}\}$ and $M_j = \max\{0, a_j^{(1)}, ..., a_j^{(S-1)}\}$.

---

[4] In [4], S is always a power of 2, but any $S \geq 2$ works.
[5] The acronyms $\mathcal{F}$ and $\mathcal{T}$ refer to "**f**ull" and "**t**runcated" ranges, respectively.

It is clear that Variant $\mathcal{F}$ and Variant $\mathcal{T}$ are mutually exclusive: in Variant $\mathcal{T}$ the ephemeral secret $\mathbf{b}$ is sampled from a set that is dependent on the private keys $\mathbf{a}^{(i)}$, whereas for Variant $\mathcal{F}$ to work it is required that this sampling is done completely independently.

2. The second improvement is more significant and modifies the "Fiat–Shamir with aborts" transform as follows: assume the identification scheme uses s-bit challenges (corresponding to a probability of 2^{-s} that an attacker can cheat), and that each execution has probability of rejection ε. The SeaSign approach to attain security level λ is to simultaneously obtain $t = \lceil \lambda/s \rceil$ non-rejected executions of the identification protocol which happens with probability $(1 - \varepsilon)^t$. Our approach increases the total number of challenges, but allows the prover to refuse answering a fixed number u of them, since this tolerates much higher rejection probabilities at the cost of a relatively small increase in public-key and signature size.

We now provide more details on each of the above ideas.

3.2 Identification Scheme

Parameters. Integers $S \geq 2$ and $\delta \geq 1$.

Keys. Like in SeaSign (Sect. 2.2).

Identification. Using Alice's key pair $(\underline{\mathbf{a}}, [\underline{\mathbf{a}}]E_0)$, a $(\log_2 S)$-bit identification protocol can be constructed as follows:

Variant $\mathcal{F}$	Variant $\mathcal{T}$
Alice samples a vector $\mathbf{b}$ uniformly random from the set ...	
$I = \left[-(\delta+1)B; (\delta+1)B \right]^n \subseteq \mathbb{Z}^n$.	$I = \prod\limits_{j=1}^{n} \left[-\delta B + m_j; \delta B + M_j \right] \subseteq \mathbb{Z}^n$, where $m_j = \min\{0, a_j^{(1)}, ..., a_j^{(S-1)}\}$; $M_j = \max\{0, a_j^{(1)}, ..., a_j^{(S-1)}\}$.
She then computes $E = [\mathbf{b}]E_0$ and commits to E. On challenge $c \in \{0, ..., S-1\}$, she computes $\mathbf{r} = \mathbf{b} - \mathbf{a}^{(c)}$ (where $\mathbf{a}^{(0)}$ is defined as $\mathbf{0}$).	
If $c = 0$ or $\mathbf{r} \in [-\delta B; \delta B]^n$,	If $\mathbf{r} \in [-\delta B; \delta B]^n$, ...
... then she reveals $\mathbf{r}$; else she rejects the challenge. Bob verifies that $[\mathbf{r}]E_c = E$.	

Lemma 1. *The distribution of __revealed__ vectors $\mathbf{r}$ is independent of $\mathbf{a}^{(c)}$.*

Proof. This is trivial in Variant $\mathcal{F}$ in the event $c = 0$. For the other cases, note that I is constructed such that $\mathbf{r} = \mathbf{b} - \mathbf{a}^{(c)}$ is uniformly distributed on a set containing $\Delta := [-\delta B; \delta B]^n$, no matter what $\mathbf{a}^{(c)}$ is. Therefore, the distribution of $\mathbf{r}$ conditioned on the event $\mathbf{r} \in \Delta$ is uniform on Δ independently of $\mathbf{a}^{(c)}$.   □

Remark 1. Lemma 1 only talks about the conditional distribution of $\mathbf{r}$ *if* it is revealed. Note that in Variant $\mathcal{T}$, the probability *that* it can be revealed is still correlated to the entries of $\mathbf{a}^{(c)}$, which may have security implications. We show in Sect. 3.3 how to get around this issue in a signature scheme.

3.3   Signature Scheme

Our improved signature scheme is essentially the "Fiat–Shamir with aborts" construction also used in SeaSign (see Sect. 2.2), except that we allow the signer to reject a few challenges in each signature. The resulting scheme is parameterized by two integers $t \geq 0$, denoting the number of challenges the signer must answer correctly, and $u \geq 0$, the number of challenges she may additionally refuse to answer.

Write ID for (one of the variants of) the identification scheme in Sect. 3.2.

Keys. Alice's identity key consists of a key pair $(\underline{\mathbf{a}}, [\mathbf{a}]E_0)$ as in ID.

Signing. To sign a message m, Alice first generates a list $\mathbf{b}_1, ..., \mathbf{b}_{t+u}$ of random vectors, each sampled as the vector $\mathbf{b}$ in ID. She computes the corresponding public elements $[\mathbf{b}_1]E_0, ..., [\mathbf{b}_{t+u}]E_0$ and hashes them together with the message m to obtain a list of challenges $c_1, ..., c_{t+u} \in \{0, ..., S - 1\}$. To produce her signature, she then traverses the tuples $(\mathbf{b}_i, c_i)$ in a random order, computing the correct response $\mathbf{r}_i = \mathbf{b}_i - \mathbf{a}^{(c_i)}$ (as in ID) if possible and a rejection ✗ otherwise. Once t successful responses have been generated, the remaining challenges are all rejected in order not to leak any information about the rejection probability; cf. Remark 1.[6] Finally, the signature is

$$([\mathbf{b}_1]E_0, ..., [\mathbf{b}_{t+u}]E_0; \ \mathbf{r}_1, ..., \mathbf{r}_{t+u}),$$

where exactly u of the $\mathbf{r}_i$ equal ✗. (If less than t challenges could be answered, Alice aborts and retries the whole signing process with new values of $\mathbf{b}_i$.)

Verification. This again is standard: Bob first checks that at most u of the $t + u$ values $\mathbf{r}_i$ are ✗. He then recomputes the challenges $c_1, ..., c_{t+u}$ by hashing the message m together with the ephemeral elements $[\mathbf{b}_i]E_0$ and verifies that $[\mathbf{r}_i]E_{c_i} = [\mathbf{b}_i]E_0$ for all $i \in \{1, ..., t + u\}$ with $\mathbf{r}_i \neq$ ✗.

---

[6] This is why the tuples are processed in a random order: Proceeding sequentially and rejecting the remaining tail still leaks, since the number of ✗ at the end would be correlated to the rejection probability.

Remark 2. The signatures can be shortened further: Sending those $[\mathbf{b}_i]E_0$ with $\mathbf{r}_i \neq \boldsymbol{X}$ is wasteful. It is enough to send the hash H of all ephemeral elements $[\mathbf{b}_i]E_0$ instead, since Bob can extract c_i from H, recompute $[\mathbf{b}_i]E_0$ as $[\mathbf{r}_i]E_{c_i}$, and verify in the end that the hash H was indeed correct.

Remark 3. As mentioned earlier, one can reduce the public-key size by using a Merkle tree, but this does not significantly alter the computation time for any part of the protocol. Given that the main focus of our adjustments to SeaSign is speeding it up, we will therefore not investigate this avenue any further.

Security. The proof for the security for this scheme is completely analogous to the original SeaSign scheme. This follows from Lemma 1 and the fact that there are always a fixed number u of $\boldsymbol{X}$ per signature in random positions. Instead of reproducing the proof here, we refer the reader to [4].

4 Analysis and Results

In order to quantify our speed-ups compared to the original SeaSign scheme, we analyze our adjustments in the same context as [4]. This means that $(n, B) = (74, 5)$ and $\log_2 p \approx 512$. Furthermore we will require 128 bits of security and will let S range through powers of two between 2 and 2^{16}.

As mentioned before, Variant $\mathcal{F}$ and Variant $\mathcal{T}$ are mutually exclusive. For this reason, we computed the results for both cases to compare which performs better under given conditions. Variant $\mathcal{T}$ clearly converges to the original SeaSign scheme rapidly for growing S, while Variant $\mathcal{F}$ always keeps at least a little bit of advantage. It is clear that from a certain value of S onward, Variant $\mathcal{F}$ will always be better. For small S however, Variant $\mathcal{T}$ will outperform Variant $\mathcal{F}$ rather significantly for average-case key vectors.

We now discuss how to optimize the parameters (t, u, δ) for a given S. The main cost metric is the *expected* signing time[7]

$$\delta \cdot (t + u)/q,$$

where q is the probability of a full signing attempt being successful (i.e., at most u rejections $\boldsymbol{X}$). This optimization problem depends on two random variables:

- The number Z of challenges that an *attacker* can successfully answer even though he cannot break the underlying isogeny problems.
- The number A of challenges that *Alice* can answer without leaking, i.e., the number of non-rejected challenges.

---

[7] Other optimizations could look at the sum of signing and verification time, or even take into account key generation time, but we will not delve into those options.

Since the $t + u$ challenges are independent, both Z and A are binomially distributed with count $t + u$. Let $T_{k,\alpha}$ denote the tail cumulative distribution function of $\text{Bin}_{k,\alpha}$, i.e.,

$$T_{k,\alpha}(x) = \sum_{i=x}^{k} \binom{k}{i} \alpha^i (1 - \alpha)^{k-i},$$

which is the probability that a $\text{Bin}_{k,\alpha}$-distributed variable attains a value of at least x. The success probability for an attacker is $1/S$, since he knows the correct answer to at most one of S challenges c. In order to achieve 128 bits of security, it is required that

$$\Pr[Z \geq t] = T_{t+u,1/S}(t) \leq 2^{-128}.$$

This condition implies that for fixed S and t, there is a maximal value $u_{max}(t)$ for u, the number of allowed rejections ✗, regardless of δ.

Let $\sigma(\delta)$ denote Alice's probability of being able to answer (i.e., not reject ✗) a single challenge for a given value of δ; hence $A \sim \text{Bin}_{t+u,\sigma(\delta)}$. In order to find the optimal (u, δ) for a given t, we need to minimize the expression

$$\delta \cdot (t + u)/q(t, u, \delta),$$

where

$$q(t, u, \delta) = \Pr[A \geq t] = T_{t+u,\sigma(\delta)}(t)$$

is the probability of a full signing attempt being successful. The function σ depends on the variant ($\mathcal{F}$ or $\mathcal{T}$). In case of Variant $\mathcal{F}$ we have

$$\sigma(\delta) = \frac{1}{S} + \frac{S-1}{S} \left(\frac{2\delta B + 1}{2(\delta + 1)B + 1} \right)^n.$$

For Variant $\mathcal{T}$, the function depends on the private keys in use. With fixed private keys $a^{(1)}, ..., a^{(S-1)}$ and the notation $m_j = \min\{0, a_j^{(1)}, ..., a_j^{(S-1)}\}$ and $M_j = \max\{0, a_j^{(1)}, ..., a_j^{(S-1)}\}$ as before, the formula becomes

$$\sigma(\delta) = \prod_{j=1}^{n} \frac{2\delta B + 1}{2\delta B + 1 - m_j + M_j}.$$

For our analysis we work with the expected probability over all possible keys.

Our results for the optimization problem can be found in Table 1. The sage [14] code that computes these values can be found in Appendix A; it takes about twelve minutes on a single core. We are quite confident that the values in Table 1 are optimal, but cannot strictly claim so since we have not *proven* that the conditions used in the script to terminate the search capture all optimal values, although this seems reasonable to assume.

There are two major differences in the way we present our data compared to [4]. First of all, we list the *expected* signing time instead of a single signing *attempt*, which represents the real cost more accurately. Second, we express the time in equivalents of "normal" CSIDH operations instead of in wall-clock time,

Table 1. Parameters for our improved SeaSign variants, optimizing for signing time. All of these choices provide ≥ 128 bits of security (of course assuming that the underlying isogeny problems are hard). Gray lines with variant "—" refer to the original parameter selection methodology suggested in [4]. The signature sizes make use of the observation in Remark 2. The "CSIDHs" columns express the computational load in terms of equivalents of a "normal" CSIDH operation, i.e., with exponents in $[-B; B]^n$, making use of the assumption that the cost is linear in the 1-norm of the input vector. Using current implementations [1,9], computing one "CSIDH"-512 takes approximately 40 ms of wall-clock time on a standard processor. Finally, the rightmost column shows the speed-up in signing and verification times compared to the original SeaSign scheme.

S	t	u	δ	Var.	Public-key bytes	Signature bytes	Expected signing attempts	Expected signing CSIDHs	Expected verifying CSIDHs	Speed-up factors
2^1	128	0	9472	—	64 b	19600 b	2.718	3295480	1212416	
2^1	337	79	114	$\mathcal{T}$	64 b	36838 b	1.058	50175	38418	65.7 | 31.6
2^2	64	0	4736	—	192 b	9216 b	2.718	823818	303104	
2^2	144	68	133	$\mathcal{T}$	192 b	18256 b	1.063	29962	19152	27.5 | 15.8
2^3	43	0	3182	—	448 b	5967 b	2.718	371862	136826	
2^3	83	56	141	$\mathcal{T}$	448 b	11695 b	1.078	21119	11703	17.6 | 11.7
2^4	32	0	2368	—	960 b	4320 b	2.718	205928	75776	
2^4	59	58	119	$\mathcal{F}$	960 b	9376 b	1.076	14985	7021	13.7 | 10.8
2^5	26	0	1924	—	1984 b	3442 b	2.717	135937	50024	
2^5	43	50	111	$\mathcal{F}$	1984 b	7301 b	1.085	11198	4773	12.1 | 10.5
2^6	22	0	1628	—	4032 b	2866 b	2.717	97322	35816	
2^6	33	42	108	$\mathcal{F}$	4032 b	5835 b	1.089	8824	3564	11.0 | 10.0
2^7	19	0	1406	—	8128 b	2440 b	2.717	72585	26714	
2^7	26	32	113	$\mathcal{F}$	8128 b	4550 b	1.107	7254	2938	10.0 | 9.1
2^8	16	0	1184	—	16320 b	2020 b	2.717	51469	18944	
2^8	22	30	106	$\mathcal{F}$	16320 b	4028 b	1.114	6139	2332	8.4 | 8.1
2^9	15	0	1110	—	32704 b	1883 b	2.717	45235	16650	
2^9	19	28	101	$\mathcal{F}$	32704 b	3609 b	1.121	5321	1919	8.5 | 8.7
2^{10}	13	0	962	—	65472 b	1609 b	2.717	33974	12506	
2^{10}	17	31	88	$\mathcal{F}$	65472 b	3593 b	1.113	4703	1496	7.2 | 8.4
2^{11}	12	0	888	—	131008 b	1473 b	2.716	28946	10656	
2^{11}	15	27	89	$\mathcal{F}$	131008 b	3155 b	1.126	4208	1335	6.9 | 8.0
2^{12}	11	0	814	—	262080 b	1340 b	2.716	24322	8954	
2^{12}	13	18	106	$\mathcal{F}$	262080 b	2413 b	1.165	3828	1378	6.4 | 6.5
2^{13}	10	0	740	—	524224 b	1207 b	2.716	20099	7400	
2^{13}	12	20	94	$\mathcal{F}$	524224 b	2436 b	1.153	3467	1128	5.8 | 6.6
2^{14}	10	0	740	—	1048512 b	1208 b	2.716	20099	7400	
2^{14}	11	19	92	$\mathcal{F}$	1048512 b	2276 b	1.157	3193	1012	6.3 | 7.3
2^{15}	9	0	666	—	2097088 b	1075 b	2.716	16279	5994	
2^{15}	10	15	100	$\mathcal{F}$	2097088 b	1934 b	1.191	2977	1000	5.5 | 6.0
2^{16}	8	0	592	—	4194240 b	944 b	2.716	12861	4736	
2^{16}	10	22	79	$\mathcal{F}$	4194240 b	2369 b	1.147	2898	790	4.4 | 6.0

which makes the results independent of a concrete choice of CSIDH implementation and eases comparison with other work.

Unsurprisingly, the biggest speed-up can be seen for the basic SeaSign scheme (i.e., $S = 2$), since that is where the largest δ could be found. The expected signing time is reduced by a factor of 65, whereas verification is sped up by a factor of roughly 31, at the cost of doubling the signature size. As predicted, Variant $\mathcal{F}$ outperforms Variant $\mathcal{T}$ from a certain point onward, which apparently is for $S \geq 2^4$. The case $S = 2^{16}$ gains a factor of 4.4 in the expected signing time and 6.0 in verification time. Note though that it only has 2.7% faster signing and 21% faster verification than the case $S = 2^{15}$ (which uses public keys half as big), which further emphasizes the importance of choosing the right trade-offs. Perhaps unsurprisingly, taking $u = u_{max}(t)$ often gives the best (expected) signing times, although this is not always the case: for instance, for $S = 2^{16}$ we have $u_{max}(10) = 29$, but $u = 22$ with a bigger δ yields (slightly) better results.

Acknowledgements. We are thankful to Steven Galbraith for his observation about shorter signatures in Remark 2, and to Taechan Kim for pointing out an error in an earlier version of the script in Appendix A.

A   Script for Table 1

```
#!/usr/bin/env sage
RR = RealField(1000)

secbits = 128
pbits = 512
csidhn, csidhB = 74, 5
isz = lambda d: 2*d*csidhB+1     # interval size
sigsize = lambda S, t, u, delta, var = '0': ceil(1/8 * (0
    + ceil(min(t+u, u*log(t+u,2), t*log(t+u,2)))      # indices of rejections
    + ceil(log(S,2)*(t+u))                            # hash of ephemeral public keys
    + pbits*u                                         # rejected ephemeral public keys
    + t*ceil(log(isz(delta+(var=='F'))**csidhn,2))))  # revealed secret keys
pksize = lambda t, S: ceil(1/8 * (S-1)*pbits)


def Bin(n, p, k):     # Pr[ Bin_n,p >= k ]
    return sum(RR(1) * binomial(n, i) * p**i * (1-p)**(n-i) for i in range(k, n+1))


@cached_function
def joint_minmax_cdf(n, x, y, a, b):
    # Pr that min and max of n independent uniformly random
    # integers in [a;b] satisfy min <= x and max <= y.
    if x < a or y < a: return 0
    if y > b: y = b
    return RR((y-a+1)/(b-a+1))**n - (RR((y-x)/(b-a+1))**n if x < y else 0)


@cached_function
def joint_minmax(n, x, y, a, b):
    # Pr that min and max of n independent uniformly random
    # integers in [a;b] satisfy min = x and max = y.
    F = lambda xx, yy: joint_minmax_cdf(n, xx, yy, a, b)
    return F(x,y) - F(x-1,y) - F(x,y-1) + F(x-1,y-1)


def prob_accept_original(delta, S):
    # sample r from [-(delta+1)*B, (delta+1)*B];
    # reject r and a_c-r outside [-delta*B; +delta*B]
    return (isz(delta) / isz(delta+1)) ** csidhn # entries are independent
```

```
def prob_accept_full(delta, S):
    # sample r from [-(delta+1)*B, (delta+1)*B];
    # reject a_c-r outside [-delta*B; +delta*B]
    prob = (isz(delta) / isz(delta+1)) ** csidhn # entries are independent
    prob = 1/S*RR(1) + (S-1)/S*prob # can always reveal r
    return prob

def prob_accept_truncate(delta, S):
    prob = RR(0)
    for x in range(-csidhB, csidhB + 1):
        for y in range(x, csidhB + 1):
            # Pr[min and max coeffs of S-1 secret keys are x and y]
            weight = joint_minmax(S-1, x, y, -csidhB, +csidhB)
            # sample from [min(0,x)-delta*B, max(0,y)+delta*B];
            # reject outside [-delta*B; +delta*B]
            prob += weight * isz(delta) / (isz(delta) + max(0,y) - min(0,x))
    return prob ** csidhn # entries are independent

@cached_function
def max_u(t, S): # largest possible u for given S,t
    u, F = 1, lambda u: Bin(t+u, 1/S, t)
    while F(u) <= 2**-secbits: u *= 2
    lo, hi = u//2, u+1
    while hi - lo > 1:
        m = (lo+hi+1)//2
        if F(m) <= 2**-secbits: lo = m
        else: hi = m
    return lo

def prob_sign(t, u, sigma):
    return Bin(t+u, sigma, t)

def exp_csidhs_sign(t, u, delta, S, prob):
    pr_single = prob(delta, S)
    pr_all = prob_sign(t, u, pr_single)
    return (t+u) * delta / pr_all

def csidhs_verif(t, delta):
    return t * delta


for s in range(1, 17):
    S = 2**s

    t = ceil(secbits/log(S,2)) - 1
    last_umax = -1

    best_time, no_progress = 1./0, 0
    while True:

        if no_progress >= max(16, t/8): break #XXX hack
        t += 1

        if Bin(t + 4*t, 1/S, t) < 2**-secbits: umax = 4*t #XXX hack
        else: umax = max_u(t,S)

        no_progress_inner = True

        for variant in ('OTF' if t == ceil(secbits/log(S,2)) else 'TF'):

            for u in ([0] if variant == 'O' else reversed(range(last_umax+1, umax+1))):

                print >>sys.stderr, log(S,2), variant, t, u, no_progress

                prob = {'O': prob_accept_original,
                        'F': prob_accept_full,
                        'T': prob_accept_truncate}[variant]
```

```
@cached_function
def f(x): return exp_csidhs_sign(t, u, x, S, prob)

if variant == '0':
    delta = csidhn * t
else:
    _, delta = find_local_minimum(f, 1, 2**24, tol=1)
    delta = min((floor(delta), ceil(delta)), key = f)

if f(delta) < best_time:
    print ('logS={:2d} t={:3d} u={:3d} delta={:4d} {} ~> ' \
           'pksize={:9,d}b sigsize={:7,d}b ' \
           'tries={:8.6f} signCSIDHs={:9,d} verifCSIDHs={:9,d}') \
           .format(log(S,2), t, u, delta, variant,
                   pksize(t,S),
                   sigsize(S, t, u, delta, variant),
                   float(1 / prob_sign(t, u, prob(delta, S))),
                   round(f(delta)),
                   csidhs_verif(t, delta))
    best_time = f(delta)
    no_progress_inner = False

no_progress = no_progress + 1 if no_progress_inner else 0

last_umax = umax
```

References

1. Castryck, W., Lange, T., Martindale, C., Panny, L., Renes, J.: CSIDH: an efficient post-quantum commutative group action. In: Peyrin, T., Galbraith, S. (eds.) ASIA-CRYPT 2018. LNCS, vol. 11274, pp. 395–427. Springer, Cham (2018). https://doi.org/10.1007/978-3-030-03332-3_15
2. Couveignes, J.M.: Hard homogeneous spaces. IACR Cryptology ePrint Archive 2006/291 (1997). https://ia.cr/2006/291
3. De Feo, L.: Mathematics of isogeny based cryptography (2017). https://defeo.lu/ema2017/poly.pdf
4. De Feo, L., Galbraith, S.D.: SeaSign: compact isogeny signatures from class group actions. IACR Cryptology ePrint Archive 2018/824 (2018). https://ia.cr/2018/824
5. Fiat, A., Shamir, A.: How to prove yourself: practical solutions to identification and signature problems. In: Odlyzko, A.M. (ed.) CRYPTO 1986. LNCS, vol. 263, pp. 186–194. Springer, Heidelberg (1987). https://doi.org/10.1007/3-540-47721-7_12
6. Jao, D., et al.: SIKE. Submission to [10]. http://sike.org
7. Jao, D., De Feo, L.: Towards quantum-resistant cryptosystems from supersingular elliptic curve isogenies. In: Yang, B.-Y. (ed.) PQCrypto 2011. LNCS, vol. 7071, pp. 19–34. Springer, Heidelberg (2011). https://doi.org/10.1007/978-3-642-25405-5_2
8. Lyubashevsky, V.: Fiat-Shamir with aborts: applications to lattice and factoring-based signatures. In: Matsui, M. (ed.) ASIA-CRYPT 2009. LNCS, vol. 5912, pp. 598–616. Springer, Heidelberg (2009). https://doi.org/10.1007/978-3-642-10366-7_35
9. Meyer, M., Reith, S.: A faster way to the CSIDH. In: Chakraborty, D., Iwata, T. (eds.) INDOCRYPT 2018. LNCS, vol. 11356, pp. 137–152. Springer, Cham (2018). https://doi.org/10.1007/978-3-030-05378-9_8. https://ia.cr/2018/782
10. National Institute of Standards and Technology. Post-quantum cryptography standardization, December 2016. https://csrc.nist.gov/Projects/Post-Quantum-Cryptography/Post-Quantum-Cryptography-Standardization

11. Rostovtsev, A., Stolbunov, A.: Public-key cryptosystem based on isogenies. IACR Cryptology ePrint Archive 2006/145 (2006). https://ia.cr/2006/145
12. Shor, P.W.: Polynomial-time algorithms for prime factorization and discrete logarithms on a quantum computer. SIAM J. Comput. **26**(5), 1484–1509 (1997). https://arxiv.org/abs/quant-ph/9508027
13. Stolbunov, A.: Constructing public-key cryptographic schemes based on class group action on a set of isogenous elliptic curves. Adv. Math. Commun. **4**(2), 215–235 (2010)
14. The Sage Developers. SageMath, the sage mathematics software system (version 8.4) (2018). https://sagemath.org

Genus Two Isogeny Cryptography

E. V. Flynn[1] and Yan Bo Ti[2(✉)]

[1] Mathematical Institute, Oxford University, Oxford, UK
flynn@maths.ox.ac.uk
[2] Mathematics Department, University of Auckland, Auckland, New Zealand
yanbo.ti@gmail.com

Abstract. We study (ℓ, ℓ)-isogeny graphs of principally polarised supersingular abelian surfaces (PPSSAS). The (ℓ, ℓ)-isogeny graph has cycles of small length that can be used to break the collision resistance assumption of the genus two isogeny hash function suggested by Takashima. Algorithms for computing $(2, 2)$-isogenies on the level of Jacobians and $(3, 3)$-isogenies on the level of Kummers are used to develop a genus two version of the supersingular isogeny Diffie–Hellman protocol of Jao and de Feo. The genus two isogeny Diffie–Hellman protocol achieves the same level of security as SIDH but uses a prime with a third of the bit length.

Keywords: Post-quantum cryptography ·
Isogeny-based cryptography · Cryptanalysis · Key exchange ·
Hash function

1 Introduction

Isogeny-based cryptography involves the study of isogenies between abelian varieties. The first proposal was an unpublished manuscript of Couveignes [6] that outlined a key-exchange algorithm set in the isogeny graph of elliptic curves. This was rediscovered by Rostovtsev and Stolbunov [18]. A hash function was developed by Charles, Goren and Lauter [4] that uses the input to the hash to generate a path in the isogeny graph and outputs the end point of the path. Next in the line of invention is the Jao–de Feo cryptosystem [12] which relies on the difficulty of finding isogenies with a given degree between supersingular elliptic curves. A key exchange protocol, called the Supersingular Isogeny Diffie–Hellman key exchange (SIDH), based on this hard problem, was proposed in the same paper. The authors proposed working with 2-isogenies and 3-isogenies for efficiency.

Elliptic curves are principally polarised abelian varieties of dimension one, hence we can turn to principally polarised abelian varieties of higher dimension when looking to generalise isogeny-based cryptosystems. As noted by Takashima elliptic curves have three 2-isogenies but abelian surfaces (abelian varieties of dimension 2) have fifteen $(2, 2)$-isogenies. Hence, this motivates the use of abelian surfaces for use in these cryptosystems.

In this work, we will focus on principally polarised supersingular abelian varieties of dimension two, which we call principally polarised supersingular abelian

© Springer Nature Switzerland AG 2019
J. Ding and R. Steinwandt (Eds.): PQCrypto 2019, LNCS 11505, pp. 286–306, 2019.
https://doi.org/10.1007/978-3-030-25510-7_16

surfaces (PPSSAS) and consider their application to cryptography. The two challenges before us are: to understand the isogeny graphs of PPSSAS, and to have efficient algorithms to compute isogenies between principally polarised abelian surfaces (PPAS) in general.

In this work, we will examine the structure of the (ℓ, ℓ)-isogeny graph of PPSSAS and show that the genus two hash mentioned above is no longer collision resistant. This will be presented in Sect. 2. The realisation of the genus two version of SIDH will make up Sect. 3 and we will examine its security in Sect. 4.

Due to space restrictions, we will assume knowledge of abelian varieties and some of their properties. Assiduous readers can refer to [16] and [15] for definitions and background.

2   PPSSAS Graph

Let p and ℓ be distinct primes. In this section, we will examine the structure of the graph $\mathcal{G}_{p,\ell}$, where the vertices are isomorphism classes of PPSSAS over $\overline{\mathbb{F}}_p$, and edges are present between two vertices if they are (ℓ, ℓ)-isogenous. We will see that the PPSSAS graph has a regular and repeating substructure that we can identify. This can be seen explicitly in the subgraphs of the full isogeny graph presented in Appendix A.

2.1   Morphisms to Subgroups

One of the key tools in studying isogenies between abelian varieties is the correspondence between subgroups and isogenies. This subsection explains the properties a subgroup needs to have in order to correspond to an appropriate isogeny.

The first result allows us to restrict our attention to Jacobians of hyperelliptic curves of genus two or some reducible product of two elliptic curves.

Theorem 1. *If $A/\overline{\mathbb{F}}_p$ is a PPAS, then $A \cong J_H$ for some smooth (hyperelliptic) genus two curve H, or $A \cong E_1 \times E_2$ where E_i are elliptic curves.*

Proof. Use [11, Theorem 3.1] which says that A is isomorphic over $\mathbb{F}_{p^n}$ (for some n) to the two cases in the theorem, or to the restriction of scalars of a polarized elliptic curve over a quadratic extension of $\mathbb{F}_{p^n}$. Since we are working over $\overline{\mathbb{F}}_p$, the latter case is absorbed into the second case. □

Given an abelian variety A, the *dual variety* $A^\vee$ exists and is unique up to isomorphism. An ample divisor $\mathcal{L}$ of A defines an isogeny $\phi_{\mathcal{L}} : A \to A^\vee$ known as the *polarisation* of A. If the polarisation is an isomorphism, then we say that it is *principal*.

There is a non-degenerate alternating pairing, known as the *Weil pairing*, on an abelian variety A over k

$$e_m : A[m](\overline{k}) \times A^\vee[m](\overline{k}) \to \overline{k}^*,$$

where $A[m]$ is the m-torsion subgroup of A.

Being non-degenerate, the Weil pairing is non-trivial on the entire torsion subgroup. But there are subgroups in the torsion subgroup onto which the Weil pairing acts trivially when restricted. We give them a special name:

Definition 1. *A subgroup S of $A[m]$ is proper if $A[n] \nsubseteq S$ for any $1 < n \le m$.*

Let A be an abelian variety over $\mathbb{F}_p$, and let m be a positive integer co-prime with p. We say a proper subgroup S of $A[m]$ is maximal m-isotropic if

(1) the m-Weil pairing on $A[m]$ restricts trivially to S, and
(2) S is not properly contained in any other subgroup of $A[m]$ satisfying (1).

We call the first condition the *isotropic condition*. Note that the definition for a maximal isotropic subgroup does not include kernels of isogenies that factor through the multiplication-by-n map.

The following result then illustrates the preservation of principal polarisations under isogenies whose kernels are isotropic.

Proposition 1. *Let H be a hyperelliptic curve of genus two over $\mathbb{F}_q$. Let K be a finite, proper, $\mathbb{F}_q$-rational subgroup of $J_H(\mathbb{F}_q)$. There exists a PPAS A over $\mathbb{F}_q$, and an isogeny $\phi : J_H \to A$ with kernel K, if and only if K is a maximal m-isotropic subgroup of $J_H[m]$ for some positive integer m.*

Proof. The quotient $J_H \to J_H/K$ always exists as an isogeny between abelian varieties [19, III.3.12]. Since J_H is the Jacobian of a hyperelliptic curve, it has a principal polarisation λ. Now consider the polarisation $\mu = [\deg \phi] \circ \lambda$ on J_H, then we certainly have $K = \ker \phi \subseteq \ker \mu$, and since K is isotropic, we use [15, Theorem 16.8] to get a polarisation λ' on J_H/K. Using [15, Remark 16.9], we have that $\deg \lambda' = 1$ and so J_H/K is a PPAS.

Furthermore, by Theorem 1, we have that A is the Jacobian of a hyperelliptic curve of genus two or a product of two elliptic curves. $\square$

Using the results above, we can focus on the type of subgroups of the torsion group that correspond to the isogenies we would like to investigate. We will denote by C_n the cyclic group of order n.

Lemma 1. *Let A be a PPAS. If K is a maximal ℓ^n-isotropic subgroup, then it cannot be cyclic.*

Proof. Suppose that K is cyclic, then K is trivial on the pairing from the alternating property. It can then be shown that K is contained in $C_{\ell^n}^2$, which is also isotropic and so K cannot be maximal. $\square$

Proposition 2. *Let A be a PPAS. Then the maximal ℓ^n-isotropic subgroups of $A[\ell^n]$ are isomorphic to*

$$C_{\ell^n} \times C_{\ell^n} \quad or \quad C_{\ell^n} \times C_{\ell^{n-k}} \times C_{\ell^k}$$

where $1 \le k \le \lfloor n/2 \rfloor$.

Proof. We see, from Lemma 1 and the fact that maximal isotropic subgroups must be proper, that K must have rank 2 or 3. Suppose that K has rank 2, then it can be shown that to be maximal, K must have the structure $C_{\ell^n} \times C_{\ell^n}$ by repeated inclusion.

Let $C_{\ell^a} \times C_{\ell^b} \times C_{\ell^c} \times C_{\ell^d}$ be a subgroup of $A[\ell^n]$. To simplify notation, we write this as $[a, b, c, d]$. Without loss of generality, we can take $a \geq b \geq c \geq d$. Then we have that the dual is $[n-a, n-b, n-c, n-d]$ (since the composition with the original isogeny is multiplication-by-ℓ^n) and $n - a \leq n - b \leq n - c \leq n - d$. Hence to get the symmetry as specified by [16, pg. 143, Thm. 1], we must have that $n - a = d$ and $n - b = c$. Since we must have that one of the indices is zero, we take $d = 0$ and the result follows. $\qquad\square$

This result narrows down the subgroups that we need to study in order to study sequences of (ℓ, ℓ)-isogenies between PPAS.

2.2 Number of Neighbours in an (ℓ, ℓ)-isogeny Graph

In this section, we will consider the structure of an (ℓ, ℓ)-isogeny graph, $\mathcal{G}_{p,\ell}$. We do so by computing the number of neighbours that each vertex is connected to. Also, we will see that the number of paths between each vertex can vary according to the structure of the kernel.

We approach this question by choosing an arbitrary PPAS and considering isogenies emanating from this surface. Then the nascent isogeny graph is a rooted graph at the chosen surface. The first result counts the number of elements n steps from the root.

Theorem 2. *Let A be a PPAS, ℓ be a prime different from p and $n > 2$. Then the number of ℓ^n-maximal isotropic subgroup of $A[\ell^n]$ is*

$$\ell^{2n-3}(\ell^2 + 1)(\ell + 1)\left(\ell^n + \ell\frac{\ell^{n-2} - 1}{\ell - 1} + 1\right)$$

if n is even, and

$$\ell^{2n-3}(\ell^2 + 1)(\ell + 1)\left(\ell^n + \frac{\ell^{n-1} - 1}{\ell - 1}\right)$$

if n is odd.

The proof of the theorem follows by summing the number of maximal isotropic subgroups which is given in the following proposition.

Proposition 3. *Let A be a PPAS. Let $N(a, b, c)$ be the number of maximal isotropic subgroups of A isomorphic to $C_{\ell^a} \times C_{\ell^b} \times C_{\ell^c}$. Then*

1. *$N(n, n - a, a) = \ell^{3n-2a-4}(\ell^2 + 1)(\ell + 1)^2$, where $1 \leq a < n/2$;*
2. *$N(n, n, 0) = \ell^{3n-3}(\ell^2 + 1)(\ell + 1)$;*
3. *$N(2k, k, k) = \ell^{4k-3}(\ell^2 + 1)(\ell + 1)$.*

Proof. We will prove this for the second case. Note that this is equivalent to finding a subgroup isomorphic to $C_{\ell^n}^2$ in $A[\ell^n] \cong C_{\ell^n}^4$ which satisfies the isotropic condition.

So we need to find 2 elements in $C_{\ell^n}^4$ that have full order, are isotropic under the Weil pairing and generate subgroups with trivial intersection. To make things concrete, let $\langle P_1, \ldots, P_4 \rangle = C_{\ell^n}^4$. Let us pick the first element $A \in C_{\ell^n}^4$. This involves picking a full order element in $C_{\ell^n}^4$ for which we have $\ell^{4n} - \ell^{4n-4}$ choices. Let $A = \sum [a_i] P_i$.

To pick the second element $B \in C_{\ell^n}^4$, we need to pick a full order element but also ensure that B is isotropic to A under the Weil pairing. If we write $B = \sum [b_i] P_i$, then we require that

$$e_\ell(A, B) = e_\ell(P_1, P_2)^{a_1 b_2 - a_2 b_1} \cdot e_\ell(P_1, P_3)^{a_1 b_3 - a_3 b_1} \cdot e_\ell(P_1, P_4)^{a_1 b_4 - a_4 b_1}$$
$$\cdot e_\ell(P_2, P_3)^{a_2 b_3 - a_3 b_2} \cdot e_\ell(P_2, P_4)^{a_2 b_4 - a_4 b_2} \cdot e_\ell(P_3, P_4)^{a_3 b_4 - a_4 b_3}$$
$$= 1.$$

But this is a linear condition on the selection of the b_i's. Thus this gives us $\ell^{3n} - \ell^{3n-3}$ choices[1]. But we need to pick B such that $B \notin \langle A \rangle$. Given that B has full order, we need to avoid $(\ell - 1)\ell^{3(n-1)}$ elements. Hence the total number of choices for B is

$$\ell^{3n} - \ell^{3(n-1)} - (\ell - 1)\ell^{3(n-1)}.$$

Now, we need to divide the choices we have for A and B by the number of generating pairs in a subgroup $C_{\ell^n}^2$. The total number of generating pairs is $(\ell^{2n} - \ell^{2(n-1)})(\ell^{2n} - \ell^{2(n-1)} - (\ell - 1)\ell^{2(n-1)})$. Hence the total number of maximal isotropic $C_{\ell^n}^2$ subgroups of $C_{\ell^n}^4$ is

$$\frac{(\ell^{4n} - \ell^{4n-4})(\ell^{3n} - \ell^{3(n-1)} - (\ell - 1)\ell^{3(n-1)})}{(\ell^{2n} - \ell^{2(n-1)})(\ell^{2n} - \ell^{2(n-1)} - (\ell - 1)\ell^{2(n-1)})} = \ell^{3n-3}(\ell^2 + 1)(\ell + 1).$$

The other two cases are proved similarly.   □

Now, suppose we have an isogeny which has a maximal isotropic kernel K with order ℓ^{2n}, then we can decompose this isogeny into a sequence of n (ℓ, ℓ)-isogenies:

$$A_0 \xrightarrow{\phi_1} A_1 \xrightarrow{\phi_2} A_2 \xrightarrow{\phi_3} \ldots \xrightarrow{\phi_n} A_0/K.$$

As mentioned in the introduction, this decomposition of isogenies is non-unique. This arises from kernels whose structure allows for more than one subgroup

---

[1] To see this, note that each $e_\ell(P_i, P_j) = \mu^{\alpha_{i,j}}$, where μ is an ℓ-root of unity and $\alpha_{i,j}$ is some non-zero integer. We can express the isotropic condition as

$$b_4(\alpha_{1,4} a_1 + \alpha_{2,4} a_2 + \alpha_{3,4} a_3) \equiv \begin{array}{l} \alpha_{1,2}(a_2 b_1 - a_1 b_2) + \alpha_{1,3}(a_3 b_1 - a_3 b_1) \\ +\alpha_{2,3}(a_3 b_2 - a_2 b_3) + \alpha_{1,4} a_4 b_1 \\ +\alpha_{2,4} a_4 b_2 + \alpha_{3,4} a_4 b_3 \end{array} \pmod{\ell}.$$

In the case where $(\alpha_{1,4} a_1 + \alpha_{2,4} a_2 + \alpha_{3,4} a_3) \not\equiv 0$, we have free choices for b_1, b_2, b_3 (not all divisible by ℓ) and so have $\ell^{3n} - \ell^{3n-3}$ choices.

isomorphic to $C_\ell \times C_\ell$. The key observation is that these subgroups form the kernels of ϕ_1. In that spirit, the next two lemmata will give properties for the kernels of the first isogeny.

Lemma 2. *Let A be a PPAS. Let K be a maximal isotropic subgroup of $A[\ell^n]$ which is isomorphic to $C_{\ell^n} \times C_{\ell^{n-a}} \times C_{\ell^a}$ for some $a \geq 0$. Let $\langle P, Q, R \rangle = K$ such that P, Q, R have orders $\ell^n, \ell^{n-a}, \ell^a$ respectively.*

(1) Let $P_i, Q_i, R_i \in A_i$ be elements mapped from $P = P_0, Q = Q_0, R = R_0$. Then $[\ell^{n-i-1}]P_i \in \ker \phi_{i+1}$ for all $i \geq 0$.
(2) The first (ℓ, ℓ)-isogeny must have kernel

$$\langle [\ell^{n-1}]P, [\ell^{n-a-1}]Q + [k][\ell^{a-1}]R \rangle \quad for\ 0 \leq k \leq \ell-1, \quad or \quad \langle [\ell^{n-1}]P, [\ell^{a-1}]R \rangle.$$

Proof. (1) One can show by contradiction that if there is a kernel not containing P_i, then we will have cyclic kernels, which cannot be a kernel of a (ℓ, ℓ)-isogeny by Lemma 1.

Next, let $P' \in \langle P_i \rangle$, $Q' \in \langle Q_i \rangle$, and $R' \in \langle R_i \rangle$ such that P', Q', R' all have order ℓ. Then kernels cannot be of the form $P' + Q', P' + R', Q' + R'$. Indeed, it can be shown by examining the pairing $e_\ell(P' + Q', P' + R')$ to see that one either obtains a cyclic kernel, or that the subgroup above is not isotropic.

(2) We have from the first part that $[\ell^{n-1}]P$ must be a generator of the group. The second generator must be chosen from the remaining points of order ℓ. By the isotropic condition of K, we have that they are all isotropic on the pairing as well.

$\square$

Lemma 3. *Let $G \cong C_{\ell^n} \times C_{\ell^{n-a}} \times C_{\ell^a}$ and H be abelian groups. Let*

$$\langle P \rangle \cong C_{\ell^n}, \quad \langle Q \rangle \cong C_{\ell^{n-a}}, \quad \langle R \rangle \cong C_{\ell^a}$$

be subgroups of G with trivial intersections. If $\phi : G \to H$ is a group homomorphism, with

$$\ker \phi = \langle [\ell^{n-1}]P, [\ell^{n-a-1}]Q + [k][\ell^{a-1}]R \rangle$$

for $1 \leq k \leq \ell - 1$ and $a \leq n/2$, then $H \cong C_{\ell^{n-1}} \times C_{\ell^{n-a}} \times C_{\ell^{a-1}}$.

Proof. We have that $\phi(P)$ has order ℓ^{n-1} and Q has order ℓ^{n-a}, since $[\ell^{n-a-1}]Q \notin \ker \phi$. Since the order of the kernel is ℓ^2, we must have that $H \cong C_{\ell^{n-1}} \times C_{\ell^{n-a}} \times C_{\ell^{a-1}}$. $\square$

We can now study the different isogenies that exist between two vertices on the graph. In particular, we will be counting the number of different paths between any two vertices on the graph.

We will examine the base cases first, where there is only one path between two vertices, or where two vertices are separated by two (ℓ, ℓ)-isogenies.

Proposition 4. *Let A be a PPAS, and let $K \cong (C_{\ell^n} \times C_{\ell^{n-a}} \times C_{\ell^a})$. Let $P(n, a)$ be the number of paths from A to A/K. Then*

1. $P(n,0) = 1$ for all n;
2. $P(2,1) = \ell + 1$.

Proof. 1. Since kernels of (ℓ, ℓ)-isogenies cannot be cyclic, the only possible subgroup of order ℓ^2 of $C_{\ell^n} \times C_{\ell^n}$ is $C_\ell \times C_\ell$, and there is only one choice for this subgroup.

2. Let $K = C_{\ell^2} \times C_\ell \times C_\ell$. Then from Lemma 2 (and using its notation) we must have that the first isogeny has kernel

$$\langle [\ell]P, Q + [k]R \rangle \quad \text{for } 0 \le k \le \ell - 1, \quad \text{or} \quad \langle [\ell]P, R \rangle.$$

There are $\ell + 1$ choices for the first kernel. Thereafter, there is only one choice for the second kernel and so we have a total of $\ell + 1$ paths.

$\square$

Now, we can prove the general case.

Proposition 5. *Using the notation above, where $P(n,a)$ is the number of paths in a $(C_{\ell^n} \times C_{\ell^{n-a}} \times C_{\ell^a})$-isogeny. Then $P(n,a)$ satisfies the following recursive equation:*

$$P(n,a) = 2P(n-1, a-1) + (\ell - 1)P(n-1, a),$$

where $1 \le a < n/2$, and with the following boundary conditions:

$$P(n,0) = 1, \quad P(2,1) = \ell + 1.$$

Proof. We will prove this by induction. The base cases of the induction steps are easy and the boundary conditions follow from Proposition 4. We will show the induction step.

Let us suppose that the recursive formula holds for $P(n-1, a-1)$ and $P(n-1, a)$. Now, suppose that our kernel is isomorphic to $C_{\ell^n} \times C_{\ell^{n-a}} \times C_{\ell^a}$. Since each (ℓ, ℓ)-isogeny has a kernel of the form $C_\ell \times C_\ell$, we have, from Lemma 2(2), that the first isogeny must have a kernel of the form

$$\langle [\ell^{n-1}]P, [\ell^{n-a-1}]Q + [k][\ell^{a-1}]R \rangle \quad \text{for } 0 \le k \le \ell - 1, \quad \text{or} \quad \langle [\ell^{n-1}]P, [\ell^{a-1}]R \rangle.$$

It is clear that if the kernel is given by

$$\langle [\ell^{n-1}]P, [\ell^{n-a-1}]Q \rangle \quad \text{or} \quad \langle [\ell^{n-1}]P, [\ell^{a-1}]R \rangle,$$

then the residual kernel will be of the form

$$C_{\ell^{n-1}} \times C_{\ell^{n-a-1}} \times C_{\ell^a} \text{ or } C_{\ell^{n-1}} \times C_{\ell^{n-a}} \times C_{\ell^{a-1}}$$

respectively. Otherwise, if the first kernel has the form

$$\langle [\ell^{n-1}]P, [\ell^{n-a-1}]Q + [k][\ell^{a-1}]R \rangle \quad \text{for } 1 \le k \le \ell - 1,$$

the residual kernel will be of the form $C_{\ell^{n-1}} \times C_{\ell^{n-a}} \times C_{\ell^{a-1}}$ by Lemma 3. Hence we are done.

$\square$

Proposition 4 actually shows us the different paths that can exist between vertices in the graph. In particular, for kernels with rank 2, there can only be a single path between the domain and codomain. However, for kernels with rank 3, there can be a multitude of paths that exist between the domain and codomain. It can be seen that the following shapes (diamonds) are the basic paths drawn out by kernels with group structure $C_{\ell^2} \times C_\ell \times C_\ell$ for different ℓ's.

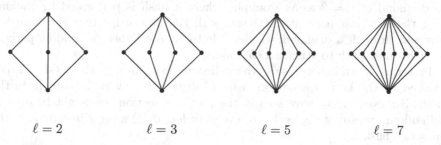

$$\ell = 2 \qquad\qquad \ell = 3 \qquad\qquad \ell = 5 \qquad\qquad \ell = 7$$

The non-uniqueness of these paths can be seen more explicitly in the example in Appendix A, where the kernel has order 256. Also in Appendix A, we will see how the diamonds fit together in the isogeny graph.

2.3 Cryptanalysis of the Isogeny-Based Hash Functions

The CGL hash function performs a random walk on the supersingular elliptic curve 2-isogeny graph. From each supersingular elliptic curve, there are three 2-isogenies emanating from that curve. The algorithm receives a binary string as input and returns an $\mathbb{F}_{p^2}$ value as output. It does so by taking a fixed base curve, discards one of the three isogenies (how this is done will not be of consequence in this discussion), and uses the first bit of the input as a choice between the remaining two isogenies. In the subsequent step, the algorithm uses the second bit to choose between the only two isogenies that does not lead back to the base curve (this is termed "no back-tracking"). Note that in this discussion, we have not mentioned how one can deterministically choose one isogeny over the other given a fixed bit, but there is a variety of ways one can "order" the isogenies. Readers are encouraged to refer to the original paper for more details.

In the genus two case of the hash function, due to the additional isogenies available to a single vertex (15 as opposed to 3), it is hoped that one can achieve a higher security level with a smaller number of steps. In [21] Takashima outlined an algorithm for obtaining a sequence of (2, 2)-isogenies without backtracking. He also implicitly suggested the generalisation of the above hash function to genus two. The genus two version of the CGL hash uses the input bits to traverse the (2, 2)-isogeny graph of PPSSAS. The algorithm begins at a pre-chosen PPSSAS and begins a walk based on the binary input to the algorithm. The walk on the graph is similar to the original CGL hash with a difference of an increased number of paths at each iteration.

Genus Two Hash Collisions. One of the main results of [4] is the proof that the CGL hash function is collision resistant. The vague intuition for this is that the supersingular elliptic curve isogeny graph is locally tree-like, i.e. there are no small cycles in a small enough subgraph. This assumption fails in the genus two case as pictured above, any diamond configuration leads to a collision in the hash. An attacker can find two pairs of bits so that the walks collide. Using the diamond of $\ell = 2$ as an example, where a hash is performed by walking along the left-most path. An attacker, with the knowledge that the hash has traversed through a diamond, will be able to choose either the middle path or the right-most path to achieve a collision.

In terms of endomorphisms, the collision resistance in the CGL hash is achieved by the lack of endomorphisms of degree 2^k, where k is small, in the graph. However, as we have seen in the previous section, we might be able to find endomorphism of degree 16 (or cycles of length 4) after 2 iterations of the genus two hash.

3   Genus Two SIDH Cryptosystem

In this section, we will construct the key exchange protocol for genus two. The scheme presented here follows the original scheme closely. Before presenting the scheme, we will review two algorithms used to select a base PPSSAS and select a key from the keyspace. We will also look briefly at the isogeny algorithms employed in the scheme.

We note that the MAGMA implementation of the scheme is extremely slow. An example is presented in Appendix B.

3.1   Selecting a Base Hyperelliptic Curve

Similar to the SIDH case, we pick primes of the form $p = 2^n \cdot 3^m \cdot f - 1$.

We consider a base hyperelliptic curve given by

$$H : y^2 = x^6 + 1.$$

It can be shown that the Jacobian of H is supersingular since it is the double cover of the supersingular elliptic curve $y^2 = x^3 + 1$, which is supersingular over $\mathbb{F}_p$, since $p \equiv 2 \pmod{3}$. We then take a random sequence of Richelot isogenies to obtain a random PPSSAS.

3.2   Selection of Secrets

Our aim is to use scalars to encode the secret kernel to be used by the two parties of the key exchange as this allows for a compact representation of the secret.

Firstly, let $H/\mathbb{F}_q$ be a hyperelliptic curve of genus two and let J_H be its Jacobian. The secret kernels will be maximal isotropic subgroups of $J_H[\ell^n]$ of order ℓ^{2n}. As seen in Sect. 2, the kernels will have structure $C_{\ell^n} \times C_{\ell^{n-k}} \times C_{\ell^k}$, where $0 \leq k < n/2$. Hence they should be generated by three points: Q_1, Q_2 and Q_3. Furthermore, to fulfil the condition of isotropy, we also require that the generators satisfy

$$e_{\ell^n}(Q_1, Q_2) = e_{\ell^n}(Q_1, Q_3) = e_{\ell^n}(Q_2, Q_3) = 1.$$

Our approach is summarised by the following steps:

Pre-computation:

Step 1: Find generators for $J_H[\ell^n]$. Name them P_1, P_2, P_3, P_4.

Step 2: Find the values $\alpha_{i,j}$ such that $e_{\ell^n}(P_i, P_j) = e_{\ell^n}(P_1, P_2)^{\alpha_{i,j}}$.

Secret selection:

Step 3: Pick some $r_1, r_2, r_3, r_4 \in [1, \dots, \ell^n - 1]^4$ such that they are not simultaneously divisible by ℓ.

Step 4: Pick a random[2] $0 \leq k < n/2$ and compute s_1, s_2, s_3, s_4 and t_1, t_2, t_3, t_4 by solving the two linear congruences

$$\begin{pmatrix} r_1 s_2 - r_2 s_1 + \alpha_{1,3}(r_1 s_3 - r_3 s_1) \\ +\alpha_{1,4}(r_1 s_4 - r_4 s_1) + \alpha_{2,3}(r_2 s_3 - r_3 s_2) \\ +\alpha_{2,4}(r_2 s_4 - r_4 s_2) + \alpha_{3,4}(r_3 s_4 - r_4 s_3) \end{pmatrix} \equiv 0 \quad \mod \ell^k$$

$$\begin{pmatrix} r_1 t_2 - r_2 t_1 + \alpha_{1,3}(r_1 t_3 - r_3 t_1) \\ +\alpha_{1,4}(r_1 t_4 - r_4 t_1) + \alpha_{2,3}(r_2 t_3 - r_3 t_2) \\ +\alpha_{2,4}(r_2 t_4 - r_4 t_2) + \alpha_{3,4}(r_3 t_4 - r_4 t_3) \end{pmatrix} \equiv 0 \quad \mod \ell^{n-k}$$

Step 5: Output $(s_1, \dots, s_4, r_1, \dots, r_4, t_1, \dots, t_4)$ as the secret scalars which will give the generators of the kernel:

$$Q_1 = \sum [s_i] P_i, \quad Q_2 = \sum [r_i] P_i, \quad Q_3 = \sum [t_i] P_i.$$

Remark 1. Note the following:

(i) Step 1 can be performed using standard group theoretic algorithms.

(ii) Step 2 performs discrete logarithm computations modulo a 2 and 3-smooth modulus and so is extremely efficient by using the Silver–Pohlig–Hellman algorithm [8, §13.2].

(iii) In Step 4, we pick a random solution in the solution space for r_i and t_i. It can be shown that this ensures that the isotropic condition is upheld.

3.3   Isogeny Algorithms

Computing an ℓ-isogeny between elliptic curves can be done with a complexity of $O(\ell)$. The general method to compute the codomains of this isogeny or to map points under the isogeny is to use Vélu's formula [25]. However, the efficient computation of arbitrary isogenies between abelian varieties of dimension greater than 1 is lacking. Here, we will present algorithms for computing the codomains of $(2, 2)$ and $(3, 3)$-isogenies and show how we can map subgroups under these isogenies. The speed-ups come from the use of simpler representations in the computation: the use of hyperelliptic curves in the (2, 2) case and the use of Kummer surfaces in the (3, 3).

---

[2] This will not be a uniformly random choice if one wants to sample the entire keyspace.

Richelot Isogenies. We will use Richelot isogenies to perform our $(2,2)$-isogenies as is standard in the literature. Richelot isogenies are relatively well-understood and have been implemented in various computational algebra programs. Useful references for Richelot isogenies are [1,3,20].

Note that Richelot isogenies operate on the level of hyperelliptic curves in the sense that they are morphisms between hyperelliptic curves. The support of the elements in the kernel of a $(2, 2)$-isogeny defines a factorisation of the defining hyperelliptic curve polynomial into quadratic polynomials. One can find the hyperelliptic curve in the codomain via the Richelot correspondence. We can map points between hyperelliptic curves via this Richelot correspondence. We use this to extend the map on curves to a map on Jacobians by mapping the support of elements of the Jacobian.

(3, 3)-Isogenies over the Kummer Surface. As for $(3, 3)$-isogenies, we note that for the purposes of genus two isogeny cryptography, we do not need to map points under the isogeny but only need to map Kummer points under the isogeny since the Jacobian points that correspond to the Kummer points both generate identical subgroups.

Given an abelian variety A, the *Kummer variety* is defined by $A/\langle\pm1\rangle$. This is a quartic surface in $\mathbb{P}^3$ and computations of isogenies on the Kummer surface was the object of study of [2]. We can use the formulae[3] presented in [2] to compute the images of Kummer points under the isogeny. This has also been noted by Costello in [5].

We remark that the procedure detailed in [2, §3] is incomplete. Using the notation in [2], a last transformation is necessary as c has shifted away from 1 due to prior transformations. At that stage, we have the following:

$$(s,t,c_0,c_1,c_2,m_0,m_1,m_2,u) = (s',t',1,-1,0,-r',0,1,1).$$

We need one last transformation

$$y \mapsto (4/\lambda_1)^2 y$$

and set

$$s = \lambda_1/4, \quad r = \text{Coefficient of } x \text{ in } H_1, \quad t = \text{Coefficient of } 1 \text{ in } H_1$$

to get the (r, s, t)-parameterisation of [2, Theorem 6].

The key to forming the cubic formula which maps Kummer points to Kummer points under the $(3, 3)$-isogeny lies in the biquadratic forms on the Kummer surface from [3, pg. 23]. Given the generators of the maximal isotropic subgroup of $J_H[3]$, the authors found two cubic forms which are each invariant under translation by T_1 and T_2 respectively. The cubic forms generated spaces of dimension 8 and intersect in dimension 4, which gives an explicit description of the quartic model of the Kummer surface.

---

[3] The files containing the formulae can be found in http://www.cecm.sfu.ca/~nbruin/c3xc3/.

3.4   Genus Two SIDH

We will present the key exchange protocol in genus two for completeness. The astute reader will see that all the steps carry over from the original scheme presented in §3.2 of [14].

Set-Up. Pick a prime p of the form $p = 2^{e_A} 3^{e_B} f - 1$ where $2^{e_A} \approx 3^{e_B}$. Now, we pick a hyperelliptic curve H using the methods of Sect. 3.1 which will be defined over $\mathbb{F}_{p^2}$. We then generate the bases $\{P_1, P_2, P_3, P_4\}$ and $\{Q_1, Q_2, Q_3, Q_4\}$ which generate $J_H[2^{e_A}]$ and $J_H[3^{e_B}]$ respectively.

First Round. Alice chooses her secret scalars $(a_i)_{i=1,\dots,12}$ using the steps outlined in Sect. 3.2 and computes the isogeny $\phi_A : J_H \to J_A$ with kernel given by

$$\left\langle \sum_{i=1}^{4}[a_i]P_i, \ \sum_{i=5}^{8}[a_i]P_i, \ \sum_{i=9}^{12}[a_i]P_i \right\rangle.$$

She also needs to compute the points $\phi_A(Q_i)$ for $i = 1, 2, 3, 4$. She sends the tuple

$$(G_2(J_A), \phi_A(Q_1), \phi_A(Q_2), \phi_A(Q_3), \phi_A(Q_4))$$

to Bob, where $G_2(J_A)$ is the G_2-invariants of the hyperelliptic curve associated to J_A.

At the same time, Bob chooses his secret scalars $(b_i)_{i=1,\dots,12}$ using the steps outlined in Sect. 3.2 and computes the isogeny $\phi_B : J_H \to J_B$ which has the kernel

$$\left\langle \sum_{i=1}^{4}[b_i]P_i, \ \sum_{i=5}^{8}[b_i]P_i, \ \sum_{i=9}^{12}[b_i]P_i \right\rangle.$$

He computes the points $\phi_B(P_i)$ for $i = 1, 2, 3, 4$, and sends the tuple

$$(G_2(J_B), \phi_B(P_1), \phi_B(P_2), \phi_B(P_3), \phi_B(P_4))$$

to Alice.

Second Round. Alice will receive Bob's tuple and proceeds with computing J_B from the G_2-invariant, and the points

$$\left\langle \sum_{i=1}^{4}[a_i]\phi_B(P_i), \ \sum_{i=5}^{8}[a_i]\phi_B(P_i), \ \sum_{i=9}^{12}[a_i]\phi_B(P_i) \right\rangle.$$

This is the kernel of a $(2^{e_A}, 2^{e_A - k}, 2^k)$-isogeny $\phi_A' : J_B \to J_{BA}$. Bob will perform a similar computation and arrive at the PPSSAS J_{AB}. But since

$$J_{AB} = J_A/\phi_A(K_B) \cong J_H/\langle K_A, K_B \rangle \cong J_B/\phi_B(K_A) = J_{BA},$$

they can then use the G_2-invariants of J_{AB} and J_{BA} as their shared secret.

Remark 2. The method in [2] allows us to find $\pm\phi_B(P_i)$. However, we need the map

$$(P_1, P_2, P_3, P_4) \mapsto (\phi_B(P_1), \phi_B(P_2), \phi_B(P_3), \phi_B(P_4))$$

or

$$(P_1, P_2, P_3, P_4) \mapsto (-\phi_B(P_1), -\phi_B(P_2), -\phi_B(P_3), -\phi_B(P_4))$$

to ensure that the subgroup generated by Alice in the second round is isotropic.

To fix this problem, one could check if

$$e_{2^{e_A}}(\phi_B(P_i), \phi_B(P_j)) = e_{2^{e_A}}(P_i, P_j)^{3^{e_B}}$$

for all $1 \leq i < j \leq 4$ and negate the $\phi_B(P_i)$'s accordingly.

4   Security and Analysis

4.1   Security Estimates

In this section, we will define the computational problem needed to analyse our cryptosystem.

Let p be a prime of the form $2^n \cdot 3^n \cdot f - 1$, and fix a hyperelliptic curve of genus two H over $\mathbb{F}_{p^2}$ and let J_H denote its Jacobian. Fix bases for $J_H[2^n]$ and $J_H[3^m]$, denoting them by $\{P_i\}_{i=1,2,3,4}$ and $\{Q_i\}_{i=1,2,3,4}$ respectively.

Problem 1 (Computational Genus Two Isogeny (CG2I) Problem). Let $\phi : J_H \to J_A$ be an isogeny whose kernel is given by K. Given J_A and the images $\{\phi(Q_i)\}$, $i \in \{1, 2, 3, 4\}$, find generators for K.

This problem is conjectured to be computationally infeasible for the same reasons as listed in [14]. However, due to the higher regularity of the genus two isogeny graph, we are able to perform a smaller number of isogeny computations to achieve the same security level as compared to SIDH.

Let us look at the complexities of the algorithms one can employ against the CG2I problem, where the task is to recover the isogeny $\phi_A : J_H \to J_A$ when given J_H and J_A. We note that from Proposition 3, we have that the number of elements in the n-sphere is $\ell^{3n-3}(\ell^2 + 1)(\ell + 1) \approx \sqrt{p^3}$, hence a naive exhaustive search on the leaves of J_H has a complexity of $O(\sqrt{p^3})$. One can improve on this by considering the meet-in-the-middle search by listing all isogenies of degree ℓ^n from J_H and J_A and finding collisions in both lists. The meet-in-the-middle search has a complexity of $O(\sqrt[4]{p^3})$. One can perform better by employing a quantum computer to reduce the complexity to $O(\sqrt[6]{p^3})$ using Claw finding algorithms [23]. This compares favourably with the genus one case which has classical security of $O(\sqrt[4]{p})$, and quantum security of $O(\sqrt[6]{p})$. An example of a prime which one can use to achieve 128-bits of security is 171-bits, whereas the genus one case requires 512-bits for the same level of security.

4.2   Existing Attacks on SIDH

We will dedicate this section to examining the impact of the attacks proposed in the cryptanalysis papers [7,9,10,17,24]. We will group the attacks into two classes: Curves and points, and computing endomorphism rings.

Attacks on curves and points include the adaptive attack [9] and fault attacks [10,24]. Attacks via the computation of endomorphism rings include the methods using auxiliary points to find a subring of the endomorphism ring [17] and using the Deuring correspondence [7]. The purpose of computing the endomorphism ring is due to the result in [9] that showed a reduction, in most cases, that the SIDH problem is at most as difficult as computing the endomorphism ring. The key observation behind this result is that the isogenies tend to be short paths in the graph, and so a lattice reduction performed on the basis of the connecting ideal would yield an element that corresponds to the secret isogeny via results in [13].

Adaptive Attack. Due to the similar construction of the two protocols, the adaptive attack still carries over to the genus two version. Suppose the attacker is playing the role of Bob and sends Alice the points

$$\phi_B(P_1), \phi_B(P_2), \phi_B(P_3), \phi_B([2^{n-1}]P_4 + P_4).$$

Following the procedure detailed in [9], Bob will be able to recover the first bit of a_4. To recover the rest of the secret, one only needs to tweak the algorithm presented in the original paper.

Fault Attack. The loop-abort fault attack presented in [10] would still apply, as our protocol still requires repeated computations of isogenies of low degrees, resulting in the existence of intermediate curves which is key to the attack.

The fault injection on a point as presented in [24] relies on the recovery of the image of one random point under the secret isogeny. Intuitively, the n-torsion points of an abelian variety of genus g is a $\mathbb{Z}/n\mathbb{Z}$-module of rank 2^g. Hence the recovery of the image of one random point as in the $g = 1$ case in [24] is akin to recovering a one-dimensional subspace and the task of finding the secret isogeny is the recovery of the complementary subspace.

This approach can still work in our setting, however we will require a minimum of 2 images of random points under the isogeny. This is because the complementary subspace in our case is of dimension 2, and so we will need at least two points to span that space.

Endomorphism Ring Computations. Let E be a supersingular elliptic curve over k and let char $k = p > 0$. Then we know that $\operatorname{End} E \otimes \mathbb{Q} = B_{p,\infty}$, where $B_{p,\infty}$ is the quaternion algebra over $\mathbb{Q}$ ramified at p and ∞. Also, $\operatorname{End} E$ is a maximal order of $B_{p,\infty}$. In the case of higher genus, if A is a PPSSAV of dimension g, then we have that the endomorphism algebra is $\operatorname{End} A \otimes \mathbb{Q} = M_g(B_{p,\infty})$ [16, pg. 174, Cor. 2].

We will leave the thorough examination of the effects of endomorphism ring computations on the cryptosystem as an open problem.

5   Conclusion

We studied the (ℓ, ℓ)-isogeny graphs and cryptanalysed a genus two variant of the CGL hash function. We studied the implementation of the genus two SIDH cryptosystem by looking at the mapping of Kummer points under a $(3, 3)$-isogeny and Jacobian points under a $(2, 2)$-isogeny. We have shown that the genus two isogeny cryptosystem can be implemented, but the fact of the matter is: improvements in the algorithms need to be found before a practical implementation can be achieved.

Acknowledgements. The authors would like to thank Steven Galbraith, Lukas Zobernig, Chloe Martindale, Luca de Feo and David Kohel for enlightening discussions. In particular, we thank Steven for the idea of the cryptanalysis of the hash function. We also thank the reviewers for suggesting improvements to the paper, most of which we have tried to include.

A   Examples of Isogeny Graphs

We will consider kernels with order 256 in this example. The key to each example is to the find the number of $C_2 \times C_2$ subgroups of each kernel since this would correspond with the number of possible $(2, 2)$-isogenies. Firstly, we note that the structure of maximal isotropic subgroups of order 256 must be $C_{16} \times C_{16}$, or $C_{16} \times C_4 \times C_4$, or $C_{16} \times C_8 \times C_2$ by Proposition 2. The isogeny graphs are given in Fig. 1.

The easy case is when the kernel K_0 has the structure $C_{16} \times C_{16}$. This is because there is only one $C_2 \times C_2$ subgroup in K. Hence, there is only one isogeny path available and we have a straight line.

Now, let us consider the case when K_1 has the structure $C_{16} \times C_4 \times C_4$. We will label the isomorphism classes of the surfaces by (n), where n is a natural number. We will denote the first surface by (1).

We can represent the 3 generators of K_1 by P, Q and R, where their orders are 16, 4 and 4 respectively. There are 3 different $C_2 \times C_2$ subgroups of K given by $\langle [8]P, [2]Q \rangle$, $\langle [8]P, [2]R \rangle$ and $\langle [8]P, [2](Q + R) \rangle$ in accordance to Lemma 2. Hence, we can and will denote the $(2, 2)$-subgroups of K by the scalar preceding Q and R. For instance, the three subgroups given here are denoted by $(2, 0)$, $(0, 2)$ and $(2, 2)$.

These 3 subgroups lead to non-isomorphic surfaces labelled as $(2), (3)$ and (4). The edges are labelled by the subgroup corresponding to the isogeny.

Consider the vertex (2), and consider the $(2, 2)$-isogeny from (2) with kernel $\langle [4]P, [2]R \rangle$[4] and denote the codomain by (8). One can see that the isogeny from (1) to (8) has kernel $\langle [4]P, [2]Q, [2]R \rangle$.

---

[4] Note that we actually mean $\langle [4]\phi(P), [2]\phi(R) \rangle$, where ϕ corresponds to the $(2, 2)$-isogeny from (1). We will drop ϕ for ease of notation.

One can also map from (3) and (4) to (8) via the kernels (2,0) and (2,0). Immediately, one can spot the diamonds mentioned prior to this example. Indeed, the diamonds can be seen repeatedly in the graph.

Vertices can form tips of the diamond when there is a $C_4 \times C_2 \times C_2$ subgroup in the kernel. This is best illustrated in the next example where the kernel K_2 has structure $C_{16} \times C_8 \times C_2$. Using the notation from the previous example, K_2 will be given by $\langle P', Q', R' \rangle$, where $P' = P$, $[2]Q' = Q$ and $R' = [2]R$.

Starting from the vertex (1) again, we have the same 3 subgroups, which result in the same surfaces (2), (3) and (4). We also have that the three surfaces will all have maps into (8) as before. However, residual kernel at (2) is now isomorphic to $C_8 \times C_8$, hence we see that the isogeny path from (2) down to (18) is a straight line. The residual kernel at (4) on the other hand, is $C_8 \times C_4 \times C_2$, hence it contains $C_4 \times C_2 \times C_2$ as a subgroup and so, (4) forms the tip of another diamond.

Another thing to note about this case is that the moment R is in the kernel, we cannot have $C_4 \times C_2 \times C_2$ as a subgroup of the residual kernel. This can be observed from the diagonal right-to-left lines in Fig. 1b.

Lastly, Fig. 2 shows all the neighbours which are two (2, 2)-isogenies away. So the top vertex is connected to each of the middle and bottom vertices by an isogeny of degree 4 and 16 respectively. The diamonds corresponding to kernels with the structure $C_4 \times C_2 \times C_2$, (though contorted) are present and its number is as predicted in Proposition 3.

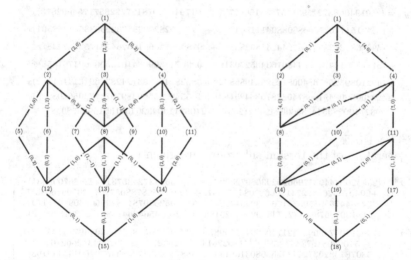

(a) Kernel has structure $C_{16} \times C_4 \times C_4$.   (b) Kernel has structure $C_{16} \times C_8 \times C_2$.

Fig. 1. Isogeny subgraphs when the kernel has order 256.

Fig. 2. Isogeny graph from an arbitrary vertex showing 2 layers of isogenies.

B   Implementation

We have implemented the key exchange scheme in MAGMA using p of 100-bits. This yields a classical security of 75-bits and a quantum security of 50-bits. The first round of the key exchange which required the mapping of points took 145.7 s for Alice and 145.41 s for Bob. The second round of the key exchange took 74.8 s for Alice and 72.29 s for Bob.

The implementation took parameters $e_A = 51$ and $e_B = 32$, and $f = 1$ with

$$p = 4172630516011578626876079341567.$$

The base hyperelliptic curve is defined by

$$H : y^2 = (38019406837215931757454156477 5i + 1017916559181277226571754002873)x^6$$
$$+ (36421517102766088088041115049 56i + 144909282502887329503355336850 1)x^5$$
$$+ (49066823138362447944241802829 6i + 3978975720631052645817531474 33)x^4$$
$$+ (57740951447471244861634352793 1i + 1029071839968410755001691761 655)x^3$$
$$+ (40210895258768400812396249868 22i + 3862824071831242831691614151 192)x^2$$
$$+ (29306799946196874037876864251 53i + 1855492455663897070774056208 936)x$$
$$+ 29827400283544785606249472126 57i + 2106211304320458155169465303 811$$

where $i^2 = -1$ in $\mathbb{F}_{p^2}$.

The generators of the torsion subgroups are given by

$$P_1 = \begin{pmatrix} x^2 + (2643268744935796625293669726227i + 13735594372435731040368670955 31)x \\ + 20407662634727412966290841723 57i + 41483369878805720742059996660 55, \\ + (2643644763015937217035303914167 i + 31020526897811829950440900811 79)x \\ + 18139366788512227462025965251 86i + 32920456486411309193331330172 18 \end{pmatrix},$$

$$P_2 = \begin{pmatrix} x^2 + (15061200799092632174926643259 98i + 12284157551831850904697886088 52)x \\ + 51094081672353821002441302281 4i + 32592780521393094312662164619 2, \\ + (15807813820372443925368031651 34i + 38878349227209545737501494461 63)x \\ + 16757335039355513696075241508 2i + 12251357810407421135728604974 57 \end{pmatrix},$$

$$P_3 = \begin{pmatrix} x^2 + (35057817678791868788329181344 39i + 19042727531810818525233349801 36)x \\ + 64697958988346132328090633896 2i + 40346647046094746109879657069 0, \\ + (31131134663622057935052438727 9i + 10188063705829807090021974932 73)x \\ + 14080048698953325872639947999 89i + 18498261497256933122830868888 29 \end{pmatrix},$$

$$P_4 = \begin{pmatrix} x^2 + (26343147864478195100806659494014i + 72540633574927805301023935272)x \\ +15319665321637235784288271430067i + 14302990368694446800715409581 09, \\ +(39571360239630643404860297241 24i + 30434823040861445670969781 3720)x \\ +88836486727672932 62 09394828038i + 2453132774156594607548927379151 \end{pmatrix},$$

$$Q_1 = \begin{pmatrix} x^2 + (26308520634811144249410318474 50i + 6619970040259422441 4830947 4867)x \\ +49730048867515193197021568 7005i + 75956323361686550950309496398 4, \\ +(17119904176260119642353689957 95i + 33705425282256825917 75373090846)x \\ +24092469604303535035201751767 54i + 1486115372404013153540282992605 \end{pmatrix},$$

$$Q_2 = \begin{pmatrix} x^2 + (95043282961744369647577255188 4i + 380976622923188369170746945 0961)x \\ +129388673102344467760710676378 3i + 215204408326901665315858826 2237, \\ +(36137651249829978523455580063 02i + 41660672856319982178735608467 41)x \\ +24948775499708669140939804 00340i + 3422166823321314392366398023265 \end{pmatrix},$$

$$Q_3 = \begin{pmatrix} x^2 + (18679094737438074248796337 296 41i + 356101797346565520153144598651 7)x \\ +614550355856817299796257158 420i + 37138188654065102989637260730 88, \\ +(84656550479653169476065229266 1i + 243014947674736028558572549178 9)x \\ +38271025076183622817535267350 86i + 8788436826079659618324972589 82 \end{pmatrix},$$

$$Q_4 = \begin{pmatrix} x^2 + (2493766102609911097717660796 748i + 247455915099714654469886873508 1)x \\ +843886014491849541025676396 448i + 27006747538039826586748111156 56, \\ +(24571090031163023001803040011 13i + 300075482504820765517164136114 2)x \\ +25605201982250874011832488329 55i + 2490028703281853247425401658313 \end{pmatrix}.$$

The secret scalars of Alice and Bob are

$\alpha_1 = 937242395764589$,	$\alpha_2 = 282151393547351$,	$\alpha_3 = 0$,	$\alpha_4 = 0$,
$\alpha_5 = 0$,	$\alpha_6 = 0$,	$\alpha_7 = 1666968036125619$,	$\alpha_8 = 324369560360356$,
$\alpha_9 = 0$,	$\alpha_{10} = 0$,	$\alpha_{11} = 0$,	$\alpha_{12} = 0$,
$\beta_1 = 103258914945647$,	$\beta_2 = 1444900449480064$,	$\beta_3 = 0$,	$\beta_4 = 0$,
$\beta_5 = 0$,	$\beta_6 = 0$,	$\beta_7 = 28000236972265$,	$\beta_8 = 720020678656772$,
$\beta_9 = 0$,	$\beta_{10} = 0$,	$\beta_{11} = 0$,	$\beta_{12} = 0$,

Using their secret scalars, they will obtain the following pair of hyperelliptic curves

$$\begin{aligned} H_A : y^2 = {} & (34047030045874958215961176965058i + 40333618126043548010579938 2459)x^6 \\ & + (30015840864247629380622762223 40i + 311047190480692260305532924751 0)x^5 \\ & + (10171993106272309835115864633 32i + 15991896986314333726508575440 71)x^4 \\ & + (24695620123390929453983656786 89i + 11545664726152368274164676245 84)x^3 \\ & + (84187423865805302301385741620 0i + 4224108156439043197291319594 69)x^2 \\ & + (35075842271804269761097720529 62i + 2331298266595569462657798736063)x \\ & + 27298166205209051755907581870 19i + 37487040066451290004985635147 34, \end{aligned}$$

$$\begin{aligned} H_B : y^2 = {} & (34343946890747526635795108965 30i + 3258819610341997123576600332954)x^6 \\ & + (3350255113820895191389143565973i + 26818924894486594289304672 20147)x^5 \\ & + (2958298818675004062047066758264i + 9047693620793210554250767283 09)x^4 \\ & + (2701255487608026975177181091075i + 7870331200150121461421861825 56)x^3 \\ & + (35236758116710920224917644660 22i + 2804841353558342542840805561369)x^2 \\ & + (3238151513550798796238052565124i + 3437885792433773163395130700555)x \\ & + 1829327374163410097298853068766i + 34534895169444063163962714851 72. \end{aligned}$$

The auxiliary points computed are the following

$$\phi_B(P_1) = \pm \begin{pmatrix} x^2 + (57696747003522438444707169185 9i + 39055912331691419936017033810 59)x \\ +14976084511258721758524483591 37i + 26229380933247876792294133204 05, \\ (2205483026731282488507766835920i + 18876318955336669751709604986 04)x \\ +22704381367194868281470967681 68i + 10988930791405119751197407891 84 \end{pmatrix},$$

$$\phi_B(P_2) = \pm \begin{pmatrix} x^2 + (2002807208424762458028352734 43i + 3878472110821865480924821702 529)x \\ +4766280318107577344887407192 90i + 2957584612454518004162519574 871, \\ (3949908621907714361071815553277i + 63063932362073596663671832104 3)x \\ +9015976423853241579257009768 89i + 2429302320101537821240219151 082 \end{pmatrix},$$

$$\phi_B(P_3) = \pm \begin{pmatrix} x^2 + (4133157753622694250606077231 439i + 2486410359530824865039464484 854)x \\ +2178006463745651824830649066 26i + 1249364962732904443349026898 84, \\ (12654902465945371726616464990 03i + 2130834160349159007051974433 128)x \\ +25802866809874256010007380109 69i + 5780466101921461146984665305 08 \end{pmatrix},$$

$$\phi_B(P_4) = \pm \begin{pmatrix} x^2 + (6601102003779684073844190837i + 8710635072963118478554914007 4)x \\ +23303393342511305368718930396 27i + 1494511552650494479113393669 713, \\ (17063142627028927741094461459 89i + 3539074449728790590891503255 545)x \\ +19506194536813819323291061300 08i + 6851709156707418584307749200 61 \end{pmatrix},$$

$$\phi_A(Q_1) = \begin{pmatrix} x^2 + (3464040394311932964693107348 618i + 1234121484161567611101667399 525)x \\ +17895775393232773855271038385i + 3856858968014591645005318326 985, \\ (2432835950855765586938146638 349i + 3267484715628220519231772140 55)x \\ +98538613755178934876027713807 6i + 1179835886991851012234054275 735 \end{pmatrix},$$

$$\phi_A(Q_2) = \begin{pmatrix} x^2 + (36338270096097826108869629350 1i + 3499548729039922528103431054 749)x \\ +38325125233825477164180751955 17i + 3364204966204284852762530333 038, \\ (30438171015966076121868088851 16i + 4027557567198565187096133171 734)x \\ +40871766319171660663568861985 18i + 1327157646340760346840638146 328 \end{pmatrix},$$

$$\phi_A(Q_3) = \begin{pmatrix} x^2 + (3946684136660787881888285451 015i + 1250236853749119184502604023 717)x \\ +33581526134833765878728676747 03i + 4672522011510763890555248094 76, \\ (15629207843681052454991327577 75i + 9879208230759468502336446004 97)x \\ +16750057582828713370107986050 79i + 1490924669195823363601763347 629 \end{pmatrix},$$

$$\phi_A(Q_4) = \begin{pmatrix} x^2 + (16294082425577501557293307597 72i + 3235283387810139201773539373 655)x \\ +13413806694903683434507043166 76i + 1454971022788254094961980229 605, \\ (23936759862475240326635668723 48i + 3412019204974086421616096641 702)x \\ +18903496968565042343202833185 45i + 8416990613472152346312100120 75 \end{pmatrix}.$$

This allows for both parties to compute the final isogeny to obtain

$$\begin{pmatrix} 10550181501975738539472491986 25i + 2223713843055934677989300194 259, \\ 8190605807295720135080065372 32i + 3874192400826551831686249391 528, \\ 16588859753516044944861384828 83i + 3931354413698538292465352257 393 \end{pmatrix}$$

as their common G_2-invariants.

References

1. Bruin, N., Doerksen, K.: The arithmetic of genus two curves with (4, 4)-split Jacobians. Can. J. Math. **63**, 992–1024 (2009)
2. Bruin, N., Flynn, E.V., Testa, D.: Descent via (3, 3)-isogeny on Jacobians of genus 2 curves. Acta Arithmetica **165** (2014)
3. Cassels, J.W.S., Flynn, E.V.: Prolegomena to a Middlebrow Arithmetic of Curves of Genus 2. London Mathematical Society Lecture Note Series. Cambridge University Press, Cambridge (1996)
4. Charles, D.X., Lauter, K.E., Goren, E.Z.: Cryptographic hash functions from expander graphs. J. Cryptol. **22**(1), 93–113 (2009)

5. Costello, C.: Computing supersingular isogenies on kummer surfaces. In: Peyrin, T., Galbraith, S. (eds.) ASIACRYPT 2018. LNCS, vol. 11274, pp. 428–456. Springer, Cham (2018). https://doi.org/10.1007/978-3-030-03332-3_16

6. Couveignes, J.M.: Hard homogeneous spaces. Cryptology ePrint Archive, Report 2006/291 (2006). http://eprint.iacr.org/2006/291

7. Eisenträger, K., Hallgren, S., Lauter, K., Morrison, T., Petit, C.: Supersingular isogeny graphs and endomorphism rings: reductions and solutions. In: Nielsen, J.B., Rijmen, V. (eds.) EUROCRYPT 2018. LNCS, vol. 10822, pp. 329–368. Springer, Cham (2018). https://doi.org/10.1007/978-3-319-78372-7_11

8. Galbraith, S.D.: Mathematics of Public Key Cryptography, 1st edn. Cambridge University Press, New York (2012)

9. Galbraith, S.D., Petit, C., Shani, B., Ti, Y.B.: On the security of supersingular isogeny cryptosystems. In: Cheon, J.H., Takagi, T. (eds.) ASIACRYPT 2016. LNCS, vol. 10031, pp. 63–91. Springer, Heidelberg (2016). https://doi.org/10.1007/978-3-662-53887-6_3

10. Gélin, A., Wesolowski, B.: Loop-abort faults on supersingular isogeny cryptosystems. In: Lange, T., Takagi, T. (eds.) PQCrypto 2017. LNCS, vol. 10346, pp. 93–106. Springer, Cham (2017). https://doi.org/10.1007/978-3-319-59879-6_6

11. Gonzalez, J., Guàrdia, J., Rotger, V.: Abelian surfaces of GL[2]-type as Jacobians of curves. Acta Arithmetica **116**, 263–287 (2005)

12. Jao, D., De Feo, L.: Towards quantum-resistant cryptosystems from supersingular elliptic curve isogenies. In: Yang, B.-Y. (ed.) PQCrypto 2011. LNCS, vol. 7071, pp. 19–34. Springer, Heidelberg (2011). https://doi.org/10.1007/978-3-642-25405-5_2

13. Kohel, D., Lauter, K., Petit, C., Tignol, J.: On the quaternion ℓ-isogeny path problem. LMS J. Comput. Math. **17**(Special issue A), 418–432 (2014)

14. De Feo, L., Jao, D., Plût, J.: Towards quantum-resistant cryptosystems from supersingular elliptic curve isogenies. J. Math. Cryptol. **8**(3), 209–247 (2014)

15. Milne, J.S.: Abelian varieties. In: Cornell, G., Silverman, J.H. (eds.) Arithmetic Geometry, pp. 103–150. Springer, New York (1986). https://doi.org/10.1007/978-1-4613-8655-1_5

16. Mumford, D.: Abelian Varieties, Tata Institute of Fundamental Research Studies in Mathematics, vol. 5. Tata Institute of Fundamental Research, Bombay (2008)

17. Petit, C.: Faster algorithms for isogeny problems using torsion point images. In: Takagi, T., Peyrin, T. (eds.) ASIACRYPT 2017. LNCS, vol. 10625, pp. 330–353. Springer, Cham (2017). https://doi.org/10.1007/978-3-319-70697-9_12

18. Rostovtsev, A., Stolbunov, A.: Public-key cryptosystem based on isogenies. Cryptology ePrint Archive, Report 2006/145 (2006). http://eprint.iacr.org/

19. Serre, J.P.: Algebraic Groups and Class Fields. Graduate Texts in Mathematics, vol. 117. Springer, New York (1988). https://doi.org/10.1007/978-1-4612-1035-1. Translated from the French

20. Smith, B.: Explicit endomorphisms and correspondences. Ph.D. thesis, University of Sydney (2005)

21. Takashima, K.: Efficient algorithms for isogeny sequences and their cryptographic applications. In: Takagi, T., Wakayama, M., Tanaka, K., Kunihiro, N., Kimoto, K., Duong, D.H. (eds.) Mathematical Modelling for Next-Generation Cryptography. MI, vol. 29, pp. 97–114. Springer, Singapore (2018). https://doi.org/10.1007/978-981-10-5065-7_6

22. Takashima, K., Yoshida, R.: An algorithm for computing a sequence of richelot isogenies. Bull. Korean Math. Soc. **46**, 789–802 (2009)

23. Tani, S.: Claw finding algorithms using quantum walk. arXiv e-prints (2007)

24. Ti, Y.B.: Fault attack on supersingular isogeny cryptosystems. In: Lange, T., Takagi, T. (eds.) PQCrypto 2017. LNCS, vol. 10346, pp. 107–122. Springer, Cham (2017). https://doi.org/10.1007/978-3-319-59879-6_7
25. Vélu, J.: Isogénies entre courbes elliptiques. C.R. Acad. Sci. Paris, Série A. **273**, 238–241 (1971)

On Lions and Elligators: An Efficient Constant-Time Implementation of CSIDH

Michael Meyer[1,2(✉)], Fabio Campos[1], and Steffen Reith[1]

[1] Department of Computer Science, University of Applied Sciences,
Wiesbaden, Germany
{Michael.Meyer,FabioFelipe.Campos,Steffen.Reith}@hs-rm.de
[2] Department of Mathematics, University of Würzburg,
Würzburg, Germany

Abstract. The recently proposed CSIDH primitive is a promising candidate for post quantum static-static key exchanges with very small keys. However, until now there is only a variable-time proof-of-concept implementation by Castryck, Lange, Martindale, Panny, and Renes, recently optimized by Meyer and Reith, which can leak various information about the private key. Therefore, we present an efficient constant-time implementation that samples key elements only from intervals of nonnegative numbers and uses dummy isogenies, which prevents certain kinds of side-channel attacks. We apply several optimizations, e.g. Elligator and the newly introduced SIMBA, in order to get a more efficient implementation.

Keywords: CSIDH · Isogeny-based cryptography ·
Post-quantum cryptography · Constant-time implementation

1 Introduction

Isogeny-based cryptography is the most juvenile family of the current proposals for post-quantum cryptography. The first cryptosystem based on the hardness of finding an explicit isogeny between two given isogenous elliptic curves over a finite field was proposed in 1997 by Couveignes [10], eventually independently rediscovered by Rostovtsev and Stolbunov [19] in 2004, and therefore typically called CRS. Childs, Jao, and Soukharev [7] showed in 2010 that CRS can be broken using a subexponential quantum algorithm by solving an abelian hidden shift problem. To avoid this attack, Jao and De Feo [13] invented a new isogeny-based scheme SIDH (supersingular isogeny Diffie-Hellman) that works with supersingular curves over $\mathbb{F}_{p^2}$. The current state-of-the-art implementation is SIKE [12], which was submitted to the NIST post-quantum cryptography competition [17].

De Feo, Kieffer and Smith optimized CRS in 2018 [11]. Their ideas led to the development of CSIDH by Castryck, Lange, Martindale, Panny, and Renes [6],

This work was partially supported by Elektrobit Automotive, Erlangen, Germany.

© Springer Nature Switzerland AG 2019
J. Ding and R. Steinwandt (Eds.): PQCrypto 2019, LNCS 11505, pp. 307–325, 2019.
https://doi.org/10.1007/978-3-030-25510-7_17

who adapted the CRS scheme to supersingular curves and isogenies defined over a prime field $\mathbb{F}_p$. They implemented the key exchange as a proof-of-concept, which is efficient, but does not run in constant time, and can therefore leak information about private keys. We note that building an efficient constant-time implementation of CSIDH is not as straightforward as in SIDH, where, speaking of running times, only one Montgomery ladder computation depends on the private key (see [9]).

In this paper we present a constant-time implementation of CSIDH with many practical optimizations, requiring only a small overhead of factor 3.03 compared to the fastest variable-time implementation from [14].

Organization. The rest of this paper is organized as follows. The following section gives a brief algorithmic introduction to CSIDH [6]. Leakage scenarios based on time, power analysis, and cache timing are presented in Sect. 3. In Sect. 4, we suggest different methods on how to avoid these leakages and build a constant-time implementation. Section 5 contains a straightforward application of our suggested methods, and various optimizations. Thereafter, we provide implementation results in Sect. 6 and give concluding remarks in Sect. 7. Appendices A and B give more details about our implementations and algorithms.

Note that there are two different notions of constant-time implementations, as explained in [3]. In our case, it suffices to work with the notion that the running time does not depend upon the choice of the private key, but may vary due to randomness. The second notion specifies strict constant time, meaning that the running time must be the same every time, independent from private keys or randomness. Throughout this paper, 'constant time' refers to the first notion described above.

Related Work. In [3], Bernstein, Lange, Martindale, and Panny describe constant-time implementations in the second notion from above, which is required for quantum attacks. In this paper, we follow the mentioned different approach for an efficient constant-time implementation, but reuse some of the techniques from [3].

2   CSIDH

We only cover the algorithmic aspects of CSIDH here, and refer to [6] for the mathematical background and a more detailed description.

We first choose a prime of the form $p = 4 \cdot \ell_1 \cdot \ldots \cdot \ell_n - 1$, where the ℓ_i are small distinct odd primes. We work with supersingular curves over $\mathbb{F}_p$, which guarantees the existence of points of the orders ℓ_i, that enable us to compute ℓ_i-isogenies from kernel generator points by Vélu-type formulas [20].

A private key consists of a tuple $(e_1, \ldots, e_n)$, where the e_i are sampled from an interval $[-B, B]$. The absolute value $|e_i|$ specifies how many ℓ_i-isogenies have to be computed, and the sign of e_i determines, whether points on the current

---

Algorithm 1. Evaluating the class group action.

Input : $a \in \mathbb{F}_p$ such that $E_a : y^2 = x^3 + ax^2 + x$ is supersingular, and a list of integers $(e_1, ..., e_n)$ with $e_i \in \{-B, ..., B\}$ for all $i \leq n$.

Output: $a' \in \mathbb{F}_p$, the curve parameter of the resulting curve $E_{a'}$.

```
 1  while some eᵢ ≠ 0 do
 2  │   Sample a random x ∈ 𝔽ₚ.
 3  │   Set s ← +1 if x³ + ax² + x is a square in 𝔽ₚ, else s ← −1.
 4  │   Let S = {i | sign(eᵢ) = s}.
 5  │   if S = ∅ then
 6  │   └   Go to line 2.
 7  │   P = (x : 1), k ← ∏ᵢ∈S ℓᵢ, P ← [(p + 1)/k]P.
 8  │   foreach i ∈ S do
 9  │   │   K ← [k/ℓᵢ]P.
10  │   │   if K ≠ ∞ then
11  │   │   │   Compute a degree-ℓᵢ isogeny φ : Eₐ → Eₐ′ with ker(φ) = ⟨K⟩.
12  │   │   └   a ← a′, P ← φ(P), k ← k/ℓᵢ, eᵢ ← eᵢ − s.
```

---

curve or on its twist have to be used as kernel generators. One can represent this graphically: Over $\mathbb{F}_p$, the supersingular ℓ_i-isogeny graph consists of distinct cycles. Therefore, we have to walk $|e_i|$ steps through the cycle for ℓ_i, and the sign of e_i tells us the direction.

Since this class group action is commutative, it allows a basic Diffie-Hellman-type key exchange: Starting from a supersingular curve E_0, Alice and Bob choose a private key as described above, and compute their public key curves E_A resp. E_B via isogenies, as described in Algorithm 1. Then Alice repeats her computations, this time starting at the curve E_B, and vice versa. Both parties then arrive at the same curve E_{AB}, which represents their shared secret. Furthermore, public keys can be verified efficiently in CSIDH (see [6]). Therefore, a static-static key-exchange is possible.

However, the quantum security is still an open problem. For our implementation we use CSIDH-512, the parameter set from [6], that is conjectured to satisfy NIST security level 1. In the light of the subexponential quantum attack on CRS and CSIDH [7], more analysis on CSIDH has been done in [3–5].

3   Leakage Scenarios

It is clear and already mentioned in [6] that the proof-of-concept implementation of CSIDH is not side-channel resistant. In this paper we focus on three scenarios that can leak information on the private key. Note that the second scenario features a stronger attacker. Further, there will of course be many more scenarios for side-channel attacks.

Timing Leakage. As the private key in CSIDH specifies how many isogenies of each degree have to be computed, it is obvious that this (up to additional effort for point multiplications due to the random choice of points) determines the running time of the algorithm. As stated in [14], the worst case running time occurs for the private key $(5, 5, \ldots, 5)$, and takes more than 3 times as much as in the average case. The other extreme is the private key $(0, 0, \ldots, 0)$, which would require no computations at all. However, in a timing-attack protected implementation, the running time should be independent from the private key.

Power Analysis. Instead of focusing on the running time, we now assume that an attacker can measure the power consumption of the algorithm. We further assume that from the measurement, the attacker can determine blocks which represent the two main primitives in CSIDH, namely point multiplication and isogeny computation, and can separate these from each other. Now assume that the attacker can separate the loop iterations from each other. Then the attacker can determine which private key elements share the same sign from the isogeny blocks that are performed in the same loop, since they have variable running time based on the isogeny degree. This significantly reduces the possible key space and therefore also the complexity of finding the correct key.

Cache Timing Attacks. In general, data flow from the secret key to branch conditions and array indices must be avoided in order to achieve protection against cache timing attacks [1]. Our implementation follows these guidelines to avoid vulnerabilities against the respective possible attacks.

4   Mitigating Leakage

In this section we give some ideas on how to fix these possible leakages in an implementation of CSIDH. We outline the most important ideas here, and give details about how to implement them efficiently in CSIDH-512 in Sect. 5.

Dummy Isogenies. First, it seems obvious that one should compute a constant number of isogenies of each degree ℓ_i, and only use the results of those required by the private key, in order to obtain a constant running time. However, in this case additional multiplications are required, if normal isogenies and unused isogenies are computed in the same loop[1]. We adapt the idea of using dummy isogenies from [14] for that cause. Meyer and Reith propose to design dummy isogenies, which instead of updating the curve parameters and evaluating the curve point P, compute $[\ell_i]P$ in the degree-ℓ_i dummy isogeny. Since the isogeny algorithm computes $[\frac{\ell_i - 1}{2}]K$ for the kernel generator K, one can replace K by P there, and perform two more differential additions to compute $[\ell_i]P$. The curve parameters remain unchanged.

---

[1] This is required, since otherwise, an attacker in the second leakage scenario can determine the private key easily.

In consequence, a dummy isogeny simply performs a scalar multiplication. Therefore, the output point $[\ell_i]P$ then has order not divisible by ℓ_i, which is important for using this point to compute correct kernel generators in following iterations. Further, one can design the isogeny and dummy isogeny algorithms for a given degree ℓ_i such that they perform the same number and sequence of operations with only minor computational overhead compared to the isogenies from [14]. This is important to make it hard for side-channel attackers to distinguish between those two cases, since conditionally branching can be avoided with rather small overhead.

Balanced vs. Unbalanced Private Keys. Using dummy isogenies to spend a fixed time on isogeny computations in not enough for a constant-time implementation, however. Another problem lies in the point multiplications in line 7 and 9 of Algorithm 1. We use an observation from [14] to illustrate this. They consider the private keys $(5, 5, 5, \ldots)$ and $(5, -5, 5, -5, \ldots)$ and observe that for the first key, the running time is 50% higher than for the second key. The reason for this is that in the first case in order to compute one isogeny of each degree, the multiplication in line 7 is only a multiplication by 4, and the multiplication in line 9 has a factor of bitlength 509 in the first iteration, 500 in the second iteration, and so on.

For the second key, we have to perform one loop through the odd i and one through the even i in order two compute one isogeny of each degree ℓ_i. Therefore, the multiplications in line 7 are by 254 resp. 259 bit factors, while the bitlengths of the factors in the multiplications in line 9 are $252, 244, \ldots$, resp. 257, 248, and so on (see Fig. 1). In total, adding up the bitlengths of all factors, we can measure the cost of all point multiplications for the computation of one isogeny per degree, where we assume that the condition in line 10 of Algorithm 1 never fails, since one Montgomery ladder step is performed per bit. For the first key, we end up with 16813 bits, while for the second key we only have 9066 bits.

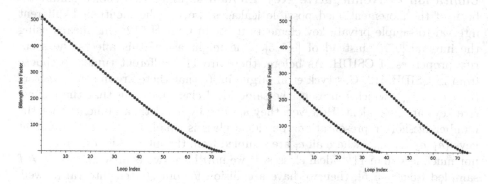

Fig. 1. Bitlengths of factors for computing one isogeny per degree for the keys $(5, 5, \ldots, 5)$ (left) and $(5, -5, 5, -5, \ldots)$ (right).

This can be generalized to any private key: The more the key elements (or the products of the respective ℓ_i) are unbalanced, i.e. many of them share the same sign, the more the computational effort grows, compared to the perfectly balanced case from above. This behavior depends on the private key and can therefore leak information. Hence, it is clear that we have to prevent this in order to achieve a constant-time implementation.

One way to achieve this is to use constant-time Montgomery ladders that always run to the maximum bitlength, no matter how large the respective factor is. However, this would lead to a massive increase in running time. Another possibility for handling this is to only choose key elements of a fixed sign. Then we have to adjust the interval from which we sample the integer key elements, e.g. from $[-5, 5]$ to $[0, 10]$ in CSIDH-512. This however doubles the computational effort for isogenies (combined normal and dummy isogenies). We will return to this idea later.

Determining the Sign Distribution. In our second leakage scenario, an attacker might determine the sign distribution of the key elements by identifying blocks of isogeny resp. dummy isogeny computations. One way of mitigating this attack would be to let each degree-ℓ_i isogeny run as long as a ℓ_{max}-isogeny, where ℓ_{max} is the largest ℓ_i. As used in [3], this is possible because of the Matryoshka-doll structure of the isogeny algorithms. This would allow an attacker in the second leakage scenario to only determine the number of positive resp. negative elements, but not their distribution, at the cost of a large increase of computational effort. We can also again restrict to the case that we only choose nonnegative (resp. only nonpositive) key elements. Then there is no risk of leaking information about the sign distribution of the elements, since in this setting the attacker knows this beforehand, at the cost of twice as many isogeny computations.

Limitation to Nonnegative Key Elements. Since this choice eliminates both of the aforementioned possible leakages, we use the mentioned different interval to sample private key elements from. In CSIDH-512, this means using the interval $[0, 10]$ instead of $[-5, 5]$. One might ask if this affects the security properties of CSIDH. As before, there are 11^{74} different tuples to choose from in CSIDH-512. Castryck et al. argue in [6] that there are multiple vectors $(e_1, e_2, \ldots, e_n)$, which represent the same ideal class, meaning that the respective keys are equivalent. However, they assume by heuristic arguments that the number of short representations per ideal class is small, i.e. the 11^{74} different keys $(e_1, e_2, \ldots, e_n)$, where all e_i are sampled from the interval $[-5, 5]$, represent not much less than 11^{74} ideal classes. If we now have two equivalent keys $e \neq f$ sampled from $[-5, 5]$, then we have a collision for our shifted interval as well, since shifting all elements of e and f by $+5$ results in equivalent keys $e' \neq f'$ with elements in $[0, 10]$, and vice versa. Therefore, our shifted version is equivalent to CSIDH-512 as defined in [6][2].

In the following sections we focus on optimized implementations, using the mentioned countermeasures against attacks, i.e. sampling key elements from the interval $[0, 10]$ and using dummy isogenies.

5   Efficient Implementation

5.1   Straightforward Implementation

First, we describe the straightforward implementation of the evaluation of the class group action in CSIDH-512 with the choices from above, before applying various optimizations. We briefly go through the implementation aspects of the main primitives, i.e. point multiplications, isogenies and dummy isogenies, and explain why this algorithm runs in constant time, and does not leak information about the private key.

Parameters. As described in [6], we have a prime number $p = 4 \cdot \ell_1 \cdot \ell_2 \cdot \ldots \cdot \ell_n - 1$, where the ℓ_i are small distinct odd primes. We further assume that we have $\ell_1 > \ell_2 > \ldots > \ell_n$. In CSIDH-512 we have $n = 74$, and we sample the elements of private keys $(e_1, e_2, \ldots, e_n)$ from $[0, 10]$.

Handling the Private Key. Similar to the original implementation of Castryck et al., we copy the elements of the private key in an array $e = (e_1, e_2, \ldots, e_n)$, where e_i determines how many isogenies of degree ℓ_i we have to compute. Furthermore, we set up another array $f = (10-e_1, 10-e_2, \ldots, 10-e_n)$, to determine how many dummy isogenies of each degree we have to compute. As we go through the algorithm, we compute all the required isogenies and dummy isogenies, reducing e_i resp. f_i by 1 after each degree-ℓ_i isogeny resp. dummy isogeny. We therefore end up with a total of 10 isogeny computations (counting isogenies and dummy isogenies) for each ℓ_i.

Sampling Random Points. In Algorithm 2 line 3, we have to find curve points on the current curve that are defined over $\mathbb{F}_p$ instead of $\mathbb{F}_{p^2} \setminus \mathbb{F}_p$. As in [6] this can be done by sampling a random $x \in \mathbb{F}_p$, and computing y^2 by the curve equation $y^2 = x^3 + ax^2 + x$. We then check if y is defined over $\mathbb{F}_p$ by a Legendre symbol computation, i.e. by checking if $(y^2)^{(p-1)/2} \equiv 1 \pmod{p}$. If this is not the case, we simply repeat this procedure until we find a suitable point. Note that we require the curve parameter a to be in affine form. Since a will typically be in projective form after isogeny computations, we therefore have to compute the affine parameter each time before sampling a new point.

---

[2] One could also think of using the starting curve E', which is the result of applying the key $(5, 5, \ldots, 5)$ to the curve E_0. Then for a class group action evaluation using key elements from $[-5, 5]$ and the starting curve E' is equivalent to using key elements from $[0, 10]$ and the starting curve E_0.

Algorithm 2. Constant-time evaluation of the class group action in CSIDH-512.

Input : $a \in \mathbb{F}_p$ such that $E_a : y^2 = x^3 + ax^2 + x$ is supersingular, and a list of integers $(e_1, ..., e_n)$ with $e_i \in \{0, 1, .., 10\}$ for all $i \leq n$.

Output: $a' \in \mathbb{F}_p$, the curve parameter of the resulting curve $E_{a'}$.

1 Initialize $k = 4$, $e = (e_1, ..., e_n)$ and $f = (f_1, ..., f_n)$, where $f_i = 10 - e_i$.
2 **while** some $e_i \neq 0$ or $f_i \neq 0$ **do**
3   Sample random values $x \in \mathbb{F}_p$ until we have some x where $x^3 + ax^2 + x$ is a square in $\mathbb{F}_p$.
4   Set $P = (x : 1)$, $P \leftarrow [k]P$, $S = \{i \mid e_i \neq 0$ or $f_i \neq 0\}$.
5   **foreach** $i \in S$ **do**
6   Let $m = \prod_{j \in S, j > i} \ell_i$.
7   Set $K \leftarrow [m]P$.
8   **if** $K \neq \infty$ **then**
9   **if** $e_i \neq 0$ **then**
10   Compute a degree-ℓ_i isogeny $\varphi : E_a \rightarrow E_{a'}$ with $ker(\varphi) = \langle K \rangle$.
11         $a \leftarrow a'$, $P \leftarrow \varphi(P)$, $e_i \leftarrow e_i - 1$.
12   **else**
13   Compute a degree-ℓ_i dummy isogeny:
14         $a \leftarrow a$, $P \leftarrow [\ell_i]P$, $f_i \leftarrow f_i - 1$.
15   **if** $e_i = 0$ *and* $f_i = 0$ **then**
16   Set $k \leftarrow k \cdot \ell_i$.

Elliptic Curve Point Multiplications. Since we work with Montgomery curves, using only projective XZ-coordinates, and projective curve parameters $a = A/C$, we can use the standard Montgomery ladder as introduced in [15], adapted to projective curve parameters as in [9]. This means that per bit of the factor, one combined doubling and differential addition is performed.

Isogenies. For the computation of isogenies, we use the formulas presented by Meyer and Reith in [14]. They combine the Montgomery isogeny formulas by Costello and Hisil [8], and Renes [18] with the twisted Edwards formulas by Moody and Shumow [16], in order to obtain an efficient algorithm for the isogeny computations in CSIDH. For a ℓ_i-isogeny, this requires a point K of order ℓ_i as kernel generator, and the projective parameters A and C of the current curve. It outputs the image curve parameters A' and C', and the evaluation of the point P. As mentioned before, the algorithm computes all multiples of the point K up to the factor $\frac{\ell_i - 1}{2}$. See e.g. [3] for more details.

Dummy Isogenies. As described before, we want the degree-ℓ_i dummy isogenies to output the scalar multiple $[\ell_i]P$ instead of an isogeny evaluation of P. Therefore, we interchange the points K and P in the original isogeny algorithm, such that it computes $[\frac{\ell_i-1}{2}]P$. We then perform two more differential additions, i.e. compute $[\frac{\ell_i+1}{2}]P$ from $[\frac{\ell_i-1}{2}]P$, P, and $[\frac{\ell_i-3}{2}]P$, and compute $[\ell_i]P$ from $[\frac{\ell_i+1}{2}]P$, $[\frac{\ell_i-1}{2}]P$, and P.

As mentioned before, we want isogenies and dummy isogenies of degree ℓ_i to share the same code in order to avoid conditionally branching. Hence, the two extra differential additions are also performed in the isogeny algorithm, without using the results. In our implementation, a conditional point swapping based on a bitmask ensures that the correct input point is chosen. This avoids conditionally branching that depends on the private key in line 9 of Algorithm 2 (and lines 11 and 27 of Algorithm 5).

If one is concerned that a side-channel attacker can detect that the curve parameters A and C are not changed for some time (meaning that a series of dummy isogenies is performed), one could further rerandomize the projective representation of the curve parameter A/C by multiplying A and C by the same random number[3] $1 < \alpha < p$.

5.2 Running Time

We now explain why this algorithm runs in constant time. As already explained, we perform 10 isogeny computations (counting isogenies and dummy isogenies) for each degree ℓ_i. Furthermore, isogenies and dummy isogenies have the same running time, since they share the same code, and conditionally branching is avoided. Therefore the total computational effort for isogenies is constant, independent from the respective private key. We also set the same condition (line 8 of Algorithm 2) for the kernel generator for the computation of a dummy isogeny, in order not to leak information.

Sampling random points and finding a suitable one doesn't run in constant time in Algorithm 2. However, the running time only depends on randomly chosen values, and does not leak any information on the private key.

Now for simplicity assume that we always find a point of full order, i.e. a point that can be used to compute one isogeny of each degree ℓ_i. Then it is easy to see that the total computational effort for scalar multiplications in Algorithm 2 is constant, independent from the respective private key. If we now allow random points, we will typically not satisfy the condition in line 8 of Algorithm 2 for all i. Therefore, additional computations (sampling random points, and point multiplications) are required. However, this does not leak information about the private key, since this only depends on the random choice of curve points, but not on the private key.

Hence, we conclude that the implementation of Algorithm 2 as described here prevents the leakage scenarios considered in Sect. 3. It is however quite slow compared to the performance of variable-time CSIDH-512 in [6,14]. In the following section, we focus on how to optimize and speed up the implementation.

---

[3] One could actually use an intermediate value $\alpha \in \mathbb{F}_p \setminus \{0, 1\}$ of the isogeny computation, since the factor is not required to be truly random.

5.3   Optimizations

Sampling Points with Elligator. In [3] Bernstein, Lange, Martindale, and Panny pointed out that Elligator [2], specifically the Elligator 2 map, can be used in CSIDH to be able to choose points over the required field of definition. Since we only need points defined over $\mathbb{F}_p$, this is especially advantageous in our situation. For $a \neq 0$ the Elligator 2 map works as follows (see [3]):

- Sample a random $u \in \{2, 3, \ldots, (p-1)/2\}$.
- Compute $v = a/(u^2 - 1)$.
- Compute e, the Legendre symbol of $v^3 + av^2 + v$.
- If $e = 1$, output v. Otherwise, output $-v - a$.

Therefore, for all $a \neq 0$, we can replace the search for a suitable point in line 3 of Algorithm 2, at the cost of an extra inversion. However, as explained by Bernstein et al., one can precompute $1/(u^2 - 1)$ for some values of u, e.g. for $u \in \{2, 3, 4, \ldots\}$. Then the cost is essentially the same as for the random choice of points, but we always find a suitable point this way, compared to the probability of $1/2$ when sampling random points. This could, however, potentially lead to the case that we cannot finish the computation: Consider that we only have one isogeny of degree ℓ_i left to compute, but for all of the precomputed values of u, the order of the corresponding point is not divided by ℓ_i. Then we would have to go back to a random choice of points to finish the computation. However, our experiments suggest that it is enough to have 10 precomputed values. Note that the probability for actually finding points of suitable order appears to be almost unchanged when using Elligator instead of random points, as discussed in [3].

For $a = 0$, Bernstein et al. also show how to adapt the Elligator 2 map to this case, but also argue that one could precompute a point of full order (or almost full order, i.e. divided by all ℓ_i) and simply use this point whenever $a = 0$. We follow their latter approach.

SIMBA (Splitting Isogeny Computations into Multiple Batches). In Sect. 4, we analyzed the running time of variable-time CSIDH-512 for the keys $e_1 = (5, 5, \ldots, 5)$ and $e_2 = (5, -5, 5, -5, \ldots)$. For the latter, the algorithm is significantly faster, because of the smaller multiplications during the loop (line 9 of Algorithm 1), see Fig. 1. We adapt and generalize this observation here, in order to speed up our constant-time implementation.

Consider for our setting the key $(10, 10, \ldots, 10)$ and that we can again always choose points of full order. To split the indices in two sets (exactly as Algorithm 1 does for the key e_2), we define the sets $S_1 = \{1, 3, 5, \ldots, 73\}$ and $S_2 = \{2, 4, 6, \ldots, 74\}$. Then the loops through the ℓ_i for $i \in S_1$ resp. $i \in S_2$ require significantly smaller multiplications, while only requiring to compute $[4k]P$ with $k = \prod_{i \in S_2} \ell_i$ resp. $k = \prod_{i \in S_1} \ell_i$ beforehand. We now simply perform 10 loops for each set, and hence this gives exactly the same speedup over Algorithm 2, as Algorithm 1 gives for the key e_2 compared to e_1, by using two batches of indices instead of only one.

One might ask if splitting the indices in two sets already gives the best speedup. We generalize the observation from above, now splitting the indices into m batches, where $S_1 = \{1, m+1, 2m+1, \ldots\}$, $S_2 = \{2, m+2, 2m+2, \ldots\}$, and so on[4]. Before starting a loop through the indices $i \in S_j$ with $1 \leq j \leq m$, one now has to compute $[4k]P$ with $k = \prod_{h \notin S_j} \ell_h$. The number and size of these multiplications grows when m grows, so we can expect that the speedup turns into an increasing computational effort when m is too large.

To find the best choice for m, we computed the total number of Montgomery ladder steps during the computation of one isogeny of each degree in CSIDH-512 for different m, with the assumptions from above. We did not take into account here that when m grows, we will have to sample more points (which costs at least one Legendre symbol computation each), since this depends on the cost ratio between Montgomery ladder steps and Legendre symbol computations in the respective implementation. Table 1 shows that the optimal choice should be around $m = 5$.

Table 1. Number of Montgomery ladder steps for computing one isogeny of each degree in CSIDH-512 for different numbers of batches m.

m	1	2	3	4	5	6	7
Ladder steps	16813	9066	6821	5959	5640	5602	5721

If we now come back to the choice of points through Elligator, the assumption from above does not hold anymore, and with very high probability, we will need more than 10 loops per index set. Typically, soon after 10 loops through each batch the large degree isogenies will be finished, while there are some small degree isogenies left to compute. In this case our optimization backfires, since in this construction, the indices of the missing ℓ_i will be distributed among the m different batches. We therefore need large multiplications in order to only check a few small degrees per set. Hence it is beneficial to define a number $\mu \geq 10$, and merge the batches after μ steps, i.e. simply going back to Algorithm 2 for the computation of the remaining isogenies. We dub this construction SIMBA-m-μ.

Sampling Private Key Elements from Different Intervals. Instead of sampling all private key elements from the interval $[0, 10]$, and in total computing 10 isogenies of each degree, one could also consider to choose the key elements from different intervals for each isogeny degree, as done in [11]. For a private key $e = (e_1, e_2, \ldots, e_n)$, we can choose an interval $[0, B_i]$ for each e_i, in order to e.g. reduce the number of expensive large degree isogenies at the cost of computing

---

[4] Note that in [3] a similar idea is described. However, in their algorithm only two isogeny degrees are covered in each iteration. Our construction makes use of the fact that we restrict to intervals of nonnegative numbers for sampling the private key elements.

more small degree isogenies. We require $\prod_i (B_i+1) \approx 11^{74}$, in order to obtain the same security level as before. For the security implication of this choice, similar arguments as in Sect. 4 apply.

Trying to find the optimal parameters B_i leads to a large integer optimization problem, which is not likely to be solvable exactly. Therefore, we heuristically searched for parameters likely to improve the performance of CSIDH-512. We present them in Sect. 6 and Appendix A.

Note that if we choose $B = (B_1, \ldots, B_n)$ differently from $B = (10, 10, \ldots, 10)$, the benefit of our optimizations above will change accordingly. Therefore, we changed the parameters m and μ in our implementation according to the respective B.

Skip Point Evaluations. As described before, the isogeny algorithms compute the image curve parameters, and push a point P through the isogeny. However, in the last isogeny per loop, this is unnecessary, since we choose a new point after the isogeny computation anyway. Therefore, it saves some computational effort, if we skip the point evaluation part in these cases.

Application to Variable-Time CSIDH. Note that many of the optimizations from above are also applicable to variable-time CSIDH-512 implementations as in [14] or [6]. We could therefore also speed up the respective implementation results using the mentioned methods.

6   Implementation Results

We implemented our optimized constant-time algorithm in C, using the implementation accompanying [14], which is based on the implementation from the original CSIDH paper by Castryck et al. [6]. For example the implementation of the field arithmetic in assembly is the one from [6]. Our final algorithm, containing all the optimizations from above, can be found in Appendix B.

Since we described different optimizations that can influence one another, it is not straightforward to decide which parameters B, m, and μ to use. Therefore, we tested various choices and combinations of parameters B, m, and μ, assuming $\ell_1 > \ell_2 > \ldots > \ell_n$. The parameters and implementation results can be found in Appendix A. The best parameters we found are given by

$$B = [5,7,7,7,7,7,7,7,7,7,7,7,7,7,7,7,7,7,7,7,7,8,8,8,8,8,8,8,11,11,11,$$
$$11,11,11,11,11,11,11,11,11,11,11,11,11,11,11,13,13,13,13,13,13,13$$
$$13,13,13,13,13,13,13,13,13,13,13,13,13,13,13,13,13,13,13,13]$$

using SIMBA-5-11, where the key element e_i is chosen from $[0, B_i]$. We do not claim that these are the best parameters; there might be better choices that we did not consider in our experiments.

We further tried to rearrange the order of the primes ℓ_i in the different loops. As pointed out in [14], it is beneficial to go through the ℓ_i in descending order. However, if we suppress isogeny point evaluations in the last iteration per loop, this means that these savings refer to small ℓ_i, and therefore the impact of this is rather small. Hence, we put a few large primes at the end of the loops, therefore requiring more computational effort for point multiplications, which is however in some situations outweighed by the larger savings from not evaluating points.

In this way, the best combination we found for CSIDH-512 is $\ell_1 = 349$, $\ell_2 = 347$, $\ell_3 = 337, \ldots, \ell_{69} = 3, \ell_{70} = 587, \ell_{71} = 373, \ell_{72} = 367, \ell_{73} = 359$, and $\ell_{74} = 353$, using SIMBA-5-11 and B from above, where the B_i are swapped accordingly to the ℓ_i.

Table 2. Performance of one class group action evaluation in CSIDH-512 with the mentioned parameters. All timings were measured on an Intel Core i7-6500 Skylake processor running Ubuntu 16.04 LTS, averaged over 1 000 runs.

Clock cycles $\times 10^8$	Wall clock time
3.145	121.3 ms

In Table 2, we give the cycle count and running time for the implementation using the parameters from above. The code is freely available at https://zenon. cs.hs-rm.de/pqcrypto/constant-csidh-c-implementation.

To give a comparison that mainly shows the impact of SIMBA and the different choice of B, we also ran the straightforward implementation according to Algorithm 2 with $B = [10, 10, \ldots, 10]$, also using Elligator. In this case, we measured 621.5 million clock cycles in the same setting as above.

Compared to the performance of the variable-time implementation from [14], the results from Table 2 mean a slowdown of factor 3.03. However, as mentioned, also the variable-time implementation can benefit from the optimizations from this paper, so this comparison should not be taken too serious.

7 Conclusion

We present the first implementation of CSIDH that prevents certain side-channel attacks, such as timing leakages. However, there might be more leakage models, depending on how powerful the attacker is. There is also more work to be done on making this implementation as efficient as possible. It may e.g. be possible to find a CSIDH-friendly prime p that allows for faster computations in $\mathbb{F}_p$.

Also the security features of CSIDH remain an open problem. More analysis on this is required, to show if the parameters are chosen correctly for the respective security levels.

We note that our results depend on the parameters from CSIDH-512. However, it is clear that the described optimizations can be adapted to other parameter sets and security levels as well.

Acknowledgments. This work was partially supported by Elektrobit Automotive, Erlangen, Germany. We thank Joost Renes for answering some questions during the preparation of this work, and the anonymous reviewers for their helpful and valuable comments.

A   Implementation Results

We tested several parameters in a dynamical implementation, as explained in the paper. The setting is the same as in Sect. 6. For the parameters $B_0, \ldots, B_4$ we chose

$$B_0 = [10, 10, 10, ..., 10],$$

$$B_1 = [1, 6, 6, 6, 6, 6, 6, 6, 6, 6, 6, 6, 6, 6, 6, 6, 6, 6, 6, 6, 6, 6, 8, 8, 8, 8, 8, 8, 8,$$
$$12, 12, 12, 12, 12, 12, 12, 12, 12, 12, 12, 12, 12, 12, 14, 14, 14, 14, 14,$$
$$14, 14, 14, 14, 14, 14, 14, 14, 14, 14, 14, 14, 14, 14, 14, 14, 14, 14, 14,$$
$$14, 14, 14, 14, 14, 14, 14, 14],$$

$$B_2 = [5, 7, 7, 7, 7, 7, 7, 7, 7, 7, 7, 7, 7, 7, 7, 7, 7, 7, 7, 7, 7, 7, 8, 8, 8, 8, 8, 8, 8,$$
$$11, 11, 11, 11, 11, 11, 11, 11, 11, 11, 11, 11, 11, 11, 11, 11, 11, 11, 13,$$
$$13, 13, 13, 13, 13, 13, 13, 13, 13, 13, 13, 13, 13, 13, 13, 13, 13, 13, 13,$$
$$13, 13, 13, 13, 13, 13, 13, 13],$$

$$B_3 = [2, 4, 4, 4, 4, 4, 4, 4, 4, 4, 4, 4, 4, 4, 6, 6, 6, 6, 6, 6, 6, 6, 6, 6, 10, 10,$$
$$10, 10, 10, 10, 10, 10, 10, 10, 10, 16, 16, 16, 16, 16, 16, 16, 16, 16, 16,$$
$$16, 16, 16, 16, 16, 16, 16, 16, 16, 16, 16, 16, 16, 16, 16, 16, 16, 16, 16,$$
$$16, 16, 16, 16, 16, 16, 16, 16, 16], \text{ and}$$

$$B_4 = [2, 2, 2, 2, 2, 2, 2, 2, 2, 2, 2, 2, 2, 2, 2, 2, 2, 2, 2, 2, 2, 2, 2, 2, 12, 20, 20,$$
$$20, 20, 20, 20, 20, 20, 20, 20, 20, 20, 20, 20, 20, 20, 20, 20, 20, 20, 20,$$
$$20, 20, 20, 20, 20, 20, 20, 20, 20, 20, 20, 20, 20, 20, 20, 20, 20, 20, 20,$$
$$20, 20, 20, 20, 20, 20, 20, 20, 20].$$

In an earlier version of our implementation we measured many different combinations with different m and μ, running SIMBA-m-μ as described above, averaging the running time over 1 000 runs per parameter set, given in 10^6 clock cycles. For each B_i, we present the three best combinations we found in the Table 3.

Table 3. Performance of one class group action evaluation in CSIDH-512 with different combinations of parameters. All timings are given in 10^6 clock cycles, and were measured on an Intel Core i7-6500 Skylake processor running Ubuntu 16.04 LTS, averaged over 1 000 runs.

B	1st		2nd		3rd	
0	$\mu = 10$ $m = 5$	338.1	$\mu = 10$ $m = 6$	343.5	$\mu = 11$ $m = 5$	343.7
1	$\mu = 12$ $m = 4$	329.3	$\mu = 14$ $m = 4$	330.6	$\mu = 13$ $m = 4$	330.8
2	$\mu = 11$ $m = 5$	326.5	$\mu = 12$ $m = 5$	327.0	$\mu = 11$ $m = 4$	327.6
3	$\mu = 16$ $m = 4$	333.8	$\mu = 17$ $m = 4$	337.6	$\mu = 16$ $m = 3$	339.3
4	$\mu = 20$ $m = 3$	397.5	$\mu = 20$ $m = 4$	399.0	$\mu = 21$ $m = 3$	399.5

We further tried to rearrange the order of the primes ℓ_i in the different loops, as described in Sect. 6. However, the fastest parameter set from above was the best choice in all our tests.

B   Algorithms

In this section we describe our constant-time algorithm, containing the optimizations from above. We split the application of SIMBA in two parts: SIMBA-I splits the isogeny computations in m batches, and SIMBA-II merges them after μ rounds. Note that in our implementation, it is actually not required to generate all the arrays from SIMBA-I.

Algorithm 5 shows the full class group action evaluation. Due to many loops and indices, it looks rather complicated. We recommend to additionally have a look at our implementation, provided in Sect. 6.

Algorithm 3. SIMBA-I.

Input : $e = (e_1, ..., e_n)$, $B = (B_1, ..., B_n)$, m.
Output: $e^i = (e_1^i, ..., e_n^i)$, $f^i = (f_1^i, ..., f_n^i)$, k_i for $i \in \{0, ..., m-1\}$.

1 Initialize $e^i = f^i = (0, 0, ..., 0)$ and $k_i = 4$ for $i \in \{0, ..., m-1\}$
2 foreach $i \in \{1, ..., n\}$ do
3 $\quad e_i^{i\%m} \leftarrow e_i$
4 $\quad f_i^{i\%m} \leftarrow B_i - e_i$
5 $\quad$ foreach $j \in \{1, ..., m\}$ do
6 $\quad\quad$ if $j \neq (i\%m)$ then
7 $\quad\quad\quad k_i \leftarrow k_i \cdot \ell_i$

Algorithm 4. SIMBA-II.

Input : $e^i = (e_1^i, ..., e_n^i)$ and $f^i = (f_1^i, ..., f_n^i)$ for $i \in \{0, ..., m-1\}$, m.
Output: $e = (e_1, ..., e_n)$, $f = (f_1, ..., f_n)$, and k.

1 Initialize $e = f = (0, 0, ..., 0)$, and $k = 4$.
2 foreach $i \in \{1, ..., n\}$ do
3 $\quad e_i \leftarrow e_i^{i\%m}$
4 $\quad f_i \leftarrow f_i^{i\%m}$
5 $\quad$ if $e_i = 0$ and $f_i = 0$ then
6 $\quad\quad k \leftarrow k \cdot \ell_i$

Algorithm 5. Constant-time evaluation of the class group action in CSIDH-512.

Input : $a \in \mathbb{F}_p$ such that $E_a : y^2 = x^3 + ax^2 + x$ is supersingular, a list of integers $(e_1, ..., e_n)$ with $0 \le e_i \le B_i$ for all $i \le n$, $B = (B_1, ..., B_n)$, m, μ.

Output: $a' \in \mathbb{F}_p$, the curve parameter of the resulting curve $E_{a'}$.

```
1   Run SIMBA-I(e, B, m).
2   foreach i ∈ {1, ..., μ} do
3       foreach j ∈ {1, ..., m} do
4           Run Elligator to find a point P, where y_P ∈ F_p.
5           P ← [k_j]P
6           S = {ι | e_ι^j ≠ 0 or f_ι^j ≠ 0}
7           foreach ι ∈ S do
8               α = ∏_{κ∈S,κ>ι} ℓ_κ
9               K ← [α]P.
10              if K ≠ ∞ then
11                  if e_ι^j ≠ 0 then
12                      Compute a degree-ℓ_ι isogeny φ : E_a → E_{a'} with
                        ker(φ) = ⟨K⟩.
13                      a ← a', P ← φ(P), e_ι^j ← e_ι^j − 1.
14                  else
15                      Compute a degree-ℓ_ι dummy isogeny:
16                      a ← a, P ← [ℓ_ι]P, f_ι^j ← f_ι^j − 1.
17                  if e_ι^j = 0 and f_ι^j = 0 then
18                      Set k_j = k_j · ℓ_ι.

19  Run SIMBA-II(e^i and f^i for i ∈ {0, ..., m − 1}, m).
20  while some e_i ≠ 0 or f_i ≠ 0 do
21      Run Elligator to find a point P, where y_P ∈ F_p.
22      Set P = (x : 1), P ← [k]P, S = {i | e_i ≠ 0 or f_i ≠ 0}.
23      foreach i ∈ S do
24          Let m = ∏_{j∈S,j<i} ℓ_j.
25          Set K ← [m]P.
26          if K ≠ ∞ then
27              if e_i ≠ 0 then
28                  Compute a degree-ℓ_i isogeny φ : E_a → E_{a'} with ker(φ) = ⟨K⟩.
29                  a ← a', P ← φ(P), e_i ← e_i − 1.
30              else
31                  Compute a degree-ℓ_i dummy isogeny:
32                  a ← a, P ← [ℓ_i]P, f_i ← f_i − 1.
33              if e_i = 0 and f_i = 0 then
34                  Set k = k · ℓ_i.
```

References

1. Bernstein, D.J., Duif, N., Lange, T., Schwabe, P., Yang, B.Y.: High-speed high-security signatures. J. Cryptogr. Eng. **2**(2), 77–89 (2012)
2. Bernstein, D.J., Hamburg, M., Krasnova, A., Lange, T.: Elligator: elliptic-curve points indistinguishable from uniform random strings. In: Proceedings of the 2013 ACM SIGSAC Conference on Computer & Communications Security, pp. 967–980. ACM (2013)
3. Bernstein, D.J., Lange, T., Martindale, C., Panny, L.: Quantum circuits for the CSIDH: optimizing quantum evaluation of isogenies. Cryptology ePrint Archive, Report 2018/1059 (2018). https://eprint.iacr.org/2018/1059
4. Biasse, J.-F., Iezzi, A., Jacobson, M.J.: A note on the security of CSIDH. In: Chakraborty, D., Iwata, T. (eds.) INDOCRYPT 2018. LNCS, vol. 11356, pp. 153–168. Springer, Cham (2018). https://doi.org/10.1007/978-3-030-05378-9_9
5. Bonnetain, X., Schrottenloher, A.: Quantum security analysis of CSIDH and ordinary isogeny-based schemes. Cryptology ePrint Archive, Report 2018/537 (2018). https://eprint.iacr.org/2018/537
6. Castryck, W., Lange, T., Martindale, C., Panny, L., Renes, J.: CSIDH: an efficient post-quantum commutative group action. In: Peyrin, T., Galbraith, S. (eds.) ASIACRYPT 2018. LNCS, vol. 11274, pp. 395–427. Springer, Cham (2018). https://doi.org/10.1007/978-3-030-03332-3_15
7. Childs, A., Jao, D., Soukharev, V.: Constructing elliptic curve isogenies in quantum subexponential time. J. Math. Cryptol. **8**(1), 1–29 (2014)
8. Costello, C., Hisil, H.: A simple and compact algorithm for SIDH with arbitrary degree isogenies. In: Takagi, T., Peyrin, T. (eds.) ASIACRYPT 2017. LNCS, vol. 10625, pp. 303–329. Springer, Cham (2017). https://doi.org/10.1007/978-3-319-70697-9_11
9. Costello, C., Longa, P., Naehrig, M.: Efficient algorithms for supersingular isogeny Diffie-Hellman. In: Robshaw, M., Katz, J. (eds.) CRYPTO 2016. LNCS, vol. 9814, pp. 572–601. Springer, Heidelberg (2016). https://doi.org/10.1007/978-3-662-53018-4_21
10. Couveignes, J.M.: Hard homogeneous spaces. Cryptology ePrint Archive, Report 2006/291 (2006). https://eprint.iacr.org/2006/291
11. De Feo, L., Kieffer, J., Smith, B.: Towards practical key exchange from ordinary isogeny graphs. In: Peyrin, T., Galbraith, S. (eds.) ASIACRYPT 2018. LNCS, vol. 11274, pp. 365–394. Springer, Cham (2018). https://doi.org/10.1007/978-3-030-03332-3_14
12. Jao, D., et al.: Supersingular isogeny key encapsulation. Round 1 submission, NIST Post-Quantum Cryptography Standardization (2017)
13. Jao, D., De Feo, L., Plût, J.: Towards quantum-resistant cryptosystems from supersingular elliptic curve isogenies. J. Math. Cryptol. **8**(3), 209–247 (2014)
14. Meyer, M., Reith, S.: A faster way to the CSIDH. In: Chakraborty, D., Iwata, T. (eds.) INDOCRYPT 2018. LNCS, vol. 11356, pp. 137–152. Springer, Cham (2018). https://doi.org/10.1007/978-3-030-05378-9_8
15. Montgomery, P.L.: Speeding the Pollard and elliptic curve methods of factorization. Math. Comput. **48**(177), 243–264 (1987)
16. Moody, D., Shumow, D.: Analogues of Vélu's formulas for isogenies on alternate models of elliptic curves. Math. Comput. **85**(300), 1929–1951 (2016)
17. National Institute of Standards and Technology (NIST): Submission requirements and evaluation criteria for the post-quantum cryptography standardization process (2016)

18. Renes, J.: Computing isogenies between montgomery curves using the action of (0, 0). In: Lange, T., Steinwandt, R. (eds.) PQCrypto 2018. LNCS, vol. 10786, pp. 229–247. Springer, Cham (2018). https://doi.org/10.1007/978-3-319-79063-3_11
19. Rostovtsev, A., Stolbunov, A.: Public-key cryptosystem based on isogenies. Cryptology ePrint Archive, Report 2006/145 (2006). http://eprint.iacr.org/2006/145
20. Vélu, J.: Isogénies entre courbes elliptiques. C.R. Acad. Sci. Paris Série A **271**, 238–241 (1971)

Hash-Based Cryptography

Quantum Security of Hash Functions and Property-Preservation of Iterated Hashing

Ben Hamlin[(✉)] and Fang Song[(✉)]

Texas A&M University, College Station, USA
{hamlinb,fang.song}@tamu.edu

Abstract. This work contains two major parts: comprehensively studying the security notions of cryptographic hash functions against quantum attacks and the relationships between them; and revisiting whether Merkle-Damgård and related iterated hash constructions preserve the security properties of the compression function in the quantum setting. Specifically, we adapt the seven notions in Rogaway and Shrimpton (FSE'04) to the quantum setting and prove that the seemingly stronger attack model where an adversary accesses a challenger in quantum superposition does not make a difference. We confirm the implications and separations between the seven properties in the quantum setting, and in addition we construct explicit examples separating an inherently quantum notion called collapsing from several proposed properties. Finally, we pin down the properties that are preserved under several iterated hash schemes. In particular, we prove that the ROX construction in Andreeva et al. (Asiacrypt'07) preserves the seven properties in the quantum random oracle model.

Keywords: Quantum random-oracle model ·
Post-quantum security definitions · Hash functions

1   Introduction

Cryptographic hash functions, which produce a short digest on an input message efficiently, are a ubiquitous building block in modern cryptography. They are indispensable in constructing key-establishment, authentication, encryption, digital signature, cryptocurrency, and more, which constitute the backbone of a secure cyberspace. A host of cryptographic hash functions have been designed [NIS15] which have been subject to extensive cryptanalysis. Most of the constructions follow the *iterated* hash paradigm, which iterates a compression function on a small domain.

The emerging technology of quantum computing brings devastating challenges to cryptography. In addition to breaking widely deployed public-key cryptography due to Shor's efficient quantum algorithm for factoring and discrete

© Springer Nature Switzerland AG 2019
J. Ding and R. Steinwandt (Eds.): PQCrypto 2019, LNCS 11505, pp. 329–349, 2019.
https://doi.org/10.1007/978-3-030-25510-7_18

330 B. Hamlin and F. Song

logarithm, effective quantum attacks on symmetric primitives have been found in recent years that break of a variety of message authentication and authenticated encryption schemes [KLLNP16, SS17].

In this work, we revisit two fundamental threads of cryptographic hash functions in the presence of quantum attacks: modeling basic security properties and establishing their interrelations; and pinning down whether the iterated hash constructions *preserve* the security of the underlying compression functions.

A principal security property is *collision resistance*: It should be computationally infeasible to compute a *collision* (x, x') such that $H(x) = H(x')$. Two other basic properties are preimage resistance (Pre) and second-preimage resistance (Sec). Rogaway and Shrimpton extend the three and arrive at a total of seven properties to cope with various scenarios [RS04]. More specifically, they consider a family of hash functions $H : \mathcal{K} \times \mathcal{M} \to \mathcal{D}$. Conventional Pre and Sec require that under a *random* key, it is infeasible to find a preimage of a *random* digest or to find a message that forms a collision with a given *random* input. They propose two variations named *always* and *everywhere*. For example, always preimage resistance (aPre) allows an attacker to pick a key K at will, and H_K needs to be preimage resistant in the usual sense. This reflects that real-world hash functions are standalone (i.e., unkeyed), so it is important to *always* enforce the property on all members in the hash family. In a complementary vein *everywhere* preimage resistance (ePre), for instance, asks about finding a preimage on any digest (i.e., adversarially chosen as opposed to a random one) being hard. They give a comprehensive characterization of the seven properties, including both implications and separations. For instance, they show that while Coll implies standard Pre, there exist Coll hash functions that are not aPre or ePre. This motivates our first question of this work:

How do we model these properties appropriately against quantum attacks, and what are the relationships between them?

Once the appropriate quantum security notions have been nailed down, we would like to construct hash functions achieving various desired properties. The dominating design framework is *iterated* hashing, which takes a compression function on a relatively small domain and runs it iteratively, with minor variations, to process longer messages. The Merkle-Damgård construction [Mer89, Dam89] (adopted by SHA-1,2 families) and the sponge construction [BDPA07] (adopted in SHA-3) are notable examples. As a modular approach to attaining security, researchers ask whether the iterated hash preserves the security of the compression function. It is known that Merkle-Damgård is collision resistant as long as the compression function is collision resistant. However it does not preserve preimage resistance: There is a preimage-resistant compression function, such that plugging it into Merkle-Damgård fails to result in preimage-resistance. Andreeva et al. [ANPS07] study several variants of Merkle-Damgård, such as XOR-linear [BR97] and Shoup's [Sho00] hash schemes, and determine their security-preserving capabilities. In short, none of them are able to preserve all seven properties. They therefore propose a new iterated construction, *ROX*, built on XOR-linear hash, and prove that it preserves all seven properties in the random oracle model[1]. In contrast, we refer to other constructions as being in the plain model. We pose the second major question of this work:

Are iterated hashes security preserving in the quantum setting?

A positive answer will dramatically simplify the design of secure hash functions to the design of a secure compression function of a small size. Answering this question, however, could be challenging and subtle. What we prove classically often fails to carry over against quantum attacks for some fundamental reasons (e.g., no-cloning of quantum states or probabilistic analysis that has no counterpart in the quantum formalism). There has been extensive work developing tools for analyzing quantum security [Wat09, Unr12, Son14, Zha12a]. In particular, Unruh proves that Merkle-Damgård preserves collapsing, and it can be observed that collision resistance is also preserved in the quantum setting. More specific to ROX, the random oracle model faces grave difficulties in the presence of quantum adversaries [BDF+11]. For example, classically one can easily simulate a random oracle by *lazy sampling* the responses upon every query *on-the-fly*. A quantum query, which can be in *superposition* of all possible inputs seems to force the function to be completely specified at the onset. Likewise, the powerful trick of programming a random oracle, i.e., changing the outputs on some input points as long as they have not been queried before, appears impossible if quantum queries are permitted. Recently, there is progress on restoring proof techniques including programming a quantum random oracle [ARU14, Unr14, ES15, HRS16].

Our Contributions. We investigate the two questions systematically in this work. The main results are summarized below.

We formalize the seven security notions in the quantum setting[2]. Since all properties are described in simple interactive games, we face two options to modeling quantum attackers depending on whether the *interface* between the challenger and the adversary remains classical or can also be quantum. We call the latter "fully" or "strong" quantum attacks, reminiscent of an active line of work recently [BZ13, Unr14, AR17]. This stronger type of attack is more realistic in some cases than others. Our interesting finding is that which model we use makes *no* difference in this setting, by a simple observation of commutativity of some quantum operators. Namely, the security property (e.g. aPre) against a quantum adversary and classical communication with the challenger is equivalent to that where the access to the challenger can be quantum too.

We depict the landscape of the seven notions in the quantum setting as well as the collapsing property, by fully determining their relationships (Fig. 2a). For most of the existing implications and separations in [RS04], we apply a general lifting tool in [Son14] to make analogous conclusions in the quantum setting.

---

[1] The compression function is not given as a random oracle. Rather apart from the compression function, the construction has access to a public random function that is given as a black-box.

[2] Some standard notions have appeared in the literature before [HRS16].

We construct new examples to separate collapsing from our quantum notions of aSecQ and eSecQ, and derive other relations by transitivity. Unruh's separation example between collapsing and collision resistance [Unr16b] is the only one that is relative to an oracle.

We determine the security-preserving capabilities of various iterated hash constructions. We show that the results in [ANPS07] (other than ROX) can be "lifted" into a quantum setting. As to ROX, we adapt techniques of programming a quantum random oracle and show that ROX preserves all security properties we consider in this work.

Discussion. As Andreeva et al. remarked in their work, ROX is proven secure in the random oracle model. Can we design an iterated hash that is all-preserving in the plain model? Recently there is another quantum notion extending collision resistance proposed in [AMRS18] termed *Bernoulli-preserving*. It implies collapsing and appears stronger. Do the iterated hash constructions preserve collapsing and Bernoulli-preserving of the compression function? Another interesting future direction is to investigate whether iterated hash can be *amplifying*, especially with the assistance of a random oracle such as in ROX. Finally, we consider variants of the Merkle-Damgård and Merkle Tree constructions. Less is known about the versatile sponge construction in terms of security-preserving of round functions. It has been shown very recently that the sponge is collapsing assuming the round functions are truly random [CBH+18].

2   Preliminaries

Notations. Hash-function properties are formulated as games with a challenger C and an adversary A. C and A perform one or more rounds of communication, after which C outputs a bit indicating whether A "won". Our proofs take the form of reductions, where winning the game allows us to create an adversary to win another game that is supposed to be hard. Following on [Son14], we formalize a reduction as a tuple $(\mathcal{G}^{\mathrm{int}}, \mathcal{T}, \mathcal{G}^{\mathrm{ext}})$ where $\mathcal{G}^{\mathrm{ext}}$ is the game that is assumed to be hard, $\mathcal{G}^{\mathrm{int}}$ is the game we would like to show to be secure, and $\mathcal{T}$ transforms an adversary A for $\mathcal{G}^{\mathrm{int}}$ into one for $\mathcal{G}^{\mathrm{ext}}$. If $\mathcal{T}$ is efficient and maintains A's success probability up to a negligible difference, showing the existence of a reduction is a proof by contradiction that $\mathcal{G}^{\mathrm{int}}$ is hard.

We are concerned primarily with quantum adversaries. These are adversaries that run in polynomial time on a quantum computer (QPT). We call the probability that this adversary succeeds its "advantage", denoted by $\mathrm{Adv}_H^{\mathrm{prop}}(A)$, where H is a hash function. By $\mathrm{Adv}_H^{\mathrm{prop}}$, we mean the maximum advantage over QPT adversaries. When discussing concrete security, we say that H is (t, ε)-prop if for all adversaries A running in time at most t, $\mathrm{Adv}_H^{\mathrm{prop}} A \leq \varepsilon$. When the interaction between C and an adversary has two rounds, we sometimes refer to an adversary as having two parts (A, B). In this case, they share a state register S, which the challenger may not read or modify. By convention, we use capital letters to indicate quantum registers. Measuring a quantum register $(\mathcal{M}(\cdot))$ results in a classical value, which we denote with the corresponding lowercase letter.

We assume there exists a security parameter n for each hash function that corresponds to the size of a key. A probability is negligible, denoted $negl(n)$, if it is less than $\frac{1}{poly(n)}$, where $poly(\cdot)$ is any polynomial function. By τ_H, we mean the time required to compute H. We indicate sampling from a distribution or receiving a result from a probabilistic algorithm by $x \leftarrow S$. When S is a set, this indicates uniform sampling, unless otherwise noted.

Quantum Random Oracles. One goal of this paper is to translate results about the ROX construction from the classical (RO) to the quantum (QRO) random oracle model. In general, results proven in the classical RO model do not necessarily carry over to a quantum setting, and even when they do, the techniques often need to be modified.

Even efficiently simulating a random oracle—a simple task in a classical setting, since an algorithm can simply lazily answer $poly(n)$ queries—is not obviously possible in a quantum setting. A quantum query could be a superposition of exponentially many inputs, naively requiring an exponential number of samples from the oracle's codomain to simulate. Zhandry showed that it is possible to efficiently simulate a random oracle using $2q$ samples, where q is the number of queries made to the oracle (Corollary 1 of Theorem 3.1 from [Zha12b]). Whenever we refer to simulating a QRO, we refer to this technique.

Another property of classical random oracles is that they can be adaptively programmed. That is, even after a polynomial number of queries have been made, the algorithm simulating the oracle can change the output of the oracle at some input points, since it is unlikely that A has seen the output at those points. However, a single quantum query in superposition can "see" the output at all points of the domain. We use a technique for programming a quantum random oracle from [ES15], which defines a "witness-search" game in which an adversary must guess a "witness" $\hat{w}$ with $P(\hat{w}) = 1$, given some predicate P and public information pk chosen by the challenger, given that the challenger knows a witness w. The probability that any QPT adversary detects adaptive programming at a point x with $P(\hat{w}) = 1$ is at most his success probability in witness search.

Standard Hash-Function Security. Rogaway and Shrimpton [RS04] identify seven properties of hash functions. These consist of the standard collision resistance (Coll), preimage resistance (Pre), and second-preimage resistance (Sec), as well as two stronger variants of each of the latter two—"always" (aPre, aSec) and "everywhere" (ePre, eSec)—which give the adversary more power. The following defines standard collision, preimage, and second-preimage resistance:

$$\mathrm{Adv}_H^{\mathrm{Coll}}(A) = \Pr[x \neq x' \wedge H_k(x) = H_k(x') : k \leftarrow \mathcal{K}; x, x' \leftarrow A(1^n, k)] \qquad (1)$$

$$\mathrm{Adv}_H^{\mathrm{Pre}}(A) = \Pr[H_k(x) = y : k \leftarrow \mathcal{K}; x' \leftarrow M; y = H_k(x'); x \leftarrow A(1^n, k, y)] \qquad (2)$$

$$\mathrm{Adv}_H^{\mathrm{Sec}}(A) = \Pr[x \neq x' \wedge H_k(x) = H_k(x') : k \leftarrow \mathcal{K}; x' \leftarrow M; x \leftarrow A(1^n, k, x')] \qquad (3)$$

Note that the challenger chooses the key k, and in the latter two properties, challenger chooses the target that the preimage needs to match. A successful adversary needs to work with non-negligible probability regardless of what the challenger chooses. One way to create a stronger property would be to relax this requirement on either the key or the preimage target.

Allowing the adversary to choose the key results in the "always" variants of preimage and second-preimage resistance. Here, the adversary is given as a pair of algorithms (A, B): A is responsible for choosing the key, and B is responsible for guessing the preimage.

$$\mathrm{Adv}_H^{\mathrm{aPre}}(A, B) = \Pr[H_k(x) = y$$
$$: k, S \leftarrow A(1^n); x' \leftarrow M; y = H_k(x'); x \leftarrow B(1^n, S, y)] \qquad (4)$$
$$\mathrm{Adv}_H^{\mathrm{aSec}}(A, B) = \Pr[x \neq x' \wedge H_k(x) = H_k(x')$$
$$: k, S \leftarrow A(1^n); x' \leftarrow M; x \leftarrow B(1^n, S, x')] \qquad (5)$$

Alternatively, allowing the adversary to choose the target the preimage must match before knowing the key results in the "everywhere" variants of these properties:

$$\mathrm{Adv}_H^{\mathrm{ePre}}(A, B) = \Pr[H_k(x) = y : y, S \leftarrow A(1^n); k \leftarrow \mathcal{K}; x \leftarrow B(1^n, S, k)] \qquad (6)$$
$$\mathrm{Adv}_H^{\mathrm{eSec}}(A, B) = \Pr[x \neq x' \wedge H_k(x) = H_k(x')$$
$$: x', S \leftarrow A(1^n); k \leftarrow \mathcal{K}; x \leftarrow B(1^n, S, k)] \qquad (7)$$

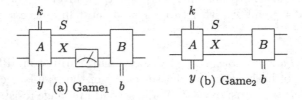

Fig. 1. Games defining the CLAPS property.

A standard quantum-only property is called "collapsing" [Unr16b, Unr16a] (CLAPS). Let $y \in \mathcal{D}$ be an element of the digest space of H_k. CLAPS captures the idea that it should be difficult for an adversary to produce a "useful" superposition of elements of the set $H_k^{-1}(y) \subseteq \mathcal{M}$. If a hash function is not collapsing, an adversary may be able to find some input-output pair with desirable properties even if it can succeed with only negligible advantage in the Coll game.

An adversary for CLAPS is a pair of QPT algorithms (A, B). On input k, A outputs quantum registers S, X and a classical register y. We call the adversary "correct" if $\Pr[H_k(\mathcal{M}(X)) = y] = 1$, and we restrict our attention to correct adversaries. On input S, X, B outputs a classical bit b that represents a guess whether X has been measured. The collapsing advantage $\mathrm{Adv}_H^{\mathrm{CLAPS}}(A, B) = |\Pr[b = 1 : \mathrm{Game1}] - \Pr[b = 1 : \mathrm{Game2}]|$, where $\mathrm{Game1}, 2$ are as shown in Fig. 1.

3 Quantum Security Properties of Hash Functions

We adapt the above notions from [RS04] to a quantum setting by allowing the adversary to be QPT, rather than PPT, as in the original definitions. The hash function is public, so he can make superposition queries to it, but all interactions with the challenger are classical. With the exception of the $poly(n)$-qubit state register S, we assume that the adversary measures all of its wires before outputting them. We call these variants CollQ, PreQ, etc.

It would be natural to ask whether stronger properties result from allowing the *interface* between the adversary and the challenger to be quantum. In other words, the adversary does not measure its wires before outputting them. At the end, the challenger measures all registers to determine whether the adversary has succeeded. These properties, which we call "strongly quantum" (SQ), are defined as follows, where K, Y, and X' are quantum registers:

$$\mathrm{Adv}_H^{\mathrm{CollSQ}}(A) = \Pr[x \neq x' \wedge H_k(x) = H_k(x') \\ : k \leftarrow \mathcal{K}; X, X' \leftarrow A(1^n, k); x, x' \leftarrow \mathcal{M}(X, X')] \tag{8}$$

$$\mathrm{Adv}_H^{\mathrm{PreSQ}}(A) = \Pr[H_k(x) = y \\ : k \leftarrow \mathcal{K}; x' \leftarrow M; y = H_k(x'); X \leftarrow A(1^n, k, y); x \leftarrow \mathcal{M}(X)] \tag{9}$$

$$\mathrm{Adv}_H^{\mathrm{SecSQ}}(A) = \Pr[x \neq x' \wedge H_k(x) = H_k(x') \\ : k \leftarrow \mathcal{K}; x' \leftarrow M; X \leftarrow A(1^n, k, x'); x \leftarrow \mathcal{M}(X)] \tag{10}$$

$$\mathrm{Adv}_H^{\mathrm{aPreSQ}}(A) = \Pr[H_k(x) = y \\ : K, S \leftarrow A(1^n); x' \leftarrow M; Y = U_{H(x')}(K \otimes |0\rangle); \\ X \leftarrow B(1^n, S, Y); k, x \leftarrow \mathcal{M}(K, X)] \tag{11}$$

$$\mathrm{Adv}_H^{\mathrm{aSecSQ}}(A) = \Pr[x \neq x' \wedge H_k(x) = H_k(x') \\ : K, S \leftarrow A(1^n); x' \leftarrow M; X \leftarrow B(1^n, S, x'); k, x \leftarrow \mathcal{M}(K, X)] \tag{12}$$

$$\mathrm{Adv}_H^{\mathrm{ePreSQ}}(A) = \Pr[H_k(x) = y \\ : Y, S \leftarrow A(1^n); k \leftarrow \mathcal{K}; X \leftarrow B(1^n, S, k); x, y \leftarrow \mathcal{M}(X, Y)] \tag{13}$$

$$\mathrm{Adv}_H^{\mathrm{eSecSQ}}(A) = \Pr[x \neq x' \wedge H_k(x) = H_k(x')$$
$$: X', S \leftarrow A(1^n); k \leftarrow \mathcal{K}; X \leftarrow B(1^n, S, k); x, x' \leftarrow \mathcal{M}(X, X')] \tag{14}$$

In (11), $U_{H(x')}$ is quantum gate that acts as $U_{H(x')} : |k\rangle |y\rangle \mapsto |k\rangle |y \oplus H_k(x')\rangle$. In other words, given a key register K in superposition, it outputs a superposition of digests for x'.

It is easy to see that CollSQ, PreSQ, and SecSQ(8, 9, and 10) are equivalent to their counterparts (1, 2, and 3) defined above: The challenger immediately measures the adversary's output registers, so without loss of generality, we may assume that the adversary measures all output registers itself.

As it happens, the other SQ properties (11–14) are equivalent to the above versions (4–7) as well. Intuitively, this is because, although A can put a superposition of values on its output register, the challenger never gives this register to B. If the challenger did so, it would be unable to check whether the adversary had won, since it would no longer have a copy of that register. Hence, the quantum "interface" with the challenger gives the adversary no additional power in this case.

A more formal proof requires us to show the equivalence of two quantum circuits. We give the full proof for aPreQ $\equiv$ aPreSQ in Appendix B. The proofs for aSecQ, ePreQ, and eSecQ are similar, but slightly more straightforward, in that they do not require Lemma 8.

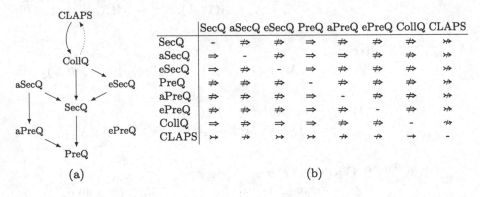

	SecQ	aSecQ	eSecQ	PreQ	aPreQ	ePreQ	CollQ	CLAPS
SecQ	-	$\nRightarrow$	$\nRightarrow$	$\Rightarrow$	$\nRightarrow$	$\nRightarrow$	$\nRightarrow$	$\twoheadrightarrow$
aSecQ	$\Rightarrow$	-	$\nRightarrow$	$\Rightarrow$	$\Rightarrow$	$\nRightarrow$	$\nRightarrow$	$\twoheadrightarrow$
eSecQ	$\Rightarrow$	$\nRightarrow$	-	$\Rightarrow$	$\nRightarrow$	$\nRightarrow$	$\nRightarrow$	$\twoheadrightarrow$
PreQ	$\nRightarrow$	$\nRightarrow$	$\nRightarrow$	-	$\nRightarrow$	$\nRightarrow$	$\nRightarrow$	$\twoheadrightarrow$
aPreQ	$\nRightarrow$	$\nRightarrow$	$\nRightarrow$	$\Rightarrow$	-	$\nRightarrow$	$\nRightarrow$	$\twoheadrightarrow$
ePreQ	$\nRightarrow$	$\nRightarrow$	$\nRightarrow$	$\Rightarrow$	$\nRightarrow$	-	$\nRightarrow$	$\twoheadrightarrow$
CollQ	$\Rightarrow$	$\nRightarrow$	$\Rightarrow$	$\Rightarrow$	$\nRightarrow$	$\nRightarrow$	-	$\rightsquigarrow$
CLAPS	$\twoheadrightarrow$	$\nrightarrow$	$\twoheadrightarrow$	$\twoheadrightarrow$	$\nrightarrow$	$\nrightarrow$	$\rightarrow$	-

(a)	(b)

Fig. 2. The relationships between the properties defined in Sect. 3. In Fig. 2a, solid arrows indicate implications. Everywhere an arrow (or a transitive implication) is absent indicates a separation. In Fig. 2b, $\rightarrow$ and $\nrightarrow$ are implications with explicit proofs, and $\twoheadrightarrow$ and $\nrightarrow\!\!\!\rightarrow$ hold by transitivity, $\Rightarrow$ and $\nRightarrow$ indicate quantumly "lifted" classical reductions. The dotted arrow in Fig. 2a and $\rightsquigarrow$ in Fig. 2b indicate that only a relativized separation has been shown [Unr16b].

4 Relations of Quantum Security Properties

In this section, we examine the relationships among the properties in Sect. 3. Figure 2 illustrates these graphically. The relationships among the properties with classical analogs carry over from the classical setting, based on the framework from [Son14]. The following is a sufficient criterion for "lifting" a reduction from a classical to a quantum setting:

Lemma 1 (Corrollary 4.6 from [Son14]). *Let* $\mathcal{R} = (\mathcal{G}^{ext}, \mathcal{T}, \mathcal{G}^{int})$ *be a black-box reduction that holds for* PPT *machines, and suppose the following:*

1. $\mathcal{G}^{int}(A)$ *and* $\mathcal{G}^{ext}(A)$ *are defined for* QPT A;
2. $|Adv_{(}^{\mathcal{G}^{int}} A) - Adv^{\mathcal{G}^{ext}}(\mathcal{T}(A))| \leq negl(n)$ *for all* QPT A;
3. *when* $\mathcal{T}$ *runs* A, *it runs it "in a straight line until completion," i.e., as an honest challenger would; and*
4. *for all* A, A' *with* $Adv^{\mathcal{G}^{int}}(A) = Adv^{\mathcal{G}^{ext}}(A')$, $Adv^{\mathcal{G}^{ext}}(\mathcal{T}(A)) = Adv^{\mathcal{G}^{ext}}(\mathcal{T}(A'))$.

Then $\mathcal{R}$ *holds for* QPT *machines as well.*

All the classical implication proofs from [RS04] ($\Rightarrow$ from Fig. 2b) satisfy the hypotheses in Lemma 1, and thus that these proofs can be lifted into a quantum setting. For example, the standard proof that Coll → eSec involves creating a reduction ($\mathcal{G}^{ext} = $ Coll, $\mathcal{T}, \mathcal{G}^{int} = $ eSec) where $\mathcal{T}$ is defined as follows:

$$\mathcal{T} : A \mapsto A'$$

1. Sample $x \leftarrow \mathcal{M}$ and send it to the challenger.
2. Receive k from $\mathcal{C}$.
3. Run $A(1^n, k, x)$ to get x' and send (x, x') to the challenger.

Note that $\mathcal{T}$ could be applied to a quantum A for eSecQ as easily as a classical one for eSec, and the result, $\mathcal{T}(A)$ finds a collision in the CollQ game. This is guaranteed due to the classical "interface" in the definitions from Sect. 3. Moreover, it runs A as normal. So hypotheses 1 and 3 from Lemma 1 hold. Hypothesis 2 holds as well, since the success probabilities of A and $\mathcal{T}(A)$ are the same Hypothesis 4 captures the idea that the success probability of $\mathcal{T}(A)$ depends only on the success probability of A, not some specific facet of its internal behavior. This is easily seen to be the case here.

The classical separations from [RS04] ($\nRightarrow$ from Fig. 2b) can also be lifted in a similar fashion. For example, the proof that Coll does not imply aSec runs as follows: Suppose that H is Coll. We define a new function H' such that if $k \neq 0$, $H'_k(x) = H_k(x)$, but $H_0(x) = 0$. There is a trivial attack for aSec on H': The adversary simply chooses $k = 0$ and outputs any $x' \neq x$ as a second preimage. Finally, we show that H' is still collision resistant using a simple reduction. The first half of this proof (the attack) is clearly as possible on a quantum computer as it is on a classical one. In fact, the structure of the properties from Sect. 3

(excluding CLAPS)—where the adversary is given classical input and must produce classical output—guarantees this. Moreover, as with the implication proofs, the reductions in the separation proofs satisfy the hypotheses in Lemma 1. So we conclude that these separations hold in a quantum setting as well.

We additionally examine the relationships between collapsing and each of the standard properties. Unruh shows in [Unr16b] that collapsing implies collision resistance, and this proof applies to CollQ as well. This leads to the transitive implications from CLAPS in Fig. 2b. We find that CLAPS does *not* imply aPreQ, aSecQ, or ePreQ. The proofs of these separations are given in Appendix A.

5   Quantum Security Preservations of Itcrated Hash Constructions

In this section, we consider whether several standard iterated hash constructions, including one in the random oracle model (ROX), preserve the quantum-safe properties from Sect. 3. The constructions we consider are the same as those considered in [ANPS07], and we find that they preserve (and fail to preserve) the quantum analogs of the same properties that [ANPS07] show they do classically. In the case of the standard constructions, we omit explicit proofs, instead using the lifting framework we introduced in Sect. 4. The proofs for ROX, meanwhile, are more subtle, since they must be adapted to the quantum random oracle model. We give explicit proofs in the most interesting of these cases.

Andreeva et al. discuss eleven standard iterated hash constructions, proving exhaustively (with a few exceptions) which of the seven classical properties from [RS04] they preserve. These proofs are amenable to being "lifted" to a quantum setting by reasoning similar to that in Sect. 4: Each implication proof uses a reduction that satisfies the hypotheses of Lemma 1. Each separation combines an attack, which is still possible in a quantum setting given the nature of the games we consider, and a reduction, which also satisfies the hypotheses.

In contrast, we cannot use Lemma 1 to lift the proofs for the random-oracle model construction ROX. In particular, the reductions used cannot claim to run A identically to an honest challenger, since they must simulate a pair of random oracles. This violates Hypothesis 3 of the lemma. Although the same results hold, the proofs must be explicitly adapted, which we do below.

5.1 ROX Preserves All Quantum Properties

Definition 1 (ROX). $ROX_k^{(H)} = \overline{ROX}_k^{(H)} \circ pad_{ROX}$

$$pad_{ROX} : \{0,1\}^* \quad \to (\{0,1\}^b)^*$$
$$x \qquad\qquad \mapsto trunc_b(x \| RO_2(\bar{x}, |x|, 1) \| RO_2(\bar{x}, |x|, 2) \| \dots)$$

$$\overline{ROX}_k^{(H)} : (\{0,1\}^b)^* \to \{0,1\}^d$$
$$\Lambda \qquad\qquad \mapsto IV$$

$$x_1 \| \dots \| x_i \mapsto H_k(x_i \| \overline{ROX}_k^{(H)}(x_1 \| \dots \| x_{i-1}) \oplus RO_1(\bar{x}, k, \nu(i)))$$

where Λ is the empty string; $\nu(i)$ is the largest integer such that $2^{\nu(i)}$ divides i; $\bar{x}$ is the first n bits of x; $IV \in \{0,1\}^d$ is a fixed string; and

- $H : \{0,1\}^n \times \{0,1\}^m \to \{0,1\}^d$, where $b = m - d > 0$ is the block size, and $d \geq 2b$;
- $RO_1 : \{0,1\}^{2n+\log L} \to \{0,1\}^d$ and $RO_2 : \{0,1\}^{n+2\log L} \to \{0,1\}^{2n}$ are random oracles, where L is the maximum input size in blocks; and
- $trunc_b$ truncates its input to a multiple of b bits;

We denote the block length of x as $\ell(x) = \lceil (|x| + 2n)/b \rceil$, the number of padding blocks as $1 \leq q_2(x) \leq \lceil \frac{b+2n-1}{2n} \rceil$, and the total oracle queries as $q(x) = \ell(x) + q_2(x)$.

Andreeva et al. [ANPS07] describe an iterated hash called ROX (Definition 1) that preserves all of the classical properties discussed in [RS04]. In addition to a compression function, ROX relies on two random oracles ($RO_{1,2}$), although it does not rely on this fact for all proofs. Specifically, ROX preserves aPre, Pre, aSec, and Sec in the random oracle (RO) model, and Coll, ePre, and eSec in the standard model.

We show that ROX also preserves the quantum analogs of these properties. Andreeva et al.'s standard-model proofs carry over nearly unchanged for CollQ, ePreQ, and eSecQ carry over nearly unchanged, so we omit those proofs. We show that ROX preserves aPreQ, PreQ, aSecQ, and SecQ, replacing the classical RO model with the QRO model.

We begin by stating the existence of some constructions using ROX that will be useful in our proofs. The full constructions are given in Appendix C.

Lemma 2 (Extracting collisions on H_k from collisions on $ROX_k^{(H)}$). Given $\hat{x}, \hat{x}' \in dom(ROX_k^{(H)})$ with $\hat{x} \neq \hat{x}'$ and $ROX_k^{(H)}(\hat{x}) = ROX_k^{(H)}(\hat{x}')$, we can extract $x, x' \in dom(H_k)$ with $x \neq x'$ and $H_k(x) = H_k(x')$ except with probability $\frac{1}{2^n}$ using $\ell(\hat{x}) + \ell(\hat{x}')$ applications of H and $q(\hat{x}) + q(\hat{x}')$ oracle queries.

Lemma 3 (Embedding inputs for H_k into inputs for $ROX^{(H)}$). Given an input x for H_k and an index i, we can create an input $\hat{x}$ for $ROX_k^{(H)}$ such that the input to the ith application of H_k is x using i calls to H and at most $\lceil \frac{b+2n-1}{2n} \rceil + i$ oracle queries. Moreover, an adversary A making q queries notices the change with probability at most $O(q^2/2^n)$.

Lemma 4 (Extracting a preimage under H from a preimage under $ROX^{(H)}$). *Given a key k and a message $\hat{x} \in \{0,1\}^*$ with $ROX_k^{(H)}(\hat{x}) = y$, we can generate a message $x \in \mathcal{M}$ with $H_k(x) = y$ using $\ell(x) - 1$ calls to H and $q(x)$ oracle queries.*

We are now ready to prove that ROX preserves the properties from Sect. 3 in the QRO model. To conserve space, we only summarize our proofs here, providing the full proofs in Appendix D.

Theorem 1 (ROX preserves aPreQ). *If H is (t', ε')-aPreQ, then $ROX^{(H)}$ is (t, ε)-aPreQ with*

$$t = t' - poly(n)\tau_H; \; \varepsilon = \varepsilon' + O(q^2/2^d)$$

Proof Summary. We use a preimage target y for H as a preimage target for $ROX^{(H)}$. In the classical proof, y is correctly distributed because an adversary would have to guess correctly some random points to query $RO_{1,2}$. This argument fails in the quantum setting. We instead use QRO programming to show that y appears correctly distributed to a quantum adversary.

Theorem 2 (ROX preserves PreQ). *If H is (t', ε')-PreQ then $ROX^{(H)}$ is (t, ε)-PreQ, where*

$$t = t - poly(n)\tau_H; \; \varepsilon' = \varepsilon + O(q^2/2^d)$$

Proof Summary. An adversary for PreQ on $ROX^{(H)}$ can be run using a preimage target y for H, since y will appear to be correctly distributed. The argument is the same as that in the proof of Theorem 1, so we omit it here for brevity.

Theorem 3 (ROX preserves aSecQ). *If H is (t', ε')-aSecQ then $ROX^{(H)}$ is (t, ε)-aSecQ with*

$$t = t' - poly(n)\tau_H; \; \varepsilon = poly(n)\varepsilon'/(1 - 1/2^n)(1 - poly(n)/2^n)$$

Proof Summary. We embed a second-preimage target for H into a second-preimage target for $ROX^{(H)}$ by adaptively programming $RO_{1,2}$. We argue that reprogramming the random oracles in this way is imperceptible to the adversary.

Theorem 4 (ROX preserves SecQ). *If H is $(t'\varepsilon')$-SecQ then $ROX^{(H)}$ is (t, ε)-SecQ, where*

$$t = t' - poly(n)\tau_H; \; \varepsilon = poly(n)\varepsilon'/(1 - 1/2^n)(1 - poly(n)/2^n)$$

Proof Summary. Similarly to Theorem 3, here we embed a second-preimage target for H into one for $ROX^{(H)}$ by programming $RO_{1,2}$. Since we do not need to program adaptively, however, the programming is straightforward. The proof is similar to that of Theorem 3, so we omit it here for brevity.

A   CLAPS Separation Proofs

Here we show that CLAPS does not imply aPreQ, aSecQ, or ePreQ, completing the diagram in Fig. 2.

A.1   CLAPS ↛ aPreQ

Theorem 5. *If a collapsing function family exists, then there is a function family H that is (t, ε)-CLAPS with negligible ε, but with $Adv_H^{aPreQ} = 1$.*

Proof Summary. Since the key k in the collapsing game is chosen uniformly at random, a collapsing function can have a constant number of "bad" keys that, for example, result in a constant function H_k. Finding a preimage for such a function is obviously trivial. Given a collapsing function F, we exhibit a function H that is collapsing, but for which $Adv_H^{aPreQ} = 1$.

Proof. Suppose $F : \{0,1\}^n \times \{0,1\}^m \to \{0,1\}^d$ is (t, ε)-CLAPS, and define H as follows:

$$H_k(x) = \begin{cases} 0^d & \text{if } k = 0^n \\ F_k(x) & \text{o.w.} \end{cases}$$

Lemma 5. *H is (t, ε')-CLAPS, where $\varepsilon' = \varepsilon - \frac{1}{2^n}$.*

The obvious adversary suffices to break aPreQ on H: A picks $k = 0^n$, and B outputs any x. Since we assume ε to be negligible, ε' is negligible as well, and the theorem is immediate from Lemma 5.

Proof (Proof of Lemma 5). Let (A, B) be a correct QPT adversary with $Adv_H^{CLAPS}(A, B) = \varepsilon'$. We construct a correct QPT adversary (A', B') for F as follows:

Constructing (A', B') from (A, B)

$A'(1^n, k)$:

$B'(1^n, S, X)$:

1. If $k = 0^n$, FAIL. Otherwise...
2. Run $A(1^n, k)$ to get S, X, y with $\Pr[H_k(\mathcal{M}(X)) = y] = 1$.
3. Send the challenger S, X, y.

1. Run $B(1^n, S, X)$ to get b.
2. Send b to the challenger.

We claim that (A', B') is correct: If A' does not fail, then $k \neq 0^n$, and by the premise that (A, B) is correct, $\Pr[F_k(\mathcal{M}(X)) = y] = \Pr[H_k(\mathcal{M}(X)) = y | k \neq 0] = 1$.

Suppose A' doesn't fail, and the challenger for (A', B') is running Game$_1$. Then B receives $S, \mathcal{M}(X)$, and (A, B) sees Game$_1$. On the other hand, if the challenger for (A', B') is running Game$_2$, X is unmeasured, and (A, B) sees Game$_2$.

Since the probability that A' fails is $\Pr[k = 0^n] = \frac{1}{2^n}$, $Adv_F^{CLAPS}(A', B') \geq \varepsilon' - \frac{1}{2^n}$. Therefore $Adv_H^{CLAPS} \leq Adv_F^{CLAPS} + \frac{1}{2^n} = negl(n)$.

A.2   CLAPS ↛ aSecQ

Theorem 6. *If a collapsing function family exists, then there is a function family H that is (t,ε)-CLAPS with negligible ε, but with $Adv_H^{aSec} = 1$.*

Proof Summary. This proof uses the same H as the proof of Theorem 5. Given a collapsing function F, this H is also collapsing, but has a single "bad" key $\hat{k}$ s.t. $H_{\hat{k}}(x) = 0^d$, $\forall x \in \{0,1\}^m$. If an adversary can control the key and chooses $\hat{k}$, then whichever x the challenger picks, any other element of $dom(H_k)$ is a second preimage. Since the proof is identical to Theorem 5, we omit it for brevity.

A.3   CLAPS ↛ ePreQ

Theorem 7. *If a collapsing function family exists, then there is a function family H that is (t,ε)-CLAPS with negligible ε, but $Adv_H^{ePre} = 1$.*

Proof Summary. If the image $\hat{y}$ of some element x in the domain of H is fixed, regardless of the key k, then an adversary can find a preimage of an element y of his choice easily: All he must do is choose $y = \hat{y}$, and whatever k the adversary picks, x is a preimage. But if x is the only preimage of y, this property does not help in creating superpositions of preimages to use in the collapsing game. So H may still be collapsing.

Proof. Suppose $F : \{0,1\}^n \times \{0,1\}^m \to \{0,1\}^{d-1}$ is (t,ε)-CLAPS. We define a new function $H : \{0,1\}^n \times \{0,1\}^m \to \{0,1\}^d$ as follows:

$$H_k(x) = \begin{cases} 0^d & \text{if } x = 0^m \\ 1\|F_k(x) & \text{o.w.} \end{cases}$$

Lemma 6. *H is (t,ε)-CLAPS.*

The obvious adversary suffices to break ePreQ on H: A picks $y = 0^d$ and B outputs 0^m. Thus, the theorem is immediate from Lemma 6.

Proof (Proof of Lemma 6). Let (A,B) be a correct QPT adversary with $Adv_H^{CLAPS}(A,B) = \varepsilon'$. We construct a QPT adversary (A',B') for F as follows:

Constructing (A',B') from (A,B)	
$A'(1^n,k)$:	$B'(1^n,S,X)$:
1. Run $A(1^n,k)$ to get S,X,y with $\Pr[H_k(\mathcal{M}(X)) = y] = 1$.	1. Run $B(S,X,y)$ to get b.
	2. Send b to the challenger.
2. Measure $\mathcal{M}_F(X)$ to get y'.	
3. Send S,X,y' to the challenger.	

(A', B') is correct by construction. We claim that $\mathrm{Adv}_F^{CLAPS}(A', B') \geq \epsilon$. Consider the following cases:

1. Suppose $y = 0^d$. Then by the premise that (A, B) is correct, $X = |0^m\rangle$, since 0^m is the only preimage of 0^d. In this case $\mathrm{Game}_1 = \mathrm{Game}_2$, since $X = \mathcal{M}(X)$, so $|\Pr[b = 1 : \mathrm{Game}_1] - \Pr[b = 1 : \mathrm{Game}_2]| = 0$ for both (A, B) and (A', B').
2. Suppose $y \neq 0^d$, and the challenger for (A, B) is running Game_1. Then B receives $\mathcal{M}(X)$, so B sees Game_2.
3. Suppose $y \neq 0^d$, and the challenger for (A, B) is running Game_2. By the premise that (A, B) is correct, when A produces X,

$$X = \sum_{x \in H^{-1}(y)} \alpha_x |x\rangle = |1\rangle \left(\sum_{x \in F^{-1}(y')} \alpha_x |x\rangle \right)$$

So the measurement at step 2 of A' does not collapse X. Hence, B sees Game_2.

Therefore $\mathrm{Adv}_F^{CLAPS}(A', B') = \varepsilon'$.

B   aPreQ ≡ aPreSQ

Theorem 8. *Equations 4 and 11 are equivalent. I.e.,* $Adv_H^{aPreQ} = Adv_H^{aPreSQ}$

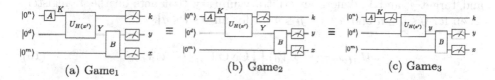

(a) Game₁   (b) Game₂   (c) Game₃

Fig. 3. Three equivalent games showing that measuring the K wire before the end does not change the aPreSQ game—hence aPreSQ and aPreQ are equivalent. Figure a is the same as aPreSQ; Fig. c is functionally equivalent to aPreQ; and Fig. b is intermediate between the two. The state register S from Eqs. 4 and 11 is omitted for clarity.

Proof (Proof of Theorem 8).
    Let each part A, B of the adversary be a unitary operator and let $n = \lceil \lg |\mathcal{K}| \rceil$ be the size of a key, $m = \lceil \lg |\mathcal{M}| \rceil$ be the size of a message, and $d = \lceil \lg |\mathcal{D}| \rceil$ be the size of a digest. We illustrate the circuits for three games in Fig. 3.

Lemma 7. *Game 1 is equivalent to Game 2.*

Lemma 8. *Game 2 is equivalent to Game 3.*

We claim that the theorem follows from Lemmas 7 and 8. Note that Game 1 is exactly the aPreSQ game, as defined in Eq. 11. In Game 3, the output of A and B, with the exception of the state register S, are measured immediately, so without loss of generality, we may assume that their output is classical. Thus Game 3 is equivalent to the aPreQ game (Eq. 4).

In the following two proofs, let $\mathcal{M}_n$ denote measuring the first n qubits in the standard basis and leaving the rest untouched. In other words,

$$\mathcal{M}_n(\rho) = \sum_{x \in \{0,1\}^n} (|x\rangle \langle x| \otimes \mathbb{I}) \rho (|x\rangle \langle x| \otimes \mathbb{I}) \tag{15}$$

Proof (Proof of Lemma 7).
It suffices to show that for any unitary B and all $x \in \{0,1\}^n$, $(|x\rangle \langle x| \otimes \mathbb{I})$ commutes with $(\mathbb{I}_n \otimes B)$. This is immediate, since $(\mathbb{I}_n \otimes B)(|x\rangle \langle x| \otimes \mathbb{I}) = |x\rangle \langle x| \otimes B$.

Proof (Proof of Lemma 8).
We must show that $U_{H(x')}$ commutes with $\mathcal{M}_n$. Since

$$U_{H(x')} : |K\rangle |Y\rangle \mapsto |K\rangle |H_k(x') \oplus Y\rangle$$

is a unitary operator that leaves the K register untouched, it can be viewed as using the K register solely as control bits for CNOT gates, interspersed with unitaries on the Y register. Let $\text{CNOT}_{i,j}$ denote a CNOT gate with control i and target j, and V denote an arbitrary unitary that acts on the Y register. Then for $0 \le i_\ell \le n$ and $n+1 \le j_\ell \le n+d$ for all $0 \le \ell \le q]$,

$$U_{H(x')} = (\mathbb{I}^n \otimes V_0) \prod_{\ell=1}^{q} \text{CNOT}_{i_\ell, j_\ell} (\mathbb{I}^n \otimes V_\ell) \tag{16}$$

Given the definition of $\mathcal{M}_n$ in Eq. 15, we must show all the factors in Eq. 16 commute with $|x\rangle \langle x| \otimes \mathbb{I}_d$. Clearly this is the case for $\mathbb{I}^n \otimes V_\ell$, by the same reasoning as in the proof of Lemma 7. Similarly, it is well known that measurement of the control qubit commutes with CNOT.

C   ROX Constructions

C.1   Extracting Compression-Function Collisions (Lemma 2)

Proof (Proof of Lemma 2). We claim that the following procedure extracts a compression-function with overwhelming probability:

EXTRACT-COLLISION$(k, \hat{x}, \hat{x}')$

1. Let $b_1 \| \ldots \| b_\ell = \mathrm{pad}_{\mathrm{ROX}}(\hat{x})$ and $b'_1 \| \ldots \| b'_{\ell'} = \mathrm{pad}_{\mathrm{ROX}}(\hat{x}')$.
2. Let $x_i = b_i \| \overline{\mathrm{ROX}}_k^{(H)}(b_1 \| \ldots \| b_{i-1})$ and $x'_i = b'_i \| \overline{\mathrm{ROX}}_k^{(H)}(b'_1 \| \ldots \| b'_{i-1})$.
3. For $i = 0$ to $\min(\ell, \ell') \ldots$
4. If $x_{\ell-i} \neq x'_{\ell'-i}$, output $(x = x_{\ell-i}, x' = x'_{\ell'-i}, i^* = \ell - i)$.

Let $\bar{x}, \bar{x}'$ and be the first n bits of $\hat{x}, \hat{x}'$, and λ, λ' be their respective lengths. We must show that there always exists a colliding pair (x, x'). We consider two cases:

- *Case i.* Suppose $\bar{x} \neq \bar{x}'$ or $\lambda \neq \lambda'$. Then since x_ℓ and $x'_{\ell'}$ each contains at least one full output from RO_2, $x_\ell \neq x'_{\ell'}$ except with probability $\delta = \frac{1}{2^n}$. In this case the inputs to the last application of H_k form a collision for H_k.
- *Case ii.* Otherwise, $\bar{x} = \bar{x}'$ and $\lambda = \lambda'$. In this case, the padding applied to $\hat{x}$ and $\hat{x}'$ will be identical. But the mask schedule taken from RO_1 will be identical as well. So since $\hat{x} \neq \hat{x}'$, there must be block pair, $(b_{i^*}, b'_{i'^*})$ on which they differ. Since the masks and padding match, these form a collision for H_k.

C.2   Embedding Messages (Lemma 3)

Proof (Proof of Lemma 3). Let $h \| g = x$, where $|h| = b$ and $|g| = d$, and define the following procedure:

EMBED-MESSAGE(x, i)

1. Generate a random message $\hat{x}$ of length $\lambda \geq bi$.
2. If $i = 1$, let $\bar{x}$ be the first n bits of x, adding bits from $\hat{x}$, starting with the $(m+1)$st, if x isn't long enough. Otherwise, let $\bar{x}$ be the first n bits of $\hat{x}$.
3. Let $h_1 \| \ldots \| h_\ell = \mathrm{pad}_{\mathrm{ROX}}(\hat{x})$ with $|h_j| = b$.
4. Evaluate $\mu_i = \overline{\mathrm{ROX}}_k^{(H)}(x_1 \| \ldots \| x_{i-1})$.
5. Program $\mathrm{RO}_1(\bar{x}, k, \nu(i))$ with $g \oplus \mu_i$.
6. Program the $q' \leq q_2(\hat{x})$ outputs of RO_2 contained in h_i with x.
7. Let $\hat{x}'$ be the first λ bits of $h_1 \| \ldots \| h_{i-1} \| h \| h_{i+1} \| \ldots \| h_\ell$.
8. Output $\hat{x}'$.

In steps 5 and 6, the above procedure requires us to program a random oracle. To do so, we invoke witness search from [ES15], where a witness is some image of $\mathrm{RO}_{1,2}$ corresponding to an input that starts with $\bar{x}$. Since $\bar{x}$ is chosen at random, and since the codomains of $\mathrm{RO}_{1,2}$ are much larger than their domains, the random search problem in [HRS16] can be reduced to this, with 2^n marked items in a set of $2^{b-n} \geq 2^n$, so the success probability is $O(q^2/2^n)$.

C.3   Extracting Compression-Function Preimages (Lemma 4)

Proof (Proof of Lemma 4). We claim that the following procedure extracts a collision-function preimage with overwhelming probability:

$$\text{EXTRACT-PREIMAGE}(k, \hat{x})$$

1. Evaluate $\text{ROX}_k^{(H)}(x)$ up to the last application of H_k. Namely let

$$x_1 \| \dots \| x_\ell = \text{pad}_{\text{ROX}}(x)$$
$$x = x_\ell \| \overline{\text{ROX}}_k^{(H)}(x_1 \| \dots \| x_{\ell-1}) \oplus \text{RO}_1(\hat{x}, k, \ell)$$

2. Output x.

By construction, $H_k(x) = y$ as desired. The only calls to H and RO_1, RO_2 are in the partial computation of $\text{ROX}^{(H)}(x)$. Since we omit one call to H, the procedure calls it $\ell(x) - 1$ times.

D   ROX Property-Preservation Proofs

D.1   ROX Preserves aPreQ

Proof (Proof of Theorem 1). Let (A, B) be a (t, ε) quantum adversary for aPreQ on $\text{ROX}^{(H)}$, making $q = poly(n)$ oracle queries. We construct an adversary (A', B') for H using an additional $poly(n)$ oracle queries:

Constructing (A', B') from (A, B)

$A'(1^n)$:

1. Run $k, S \leftarrow A^{\text{RO}_{1,2}}(1^n)$, simulating quantum oracles $\text{RO}_{1,2}$.
2. Output k, S.

$B'(1^n, S, y)$:

1. Run $x \leftarrow B^{\text{RO}_{1,2}}(1^n, S, y)$.
2. Run $\text{EXTRACT-PREIMAGE}(k, x)$ to obtain a preimage x' for y under H_k.
3. Output x'.

By Lemma 4, if $\text{ROX}^{(H_k)}(x) = y$, then $H_k(x') = y$, and A' wins the aPreQ-game. Note that $y = H_k(g' \| h')$ for $g' \| h'$ chosen at random, while A would expect a $\hat{y}$ to be $H_k(g \| h)$, where g contains at least $2b$ bits of $\text{RO}_2(\bar{x}, \cdot)$, and $h = d \oplus \text{RO}_1(\bar{x}, \cdot)$ for some d. The view of (A, B) in the simulated run in (A', B') is thus identical to the real aPreQ-game, unless (A, B) can distinguish y and $\hat{y}$ using at most q queries. We show that A can distinguish them with probability at most $q^2/2^n$. Hence $\text{Adv}_H^{\text{aPreQ}}(A', B') \geq \varepsilon - q^2/2^n$.

We argue that if some challenger that knew x were to reprogram $\text{RO}_{1,2}$ on inputs corresponding to x, no algorithm would be able to discover this except with negligible probability. In the Witness-Search game from [ES15], let $P(w)$ output 1 if and only if $RO_2(w,|x|,j) = g$ and $\overline{ROX}_k^{(H)}(x_1\|\ldots\|x_\ell)\oplus RO_1(w,k,i) = h$ for some $1 \leq i,j \leq |x|$. Next, let $w = \bar{x}$ and $pk = (k,|x|)$. This amounts to finding a preimage with a suffix from a set in a random function. Hence $\mathrm{Adv}_{\mathrm{Samp}}^{WS}(A) \leq O(q^2/2^d)$ by reducing a random search problem developed in [HRS16] to it. Thus we can safely reprogram $RO_{1,2}$ at points corresponding to P being true, and h,g are indistinguishable from the random values supplied by B'.

D.2   ROX Preserves aSecQ

Proof (Proof of Theorem 3). Let (A,B) be a (t,ε) adversary for aSecQ on $ROX^{(H)}$ making $q = poly(n)$ oracle queries. We construct an adversary (A',B') for H, using an additional $\left\lceil \frac{b+2n-1}{2n} \right\rceil + poly(n)$ oracle queries:

Constructing (A',B') from (A,B)

$A'(1^n)$:

1. Run $k,S \leftarrow A^{RO_{1,2}}(1^n)$, simulating quantum oracles $RO_{1,2}$.
2. Output k,S.

$B'(1^n,S,x)$:

1. Choose an index $i \leq poly(n)$.
2. Run EMBED-MESSAGE(x,i) to get $\hat{x} \in dom(ROX_k^{(H)})$ with x embedded as the input to the ith application of H_k.
3. Run $B^{RO_{1,2}}(1^n,S,\hat{x}')$, to get $\hat{x}'$.
4. Run EXTRACT-COLLISION$(k,\hat{x},\hat{x}')$ to get (x,x',i^*).
5. If $i^* \neq i$, FAIL. Output x'.

By Lemma 3, EMBED-MESSAGE adds an additional $i = poly(n)$ applications of H and an additional $\left\lceil \frac{b+2n-1}{2n} \right\rceil + i$ oracle queries and alters the success probability of A by at most $O(q/2^n) = poly(n)/2^n$, where $q = poly(n)$ is the number of queries A makes. By Lemma 2, EXTRACT-COLLISION adds $\ell(\hat{x}) + \ell(\hat{x}') = poly(n)$ applications of H and $q(\hat{x}) + q(\hat{x}') = poly(n)$ oracle queries and fails w.p. $\frac{1}{2^n}$. Assuming both succeed, $i = i^*$ w.p. $\frac{1}{poly(n)}$. Hence $\mathrm{Adv}_H^{\mathrm{aSecQ}}(A',B') \geq \varepsilon(1 - q/2^n)(1 - 1/2^n)/poly(n)$.

References

[AMRS18] Alagic, G., Majenz, C., Russell, A., Song, F.: Quantum-secure message authentication via blind-unforgeability. arXiv preprint arXiv:1803.03761 (2018)

[ANPS07] Andreeva, E., Neven, G., Preneel, B., Shrimpton, T.: Seven-property-preserving iterated hashing: ROX. In: Kurosawa, K. (ed.) ASIACRYPT 2007. LNCS, vol. 4833, pp. 130–146. Springer, Heidelberg (2007). https://doi.org/10.1007/978-3-540-76900-2_8

[AR17] Alagic, G., Russell, A.: Quantum-secure symmetric-key cryptography based on hidden shifts. In: Coron, J.-S., Nielsen, J.B. (eds.) EUROCRYPT 2017. LNCS, vol. 10212, pp. 65–93. Springer, Cham (2017). https://doi.org/10.1007/978-3-319-56617-7_3

[ARU14] Ambainis, A., Rosmanis, A., Unruh, D.: Quantum attacks on classical proof systems: the hardness of quantum rewinding. In: 2014 IEEE 55th Annual Symposium on Foundations of Computer Science (FOCS), pp. 474–483. IEEE (2014)

[BDF+11] Boneh, D., Dagdelen, Ö., Fischlin, M., Lehmann, A., Schaffner, C., Zhandry, M.: Random oracles in a quantum world. In: Lee, D.H., Wang, X. (eds.) ASIACRYPT 2011. LNCS, vol. 7073, pp. 41–69. Springer, Heidelberg (2011). https://doi.org/10.1007/978-3-642-25385-0_3

[BDPA07] Bertoni, G., Daemen, J., Peeters, M., Van Assche, G.: Sponge functions. In: Ecrypt Hash Workshop (2007). http://sponge.noekeon.org/

[BR97] Bellare, M., Rogaway, P.: Collision-resistant hashing: towards making UOWHFs practical. In: Kaliski, B.S. (ed.) CRYPTO 1997. LNCS, vol. 1294, pp. 470–484. Springer, Heidelberg (1997). https://doi.org/10.1007/BFb0052256

[BZ13] Boneh, D., Zhandry, M.: Secure signatures and chosen ciphertext security in a quantum computing world. In: Canetti, R., Garay, J.A. (eds.) CRYPTO 2013. LNCS, vol. 8043, pp. 361–379. Springer, Heidelberg (2013). https://doi.org/10.1007/978-3-642-40084-1_21

[CBH+18] Czajkowski, J., Groot Bruinderink, L., Hülsing, A., Schaffner, C., Unruh, D.: Post-quantum security of the sponge construction. In: Lange, T., Steinwandt, R. (eds.) PQCrypto 2018. LNCS, vol. 10786, pp. 185–204. Springer, Cham (2018). https://doi.org/10.1007/978-3-319-79063-3_9

[Dam89] Damgård, I.B.: A design principle for hash functions. In: Brassard, G. (ed.) CRYPTO 1989. LNCS, vol. 435, pp. 416–427. Springer, New York (1990). https://doi.org/10.1007/0-387-34805-0_39

[ES15] Eaton, E., Song, F.: Making existential-unforgeable signatures strongly unforgeable in the quantum random-oracle model. In: 10th Conference on the Theory of Quantum Computation, Communication and Cryptography, TQC 2015. LIPIcs, vol. 44, pp. 147–162. Schloss Dagstuhl (2015). https://eprint.iacr.org/2015/878

[HRS16] Hülsing, A., Rijneveld, J., Song, F.: Mitigating multi-target attacks in hash-based signatures. In: Cheng, C.-M., Chung, K.-M., Persiano, G., Yang, B.-Y. (eds.) PKC 2016. LNCS, vol. 9614, pp. 387–416. Springer, Heidelberg (2016). https://doi.org/10.1007/978-3-662-49384-7_15

[KLLNP16] Kaplan, M., Leurent, G., Leverrier, A., Naya-Plasencia, M.: Breaking symmetric cryptosystems using quantum period finding. In: Robshaw, M., Katz, J. (eds.) CRYPTO 2016. LNCS, vol. 9815, pp. 207–237. Springer, Heidelberg (2016). https://doi.org/10.1007/978-3-662-53008-5_8

[Mer89] Merkle, R.C.: One way hash functions and DES. In: Brassard, G. (ed.) CRYPTO 1989. LNCS, vol. 435, pp. 428–446. Springer, New York (1990). https://doi.org/10.1007/0-387-34805-0_40

[NIS15] Secure hash standard (SHS) & SHA-3 standard. FIPS PUB 180–4 & 202 (2015). http://nvlpubs.nist.gov/nistpubs/FIPS/NIST.FIPS.180-4.pdf. http://nvlpubs.nist.gov/nistpubs/FIPS/NIST.FIPS.202.pdf

[RS04] Rogaway, P., Shrimpton, T.: Cryptographic hash-function basics: definitions, implications, and separations for preimage resistance, second-preimage resistance, and collision resistance. In: Roy, B., Meier, W. (eds.) FSE 2004. LNCS, vol. 3017, pp. 371–388. Springer, Heidelberg (2004). https://doi.org/10.1007/978-3-540-25937-4_24

[Sho00] Shoup, V.: A composition theorem for universal one-way hash functions. In: Preneel, B. (ed.) EUROCRYPT 2000. LNCS, vol. 1807, pp. 445–452. Springer, Heidelberg (2000). https://doi.org/10.1007/3-540-45539-6_32

[Son14] Song, F.: A note on quantum security for post-quantum cryptography. In: Mosca, M. (ed.) PQCrypto 2014. LNCS, vol. 8772, pp. 246–265. Springer, Cham (2014). https://doi.org/10.1007/978-3-319-11659-4_15

[SS17] Santoli, T.: Schaffner, Christian: using Simon's algorithm to attack symmetric-key cryptographic primitives. Quantum Inf. Comput. **17**(1&2), 65–78 (2017)

[Unr12] Unruh, D.: Quantum proofs of knowledge. In: Pointcheval, D., Johansson, T. (eds.) EUROCRYPT 2012. LNCS, vol. 7237, pp. 135–152. Springer, Heidelberg (2012). https://doi.org/10.1007/978-3-642-29011-4_10

[Unr14] Unruh, D.: Quantum position verification in the random oracle model. In: Garay, J.A., Gennaro, R. (eds.) CRYPTO 2014. LNCS, vol. 8617, pp. 1–18. Springer, Heidelberg (2014). https://doi.org/10.1007/978-3-662-44381-1_1

[Unr16a] Unruh, D.: Collapse-binding quantum commitments without random oracles. In: Cheon, J.H., Takagi, T. (eds.) ASIACRYPT 2016. LNCS, vol. 10032, pp. 166–195. Springer, Heidelberg (2016). https://doi.org/10.1007/978-3-662-53890-6_6

[Unr16b] Unruh, D.: Computationally binding quantum commitments. In: Fischlin, M., Coron, J.-S. (eds.) EUROCRYPT 2016. LNCS, vol. 9666, pp. 497–527. Springer, Heidelberg (2016). https://doi.org/10.1007/978-3-662-49896-5_18

[Wat09] Watrous, J.: Zero-knowledge against quantum attacks. SIAM J. Comput. **39**(1), 25–58 (2009)

[Zha12a] Zhandry, M.: How to construct quantum random functions. In: FOCS 2012, pp. 679–687. IEEE (2012)

[Zha12b] Zhandry, M.: Secure identity-based encryption in the quantum random oracle model. In: Safavi-Naini, R., Canetti, R. (eds.) CRYPTO 2012. LNCS, vol. 7417, pp. 758–775. Springer, Heidelberg (2012). https://doi.org/10.1007/978-3-642-32009-5_44

Improved Quantum
Multicollision-Finding Algorithm

Akinori Hosoyamada[1,2(✉)], Yu Sasaki[1], Seiichiro Tani[3], and Keita Xagawa[1]

[1] NTT Secure Platform Laboratories, NTT Corporation,
3-9-11, Midori-cho, Musashino-shi, Tokyo 180-8585, Japan
{hosoyamada.akinori,sasaki.yu,xagawa.keita}@lab.ntt.co.jp
[2] Department of Information and Communication Engineering, Nagoya University,
Furo-cho, Chikusa-ku, Nagoya 464-8603, Japan
[3] NTT Communication Science Laboratories, NTT Corporation,
3-1, Morinosato-Wakamiya, Atsugi-shi, Kanagawa 243-0198, Japan
tani.seiichiro@lab.ntt.co.jp

Abstract. The current paper improves the number of queries of the previous quantum multi-collision finding algorithms presented by Hosoyamada *et al.* at Asiacrypt 2017. Let an l-collision be a tuple of l distinct inputs that result in the same output of a target function. In cryptology, it is important to study how many queries are required to find l-collisions for random functions of which domains are larger than ranges. The previous algorithm finds an l-collision for a random function by recursively calling the algorithm for finding $(l-1)$-collisions, and it achieves the average quantum query complexity of $O(N^{(3^{l-1}-1)/(2\cdot 3^{l-1})})$, where N is the range size of target functions. The new algorithm removes the redundancy of the previous recursive algorithm so that different recursive calls can share a part of computations. The new algorithm finds an l-collision for random functions with the average quantum query complexity of $O(N^{(2^{l-1}-1)/(2^l-1)})$, which improves the previous bound for all $l \geq 3$ (the new and previous algorithms achieve the optimal bound for $l = 2$). More generally, the new algorithm achieves the average quantum query complexity of $O\left(c_N^{3/2} N^{\frac{2^{l-1}-1}{2^l-1}}\right)$ for a random function $f\colon X \to Y$ such that $|X| \geq l \cdot |Y|/c_N$ for any $1 \leq c_N \in o(N^{\frac{1}{2^l-1}})$. With the same query complexity, it also finds a multiclaw for random functions, which is harder to find than a multicollision.

Keywords: Post-quantum cryptography · Quantum algorithm · Multiclaw · Multicollision

1 Introduction

Post-quantum cryptography has recently been discussed very actively in the cryptographic community. Quantum computers would completely break many

© Springer Nature Switzerland AG 2019
J. Ding and R. Steinwandt (Eds.): PQCrypto 2019, LNCS 11505, pp. 350–367, 2019.
https://doi.org/10.1007/978-3-030-25510-7_19

classical public-key cryptosystems. In response, NIST is now conducting a standardization to select new public-key cryptosystems that resist attacks with quantum computers. Given this background, it is now important to investigate how quantum computers can impact on other cryptographic schemes including cryptographic hash functions.

A multicollision for a function f denotes multiple inputs to f such that they are mapped to the same output value. In particular, an l-collision denotes a tuple of l distinct inputs $x_1, x_2, \cdots, x_l$ such that $f(x_1) = f(x_2) = \cdots = f(x_l)$.

A multicollision is an important object in cryptography. Lower bounds on the complexity of finding a multicollision are sometimes used to derive security bounds in the area of provable security (e.g., security bounds for the schemes based on the sponge construction [JLM14]). In a similar context, the complexity of finding a multicollision directly impacts on the best cryptanalysis against some constructions. Furthermore, multicollisions can be used as a proof-of-work for blockchains. In digital payment schemes, a coin must be a bit-string the validity of which can be easily checked but which is hard to produce. A micropayment scheme, MicroMint [RS96], defines coins as 4-collisions for a function. If 4-collisions can be produced quickly, a malicious user can counterfeit coins. Some recent works prove the security of schemes and protocols based on the assumption that there exist functions for which it is hard to find multicollisions [BKP18, BDRV18, KNY18].

Hosoyamada et al. [HSX17] provided a survey of multicollision finding algorithms with quantum computers. They first showed that an l-collision can be produced with at most $O(N^{1/2})$ queries on average to the target random function with range size N by iteratively applying the Grover search [Gro96, BBHT98] l times. They also reported that a combination of Zhandry's algorithm with $l = 3$ [Zha15] and Belovs' algorithm [Bel12] achieves $O(N^{10/21})$ for $l = 3$, which is faster than the simple application of Grover's algorithm. Finally, Hosoyamada et al. presented their own algorithm that recursively applies the collision finding algorithm by Brassard, Høyer, and Tapp [BHT98]. Their algorithm achieves the average query complexity of $O(N^{(3^{l-1}-1)/(2 \cdot 3^{l-1})})$ for every $l \geq 2$. For $l = 3$ and $l = 4$, the complexities are $O(N^{4/9})$ and $O(N^{13/27})$, respectively, and the algorithm works as follows.

- To search for 3-collisions, it first iterates the $O(N^{1/3})$-query quantum algorithm for finding a 2-collision $O(N^{1/9})$ times. Then, it searches for the preimage of any one of the $O(N^{1/9})$ 2-collisions by using Grover's algorithm, which runs with $O(N^{4/9})$ queries.
- To search for 4-collisions, it iterates the $O(N^{4/9})$-query quantum algorithm for finding a 3-collision $O(N^{1/27})$ times. Then, it searches for the preimage of any one of the $O(N^{1/27})$ 3-collisions with $O(N^{13/27})$ queries.

As demonstrated above, the recursive algorithm by Hosoyamada et al. [HSX17] runs the $(l-1)$-collision algorithm multiple times, but in each invocation, the algorithm starts from scratch. This fact motivates us to consider reusing the computations when we search for multiple $(l-1)$-collisions.

Our Contributions. In this paper, we improve the quantum query complexity of the previous multicollision finding algorithm by removing the redundancy of the algorithm. Consider the problem of finding an l-collision of a random function $f \colon X \to Y$, where $l \geq 2$ is an integer constant and $|Y| = N$. In addition, suppose that there exists a parameter $c_N \geq 1$ such that $c_N = o(N^{\frac{1}{2^l-1}})$ and $|X| \geq l \cdot |Y|/c_N$. Then, the new algorithm achieves the average quantum query complexity of $O\left(c_N^{3/2} N^{\frac{2^{l-1}-1}{2^l-1}}\right)$. In particular, if we can take c_N as a constant, then our algorithm can find an l-collision of a random function with $O\left(N^{\frac{2^{l-1}-1}{2^l-1}}\right)$ queries on average, which improves the previous quantum query complexity $O\left(N^{\frac{3^{l-1}-1}{2 \cdot 3^{l-1}-1}}\right)$ [HSX17] and matches with the lower bound proved by Liu and Zhandry [LZ18].

The complexities for small l's are listed in Table 1. A comparison between them can be found in Fig. 1. Our algorithm finds a 2-collision, 3-collision, 4-collision, and 5-collision of SHA3-512 with $2^{170.7}$, $2^{219.4}$, $2^{238.9}$, and $2^{247.7}$ quantum queries, respectively, up to a constant factor (Table 2).

Moreover, our new algorithm finds multiclaws for random functions, which are harder to find than multicollisions: An l-claw for functions $f_i \colon X_i \to Y$ for $1 \leq i \leq l$ is defined as a tuple $(x_1, \ldots, x_l) \in X_1 \times \cdots \times X_l$ such that $f_i(x_i) = f_j(x_j)$ for all (i,j). If there exists a parameter $c_N \geq 1$ such that $c_N = o(N^{\frac{1}{2^l-1}})$ and $|X_i| \geq |Y|/c_N$ for each i, our quantum algorithm finds an l-claw for random functions f_i's with $O\left(c_N^{3/2} N^{\frac{2^{l-1}-1}{2^l-1}}\right)$ quantum queries on average. In particular, if we can take c_N as a constant, then our algorithm can find an l-claw with $O\left(N^{\frac{2^{l-1}-1}{2^l-1}}\right)$ quantum queries.

In this paper, we do not provide the analyses of other complexity measures such as time/space complexity and the depth of quantum circuits, but it is not difficult to show with analyses similar to those in Ref. [HSX17] that the space complexity and the circuit depth are the same order as the query complexity up to a polylogarithmic factor.

Hereafter, we only consider *average* quantum query complexity over random functions as the performance of algorithms unless stated otherwise.

Paper Outline. The remaining of this paper is organized as follows. In Sect. 2, we describe notations, definitions and settings. In Sect. 3, we review previous works related to the multicollision-finding problem. In Sect. 4, we provide our new quantum algorithm and its complexity analysis. In Sect. 5, we conclude this paper.

Concurrent Work. Very recently, Liu and Zhandry [LZ18] showed that for every integer constant $l \geq 2$, $\Theta\left(N^{\frac{1}{2}(1-\frac{1}{2^l-1})}\right)$ quantum queries are both neces-

Table 1. Query complexities of l-collision finding quantum algorithms. Each fraction denotes the logarithm of the number of queries to the base N. The query complexity asymptotically approaches $1/2$ as l increases.

l	2	3	4	5	6	7	8
[HSX17]: $\frac{3^{l-1}-1}{2\cdot 3^{l-1}}$	$\frac{1}{3}$	$\frac{4}{9}$	$\frac{13}{27}$	$\frac{40}{81}$	$\frac{121}{243}$	$\frac{364}{729}$	$\frac{1093}{2187}$
Ours: $\frac{2^{l-1}-1}{2^{l}-1}$	$\frac{1}{3}$	$\frac{3}{7}$	$\frac{7}{15}$	$\frac{15}{31}$	$\frac{31}{63}$	$\frac{63}{127}$	$\frac{127}{255}$

l	2	3	4	5	6	7	8
[HSX17]: $\frac{3^{l-1}-1}{2\cdot 3^{l-1}}$	0.3333..	0.4444.	0.4814..	0.4938..	0.4979..	0.4993..	0.4997..
Ours: $\frac{2^{l-1}-1}{2^{l}-1}$	0.3333..	0.4285..	0.4666..	0.4838..	0.4920..	0.4960..	0.4980..

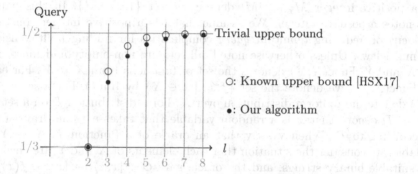

Fig. 1. Quantum query complexity for finding an l-collision. "Query" denotes the logarithm of the number of queries to the base N.

Table 2. The number of queries required to find an l-collision of SHA3-512. The numbers in the first row are obtained from the concrete bound given in [HSX17, Thm.5.1], and those in the second row are obtained from the concrete bound given in Theorem 2 with $k = 2$.

l	2	3	4	5
[HSX17, Thm 5.1]	2^{179}	2^{238}	2^{260}	2^{268}
Ours, Theorem 2	2^{181}	2^{230}	2^{250}	2^{259}

sary and sufficient to find a l-collision with constant probability, for a random function. That is, they gave an improved upper bound and a new lower bound on the average case. The comparisons are summarized as follows:

- Liu and Zhandry consider the l-collision case that $|X| \geq l|Y|$, where X is the domain and Y is the range. We treat the case that $|X| \geq \frac{l}{c_N}|Y|$ holds for any positive value $c_N \geq 1$ which is in $o(N^{\frac{1}{2^l-1}})$. We also consider the *multiclaw* case.

- Their exponent $\frac{1}{2}(1 - \frac{1}{2^l-1})$ is the same as ours $\frac{2^{l-1}-1}{2^l-1}$.
- They give the upper bound $O(N^{\frac{1}{2}(1-\frac{1}{2^l-1})})$, while we give $O(c_N^{3/2} N^{\frac{1}{2}(1-\frac{1}{2^l-1})})$. When c_N is a constant, our bound matches their bound.
- They give a lower bound, which matches with their and our upper bound.

We finally note that our result on an improved l-collision finding algorithm for the case $|X| \geq l|Y|$ with query complexity $O\left(N^{\frac{1}{2}(1-\frac{1}{2^l-1})}\right)$ is reported in the Rump Session of Asiacrypt 2017.

2 Preliminaries

For a positive integer M, let $[M]$ denote the set $\{1, \ldots, M\}$. In this paper, N denotes a positive integer. We assume that l is a positive integer constant. We focus on reducing quantum *query* complexities for finding multicollisions and multiclaws. Unless otherwise noted, all sets are non-empty and finite. For sets X and Y, $\mathsf{Func}(X, Y)$ denotes the set of functions from X to Y. For each $f \in \mathsf{Func}(X, Y)$, we denote the set $\{f(x) \mid x \in X\}$ by $\mathsf{Im}(f)$. For a set X, let $U(X)$ denote the uniform distribution over X. For a distribution $\mathcal{D}$ on a set X, let $x \sim \mathcal{D}$ denote that x is a random variable that takes a value drawn from X according to $\mathcal{D}$. When we say that an oracle of a function $f \colon X \to Y$ is available, we consider the situation that each elements of X and Y are encoded into suitable binary strings, and the oracle gate $O_f \colon |x, z\rangle \mapsto |x, z \oplus f(x)\rangle$ is available.

An *l-collision* for a function $f \colon X \to Y$ is a tuple of elements $(x_1, \ldots, x_l, y)$ in $X^\ell \times Y$ such that $f(x_i) = f(x_j) = y$ and $x_i \neq x_j$ for all $1 \leq i \neq j \leq l$. An l-collision is simply called a *collision* for $l = 2$, and called a *multicollision* for $l \geq 3$. Moreover, an *l-claw* for functions $f_i \colon X_i \to Y$ for $1 \leq i \leq l$ is a tuple $(x_1, \ldots, x_l, y) \in X_1 \times \cdots \times X_l \times Y$ such that $f_1(x_1) = \cdots = f_l(x_l) = y$. An l-claw is simply called a *claw* for $l = 2$, and called a *multiclaw* for $l \geq 3$.

The problems of finding multicollisions or multiclaws are often studied in the contexts of both cryptography and quantum computation, but the problem settings of interest change depending on the contexts. In the context of quantum computation, most problems are studied in the *worst case*, and an algorithm is said to (efficiently) solve a problem only when it does (efficiently) for all functions. On the other hand, most problems in cryptography are studied in the *average case*, since randomness is one of the most crucial notions in cryptography. In particular, we say that an algorithm (efficiently) solves a problem if it does so with a high probability on average over randomly chosen functions.

This paper focuses on the settings of interest in the context of cryptography. Formally, our goal is to solve the following two problems.

Problem 1 (Multicollision-finding problem, average case). Let $l \geq 2$ be a positive integer constant, and X, Y denote non-empty finite sets. Suppose that a function

$F\colon X \to Y$ is chosen uniformly at random and given as a quantum oracle. Then, find an l-collision for F.

Problem 2 (Multiclaw-finding problem, average case). Let $l \geq 2$ be a positive integer constant, and $X_1, \ldots, X_l, Y$ denote non-empty finite sets. Suppose that functions $f_i\colon X_i \to Y(1 \leq i \leq l)$ are chosen independently and uniformly at random, and given as quantum oracles. Then, find an l-claw for $f_1, \ldots, f_l$.

Roughly speaking, Problem 1 is easier to solve than Problem 2. Suppose that $F\colon X \to Y$ is a function, and we want to find an l-collision for F. Let $X_1, \ldots, X_l$ be subsets of X such that $X_i \cap X_j = \emptyset$ for $i \neq j$ and $\bigcup_i X_i = X$. If $(x_1, \ldots, x_l, y)$ is an l-claw for $F|_{X_1}, \ldots, F|_{X_l}$, then it is obviously an l-collision for F. In general, an algorithm for finding an l-claw can be converted into one for finding an l-collision. To be precise, the following lemma holds.

Lemma 1. *Let X, Y be non-empty finite sets, and $X_1, \ldots, X_l$ be subsets of X such that $X_i \cap X_j = \emptyset$ for $i \neq j$ and $\bigcup_i X_i = X$. If there exists a quantum algorithm $\mathcal{A}$ that solves Problem 2 for the sets $X_1, \ldots, X_l, Y$ by making at most q quantum queries with probability at least p, then there exists a quantum algorithm $\mathcal{B}$ that solves Problem 1 for the sets X, Y by making at most q quantum queries with probability at least p.*

How to measure the size of a problem also changes depending on which context we are in. In the context of cryptography, the problem size is often regarded as the size of the range of functions in the problem rather than the size of the domains, since the domains of cryptographic functions such as hash functions are much larger than their ranges. Hence, we regard the range size $|Y|$ as the size of Problem 1 (and Problem 2) when we analyze the complexity of quantum algorithms.

In the context of quantum computation, there exist previous works on problems related to ours [Bel12, Amb04, Tan09, BDH+01] (element distinctness problem, for example), but those works usually focus on the worst case complexity and regard the domain sizes of functions as the problem size. In particular, there does not exist any previous work that studies multiclaw-finding problem for general l in the average case, to the best of authors' knowledge.

3 Previous Works

3.1 The Grover Search and Its Generalization

As a main tool for developing quantum algorithms, we use the quantum database search algorithm that was originally developed by Grover [Gro96] and later generalized by Boyer, Brassard, Høyer, and Tapp [BBHT98]. Below we introduce the generalized version.

Theorem 1. *Let X be a non-empty finite set and $f\colon X \to \{0, 1\}$ be a function such that $t/|X| < 17/81$, where $t = |f^{-1}(1)|$. Then, there exists a quantum* *algorithm* BBHT *that finds* x *such that* $f(x) = 1$ *with an expected number of quantum queries to* f *at most*

$$\frac{4|X|}{\sqrt{(|X| - t)t}} \leq \frac{9}{2} \cdot \sqrt{\frac{|X|}{t}}.$$

If $f^{-1}(1) = \emptyset$, *then* BBHT *runs forever.*

Theorem 1 implies that we can find l-collisions and l-claws for random functions with $O(\sqrt{N})$ quantum queries, if the sizes of range(s) and domain(s) of function(s) are $\Theta(N)$: Suppose that we are given random functions $f_i \colon X_i \to Y$ for $1 \leq i \leq l$, where $|X_1|, \ldots, |X_l|$, and $|Y|$ are all in $\Theta(N)$, and we want to find an l-claw for those functions. Take an element $y \in Y$ randomly, and define $F_i \colon X_i \to \{0, 1\}$ for each i by $F_i(x) = 1$ if and only if $f_i(x) = y$. Then, effectively, by applying BBHT to each F_i, we can find $x_i \in X_i$ such that $f_i(x_i) = y$ for each i with $O(\sqrt{N})$ quantum queries with a constant probability. Similarly we can find an l-collision for a random function $F \colon [N] \to [N]$ with $O(\sqrt{N})$ quantum queries. In particular, $O(\sqrt{N})$ is a trivial upper bound of Problems 1 and 2.

3.2   The BHT Algorithm

Brassard, Høyer, and Tapp [BHT98] developed a quantum algorithm that finds 2-claws (below we call it BHT).[1] BHT finds a claw for two one-to-one functions $f_1 \colon X_1 \to Y$ and $f_2 \colon X_2 \to Y$ as sketched in the following. For simplicity, here we assume $|X_1| = |X_2| = |Y| = N$. Under this setting, BHT finds a 2-claw with $O(N^{1/3})$ quantum queries.

Rough Sketch of BHT:

1. **Construction of a list L.** Take a subset $S \subset X_1$ of size $N^{1/3}$ arbitrarily. For each $x \in S$, compute the value $f_1(x)$ by making a query and store the pair $(x, f_1(x))$ in a list L.
2. **Extension to a claw.** Define a function $F_L \colon X_2 \to \{0, 1\}$ by $F_L(x') = 1$ if and only if the value $f_2(x') \in Y$ appears in the list L (i.e., there exists $x_1 \in S$ such that $f_2(x') = f_1(x_1)$). Apply BBHT to F_L and find $x_2 \in X_2$ such that $f_2(x_2)$ appears in L.
3. **Finalization.** Find $(x_1, f_1(x_1)) \in L$ such that $f_1(x_1) = f_2(x_2)$, and then output (x_1, x_2).

---

[1] As in our case, the BHT algorithm also focus on only quantum query complexity. Although it runs in time $\tilde{O}(N^{1/3})$ on an idealized quantum computer, it requires $\tilde{O}(N^{1/3})$ qubits to store data in quantum memories. Recently Chailloux et al. [CNS17] has developed a quantum 2-collision finding algorithm that runs in time $\tilde{O}(N^{2/5})$, which is polynomially slower than the BHT algorithm but requires only $O(\log N)$ quantum memories.

Quantum Query Complexity. BHT finds a claw with $O(N^{1/3})$ quantum queries. In the first step, the list L is constructed by making $N^{1/3}$ queries to f_1. In the second step, since $|F_L^{-1}(1)| = |f_2^{-1}(f_1(S))|$ is equal to $N^{1/3}$, BBHT finds x_2 with $O(\sqrt{N/N^{1/3}}) = O(N^{1/3})$ quantum queries to f_2 (note that we can evaluate F_L by making one query to f_2). The third step does not require queries. Therefore BHT finds a collision by making $O(N^{1/3})$ quantum queries in total in the worst case.

Extension to a Collision-Finding Algorithm. It is not difficult to show that BHT works for random functions. Thus, BHT can be extended to the quantum collision-finding algorithm as mentioned in Sect. 2. Suppose we want to find a (2-)collision for a random function $F\colon X \to Y$. Here we assume $|X| = 2N$ and $|Y| = N$ for simplicity. Now, choose a subset $X_1 \subset X$ of size N arbitrarily and let $X_2\colon = X\backslash X_1$. Then we can find a collision for F by applying the BHT algorithm introduced above to the functions $F|_{X_1}$ and $F|_{X_2}$, since a claw for them becomes a collision for F.

3.3 The HSX Algorithm

Next, we introduce a quantum algorithm for finding multicollisions that was developed by Hosoyamada, Sasaki, and Xagawa [HSX17] (the algorithm is designed to find only multicollisions, and cannot find multiclaws). Below we call their algorithm HSX.

The main idea of HSX is to apply the strategy of BHT recursively: To find an l-collision, HSX calls itself recursively to find many $(l-1)$-collisions, and then extend any one of those $(l-1)$-collisions to an l-collision by applying BBHT.

Rough Sketch of HSX: In what follows, N denotes $|Y|$. Let us denote HSX(l) by the HSX algorithm for finding l-collisions. HSX(l) finds an l-collision for a random function $f\colon X \to Y$ with $|X| \geq l \cdot |Y|$ as follows.

Recursive call to construct a list L_{l-1}. Apply HSX($l-1$) to f $N^{1/3^{l-1}}$ times to obtain $N^{1/3^{l-1}}$ many $(l-1)$-collisions. Store those $(l-1)$-collisions in a list L_{l-1}.
Extension to an l-collision. Define $F_{l-1}\colon X \to \{0,1\}$ by $F_{l-1}(x') = 1$ if and only if there exists an $(l-1)$-collision $(x_1,\ldots,x_{l-1},y) \in L_{l-1}$ such that $(x_1,\ldots,x_{l-1},x',y)$ forms an l-collision for f, i.e., $f(x') = y$ and $x' \neq x_i$ for $1 \leq i \leq l-1$. Apply BBHT to F_{l-1} to find $x_l \in X$ such that $F_{l-1}(x_l) = 1$.
Finalization. Find $(x_1,\ldots,x_{l-1},y) \in L_{l-1}$ such that $F_{l-1}(x_l) = y$. Output $(x_1,\ldots,x_{l-1},x_l,y)$.

Quantum Query Complexity. HSX finds a l-collision with $O(N^{(3^{l-1}-1)/2\cdot3^{l-1}})$ quantum queries on average, which can be shown by induction as follows. For 2-collisions, HSX(2) matches the BHT algorithm. For general $l \geq 3$, suppose that HSX($l-1$) finds an $(l-1)$-collision with $O(N^{(3^{l-2}-1)/2\cdot3^{l-2}})$ quantum queries on average. In its first step, HSX(l) makes $N^{1/3^{l-1}} \cdot O(N^{(3^{l-2}-1)/2 \cdot 3^{l-2}}) = O(N^{(3^{l-1}-1)/2 \cdot 3^{l-1}})$ quantum queries. Moreover, in its second step, HSX(l) makes $O(\sqrt{N/N^{(3^{l-2}-1)/2 \cdot 3^{l-2}}}) = O(N^{(3^{l-1}-1)/2 \cdot 3^{l-1}})$ quantum queries by using BBHT. The third step does not make quantum queries. Therefore it follows that HSX(l) makes $O(N^{(3^{l-1}-1)/2 \cdot 3^{l-1}})$ quantum queries in total.

4   New Quantum Algorithm Mclaw

This section gives our new quantum algorithm Mclaw that finds an l-claw with $O(c_N^{3/2} N^{(2^{l-1}-1)/(2^l-1)})$ quantum queries for random functions $f_i \colon X_i \to Y$ for $1 \le i \le l$, where $|Y| = N$ and there exists a real value c_N with $1 \le c_N \in o(N^{\frac{1}{2^l-1}})$ such that $\frac{N}{c_N} \le |X_i|$ holds for all i. Roughly speaking, this means that, an l-collision for a random function $f \colon X \to Y$, where $|Y| = N$ and $|X| \ge l \cdot N$, can be found with $O(N^{(2^{l-1}-1)/(2^l-1)})$ quantum queries, which improves the previous result [HSX17] (see Sect. 2).

Our algorithm assumes that $|X_1|, \ldots, |X_l|$ are less than or equal to $|Y|$. However, it can also be applied to the functions of interest in the context of cryptography, i.e., the functions of which domains are much larger than ranges, by restricting the domains of them to suitable subsets.

The main idea of our new algorithm is to improve HSX by getting rid of its redundancy: To find an l-collision, HSX recursively calls itself to find many $(l-1)$-collisions. Once HSX finds an $(l-1)$-collision $\gamma = (x_1, \ldots, x_{l-1}, y)$, it stores γ in a list L_{l-1}, *discards all the data that was used to find* γ, and then start to search for another $(l-1)$-collision γ'. It is inefficient to discard data every time an $(l-1)$-collision is found, and our new algorithm Mclaw reduces the number of quantum queries by reusing those data. We note that our algorithm Mclaw can solve the multiclaw-finding problem as well as the multicollision-finding problem.

We begin with describing our algorithm in an intuitive manner, and then give its formal description.

4.1   Intuitive Description and Complexity Analysis

We explain the idea of how to develop the BHT algorithm, how to develop a quantum algorithm to find 3-claws from BHT, and how to extend it further to the case of finding an l-claw for any l.

How to Develop the BHT Algorithm. Here we review how the BHT algorithm is developed. Let $f_1 \colon X_1 \to Y$ and $f_2 \colon X_2 \to Y$ be one-to-one functions. The goal of the BHT algorithm is to find a (2-)claw for f_1 and f_2 with $O(N^{1/3})$ quantum queries. For simplicity, below we assume that $|X_1| = |X_2| = |Y| = N$ holds. Let t_1 be a parameter that defines the size of a list of 1-claws for f_1. It will be set as $t_1 = N^{1/3}$.

First, collect t_1 many 1-claws for f_1 and store them in a list L_1. This first step makes t_1 queries. Second, extend one of 1-claws in L_1 to a 2-claw for f_1 and f_2, by using BBHT, and output the obtained 2-claw. Since BBHT makes $O(\sqrt{N/t_1})$

queries to make a 2-claw from L_1, this second step makes $O(\sqrt{N/t_1})$ queries (see Theorem 1). Overall, the above algorithm makes $q_2(t_1) = t_1 + \sqrt{N/t_1}$ quantum queries up to a constant factor. The function $q_2(t_1)$ takes its minimum value $2 \cdot N^{1/3}$ when $t_1 = N^{1/3}$. By setting $t_1 = N^{1/3}$, the BHT algorithm is obtained.

From BHT to a 3-Claw-Finding Algorithm. Next, we show how the above strategy to develop the BHT algorithm can be extended to develop a 3-claw-finding algorithm. Let $f_i \colon X_i \to Y$ be one-to-one functions for $1 \le i \le 3$. Our goal here is to find a 3-claw for f_1, f_2, and f_3 with $O(N^{3/7})$ quantum queries. For simplicity, below we assume $|X_1| = |X_2| = |X_3| = |Y| = N$. Let t_1, t_2 be parameters that define the number of 1-claws for f_1 and that of 2-claws for f_1 and f_2, respectively. (They will be fixed later.)

First, collect t_1 many 1-claws for f_1 and store them in a list L_1. This first step makes t_1 queries. Second, extend 1-claws in L_1 to t_2 many 2-claws for f_1 and f_2 by using BBHT, and store them in a list L_2. Here we do not discard the list L_1 until we construct the list L_2 of size t_2, while the HSX algorithm does. Since BBHT makes $O(\sqrt{N/t_1})$ queries to make a 2-claw from L_1, this second step makes $t_2 \cdot O(\sqrt{N/t_1})$ queries if $t_2 = o(t_1)$ (see Theorem 1). Finally, extend one of 2-claws in L_2 to a 3-claw for f_1, f_2, and f_3 by using BBHT, and output the obtained 3-claw. This final step makes $O(\sqrt{N/t_2})$ queries. Overall, the above algorithm makes $q_3(t_1, t_2) = t_1 + t_2 \cdot \sqrt{N/t_1} + \sqrt{N/t_2}$ quantum queries up to a constant factor. The function $q_3(t_1, t_2)$ takes its minimum value $3 \cdot N^{3/7}$ when $t_1 = t_2 \cdot \sqrt{N/t_1} = \sqrt{N/t_2}$, which is equivalent to $t_1 = N^{3/7}$ and $t_2 = N^{1/7}$. By setting $t_1 = N^{3/7}$ and $t_2 = N^{1/7}$, we can obtain a 3-claw finding algorithm with $O(N^{3/7})$ quantum queries.

l-**Claw-Finding Algorithm for General *l*.** Generalizing the above idea to find a 3-claw, we can find an l-claw for general l as follows. Let $f_i \colon X_i \to Y$ be one-to-one functions for $1 \le i \le l$. Our goal here is to find an l-claw for $f_1, \ldots, f_l$. For simplicity, below we assume that $|X_1| = \cdots = |X_l| = |Y| = N$ holds. Let $t_1, \ldots, t_{l-1}$ be parameters with $t_i = o(t_{i-1})$ for $i = 2, \ldots, l$.

First, collect t_1 many 1-claws for f_1 and store them in a list L_1. This first step makes t_1 queries. In the i-th step for $2 \le i \le l-1$, extend t_i many $(i-1)$-claws in L_{i-1} to t_i many i-claws for $f_1, \ldots, f_i$ by using BBHT, and store them in a list L_i. Here we do not discard the list L_{i-1} until we construct the list L_i of size t_i. Since BBHT makes $O(\sqrt{N/t_{i-1}})$ queries to make an i-claw from L_{i-1}, the i-th step makes $t_i \cdot O(\sqrt{N/t_{i-1}})$ queries. Finally, extend one of $(l-1)$-claws in L_{l-1} to an l-claw for $f_1, \ldots, f_l$ by using BBHT, and output the obtained l-claw. This final step makes $O(\sqrt{N/t_{l-1}})$ queries. Overall, this algorithm makes $q_l(t_1, \ldots, t_{l-1}) = t_1 + t_2 \cdot \sqrt{N/t_1} + \cdots + t_{l-1} \cdot \sqrt{N/t_{l-2}} + \sqrt{N/t_{l-1}}$ quantum queries up to a constant factor. The function $q_l(t_1, \ldots, t_{l-1})$ takes its minimum value $l \cdot N^{(2^{l-1}-1)/(2^l-1)}$ when $t_1 = t_2 \cdot \sqrt{N/t_1} = \cdots = t_{l-1} \cdot \sqrt{N/t_{l-2}} = \sqrt{N/t_{l-1}}$, which is equivalent to $t_i = N^{(2^{l-i}-1)/(2^l-1)}$. By setting $t_i = N^{(2^{l-i}-1)/(2^l-1)}$, we can find an l-claw with $O(N^{(2^{l-1}-1)/(2^l-1)})$ quantum queries. Our new quantum algorithm Mclaw is developed based on the above strategy for random functions.

4.2   Formal Description

Here we formally describe our quantum multiclaw-finding algorithm Mclaw. A formal complexity analysis of Mclaw is given in the next subsection, and this subsection only describes how the algorithm works.

Let N be a sufficiently large integer and suppose that $|Y| = N$ holds. Below we assume that $|X_i| \leq |Y|$ holds for all i. This is a reasonable assumption since, if there is an algorithm that solves Problem 2 in the case that $|X_i| \leq |Y|$ holds for all i, then we can also solve the problem in other cases: If $|X_i| > |Y|$ holds for some i, take a subset $S_i \subset X_i$ such that $|S_i| = |Y|$ and find an l-claw for $f_1, \ldots, f_{i-1}, f_i|_{S_i}, f_{i+1}, \ldots, f_l$. Then the l-claw is also an l-claw for $f_1, \ldots, f_l$.

Here we introduce a corollary that follows from Theorem 1.

Corollary 1. *Let X, Y be non-empty finite sets, $f : X \to Y$ be a function, and $L' \subset Y$ be a non-empty subset. Then there exists a quantum algorithm MTPS that finds x such that $f(x) \in L'$ with an expected number of quantum queries to f at most $9\sqrt{5|X|/|f^{-1}(L')|}$.*

Let $F_{L'} : \{1, \ldots, 5\} \times X \to \{0, 1\}$ be the boolean function defined by $F_{L'}(\alpha, x) = 1$ if and only if $\alpha = 1$ and $f(x) \in L'$. A quantum circuit that computes $F_{L'}$ can be implemented with two oracle calls to f. Then, run BBHT on $F_{L'}$. Since $|\{1, \ldots, 5\} \times X| = 5|X|$ and $|F_{L'}^{-1}(1)| \leq |X| \leq 17/81 \cdot |\{1, \ldots, 5\} \times X|$ always hold, we can show that the corollary follows from Theorem 1.

Our algorithm is parametrized by a positive integer $k \geq 2$, and we denote the algorithm for the parameter k by Mclaw_k. Mclaw_k can be applied in the situation that there exists a parameter $c_N \geq 1$ such that c_N is in $o(N^{\frac{1}{2^l-1}})$ and $|X_i| \geq |Y|/c_N$ holds for each i. We impose an upper limit on the number of queries that Mclaw_k is allowed to make: We design Mclaw_k in such a way that it immediately stops and aborts if the number of queries made reaches the limit specified by the parameter $\mathsf{Qlimit}_k := k \cdot 169 l c_N^{3/2} \cdot N^{\frac{2^{l-1}-1}{2^l-1}}$. The upper limit Qlimit_k is necessary to prevent the algorithm from running forever, and to make the expected value of the number of queries converge. We also define the parameters controlling the sizes of the lists:

$$N_i := \begin{cases} \frac{N}{4c_N} & (i = 0), \\ N^{\frac{2^{l-i}-1}{2^l-1}} & (i \geq 1). \end{cases} \qquad (1)$$

For ease of notation, we define L_0 and L_0' as $L_0 = L_0' = Y$. Then, Mclaw_k is described as in Algorithm 1.

4.3   Formal Complexity Analysis

This section gives a formal complexity analysis of Mclaw_k. The goal of this section is to show the following theorem.

Algorithm 1. Mclaw$_k$

Require: Randomly chosen functions $f_1, \ldots, f_l$ ($f_i \colon X_i \to Y$ and $|X_i| \leq |Y|$)).
Ensure: An l-claw for $f_1, \ldots, f_l$ or $\bot$.
Stop condition: If the number of queries reaches Qlimit$_k$, stop and output $\bot$.
$\quad L_1, \ldots, L_l \leftarrow \emptyset,\ L_1', \ldots, L_l' \leftarrow \emptyset.$
$\quad$ **for** $i = 1$ to l **do**
$\qquad$ **for** $j = 1$ to $\lceil 4c_N \cdot N_i \rceil$ **do**
$\qquad\quad$ **if** $i = 1$ **then**
$\qquad\qquad$ Take $x_j \in X_1$ that does not appear in L_1, $y \leftarrow f_1(x_j)$.
$\qquad\quad$ **else**
$\qquad\qquad$ Find $x_j \in X_i$ whose image $y \colon = f_i(x_j)$ is in L_{i-1}' by running MTPS on f_i
$\qquad\qquad$ and L_{i-1}'. $\qquad\qquad\qquad\qquad\qquad\qquad\qquad$ //multiple queries are made
$\qquad\quad$ **end if**
$\qquad\quad L_i \leftarrow L_i \cup \{(x^{(1)}, \ldots, x^{(i-1)}, x_j, y)\},\ L_i' \leftarrow L_i' \cup \{y\}.$
$\qquad\quad L_{i-1} \leftarrow L_{i-1} \setminus \{(x^{(1)}, \ldots, x^{(i-1)}, y)\},\ L_i' \leftarrow L_{i-1}' \setminus \{y\}.$
$\qquad$ **end for**
$\quad$ **end for**
$\quad$ Return an element $(x^{(1)}, \ldots, x^{(l)}; y) \in L_l$ as an output.

Theorem 2. *Assume that there exists a parameter $c_N \geq 1$ such that c_N is in $o(N^{\frac{1}{2^l-1}})$ and $|X_i| \geq \frac{1}{c_N}|Y|$ holds for each i. If $|Y| = N$ is sufficiently large, Mclaw$_k$ finds an l-claw with a probability at least*

$$1 - \frac{1}{k} - \frac{2l}{N} - l \cdot \exp\left(-\frac{1}{15} \cdot \frac{N^{\frac{1}{2^l-1}}}{c_N}\right), \tag{2}$$

by making at most

$$\text{Qlimit}_k = k \cdot 169 l c_N^{3/2} \cdot N^{\frac{2^{l-1}-1}{2^l-1}} \tag{3}$$

quantum queries, where k is any positive integer 2 or more.

This theorem shows that, for each integer $k \geq 2$, Mclaw$_k$ finds an l-claw with a constant probability by making $O\left(c_N^{3/2} N^{\frac{2^{l-1}-1}{2^l-1}}\right)$ queries.

For later use, we show the following lemma.

Lemma 2. *Let X, Y be non-empty finite sets such that $|X| \leq |Y|$. Suppose that a function $f \colon X \to Y$ is chosen uniformly at random. Then*

$$\Pr_{f \sim U(\text{Func}(X,Y))}\left[|\text{Im}(f)| \geq \frac{|X|}{2} - \sqrt{|X| \ln |Y|/2}\right] \geq 1 - \frac{2}{|Y|} \tag{4}$$

holds.

Proof. Note that, for each $x \in X$, $f(x)$ is the random variable that takes value in Y. Moreover, $\{f(x)\}_{x \in X}$ is the set of independent random variables. Let us define a function $\Phi\colon Y^{\times|X|} \to \mathbb{N}$ by $\Phi(y_1,\ldots,y_{|X|}) = \left|Y\backslash\{y_i\}_{1\le i\le|X|}\right|$. Then Φ is 1-Lipschitz, i.e.,

$$\left|\Phi(y_1,\ldots,y_{i-1},y_i,y_{i+1},\ldots,y_{|X|}) - \Phi(y_1,\ldots,y_{i-1},y_i',y_{i+1},\ldots,y_{|X|})\right| \le 1 \quad (5)$$

holds for arbitrary choices of elements $y_1,\ldots,y_{|X|}$, and y_i' in Y. Now we apply the following theorem to Φ.

Theorem 3 (McDiarmid's Inequality (Theorem 13.7 in [MU17])). *Let M be a positive integer, and $\Phi\colon Y^{\times M}\colon \to \mathbb{N}$ be a 1-Lipschitz function. Let $\{y_i\}_{1\le i\le M}$ be the set of independent random variables that take values in Y. Let μ denote the expectation value $\mathbf{E}_{y_1,\ldots,y_M}\left[\Phi(y_1,\ldots,y_M)\right]$. Then*

$$\Pr_{y_1,\ldots,y_M}\left[\Phi(y_1,\ldots,y_M) \ge \mu + \lambda\right] \le 2e^{-2\lambda^2/M} \quad (6)$$

holds.

Apply the above theorem with $M = |X|$, $\lambda = \sqrt{|X|\ln|Y|/2}$, and $y_x = f(x)$ for each $x \in X$ (here we identify X with the set $\{1,\ldots,|X|\}$). Then, since $\mathbf{E}\left[\Phi(y_1,\ldots,y_M)\right] = |Y|\left(1 - 1/|Y|\right)^{|X|}$ holds, we have that

$$\Pr_{f\sim U(\mathrm{Func}(X,Y))}\left[\Phi(y_1,\ldots,y_M) \ge |Y|\left(1 - 1/|Y|\right)^{|X|} + \sqrt{|X|\ln|Y|/2}\right] \le \frac{2}{|Y|}.$$

In addition, it follows that

$$|Y|\left(1 - 1/|Y|\right)^{|X|} \le |Y|e^{-|X|/|Y|} \le |Y|\left(1 - \frac{|X|}{|Y|} + \frac{1}{2}\left(\frac{|X|}{|Y|}\right)^2\right)$$

$$= |Y| - |X|\left(1 - \frac{1}{2}\frac{|X|}{|Y|}\right) \le |Y| - \frac{|X|}{2}, \quad (7)$$

where we used the assumption that $|X| \le |Y|$ for the last inequality. Since $\Phi(y_1,\ldots,y_M) = |Y\backslash\mathrm{Im}(f)|$ and $|\mathrm{Im}(f)| = |Y| - |Y\backslash\mathrm{Im}(f)|$ hold, it follows that $|\mathrm{Im}(f)|$ is at least

$$|Y| - \left(|Y| - \frac{|X|}{2} + \sqrt{|X|\ln|Y|/2}\right) = \frac{|X|}{2} - \sqrt{|X|\ln|Y|/2} \quad (8)$$

with a probability at least $1 - \frac{2}{|Y|}$, which completes the proof. $\qquad\square$

Proof (of Theorem 2). We show that Eq. 2 holds. Let us define $\mathsf{good}^{(i)}$ to be the event that

$$|\mathrm{Im}(f_i) \cap L_{i-1}'| \ge N_{i-1} \quad (9)$$

holds just before Mclaw_k starts to construct i-claws. (Intuitively, under the condition that $\mathsf{good}^{(i)}$ occurs, the number of queries does not become too large.) We show the following claim.

Claim. For sufficiently large N,

$$\Pr\left[\text{good}^{(i)}\right] \geq 1 - \frac{2}{N} - \exp\left(-\frac{1}{15} \cdot \frac{N_{i-1}}{c_N}\right). \tag{10}$$

holds.

Proof. In this proof we consider the situation that Mclaw_k has finished to make L_{i-1} and before starting to make i-claws. In particular, we assume that $|L_{i-1}| = |L'_{i-1}| = \lceil 4c_N N_{i-1}\rceil$.

Let $\text{pregood}^{(i)}$ be the event that $|\text{Im}(f_i)| \geq \lceil N/3c_N\rceil$ holds. Since c_N is in $o(N^{\frac{1}{2^i-1}})$, we have that $\frac{|X_i|}{2} - \sqrt{|X_i|\ln|Y|/2} \geq \left\lceil\frac{N}{3c_N}\right\rceil$ holds for sufficiently large N. Hence

$$\Pr\left[\text{pregood}^{(i)}\right] \geq 1 - \frac{2}{|Y|} \tag{11}$$

follows from Lemma 2.

Let us identify X_i and Y with the sets $\{1,\ldots,|X_i|\}$ and $\{1,\ldots,|Y|\}$, respectively. Let B_j be the j-th element in $\text{Im}(f_i)$. Let χ_j be the indicator variable that is defined by $\chi_j = 1$ if and only if $B_j \in L'_{i-1}$, and define a random variable χ by $\chi := \sum_j \chi_j$. Then χ follows the hypergeometric distribution. We use the following theorem as a fact.

Theorem 4 (Theorem 1 in [HS05]). *Let $K = K(n_1, n, m)$ denote the hypergeometric random variable describing the process of counting how many defectives are selected when n_1 items are randomly selected without replacement from n items among which there are m defective ones. Let $\lambda \geq 2$. Then*

$$\Pr\left[K - \mathbf{E}[K] < -\lambda\right] < e^{-2\alpha_{n_1,n,m}(\lambda^2-1)} \tag{12}$$

holds, where

$$\alpha_{n_1,m,n} = \max\left(\left(\frac{1}{n_1+1} + \frac{1}{n-n_1+1}\right), \left(\frac{1}{m+1} + \frac{1}{n-m+1}\right)\right). \tag{13}$$

Apply the above theorem with $n_1 = \lceil N/3c_N\rceil$, $n = N$, and $m = |L'_{i-1}| = \lceil 4c_N N_{i-1}\rceil$, for the random variable χ under the condition that $|\text{Im}(f_i)| = \lceil N/3c_N\rceil$ holds. Let equal denote the event that $|\text{Im}(f_i)| = \lceil N/3c_N\rceil$ holds. Then $\mathbf{E}[\chi|\text{equal}] = \frac{n_1 m}{n} \geq \frac{4}{3}N_{i-1}$ holds, and we have that

$$\Pr\left[\chi - \mathbf{E}[\chi|\text{equal}] < -\frac{1}{4}\mathbf{E}[\chi|\text{equal}]\,\Big|\,\text{equal}\right]$$

$$\leq \exp\left(-2\left(\frac{1}{m+1} + \frac{1}{n-m+1}\right)\left((\mathbf{E}[\chi|\text{equal}]/4)^2 - 1\right)\right)$$

$$\leq \exp\left(-\frac{1}{15m}(\mathbf{E}[\chi|\text{equal}])^2\right) \leq \exp\left(-\frac{1}{15} \cdot \frac{N_{i-1}}{c_N}\right) \tag{14}$$

for sufficiently large N, where we use $c_N = o(N^{\frac{1}{2^l-1}})$ in evaluating $\alpha_{n_1,m,n}$. Hence

$$\Pr\left[\chi \geq N_{i-1}|\text{equal}\right] \geq 1 - \exp\left(-\frac{1}{15} \cdot \frac{N_{i-1}}{c_N}\right) \tag{15}$$

holds, which implies that

$$
\begin{aligned}
\Pr\left[|\text{Im}(f_i) \cap L'_{i-1}| \geq N_{i-1}\Big|\text{pregood}^{(i)}\right] &= \Pr\left[\chi \geq N_{i-1}\Big|\text{pregood}^{(i)}\right] \\
&\geq \Pr\left[\chi \geq N_{i-1}|\text{equal}\right] \\
&\geq 1 - \exp\left(-\frac{1}{15} \cdot \frac{N_{i-1}}{c_N}\right).
\end{aligned} \tag{16}
$$

Therefore we have that

$$
\begin{aligned}
\Pr\left[\text{good}^{(i)}\right] &> \Pr\left[\text{good}^{(i)}\Big|\text{pregood}^{(i)}\right] \cdot \Pr\left[\text{pregood}^{(i)}\right] \\
&= \Pr\left[|\text{Im}(f_i) \cap L'_{i-1}| \geq N_{i-1}\Big|\text{pregood}^{(i)}\right] \cdot \Pr\left[\text{pregood}^{(i)}\right] \\
&\geq \left(1 - \frac{2}{|Y|}\right)\left(1 - \exp\left(-\frac{1}{15} \cdot \frac{N_{i-1}}{c_N}\right)\right) \\
&\geq 1 - \frac{2}{|Y|} - \exp\left(-\frac{1}{15} \cdot \frac{N_{i-1}}{c_N}\right),
\end{aligned} \tag{17}
$$

which completes the proof. $\qquad\square$

Let good denote the event $\text{good}^{(1)} \wedge \cdots \wedge \text{good}^{(l)}$. Then we can show the following claim.

Claim. For sufficiently large N, it holds that

$$\mathbf{E}\left[Q \mid \text{good}\right] \leq \frac{1}{k}\text{Qlimit}_k, \tag{18}$$

where Q is the total number of queries made by Mclaw_k.

Proof. Let us fix i and j. Let $Q_j^{(i)}$ denote the number of queries made by Mclaw_k in the j-th search to construct i-claws, and $Q^{(i)}$ denote $\sum_j Q_j^{(i)}$. In the j-th search to construct i-claws, we search X_i for x with $f_i(x) \in L'_{i-1}$, where there exist at least $|L'_{i-1} \cap \text{Im}(f_i)| \geq N_{i-1} - j + 1$ answers in X_i under the condition that $\text{good}^{(i)}$ occurs. From Corollary 1, the expected value of the number of queries made by MTPS in the j-th search to construct i-claws is upper bounded by

$$9\sqrt{5|X_i|/|f_i^{-1}(L'_{i-1})|} \leq 9\sqrt{5|X_i|/|L'_{i-1} \cap \text{Im}(f_i)|} \leq 21\sqrt{N/N_{i-1}} \tag{19}$$

for each j under the condition that $\text{good}^{(i)}$ occurs, for sufficiently large N (we used the condition that $N_{i-1} = \omega(c_N N_i)$ holds for the last inequality).

Hence it follows that

$$\mathbf{E}\left[Q^{(i)} \mid \text{good}^{(i)}\right] = \mathbf{E}\left[\sum_j Q_j^{(i)} \mid \text{good}^{(i)}\right] = \sum_j \mathbf{E}\left[Q_j^{(i)} \mid \text{good}^{(i)}\right]$$

$$\leq \sum_{1 \leq j \leq \lceil 4 c_N N_i \rceil} 21\sqrt{N/N_{i-1}} \leq \begin{cases} 169 c_N^{3/2} N^{\frac{2^{l-1}-1}{2^l-1}} & (i=1) \\ 85 c_N N^{\frac{2^{l-1}-1}{2^l-1}} & (i \geq 2) \end{cases}$$

for sufficiently large N. Hence we have that $\mathbf{E}[Q \mid \text{good}] = \sum_i \mathbf{E}\left[Q^{(i)} \mid \text{good}^{(i)}\right]$ is upper bounded by

$$169 c_N^{3/2} N^{\frac{2^{l-1}-1}{2^l-1}} + \sum_{i=2}^{l} 85 c_N N^{\frac{2^{l-1}-1}{2^l-1}} \leq 169 l c_N^{3/2} \cdot N^{\frac{2^{l-1}-1}{2^l-1}} = \frac{1}{k}\mathsf{Qlimit}_k,$$

which completes the proof.   □

From the above claims, it follows that $\mathbf{E}[Q]$ is upper-bounded by

$$\mathbf{E}[Q \mid \text{good}] + \mathbf{E}[Q \mid \neg\text{good}]\Pr[\neg\text{good}] \leq \left(\frac{1}{k} + \Pr[\neg\text{good}]\right) \cdot \mathsf{Qlimit}_k, \quad (20)$$

and $\Pr[\neg\text{good}]$ is upper-bounded by $\sum_i \Pr\left[\neg\text{good}^{(i)}\right]$, which is further upper-bounded by

$$\sum_i \left(\frac{2}{N} + \exp\left(-\frac{1}{15} \cdot \frac{N_{i-1}}{c_N}\right)\right) \leq \frac{2l}{N} + l \cdot \exp\left(-\frac{1}{15} \cdot \frac{N^{\frac{1}{2^l-1}}}{c_N}\right). \quad (21)$$

From Markov's inequality, the probability that Q reaches Qlimit_k is at most

$$\Pr\left[Q \geq \mathsf{Qlimit}_k\right] \leq \frac{\mathbf{E}[Q]}{\mathsf{Qlimit}_k} \leq \frac{1}{k} + \Pr[\neg\text{good}]. \quad (22)$$

The event "Q does not reach Qlimit_k" implies that Mclaw_k finds an l-claw. Thus, from Eqs. 21 and 22, the probability that Mclaw_k finds an l-claw is lower-bounded by

$$1 - \frac{1}{k} - \frac{2l}{N} - l \cdot \exp\left(-\frac{1}{15} \cdot \frac{N^{\frac{1}{2^l-1}}}{c_N}\right), \quad (23)$$

which completes the proof.

□

5   Conclusion

This paper has developed a new quantum algorithm to find multicollisions of random functions. Our new algorithm finds an l-collision of a random function $F: [N] \to [N]$ with $O\left(N^{(2^{l-1}-1)/(2^l-1)}\right)$ quantum queries on average, which improves the previous upper bound $O(N^{(3^{l-1})/(2 \cdot 3^{l-1})})$ by Hosoyamada et al. [HSX17]. In fact, our algorithm can find an l-claw of random functions $f_i: [N] \to [N]$ for $1 \leq i \leq l$ with the same average complexity $O\left(N^{(2^{l-1}-1)/(2^l-1)}\right)$. In describing the algorithm, we assumed for ease of analysis and understanding that intermediate measurements were allowed. However, it is easy to move all measurements to the final step of the algorithm by the standard techniques. In this paper, we focused only on query complexity, and did not provide the analyses of other complexity measures. However, it is not difficult to show that the space complexity and the depth of quantum circuits are both bounded by $\tilde{O}\left(N^{(2^{l-1}-1)/(2^l-1)}\right)$. For applications to cryptanalyses, it is of interest to further study time-and-memory-efficient variants.

References

Amb04. Ambainis, A.: Quantum walk algorithm for element distinctness. In: Proceedings of the 45th Annual IEEE Symposium on Foundations of Computer Science, FOCS 2004, Rome, Italy, 17–19 October 2004, pp. 22–31 (2004)

BBHT98. Boyer, M., Brassard, G., Høyer, P., Tapp, A.: Tight bounds on quantum searching. Fortschr. Physik Prog. Phys. **46**(4–5), 493–505 (1998)

BDH+01. Buhrman, H., et al.: Quantum algorithms for element distinctness. In: Proceedings of the 16th Annual IEEE Conference on Computational Complexity, Chicago, Illinois, USA, 18–21 June 2001, pp. 131–137 (2001)

BDRV18. Berman, I., Degwekar, A., Rothblum, R.D., Vasudevan, P.N.: Multi-collision resistant hash functions and their applications. In: Nielsen, J.B., Rijmen, V. (eds.) EUROCRYPT 2018. LNCS, vol. 10821, pp. 133–161. Springer, Cham (2018). https://doi.org/10.1007/978-3-319-78375-8_5

Bel12. Belovs, A.: Learning-graph-based quantum algorithm for k-distinctness. In: 53rd Annual IEEE Symposium on Foundations of Computer Science, FOCS 2012, New Brunswick, NJ, USA, 20–23 October 2012, pp. 207–216 (2012)

BHT98. Brassard, G., Høyer, P., Tapp, A.: Quantum cryptanalysis of hash and claw-free functions. In: Lucchesi, C.L., Moura, A.V. (eds.) LATIN 1998. LNCS, vol. 1380, pp. 163–169. Springer, Heidelberg (1998). https://doi.org/10.1007/BFb0054319

BKP18. Bitansky, N., Kalai, Y.T., Paneth, O.: Multi-collision resistance: a paradigm for keyless hash functions. In: Proceedings of the 50th Annual ACM Symposium on Theory of Computing, STOC 2018, Los Angeles, CA, USA, 25–29 June 2018, pp. 671–684 (2018)

CNS17. Chailloux, A., Naya-Plasencia, M., Schrottenloher, A.: An efficient quantum collision search algorithm and implications on symmetric cryptography. In: Takagi, T., Peyrin, T. (eds.) ASIACRYPT 2017. LNCS, vol. 10625, pp. 211–240. Springer, Cham (2017). https://doi.org/10.1007/978-3-319-70697-9_8

Gro96. Grover, L.K.: A fast quantum mechanical algorithm for database search. In: Proceedings of the Twenty-Eighth Annual ACM Symposium on the Theory of Computing, Philadelphia, Pennsylvania, USA, 22–24 May 1996, pp. 212–219 (1996)

HS05. Hush, D., Scovel, C.: Concentration of the hypergeometric distribution. Stat. Prob. Lett. **75**(2), 127–132 (2005)

HSX17. Hosoyamada, A., Sasaki, Y., Xagawa, K.: Quantum multicollision-finding algorithm. In: Takagi, T., Peyrin, T. (eds.) ASIACRYPT 2017. LNCS, vol. 10625, pp. 179–210. Springer, Cham (2017). https://doi.org/10.1007/978-3-319-70697-9_7

JLM14. Jovanovic, P., Luykx, A., Mennink, B.: Beyond $2^{c/2}$ security in sponge-based authenticated encryption modes. In: Sarkar, P., Iwata, T. (eds.) ASIACRYPT 2014. LNCS, vol. 8873, pp. 85–104. Springer, Heidelberg (2014). https://doi.org/10.1007/978-3-662-45611-8_5

KNY18. Komargodski, I., Naor, M., Yogev, E.: Collision resistant hashing for paranoids: dealing with multiple collisions. In: Nielsen, J.B., Rijmen, V. (eds.) EUROCRYPT 2018. LNCS, vol. 10821, pp. 162–194. Springer, Cham (2018). https://doi.org/10.1007/978-3-319-78375-8_6

LZ18. Liu, Q., Zhandry, M.: On finding quantum multi-collisions. In: Proceedings of EUROCRYPT 2019 (2018)

MU17. Mitzenmacher, M., Upfal, E.: Probability and Computing: Randomization and Probabilistic Techniques in Algorithms and Data Analysis. Cambridge University Press, Cambridge (2017)

RS96. Rivest, R.L., Shamir, A.: PayWord and MicroMint: two simple micropayment schemes. In: Proceedings of the International Workshop on Security Protocols, Cambridge, United Kingdom, 10–12 April 1996, pp. 69–87 (1996)

Tan09. Tani, S.: Claw finding algorithms using quantum walk. Theor. Comput. Sci. **410**(50), 5285–5297 (2009)

Zha15. Zhandry, M.: A note on the quantum collision and set equality problems. Quantum Inf. Comput. **15**(7&8), 557–567 (2015)

Code-Based Cryptography

Preventing Timing Attacks Against RQC Using Constant Time Decoding of Gabidulin Codes

Slim Bettaieb[1], Loïc Bidoux[1], Philippe Gaborit[2]([✉]), and Etienne Marcatel[3]

[1] Worldline, ZI Rue de la pointe, 59113 Seclin, France
[2] University of Limoges, XLIM-DMI, 123, Av. Albert Thomas,
87060 Limoges, France
philippe.gaborit@unilim.fr
[3] Atos, 68 avenue Jean Jaurès, 78340 Les Clayes-sous-Bois, France

Abstract. This paper studies the resistance of the code-based encryption scheme RQC to timing attacks. We describe two chosen ciphertext timing attacks that rely on a correlation between the weight of the error to be decoded and the running time of Gabidulin code's decoding algorithm. These attacks are of theoretical interest as they outperform the best known algorithm to solve the rank syndrome decoding problem in term of complexity. Nevertheless, they are quite impracticable in real situations as they require a huge number of requests to a timing oracle. We also provide a constant-time algorithm for the decoding of Gabidulin codes that prevent these attacks without any performance cost for honest users.

Keywords: RQC · Gabidulin decoding · Timing attack · Rank metric

1 Introduction

RQC [2,3] is a code-based IND-CCA2 public key encryption scheme submitted to the NIST's post-quantum cryptography standardization project. It features attractive parameters and its security only relies on the rank syndrome decoding problem without any additional assumption regarding the indistinguishability of the considered family of codes. RQC relies on Gabidulin codes which were introduced in 1985 in [6]. The latter are the analogs of the Reed-Solomon codes for the rank metric and can be thought as the evaluation of q-polynomials of bounded degree on the coordinates of a vector over $\mathbb{F}_{q^m}$. Gabidulin decoding can be performed efficiently using the Welch-Berlekamp like algorithm proposed by Loidreau [9]. Hereafter, we study the resistant of RQC to timing attacks.

Contributions. In this paper, we present two timing attacks against RQC. In addition, we also describe a constant time decoding algorithm for Gabidulin codes that prevent these attacks without any performance cost for honest users.

© Springer Nature Switzerland AG 2019
J. Ding and R. Steinwandt (Eds.): PQCrypto 2019, LNCS 11505, pp. 371–386, 2019.
https://doi.org/10.1007/978-3-030-25510-7_20

Paper organisation. In Sect. 2, we introduce the rank metric, Loidreau's algorithm for the decoding of Gabidulin codes as well as the RQC cryptosystem. Next, in Sect. 3, we highlight the correlation between the rank of the error to be decoded and the decoding time of Loidreau's algorithm. This correlation is the keystone of the timing attacks described in Sect. 4. To finish, countermeasures to these attacks are presented in Sect. 5.

2   Preliminaries

In this section, we present some preliminaries regarding the rank metric (Sect. 2.1), Gabidulin codes (Sect. 2.2) and the RQC cryptosystem (Sect. 2.3).

2.1   Rank Metric

Let q be a power of a prime p, m an integer, $\mathbb{F}_{q^m}$ a finite field and $\beta = (\beta_1, \cdots, \beta_m)$ a basis of $\mathbb{F}_{q^m}$ over $\mathbb{F}_q$. Any vector $\mathbf{x} \in \mathbb{F}_{q^m}^n$ can be associated to the matrix $\mathbf{M_x} \in \mathcal{M}_{m,n}(\mathbb{F}_q)$ by expressing its coordinates in β.

Definition 1 (Rank weight). *Let $\mathbf{x} = (x_1, \cdots, x_n) \in \mathbb{F}_{q^m}^n$ be a vector, the rank weight of $\mathbf{x}$, denoted $\omega(\mathbf{x})$, is defined as the rank of the matrix $\mathbf{M_x} = (x_{i,j})$ where $x_j = \sum_{i=1}^m x_{i,j}\beta_i$. The set of words of weight w in $\mathbb{F}_{q^m}^n$ is denoted $\mathcal{S}_w^n$.*

Definition 2 (Support). *The support of $\mathbf{x} \in \mathbb{F}_{q^m}^n$, denoted $\mathrm{Supp}(\mathbf{x})$, is the $\mathbb{F}_q$-linear space of $\mathbb{F}_{q^m}$ spanned by the coordinates of $\mathbf{x}$. Formally, $\mathrm{Supp}(\mathbf{x}) = \langle x_1, \ldots, x_n \rangle_{\mathbb{F}_q}$.*

Definition 3 ($\mathbb{F}_{q^m}$-linear code). *An $\mathbb{F}_{q^m}$-linear $[n, k]$ code $\mathcal{C}$ of length n and dimension k is a linear subspace of $\mathbb{F}_{q^m}^n$ of dimension k.*

Definition 4 (Generator Matrix). *A matrix $\mathbf{G} \in \mathbb{F}_{q^m}^{k \times n}$ is a generator matrix for the $[n, k]$ code $\mathcal{C}$ if $\mathcal{C} = \{\mathbf{xG} \mid \mathbf{x} \in \mathbb{F}_{q^m}^k\}$.*

Definition 5 (Parity-Check Matrix). *A matrix $\mathbf{H} \in \mathbb{F}_{q^m}^{(n-k) \times n}$ is a parity-check matrix for the $[n, k]$ code $\mathcal{C}$ if $\mathcal{C} = \{\mathbf{x} \in \mathbb{F}_{q^m}^n \mid \mathbf{Hx}^\top = \mathbf{0}\}$. The vector $\mathbf{Hx}^\top \in \mathbb{F}_{q^m}^{n-k}$ is called the syndrome of $\mathbf{x}$.*

2.2   Gabidulin Codes

Gabidulin codes were introduced in 1985 in [6]. They can be seen as the evaluation of q-polynomials of bounded degree on the coordinates of a vector over $\mathbb{F}_{q^m}$. The notion of q-polynomial was introduced by Ore in [10].

Definition 6 (q-polynomials). *A q-polynomial over $\mathbb{F}_{q^m}$ is a polynomial defined as $P(X) = \sum_{i=0}^r p_i X^{q^i}$ with $p_i \in \mathbb{F}_{q^m}$ and $p_r \neq 0$. The q-degree of a q-polynomial P is denoted $\deg_q(P)$.*

Definition 7 (Gabidulin codes). *Let* $k, n, m \in \mathbb{N}$ *such that* $k \leqslant n \leqslant m$. *Let* $\mathbf{g} = (g_1, \ldots, g_n)$ *be a* $\mathbb{F}_q$-*linearly family of vectors of* $\mathbb{F}_{q^m}$. *The Gabidulin code* $\mathcal{G}_\mathbf{g}(n, k, m)$ *is the* $[n, k]_{q^m}$ *code defined as* $\{P(\mathbf{g}) \mid \deg_q(P) < k\}$ *where* $P(\mathbf{g})$ *denotes the evaluation of the coordinates of* $\mathbf{g}$ *by the* q-*polynomial* P.

Gabidulin codes can efficiently decode up to $\lfloor \frac{n-k}{2} \rfloor$ errors [6]. In such cases, the algorithm considered hereafter in this paper features no decoding failure. It has been proposed by Loidreau in [9] and later improved in [5]. It is based on the resolution of the Linear Reconstruction Problem (see [5,9] for further details).

Definition 8 (Decoding$(\mathbf{y}, \mathcal{G}_\mathbf{g}, t)$). *Find, if it exists,* $\mathbf{c} \in \mathcal{G}_\mathbf{g}$ *and* $\mathbf{e}$ *with* $\omega(\mathbf{e}) \leq t$ *such that* $\mathbf{y} = \mathbf{c} + \mathbf{e}$.

Definition 9 (Reconstruction$(\mathbf{y}, \mathbf{g}, k, t)$). *Find a tuple* (V, N) *where* V *is a non-zero* q-*polynomial with* $\deg_q(V) \leq t$ *and* N *is a* q-*polynomial with* $\deg_q(N) \leq k + t - 1$ *such that* $V(y_i) = N(g_i)$ *with* $1 \leq i \leq n$.

Theorem 1 ([9]). *If* (V, N) *is a solution of* **Reconstruction**$(\mathbf{y}, \mathbf{g}, k, t)$ *and* $t \leq \lfloor \frac{(n-k)}{2} \rfloor$, *then* $(\mathbf{c}, \mathbf{e}) = (f(\mathbf{g}), \mathbf{y} - \mathbf{c})$ *with* f *defined as the left euclidean division of* N *by* V *in the ring of* q-*polynomials is a solution of* **Decoding**$(\mathbf{y}, \mathbf{g}, k, t)$.

As stated in [2], one can solve **Reconstruction**$(\mathbf{y}, \mathbf{g}, k, t)$ by constructing by recurrence two pairs of q-polynomials (N_0, V_0) and (N_1, V_1) satisfying the interpolation conditions of the problem $V(y_i) = N(g_i), 1 \leq i \leq n$ at each step i and such that at least one of the pairs satisfies the final degree conditions $\deg_q(V) \leq t$ and $\deg_q(N) \leq k+t-1$. See Algorithm 5 (from [5], Sect. 4, Algorithm 5) hereafter for additionnal details.

Theorem 2 ([5]). *The complexity of solving the* **Decoding**$(\mathbf{y}, \mathcal{G}_\mathbf{g}, t)$ *problem using Algorithm 5 is* $\mathcal{O}(n^2)$ *operations in* $\mathbb{F}_{q^m}$.

2.3 The RQC Public Key Encryption Scheme

RQC [2,3] is a code-based IND-CCA2 encryption scheme whose security relies on the rank syndrom decoding problem [4,7] without any additionnal assumption regarding the indistinguishability of the family of codes used. It is based on an IND-CPA PKE construction (described in Fig. 1) on top of which the HHK transformation [8] is applied in order to obtain an IND-CCA2 KEM. Standard transformations are then applied in order to get an IND-CCA2 encryption scheme. RQC uses a Gabidulin code of generator matrix $\mathbf{G}$ denoted $\mathcal{C}$ and a random double-circulant $[2n, n]$ code of parity-check matrix $(\mathbf{1}, \mathbf{h})$.

RQC correctness relies on the decoding capability of the Gabidulin code $\mathcal{C}$. Indeed, Decrypt (sk, Encrypt (pk, $\mathbf{m}$)) = $\mathbf{m}$ when $\mathbf{v} - \mathbf{u} \cdot \mathbf{y}$ is correctly decoded namely whenever $\omega(\mathbf{x} \cdot \mathbf{r}_2 - \mathbf{y} \cdot \mathbf{r}_1 + \mathbf{e}) \leq \lfloor \frac{(n-k)}{2} \rfloor$.

- Setup(1^λ): Generates and outputs the global parameters **param** = $(n, k, \delta, w, w_r, w_e)$.
- KeyGen(param): Samples $\mathbf{h} \xleftarrow{\$} \mathbb{F}_{q^m}^n$, $\mathbf{G} \in \mathbb{F}_{q^m}^{k \times n}$ a generator matrix of $\mathcal{C}$, $\mathbf{x} \xleftarrow{\$} \mathcal{S}_w^n$, $\mathbf{y} \xleftarrow{\$} \mathcal{S}_w^n$ such that Supp($\mathbf{x}$) = Supp($\mathbf{y}$). Sets sk = ($\mathbf{x}, \mathbf{y}$), pk = ($\mathbf{G}, \mathbf{h}, \mathbf{s} = \mathbf{x} + \mathbf{h} \cdot \mathbf{y}$) and returns (pk, sk).
- Encrypt(pk, m): Generates $\mathbf{r}_1 \xleftarrow{\$} \mathcal{S}_{w_r}^n$, $\mathbf{r}_2 \xleftarrow{\$} \mathcal{S}_{w_r}^n$, $\mathbf{e} \xleftarrow{\$} \mathcal{S}_{w_r}^n$ such that Supp($\mathbf{r}_1$) = Supp($\mathbf{r}_2$) = Supp($\mathbf{r}_3$). Sets $\mathbf{u} = \mathbf{r}_1 + \mathbf{h} \cdot \mathbf{r}_2$ and $\mathbf{v} = \mathbf{mG} + \mathbf{s} \cdot \mathbf{r}_2 + \mathbf{e}$ and returns $\mathbf{c} = (\mathbf{u}, \mathbf{v})$.
- Decrypt(sk, c): Returns $\mathcal{C}$.Decode($\mathbf{v} - \mathbf{u} \cdot \mathbf{y}$).

Fig. 1. Description of the IND-CPA version of RQC [2].

3 Correlation Between Decoding Time and Error Rank

In this section, we show that there exists a correlation between the rank of the error to be decoded and the running time of Algorithm 5. This observation is summarized in Theorem 3. We start by introducing a simpler version of Loidreau's algorithm (Sect. 3.1) and then we prove the aforementioned theorem (Sect. 3.2). Next, we describe an oracle that computes the rank of the error to be decoded using the running time of the decoding algorithm (Sect. 3.3).

3.1 A Simpler Decoding Algorithm

In order to solve the **Reconstruction**($\mathbf{y}, \mathbf{g}, k, t$) problem, Loidreau's algorithm performs a q-polynomial interpolation. We denote by *nominal case, dummy interpolation case* and *early end case* the three scenarios that may occur during the interpolation step (see Algorithm 5). The *early end case* is quite subtle as it performs two operations simultaneously. First, it checks the discrepancy vector to detect if the current q-polynomials are an admissible solution which can happen whenever the rank of the error to be decoded is inferior to the decoding capacity of the code. In addition, if a nominal interpolation can't be performed using the ith coordinate of the discrepancy vector (see *nominal case* below) but can be performed using one of its jth coordinate where $j > i$, then the ith and j^{th} coordinates of the discrepancy vector are swapped. The *nominal case* corresponds to the expected interpolation which requires to inverse $u_{1,i}$ to be performed. If both $u_{1,i} = 0$ and $u_{0,i} = 0$, a *dummy interpolation case* will be performed.

As both the *dummy interpolation case* and the *early end case* handle situations where $u_{1,i} = 0$, the considered algorithm can be simplified by merging them together. Indeed, one can see that the dummy interpolation is using $\lambda_0 = \lambda_1 = 0$ which mean that no interpolation is actually performed at this step even if the q-degrees of the q-polynomials are increased. As a consequence, by modifying the *early end case* condition to $u_{1,j} = 0$ only (see Algorithm 6), one can handle these two cases simultaneously. In fact, the *dummy interpolation cases* will be delayed to the end of the algorithm during the swap step but will never be performed as an admissible solution will be found as some point before we had to handle these cases. This is due to the fact that the dummy interpolation only increase the q-degrees of the q-polynomials without making any progress with respect to error correction. Therefore, our simpler algorithm always returns the q-polynomials of *minimal q-degrees* solving the reconstruction problem while the original algorithm may return any admissible solution.

The constant time decoding algorithm proposed in Sect. 5 is based on our simpler algorithm. Hereafter, the term decoding algorithm refers to Algorithm 6.

3.2 From Decoding Time to Error Weight

The decoding algorithm performs successive interpolations until the solution is found. As the *early end case* may end the main loop prematurely, the running time of the algorithm may vary. Theorem 3 formalizes this observation as it shows that there exists a correlation between the rank of the error to be decoded and the decoding time of the Gabidulin code whenever the rank of the considered error is smaller than the error correcting capacity $\lfloor \frac{n-k}{2} \rfloor$.

Theorem 3. *Let $\mathbf{G}$ be the generator matrix of a Gabidulin code $\mathcal{G}_\mathbf{g}(n, k, m)$, $\mathbf{m} \in \mathbb{F}_{q^m}^k$, $\mathbf{e} \in \mathbb{F}_{q^m}^n$ such that $\omega(\mathbf{e}) = t$ with $t \leq \lfloor \frac{n-k}{2} \rfloor$ and $\mathbf{y} = \mathbf{mG} + \mathbf{e}$. Then, Algorithm 6 will perform exactly $2t$ interpolation steps when solving* $\mathbf{Decoding}(\mathbf{y}, \mathcal{G}_\mathbf{g}, t)$.

Proof. The proof of Theorem 3 follows from Lemmas 1 and 2.

Lemma 1. *Under the same hypotheses as Theorem 3, Algorithm 6 will perform at least $2t$ interpolation steps when solving* $\mathbf{Decoding}(\mathbf{y}, \mathcal{G}_\mathbf{g}, t)$.

Proof. In order to retrieve an error $\mathbf{e}$, one needs to find a q-polynomial V_1 such that $V_1(\mathbf{e}) = 0$. If $\omega(\mathbf{e}) = t$, then one have $\deg_q(V_1) \geq t$. As $\deg_q(V_1) \geq u$ if $2u$ interpolations steps have been performed (from propostion 12 of [5]), it follows that Algorithm 6 will perform at least $2t$ interpolation steps.

Lemma 2. *Under the same hypotheses as Theorem 3, Algorithm 6 will perform at most $2t$ interpolation steps when solving* $\mathbf{Decoding}(\mathbf{y}, \mathcal{G}_\mathbf{g}, t)$.

Proof. Let $n' = k + 2t$ and $\mathbf{e}' = (e_1, \ldots, e_{n'})$ be a shortened error such that $\mathsf{Supp}(\mathbf{e}') = \mathsf{Supp}(\mathbf{e})$. It is always possible to construct $\mathbf{e}'$ from $\mathbf{e}$ using a coordinates permutation followed by a truncation. Let $\mathcal{G}_{\mathbf{g}'}(n', k, m)$ be the shortened Gabidulin code generated by the matrix $\mathbf{G}'$ using the vector $\mathbf{g}' = (g_1, \ldots, g_{n'})$. As the error decoding capacity of $\mathcal{G}_{\mathbf{g}'}(n', k, m)$ is equal to $t = \lfloor \frac{n'-k}{2} \rfloor$, the vector $\mathbf{y}' = (y_1, \ldots, y_{n'}) = \mathbf{mG}' + \mathbf{e}'$ can be decoded using Algorithm 6 in at most $2t$ interpolation steps. Let (N_1', V_1') be the solution retuned by Algorithm 6, then every vector in $\mathsf{Supp}(\mathbf{e}')$ is a root of V_1' as well as every vector in $\mathsf{Supp}(\mathbf{e})$ because $\mathsf{Supp}(\mathbf{e}') = \mathsf{Supp}(\mathbf{e})$. It follows that (N_1', V_1') is a solution of the decoding problem induced by $\mathcal{G}_\mathbf{g}(n, k, m)$ and $\mathbf{y}$. As Algorithm 6 outputs the q-polynomials of minimal q-degrees solving the reconstruction problem, decoding $\mathcal{G}_\mathbf{g}(n, k, m)$ is equivalent to decoding $\mathcal{G}_{\mathbf{g}'}(n', k, m)$ therefore Algorithm 6 will perform at most $2t$ interpolation steps when solving $\mathbf{Decoding}(\mathbf{y}, \mathcal{G}_\mathbf{g}, t)$.

Corollary 1. *Let* $\mathbf{G}$ *be the generator matrix of a Gabidulin code* $\mathcal{G}_{\mathbf{g}}(n,k,m)$, $\mathbf{m} \in \mathbb{F}_{q^m}^k$, $\mathbf{e} \in \mathbb{F}_{q^m}^n$ *such that* $\omega(\mathbf{e}) = t$ *with* $t \leq \lfloor \frac{n-k}{2} \rfloor$ *and* $\mathbf{y} = \mathbf{m}\mathbf{G} + \mathbf{e}$, *then it is possible to find* $\omega(\mathbf{e})$ *from the running time of Algorithm 6.*

3.3   Error Weight Oracle for Gabidulin Codes and RQC

Let $O_{\text{Time}}^{\text{Gab}}$ and $O_{\text{Time}}^{\text{RQC}}$ denote two timing oracles that return the running time of either the Gabidulin decoding algorithm or the RQC Decapsulate step. Following Corollary 1, we now explain how to construct two oracles denoted $O_{\omega(\mathbf{e})}^{\text{Gab}}$ and $O_{\omega(\mathbf{e})}^{\text{RQC}}$ that return the rank $\omega(\mathbf{e})$ of the decoded error using respectively $O_{\text{Time}}^{\text{Gab}}$ and $O_{\text{Time}}^{\text{RQC}}$. The oracle $O_{\omega(\mathbf{e})}^{\text{Gab}}$ takes as input a Gabidulin code $\mathcal{G}$ and a vector $\mathbf{y}$ while the oracle $O_{\omega(\mathbf{e})}^{\text{RQC}}$ takes as input an RQC public key pk (which implicitly defines a Gabidulin code) and a ciphertext ct.

Each oracle features an initialization step Init (see Algorithm 1) and an evaluation step Eval (see Algorithm 2). The Init step computes the expected running times required to decode an error $\mathbf{e}$ of given weight w for all $w \in [0,t]$. To this end, requests $O_{\text{Time}}^{\text{Gab}}$ $(\mathcal{G}, \mathbf{e})$ (respectively $O_{\text{Time}}^{\text{RQC}}$ $(\text{pk}, (0, \mathbf{e}))$ are made using the message $\mathbf{m} = 0$ (respectively $\mathbf{m} = \mathbf{r}_1 = \mathbf{r}_2 = 0$) along with errors $\mathbf{e}$ of weight $i \in [0,t]$. The Eval step uses these expected running times $\mathbf{T}$ to output the rank of the error $\omega(\mathbf{e})$ by returning the index i such that $|\text{time} - \mathbf{T}_i|$ is minimal where time denotes the result given by $O_{\text{Time}}^{\text{Gab}}$ $(\mathcal{G}, \mathbf{y})$ or $O_{\text{Time}}^{\text{RQC}}$ (pk, ct). The complexity of a $O_{\omega(\mathbf{e})}^{\text{Gab}}$ (respectively $O_{\omega(\mathbf{e})}^{\text{RQC}}$) request is equal to the complexity of a Gabidulin decoding (respectively an RQC decapsulation) namely $O(n^2)$ operations in $\mathbb{F}_{q^m}$.

Algorithm 1. Init step of $O_{\omega(\mathbf{e})}^{\text{Gab}}$ and $O_{\omega(\mathbf{e})}^{\text{RQC}}$

Input: $\begin{cases} \text{A Gabidulin code } \mathcal{G}(n,k,m) \text{ and access to } O_{\text{Time}}^{\text{Gab}} \text{ for } O_{\omega(\mathbf{e})}^{\text{Gab}} \\ \text{A public key pk and access to } O_{\text{Time}}^{\text{RQC}} \text{ for } O_{\omega(\mathbf{e})}^{\text{RQC}} \end{cases}$
A precision parameter param

Output: An array $\mathbf{T}$ of expected running times

1: $\mathbf{T} \longleftarrow (0, \cdots, 0) \in \mathbb{R}^{t+1}$
2: **for** $i \in \{0, \cdots, t\}$ **do**
3:     **for** $j \in \{1, \cdots, \text{param}\}$ **do**
4:         $\mathbf{e} \xleftarrow{\$} S_i^n$
5:         time $\longleftarrow \begin{cases} O_{\text{Time}}^{\text{Gab}} (\mathcal{G}, \mathbf{e}) \text{ for } O_{\omega(\mathbf{e})}^{\text{Gab}} \\ O_{\text{Time}}^{\text{RQC}} (\text{pk}, (0, \mathbf{e}) \text{ for } O_{\omega(\mathbf{e})}^{\text{RQC}} \end{cases}$
6:         $\mathbf{T}_{i+1} \longleftarrow \mathbf{T}_{i+1} + \text{time}$
7:     $\mathbf{T}_{i+1} \longleftarrow \mathbf{T}_{i+1} / \text{param}$
8: **return** $\mathbf{T}$

In order for these oracles to be useful, each difference $\mathbf{T}_{i+1} - \mathbf{T}_i$ have to be large enough to be accurately measured. Experimental results (see Sect. 5,

---

Algorithm 2. Eval step of $O^{\mathrm{Gab}}_{\omega(\mathbf{e})}$ and $O^{\mathrm{RQC}}_{\omega(\mathbf{e})}$

Input: $\begin{cases} \text{A Gabidulin code } \mathcal{G}(n,k,m) \text{ and a vector } \mathbf{y} \text{ for } O^{\mathrm{Gab}}_{\omega(\mathbf{e})} \\ \text{A public key pk and a ciphertext ct for } O^{\mathrm{RQC}}_{\omega(\mathbf{e})} \end{cases}$
An array $\mathbf{T}$ of expected running times from the Init step

Output: The rank $\omega(\mathbf{e})$ of the decoded error

1: $\text{time} \longleftarrow \begin{cases} O^{\mathrm{Gab}}_{\mathrm{Time}}(\mathcal{G},\mathbf{y}) \text{ for } O^{\mathrm{Gab}}_{\omega(\mathbf{e})} \\ O^{\mathrm{RQC}}_{\mathrm{Time}}(\mathrm{pk},\mathrm{ct}) \text{ for } O^{\mathrm{RQC}}_{\omega(\mathbf{e})} \end{cases}$

2: **return** i such that $|\text{time} - \mathbf{T}_i|$ is minimum

---

Fig. 2) shows that for the considered machine, $\mathbf{T}_{i+1} - \mathbf{T}_i$ amounts for 6.6×10^4 CPU cycles (approximately 0.02 ms) for $O^{\mathrm{RQC}}_{\omega(\mathbf{e})}$ in average. Such values allow timing attacks to be performed locally but would hardly be sufficient to allow an adverdary to perform a remote attack due to the variability of the network transfer times. Nevertheless, we assume hereafter that the existence of such an oracle is a potential threat for RQC and thus we choose to address it properly.

4 Timing Attacks Against RQC

In this section, we present two side-channel chosen ciphertext attacks against RQC. These attacks outperform the best known algorithm to solve the rank syndrome decoding problem [4] in term of complexity. Nonetheless, they require a huge number of requests to $O^{\mathrm{RQC}}_{\omega(\mathbf{e})}$ therefore are quite unpracticable in real situations. We start by giving an overview of the attacks (Sect. 4.1) then we describe two support recovery algorithms (Sects. 4.2 and 4.3) that relies on $O^{\mathrm{RQC}}_{\omega(\mathbf{e})}$ in order to bring the aforementioned improvement. Next, we present the complexity and the bandwidth cost of these attacks with respect to RQC parameters (Sect. 4.4).

4.1 Overview of the Attacks

The two attacks presented hereafter follow the same pattern. First, a support recovery algorithm is used to find $\mathbf{F} = \mathsf{Supp}(\mathbf{x}) = \mathsf{Supp}(\mathbf{y})$ then a linear system is solved in order to retrieve $\mathbf{x}$ and $\mathbf{y}$ thus revealing the secret key.

The support recovery algorithm makes several requests to $O^{\mathrm{RQC}}_{\omega(\mathbf{e})}$ in order to find the support of $\mathbf{y}$. All these requests are constructed such that $\mathbf{m} = 0$, $\mathbf{r}_1 = 1$ and $\mathbf{r}_2 = 0$ namely the considered ciphertexts are of the form $(1, \mathbf{e})$. Recall from Sect. 2.3 that decrypting a RQC ciphertext implies to decode $\mathbf{m}\mathbf{G} + \mathbf{x}\cdot\mathbf{r}_2 - \mathbf{y}\cdot\mathbf{r}_1 + \mathbf{e}$. In this case, this will reduce to decoding $\mathbf{e} - \mathbf{y}$. The support recovery algorithm uses this particular form in order to retrieve $\mathbf{F} = \mathsf{Supp}(\mathbf{y})$.

Once the support $\mathbf{F}$ is known, one only need to solve the linear system $(1 \; \mathbf{h}) \cdot (\mathbf{x} \; \mathbf{y})^\top = \mathbf{s}$ to find $\mathbf{x}$ and $\mathbf{y}$ as explained in [4]. This system can be obtained from the public key and features nm equations over $\mathbb{F}_q$ as well as $2wn$ unknowns over $\mathbb{F}_q$ because $\dim(\mathbf{F}) = w$. Given the RQC parameters, this system is always solvable and the secret key $\mathsf{sk} = (\mathbf{x}, \mathbf{y})$ is its unique solution.

4.2 Simple Support Recovery Algorithm

The simple support recovery strategy (see Algorithm 3) tests all the elements $\alpha \in \mathbb{F}_{q^m}$ and checks whether they belong to the support $\mathbf{F}$ in order to retrieve one of its basis $(F_1, \cdots, F_w)$. To this end, a function $\psi : \mathbb{F}_{q^m} \longrightarrow \mathbb{F}_{q^m}$ that deterministically enumerates the elements of $\mathbb{F}_{q^m}$ is defined. In addition, errors of the form $\mathbf{e} = (\alpha, 0, \cdots, 0) \in \mathbb{F}_{q^m}^n$ are considered. One can see that if $\mathsf{Supp}(\mathbf{e}) \subset \mathsf{Supp}(\mathbf{y})$, then $\omega(\mathbf{e} - \mathbf{y}) = w$ otherwise $\omega(\mathbf{e} - \mathbf{y}) = w + 1$. Using $O^{\mathrm{RQC}}_{\omega(\mathbf{e})}$, one can retrieve the rank of $\mathbf{e} - \mathbf{y}$ thus learning if $\alpha \in \mathbf{F}$ or not.

Algorithm 3. Simple support recovery

Input: A public key pk and access to $O^{\mathrm{RQC}}_{\omega(\mathbf{e})}$
  The oracle precision parameter param

Output: $\mathbf{F} = \mathsf{Supp}(\mathbf{x}) = \mathsf{Supp}(\mathbf{y})$

1: $\mathbf{T} \longleftarrow O^{\mathrm{RQC}}_{\omega(\mathbf{e})}.\mathsf{Init}(\mathsf{pk}, \mathsf{param})$
2: $\mathbf{F} \longleftarrow \langle 0 \rangle_{\mathbb{F}_q}$
3: $\alpha \longleftarrow 0 \in \mathbb{F}_{q^m}$
4: **while** $\dim(\mathbf{F}) < w$ **do**
5:     $\alpha \longleftarrow \psi(\alpha)$
6:     $\mathbf{e} \longleftarrow (\alpha, 0, \cdots, 0) \in \mathbb{F}_{q^m}^n$
7:     $\omega \longleftarrow O^{\mathrm{RQC}}_{\omega(\mathbf{e})}.\mathsf{Eval}(\mathbf{T}, \mathsf{pk}, (1, \mathbf{e}))$
8:     **if** $\omega = w$ **then**
9:         $\mathbf{F} \longleftarrow \mathbf{F} + \langle \alpha \rangle_{\mathbb{F}_q}$
10: **return** $\mathbf{F}$

Algorithm 3 requires $O(q^m)$ requests to the $O^{\mathrm{RQC}}_{\omega(\mathbf{e})}$ oracle therefore its complexity is $O(n^2 q^m)$ operations in $\mathbb{F}_{q^m}$.

4.3 Advanced Support Recovery Algorithm

The advanced support recovery strategy (see Algorithm 4) is a generalization of the simple one in which we no longer consider errors of weigth $\omega(\mathbf{e}) = 1$ but rather errors of weight $\omega(\mathbf{e}) = t - w$. Instead of only checking if $\alpha \in \mathsf{Supp}(\mathbf{y})$, we look for any linear combination of the error's coordinates belonging to $\mathsf{Supp}(\mathbf{y})$ therefore speeding-up the algorithm. Without loss of generality, we only consider the case $q = 2$ since it matches the parameters used in RQC.

Given $\mathbf{a} \in \mathbb{F}_{q^m}^n$, let $(\overline{a}_1, \cdots, \overline{a}_{\omega(\mathbf{a})}) \in \mathbb{F}_{q^m}^{\omega(\mathbf{a})}$ denotes a basis of $\mathsf{Supp}(\mathbf{a})$. As $\omega(\mathbf{e}) = t - w$ and $\omega(\mathbf{y}) = w$, if $\omega(\mathbf{e} - \mathbf{y}) < t$ then there exists at least one non trivial linear combination of the vectors $(\overline{e}_i)_{i \in [1,t-w]}$ such that:

$$\sum_{i=1}^{t-w} \lambda_i \overline{e}_i = \sum_{j=1}^{w} \mu_j \overline{y}_j \in Supp(\mathbf{y})$$

The remaining of the algorithm compute the λ_i of such expressions thus retrieving a vector in the support $\mathbf{F}$. Each oracle request may lead to the discovery of $\Delta = \omega(\mathbf{e}) + \omega(\mathbf{y}) - \omega(\mathbf{e} - \mathbf{y}) = \dim(\ker(\overline{y}_1 \cdots \overline{y}_w \, \overline{e}_1 \cdots \overline{e}_{t-w}))$ elements of $\mathbf{F}$ although Δ will be equal to 1 with overwhelming probability.

Let $\mathbf{M}_i \in \mathcal{M}_{m,w+i}(\mathbb{F}_q)$ be the matrices defined as $\mathbf{M}_i = (\overline{y}_1 \cdots \overline{y}_w \, \overline{e}_1 \cdots \overline{e}_i)$ for $i \in [1, t-w]$ and $d = \min \{i \mid \mathrm{rank}(\mathbf{M}_i) < w + i\}$. By construction, $\lambda_d = 1$. For $i \in [1,d]$, let $\mathbf{M}_{d,i} \in \mathcal{M}_{m,w+d}(\mathbb{F}_q)$ be the matrices defined as $\mathbf{M}_{d,i} = (\overline{y}_1 \cdots \overline{y}_w \, \overline{e}_1 \cdots \overline{e}_{i-1} \, 0 \, \overline{e}_{i+1} \cdots \overline{e}_d)$. If $\mathrm{rank}(\mathbf{M}_d) = \mathrm{rank}(\mathbf{M}_{d,i})$, then $\lambda_i = 1$. By performing this test for all $i \in [1,d]$, one can retrieve $\sum_{i=1}^{d} \lambda_i \overline{e}_i \in Supp(\mathbf{y})$.

Hereafter, we assume for simplicity that $\mathrm{rank}(\mathbf{e}) = t - w$ as it happens with high probability and can be enforced at no cost by tweaking the algorithm. The complexity of algorithm 4 is $O\left(wn^2/p\right)$ where p denotes the probability to find a non trivial intersection between $\mathsf{Supp}(\mathbf{e})$ and $\mathsf{Supp}(\mathbf{y})$ namely $p = P\left(\omega(\mathbf{e} - \mathbf{y}) < t \mid \omega(\mathbf{y}) = w \wedge \omega(\mathbf{e}) = t - w\right)$. The quantity $1 - p$ represents the probability to pick the coordinates of $\mathbf{e}$ linearly independant from the coordinates of $\mathbf{y}$ knowing that $\omega(\mathbf{e}) = t - w$ and $\omega(\mathbf{y}) = w$. For each coordinate e_i, one have $q^m - q^{w+i}$ ways to pick it correctly amongst $q^m - q^i$ potential choices therefore:

$$1 - p = \prod_{i=0}^{t-w-1} \frac{q^m - q^{w+i}}{q^m - q^i} = \prod_{i=0}^{w-1} \frac{1}{q^m - q^i} \times \prod_{i=t-w}^{t-1} \frac{q^m - q^i}{1}$$

When considering the RQC parameters, one can approximate the complexity of Algorithm 4 as $O\left(wn^2 q^{m-t}\right)$ operations in $\mathbb{F}_{q^m}$.

4.4   Attacks Complexity and Bandwith Cost

As the linear system solving step of the attack is negligible with respect to the support recovery one, the attacks complexity is equal to the complexity of Algorithms 3 and 4. Hereafter, we briefly describe a small improvement for these algorithms relying on the fact that $1 \in \mathsf{Supp}(\mathbf{y})$ in RQC. Indeed, one should note that if $a \notin \mathsf{Supp}(\mathbf{y})$, then $\forall \lambda \in \mathbb{F}_q, a + \lambda \notin \mathsf{Supp}(\mathbf{y})$. Thus, by setting $\mathbf{F} = \langle 1 \rangle_{\mathbb{F}_q}$ at the beginning of the algorithms, one can choose error's coordinates from $\mathbb{F}_{q^m}/\langle 1 \rangle_{\mathbb{F}_q}$ instead of $\mathbb{F}_{q^m}$. Consequently, the simple attack has a complexity of $O(n^2 q^{m-1})$ operations in $\mathbb{F}_{q^m}$ and requires $O(q^{m-1})$ requests to the $O_{\omega(\mathbf{e})}^{\mathrm{RQC}}$ oracle. Similarly, the advanced attack has a complexity of $O(wn^2 q^{m-t-1})$ operations in $\mathbb{F}_{q^m}$ and requires $O(q^{m-t-1})$ requests to the $O_{\omega(\mathbf{e})}^{\mathrm{RQC}}$ oracle.

Table 1 presents the complexity and number of requests required to perform the attacks with respect to RQC parameters. One can see that both attacks outperform the best known algorithm to solve the rank syndrome decoding problem [4]. Nevertheless, they both require a huge number of requests to the $O_{\omega(\mathbf{e})}^{\mathrm{RQC}}$ oracle therefore are quite unpracticable in real situations.

Algorithm 4. Advanced support recovery

Input: A public key pk and access to $O_{\omega(\mathbf{e})}^{\mathrm{RQC}}$
$\qquad$ The oracle precision parameter param

Output: $\mathbf{F} = \mathsf{Supp}(\mathbf{x}) = \mathsf{Supp}(\mathbf{y})$

1: $\mathbf{T} \longleftarrow O_{\omega(\mathbf{e})}^{\mathrm{RQC}}.\mathsf{Init}(\mathsf{pk}, \mathsf{param})$
2: $\mathbf{F} \longleftarrow \langle 0 \rangle_{\mathbb{F}_q}$
3: **while** $\dim(\mathbf{F}) < w$ **do**
4: $\quad \mathbf{e} \xleftarrow{\$} \mathcal{S}_{t-w}^n$
5: $\quad \omega \longleftarrow O_{\omega(\mathbf{e})}^{\mathrm{RQC}}.\mathsf{Eval}(\mathbf{T}, \mathsf{pk}, (1, \mathbf{e}))$
6: $\quad$ **if** $\omega < t$ **then**
7: $\quad\quad \Delta \longleftarrow t - \omega$
8: $\quad\quad d \longleftarrow 0$
9: $\quad\quad \omega' \longleftarrow 0$
10: $\quad\quad$ **for** $k \in \{1, \cdots, \Delta\}$ **do**
$\qquad\qquad\qquad$ ▷ Compute d
11: $\quad\quad\quad$ **repeat**
12: $\quad\quad\quad\quad d \longleftarrow d + 1$
13: $\quad\quad\quad\quad \omega' \longleftarrow \omega' + 1$
14: $\quad\quad\quad\quad \mathbf{e}' \longleftarrow (\overline{e}_1, \cdots, \overline{e}_d, 0, \cdots, 0) \in \mathbb{F}_{q^m}^n$
15: $\quad\quad\quad$ **until** $O_{\omega(\mathbf{e})}^{\mathrm{RQC}}.\mathsf{Eval}(\mathbf{T}, \mathsf{pk}, (1, \mathbf{e}')) < w + \omega'$
$\qquad\qquad\qquad$ ▷ Compute λ
16: $\quad\quad\quad \lambda_d \longleftarrow 1$
17: $\quad\quad\quad$ **for** $i \in \{1, \cdots, d-1\}$ **do**
18: $\quad\quad\quad\quad \mathbf{e}' \longleftarrow (\overline{e}_1, \cdots, \overline{e}_{i-1}, 0, \overline{e}_{i+1}, \cdots, \overline{e}_d, 0, \cdots, 0) \in \mathbb{F}_{q^m}^n$
19: $\quad\quad\quad\quad$ **if** $O_{\omega(\mathbf{e})}^{\mathrm{RQC}}.\mathsf{Eval}(\mathbf{T}, \mathsf{pk}, (1, \mathbf{e}')) = w + \omega' - 1$ **then**
20: $\quad\quad\quad\quad\quad \lambda_i \longleftarrow 1$
21: $\quad\quad\quad\quad$ **else**
22: $\quad\quad\quad\quad\quad \lambda_i \longleftarrow 0$
23: $\quad\quad\quad \mathbf{F} \longleftarrow \mathbf{F} + \langle \sum_{i=1}^{d} \lambda_i \overline{e}_i \rangle_{\mathbb{F}_q}$
24: $\quad\quad\quad \overline{e}_d \longleftarrow 0$
25: $\quad\quad\quad \omega' \longleftarrow \omega' - 1$
26: **return** $\mathbf{F}$

Table 1. Attacks complexity and bandwith cost against RQC

	Complexity			Requests		
	128	192	256	128	192	256
RSD solving [4]	2^{132}	2^{203}	2^{257}	0	0	0
Simple attack (Sect. 4.2)	2^{101}	2^{126}	2^{152}	2^{88}	2^{112}	2^{138}
Advanced attack (Sect. 4.3)	2^{73}	2^{86}	2^{106}	2^{58}	2^{70}	2^{90}

5   Preventing Timing Attacks Against RQC

In this section, we explain how to prevent timing attacks against RQC using either a constant time decoding algorithm for Gabidulin codes (Sect. 5.1) or a countermeasure based on the IND-CCA2 property of RQC (Sect. 5.2). Interestingly, these two strategies can be implemented without any additional performance cost for honest users.

5.1   Constant Time Decoding of Gabidulin Codes

Algorithm 7 provides a constant-time implementation of the reconstruction algorithm and as such can be used as a countermeasure to the timing attacks against RQC. The main idea is to perform operations on dummy q-polynomials (lines 2–5) whenever required (lines 6–17) while ensuring that every operations is performed on a q-polynomial of correct q-degree with respect to a nominal case (lines 25–34). As a result, given a Gabidulin code $\mathcal{G}_{\mathbf{g}}(n, k, m)$, and an error $\mathbf{e} \in \mathbb{F}_{q^m}^n$ such that $\omega(\mathbf{e}) = t$ with $t \leq \lfloor \frac{n-k}{2} \rfloor$, Algorithm 7 will perform exactly $2 \times \lfloor \frac{n-k}{2} \rfloor$ interpolation steps whatever the value of t is.

Figure 2 compares the running time of Algorithms 6 and 7 when they are respectively used to decode Gabidulin codes or used as part of the Decapsulate step of RQC. We have performed 10 000 tests for each error weight using a computer equiped with an Intel Core i7-7820X CPU @ 3.6 GHz and 16 GB of memory. On average (excluding the case $\omega(\mathbf{e}) = 0$ which is discussed below), $\mathbf{T}_{i+1} - \mathbf{T}_i$ is reduced from 6.6×10^4 to 5.6×10^3 CPU cycles (approximately 2 μs) for $O_{\omega(\mathbf{e})}^{\mathrm{RQC}}$. The average standard deviation to the running time observed for each error weight when using Algorithm 7 is equal to 1.4×10^4 CPU cycles. Therefore, $O_{\omega(\mathbf{e})}^{\mathrm{RQC}}$ cannot be used to distinguish $\omega(\mathbf{e})$ in a reliable way anymore thus rendering the aforementioned timing attacks even more impracticable.

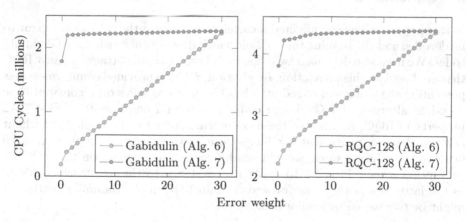

Fig. 2. Running time (CPU cycles) of Gabidulin code decoding and RQC-128 Decapsulate step with respect to different error weights $\omega(\mathbf{e})$ using Algorithms 6 and 7

By analyzing Fig. 2, one immediately sees that the special case $\omega(\mathbf{e}) = 0$ is an outlier with respect to the running time of Algorithm 7. This is presumably due to the fact that the involved q-polynomials have many coefficients equal to zero which speeds the q-polynomial update step of the decoding. This case does not appear to be concerning as it seems hard to retrieve information regarding the support $\mathbf{F}$ whenever $\omega(\mathbf{x} \cdot \mathbf{r}_2 - \mathbf{y} \cdot \mathbf{r}_1 + \mathbf{e}) = 0$. One may exploit this special case by trying to find errors $\mathbf{e}$ such that $\mathbf{e} - \mathbf{y} = 0$ (with $\mathbf{r}_1 = 1$ and $\mathbf{r}_2 = 0$) nonetheless such an attack would have a complexity of $O(q^{\omega n})$ operations in $\mathbb{F}_{q^m}$ which is worse than solving the rank syndrome decoding problem.

The running time of Algorithm 7 is similar to the running-time required to decode an error of weight $\omega(\mathbf{e}) = \lfloor \frac{n-k}{2} \rfloor$ using Algorithm 6. As the weight of the error $\mathbf{x} \cdot \mathbf{r}_2 - \mathbf{y} \cdot \mathbf{r}_1 + \mathbf{e}$ used in RQC is equal to the error correction capacity of the considered Gabidulin code, our constant time algorithm can be used without any additional performance cost for honest users.

5.2 Countermeasure Based on RQC IND-CCA2 Property

RQC being an IND-CCA2 encryption scheme, any attempt to modify one of its ciphertexts will be detected and the Decapsulate step will end-up by an Abort. Thus, by using standard techniques when implementing the Abort behaviour, the aforementioned timing attacks can be prevented. Indeed, one may choose to not respond to invalid requests therefore preventing the adversary to perform any time measurement. Alternatively, one can wait a randomly chosen amount of time before sending its response thus forcing an adversary to perform a huge number of requests in order to get any reliable time measurement. As both of these strategies intervene after an Abort case is detected, they can be implemented without any additional performance cost for honest users.

6   Conclusion

In this paper, we have highlighted a correlation between the rank of the error to be decoded and the running time of Loidreau's decoding algorithm for Gabidulin codes. We have also described two chosen ciphertext timing attacks against RQC that are based on this correlation. In addition, we have provided countermeasures preventing the aforementionned attacks. The first one relies on a constant time decoding algorithm for Gabidulin codes and second one uses the IND-CCA2 property of RQC. As both of these countermeasures can be deployed without additional performance cost for honest users, we suggest to implement both of them. In a future work, we will conduct a similar analysis on the HQC [1] encryption scheme in order to study its resistance to timing attacks. Indeed, as the latter shares the same framework than RQC in the Hamming setting, it might be threatened by similar attacks.

A   Original Reconstruction Algorithm

Algorithm 5. Original reconstruction algorithm [9, 5]

Input: $k, n \in \mathbb{N}, k \le n$
$\qquad \mathbf{g} = (g_1, \cdots, g_n) \in \mathbb{F}_{q^m}^n, \mathbb{F}_q$-linearly independent elements
$\qquad \mathbf{y} = (y_1, \cdots, y_n) \in \mathbb{F}_{q^m}^n$

Output: (N_1, V_1), solution to **Reconstruction**$(\mathbf{y}, \mathbf{g}, k, t)$.

    ▷ Initialization step
1:   $N_0(X) \longleftarrow \mathcal{A}_{\langle g_1, \cdots, g_k \rangle_{\mathbb{F}_q}}$
2:   $V_0(X) \longleftarrow 0$
3:   $N_1(X) \longleftarrow \mathcal{I}_{[g_1, \cdots, g_k],[y_1, \cdots, y_k]}$
4:   $V_1(X) \longleftarrow 1$
5:   $\mathbf{u}_0 \longleftarrow N_0\{\mathbf{g}\} - V_0\{\mathbf{y}\}$
6:   $\mathbf{u}_1 \longleftarrow N_1\{\mathbf{g}\} - V_1\{\mathbf{y}\}$

    ▷ Interpolation step
7:   **for** $i \in \{k+1, \cdots, n\}$ **do**
8:      $j \longleftarrow i$ ▷ Early-end case
9:      **while** $j \le n$ **and** $u_{1,j} = 0$ **and** $u_{0,j} \ne 0$ **do**
10:        $j \longleftarrow j + 1$
11:      **if** $j = n + 1$ **then**
12:        break
13:      **else**
14:        $u_{0,i} \longleftrightarrow u_{0,j}$
15:        $u_{1,i} \longleftrightarrow u_{1,j}$

    ▷ q-polynomials update
16:      **if** $u_{1,i} \ne 0$ **then**   ▷ Nominal case
17:        $\lambda_1 \longleftarrow \frac{\theta(u_{1,i})}{u_{1,i}}$
18:        $\lambda_0 \longleftarrow \frac{u_{0,i}}{u_{1,i}}$
19:      **else if** $u_{0,i} = 0$ **then**   ▷ Dummy interpolation case
20:        $\lambda_1 \longleftarrow 0$
21:        $\lambda_0 \longleftarrow 0$
22:      $N_1' \longleftarrow (X - \lambda_1) \cdot N_1$
23:      $V_1' \longleftarrow (X - \lambda_1) \cdot V_1$
24:      $N_0' \longleftarrow N_0 - \lambda_0 \cdot N_1$
25:      $V_0' \longleftarrow V_0 - \lambda_0 \cdot V_1$

    ▷ q-polynomials swap
26:      $N_0 \longleftarrow N_1'$
27:      $V_0 \longleftarrow V_1'$
28:      $N_1 \longleftarrow N_0'$
29:      $V_1 \longleftarrow V_0'$

    ▷ Discrepancies update
30:      **for** $j \in \{i+1, \cdots, n\}$ **do**
31:        $u_{0,j}' \longleftarrow \theta(u_{1,j}) - \lambda_1 \cdot u_{1,j}$
32:        $u_{1,j}' \longleftarrow u_{0,j} - \lambda_0 \cdot u_{1,j}$
33: **return** (N_1, V_1)

B   Simpler Reconstruction Algorithm

Algorithm 6. Simpler reconstruction algorithm (§3.1)

Input: $k, n \in \mathbb{N}, k \leq n$
        $\mathbf{g} = (g_1, \cdots, g_n) \in \mathbb{F}_{q^m}^n, \mathbb{F}_q$-linearly independent elements
        $\mathbf{y} = (y_1, \cdots, y_n) \in \mathbb{F}_{q^m}^n$

Output: (N_1, V_1), solution to **Reconstruction**$(\mathbf{y}, \mathbf{g}, k, t)$.

    ▷ Initialization step
1: $N_0(X) \longleftarrow \mathcal{A}_{\langle g_1, \cdots, g_k \rangle_{\mathbb{F}_q}}$
2: $V_0(X) \longleftarrow 0$
3: $N_1(X) \longleftarrow \mathcal{I}_{[g_1, \cdots, g_k],[y_1, \cdots, y_k]}$
4: $V_1(X) \longleftarrow 1$
5: $\mathbf{u}_0 \longleftarrow N_0\{\mathbf{g}\} - V_0\{\mathbf{y}\}$
6: $\mathbf{u}_1 \longleftarrow N_1\{\mathbf{g}\} - V_1\{\mathbf{y}\}$

    ▷ Interpolation step
7: **for** $i \in \{k+1, \ldots, n\}$ **do**
8:     $j \longleftarrow i$ ▷ Early-end case
9:     **while** $j \leq n$ **and** $u_{1,j} = 0$ **do**
10:       $j \longleftarrow j + 1$
11:     **if** $j = n + 1$ **then**
12:       break
13:     **else**
14:       $u_{0,i} \longleftrightarrow u_{0,j}$
15:       $u_{1,i} \longleftrightarrow u_{1,j}$

    ▷ q-polynomials update
16:     $\lambda_1 \longleftarrow \frac{\theta(u_{1,i})}{u_{1,i}}$ ▷ Nominal case
17:     $\lambda_0 \longleftarrow \frac{u_{0,i}}{u_{1,i}}$
18:     $N_1' \longleftarrow (X - \lambda_1) \cdot N_1$
19:     $V_1' \longleftarrow (X - \lambda_1) \cdot V_1$
20:     $N_0' \longleftarrow N_0 - \lambda_0 \cdot N_1$
21:     $V_0' \longleftarrow V_0 - \lambda_0 \cdot V_1$

    ▷ q-polynomials swap
22:     $N_0 \longleftarrow N_1'$
23:     $V_0 \longleftarrow V_1'$
24:     $N_1 \longleftarrow N_0'$
25:     $V_1 \longleftarrow V_0'$

    ▷ Discrepancies update
26:     **for** $j \in \{i+1, \cdots, n\}$ **do**
27:       $u_{0,j}' \longleftarrow \theta(u_{1,j}) - \lambda_1 \cdot u_{1,j}$
28:       $u_{1,j}' \longleftarrow u_{0,j} - \lambda_0 \cdot u_{1,j}$

29: **return** (N_1, V_1)

C   Constant-Time Reconstruction Algorithm

Algorithm 7. Constant-time reconstruction algorithm (§5)

Input: $k, n \in \mathbb{N}, k \leq n$
   $\mathbf{g} = (g_1, \cdots, g_n) \in \mathbb{F}_{q^m}^n, \mathbb{F}_q$-linearly independent elements
   $\mathbf{y} = (y_1, \cdots, y_n) \in \mathbb{F}_{q^m}^n$

Output: (N_1, V_1), solution to **Reconstruction**$(\mathbf{y}, \mathbf{g}, k, t)$.

1: ▷ Classical initialization step (see Algorithm 6, lines 1 - 6)

   ▷ Constant-time initialization step
2: $d \longleftarrow ((n-k)/2 \equiv 0 \bmod 2)\ ?\ k+t-1\ :\ k+t$
3: $N_2, N_3, V_2, V_3 \xleftarrow{\$} \{\ q\text{-polynomials of } q\text{-deg } d\ \}$
4: $c_0, c_1 \xleftarrow{\$} \mathbb{F}_{q^m} \backslash \{0\}$
5: $b \longleftarrow 0$

   ▷ Interpolation step
6: **for** $i \in \{k+1, \cdots, n\}$ **do**
7:    $i' \longleftarrow n+1$ ▷ "Early-end" case
8:    **for** $j \in \{i, \cdots, n\}$ **do**
9:       $r \longleftarrow \mathsf{isZero}(u_{1,j})$
10:      $i' \longleftarrow (1-r)j + ri'$
11:    **if** $i' = n+1$ **or** $b = 1$ **then**
12:       $b \longleftarrow 1$
13:       $u_{0,i} \longleftarrow c_0$
14:       $u_{1,i} \longleftarrow c_1$
15:    **else**
16:       $u_{0,i} \longleftrightarrow u_{0,i'}$
17:       $u_{1,i} \longleftrightarrow u_{1,i'}$

   ▷ q-polynomials update
18:   $\lambda_1 \longleftarrow \frac{\theta(u_{1,i})}{u_{1,i}}$
19:   $\lambda_0 \longleftarrow \frac{u_{0,i}}{u_{1,i}}$
20:   **if** $b = 0$ **then**   ▷ Classical nominal case
21:      $N_1' \longleftarrow (X - \lambda_1) \cdot N_1$
22:      $V_1' \longleftarrow (X - \lambda_1) \cdot V_1$
23:      $N_0' \longleftarrow N_0 - \lambda_0 \cdot N_1$
24:      $V_0' \longleftarrow V_0 - \lambda_0 \cdot V_1$
25:   **else if** $i - k \equiv 0 \bmod 2$ **then**   ▷ Constant-time nominal case
26:      $N_1 \longleftarrow (X - \lambda_1) \cdot N_1$
27:      $V_1 \longleftarrow (X - \lambda_1) \cdot V_1$
28:      $N_0' \longleftarrow N_2 - \lambda_0 \cdot N_3$
29:      $V_0' \longleftarrow V_2 - \lambda_0 \cdot V_3$
30:   **else**
31:      $N_1' \longleftarrow (X - \lambda_1) \cdot N_3$
32:      $V_1' \longleftarrow (X - \lambda_1) \cdot V_3$
33:      $N_0' \longleftarrow N_2 - \lambda_0 \cdot N_3$
34:      $V_0' \longleftarrow V_2 - \lambda_0 \cdot V_3$

35:   ▷ Classical q-polynomials swap (see Algorithm 6, lines 22 - 25)
36:   ▷ Classical discrepancies update (see Algorithm 6, lines 26 - 28)
37: **return** (N_1, V_1)

References

1. Aguilar-Melchor, C., et al.: Hamming Quasi-Cyclic (HQC) (2017)
2. Aguilar-Melchor, C., et al.: Rank Quasi-Cyclic (RQC) (2017)
3. Aguilar-Melchor, C., Blazy, O., Deneuville, J.-C., Gaborit, P., Zémor, G.: Efficient encryption from random quasi-cyclic codes. IEEE Transact. Inf. Theory **64**(5), 3927–3943 (2018)
4. Aragon, N., Gaborit, P., Hauteville, A., Tillich, J.P.: A new algorithm for solving the rank syndrome decoding problem. In: 2018 IEEE International Symposium on Information Theory (ISIT), pp. 2421–2425 (2018)
5. Augot, D., Loidreau, P., Robert, G.: Generalized Gabidulin codes over fields of any characteristic. Des. Codes Crypt. **86**(8), 1807–1848 (2018)
6. Gabidulin, E.M.: Theory of codes with maximum rank distance. Problemy Peredachi Informatsii **21**(1), 3–16 (1985)
7. Gaborit, P., Zémor, G.: On the hardness of the decoding and the minimum distance problems for rank codes. IEEE Transact. Inf. Theory **62**(12), 7245–7252 (2016)
8. Hofheinz, D., Hövelmanns, K., Kiltz, E.: A modular analysis of the Fujisaki-Okamoto transformation. In: Kalai, Y., Reyzin, L. (eds.) TCC 2017. LNCS, vol. 10677, pp. 341–371. Springer, Cham (2017). https://doi.org/10.1007/978-3-319-70500-2_12
9. Loidreau, P.: A Welch–Berlekamp like algorithm for decoding Gabidulin codes. In: Ytrehus, Ø. (ed.) WCC 2005. LNCS, vol. 3969, pp. 36–45. Springer, Heidelberg (2006). https://doi.org/10.1007/11779360_4
10. Ore, O.: On a special class of polynomials. Transact. Am. Math. Soc. **35**(3), 559–584 (1933)

A Traceable Ring Signature Scheme Based on Coding Theory

Pedro Branco[✉] and Paulo Mateus

Department of Mathematics, SQIG-Instituto de Telecomunicações,
IST-Universidade de Lisboa, Lisbon, Portugal
pmbranco@math.tecnico.ulisboa.pt

Abstract. Traceable ring signatures are a variant of ring signatures which allows the identity of a user to be revealed, when it signs two different messages with respect to the same group of users. It has applications in e-voting and in cryptocurrencies, such as the well-known Monero. We propose the first traceable ring signature scheme whose security is based on the hardness of the Syndrome Decoding problem, a problem in coding theory which is conjectured to be unsolvable by both classical and quantum algorithms. To construct the scheme, we use a variant of Stern's protocol and, by applying the Fiat-Shamir transform to it in an ingenious way, we obtain a ring signature that allows traceability. We prove that the resulting protocol has the standard security properties for traceable ring signatures in the random oracle model: tag-linkability, anonymity and exculpability. As far as we know, this is the first proposal for a traceable ring signature scheme in the post-quantum setting.

Keywords: Traceable ring signature scheme ·
Code-based cryptography · Stern's protocol

1 Introduction

With the National Institute of Standards and Technology (NIST) decision to standardize quantum-resilient protocols, post-quantum cryptography has become a hot topic in the cryptographic community. However post-quantum signature schemes, particularly signatures based on coding theory, are still underdeveloped. Although most of the operations are relatively efficient and easy to implement (even in hardware), code-based signature schemes consume too much memory for practical purposes. If we consider signature schemes with additional properties, the scenario is even worse since most of these schemes do not even have an equivalent version based on hard problems from coding theory. In this paper, we focus on the latter problem by developing a traceable ring signature scheme whose security is based on the Syndrome Decoding (SD) problem, a problem in coding theory which is believed to be hard for both classical and quantum computers. As far as we know, this is the first code-based traceable ring signature scheme to be proposed and the first one in the post-quantum setting.

© Springer Nature Switzerland AG 2019
J. Ding and R. Steinwandt (Eds.): PQCrypto 2019, LNCS 11505, pp. 387–403, 2019.
https://doi.org/10.1007/978-3-030-25510-7_21

Traceable Ring Signature Schemes. Ring signatures [22] allow for a user from a group to sign messages on behalf of the group such that a verifier is not able to trace the identity of the actual signer. Although in most cases anonymity is of great importance and should be preserved, in some applications it may become a problem, in the sense that a dishonest user can take advantage of the anonymity to its own interest. Consider, for example, an election where someone votes once and then tries to create a second vote, claiming to be someone else. From this example we can see that, in some cases, we may want to reveal the identity of abusive users. A trivial solution is to use a group signature scheme [13] (and for which there are code-based versions [2,3]), where a group manager has much more power than the rest of the users and can open signatures issued by the users of the group. However, in this case, the group manager would have to open all signatures in order to identify those issued by an abusive user, jeopardizing anonymity of honest users.

Traceable ring signatures [19] are ring signatures where the identity of a user may be revealed, in the case it signs two messages with respect to the same group of users and the same issue. In this context, an issue may be an election or a transaction, for example. Traceable ring signature schemes solve the problem presented in the previous paragraph: an abusive user in an election gets caught without compromising the anonymity of the other users. Traceable ring signature schemes have also found a lot of applications in e-cash and cryptocurrencies in the last years. In fact, one of the most famous cryptocurrencies nowadays, Monero [26], uses a variant of the scheme by Fujisaki and Suzuki [19].

Traceable ring signature schemes are closely related to linkable ring signature schemes [20]. Linkable ring signature schemes also allow a verifier to know if two signatures were issued by the same user in a group of users, but its anonymity is kept preserved no matter the number of signatures issued by this user, unlike traceable ring signature schemes where its identity is revealed.

Previous traceable ring signature schemes were all based on the hardness of the discrete logarithm problem [5,18,19] which can be solved by Shor's algorithm [23] using a quantum computer. Hence, the advent of a practical quantum computer would turn Monero (with a market value of billions of dollars) and other cryptocurrencies obsolete.

To overcome this problem, we base the security of our traceable ring signature scheme on the syndrome decoding problem. This is a classical problem in coding theory that is conjectured to be hard, even for quantum computers. By basing the security of cryptographic primitives on this problem, we can design new protocols that are conjectured to be robust against quantum adversaries. Therefore, as far as we are aware, the traceable ring signature scheme presented in this work is the first that is conjectured to be suitable for the post-quantum era.

Our Contribution and Techniques. The major contribution of this paper is the construction of a traceable ring signature scheme based on the SD problem. To develop the new traceable ring signature scheme, we build on top of a recently proposed code-based linkable ring signature scheme [10]. More precisely, we consider the GStern's protocol, a variant of the famous Stern's protocol [24], that decides the General Syndrome Decoding (GSD). This protocol allows a prover to prove the knowledge of a error vector $\mathbf{e}$ for two instances of the Syndrome Decoding $(\mathbf{H}, \mathbf{s})$ and $(\mathbf{G}, \mathbf{r})$ for an appropriate choice of parameters. After applying the construction by Cramer, Damgård and Shoemakers [14] for the OR relation, we obtain a proof of knowledge protocol $(\binom{N}{1}$-GStern's protocol) where the prover proves that it knows a witness for one of several instances of the GSD problem.

Let $(\mathbf{H}, \mathbf{s}_i)$ be the public key of a party $\mathcal{P}_i$ and $\mathbf{e}_i$ its secret key, such that $\mathbf{He}_i^T = \mathbf{s}_i^T$ and $\mathbf{e}_i$ has small weight. To sign a message using the scheme, a user collects the public keys of the elements in the ring. Let $(\mathbf{H}, \mathbf{s}_1, \dots, \mathbf{s}_N)$ (the matrix $\mathbf{H}$ is common to every party's public key) be the public keys of the users in the ring. The signer computes $\widetilde{\mathbf{H}}\mathbf{e}_i^T = \mathbf{r}_i^T$, where $\widetilde{\mathbf{H}}$ is a matrix computed using a random oracle and that depends on the ring of users. It creates random vectors $\mathbf{r}_1, \dots, \mathbf{r}_{i-1}, \mathbf{r}_{i+i}, \dots, \mathbf{r}_N$ for each user of the ring. Since these vectors must be random, the user computes them using a hash function and depending on the message. Now, the user creates a signature by applying the Fiat-Shamir [17] to the $\binom{N}{1}$-GStern's protocol on input $(\mathbf{H}, \mathbf{s}_1, \dots, \mathbf{s}_N, \widetilde{\mathbf{H}}, \mathbf{r}_1, \dots, \mathbf{r}_N)$. Suppose that some user $\mathcal{P}_i$ signs creates two signatures for two different messages. Traceability will be possible by checking for which i, $\mathbf{r}_i = \mathbf{r}_i'$ where $\mathbf{r}_i$ is part of one signature and $\mathbf{r}_i'$ is part of the other.

We prove the usual security properties for traceable ring signature schemes in the Random Oracle Model: tag-linkability, anonymity and exculpability.

2 Notation and Preliminaries

We begin by presenting some notation. We will use bold lower cases to denote vectors (like $\mathbf{x}$) and bold capital letters to denote matrices (like $\mathbf{H}$). We denote the usual Hamming weight of a vector $\mathbf{x}$ by $w(\mathbf{x})$. If $\mathcal{A}$ is an algorithm, we denote $y \leftarrow \mathcal{A}(x)$ the output y when running $\mathcal{A}$ with input x. If S is a finite set, $|S|$ denotes its cardinality and $y \leftarrow_\$ S$ means that y was chosen uniformly at random from S. By $\mathsf{negl}(n)$ we denote a function F that is negligible on the parameter n, i.e., $F < 1/\mathsf{poly}(n)$ where $\mathsf{poly}(n)$ represents any polynomial in n. The acronym PPT means probabilistic polynomial-time.

Due to the lack of space, we refer the reader to Appendix A for a brief introduction on sigma protocols[1], the Fiat-Shamir transform [17], the Cramer-Damgård-Shoenmakers (CDS) construction for the OR relation [14] and the original Stern's protocol [24].

2.1 Hard Problems in Coding Theory

We present the search version of the Syndrome Decoding (SD) problem, a hard problem in coding theory, proven to be NP-complete [7] in the worst-case. The problem states that it is hard to decode a random linear code. Recall that a k-dimensional code $\mathcal{C}$ of length n can be represented by its parity-check matrix $\mathbf{H} \in \mathbb{Z}_2^{(n-k) \times n}$.

---

[1] We refer the reader to [15] for a more detailed introduction on sigma protocols.

Problem 1 (Syndrome Decoding). *Given* $\mathbf{H} \in \mathbb{Z}_2^{(n-k)\times n}$, $\mathbf{s} \in \mathbb{Z}_2^{n-k}$ *and* $t \in \mathbb{N}$, *find* $\mathbf{e} \in \mathbb{Z}_2^n$ *such that* $w(\mathbf{e}) \leq t$ *and* $\mathbf{H}\mathbf{e}^T = \mathbf{s}^T$.

The problem is also widely believed to be hard on the average-case since the best known generic decoding classical and quantum attacks still take exponential time [6,8,11,12,21] and, when $\mathbf{e}$ is chosen uniformly at random from the set of vectors with weight t and the matrix $\mathbf{H}$ is chosen uniformly at random from $\mathbb{Z}_2^{(n-k)\times n}$, the statistical distance between $(\mathbf{H}, \mathbf{H}\mathbf{e}^T)$ and the uniform distribution over $\mathbb{Z}_2^{(n-k)\times n} \times \mathbb{Z}_2^{n-k}$ is negligible [16].

Next, we present a lemma which will be useful to prove the completeness of the proposed protocols. It states that the equation $\mathbf{H}\mathbf{x}^T = \mathbf{s}^T$ will most likely have a solution (not necessarily with $w(\mathbf{x}) \leq t$) with $\mathbf{H}$ and $\mathbf{s}$ chosen at random.

Lemma 2. *Let* $n, k' \in \mathbb{N}$ *such that* $k' \leq n/2$. *Given* $\mathbf{H} \leftarrow_{\$} \mathbb{Z}_2^{k'\times n}$ *and* $\mathbf{s} \leftarrow_{\$} \mathbb{Z}_2^{k'}$, *the probability of existing a vector* $\mathbf{x} \in \mathbb{Z}_2^n$ *such that* $\mathbf{H}\mathbf{x}^T = \mathbf{s}^T$ *is, at least,* $1 - \mathsf{negl}(n)$.

The proof is presented in Appendix B.1

Corollary 3. *Let* $n, k' \in \mathbb{N}$ *such that* $k' \leq n/4$. *Given* $\mathbf{H}, \mathbf{G} \leftarrow_{\$} \mathbb{Z}_2^{k'\times n}$ *and* $\mathbf{s}, \mathbf{r} \leftarrow_{\$} \mathbb{Z}_2^{k'}$, *the probability that there is a vector* $\mathbf{x} \in \mathbb{Z}_2^n$ *such that* $\mathbf{H}\mathbf{x}^T = \mathbf{s}^T$ *and* $\mathbf{G}\mathbf{x}^T = \mathbf{r}^T$ *is* $1 - \mathsf{negl}(n)$.

The Corollary can be easily proved by observing that

$$\binom{\mathbf{H}}{\mathbf{G}}\mathbf{x}^T = \binom{\mathbf{s}^T}{\mathbf{r}^T}$$

is a special case of the previous lemma.

For our purpose, we want the equation $\mathbf{H}\mathbf{x}^T = \mathbf{s}^T$ to have solutions, where $\mathbf{H} \in \mathbb{Z}_2^{(n-k)\times n}$. Hence, we just need to consider $n - k = k' \leq n/4$, that is, $k \geq 3n/4$. To this end, we take $k = 3n/4$.

We now present the Generalized Syndrome Decoding (GSD) problem.

Problem 4. *Given* $\mathbf{H}, \mathbf{G} \in \mathbb{Z}_2^{(n-k)\times n}$, $\mathbf{s}, \mathbf{r} \in \mathbb{Z}_2^{n-k}$ *and* $t \in \mathbb{N}$, *find* $\mathbf{e} \in \mathbb{Z}_2^n$ *such that* $w(\mathbf{e}) \leq t$, $\mathbf{H}\mathbf{e}^T = \mathbf{s}^T$ *and* $\mathbf{G}\mathbf{e}^T = \mathbf{r}^T$.

Note that the SD problem can be trivially reduced to GSD, by choosing as inputs of the reduction $\mathbf{H} = \mathbf{G}$ and $\mathbf{s} = \mathbf{r}$, and so GSD is a NP-complete language.

The next protocol is a proof of knowledge protocol for the GSD problem. We will call GStern's protocol to the protocol presented in Algorithm 1.[2]

In the protocol, presented in Algorithm 1, observe that, when $b = 1$, $\mathcal{V}$ can check that c_1 was honestly computed by verifying whether $\mathbf{H}(\mathbf{y}+\mathbf{e})^T+\mathbf{s}^T = \mathbf{H}\mathbf{y}^T$ and $\mathbf{G}(\mathbf{y}+\mathbf{e})^T+\mathbf{r}^T = \mathbf{G}\mathbf{y}^T$. Also, the verifier can check that it is the same error vector $\mathbf{e}$ that was used to compute the syndrome vectors $\mathbf{s}$ and $\mathbf{r}$.

---

[2] The name GStern's protocol comes from Generalized Stern's protocol.

Algorithm 1. GStern's protocol

---

1. **Public information:** $\mathbf{H}, \mathbf{G} \in \mathbb{Z}_2^{(n-k) \times n}$ and $\mathbf{s}, \mathbf{r} \in \mathbb{Z}_2^{n-k}$.
2. **Secret information:** $\mathbf{e} \in \mathbb{Z}_2^n$ such that $\mathbf{H}\mathbf{e}^T = \mathbf{s}^T$, $\mathbf{G}\mathbf{e}^T = \mathbf{r}^T$ and $w(\mathbf{e}) = t$.
3. **Prover's commitment:**
   - $\mathcal{P}$ chooses $\mathbf{y} \leftarrow_\$ \mathbb{Z}_2^n$ and a permutation δ;
   - $\mathcal{P}$ computes $c_1 = h(\delta, \mathbf{H}\mathbf{y}^T, \mathbf{G}\mathbf{y}^T)$, $c_2 = h(\delta(\mathbf{y}))$ and $c_3 = h(\delta(\mathbf{y} + \mathbf{e}))$;
   - $\mathcal{P}$ sends c_1, c_2 and c_3.
4. **Verifier's Challenge:** $\mathcal{V}$ sends $b \leftarrow_\$ \{0, 1, 2\}$.
5. **Prover's answer:**
   - If $b = 0$, $\mathcal{P}$ reveals $\mathbf{y}$ and δ;
   - If $b = 1$, $\mathcal{P}$ reveals $\mathbf{y} + \mathbf{e}$ and δ;
   - If $b = 2$, $\mathcal{P}$ reveals $\delta(\mathbf{y})$ and $\delta(\mathbf{e})$.
6. **Verifier's verification:**
   - If $b = 0$, $\mathcal{V}$ checks if $h(\delta, \mathbf{H}\mathbf{y}^T, \mathbf{G}\mathbf{y}^T) = c_1$ and $h(\delta(\mathbf{y})) = c_2$;
   - If $b = 1$, $\mathcal{V}$ checks if $h(\delta, \mathbf{H}(\mathbf{y}+\mathbf{e})^T + \mathbf{s}^T, \mathbf{G}(\mathbf{y}+\mathbf{e})^T + \mathbf{r}^T) = c_1$ and $h(\delta(\mathbf{y} + \mathbf{e})) = c_3$;
   - If $b = 2$, $\mathcal{V}$ checks if $h(\delta(\mathbf{y})) = c_2$, $h(\delta(\mathbf{y}) + \delta(\mathbf{e})) = c_3$ and $w(\delta(\mathbf{e})) = t$.

The protocol is proven to be complete, special sound and honest-verifier zero-knowledge (HVZK) [10]. Nevertheless, we sketch the proof here. It is easy to see that, from two valid transcripts $(com, ch, resp)$ and $(com, ch', resp')$ of GStern's protocol, with $ch \neq ch'$, there is a simulator that can extract a valid witness. For instance, when $ch = 0$ and $ch' = 1$, the simulator can extract the secret $\mathbf{e}$ from $\mathbf{y}$ and $\mathbf{y} + \mathbf{e}$. In a similar way, it can always extract $\mathbf{e}$ in the other two cases. To prove HVZK, note that: (i) when $b = 0$, the simulator just has to reveal a random vector $\mathbf{y}$ and a random permutation δ; (ii) when $b = 1$, the simulator has to reveal a vector $\mathbf{x}$ such that $\mathbf{H}\mathbf{x}^T = \mathbf{s}^T$ (but not necessarily with $w(\mathbf{x}) = t$). Note that this is possible due to Corollary 3; finally, (iii) when $b = 2$, the simulator just has to reveal a vector with weight t.

To build our signature scheme, we apply the CDS construction [14] to GStern's protocol. We will call the resulting protocol $\binom{N}{1}$-GStern's protocol. We assume that the matrices $\mathbf{H}$ and $\mathbf{G}$, and t are the same for every instance of the GSD problem. In the following, com, ch and $resp$ are commitments, challenges and responses, respectively, of GStern's protocol repeated $\mathcal{O}(1/\epsilon)$ times. Moreover, the challenges are expressed as bit strings. The protocol is presented in Algorithm 2.

The $\binom{N}{1}$-GStern's protocol is a PoK that is complete, special sound and HVZK. This fact is a direct consequence of the results in [14]. We briefly give the sketch of the proof.

Suppose that the prover has a secret for instance j. To prove completeness, note that a honest prover can always create valid transcript for instance j. This follows from the completeness of GStern's protocol. It can also create valid transcripts for the other instances from the HVZK of GStern's protocol. Thus, a prover holding a secret for instance j can always create valid transcripts for $\binom{N}{1}$-GStern's protocol.

Algorithm 2. $\binom{N}{1}$-GStern's protocol

---

1. **Public   information:** N instances   of   the   GSD   problem $(\mathbf{H}, \mathbf{s}_1, \ldots, \mathbf{s}_N, \mathbf{G}, \mathbf{r}_1, \ldots, \mathbf{r}_N, t)$
2. **Secret information:** $\mathbf{e} \in \{0,1\}^n$ such that $w(\mathbf{e}) = t$, $\mathbf{H}\mathbf{e}^T = \mathbf{s}_i^T$ and $\mathbf{G}\mathbf{e}^T = \mathbf{r}_i^T$ for some $i \in \{1, \ldots, N\}$.
3. **Prover's commitment:**
   - $\mathcal{P}^*$ simulates transcripts $(com_j, ch_j, resp_j)$ using the simulator $\mathcal{S}$ for $j \neq i$ according to GStern's protocol;
   - $\mathcal{P}^*$ computes com_i according to GStern's protocol;
   - $\mathcal{P}^*$ sends $com_1, \ldots, com_N$.
4. **Verifier's challenge:** $\mathcal{V}$ sends $b \leftarrow_\$ C$.
5. **Prover's answer:**
   - $\mathcal{P}$ computes $ch_i = b + \sum_{j \neq i} ch_j$;
   - $\mathcal{P}$ computes $resp_i$ according to com_i and ch_i;
   - Sends $(com_j, ch_j, resp_j)$ for every j.
6. **Verifier's verification:**
   - $\mathcal{V}$ checks that $(com_j, ch_j, resp_j)$ is valid according to GStern's protocol, for every j;
   - $\mathcal{V}$ checks that $b = \sum_j ch_j$;
   - $\mathcal{V}$ accepts if it passes all the verification tests.

As usual, to prove special soundness of $\binom{N}{1}$-GStern's protocol, the simulator runs the prover and gets two valid transcripts $(Com, Ch, Resp)$ and $(Com, Ch', Resp')$, where $Com = \{com_i\}_i$, $Ch = \{ch_i\}_i$, $Ch' = \{ch'_i\}_i$, $Resp = \{resp_i\}_i$, $Resp' = \{resp'_i\}_i$, $\sum_i ch_i = b$ and $\sum_i ch'_i = b'$. Suppose that the prover has the secret for the instance j. Then $ch_i = ch'_i$ and $resp_i = resp'_i$ for every $i \neq j$. Also, $ch_j \neq ch'_j$ and $resp_j \neq resp'_j$, except with negligible probability. Thus, by the special soundness of the GStern's protocol, the simulator can extract a valid witness for instance j from these transcripts.

To prove HVZK, we have to show that there is a simulator capable of creating valid transcripts for $\binom{N}{1}$-GStern's protocol, even when not holding a witness for any of the instances. But observe that, by the HVZK property of the GStern's protocol, the simulator can create valid transcripts for each of the instances. Hence, a valid transcript for $\binom{N}{1}$-GStern's protocol follows from these transcripts of GStern's protocol.

Therefore, we can use the Fiat-Shamir transform to create a secure signature scheme [1].

2.2   Traceable Ring Signature Schemes

We present the definition of traceable ring signature scheme along with the security model we consider, originally presented in [19]. In the following, let $\overline{\mathbf{pk}} = (\mathsf{pk}_1, \ldots, \mathsf{pk}_N)$, *issue* be a string denoting the goal of the signature (for example, an election or a transaction) and $L = (issue, \overline{\mathbf{pk}})$. We will call L the tag of the signature.

Definition 5. A *traceable ring signature scheme* is defined by a tuple of algorithms (*KeyGen, Sign, Ver, Trace*) where:

- (pk, sk) ← *KeyGen*(1^κ) is a PPT algorithm that takes as input a security parameter κ and outputs a pair of public and secret keys (pk, sk);
- σ ← *Sign*(sk$_i$, L, M) is a PPT algorithm that takes as input a secret key sk$_i$, a tag $L = (issue, \overline{\mathbf{pk}})$ and a message to be signed M and outputs a signature σ.
- b ← *Ver*(L, M, σ) is a deterministic algorithm that takes as input a tag $L = (issue, \overline{\mathbf{pk}})$, a signature σ and a message M and outputs a bit b such that $b = 1$ if the signature is valid and $b = 0$ otherwise.
- s ← *Trace*($L, M_1, \sigma_1, M_2, \sigma_2$) is a deterministic algorithm that takes as input a tag $L = (issue, \overline{\mathbf{pk}})$ and two pairs of messages and corresponding signatures (M_1, σ_1) and (M_2, σ_2) and outputs a string s that is either equal to *indep*, *linked* or to an element pk $\in \overline{\mathbf{pk}}$ such that, if σ_1 ← *Sign*(sk$_i$, L, M_1) and σ_2 ← *Sign*(sk$_j$, L, M_2), then

$$Trace(L, M_1, \sigma_1, M_2, \sigma_2) := \begin{cases} indep \text{ if } i \neq j, \\ linked \text{ else if } M_1 = M_2, \\ \mathsf{pk}_i \text{ otherwise.} \end{cases}$$

The security requirements for a traceable ring signature scheme are three: tag-linkability, anonymity and exculpability. Unforgeability comes from tag-linkability and exculpability. In the following, let κ be a security parameter, N be the number of users in the ring, $L = (issue, \overline{\mathbf{pk}})$ where $\overline{\mathbf{pk}} = (\mathsf{pk}_1, \ldots, \mathsf{pk}_N)$ are the public keys of each user and *Sign*(sk, ·) is a signing oracle that receives queries of the form (L, M) and outputs σ ← *Sign*(sk, L, M).

Tag-linkability. Informally, it must be infeasible for an adversary to create $N+1$ signatures having access to N pairs of public and secret keys. Let $\mathcal{A}$ be a PPT adversary. Consider the following game:

Game$_{\mathcal{A}}^{tagLink}(\kappa, N)$:
1 : $(L, (M_1, \sigma_1), \ldots, (M_{n+1}, \sigma_{n+1})) \leftarrow \mathcal{A}(1^\kappa)$
2 : $b_i \leftarrow Ver(L, M_i, \sigma_i)$ $\quad \forall i \in \{1, \ldots, N+1\}$
3 : $s_{i,j} \leftarrow Trace(L, M_i, \sigma_i, M_j, \sigma_j)$ $\quad \forall i, j \in \{1, \ldots, N+1\} \wedge i \neq j$
4 : **return** $b_1, \ldots, b_{N+1}, s_{1,1}, s_{1,2}, \ldots, s_{N+1,N+1}$

where $L = (issue, \mathbf{pk})$ and $\mathbf{pk} = \{\mathsf{pk}_1, \ldots, \mathsf{pk}_N\}$.

We define

$$\mathsf{Adv}_{\mathcal{A}}^{tagLink}(\kappa, N) := \Pr\left[\bigwedge_{i=1}^{N+1} b_i = 1 \wedge \bigwedge_{\substack{i,j=1 \\ i \neq j}}^{N+1} s_{i,j} = indep \right].$$

If, for all PPT adversaries $\mathcal{A}$ we have that $\mathsf{Adv}_{\mathcal{A}}^{tagLink}(\kappa, N) \leq \mathsf{negl}(\kappa, N)$ then we say that the traceable ring signature scheme is tag-linkable.

Anonymity. Informally, it must be infeasible for an adversary to know who signed the message. Let $\mathcal{A}$ be a PPT adversary. Consider the following game:

$\mathsf{Game}_{\mathcal{A}}^{anon}(\kappa, N):$
1: $(\mathsf{pk}_i, \mathsf{sk}_i) \leftarrow KeyGen(1^\kappa), \quad i = 0, 1$
2: $b \leftarrow_\$ \{0, 1\}$
3: $b' \leftarrow \mathcal{A}^{Sign(\mathsf{sk}_b, \cdot), Sign(\mathsf{sk}_0, \cdot), Sign(\mathsf{sk}_1, \cdot)}(\mathsf{pk}_0, \mathsf{pk}_1)$
4: **return** b'

where the adversary is not allowed to ask queries with different tags to $Sign(\mathsf{sk}_b, \cdot)$ nor to ask queries with the same tag to both $Sign(\mathsf{sk}_b, \cdot)$ and $Sign(\mathsf{sk}_0, \cdot)$ or to both $Sign(\mathsf{sk}_b, \cdot)$ and $Sign(\mathsf{sk}_1, \cdot)$. We do not allow this to happen to avoid the trivial attacks.

We define

$$\mathsf{Adv}_{\mathcal{A}}^{anon}(\kappa, N) := \Pr\left[b = b'\right] - \frac{1}{2}.$$

If for all PPT adversaries $\mathcal{A}$ we have that $\mathsf{Adv}_{\mathcal{A}}^{anon}(\kappa, N) \leq \mathsf{negl}(\kappa, N)$ then we say that the traceable ring signature scheme is anonymous.

Exculpability. Informally, it must be infeasible for an adversary $\mathcal{A}$ to produce two pairs of messages and respective signatures that seem to be issued by some user i, without knowledge of the secret key. In this case, we say that $\mathcal{A}$ frames user i. Let $\mathcal{A}$ be a PPT adversary. Consider the following game:

$\mathsf{Game}_{\mathcal{A}}^{exc}(\kappa, N):$
1: $(\mathsf{pk}, \mathsf{sk}) \leftarrow KeyGen(1^\kappa)$
2: $(L, M_1, \sigma_1), (L, M_2, \sigma_2) \leftarrow \mathcal{A}^{Sign(\mathsf{sk}, \cdot)}(\mathsf{pk})$
3: $s \leftarrow Trace(L, M_1, \sigma_1, M_2, \sigma_2)$
4: **return** s

where $Ver(L, M_1, \sigma_1) = 1$, $Ver(L, M_2, \sigma_2) = 1$, $\mathsf{pk} \in \overline{\mathsf{pk}}$ and at least one of the signatures must not be linked[3] to any query to $Sign(\mathsf{sk}, \cdot)$ made by $\mathcal{A}$ (to avoid the trivial attacks).

We define

$$\mathsf{Adv}_{\mathcal{A}}^{exc}(\kappa, N) := \Pr\left[s = \mathsf{pk}\right].$$

If for all PPT adversaries $\mathcal{A}$ we have that $\mathsf{Adv}_{\mathcal{A}}^{exc}(\kappa, N) \leq \mathsf{negl}(\kappa, N)$ then we say that the traceable ring signature scheme is exculpable.

Unforgeability comes directly from the properties of tag-linkability and exculpability, as the next theorem states.

Theorem 6. ([19]). *Assume that a traceable ring signature scheme is tag-linkable and exculpable, then it is unforgeable.*

---

[3] That is, at least one of the messages (M_1 or M_2) was not asked in a query to the oracle $Sign(\mathsf{sk}, \cdot)$.

3   A Code-Based Traceable Ring Signature Scheme

In this section we propose a new traceable ring signature scheme based on the
SD problem.

The scheme is presented in Algorithm 3. In a nutshell, the traceable ring
signature scheme is obtained by applying the Fiat-Shamir transform to the $\binom{N}{1}$-
GStern's protocol. To achieve traceability, we construct a set of random syn-
dromes $\mathbf{r}_1 \ldots, \mathbf{r}_N$ of a random matrix $\widetilde{\mathbf{H}}$ (generated via a cryptographic hash
function g and depending on the tag L), where one of the $\mathbf{r}_i$ is the syndrome of
the secret vector known by the actual signer. When signing two different messages with respect to the same tag, this syndrome will be the same in both
signatures and, thus, we can identify the signer of the message. To prevent the
signer from cheating when signing, we force it to generate the other syndromes
with another cryptographic hash function f in such a way that the verifier will
be able to check that these syndromes were honestly and randomly generated.

The new traceable ring signature scheme is presented in Algorithm 3. In
the following, let $\overline{\mathbf{pk}} = (\mathsf{pk}_1, \ldots, \mathsf{pk}_N)$ be the set of public keys of the users
$\mathcal{P}_1, \ldots, \mathcal{P}_N$ in the ring and $L = (issue, \overline{\mathbf{pk}})$ be a tag. Let $\overline{\mathbf{s}} = (\mathbf{s}_1, \ldots, \mathbf{s}_N)$,
$\overline{\mathbf{r}} = (\mathbf{r}_1, \ldots, \mathbf{r}_N)$ and $\mathbf{H}$ be a parity-check matrix of a random code.

Let $f, \tilde{f}, g$ and h be four different cryptographic hash functions (modeled as
random oracles). The function h is the one used in the $\binom{N}{1}$-GStern's protocol,
$\tilde{f}$ is the one used in the Fiat-Shamir transform, $g : \mathbb{Z}_2^* \to \mathbb{Z}_2^{(n-k) \times n}$ is used to
compute a matrix from the issue L and $f : \mathbb{Z}_2^* \to \mathbb{Z}_2^{n-k}$ is used to compute
random syndromes to allow traceability (as mentioned before). By $f^i(x)$ we
denote the function f applied i times on input x.

Note that, by Corollary 3, the probability that the prover cannot simulate
transcripts for the keys that it does not know is negligible since it can easily find
a solution $\mathbf{x} \in \mathbb{Z}_2^n$ for an equation of the type $\mathbf{H}\mathbf{x}^T - \mathbf{s}^T$ where $\mathbf{H} \in \mathbb{Z}_2^{(n-k) \times n}$
and $\mathbf{s} \in \mathbb{Z}_2^{n-k}$ (when $k = 3n/4$). Thus, Corollary 3 guarantees the correctness of
the protocol.

4   Security Analysis

In this section we give the security proofs for the proposed traceable ring signature scheme. Recall that unforgeability for the scheme follows from the tag-
linkability and exculpability properties. We begin by proving tag-linkability for
our scheme, but first we present two lemmas. Detailed proofs are in the full
version of this paper.

Lemma 7. *Given a valid signature* (L, M, σ)*, the probability that*

$$\left| \{ i \in \mathbb{N} : \exists \mathbf{e} \in \mathbb{Z}_2^n \quad w(\mathbf{e}) = t \wedge \mathbf{H}\mathbf{e}^T = \mathbf{s}_i^T \wedge \widetilde{\mathbf{H}}\mathbf{e}^T = \mathbf{r}_i^T \} \right| = 1$$

is $1 - \mathsf{negl}(n)$*.*

Algorithm 3. A new traceable ring signature scheme

---

1. **Parameters:** $n, k, t \in \mathbb{N}$ such that $k = 3n/4$, $\mathbf{H} \leftarrow_s \{0,1\}^{(n-k) \times n}$
2. **Key Generation:** Each user $\mathcal{P}_i$:
   - Chooses $\mathbf{e}_i \leftarrow_s \{0,1\}^n$ such that $w(\mathbf{e}_i) = t$
   - Computes $\mathbf{s}_i^T = \mathbf{H}\mathbf{e}_i^T$

     Public key of user $\mathcal{P}_i$: $\mathbf{H}, \mathbf{s}_i$

     Secret key of user $\mathcal{P}_i$: $\mathbf{e}_i$ such that $w(\mathbf{e}_i) = t$ and $\mathbf{H}\mathbf{e}_i^T = \mathbf{s}_i^T$
3. **Sign:** To sign message M, user $\mathcal{P}_i$:
   - Computes matrix $g(L) = \widetilde{\mathbf{H}}$ and $\widetilde{\mathbf{H}}\mathbf{e}_i^T = \mathbf{r}_i^T$;
   - Sets $A_0 = \mathbf{r}_i + f(M) + \cdots + f^i(M)$;
   - Compute $\mathbf{r}_j = A_0 + f(M) + f^2(M) + \cdots + f^j(M)$, for $j \neq i$;
   - Applies the Fiat-Shamir transform to $\binom{N}{1}$-GStern's protocol on input $(\mathbf{H}, \bar{\mathbf{s}}, \widetilde{\mathbf{H}}, \bar{\mathbf{r}})$ where $\bar{\mathbf{s}} = (\mathbf{s}_1, \ldots, \mathbf{s}_N)$ and $\bar{\mathbf{r}} = (\mathbf{r}_1, \ldots, \mathbf{r}_N)$:
     - Computes the commitments Com according to $\binom{N}{1}$-GStern's protocol;
     - Simulates the verifier's challenge as $Ch = \bar{f}(Com, M)$;
     - Computes the corresponding responses $Resp$ according to $\binom{N}{1}$-GStern's protocol;
     - Outputs the transcript $T = (Com, Ch, Resp)$.
   - Outputs the signature (L, M, σ) where $\sigma = (A_0, Com, Resp)$.
4. **Verify:** To verify, the verifier:
   - Computes $\mathbf{r}_j = A_0 + f(M) + f^2(M) + \cdots + f^j(M)$ for all $j \in \{1, \ldots, N\}$;
   - Computes $Ch = \bar{f}(Com, M)$;
   - Verifies that $T = (Com, Ch, Resp)$ is a valid transcript, according to $\binom{N}{1}$-GStern's protocol.
5. **Trace:** Given two signatures (L, M, σ) and (L, M', σ') where $\sigma = (A_0, Com, Resp)$ and $\sigma' = (A_0', Com', Resp')$ such that $Ver(L, M, \sigma) = 1$ and $Ver(L, M', \sigma') = 1$, the verifier:
   - Computes $\mathbf{r}_j = A_0 + f(M) + f^2(M) + \cdots + f^j(M)$ and $\mathbf{r}_j' = A_0' + f(M') + f^2(M') + \cdots + f^j(M')$ for all j;
   - Checks if $\mathbf{r}_j = \mathbf{r}_j'$. If this happens, it stores pk_j in a list $traceList$, which is initially empty, for all j;
   - Outputs the only $\mathsf{pk}_i \in traceList$ if $|traceList| = 1$; else if $traceList = \overline{\mathsf{pk}} = \{\mathsf{pk}_1, \ldots, \mathsf{pk}_N\}$ it outputs $linked$; else it outputs $indep$.

Lemma 8. *Given two valid signatures (L, M, σ) and (L, M', σ') such that they are independent (that is, $Trace(L, M, \sigma, M', \sigma') = indep$) the probability that $|traceList| > 1$ is $\mathsf{negl}(n)$.*

Theorem 9. (Tag-linkability). *The traceable ring signature scheme proposed is tag-linkable in the ROM.*

Before proving anonymity, note that, given an instance of the SD problem where we know the position of $t/2$ non-null coordinates of the error vector, this is still an instance of the SD problem, for an appropriate choice of parameters. So, it is still a hard problem to find the rest of the $t/2$ non-null positions of the error vector. We briefly sketch the reduction here: suppose that we have an algorithm $\mathcal{A}$ that solves the SD problem knowing $t/2$ positions of the error vector. The algorithm that breaks the SD problem receives as input $(\mathbf{H}, \mathbf{s}^T = \mathbf{H}\mathbf{e}^T, t/2)$.

Then it computes a new matrix $\mathbf{H}' = (\mathbf{H}|\mathbf{R})$ where $\mathbf{R} \leftarrow_{\$} \mathbb{Z}_2^{(n-k) \times t/2}$ and it computes the vector $\mathbf{s}' = \mathbf{s} + \mathbf{R}(1, \ldots 1)^T$ where $(1, \ldots, 1)$ has size $t/2$. Now we call the algorithm $\mathcal{A}$ on input $\mathbf{H}', \mathbf{s}', t/2$ and the last positions of the error vector. The reduction is obviously not tight. We take in account this fact when proposing parameters for the scheme.

We now turn our attention to the anonymity of the scheme. In order to prove anonymity for the proposed traceable ring signature scheme, we reduce a variant of the decision version of the GSD problem to the problem of breaking the anonymity of the scheme. This variant is the GSD problem when $t/2$ positions of the error vector are known. Note that this does not threat the security since, even when knowing half of the positions of the error vector, the GSD problem is still computationally hard.

We need to know $t/2$ positions of the error vector because of following technical reason: we know how the algorithm that breaks the anonymity behaves when it is given two valid public keys or when it is given two random values as public keys. However, we do not know how it behaves when it is given one valid public key and one random value as public key. More precisely, given a tuple $(\mathbf{H}, \mathbf{s}, \mathbf{G}, \mathbf{r}, t)$, we do not know if this represents a valid public key of the signature scheme or if it is a random tuple. However, if we know part of the secret, we are able to construct another tuple $(\mathbf{H}, \mathbf{s}', \mathbf{G}, \mathbf{r}', t)$ that is a GSD tuple, if $(\mathbf{H}, \mathbf{s}, \mathbf{G}, \mathbf{r}, t)$ is a GSD tuple, or that is a random tuple, otherwise.

Theorem 10. (Anonymity). *The traceable ring signature scheme proposed is anonymous in the ROM, given that the language*

$$GSD = \left\{ (\mathbf{H}, \mathbf{s}, \mathbf{G}, \mathbf{r}, t) : \exists \mathbf{e} \in \mathbb{Z}_2^n \quad w(\mathbf{e}) \leq t \wedge \mathbf{H}\mathbf{e}^T = \mathbf{s}^T \wedge \mathbf{G}\mathbf{e}^T = \mathbf{r}^T \right\}$$

is hard to decide knowing $t/2$ positions of the error.

Finally, we prove that our scheme is exculpable.

Theorem 11. (Exculpability). *The traceable ring signature scheme proposed is exculpable in the ROM and given that the GSD problem is hard.*

5   Parameters and Key Size

To conclude, we propose parameters for the scheme and analyze its signature and key size. For the cheating probability of GStern's protocol to be approximately 2^{-128}, it has to be iterated 220 times. Recall that anonymity for our traceable ring signature scheme is proven when knowing $t/2$ positions of the error vector. Hence, to yield the standard security of approximately 128 bits for signature schemes according to the generic decoding attack in [6], we consider a code with $n = 4150$, $k = 3n/4$ and $t = 132$ (similar to [12]). Note that a code with these parameters has a security of approximately 128 bits even when knowing $t/2$ positions of the error vector. This is necessary to maintain the anonymity of the scheme. Let N be the number of users in the ring.

Size of the Sigma Protocol. The $\binom{N}{1}$-GStern's protocol has approximately $8700N$ bits of exchange information in each round.

Signature Size. The signature size is approximately $240N$ kBytes. For example, for a ring with $N = 100$ users, the signature size is approximately 24 MBytes.

Public Key size. The public key is approximately $12918950 + 1037$ bits, which is linear in the number of users in the ring. For example, for a ring with $N = 100$ users, the public key has size approximately 1.6 MBytes.

6 Conclusion

Traceable ring signature schemes have a wide range of applications. Currently they are used in the implementation of Monero, one of the most famous cryptocurrencies, but they also have other applications, such as, in e-voting. However, the constructions for traceable ring signatures that exist in the literature are all based on the discrete logarithm problem and, thus, they can be broken using Shor's algorithm.

We proposed the first traceable ring signature whose security does not rely on the discrete logarithm problem, but rather on the SD problem, a problem that is conjectured to be unsolvable in polynomial time by any classical or quantum computer. Our construction is conjectured to be robust to quantum attacks. We proved the usual security properties for traceable ring signature schemes in the ROM.

However, the key and signature size of the protocol are too large for some applications. This is a common problem to all code-based cryptosystems. Finding new techniques to reduce the key and the signature size of code-based signature schemes is an obvious direction for future work.

We also leave as an open question to prove the security of the protocol in the Quantum Random Oracle Model (QROM) [9], where the parties can query random oracles in superposition. Note that our proofs do not apply to the quantum setup. For example, observe that the proof of exculpability uses a rewind technique and the problem of quantum rewind is more subtle than in the classical setup [4]. Also, Unruh [25] proved that the Fiat-Shamir transform can be applied to obtain secure signature schemes in the QROM, under certain conditions. However these results are not known to hold for the case of ring signatures constructed using the Fiat-Shamir transform.

Acknowledgments. The first author would like to thank the support from DP-PMI and FCT (Portugal) through the grant PD/BD/135181/2017.

This work is funded by FCT/MEC through national funds and when applicable co-funded by FEDER – PT2020 partnership agreement under the project UID/EEA/50008/2013, and IT internal project QBigData, FCT through national funds, by FEDER, through COMPETE 2020, and by Regional Operational Program of Lisbon, under projects Confident PTDC/EEI-CTP/4503/2014, QuantumMining POCI-01-0145-FEDER-031826 and Predict PTDC/CCI-CIF/ 29877/2017. It was funded by European project H2020-SU-ICT-2018-2020.

A   Sigma Protocols

A.1   Fiat-Shamir Transform

A sigma protocol $(\mathcal{P}, \mathcal{V})$ is a three-round protocol between a prover $\mathcal{P}$ and a verifier $\mathcal{V}$ where the prover tries to convince the verifier about the validity of some statement. In this work, we are only interested in a particular case of sigma protocols which are proof of knowledge (PoK) protocols. Here, the prover $\mathcal{P}$ convinces the verifier $\mathcal{V}$, not only about the veracity of the statement, but also that $\mathcal{P}$ has a witness for it. The three rounds of any sigma protocol are the commitment (com) by the prover, the challenge (ch) by the verifier and the response $(resp)$ by the prover. A transcript $(com, ch, resp)$ is said to be valid if the verifier accepts it as a valid proof.

A PoK must have the following properties: (i) completeness, which ensures that the verifier will accept the proof with high probability if the prover has the secret; (ii) special soundness, which ensures that there is an extractor such that, given two valid transcripts $(com, ch, resp)$ and $(com, ch', resp')$ where $ch \neq ch'$, then it can extract the secret; and (iii) honest-verifier zero-knowledge (HVZK) which ensures that no information is gained by the verifier just by looking at the transcript. This is usually proven by showing the existence of a simulator that can generate transcripts that are computationally indistinguishable from transcripts generated by the interaction between the prover and the verifier. A detailed survey on sigma protocols can be found in [15].

The Fiat-Shamir transform [17] is a generic method to convert any PoK protocol that is complete, special sound and HVZK into a signature scheme. The security of the Fiat-Shamir transform is proven to be secure both in the random oracle model (ROM) [1] and in the quantum random oracle model (QROM) [25], under certain conditions.

The idea behind the Fiat-Shamir transform is that the prover simulates the challenge that is usually sent by the verifier. Since this challenge should be chosen uniformly at random, the prover sets the challenge according to a cryptographic hash function receiving as input the message to be signed and the commitment chosen previously by the prover. More precisely, given a proof of knowledge $(\mathcal{P}, \mathcal{V})$, the prover computes com, then it sets $ch = \bar{f}(com, M)$ where $\bar{f}$ is a cryptographic hash function and M is the message to be signed. Finally, it computes $resp$ such that $(com, ch, resp)$ is a valid transcript. The signature of M is $(com, resp)$. To verify the validity of the signature, one just has to compute $ch = \bar{f}(com, M)$ and check that $(com, ch, resp)$ is a valid transcript.

A.2   CDS Construction

The Cramer-Damgård-Shoenmakers (CDS) construction [14] is a generic way to construct a proof of knowledge $(\mathcal{P}^*, \mathcal{V}^*)$ where the prover proves knowledge of the solution to some subset of instances of a problem, given any PoK protocol $(\mathcal{P}, \mathcal{V})$ and a secret sharing scheme $\mathcal{SS}$.

Given N instances of a problem, let A be the set of indexes for which the prover $\mathcal{P}^*$ knows the solution. The idea behind the CDS construction is that the new prover $\mathcal{P}^*$ simulates transcripts $(com_j, ch_j, resp_j)$ for the instances it does not know the solution, that is, for $j \notin A$. For the instances that it knows the secret, it computes the commitment com_i, for $i \in A$, following the protocol $(\mathcal{P}, \mathcal{V})$. After receiving the commitments for all instances, the verifier sends a random bit string b to the prover. The string b will be interpreted as the secret in SS and the challenges ch_j, for $j \notin A$, as shares such that they form an unqualified set. Now, this set of shares can be extended to a qualified set by choosing properly the challenges ch_i, for $i \in A$. The prover then computes valid transcripts $(com_i, ch_i, resp_i)$ for $i \in A$. It can do this because it has witnesses for these instances. Finally, the prover $\mathcal{P}^*$ sends the transcripts $(com_i, ch_i, resp_i)$ for all i to the verifier. The verifier can check that these are valid transcripts and that the shares ch_i constitute a qualified set for SS.

A.3   Stern's Protocol

Stern's protocol [24] is a protocol in which, given a matrix $\mathbf{H}$ and a syndrome vector $\mathbf{s}$, a prover proves the knowledge of an error vector $\mathbf{e}$ with $w(\mathbf{e}) = t$ and syndrome $\mathbf{s}$. The protocol is presented in Algorithm 4. Here, h denotes a cryptographic hash function.

Algorithm 4. Stern's protocol

1. **Public information:** $\mathbf{H} \in \mathbb{Z}_2^{n \times (n-k)}$ and $\mathbf{s} \in \mathbb{Z}_2^{n-k}$
2. **Secret information:** $\mathbf{e} \in \mathbb{Z}_2^n$ such that $\mathbf{He}^T = \mathbf{s}^T$ and $w(\mathbf{e}) = t$.
3. **Prover's commitment:**
   - $\mathcal{P}$ chooses $\mathbf{y} \leftarrow_{\$} \mathbb{Z}_2^n$ and a permutation δ;
   - $\mathcal{P}$ computes $c_1 = h(\delta, \mathbf{Hy}^T)$, $c_2 = h(\delta(\mathbf{y}))$ and $c_3 = h(\delta(\mathbf{y} + \mathbf{e}))$;
   - $\mathcal{P}$ sends c_1, c_2 and c_3.
4. **Verifier's challenge:** $\mathcal{V}$ sends $b \leftarrow_{\$} \{0, 1, 2\}$.
4. **Prover's answer:**
   - If $b = 0$, $\mathcal{P}$ reveals $\mathbf{y}$ and δ;
   - If $b = 1$, $\mathcal{P}$ reveals $\mathbf{y} + \mathbf{e}$ and δ;
   - If $b = 2$, $\mathcal{P}$ reveals $\delta(\mathbf{y})$ and $\delta(\mathbf{e})$.
6. **Verifier's verification:**
   - If $b = 0$, $\mathcal{V}$ checks if $h(\delta, \mathbf{Hy}^T) = c_1$ and $h(\delta(\mathbf{y})) = c_2$;
   - If $b = 1$, $\mathcal{V}$ checks if $h(\delta, \mathbf{H}(\mathbf{y} + \mathbf{e})^T + \mathbf{s}^T) = c_1$ and $h(\delta(\mathbf{y} + \mathbf{e})) = c_3$;
   - If $b = 2$, $\mathcal{V}$ checks if $h(\delta(\mathbf{y})) = c_2$, $h(\delta(\mathbf{y}) + \delta(\mathbf{e})) = c_3$ and $w(\delta(\mathbf{e})) = t$.

The security of Stern's protocol is based on the hardness of the SD problem. The protocol has been proven to be complete, special sound and HVZK and, furthermore, has a cheating probability of $2/3$ [24].

B   Auxiliary Results

B.1   Proof of Lemma 2

The probability of existing a vector $\mathbf{x}$ such that $\mathbf{Hx}^T = \mathbf{s}^T$ is the probability of $\mathbf{H}$ being a matrix representing a surjective application, i.e., it is the probability of $\mathbf{H}$ being a full rank matrix. Hence, we have to compute the probability of choosing k' linearly independent vectors of size n to form the rows of $\mathbf{H}$. We have

$$\Pr\left[\exists \mathbf{x} \in \mathbb{Z}_2^n : \mathbf{Hx}^T = \mathbf{s}^T\right] = \frac{(2^n - 1)(2^n - 2)\dots(2^n - 2^{k'})}{2^{k'n}}.$$

Since $(2^n - 1) \geq (2^n - 2^{k'})$, $(2^n - 2) \geq (2^n - 2^{k'})$ and $(2^n - 2^{k'-1}) \geq (2^n - 2^{k'})$, we have that

$$\frac{(2^n - 1)(2^n - 2)(2^n - 4)\dots(2^n - 2^{k'})}{2^{k'n}} \geq \frac{\left(2^n - 2^{k'}\right)^{k'+1}}{2^{k'n}} \geq \frac{\left(2^n - 2^{k'}\right)^{k'}}{2^{k'n}}.$$

Now, note that

$$\frac{\left(2^n - 2^{k'}\right)^{k'}}{2^{k'n}} = \frac{\left(2^n(1 - 2^{k'-n})\right)^{k'}}{2^{k'n}} = \left(1 - \frac{1}{2^{n-k'}}\right)^{k'}.$$

So, it remains to show that

$$\left(1 - 1/2^{n-k'}\right)^{k'} = 1 - \mathsf{negl}(n)$$

for $k' \leq n/2$. Note that the expression decreases with k' and so it is enough to show for $k' = n/2$.

Expanding the expression on the left using the Binomial theorem we get

$$\left(1 - \frac{1}{2^{n/2}}\right)^{n/2} = \sum_{i=0}^{n/2} \binom{n/2}{i}\left(-\frac{1}{2^{n/2}}\right)^i.$$

When $i = 0$ we have

$$\binom{n/2}{i}\left(-\frac{1}{2^{n/2}}\right)^i = 1.$$

The expression is maximal when $i = n/4$. Hence, if we show that

$$\binom{n/2}{i}\left(-\frac{1}{2^{n/2}}\right)^i = \mathsf{negl}(n)$$

when $i = n/4$, then

$$\sum_{i=0}^{n/2} \binom{n/2}{i}\left(-\frac{1}{2^{n/2}}\right)^i = 1 + \sum_{i=1}^{n/2} \binom{n/2}{i}\left(-\frac{1}{2^{n/2}}\right)^i = 1 - \mathsf{negl}(n).$$

In fact, it can be proved using Stirling approximation (which is tight) for $n!$ that

$$\lim_{n \to \infty} n^b \binom{n/2}{n/4} \left(-\frac{1}{2^{n/2}} \right)^{n/4} = 0$$

for any $b \in \mathbb{N}$. Hence, we have shown that the expression $\binom{n/2}{n/4} \left(-\frac{1}{2^{n/2}} \right)^{n/4}$ goes to zero faster than any function of the form $1/n^b$, for any $b \in \mathbb{N}$. Thus, the expression is negligible in n and the result follows.   □

References

1. Abdalla, M., An, J.H., Bellare, M., Namprempre, C.: From identification to signatures via the Fiat-Shamir transform: minimizing assumptions for security and forward-security. In: Knudsen, L.R. (ed.) EUROCRYPT 2002. LNCS, vol. 2332, pp. 418–433. Springer, Heidelberg (2002). https://doi.org/10.1007/3-540-46035-7_28

2. Alamélou, Q., Blazy, O., Cauchie, S., Gaborit, P.: A practical group signature scheme based on rank metric. In: Duquesne, S., Petkova-Nikova, S. (eds.) WAIFI 2016. LNCS, vol. 10064, pp. 258–275. Springer, Cham (2016). https://doi.org/10.1007/978-3-319-55227-9_18

3. Alamélou, Q., Blazy, O., Cauchie, S., Gaborit, P.: A code-based group signature scheme. Designs Codes Crypt. **82**(1), 469–493 (2017). https://doi.org/10.1007/s10623-016-0276-6

4. Ambainis, A., Rosmanis, A., Unruh, D.: Quantum attacks on classical proof systems: the hardness of quantum rewinding. In: Proceedings of the 2014 IEEE 55th Annual Symposium on Foundations of Computer Science FOCS 2014, pp. 474–483. IEEE Computer Society, Washington, DC, USA (2014). https://doi.org/10.1109/FOCS.2014.57

5. Au, M.H., Liu, J.K., Susilo, W., Yuen, T.H.: Secure ID-based linkable and revocable-iff-linked ring signature with constant-size construction. Theor. Comput. Sci. **469**, 1–14 (2013). http://www.sciencedirect.com/science/article/pii/S0304397512009528

6. Becker, A., Joux, A., May, A., Meurer, A.: Decoding random binary linear codes in $2^{n/20}$: How $1 + 1 = 0$ improves information set decoding. In: Pointcheval, D., Johansson, T. (eds.) EUROCRYPT 2012. LNCS, vol. 7237, pp. 520–536. Springer, Heidelberg (2012). https://doi.org/10.1007/978-3-642-29011-4_31

7. Berlekamp, E.R., McEliece, R.J., van Tilborg, H.: On the inherent intractability of certain coding problems. IEEE Trans. Inf. Theory (corresp.) **24**(3), 384–386 (1978)

8. Bernstein, D.J.: Grover vs. mceliece. In: Sendrier, N. (ed.) PQCrypto 2010. LNCS, vol. 6061, pp. 73–80. Springer, Heidelberg (2010). https://doi.org/10.1007/978-3-642-12929-2_6

9. Boneh, D., Dagdelen, Ö., Fischlin, M., Lehmann, A., Schaffner, C., Zhandry, M.: Random oracles in a quantum world. In: Lee, D.H., Wang, X. (eds.) ASIACRYPT 2011. LNCS, vol. 7073, pp. 41–69. Springer, Heidelberg (2011). https://doi.org/10.1007/978-3-642-25385-0_3

10. Branco, P., Mateus, P.: A code-based linkable ring signature scheme. In: Baek, J., Susilo, W., Kim, J. (eds.) ProvSec 2018. LNCS, vol. 11192, pp. 203–219. Springer, Cham (2018). https://doi.org/10.1007/978-3-030-01446-9_12

11. Canteaut, A., Chabaud, F.: A new algorithm for finding minimum-weight words in a linear code: application to McEliece's cryptosystem and to narrow-sense bch codes of length 511. IEEE Trans. Inf. Theory **44**(1), 367–378 (1998)
12. Canto Torres, R., Sendrier, N.: Analysis of information set decoding for a sub-linear error weight. In: Takagi, T. (ed.) PQCrypto 2016. LNCS, vol. 9606, pp. 144–161. Springer, Cham (2016). https://doi.org/10.1007/978-3-319-29360-8_10
13. Chaum, D., van Heyst, E.: Group signatures. In: Davies, D.W. (ed.) EUROCRYPT 1991. LNCS, vol. 547, pp. 257–265. Springer, Heidelberg (1991). https://doi.org/10.1007/3-540-46416-6_22
14. Cramer, R., Damgård, I., Schoenmakers, B.: Proofs of partial knowledge and simplified design of witness hiding protocols. In: Desmedt, Y.G. (ed.) CRYPTO 1994. LNCS, vol. 839, pp. 174–187. Springer, Heidelberg (1994). https://doi.org/10.1007/3-540-48658-5_19
15. Damgård, I.: On σ-protocols. Lecture Notes, University of Aarhus, Department for Computer Science (2002)
16. Ezerman, M.F., Lee, H.T., Ling, S., Nguyen, K., Wang, H.: A provably secure group signature scheme from code-based assumptions. In: Iwata, T., Cheon, J.H. (eds.) ASIACRYPT 2015. LNCS, vol. 9452, pp. 260–285. Springer, Heidelberg (2015). https://doi.org/10.1007/978-3-662-48797-6_12
17. Fiat, A., Shamir, A.: How to prove yourself: practical solutions to identification and signature problems. In: Odlyzko, A.M. (ed.) CRYPTO 1986. LNCS, vol. 263, pp. 186–194. Springer, Heidelberg (1987). https://doi.org/10.1007/3-540-47721-7_12
18. Fujisaki, E.: Sub-linear size traceable ring signatures without random oracles. In: Kiayias, A. (ed.) CT-RSA 2011. LNCS, vol. 6558, pp. 393–415. Springer, Heidelberg (2011). https://doi.org/10.1007/978-3-642-19074-2_25
19. Fujisaki, E., Suzuki, K.: Traceable ring signature. In: Okamoto, T., Wang, X. (eds.) PKC 2007. LNCS, vol. 4450, pp. 181–200. Springer, Heidelberg (2007). https://doi.org/10.1007/978-3-540-71677-8_13
20. Liu, J.K., Wei, V.K., Wong, D.S.: Linkable spontaneous anonymous group signature for ad hoc groups. In: Wang, H., Pieprzyk, J., Varadharajan, V. (eds.) ACISP 2004. LNCS, vol. 3108, pp. 325–335. Springer, Heidelberg (2004). https://doi.org/10.1007/978-3-540-27800-9_28
21. May, A., Meurer, A., Thomae, E.: Decoding random linear codes in $\tilde{O}(2^{0.054n})$. In: Lee, D.H., Wang, X. (eds.) ASIACRYPT 2011. LNCS, vol. 7073, pp. 107–124. Springer, Heidelberg (2011). https://doi.org/10.1007/978-3-642-25385-0_6
22. Rivest, R.L., Shamir, A., Tauman, Y.: How to leak a secret. In: Boyd, C. (ed.) ASIACRYPT 2001. LNCS, vol. 2248, pp. 552–565. Springer, Heidelberg (2001). https://doi.org/10.1007/3-540-45682-1_32
23. Shor, P.W.: Polynomial-time algorithms for prime factorization and discrete logarithms on a quantum computer. SIAM J. Comput. **26**(5), 1484–1509 (1997). https://doi.org/10.1137/S0097539795293172
24. Stern, J.: A new identification scheme based on syndrome decoding. In: Stinson, D.R. (ed.) CRYPTO 1993. LNCS, vol. 773, pp. 13–21. Springer, Heidelberg (1994). https://doi.org/10.1007/3-540-48329-2_2
25. Unruh, D.: Post-quantum security of Fiat-Shamir. In: Takagi, T., Peyrin, T. (eds.) ASIACRYPT 2017. LNCS, vol. 10624, pp. 65–95. Springer, Cham (2017). https://doi.org/10.1007/978-3-319-70694-8_3
26. Van Saberhagen, N.: CryptoNote v 2.0 (2013)

On the Decoding Failure Rate
of QC-MDPC Bit-Flipping Decoders

Nicolas Sendrier[1] and Valentin Vasseur[1,2(✉)]

[1] Inria, Paris, France
{Nicolas.Sendrier,Valentin.Vasseur}@inria.fr
[2] Université Paris Descartes, Sorbonne Paris Cité, Paris, France

Abstract. Quasi-cyclic moderate density parity check codes [1] allow the design of McEliece-like public-key encryption schemes with compact keys and a security that provably reduces to hard decoding problems for quasi-cyclic codes.

In particular, QC-MDPC are among the most promising code-based key encapsulation mechanisms (KEM) that are proposed to the NIST call for standardization of quantum safe cryptography (two proposals, BIKE and QC-MDPC KEM).

The first generation of decoding algorithms suffers from a small, but not negligible, decoding failure rate (DFR in the order of 10^{-7} to 10^{-10}). This allows a key recovery attack that exploits a small correlation between the faulty message patterns and the secret key of the scheme [2], and limits the usage of the scheme to KEMs using ephemeral public keys. It does not impact the interactive establishment of secure communications (*e.g.* TLS), but the use of static public keys for asynchronous applications (*e.g.* email) is rendered dangerous.

Understanding and improving the decoding of QCMDPC is thus of interest for cryptographic applications. In particular, finding parameters for which the failure rate is provably negligible (typically as low as 2^{-64} or 2^{-128}) would allow static keys and increase the applicability of the mentioned cryptosystems.

We study here a simple variant of bit-flipping decoding, which we call step-by-step decoding. It has a higher DFR but its evolution can be modelled by a Markov chain, within the theoretical framework of [3]. We study two other, more efficient, decoders. One is the textbook algorithm implemented as in [3]. The other is (close to) the BIKE decoder. For all those algorithms we provide simulation results, and, assuming an evolution similar to the step-by-step decoder, we extrapolate the value of the DFR as a function of the block length. This will give an indication of how much the code parameters must be increased to ensure resistance to the GJS attack.

© Springer Nature Switzerland AG 2019
J. Ding and R. Steinwandt (Eds.): PQCrypto 2019, LNCS 11505, pp. 404–416, 2019.
https://doi.org/10.1007/978-3-030-25510-7_22

1   Introduction

Moderate Density Parity Check (MDPC) codes were introduced for cryptography[1] in [1]. They are related to Low Density Parity Check (LDPC) codes, but instead of admitting a sparse parity check matrix (with rows of small constant weight) they admit a somewhat sparse parity check matrix, typically with rows of Hamming weight $O(\sqrt{n})$ and length n. Together with a quasi-cyclic structure they allow the design of a McEliece-like public-key encryption scheme [4] with reasonable key size and a security that provably reduces to generic hard problems over quasi-cyclic codes, namely the hardness of decoding and the hardness of finding low weight codewords.

Because of these features, QC-MDPC have attracted a lot of interest from the cryptographic community. In particular, two key exchange mechanisms "BIKE" and "QC-MDPC KEM" were recently proposed to the NIST call for standardization of quantum safe cryptography[2].

The decoding of MDPC codes can be achieved, as for LDPC codes, with iterative decoders [5] and in particular with the (hard decision) bit flipping algorithm, which we consider here. Using soft decision decoding would improve performance [6], but would also increase the complexity and make the scheme less suitable for hardware and embedded device implementations, which is one of its interesting features [7]. There are several motivations for studying MDPC decoding. First, since QC-MDPC based cryptographic primitives may become a standard, it is worth understanding and improving their engineering and in particular the decoding algorithm, which is the bottleneck of their implementation. The other motivation is security. A correlation was established by Guo, Johansson and Stankovski in [2] between error patterns leading to a decoding failure and the secret key of the scheme: the sparse parity check matrix of a QC-MDPC code. This GJS attack allows the recovery of the secret by making millions of queries to a decryption oracle. To overcome the GJS attack, one must find instances of the scheme for which the Decoding Failure Rate (DFR) is negligible. This is certainly possible by improving the algorithm and/or increasing the code parameters, but the difficulty is not only to achieve a negligible DFR (a conservative target is a failure rate of the same order as the security requirements, that is typically 2^{-128}) but to prove, as formally as possible, that it is negligible when the numbers we consider are out of reach by simulation.

In this work, we recall the context and the state-of-the-art in Sect. 2, mostly results of [3] as well as some new properties. In Sect. 3 we describe a new decoder, the step-by-step bit flipping algorithm, and its probabilistic model. This algorithm is less efficient than the existing techniques, but, thanks to the model, its DFR can be estimated. Finally in Sect. 4 we compare the DFR prediction of our model with the DFR obtained with simulations. We compare this with

---

[1] MDPC were previously defined, in a different context, by Ouzan and Be'ery in 2009, http://arxiv.org/abs/0911.3262.
[2] https://csrc.nist.gov/Projects/Post-Quantum-Cryptography.

BIKE decoder simulation and try to extrapolate its behavior even when the DFR cannot be obtained by simulation.

Notation

- Throughout the paper, the matrix $\mathbf{H} \in \{0,1\}^{r \times n}$ will denote the sparse parity check matrix of a binary MDPC code of length n and dimension $k = n - r$. The rows of $\mathbf{H}$, the parity check equations, have a weight $w = O(\sqrt{n})$, and are denoted eq_i, $0 \le i < r$. The columns of $\mathbf{H}$, transposed to become row vectors, are denoted h_j, $0 \le j < n$.
- For any binary vector v, we denote v_i its i-th coordinate and $|v|$ its Hamming weight. Moreover, we will identify v with its support, that is $i \in v$ if and only if $v_i = 1$.
- Given two binary vectors u and v of same length, we will denote $u \cap v$ the set of all indices that belong to both u and v, or equivalently their component-wise product.
- The scalar product of u and v is denoted $\langle u, v \rangle \in \{0, 1\}$.
- For a random variable X we write $X \sim \text{Bin}(n, p)$ when X follows a binomial distribution:
$$\Pr[X = k] = f_{n,p}(k) = \binom{n}{k} p^k (1-p)^{n-k}.$$

- In a finite state machine, the event of going from a state S to a state T in at most I iterations is denoted:
$$S \xrightarrow{I} T.$$

2   Bit Flipping Decoding

The bit flipping algorithm takes as argument a (sparse) parity check matrix $\mathbf{H} \in \{0,1\}^{r \times n}$ and a noisy codeword $y \in \{0,1\}^n$. It flips a position if the proportion of unsatisfied equations containing that position is above some threshold. A parity check equation eq_i is unsatisfied if the scalar product $\langle eq_i, y \rangle = 1$. The proportion of unsatisfied equations involving j is $|s \cap h_j| / |h_j|$, where $s = y\mathbf{H}^T$ denotes the syndrome. In practice (see [1]), the bit flipping decoder of Algorithm 1 is parallel: the syndrome is updated after all tests and flips. The choice of a particular threshold τ depends on the context, that is $\mathbf{H}$, y, and possibly anything the algorithm can observe or compute. With an appropriate choice of threshold and assuming that $\mathbf{H}$ is sparse enough and y close enough to the code, the algorithm terminates with high probability.

2.1   QC-MDPC-McEliece

Bit flipping decoding applies in particular to quasi-cyclic moderate density parity check (QC-MDPC) codes which can be used in a McEliece-like encryption scheme [1]. In the cryptographic context, those codes are often of rate 1/2, length n, dimension $k = n/2$ (codimension $r = n/2$). The parity-check matrix has row

---

Algorithm 1. The Bit Flipping Algorithm

Require: $\mathbf{H} \in \{0,1\}^{(n-k) \times n}$, $y \in \{0,1\}^n$
  while $y\mathbf{H}^T \neq 0$ **do**
    $s \leftarrow y\mathbf{H}^T$
    $\tau \leftarrow$ threshold(*context*)
    for $j \in \{0, \dots, n-1\}$ **do**
      if $|s \cap h_j| \geq \tau |h_j|$ **then**
        $y_j \leftarrow 1 - y_j$
  return y

---

weight $w = O(\sqrt{n})$ and is regular (all columns have the same weight $d = w/2$). The bit flipping decoding corrects $t = O(\sqrt{n})$ errors. Parameters n, r, w, t must be fine-tuned so that the cryptosystem is secure and the decoding failure rate (DFR) low. The implementation of Algorithm 1 for QC-MDPC was considered in several works. Different strategies have been considered so far to choose a good threshold: relying on the value of $\max_j(|s \cap h_j| / |h_j|)$ [1], using fixed values [8] or using the syndrome weight [3,9]. The last two strategies require, for each set of parameters, a precomputation based on simulation to extract the proper threshold selection rule. For the parameters of Table 1 those algorithms typically require less than 10 iterations for a DFR that does not exceed 10^{-7}. Table 1 gives the sets of parameters of the BIKE proposal [10] to NIST. The bit flipping decoder of BIKE is slightly more elaborated. Its DFR appears to be below 10^{-10} but this is unfortunately difficult to establish from mere simulations.

Table 1. BIKE parameters (security against classical adversary)

n	r	w	t	Security
20 326	10 163	142	134	128
39 706	19 853	206	199	192
65 498	32 749	274	264	256

2.2 A Key Recovery Attack

In a recent work, Guo, Johansson, and Stankovski (GJS) [2] were able to exhibit a correlation between faulty error patterns and the secret key of the scheme (the sparse parity check matrix of the QC-MDPC code). An attacker that has access to a decryption oracle for a given secret key, may perform a key recovery attack by collecting and analyzing thousands (at least) of error patterns leading to a failure. This limits the cryptographic usage of QC-MDPC to key encapsulation mechanisms with ephemeral key. To safely extend the usage of the scheme to static keys (allowing one-pass asynchronous key exchange, for instance for email), one needs to lower the failure rate to something negligible. Depending on the adversarial model the DFR could be a small constant, like 2^{-64}, or even—considering the error-amplification method from [11]—a value which decreases exponentially with the security claim (typically $2^{-\lambda}$ for λ bits of security).

2.3 Bit Flipping Identities

More details about this section can be found in [3, part III]. We assume that the MDPC code is quasi-cyclic and regular. That means that in the parity check matrix $\mathbf{H} \in \{0,1\}^{r \times n}$, every row has the same weight w and every column has the same weight d. If $r = n/2$, which is the most common situation in cryptographic applications, then we have $w = 2d$.

We consider an instance of the decoding algorithm, the noisy codeword is denoted y and is at distance $t = O(\sqrt{n})$ of the code. With probability overwhelmingly close to 1, the corresponding error e is unique. Its syndrome is $\mathbf{s} = \mathbf{y}\mathbf{H}^T = \mathbf{e}\mathbf{H}^T$.

Definition 1. *For a parity matrix* $\mathbf{H}$ *and an error vector* e, *the number of unsatisfied parity check equations involving the position* j *is* $\sigma_j(\mathbf{e}, \mathbf{H}) = |\mathbf{h}_j \cap \mathbf{e}\mathbf{H}^T|$. *We call this quantity a* counter. *The number of equations affected by exactly* ℓ *errors is*

$$E_\ell(\mathbf{e}, \mathbf{H}) = \left|\left\{i \in \{0, \dots, r-1\}: \; |\mathrm{eq}_i \cap \mathbf{e}| = \ell\right\}\right|.$$

The quantities e and $\mathbf{H}$ are usually clear from the context. We will omit them and simply write σ_j and E_ℓ.

Proposition 1. *The following identities are verified for all* e *and all* $\mathbf{H}$:

$$\sum_{\ell \text{ odd}} E_\ell = \left|\mathbf{e}\mathbf{H}^T\right|, \qquad \sum_j \sigma_j = w\left|\mathbf{e}\mathbf{H}^T\right|, \qquad \sum_{j \in \mathbf{e}} \sigma_j = \sum_{\ell \text{ odd}} \ell E_\ell.$$

The Counter Distributions. If e is distributed uniformly among the words of weight t, we have $\sigma_j \sim \mathrm{Bin}(d, \pi_{e_j})$ with

$$\pi_1 = \sum_{\ell \text{ even}} \frac{\binom{w-1}{\ell}\binom{n-w}{t-1-\ell}}{\binom{n-1}{t-1}}, \text{ and } \pi_0 = \sum_{\ell \text{ odd}} \frac{\binom{w-1}{\ell}\binom{n-w}{t-\ell}}{\binom{n-1}{t}}. \qquad (1)$$

The above distribution is valid on average. However, the following facts are remarked in [3].

1. It does not accurately predict the counter values for an individual value of e. In fact, the counters tend to grow with the syndrome weight.
2. Even if the initial error pattern is uniformly distributed (of fixed weight), this is no longer true after the first iteration and the deviation from (1) is significant.

Conditioning the Counter Distributions with the Syndrome Weight. We denote $t = |\mathbf{e}|$ and $S = |\mathbf{eH}^T|$ the syndrome weight. A better model for σ_j is given by the distribution $\mathrm{Bin}(d, \pi'_{e_j})$ where (see [3])

$$\pi'_1 = \frac{S+X}{dt}, \pi'_0 = \frac{(w-1)S - X}{d(n-t)} \text{ with } X = \sum_{\ell \text{ odd}} (\ell - 1)E_\ell. \tag{2}$$

The above formulas depends on the codes parameters n, w, d, on the error weight $t = |\mathbf{e}|$, on the syndrome weight $S = |\mathbf{eH}^T|$ but also on the quantity $X = \sum_{\ell > 0} 2\ell E_{2\ell+1}$. Here, we wish to obtain an accurate model for the counter distribution which only depends on S and t. We must somehow get rid of X. In practice $X = 2E_3 + 4E_5 + \cdots$ is not dominant in the above formula (for relevant QC-MDPC parameters) and we will replace it by its expected value.

Proposition 2. *When* $\mathbf{e}$ *is chosen uniformly at random of weight* t *the expected value of* $X = \sum_{\ell > 0} 2\ell E_{2\ell+1}$ *given that* $S = |\mathbf{eH}^T|$ *is,*

$$\overline{X}(S, t) = \frac{S \sum_\ell 2\ell \rho_{2\ell+1}}{\sum_\ell \rho_{2\ell+1}} \text{ where } \rho_\ell = \frac{\binom{w}{\ell}\binom{n-w}{t-\ell}}{\binom{n}{t}}.$$

Remarks.

- The counter distributions above are extremely close to the observations when the error pattern $\mathbf{e}$ is uniformly distributed of fixed weight.
- The model gradually degenerates as the number of iterations grows, but remains relatively accurate in the first few iterations of Algorithm 1, that is even when $\mathbf{e}$ is not uniformly distributed.

2.4 Adaptive Threshold

Within this model, a good threshold for Algorithm 1 is $\tau = T/d$ where T is the smallest integer such that (recall that $f_{d,\pi}$ is defined in the notation)

$$t f_{d, \pi'_1}(T) \geq (n - t) f_{d, \pi'_0}(T).$$

We will use this threshold selection rule in the sequel of the paper. Note that it is very consistent with the thresholds that were empirically determined in [9] to optimize Algorithm 1.

2.5 Estimating the Syndrome Weight

The probability for a parity equation eq of weight w to be unsatisfied when the error $\mathbf{e}$ is distributed uniformly of weight t is equal to

$$\bar{\rho} = \sum_{\ell \text{ odd}} \Pr[|\mathrm{eq} \cap \mathbf{e}| = \ell] = \sum_{\ell \text{ odd}} \frac{\binom{w}{\ell}\binom{n-w}{t-\ell}}{\binom{n}{t}} = \sum_{\ell \text{ odd}} \rho_\ell$$

The syndrome weight $S = |\mathbf{e}\mathbf{H}^T|$ is equal to the number of unsatisfied equations and thus its expectation in $\bar{p}r$. For a row-regular[3] MDPC code the syndrome weight follows the binomial distribution $\mathrm{Bin}(r, \bar{p})$. However, it was remarked in [3] that for a regular MDPC code, there was a dependence between equations and the syndrome weight followed a different distribution.

In the following proposition we give the distribution of the syndrome weight when the error is uniformly distributed of weight t and the matrix $\mathbf{H}$ is regular.

Proposition 3. *Let $\mathbf{H}$ be a binary $r \times n$ row-regular matrix of row weight w. When the error $\mathbf{e}$ is uniformly distributed of weight t, the syndrome weight $S = |\mathbf{e}\mathbf{H}^T|$ follows the distribution*

$$\Pr[S = \ell] = f_{r,\bar{p}}(\ell)$$

and if $\mathbf{H}$ is regular of column weight d, we have

$$P_\ell(t) = \Pr[S = \ell \mid \mathbf{H} \text{ is regular}] = \frac{f_{r,\bar{p}}(\ell)h(\ell)}{\sum_{k \in \{0,\dots,r\}} f_{r,\bar{p}}(k)h(k)} \tag{3}$$

where for $\ell \in \{0,\dots,r\}$ (is the discrete convolution operation and $*^n$ is the n-fold iteration of the convolution with itself)*

$$h(\ell) = g_1^{*\ell} * g_0^{*(r-\ell)}(dt)$$

with, for $k \in \{0,\dots,w\}$,

$$g_1(k) = \begin{cases} \frac{\binom{w}{k}\binom{n-w}{t-k}}{\binom{n}{t}}\frac{1}{\bar{p}} & \text{if } k \text{ is odd} \\ 0 & \text{otherwise} \end{cases} \quad ; \quad g_0(k) = \begin{cases} \frac{\binom{w}{k}\binom{n-w}{t-k}}{\binom{n}{t}}\frac{1}{1-\bar{p}} & \text{if } k \text{ is even} \\ 0 & \text{otherwise} \end{cases} .$$

The above distribution takes into account the regularity but not the quasi-cyclicity. Nevertheless, experimental observation shows that it is accurate for quasi-cyclic matrices, at least in the range useful for QC-MDPC codes.

3   Step-by-Step Decoding

In Algorithm 1 the positions with a counter value above the threshold are flipped all at once. In Algorithm 2 only one position is flipped at a time. The benefit, in contrast to algorithm 1, is that we can predict the evolution of the decoder. For example, when position j with counter σ_j is flipped, the syndrome weight becomes $|\mathbf{s}| + |\mathbf{h}_j| - 2\sigma_j$. And the error weight is either increased or decreased by one.

To instantiate Algorithm 2, we will use the threshold selection rule described in Sect. 2.4 and to sample j, we uniformly pick an unverified equation then a position in this equation, that is

$$i \xleftarrow{\$} \{i, |\mathrm{eq}_i \cap \mathbf{y}| \text{ odd}\}; j \xleftarrow{\$} \mathrm{eq}_i$$

---

[3] All rows of $\mathbf{H}$ have the same weight w, no condition on the column weight.

Algorithm 2. The Step-by-Step Bit Flipping Algorithm

Require: $\mathbf{H} \in \{0,1\}^{(n-k) \times n}$, $\mathbf{y} \in \{0,1\}^n$
  while $\mathbf{y}\mathbf{H}^T \neq 0$ **do**
    $\mathbf{s} \leftarrow \mathbf{y}\mathbf{H}^T$
    $\tau \leftarrow$ threshold($context$)
    $j \leftarrow$ sample($context$)
    if $|\mathbf{s} \cap \mathbf{h}_j| \geq \tau |\mathbf{h}_j|$ **then**
      $y_j \leftarrow 1 - y_j$
  return $\mathbf{y}$

(where $x \xleftarrow{\$} X$ means we pick x uniformly at random in the set X). With this rule, and using the model for counter distributions given in Sect. 2.3, the probability to pick $j \in$ e is

$$\frac{\sum_{j' \in e} \sigma_{j'}}{\sum_{j'} \sigma_{j'}} = \frac{S+X}{wS} = \frac{1}{w}\left(1 + \frac{X}{S}\right),$$

where S in the syndrome weight and $X = 2E_2 + 4E_4 + \cdots$ is defined in Sect. 2.3. Note that this probability is slightly above $1/w$ and larger in general than t/n, the same probability when j is chosen randomly.

3.1 Modeling the Step-by-Step Decoder

We assume here that $\mathbf{H}$ is the sparse parity check matrix of a regular QC-MDPC code, with row weight w and column weight d. We model the step-by-step decoder as a finite state machine (FSM) with a state (S, t) with S the syndrome weight and t the error weight.

We consider one loop of Algorithm 2. The position j is sampled, the corresponding counter value is denoted $\sigma = |\mathbf{s} \cap \mathbf{h}_j|$ and the threshold is $T = \tau |\mathbf{h}_j| = \tau d$. There are 3 kinds of transition,

- if $\sigma < T$, then $(S, t) \to (S, t)$, with probability p
- if $\sigma \geq T$ and $j \in$ e, then $(S, t) \to (S + d - 2\sigma, t - 1)$, with probability p_σ^-
- if $\sigma \geq T$ and $j \notin$ e, then $(S, t) \to (S + d - 2\sigma, t + 1)$, with probability p_σ^+

and the transition probabilities are given in the following proposition.

Proposition 4.

$$p_\sigma^- = \frac{t\sigma f_{d,\pi_1'}(\sigma)}{wS}, p_\sigma^+ = \frac{(n-t)\sigma f_{d,\pi_0'}(\sigma)}{wS}, p = \sum_{\sigma < T}(p_\sigma^- + p_\sigma^+),$$

where $f_{d,\pi}(i) = \binom{d}{i}\pi^i(1-p)^{d-i}$ and π_0', π_1' are given in (2) in Sect. 2.3.

The above machine does not correctly take into account the situation where the algorithm is unable to find a suitable position to flip. We modify it as follows: one step of the new machine will iterate the loop until a flip occurs. We call j the flipped position and σ its counter. The possible transitions are now,

- if no high enough counter is found, then $(S,t) \to \mathrm{L}$, with probability p_L
- if $\sigma \geq T$ and $j \in \mathrm{e}$, then $(S,t) \to (S+d-2\sigma, t-1)$, with probability $p_\sigma'^-$
- if $\sigma \geq T$ and $j \notin \mathrm{e}$, then $(S,t) \to (S+d-2\sigma, t+1)$, with probability $p_\sigma'^+$

where the state L corresponds to the situation where there no position exists with a suitable counter.

Proposition 5.

$$p_\sigma'^- = p_\sigma^- \frac{1-p_L}{1-p}, p_\sigma'^+ = p_\sigma^+ \frac{1-p_L}{1-p},$$

where $p, p_\sigma^-, p_\sigma^+$ are given in Proposition 4, and

$$p_L = \left(\sum_{\sigma < T} f_{d,\pi_1'}(\sigma) \right)^t \cdot \left(\sum_{\sigma < T} f_{d,\pi_0'}(\sigma) \right)^{n-t},$$

where $f_{d,\pi}(i) = \binom{d}{i}\pi^i(1-p)^{d-i}$ and π_0', π_1' are given in (2) in Sect. 2.3.

Note. As mentionned in Sect. 2.3, we have replaced X by $\overline{X}$ (Proposition 2) in π_0', π_1' in all the results of this section.

3.2   Computing the DFR

To compute the theoretical DFR in our model, we will add another state F corresponding to a decoding failure. We assume the stochastic process we have defined in the previous section is a time-homogeneous Markov chain. For any starting state (S,t) we wish to determine with which probability the FSM reaches the failure state after an infinite number of iterations:

$$\mathrm{DFR}(S,t) = \Pr[(S,t) \xrightarrow{\infty} \mathrm{F}].$$

Since we assumed an infinite number of iterations, we need to fix an error weight above which the decoder fails, say t_{fail}. Similarly, to simplify the computation, we assume that when t is small enough, say below t_{pass} the decoder always succeeds. We have $\forall t \leq t_{\mathrm{pass}}, \Pr[(S,t) \xrightarrow{\infty} \mathrm{F}] = 0$ and $\forall t > t_{\mathrm{fail}}, \Pr[(S,t) \xrightarrow{\infty} \mathrm{F}] = 1$.

Notice that as long as $T \geq \frac{d+1}{2}$ (which is always the case here), $\forall \sigma \geq T, S_\sigma < S$ therefore these probabilities can be computed by induction with S in ascending order. Finally, the probability to successfully decode a vector y noised with a uniformly distributed error of weight t in the model is

$$\mathrm{DFR}(t) = \sum_S P_S(t)\,\mathrm{DFR}(S,t)$$

where $P_S(t)$ is the distribution of the syndrome weight given in Proposition 3.

3.3 Using t Alone for the State Is Not Enough

In the analysis of LDPC decoding, starting with Gallager's work [5], it is usually assumed that the error pattern remains uniformly distributed throughout the decoding process. This assumption greatly simplifies the analysis. It is correct for LDPC codes, but unfortunately not for MDPC codes.

Assuming uniform distribution of the error during all the decoding is equivalent to adopting a stochastic model in which the decoder state is described by the error weight alone. From our analysis, we easily derive the transition probabilities as

$$\Pr[t \to (t \pm 1)] = \sum_{S} P_S(t) \sum_{S'} \Pr[(S,t) \to (S', t \pm 1)].$$

The corresponding Markov chain can be computed. We observe a huge discrepancy. For instance, for parameters $(n, r, w, t) = (65500, 32750, 274, 264)$ the observed failure rate is in the order of 10^{-4} for the step-by-step decoder while the model predicts less than 10^{-12}. The difference is even higher for larger block size.

4 Simulation

We simulate here three algorithms:

Algorithm 1: as in [3], using the threshold selection rule of Sect. 2.3.
Algorithm 2: step-by-step bit flipping as in the model of Sect. 3.
BIKE decoder: adapted from [10].

The parameters are those of BIKE-1 Level 5 $(d - 137, w = 274, t = 264)$ with rate $1/2$ and a varying block size r.

The true BIKE decoder is tuned for $r = 32749$. We adapt it here for variable r. The BIKE decoder starts with one iteration of Algorithm 1 and ends with Algorithm 2 and a threshold $\tau = 0.5$. Between the two there is a "gray zone" step described in [10].

Let us point out that the threshold selection rule of Sect. 3 (used for Algorithms 1 and 2 and the model) is not honest. It assumes that the error weight is known throughout the computation while obviously a real decoder has no access to that information. However the main objective here was to compare the simulation and the model, and both of them "cheat". Moreover, we believe that finding the "good" threshold can always be achieved for an extra computational cost without cheating. Note finally that the BIKE algorithm outperforms the others without relying on the knowledge of the error weight.

In Fig. 1, we compare the DFR derived from our model to the one obtained by Monte Carlo simulations of the three above decoders.

While our model is slightly optimistic, the DFR curve we obtain from it follows the same evolution as the one obtained by simulation. Assuming this stays true for higher block length values, this allows us to observe the evolution

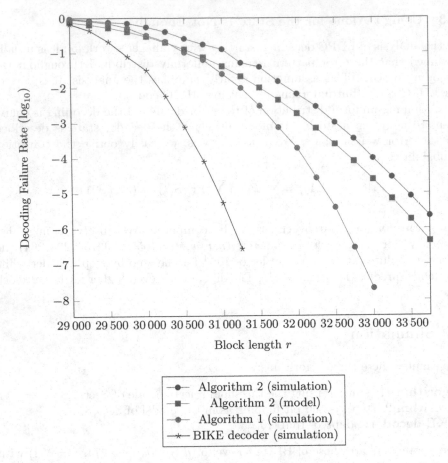

Fig. 1. DFR of the step-by-step algorithm in the models and from simulations (infinite number of iterations)

of the DFR for block lengths that are out of the reach of simulation (when the DFR becomes too small to be measured). Observing the model behavior beyond the range plotted in Fig. 1, we have noticed that the DFR evolves in two phases, in the first phase ($r < 37\,500$) it closely fits a quadratic curve and in the second phase it is linear. This ultimately linear behavior is consistent with the asymptotic analysis of [12], even though the algorithms we are considering do not clearly meet the assumptions under which this asymptotic analysis is valid.

We also observe a quadratic evolution with the algorithms that we implemented and tested. We have no indication on when or if the curve changes from quadratic to linear so our model suggests that an optimistic extrapolation of the DFR would be quadratic and a pessimistic one would be linear. We give some of those extrapolations in Table 2. We denote $p_{\text{fail}}(r)$ the DFR for block size r.

Table 2. Extrapolating QC-MDPC parameters

	(a)	(b)	(c)	(d)	(e)	(f)	(g)	(h)
Algorithm 1	−21.7		34 889	35 541	36 950	39 766	39 837	48 215
BIKE	−47.5	−57.0	32 983	33 713	34 712	37 450	37 159	44 924
Algorithm 2 (simulation)	−11.5		37 537	39 905	40 952	48 610	45 772	66 020
Algorithm 2 (model)	−13.6		37 554		41 872		50 333	

(a): linearly extrapolated value for $\log_2(p_{\text{fail}}(32\,749))$;
(b): quadratically extrapolated value for $\log_2(p_{\text{fail}}(32\,749))$;
(c): minimal r such that $p_{\text{fail}}(r) < 2^{-64}$ assuming a quadratic evolution;
(d): minimal r such that $p_{\text{fail}}(r) < 2^{-64}$ assuming a linear evolution;
(e): minimal r such that $p_{\text{fail}}(r) < 2^{-128}$ assuming a quadratic evolution;
(f): minimal r such that $p_{\text{fail}}(r) < 2^{-128}$ assuming a linear evolution;
(g): minimal r such that $p_{\text{fail}}(r) < 2^{-256}$ assuming a quadratic evolution;
(h): minimal r such that $p_{\text{fail}}(r) < 2^{-256}$ assuming a linear evolution.

5 Conclusion

We have presented here a variant of the bit flipping decoder of QC-MDPC codes, namely the step-by-step decoder. It is less efficient than the existing decoders, but can be accurately modeled by a Markov chain. If we assume that the evolution of the DFR of other related algorithms, and in particular BIKE, follow the same kind of evolution, we are able to give estimates for their DFR and also of the block size we would need to reach a low enough error rate. For BIKE-1 level 5, we estimate the DFR between 2^{-47} and 2^{-57}. As shown in Table 2, the amount by which the block size should be increased to reach a DFR of 2^{-64} or even 2^{-128} seems to be relatively limited, only 1% to 15%. This suggests that with an improvement of the decoder efficiency and a semantically secure conversion, the original BIKE parameters might not be too far from what is needed to resist to the GJS attack and allow static keys.

References

1. Misoczki, R., Tillich, J.P., Sendrier, N., Barreto, P.S.L.M.: MDPC-McEliece: new McEliece variants from moderate density parity-check codes. In: Proceedings of IEEE International Symposium Information Theory - ISIT, pp. 2069–2073 (2013)
2. Guo, Q., Johansson, T., Stankovski, P.: A key recovery attack on MDPC with CCA security using decoding errors. In: Cheon, J.H., Takagi, T. (eds.) ASIACRYPT 2016. LNCS, vol. 10031, pp. 789–815. Springer, Heidelberg (2016). https://doi.org/10.1007/978-3-662-53887-6_29
3. Chaulet, J.: Étude de cryptosystèmes à clé publique basés sur les codes MDPC quasi-cycliques. Ph.D. thesis, University Pierre et Marie Curie, March 2017
4. McEliece, R.J.: A Public-Key System Based on Algebraic Coding Theory, pp. 114–116. Jet Propulsion Lab (1978). DSN Progress Report 44
5. Gallager, R.G.: Low Density Parity Check Codes. MIT Press, Cambridge (1963)

6. Baldi, M., Santini, P., Chiaraluce, F.: Soft McEliece: MDPC code-based McEliece cryptosystems with very compact keys through real-valued intentional errors. In: Proceedings of IEEE International Symposium Information Theory - ISIT, pp. 795–799. IEEE Press (2016)

7. Heyse, S., von Maurich, I., Güneysu, T.: Smaller keys for code-based cryptography: QC-MDPC McEliece implementations on embedded devices. In: Bertoni, G., Coron, J.-S. (eds.) CHES 2013. LNCS, vol. 8086, pp. 273–292. Springer, Heidelberg (2013). https://doi.org/10.1007/978-3-642-40349-1_16

8. Chou, T.: QcBits: constant-time small-key code-based cryptography. In: Gierlichs, B., Poschmann, A.Y. (eds.) CHES 2016. LNCS, vol. 9813, pp. 280–300. Springer, Heidelberg (2016). https://doi.org/10.1007/978-3-662-53140-2_14

9. Chaulet, J., Sendrier, N.: Worst case QC-MDPC decoder for McEliece cryptosystem. In: IEEE Conference, ISIT 2016, pp. 1366–1370. IEEE Press (2016)

10. Aguilar Melchor, C., et al.: BIKE. first round submission to the NIST postquantum cryptography call, November 2017

11. Nilsson, A., Johansson, T., Stankovski Wagner, P.: Error amplification in code-based cryptography. IACR Trans. Cryptogr. Hardw. Embed. Syst. **2019**(1), 238–258 (2018)

12. Tillich, J.P.: The decoding failure probability of MDPC codes. In: 2018 IEEE International Symposium on Information Theory, ISIT 2018, 17–22 June 2018, Vail, CO, USA, pp. 941–945 (2018)

Author Index

Apon, Daniel   189

Baan, Hayo   83
Baena, John   167
Bettaieb, Slim   371
Bhattacharya, Sauvik   83
Bidoux, Loïc   371
Bindel, Nina   206
Boyen, Xavier   116
Branco, Pedro   387
Brendel, Jacqueline   206

Cabarcas, Daniel   167
Campos, Fabio   307
Couvreur, Alain   133

D'Anvers, Jan-Pieter   103
Dachman-Soled, Dana   189
Dang, Viet B.   23
de Weger, Benne   3
Decru, Thomas   271
Doulgerakis, Emmanouil   3

Farahmand, Farnoud   23
Fischlin, Marc   206
Fluhrer, Scott   83
Flynn, E. V.   286

Gaborit, Philippe   371
Gaj, Kris   23
Garcia-Morchon, Oscar   83
Goncalves, Brian   206
Gong, Huijing   189
Güneysu, Tim   65

Hamlin, Ben   329
Höltgen, Kira   65
Hosoyamada, Akinori   350

Jiang, Haodong   227

Katz, Jonathan   189

Laarhoven, Thijs   3, 83
Lequesne, Matthieu   133
Li, Qinyi   116
Ling, San   44
Liu, Zhen   153

Ma, Zhi   227
Marcatel, Etienne   371
Mateus, Paulo   387
Meyer, Michael   307

Nguyen, Duc Tri   23
Nguyen, Khoa   44

Oder, Tobias   65

Pan, Yanbin   153
Panny, Lorenz   271
Perlner, Ray   167

Rcith, Steffen   307
Rietman, Ronald   83

Saarinen, Markku-Juhani O.   83
Sasaki, Yu   350
Sendrier, Nicolas   404
Smith-Tone, Daniel   167
Song, Fang   329
Speith, Julian   65
Stebila, Douglas   206

Tani, Seiichiro   350
Ti, Yan Bo   286
Tillich, Jean-Pierre   133
Tolhuizen, Ludo   83

Vasseur, Valentin   404
Verbauwhede, Ingrid   103
Verbel, Javier   167
Vercauteren, Frederik   103, 271

Wang, Huaxiong 44

Xagawa, Keita 249, 350
Xu, Yanhong 44

Yamakawa, Takashi 249

Zhang, Zhenfei 83, 153
Zhang, Zhenfeng 227

Printed in the United States
By Bookmasters